CLINICAL PSYCHOLOGY
Scientific and Professional Dimensions

CLINICAL PSYCHOLOGY

Scientific and Professional Dimensions

PHILIP C. KENDALL
University of Minnesota

JULIAN D. NORTON-FORD
University of California at Los Angeles

John Wiley & Sons
New York   Chichester   Brisbane   Toronto   Singapore

Library of Congress Cataloging in Publication Data:

Kendall, Philip C.
   Clinical psychology.

   Includes bibliographical references and indexes.
   1. Clinical psychology.   I. Norton-Ford,
Julian D.   II. Title.

RC467.K46   616.89   81-16035
ISBN 0-471-04350-8   AACR2

Printed in the United States of America

10 9 8 7 6 5 4 3 2 1

To our wives and families,
Sue, Stella, Charles, and Jean (PCK)
Bobbi, Anne, James, Ame, and Carol (JN-F)

Preface

The impressive growth in the field of clinical psychology has led to an acute need for an integrative and comprehensive mapping of the discipline. No longer are clinical psychological endeavors restricted to any one facet of mental health. The current status of clinical psychology is quite diverse and impressive, including full involvement in the development and evaluation of therapeutic procedures; active participation in community, organizational, and medical services; ongoing research on psychological dysfunctions; creative production of theoretical and methodological advances; and a continuing involvement in clinical assessment and measurement. In each of these areas, clinical psychologists are *scientists*, trained in the methods and procedures for conducting investigations, and *professionals*, trained to provide direct services to clients. Perhaps because of the breadth of the field and the magnitude of the endeavor, few attempts at a "state of the art/science" document have appeared.

When we decided to write a text on clinical psychology, we were motivated, at the outset, to integrate the scientific aspects of the field with its more applied professional qualities. We also wanted to be comprehensive—covering all aspects of the field in an eclectic fashion and including classic as well as current citations. The task was massive. A single guiding principle helped us to reduce the annoyance of reorganization and the pains of revision—an adherence to our initial goal of integrating the scientific and professional components of clinical psychology.

The result, *Clinical Psychology: Scientific and Professional Dimensions*, is a text for advanced undergraduate students and beginning graduate students (and preparing for professional licensing exams) that addresses the many aspects of the field—each with a scientific and a professional perspective. We present the history of clinical psychology, including an identification of the "landmarks" in assessment, treatment, research, and professionalization. Our coverage of training focuses on the scientific-professional model, each aspect of which is presented independently. Our sections on assessment and intervention are separately initiated with chapters on the related scientific and professional concerns; each individual assessment chapter as well as each individual intervention chapter maintains this dual focus. Actual research experiences and clinical "hands-on" experiences are not, however, integrated with the text. These experiences, where appropriate, should be coordinated and supervised by the instructor.

We have written this text with enthusiasm. We are aware of the many questions that remain to be answered by clinical psychologists, questions as varied as the materials that this text surveys, yet our enthusiasm has not been dampened but enhanced by this greater awareness of the unresolved issues. We hope that this book will provide a similar foundation for further exploration in clinical psychology by both aspiring students and our professional colleagues.

We envision two outcomes for the careful reader. First, a clearer and relatively complete view of the multifaceted field of clinical psychology is offered. In this sense, the text surveys a vast territory, with inevitable oversights but a sufficient range to alert the reader to contemporary and historical themes and areas of discourse in clinical psychology. Second, a scientist-professional model is presented for processing the diverse issues, phenomena, and data that confront the clinical psychologist. The clarity and incisiveness of science provides an excellent complement for the creativity and social awareness of the helping professions.

Several mentors have provided a background and entree to the field and their contributions are recognized and acknowledged. Although only a sampling, the following teachers have had an impact on us in exceptionally fortunate ways: Gerald Davison, A.J. Finch, Jr., Marvin Goldfried, E.L. Hoch, Donald Kiesler, Leonard Krasner, Donald Lim, Joseph LoPiccolo, James V. McConnell, Peter J. Mikulka, W. Robert Nay, and Sheldon Starr. Both senior and peer colleagues have offered new perspectives and provided much support: Linda Berg-Cross, Lila Berman, James Butcher, Jonathan Fielding, James Framo, Norman Garmezy, Steven Hollon, Carroll Izard, Charles Kleeman, Eric Klinger, Gloria Leon, Paul Meehl, Auke Tellegen, and Marvin Zuckerman. Our students have still further enriched our experiences, contributing invaluably to our knowledge and well-being as we taught at the University of Minnesota (PCK), the University of Delaware, the San Fernando Valley Community Mental Health Centers, the California School of Professional Psychology, the California Family Study Center, Antioch University West, and the University of California at Los Angeles (JN-F). Colleagues and students were also helpful in providing comments and information that we have used in the text: Beatrice Bauer, Lauren Braswell, Gary Fischler, James Moses, David Watson, Lance Wilcox, and Carolyn Williams.

We also acknowledge and express our appreciation for the assistance and consultation that we have received from the staff at John Wiley & Sons. Our special thanks go to Jack Burton who guided our progress from the beginning, Brendan Maher who provided insightful commentaries on the entire text, and to reviewers, Harold Arkowitz and William Scholfield who have helped us sharpen our thinking and writing. We thank Cathy Starnella for guiding us through the production of our book and Kathy Bendo for her photo research. Finally, we wish to thank those who have labored hard on the preparation of the manuscript in its various stages. At the University of Minnesota, Lydia Ericson and Jo Nichols were most supportive and helpful, as were the Psychology Department secretaries (Elsie, Judy, Helen, and Mary Jo) at the University of Delaware.

The first author is most grateful to the Center for Advanced Study in the Behavioral Sciences, Stanford, California—especially its director, Gardner Lindzey—for the opportunity to work under the desirable conditions that were found there. The Center truly provided the ideal interlude, both academically and socially, for the completion of this volume. I am most grateful for financial support provided by the National Institute of Mental Health (#5-T32-MH14581-05), the John D. and Catherine T. MacArthur Foundation, and the University of Minnesota.

Philip C. Kendall
Julian D. Norton-Ford

Contents

The Empire of Light, II by Rene Magritte, 1950.

I

INTRODUCTION TO BASIC ISSUES

The Changing West by Thomas Hart Benton, 1930–31.

Every science and every inquiry, and similarly, every activity and pursuit, is thought to aim at some good.

Aristotle.

This painting traces the history of the United States during the period of time corresponding to most of the advances in clinical psychology.

1

THE NATURE AND HISTORY
OF CLINICAL PSYCHOLOGY

Nearly 50 years ago an eminent psychologist, J. McKeen Cattell (1937), reiterated a prediction that he had offered 20 years earlier: "All the professions need a science of psychology and a profession of psychology" (p. 3). Clinical psychology has evolved as a field within psychology that provides both scientific and professional expertise: expertise in the provision of professional services and in the scholarly inquiry of a science. In this chapter, the defining characteristics of clinical psychology are reviewed and clinical psychology's evolution as a science and as a profession is traced.

DEFINITIONS OF CLINICAL PSYCHOLOGY

A historical sampling of definitions of clinical psychology reveals a continuity in certain basic characteristics. In 1912, Witmer introduced the first issue of the journal *Psychological Clinics* with the following definition:

> For the methods of clinical psychology are necessarily involved whenever the status of an individual mind is determined by observation and experiment, and pedagogical treatment applied to affect a change, i.e., the development of such a mind. (p. 1)

Witmer is credited with first using the term "clinical psychology," and his statement highlights the importance of considering each *individual's* needs and status with a *scientific* methodology of observation and experiment. Witmer also proposed that clinical psychologists serve as *teachers*—"pedagogical" means "educational"—to help people develop their capabilities.

Twenty-five years later, Woodworth (1937) suggested that the term "clinical" had too many medical connotations, and advocated "personal service psychology" (p. 3) as an alternative descriptor. In Woodworth's view, the future clinical psychologist would provide "assistance to the individual in solving problems of education and vocational selection, family and social adjustments, working conditions and other aspects of life" (p. 5). Clinical psychologists were seen as professional advisors who use scientifically developed tools for testing and counseling individuals in a variety of important areas for personal adjustment.

Narrower definitions were put forth during the 1930s (Louttit, 1939) to limit clinical psychology to (1) intellectual or personality testing (leaving teaching to teachers, therapy to psychiatrists, and social counseling to social workers) or (2) research on abnormal and subnormal individuals (leaving the study of normal individuals to other areas in psychology and medicine). However, most clinical psychologists continued to favor a middle-ground position, leaning toward a broader *scientist-professional* orientation, as reflected in the definition formulated in 1935 by the American Psychological Association's Clinical Section:

> *Clinical psychology is a form of applied psychology which aims to define the behavior capacities and behavior characteristics of an individual through methods of measurement, analysis, and observation; and which, on the basis of an integration of these findings with the data received from the physical examinations and social histories, gives suggestions and recommendations for the proper adjustment of the individual. (p. 5)*

This definition underscored the *scientific* approach to evaluating individual clients' behavior patterns and capabilities, and the clinical psychologist's role as a *professional* counselor. Forty years later, Shakow (1976) "reaffirmed . . . the scientist-professional model . . . as the best training method to develop psychologists capable of practicing both a profession objectively and a science humanistically'' (p. 553).

Future definitions are likely to retain the basic threads that run through the models proposed in this first century of clinical psychology: utilization of the methods of science and the principles of psychology; provision of aid to individuals who are suffering from psychological problems through psychological evaluation and intervention; in sum, a *scientist-professional* orientation. As a result, clinical psychologists share several common attributes. They are *psychologists* because they have been trained to use the guidelines and knowledge of psychology in their professional work. They are *clinicians* because they "attempt to understand people in their natural complexity and in their continuous adaptive transformations'' (Wyatt, 1968, p. 236). They are *scientists* because they utilize the scientific method to achieve objectivity and precision in their professional work. Finally, they are *professionals* because they render important human services by helping individuals, social groups, and communities to solve psychosocial problems and to improve the quality of life.

THE CLINICAL PSYCHOLOGISTS

Boneau and Cuca (1974) reported that in the United States in 1972 there were more than 50,000 psychologists, of whom 33% identified themselves as clinical in orientation. The actual number of clinical psychologists is growing, as is the number of clinical psychologists employed in mental health facilities in the United States (see Table 1-1). The increase in clinical psychologists was one of the greatest increases relative to other mental health professionals in both 1972–1974 and

Table 1-1 Full-Time Equivalent Positions in Mental Health Facilities, United States 1972, 1974, 1976

Discipline	Number of Full-Time Equivalent Positions			Percent Change in Number	
	1972	1974	1976	1972–1974	1974–1976
Total professional patient care staff	100,886	127,160	143,105	+26.0	+12.5
Psychiatrists	12,938	14,947	15,339	+15.5	+ 2.6
Physicians, nonpsychiatrist	3,991	3,548	3,356	−11.1	− 5.4
Psychologists	9,443	12,597	15,251	+33.4	+21.1
Social workers	17,687	22,147	25,887	+25.2	+16.9
Registered nurses	31,110	34,089	39,392	+ 9.6	+15.6
Other mental health professionals	17,514	29,325	34,249	+67.4	+16.8
Physical health professionals and assistants	8,203	10,507	9,631	+28.1	− 8.3
Other patient care staff	140,379	145,722	145,358	+ 3.8	− 0.2
LPN, LVN	19,626	17,193	15,337	−12.4	−10.8
Other	120,753	128,529	130,021	+ 6.4	+ 1.2
Administrative and maintenance staff	134,719	130,142	134,795	− 3.4	+ 3.6
Total all staff	375,984	403,024	423,258	+ 7.2	+ 5.0

From M. Rosenstein and C. Taube, *National Institute of Mental Health, Staffing of Mental Health Facilities, United States, 1976.* DHEW Publication No. (ADM) 78-522, Superintendent of Documents, U.S. Government Printing Office, Washington, D.C., 1978. In the public domain.

1974–1976, although the amount of increase for all professions has dropped some over the years.

Clinical psychologists are trained and employed in more than 20 countries across the world, in addition to the United States. The number of clinical psychologists per 100,000 persons in the population ranges from more than 34 in the Netherlands and the United States, to a middle ground of 12 to 25 in Australia, Scandinavian countries (Norway, Denmark, Sweden), New Zealand, and Western European Countries (West Germany, Austria, Luxembourg), to as few as 2 (and rarely more than 10) in Greece, Ireland, Portugal, and Eastern European countries (Fichter & Wittchen, 1980). Clinical psychologists also train and work in Canada, France, Great Britain (Broadhurst, 1980), Italy, Switzerland, and the Soviet Union, although data on their numbers were unavailable at present (Table 1-2).

Clinical Psychologists: Who Are They?

In 1971, Henry, Sims, and Spray surveyed over 7000 specialists in psychotherapy residing in New York, Chicago, or Los Angeles and inquired about some of the personal characteristics of clinical psychologists, especially in comparison with their psychoanalytic, psychiatric, or social work colleagues. These professionals

Table 1-2 Clinical Psychologists Across the Globe

	Results of Present Survey			Persons Employed in Psychiatric Services per 100,000 Inhabitants[a]			
Country	Psychologists per 100,000 Inhabitants	Psychologists Practicing Psychotherapy per 100,000 Inhabitants	Psychologists Practicing Psychotherapy in Private Practice (%)	Psychologists	Social Workers	Physicians	Psychiatrists
Australia	21.7	(4.4)	5	—	—	—	—
Austria	13.7	(1.6)	40	—	—	4.8	4.3
Belgium	—	—	—	—	—	8.1	6.2
Canada	—	—	—	—	—	—	—
Czechoslovakia	12.5	1.4	0	—	—	—	—
Denmark	24.5	—	0[b]	.9	1.7	10.9	6.1
France	—	—	—	2.3	1.1	3.3	3.3
East Germany	9.9	2.0	0	—	—	—	—
West Germany	21.7	12.3	24[c]	—	14.4	4.7	4.7
Great Britain	—	13.5	5	1.5	5.5	5.3	3.4
Greece	2.2	.9	—	—	—	—	—
Ireland	9.2	1.9	4.5	—	—	—	—
Italy	(37.3)	—	—	—	—	—	—
Luxembourg	13.3	—	0	2.9	2.1	6.2	3.5

The Netherlands	34.6	(11.5)	10	2.3	7.9	6.7	6.7
New Zealand	15.8	(3.4)	2	—	—	—	—
Norway	19.7	5.4	15[d]	2.5	4.0	10.0	7.3
Poland	15.3	.5	0	.4	.2	6.1	3.5
Portugal	4.0	—	—	.1	.8	2.9	1.4
Soviet Union[f]	—	—	0	—	—	5.9	5.5
Sweden	24.7	—	5	2.6	6.5	11.2	5.6
Canton of Basel, Switzerland	—	(20.5)	89	—	—	—	—
United States	34.3	9.1	82[e]	—	—	—	—

From M. M. Fichter and H. Wittchen, Clinical psychology and psychotherapy: A survey of the present state of professionalization in 23 countries. *American Psychologist*, 1980, *35*, 16–25. Copyright 1980 by the American Psychological Association. Reprinted by permission.

Note: Dash indicates that no information was available. Figures without parentheses refer to psychologists with defined qualifications, specialization in clinical psychology or psychotherapy, and a relevant title; figures in parentheses refer to psychologists practicing psychotherapy with varying qualifications and are likely to be less accurate. Figures for West Germany are partly based on the projection of an empirical study by Fichter, Wittchen, and Dvorak (in press).

[a]Data from May (1976), whose survey of 32 countries was performed during 1968–1971. May's figures referring to Great Britain are valid for England and Wales only.

[b]Approximate.

[c]Includes 7% in part-time private practice and 17% in full-time private practice. These figures came from experts in West Germany who were not official spokespersons for the psychological association.

[d]Includes 9% in part-time private practice and 6% in full-time private practice.

[e]Includes 25% in full-time private practice and 57% in part-time private practice. Psychologists spending between 4 and 30 hours per week in private practice were counted as part time; psychologists spending more than 30 hours per week in private practice were counted as full time.

[f]These figures came from experts in the Soviet Union who were not official spokespersons for the psychological association.

were found to differ somewhat in their reasons for becoming psychotherapists, with clinical psychologists reporting their primary motives are "to understand people" (29%), and "to help people" (12.5%). The principal reasons noted by psychoanalysts were "to gain an identity" (20%) and "to help people" (18%), while psychiatrists were most attracted by gaining an identity (13.5%), gaining professional status (12.5%), and meeting practical pressures (12.5%). Social workers sought to help people (23%), to achieve "affiliation with others" (13.5%), or "to help and understand society" (9%). Both psychiatrists and psychoanalysts reported choosing their career early in life, around 14–15 years old, while clinical psychologists and social workers made the choice in their twenties after contemplating several alternatives. Teachers in college were the central influence in many psychologists' decisions to go into clinical psychology, where practicing therapists influenced social workers in their choice. However, note that this sample of therapists excludes many clinical psychologists who specialize in research, testing, teaching, or administration.

Garfield and Kurtz (1976a) surveyed a sample of 855 doctoral level clinical psychologists to obtain additional personal information. One respondent in six was a woman, no different from a survey of clinical psychologists reported in 1961 by Kelly. The average age was 46.8 years, and the average length of experience as a clinician (post Ph.D.) was 16 years. An influx of younger clinicians was evident in the finding that 30.5% of the respondents had less than 10 years postdoctoral experience. Importantly, 71% of Garfield and Kurtz's (1976a) respondents said that they would choose clinical psychology as a career if they could live their lives again, and 89% were "very" or "quite" satisfied with clinical psychology as a career. The Garfield and Kurtz sample of clinical psychologists included academicians (20%), administrators (8%), consultants (5%), and researchers (5%), in addition to clinical practitioners (59%). Apparently, this national sample of clinical psychologists with varying specialties indicated that clinical psychology is an exciting and rewarding career.

Relationship to Allied Fields in Psychology and Mental Health

Clinical psychology is but one of several specializations within the fields of psychology and mental health. In many cases, the professional roles and training of clinical psychologists overlap somewhat with that offered by the allied disciplines in psychology and mental health (Table 1-3). Each field tends to have a distinctive focus and perspective on mental health and human functioning, but the differences often diminish when professionals work together in multidisciplinary settings such as community mental health centers, hospitals, or universities. Cooperation among the disciplines does much to broaden each professional's knowledge and expertise: clinical psychologists have much to both learn and teach as they work on cross-disciplinary mental health teams.

ROLES OF THE CLINICAL PSYCHOLOGIST

Clinical psychologists are called on to fill several roles as scientists and professionals. According to the Garfield and Kurtz (1976a) survey, clinical psycholo-

Table 1-3 Clinical Psychology and Allied Mental Health Fields

The Allied Fields	Professional Practice Specialties
IN PSYCHOLOGY	
Consulting/organizational	Organizational development, industrial relations, group dynamics, human factors engineering, personnel practices and issues.
School	Psychoeducational assessment of children, academic and vocational guidance, psychological counseling
Social/personality	Research on personality, social issues, interpersonal dynamics, attribution processes, program evaluation
Experimental	Human learning and memory, animal behavior, mathematical/statistical models and techniques
Counseling/educational	Vocational assessment and counseling, personal counseling
IN MENTAL HEALTH	
Psychiatry	Medicine, psychopharmacological treatments, psychotherapy
Psychoanalysis	Long-term and intensive psychoanalysis, medicine and psychiatry (*usually*)
Social work	Social casework (e.g., investigating potential child abuse, facilitating reentry to community from hospitals); group, marital, and personal counseling; social welfare planning
Mental health nursing	Individual and group counseling, hospital administration, mental health education
Neurology	Medicine, assessment, and treatment of neuropsychological disorders
Public health	Health education, epidemiology, health services administration

gists devote the following percentages of their work time, on the average, to six basic roles: therapy and behavior modification (31%), psychological testing (10%), teaching and supervision (21.5%), consultation (5%), administration (13%), and research (10%).

Therapy

Clinical psychologists conduct *psychological* therapy, as opposed to such medical therapies as psychosurgery (operations on the brain), electroconvulsive therapy (ECT; transmitting electric currents through areas of the brain), or chemotherapy (administration of drugs). Many types of psychological therapy are utilized by clinical psychologists, and they have four common features: (1) the therapist establishes a caring and genuine relationship with the client, (2) the therapist aids the client in undertaking a psychological self-exploration, (3) the therapist and client work as a team to set goals for resolving the client's psychological problems and enhancing the client's personal functioning, and (4) the therapist teaches the client skills for coping with stress and controlling his or her own life autonomously and effectively. The following hypothetical examples illustrate these basic elements in the clinician's role as therapist.

Overcoming Depression Through Therapy   John B., a 48-year-old business executive who has been married 28 years and has four children, sought aid from a clinical psychologist because of feelings of hopelessness and fatigue. John met with the clinical psychologist for an hour each week at the clinician's office over a period of 8 months. After spending several sessions getting to know John and gaining an understanding of his strengths and problems, the clinical psychologist gradually began to challenge several self-defeating patterns of thinking and behaving that were consistently associated with painful experiences and emotions for John. For example, the clinician gave John some thought-provoking feedback by asking, "I wonder if you have noticed the parallel between yourself and how you describe your father in that you both seem to have channeled your energy into work, worrying about being a failure, and feeling angry and martyred, rather than taking the risk of reaching out and assertively developing new sources of life satisfaction?"

The clinical psychologist also used homework assignments and role playing in the sessions to help John gain a clearer perspective on himself and his life, and to teach new skills once John became ready to attempt change. For instance, John was asked to simply keep a brief written record of times during the week when he felt significantly happy or disconsolate. As discussions of these records with the clinician began to show John the ways in which he had control over his own feelings, he was asked to engage in more active homework such as thinking more positive thoughts whenever he found himself entering a period of depression. The therapy process had both peaks of heightened self-awareness and valleys of dismay for John, but the clinician's patient guidance helped him to gradually attain greater self-acceptance and to actively restructure his life and himself so as to achieve greater balance and harmony inwardly and in his relationships.

Therapy for Child and Family   Lucy R., a 5-year-old girl from a family with two older sons and an older daughter, had been placed in a residential treatment school by her parents. Lucy spoke only to herself and actively avoided physical or social contact with people while spending most of her time repeating a few ritualized behaviors such as rocking herself or biting her own arms. After extensive psychological and medical examinations, Lucy was placed in the care of a clinical psychologist while she resided in a cottage with nine other children who displayed similar dysfunctions. The clinician developed a "milieu therapy" program that was conducted 24 hours a day by the nurse and aides who supervised the cottage, including having the staff monitor and reward Lucy (with foods, toys, and social reinforcers such as praise and hugs) for small improvements in her care for herself and her interactions with others. Three times each week, the clinical psychol-

ogist met individually with Lucy to provide play therapy and more intensive training in areas such as controlling temper tantrums, responding to commands and
affection, and accomplishing toilet training. The parents observed several of
these sessions through a one-way window, and gradually began to participate actively in working with Lucy under the clinician's close guidance. After more than
a year, Lucy's parents were able to start taking her home for increasing time periods. By her seventh birthday, Lucy was speaking in short sentences and learning
to read, so she was able to join a private school specializing in emotionally disturbed children. She continued to show impairment in intellectual skills and social relationships, but perseverance by her parents and therapist enabled her to
continue to grow psychologically.

Varieties of Therapy   Clinicians use many therapeutic approaches to help many
kinds of clients. Therapy may be done with individual adults or children with a
focus on resolving unconscious personal conflicts (psychoanalytic), fostering self-
acceptance (client-centered), integrating conflicting feelings (Gestalt), bringing
meaning to life (existential), restructuring self-defeating patterns of thinking
(cognitive), teaching skills for coping and effective behavior (behavioral), or any
combination of these. Most clinical psychologists (54%) report using an *eclectic
orientation* (Garfield & Kurtz, 1976a; see also Garfield, 1980): rather than restricting themselves to just one therapy approach, they utilize any of several methods
depending on the specific needs of each client.
    Therapy is also conducted with couples who seek to improve their relation-
ships. Entire families may be seen in therapy, and clients are sometimes brought
together for group therapy. Brief therapy is also offered to people who are experiencing crises such as attempted suicide or drug overdose, both in-person and via
telephone "hotlines." Whenever and wherever people experience psychological
distress, clinical psychologists are likely to be found providing therapeutic assistance.

Assessment

Assessment is the process by which clinical psychologists observe and evaluate clients' psychological and social problems, limitations, and capabilities. As a prerequisite to therapy, clinical assessment provides answers to such key questions as
"How is this client's functioning impaired, and what ill consequences are resulting?" "What disorders or deficiencies in the client's personal functioning or social environment appear to be maintaining problems or impeding positive development?" and "What therapy interventions appear best suited to this client's
needs?"
    Assessment also contributes to clinical research, providing a scientific basis for
evaluating therapy and constructing theories of human functioning and dysfunctions. For example, a clinical psychologist who is researching the effects of several approaches to therapy for clients diagnosed as depressed could use a variety of
assessment instruments before, during, and after the therapies in order to examine the nature and effects of each therapeutic method. Clinical psychologists also
provide other professionals such as teachers, employers, or courts of law with

psychological evaluations of their students, employees, or legal charges. For example, a clinician might be asked to assess a new patient's intellectual functioning and personality patterns in order to provide data for a therapy team to use in developing a comprehensive medical, vocational, and psychological rehabilitation program.

Clinical Assessment in Action   Most clinical psychologists conduct assessment in the context of therapy or research, rather than serving exclusively as assessors (Garfield & Kurtz, 1976a). Historically, clinical psychologists have moved away from being identified as *only* assessment specialists (Kelly, 1961) toward the position of multiservice specialists in human functioning. Nevertheless, psychological assessment is an expertise for which clinical psychologists are particularly well trained, as the following example illustrates.

Dr. Horn is a clinical psychologist who works in a community mental health center, as well as serving on the staff of a psychiatric ward of a medical hospital. On a typical day, Dr. Horn spends the morning at the clinic interviewing and testing clients. She does "intake" sessions to acclimate, screen, and place new clients in the best treatment group, as well as more intensive assessments to gain an in-depth understanding of client's intellectual, neuropsychological, social, and personality capabilities and dysfunctions. A mixture of tests can be used in these assessments, including open-ended or structured interviews, standardized tests on intellectual, neuropsychological, or personality functioning, or informal simulations such as role playing a problematic situation.

In the afternoon, Dr. Horn conducts assessment with patients at the psychiatric ward. In addition to in-depth interviews and tests of psychological functioning, she and the nursing staff directly observe patients both during their daily activities at the hospital and at their homes with families and friends. Dr. Horn's assessments are used both to aid patients' therapists in understanding and working effectively with each individual patient, and to enable the hospital to evaluate the success of their inpatient treatment programs.

Teaching

Clinical psychologists serve as teachers for a variety of students. Formal courses on such topics as clinical psychology, abnormal psychology, counseling and therapy, personality, community psychology, medical psychology, research methodology, interviewing, psychological testing, and behavior modification are often taught by clinical psychologists to undergraduate and graduate students in universities, colleges, or community colleges. Informal courses in such areas as assertiveness, parenting, human sexuality, marital communication, and coping with stress are also frequently taught by clinical psychologists at clinics and counseling centers, adult education programs, or professional conventions. In addition, clinical psychologists supervise graduate and undergraduate trainees who are conducting research projects or doing field work in assessment, therapy, or consultation.

Teaching by a Clinical Psychologist   Dr. Rand is a professor at a university and he teaches workshops at a residential treatment facility for adolescents to both the staff members and residents' parents. Dr. Rand usually teaches two courses each semester, one for graduate students and one for undergraduates. In recent years, he has taught graduate seminars on personality assessment and family therapy for trainees in the clinical program. His undergraduate courses have ranged from an introductory lecture sequence on abnormal psychology to a seminar on community psychology. In the latter seminar, Dr. Rand supervised each student in a practicum placement in which they were participant-observers in local community and mental health organizations.

Dr. Rand also supervises clinical graduate students in their professional work at the university psychological clinic. Each student trainee sees clients and Dr. Rand meets with the students for two hours individually each week and two hours as a group. The supervision meetings include activities such as reviewing audiotapes of the students' assessment, therapy, or consultation interviews, conducting actual interviews with clients in which Dr. Rand "sits in" to observe and assist, discussing students' interpretations of assessment data or plans for therapy, or talking over ethical and professional issues such as client privacy or fees.

At the treatment facility, Dr. Rand teaches a series of regular inservice workshops for all staff members. Each workshop covers an approach to therapy or consultation with adolescents, families, schools, courts, or community organizations. Staff persons from several disciplines attend, including psychiatry, social work, nursing, occupational and vocational therapy, pediatrics, education, and clinical psychology, as well as nonprofessional personnel such as psychological technicians and nursing aides. Dr. Rand presents brief lectures and demonstrations, involving each person as an active participant via role playing and discussion. Dr. Rand uses a similar "experiential" format in teaching workshops on parenting, family communication, and drug use in adolescence to parents.

Consultation

Clinical psychologists offer guidance to a variety of laypersons and human service professionals by providing resources that enable these people to formulate and implement new plans for improving their groups and organizations. Such intervention is called consultation because the clinical psychologist's goal is to help the persons receiving consultation (consultees) do *their jobs* with greater satisfaction and effectiveness. As a consultant, the clinician is a facilitator who guides consultees toward creating their own improvements in the groups or organizations that they represent. For example, clinical psychologists consult with school teachers by providing psychological assessments of individual schoolchildren. The clinician's role is to provide the teacher with appropriate information and to serve as an advisor when the teacher develops plans for improving the milieu of the classroom. Clinical psychologists offer consultation to many consultees, including government officials, police officers, business executives, athletes, civic group leaders, educational administrators, mental health professionals, and many more.

Clinical Psychologists as Consultants   Dr. Baxter works in the consultation and education program of a community mental health center and part time for a psychological consulting firm. She currently consults with local chapters of several self-help groups, such as Alcoholics Anonymous, that provide support and information to people in distress. The groups are governed and administered totally by their members, but they have sought Dr. Baxter's services to help with issues such as how to increase the cohesion within the group, how to provide for the special needs of alcoholics' families, and how to acquire sources of funding. For example, in order to obtain financial support, Dr. Baxter designed a research evaluation that the state funded as a method to document the beneficial effects of their self-help programs.

Dr. Baxter also consults with the director and staff of a new treatment program at a Veterans Administration Hospital for veterans with impaired sight or hearing. She functions in two capacities here. First, Dr. Baxter uses her special background training in the psychological needs and problems of sight- and hearing-impaired persons to help the program personnel better understand and work with their clients. She also conducts psychological assessments of individual clients and discusses the findings' implications for a comprehensive treatment plan for each client. Second, Dr. Baxter holds weekly team meetings with the program's diverse staff members in order to help them develop mutual trust and cooperative channels of communication. Many disparate professions are represented, including ophthalmology, vocational rehabilitation, social work, education, audiology, internal medicine, nursing, and psychology. Dr. Baxter has assessed their individual complaints and proposals about the program and is using structured exercises to aid the staff group in working together as a team.

Administration

Some clinical psychologists serve in executive or management positions in organizations such as university or hospital psychology departments and outpatient psychological clinics. Administration involves "guidance and control of efforts of a group of individuals toward some common goal" through the use of skills in planning, organizing, assembling resources, directing, and controlling (Newman, 1950). Clinical psychologists' competencies in assessment, therapy, teaching, and consultation can serve as valuable tools for the administrator's role, but an understanding of complex political, sociological, and economic forces is also necessary (Feinberg, 1971).

A survey of 30 clinical psychologist administrators suggested that clinical training provides five special assets for an administrative position: (1) sensitivity to individual differences within and between people, (2) awareness of social and psychological forces in groups, (3) expertise in procedures for selecting and evaluating employees, (4) awareness of psychological dysfunctions that may impede employees' performance, and (5) skill in communication (Feinberg, 1971). However, an administrator cannot afford to offer more than brief crisis-oriented counseling to employees because the focus in administration is on practical business rather than on resolving emotional needs and problems. Furthermore, administrators must often make swift decisions that cannot wait for a thorough psychological assessment or research evaluation. Concern for people and an understanding of them are important in administration, but clinical training should be seen as an enhancement of, and not a substitute for, special training in administrative skills.

Two Clinical Psychologist Administrators   Dr. Young and Dr. Wallace are two administrators with clinical training. Dr. Young is the chairperson of a 30-person university psychology department. Dr. Young must resolve problems ranging from personal disputes to funding shortages, as well as overseeing the planning, implementation, and evaluation of policies for the department's current and future operations. He serves as liaison and negotiator for the psychology department with other department chairpersons, college deans, the faculty senate, the regents and community organizations on matters such as the hiring and promotion of faculty members and the allocation of university and community funds for training and research.

   Dr. Wallace is the director of an outpatient psychological clinic that involves a psychiatrist, three psychiatric social workers, nine clinical psychologists, and a public health nurse. Dr. Wallace holds weekly meetings with all staff members and monthly sessions with each one individually. He also confers regularly with the clinic's business administrator and board of directors, as well as with directors of other mental health, social service, and community organizations. A variety of administrative issues must be dealt with, including planning of policies and procedures for clinic operation, insuring quality treatment for all clients and responsiveness to community needs, coordination of services with other local agencies, fiscal planning and application for funding from the federal, state, and local governments, and resolution of conflicts among staff members.

Research

Clinical psychologists conduct many kinds of research investigations, studying such topics as the effectiveness of different approaches to therapy or consultation, the causes and consequences of psychological dysfunctions, and the accuracy of different assessment procedures. Clinical research requires a variety of competencies and roles. To see a project through from beginning to end, the clinical researcher must develop a thorough knowledge of prior relevant research and theory, a set of questions ("hypotheses") that can be tested, a systematic and accurate method for making the tests, a set of instruments for gathering the information for the tests, a meaningful and precise procedure for analyzing and interpreting this information, and a clear and accurate report of the findings and their implications.

Clinical Research in Action   Dr. Gage is on the faculty of a university psychology department. He has developed a research project that is funded by the National Institute of Mental Health, a branch of the Department of Health and Human Services. The research focus is on children who have difficulty in controlling impulses and concentrating on single activities such as reading. Dr. Gage initiated the project by carefully locating and reviewing pertinent past research studies from psychological, medical, and educational journals and books. His first study involved the development and evaluation of an assessment instrument that mea-

Table 1-4 Number and Percent Distribution of Positions (full-time, part-time, and trainee) of Psychologists in Mental Health Facilities, United States, 1976

Mental Health Facilities	Total		Number of Positions					
			Full-Time		Part-Time		Trainee	
	Number	Percent	Number	Percent	Number	Percent	Number	Percent
Total all facilities	20,536	100.0	11,973	100.0	4,661	100.0	3,902	100.0
Total psychiatric hospitals	3,964	19.3	3,073	25.7	418	9.0	473	12.1
State and county	3,291	16.0	2,725	22.8	274	5.9	292	7.5
Private mental hospitals	673	3.3	348	2.9	144	3.1	181	4.6
Total VA psychiatric services	1,572	7.7	903	7.5	184	4.0	485	12.4
Neuropsychiatric hospital	434	2.1	324	2.7	7	0.2	103	2.6
General hospital inpatient units	716	3.5	386	3.2	94	2.0	236	6.1
General hospital outpatient units	422	2.1	193	1.6	83	1.8	146	3.7

Total nonfederal general hospital psychiatric services	2,077	10.1	826	6.9	687	14.7	564	14.5
Inpatient units	748	3.6	342	2.9	238	5.1	168	4.3
Outpatient units	1,329	6.5	484	4.0	449	9.6	396	10.2
Residential treatment center for emotionally disturbed children	634	3.1	300	2.5	229	4.9	105	2.7
Freestanding outpatient clinics	6,074	29.5	2,795	23.3	2,020	43.3	1,259	32.3
Community mental health centers	5,770	28.1	3,791	31.7	1,064	22.8	915	23.4
Other	445	2.2	285	2.4	59	1.3	101	2.6
Freestanding day/night facilities	72	0.4	30	0.3	25	0.5	17	0.4
Other multi-service facilities	373	1.8	255	2.1	34	0.8	84	2.2

From M. Rosenstein and C. Taube, *National Institute of Mental Health, Staffing of Mental Health Facilities, United States, 1976*. DHEW Publication No. (ADM) 78-522, Superintendent of Documents, U.S. Government Printing Office, Washington, D.C., 1978. In the public domain.

sured children's ability to cope with uncertainty. After several preliminary test runs, Dr. Gage administered his instrument and several related (and well researched) measures of childhood functioning to a variety of children. When combined, the measures were found to be accurate in identifying children who were viewed as serious problems by their teachers and parents. Furthermore, Dr. Gage's instrument added unique information concerning the children's abilities to cope with distractions and uncertainty.

Dr. Gage's next step was to arrange to administer all the measures in a large local school system to students aged 6 to 10. All children whose scores indicated potential psychological problems were then randomly assigned to one of three groups: a *prevention* group which was given special training and practice in ways to delay impulsive responding and to cope with distractions; a *family prevention* group, which received similar training but with their families participating as well; and a *control* group, which received unstructured recreation sessions instead of the training. Dr. Gage is currently evaluating the prevention programs by following all the children's progress in school and readministering the assessment measures once every year for the next five years. He plans to examine not only how well the two prevention interventions functioned in helping the children avoid future problems but also to identify the children who need more or different help than that provided. For these children, and for children who have already run into trouble at school and at home, Dr. Gage is developing a more intensive education and therapy program that he will begin to evaluate next year. Dr. Gage has written several articles for professional journals describing his research methods and findings and plans to summarize the entire program in a future book.

SETTINGS FOR THE CLINICAL PSYCHOLOGIST

Clinical psychologists conduct their scientific and professional work in varied settings (Table 1-4), including community mental health centers, state, county, or Veterans Administration hospitals, independent outpatient clinics or private practice, general medical hospitals, residential treatment programs, universities and colleges, school systems, courts and police departments, and government and industry.

Community Mental Health Centers (CMHCs)

CMHCs are multiservice facilities designed to provide for the mental health needs of "catchment areas"—geographical regions in which between 75,000 and 200,000 people reside. CMHCs were originally mandated by the federal government in the Community Mental Health Centers Act of 1963 (Public Law 94-63) as a means to assuring that all U.S. citizens receive all necessary mental health services regardless of age, racial or ethnic background, socioeconomic status, residence, or any other personal or social factors. In 1975, amendments to P.L. 94-63 increased the number of required CMHC services from 5 to 12, adding six new areas and making one area that had been optional a necessity. Every CMHC *must* provide all 12 services to all residents of its catchment area in order to receive federal financial support: inpatient hospitalization, outpatient services, partial hospitalization, 24-hour emergency services, consultation and community education, specialized services for children, specialized services for the elderly, screening, follow-up care, transitional care, alcoholism treatment, and drug addiction treatment. Clinical psychologists play important roles as therapists, assessors, teachers, supervisors, administrators, and researchers in all CMHC areas (Bloom & Parad, 1978).

Inpatient Hospitalization   When people require 24-hour care during severe psychological upheavals they are treated as "inpatients," that is, as residents on a live-in hospital ward. Inpatient services are designed to assure that a full range of services are provided to inpatients, including group and individual therapies, occupational and recreational therapy, personal and academic education, and necessary medical treatment by physicians.

Outpatient Services   Outpatient therapy and education is provided to people who can sustain themselves independently in their natural social environments. CMHC outpatient clinics provide assessment, treatment, and appropriate referrals for adults, children, adolescents, families, couples, infants, and the aged.

Partial Hospitalization   Clients who require a supportive, educational, and therapeutic setting at any or all times during the day, but not overnight, are served by programs such as day treatment centers or weekend drop-in shelters. Partial hospitalization programs help such persons maintain their family, employment, and community ties while avoiding inpatient hospitalization.

Emergency Services   When people experience psychological crises, such as emotional breakdowns, suicide attempts, drug overdoses, or rape, the CMHC provides crisis counselors who are available 24 hours each day at telephone "hotlines" and walk-in emergency rooms, as well as to make home visits or consultation contacts with other community or mental health agencies. The crisis counselor works to reduce the client's anxiety and confusion so that he or she can think clearly and take steps to solve the immediate problem, as well as being on call to handle emergency calls or visits on a 24-hour basis.

Consultation and Community Education   CMHCs serve the community as a whole, as well as individual clients, through providing consultants who may work with (1) teachers, administrators, and psychologists in the local school system, (2) social service and mental health professionals in other local clinics and agencies, (3) community groups that deal with issues such as sexual or racial discrimination, child or sexual abuse, or alcoholism, (4) local industry and labor unions, (5) local law enforcement and correctional agencies, (6) members of the clergy, (7) public welfare agencies, (8) medical care facilities, and (9) government agencies such as city councils.

Services for Children   CMHCs must provide a full range of hospitalization, therapy, education, assessment, and outreach services (e.g., home visits) specially tailored to children's needs and problems. Some CMHCs provide services to children in special branches of their outpatient, inpatient, etc. programs, while other CMHCs offer separate child guidance clinics to insure that children receive appropriate and comprehensive services.

Services for the Elderly   CMHCs must also provide the full range of specially tailored services to persons beyond the midyears of life. In addition to services required by all adults, seniors often require special help with issues such as death and dying, loss of physical capabilities, "ageism"—discrimination against elderly people, loneliness and lack of social support systems, and retirement.

Screening Services   People often come to a CMHC without a clear idea of what services would best suit their needs. Screening services are designed to quickly but thoroughly assess the individual's problems and capabilities so as to identify the optimal educational and therapeutic interventions. By law, the emphasis is on finding appropriate placements within the CMHCs' community-based programs rather than in a mental hospital.

Follow-up Care   Clients who have ended their involvement with CMHC or other mental health facility services often face a difficult transition from the security of ongoing contact with a concerned professional to the responsibility of independent living. CMHCs provide liaison professionals, often clinical psychologists, who facilitate this adjustment by helping the client with the planning, coping, and troubleshooting required. Even a single brief phone follow-up can provide the reassurance and aid needed by many ex-clients. Follow-up is also necessary to identify persons who require further CMHC services.

Transitional Services   In order to prevent people from having to cut their ties with their community support systems by being treated as inpatients in a mental hospital, and to help former mental patients to readjust to community living, CMHCs provide appropriate living arrangements and supportive or rehabilitative services to such persons on the fringe of society. These include halfway houses and group-living homes.

Alcoholism Services   Special outpatient, inpatient, partial hospitalization, and community education services for the prevention and treatment of alcoholism are mandated for all CMHCs.

Drug Addiction Services   A full range of assessment, treatment, and prevention services for persons who have serious problems with drugs such as heroin, amphetamines, or barbiturates are also mandated for all CMHCs.

   CMHCs offer a range of services that is designed to be comprehensive, that is, to meet all needs of all community members. Although designated as recommended rather than required, four additional services are provided by most CMHCs: in-depth psychological assessment, program evaluation to demonstrate the effectiveness of all CMHC services, training to maintain and upgrade staff members' skills and morale, and research projects related to CMHC services and clients. Clinical psychologists contribute to all these areas.

Mental Hospitals

Mental hospitals are the descendants of many prior treatment institutions, such as asylums, "moral treatment" retreats, and settlement houses, all of which were at one time hailed as the panacea for mental health and subsequently found to be ineffective on a large-scale basis (Foucault, 1965; Gagnon & Davison, 1976). From the early 1900s through the 1940s, many states and counties attempted to deal with increasing numbers of persons who were considered "mentally ill" by removing them from society. These people typically came from the fringes of society, due to financial destitution or racial or cultural discrimination, and were not able to afford admittance into expensive private homes or sanitariums. They were placed in large and bulky buildings that are reminiscent of a cross between hospitals and prisons, set away from population centers in the countryside. Inside, the typical mental hospital was arranged as a series of large living areas ("wards") that held as many as 100 patients. Each ward was a self-contained unit typically composed of one or two dayrooms (long rooms substituting for a house's living room), several dormitories affording minimal privacy, a few single rooms (often used to "seclude" violent patients), a small room in which medications were locked, a nurses' office, shower and laundry rooms, and a kitchen. Conditions tended to be crowded, noisy, perceptually disorienting, cold, too bright or too dark, isolated and confining, regimented, and impersonal.

Laypersons and mental health professionals alike have voiced concern in the past 20 years that such mental hospitals are hazardous to patients' health (e.g., Goffman, 1961). However, until the advent of the CMHC, mental hospitals were the only major public institution providing housing, supervision and treatment for people who could not live independently in the community. Thousands of clinical psychologists currently work to create a therapeutic milieu within mental hospitals by providing therapy to patients in groups or on a one-to-one basis. Clinical psychologists also design and facilitate educational and social activities to help patients learn new skills and develop peer support networks. Consultation with other mental health professionals is a further contribution from clinical psychologists, particularly using the findings from psychological assessments to guide the planning of comprehensive therapeutic programs for each individual client (Wechsler, 1944). Clinicians also provide inservice training programs that bring staff members from different wards and varied fields together in an atmosphere of professional growth and cooperation.

Private Practice

Thousands of clinical psychologists work in their own offices, alone or with a group of colleagues. Such clinicians are self-employed in a "private practice." They enjoy the freedom of setting their own policies in such areas as hours, fees, and types of clients and therapies, but they are responsible for running a business as well as providing professional services. Issues such as keeping a sufficient clientele, managing bookkeeping, insurance and taxes, registering legally as a profit-making corporation, and retaining enthusiasm and accountability to clients in spite of a large caseload (the number of client cases being seen) are difficult challenges for private practice clinicians (Pressman, 1979). Clinical psychologists often form group practices with several colleagues, renting a suite of offices in a professional building, in order to create a financial and professional support system for themselves. Clinical psychologists in private practice must be licensed (Highlight 1-1), and they usually serve clients who can either afford to pay $25 to $75 per hour or who have health insurance that pays for psychotherapy provided by a psychologist. A wide range of services can be offered in private practice if the clinician has the appropriate training and experience, including therapy for adults, children, adolescents, couples, families and the elderly, assessment of clients' psychological, intellectual, or neuropsychological (brain) functioning, and consultation to industry, schools, government, or community groups. Of course, each individual clinician can offer only that subset of these services for which he or she has the necessary training and expertise.

Highlight 1-1   Licensure for Clinical Psychologists

In 1946, Virginia became the first state to officially certify clinical psychologists, and in 1951 Georgia passed legislation to license clinical psychologists. At present, clinicians are required to have certification or licensure in order to conduct assessment, therapy, or consultation without being directly supervised by a licensed mental health professional. Certification and licensure represent an attempt to protect clients by identifying clinical psychologists who are competent to provide effective services, and by prohibiting unqualified or insufficiently experienced clinicians to deliver psychological services without careful supervision.

In order to earn a license, a clinician must fulfill three criteria (Hess, 1977): (1) appropriate training background (usually a Ph.D., or Psy.D., from a graduate program approved by the American Psychological Association plus one year predoctoral internship and one or two years of supervised postdoctoral clinical experience), (2) written examination (typically a lengthy multiple-choice test given nationally to all candidates to assess their knowledge of general psychology, research methods, assessment, intervention, and ethical standards), and (3) oral examination (an interview conducted by a panel of licensed psychologists who review several work samples, such as summary reports of clinical assessments or interventions, and question the candidate to ascertain his or her skill, knowledge, and ethical conduct).

Licensing is an important professional challenge for clinicians who wish to become independent assessors, therapists, consultants, or administrators in private practice, community mental health centers, or public and private hospitals. A license is not required for teaching and research, and other important forms of credentialing exist for psychologists, such as the American Board of Professional Psychology (ABPP, a voluntary certification as a "diplomate" in one of several areas of professional practice) and the National Register of Health Service Providers in Psychology. However, licensure is necessary for the many clinical psychologists in universities, medical centers, and schools who devote some professional time to assessment, therapy, or consultation.

Although licensure is an attempt to assure that all clinicians provide quality service (Moore, 1961), Gross (1978) has concluded that the available research does *not* suggest that licensed practitioners in medicine or psychology are uniformly effective. He suggests that written and oral tests are not the best way to predict the efficacy of a clinician's actual assessment, therapy, or consultation, primarily because such tests sample a very different kind of skill than is required in real clinical work with clients. Most clinicians are probably providing effective services to their clients, but it does not appear that licensing offers a foolproof guarantee to consumers. Quality training (Matarazzo, 1977), continued self-training in consultation with clinical colleagues (Newman & Luft, 1974), and personal integrity are the best assurances of quality service. Similarly, the best way to find an effective clinician is often to rely on the evaluations of friends who have been pleased with a particular professional or on the recommendation of a current clinical psychologist or physician. Licensure remains an important milestone in most clinical psychologists' careers, signifying graduation to the status of an autonomous clinical professional.

Licensure is in danger in several states at present, due to efforts to pass legislation that would "sunset" (i.e., terminate) all licensing of mental health professionals other than medical doctors (Cummings, 1979). By 1980, licensing of psychologists had been fully terminated in Florida and South Dakota. But, South Dakata reenacted licensing in 1981. Many interest groups and rationales may be at the root of the sunsetting movement, including consumer activists who view licensure as inadequate protection, previously unlicensed counselors who wish to remove restrictions on their practices, and even factions from within the American Medical Association and the American Psychiatric Association who see sunsetting as a way to neutralize competition from psychologists in the private practice market.

A recent contrast of the private practices of psychologists and psychiatrists revealed that the clients seen by members of these two professions appear quite comparable (Webb, 1980). With respect to age, income, occupation, marital status, sex, and psychological profile, only two differences were noted in a sample of more than 12,000 patients from over 1000 psychiatrists and 200 psychologists. Psychologists tended to serve college-educated persons and clients of nonwhite ethnicities more often than psychiatrists. The services offered by private practice psychiatrists (e.g., drug treatment) versus psychologists (e.g., in-depth psychological assessment) often differ, but their clienteles and their basic service (e.g., psychotherapy) are relatively similar. Another parallel is provided by the growing interest among private practice psychologists in adopting a service model similar to that of the family practice specialty in medicine (Griswold, 1980). This represents a move toward more preventive and comprehensive services to clients.

General Medical Hospitals

Hospitals that provide a range of medical as well as psychological services are sponsored by private enterprise corporations, the Veterans Administration, and university medical centers. Clinical psychologists serve as therapists, assessors, teachers of medical staff and students, and consultants to medical personnel concerning psychological issues in medical treatment (Copeland, 1980). Three special issues confront the clinical psychologist in a medical hospital: the "medicalized ambience," the application of psychological principles and methods to physical as well as psychological health, and research pressures.

Medical hospitals are run primarily by physicians. Assessment and intervention are done with an emphasis on physical health, and personal adjustment can be overlooked or reinterpreted in ways that lead to medical rather than psychological therapies. Fortunately, many physicians have joined clinical psychologists in emphasizing the need for psychological assessments and interventions even with patients whose dysfunctions appear primarily physical.

Clinical psychologists in hospital settings have developed research and treatment programs in areas of "health psychology" such as (1) psychosocial factors in major illness (e.g., cancer), (2) psychological methods for coping with physical illness, (3) education of the public concerning good health practices, (4) psychological approaches to influencing patients to adhere to medical regimens, and (5) psychological interventions to alleviate, overcome, or prevent such health problems as smoking, pain and obesity (American Psychological Association Task Force on Health Research, 1976; Matarazzo, 1980; Olbrisch, 1977; Stachnik, 1980). Clinical psychologists are often required to acquire research grants to help pay for their salaries, equipment, and facilities, sometimes in addition to carrying a full caseload of clinical assessment and treatment. This research pressure applies to many medical professionals working in medical hospitals as well, because medical centers depend on such grants to supplement patient fees in paying for their enormous costs and to create a positive reputation for the hospital as a hub of innovative scientific work.

Residential Treatment Centers for Children and Adolescents

Facilities for housing, educating, treating, and caring for troubled children and adolescents often employ clinical psychologists to work in cottages set in an open area with, ideally, lawns, trees, and playgrounds that are easily accessible. Clinicians have been the primary assessment and treatment agents for 75 years, as well as consulting to staff members such as special education teachers, recreational and vocational counselors, physicians, social workers, and house parents (Doll, 1940; Mathews, 1942). Clinical psychologists are often administrators for residential treatment centers. For example, the Vineland Training School had its clinical research programs supervised by three famous clinical psychologists from the early 1900s. Goddard, who introduced the Stanford-Binet Intelligence Test (then the Binet-Simon test) to America in 1908, came first. Porteus, the originator of a maze test that is still used today, took over in 1919. Doll, the developer of the Vineland Social Maturity Schedule (an early measure of social competence), became director in 1925 and continued through the 1940s.

Residential settings have also been developed for juveniles who have repeatedly and/or destructively committed crimes. Juvenile correctional centers also vary in setting from prisonlike institutions to more homelike cottages, with some newer facilities taking the form of large houses right in the community (Dean & Repucci, 1974). Psychologists are called on to create a social climate that provides familylike emotional support, training in academic and social skills, and encouragement of negotiation and problem solving rather than violence or running away. While assessment and counseling of individual residents can contribute to the development of individualized rehabilitation, the development and administration of milieu programs can enhance the total living environment in a therapeutic and educational fashion. For example, clinicians have trained house parents for residential facilities to run 24-hour programs that are designed to teach the youths appropriate behavior.

Universities and Colleges

Clinical psychologists are professors on the faculties of the psychology departments at most colleges and universities across the world. As academicians, clinical psychologists teach undergraduate and graduate courses, conduct research, serve as advisors for students, and participate on administrative committees. They are also consultants to schools, mental health agencies, community groups, charitable organizations, government, and businesses. Clinical psychology faculty persons describe themselves as more concerned with social issues and the advancement of human welfare than professors from other areas in psychology, according to Lipsey's survey (1974). There is pressure to publish research reports, as in medical centers, and many commentators from within and outside clinical psychology are concerned that clinical faculty members may be sidetracked from fulfilling their responsibilities as teachers and human service providers (Bevan, 1976; Levine, 1974; Raush, 1974). However, universities and colleges provide a unique forum for scientific discovery and communication that can facilitate clinical research and practice.

Some clinical psychologists work in college or university counseling centers (Simone & Wachowiak, 1980; Williamson, 1940). Their responsibilities include psychological and vocational assessment and therapy with student clients, provision of personal development workshops to help students adjust to adulthood and independent living, and teaching courses on counseling and assessment. Clinical psychologists may also serve as counseling center administrators.

Important administrative positions in colleges and universities are sometimes held by distinguished clinical psychologists, including departmental chairpersonships, college deans, executive officers, or presidents and chancellors. For example, William Bevan, the 1981 president of the American Psychological Association, has served as Chancellor at Duke University.

School Systems

Clinical psychologists have worked in many elementary, junior high, and high schools (Cornell, 1942). Today, doctoral-level clinicians are rarely employed full time by school systems, except as administrators. More often they consult with teachers and administrators concerning issues such as special educational and therapeutic needs of "problem" students, inservice training and professional development, and the application of psychological principles to improve motivation and learning in classrooms. For example, a clinician might be asked to assess the specific skill deficits that cause "learning disabled" children to have difficulty with reading or arithmetic, and to design special remedial teaching programs for each child. Clinical psychologists frequently develop research evaluations in conjunction with such school consultations. For instance, a clinician might train teachers to use rewards to motivate students to study quietly and effectively, and then experimentally compare the classroom behavior and achievement test scores of these teachers' students with comparable students in other classes.

Clinical psychologists who stopped their graduate education at the master's degree (MA or MS) level are sometimes employed as full-time school psychologists in school systems. Although specialized training in school psychology is a major separate specialty in psychology, clinicians with experience in testing and counseling children both serve as, or work closely with school psychologists. In a recent survey of teachers, Ford and Migles (1979) found that the most highly valued roles for school psychologists were use of psychological assessment to screen students for placement in special education programs, psychological testing of individual students and recommendation of practical methods for teachers to use in meeting such students' special needs, and counseling individual students with emotional disturbances. A minority of teachers who favored "open education" methods (Silberman, 1975) also saw the school psychologist as a consultant concerning teaching practices and meetings with parents. However, school psychologists are often too flooded with requests for psychological testing to consult with teachers on more than the most practical issues.

Prisons, Courts, and Police Departments

Clinical psychologists have conducted psychological testing and counseling with individual inmates in prisons for at least 40 years (Corsini, 1945; Monahan, 1976). In the 1960s and early 1970s clinicians were asked to develop rehabilitation programs in consultation with guards and administrators to create a more secure, humane, and educational prison environment. By the mid-1970s clinical psychologists were responding to concern from both colleagues and the public by working to create alternative correctional programs such as work release projects in which prisoners can simultaneously develop vocational skills and earn a discharge. Psychologists also pioneered alternative correctional settings such as halfway houses that permit selected prisoners to live and work under supervision in the community.

Prisons tend to be highly restrictive institutions that use physical barriers, rigid rules and schedules, threats and penalties, and, secondarily, persuasion, counseling, and education to maximize orderliness and minimize the potential for harm to staff persons, prisoners, and the community (Shah, 1972). Clinical psychologists can render valuable services to prisoners, but there is the danger that clinical interventions will be seen as a further pressure and threat rather than as an opportunity to increase skills and motivation for autonomous social functioning (American Psychological Association Task Force on the Role of Psychology in the Criminal Justice System, 1978; Pallone, Hennessy & Larason, 1980).

In courts of law, clinical psychologists have, along with psychiatrists, served as "expert witnesses" to help judges and juries determine (1) whether defendants were legally "insane," and therefore not legally accountable, at the time of crimes, (2) whether defendants are competent to stand trial, as opposed to being "mentally deficient," (3) whether defendants are likely to repeat dangerous acts, and (4) other issues of competency, such as whether a prisoner may be permitted visitation rights with children of a divorced wife (Tanke & Tanke, 1979). Clinicians have not been able to accurately predict who will and who will not commit acts of violence (Monahan, 1976), nor have any mental health professionals developed foolproof methods for determining individuals' mental competency. However, clinical psychologists can provide useful consultation to legal agents by helping them to identify the psychological, interpersonal, and behavioral factors that increase or decrease the probability that a defendant is, was, or will be either competent or violent. Issues such as sanity or proper prison sentences are social policy decisions that cannot be definitively proven "right" or "wrong," and clinical psychologists can contribute only information from assessment and research rather than final answers. Both psychologists and members of the legal profession are increasingly recognizing the potential for a fruitful collaboration. The American Psychological Association's "in-house counsel," a lawyer-psychologist, offers a useful summary:

> . . . in a case involving eyewitness identification (for example), why couldn't APA decide to write a brief that was like a Psychological Bulletin article reviewing what psychologists have found out about eyewitness identification and present it to the court? We're not saying we're for the defendant. We're not saying we're against the defendant. We're not for psychologists. We're not against psychologists. We're not fighting psychiatry. We're not promoting psychology. What we're doing is saying we want to act as a genuine friend of the court. (Bersoff, 1980, p. 13)

Clinical psychologists' involvement in court process can have a research, direct intervention, and/or consultation focus. Recent investigations of legal decision-making processes such as jury procedures exemplify the research approach, with important results such as the revision of jury regulations to require equal representation by men and women (Nagel & Weitzman, 1972; Gerbasi, Zuckerman, & Reis, 1977). Innovations such as diverting certain offenders from trial or prison to probation or community rehabilitation programs have been developed by clinical psychologists from a combined intervention-research perspective (Rappaport, 1977). The psychological assessment that clinical psychologist Margaret Singer conducted with Patty Hearst during her controversial kidnapping/terrorism trial illustrates the application of research and clinical expertise to legal consultation (Freeman, 1979). Dr. Singer's clinical research on brainwashing and cults, and her skill in psychological assessment, were both required in addition to a persuasive consultation style in order to provide meaningful guidance to the legal decision makers.

Clinical psychologists also consult with law enforcement agencies, such as teaching police officers the skills used to intervene in family crises (Bard & Berkowitz, 1967) or those used to cope with anger (Novaco, 1977a). Police are frequently faced with situations in which calm counseling might alleviate a potentially harmful crisis, so clinicians have developed practical training programs that impart such information as (1) ways to differentiate between instances requiring forceful intervention versus crisis counseling, (2) how to use silent self-talk to handle anger induced by citizens, and (3) methods for clear communication and rational problem solving. Here, as in all cases where clinical psychologists consult with professionals who have their own expertise, skepticism must be dealt with by adopting a policy of "I'm only here to learn how *you* feel that psychological skills could enhance your present skills, and to work with you to adapt the psychological skills to fit your particular needs."

Government and Industry

Clinical psychologists with special training in the nuances of corporate and union politics and economics work as consultants for business, labor, and government officials and organizations (Meltzer & Stagner, 1980). In the role of an organizational psychologist, the clinician might form a private practice consulting firm that assists in personnel selection, employee motivation, or resolution of conflicts among executives. Alternatively, the clinical psychologist could serve on the staff of a government official such as a member of Congress, serving as a liaison between the politician and psychology on such major issues as national health insurance (Highlight 1-2). In government and industry, clinical psychologists focus on program evaluation, organizational development, and training in management skills, to help organizations function humanely and productively. Such organizational interventions require specialized training beyond what is typically offered in clinical psychology (more often the province of industrial/organizational psychology), but a good number of clinical psychologists have moved in this direction with advanced training.

Highlight 1-2   National Health Insurance and Clinical Psychology

Many countries provide citizens with insurance that enables them to receive health services at no charge or for reduced fees. Such national health insurance requires all citizens to pay a premium just as private insurance companies charge their clients. "Comprehensive" health insurance covers a wide range of health services such as outpatient visits for medical or psychological evaluation and treatment, hospitalization, and emergency care. The U. S. Congress appears on the verge of establishing national health insurance in the 1980s, and clinical psychologists have become active in the political arena to assure that psychology is considered a health service profession equal to medicine (Deleon, 1977; Dörken, 1977; 1980). The issue is crucial:

The future of psychology, especially clinical psychology, as a profession will be shaped by decisions being made in the federal government about the national health care system. . . . Within the next 3–5 years, it seems certain that the Congress of the United States will enact a comprehensive national health insurance program. . . . Organized psychology will either become an integral segment of our nation's health system or it will be systematically excluded, with its current serv-ices being provided by other health disciplines. (Deleon, 1977, pp. 263–265)

Clinical psychologists face an uphill battle because physicians have tradi-tionally been considered the only legitimate autonomous providers of health services in government programs such as Medicare. Once national health in-surance is in effect, most people will use insurance coverage to pay for psycho-logical therapy and assessment, so it is imperative that clinical psychologists be recognized as health care professionals if they wish to continue working as pri-vate practitioners and administrators (Cummings, 1977). Two issues will deter-mine the outcome.

WILL CLINICAL PSYCHOLOGISTS INCREASE THE COSTS OF HEALTH INSURANCE?

Government officials and medical doctors have argued that clients will overuse their insurance coverages if they can receive treatment for psychological dys-functions from clinical psychologists as well as psychiatrists (cf. Cummings, 1977). However, empirical research from three separate studies clearly indi-cates that psychologists *save* money by reducing the use of medical services, rather than adding extra costs (Cummings & Follette, 1976; Goldberg, Krantz, & Locke, 1970; Rosen & Wiens, 1979). For example, Rosen and Wiens (1979) compared 103 child and adult patients at a medical center who received psy-chotherapy at a medical psychology clinic with (1) 205 patients who were as-sessed but not treated at the clinic, (2) 60 patients who were referred but failed to come to the clinic, and (3) 100 matched patients who were neither referred to nor served by the clinic. The treated patients and those who were evaluated and then referred for appropriate treatment elsewhere showed statistically sig-nificant *decreases* in their use of outpatient medical services and prescriptions in the 12 months following psychological assessment or treatment (compared to the prior 12 months), and in their frequency of reporting medical problems. The no-shows and the control subjects did not change their usage of medical services nor their frequency of reporting medical problems. The treated or evaluated patients also decreased their use of medical inpatient hospitalization by 35%, compared to no change for the no-shows and control subjects.

It appears that appropriate therapy is, unless it becomes a substitute for medical treatment (as occurred for only a minority of patients), a boon rather than a burden for both patients and the insurance program. A large-scale ex-periment was just completed in Colorado to examine this question for Med-icare programs, with clients randomly assigned to either a physician or a clini-cal psychologist from 1976 to 1978 (Willens, 1977), as clinical psychologists continue to apply scientific rigor to demonstrating the viability of their work.

WILL THE INCLUSION OF THERAPY IN NATIONAL HEALTH INSURANCE REPRESENT A SUBSIDY TO THE RICH FROM THE POOR (Albee, 1977a)?

Some clinical research indicates that persons of lower socioeconomic status neither seek nor receive therapy as often or as effectively as more affluent people (Lorion, 1978). If this were true with national health insurance, then poor people would be paying the (proportionately) same fee as wealthier people, but they would not be receiving equivalent services in the mental health domain. However, four recent empirical investigations independently demonstrate that lower-income people *seek* and *receive* therapy services of *equal* duration and quality as do their more affluent neighbors (Cummings, 1977; Edwards, Greene, Abramowitz, & Davidson, 1979; Sharfstein, Taube, & Goldberg, 1977; Stern, 1977). For instance, Edwards et al. (1979) found that a *greater* proportion of the poorest people (annual incomes less than $5000) who required psychological services actually received therapy from community mental health centers than was true for higher-income children or adults. Furthermore, the clients' incomes had no effect on the length or effectiveness (as measured by several rating scales and psychological tests) of therapy, nor on the expertise or profession of the therapist to whom they were assigned.

These findings suggest that when therapy services are tailored to meet the individualized needs of poor as well as affluent people, and offered at an affordable fee, low-income persons are not underserved. Of course, it is imperative that psychological treatments be carefully individualized for each client, and this will require persistent effort and stringent evaluation by all clinical psychologists (APA Task Force on Continuing Evaluation in National Health Insurance, 1978; McSweeny, 1977). Clinical psychologists often do not share the cultural or socioeconomic background of minority-group or low-income clients, so extra consideration must be devoted to these persons' special needs if they are to be effectively served. The foregoing studies, and related work on innovations in treatment methods for lower socioeconomic status clients (e.g., Goldstein, 1973), suggest that clinicians *can* fill the bill.

EVOLUTION OF CLINICAL PSYCHOLOGY

As you have seeen, clinical psychologists have taken on different roles in many different settings. But the field did not begin this way. Many factors have influenced the evolution of clinical psychology, each contributing in different ways. Over the last century, the field of psychology has emerged from its sources in philosophy, physiology, sociology, and experimental sciences such as physics (Boring, 1950). Clinical psychology began to emerge as early as the 1890s, with roots in psychiatry and social work as well as in psychology (Reisman, 1966). Four parallel streams of action and ideology are apparent in the developmental history of clinical psychology: assessment, intervention, research, and professional organization. All four streams have descended from several shared antecedents in the sciences and humanities.

Antecedents

Scientific research and theory in clinical psychology has its origins in the philosophical traditions of metaphysics and empiricism and the scientific approaches of descriptive and experimental research. Professional practice in clinical psychology derives, in addition, from the heritage of earlier professions and the spirit of social reform.

Metaphysics in Philosophy   For more than 2500 years, philosophers such as Plato (428–347 B.C.), Descartes (1596–1650) and Kant (1724–1804) have taken the position that knowledge is best acquired through logical reasoning. For example, Kant postulated that certain ultimate truths ("categorical imperatives") exist that can only be established through rational analysis, not through observation of events or actions. Theories in psychology, although based in part on observations (which would be considered superfluous by metaphysical philosophers) derive in part from logical analyses that transcend the information provided by observations. For instance, *structuralism* was based on the assumption that the fundamental characteristics of the human mind could be ascertained through logical reasoning about patterns of people's actions and perceptions. In contrast, *functionalism* held that the outcomes of human actions and thoughts were more important to understand than their structure. The *gestalt* school of psychology takes yet another position, asserting that the central aspect of human experience is the tendency to organize and integrate isolated perceptions into meaningful wholes (gestalts)—to see a forest rather than many separate trees. *Behaviorism*, on the other hand, emphasized that only directly observable responses and stimuli were useful in the scientific study of humans. Each theory represents a different logical interpretation, so each offers a unique and potentially valuable perspective on human functioning. Most clinical psychologists utilize several theoretical viewpoints in scientific and professional work.

Empiricism in Philosophy   Other philosophers such as Aristotle (384–322 B.C.), Locke (1632–1704), and Hume (1711–1776) stressed the observation of actual events as the prime source of knowledge. The empiricism doctrine has had profound effects on (1) the sciences, by encouraging empirical (based on objective observation) research in addition to logical analysis and (2) the educational, medical, and psychological professions, by suggesting that people can change due to new learning experiences, rather than being inalterably the same all their lives.

Descriptive Research in Science   One method of applying empiricism to gaining systematic knowledge about the world is the observation of naturally occurring events. Such research is descriptive, in that it aims to describe phenomena accurately. Galileo's astronomical observations, Newton's discovery of gravity, Darwin's description of natural selection in species, Mendel's account of genetic transmission, and Hippocrates's ancient reports of the causes and courses of diseases all exemplify the descriptive tradition in science. Formulations that have had important impacts on psychology such as Kraepelin's (1887) classification of different psychological dysfunctions, Meyer's (1911) observation that psychological dysfunctions are often due to faulty learning, and especially Freud's (1905–1910) psychoanalytic conceptualization of personality and therapy have been derived from descriptive research.

Experimental Research in Science   Empirical research is experimental if the scientist causes a change in naturally occurring processes and then observes the resultant deviations in the processes that occur. By changing only a very limited part of the natural phenomenon, the scientist can be sure that this change is the *cause* of any resultant deviations. Experimental research thus enables not only the description but also the identification of the causes of important natural events and processes. Examples of experimental investigations that served as forerunners for clinical research include Joule's experiments that enabled Von Helmholtz to formulate the conservation of energy principle, Fechner's psychophysical experiments in which the physical stimuli for different sensory experiences were established, Pasteur's demonstration of the role of bacteria in certain diseases, and Ebbinghaus's experiments on human memory.

Professions and Professionalism Professions have existed for centuries to train and regulate people who could provide complex and specialized services such as medical treatment, legal aid, and business management (Goode, 1957). Professions evolved as people found that certain social responsibilities required greater knowledge or expertise than most people had the time, energy, or skills to acquire, and as an elite minority of people discovered that providing these services enabled them to achieve financial power and social status. Perhaps the first professionals were religious shamans and priests, and some quasi-spiritual mysticism is retained by many modern professions (Albee, 1977b): for example, physicians may be asked to decide whether or not, and how, to save people's lives, and patients may ask, or be forced, to relinquish their control over their own lives in the process. Professions serve many important social functions, and professionalism represents an attempt to render these services in order to provide maximum benefit and protection for consumers.

Social Reform The humanism of the seventeenth-century "Enlightenment" and the political reforms in the eighteenth and nineteenth centuries that represented an increase in the personal power and social rights of the common man spurred parallel reforms in mental health and social welfare (Foucault, 1965). The spirit of optimism and kindness that is exemplified by the French physician Pinel's throwing off the chains of "lunatics" in the asylum in Bicêtre was carried on through the "moral treatment" programs that he, the British philanthropist Tuke, and the American physician Todd, founded independently to replace asylums. Moral treatment involved providing a homelike haven in which psychologically distressed persons could relax, initiate positive relationships, and more rationally resolve their problems. A major impetus behind the establishment of reformed treatment facilities in dozens of states and more than a dozen countries was the persuasive crusading of Dorothea Dix, who set a model for all social activists and advocates of disadvantaged groups through her work. Settlement houses—refuges for destitute immigrants in the early 1900s—provided another early demonstration of the efficacy of humane social/educational treatment. The final spark that launched clinical psychologists as full-fledged participants in the mental health service delivery system was the founding of psychology clinics (first by the clinical psychologist Witmer at the University of Pennsylvania in 1896) and child guidance clinics (first by Fernald, a psychologist, and Healy, a psychiatrist, at the Juvenile Psychopathic Institute in Chicago in 1909).

Evolution of Assessment in Clinical Psychology

Until the 1920s, most clinical psychologists considered their primary role to be that of assessor (Louttit, 1939). Psychometric assessment, the precise quantitative measurement of human attributes and behavior, evolved from early psychological research by pioneers such as Wundt and Galton (Boring, 1950). Some landmark events through the 1960s are chronicled in Table 1-5. The landmarks are only a sampling, but they reflect the development of psychological assessment from simple tests of motor skills to more complex assessments of mental compe-

Table 1-5   Clinical Assessment: Landmarks[a]

1869	Galton publishes *Hereditary Genius*, commencing the study of individual differences that led him to later develop tests of simple abilities such as reaction time.
1890	J. M. Cattell introduces the concept of "mental tests and measurements" that aimed at discovering constancies in mental processes that differentiate among individuals.
1896	Witmer founds the first psychological clinic, University of Pennsylvania.
1905	Binet and Simon publish the first objective test of intelligence.
1915	APA recommends that only qualified psychologists use psychological tests.
1915– 1918	Psychologists develop the Army Alpha (verbal intelligence) and Beta (nonverbal intelligence) and the Personal Data Sheet (personality) to screen recruits for the armed forces during World War I.
1916	Terman revises the Binet-Simon, incorporating the IQ.
1921	Rorschach inkblot test published, representing the first major projective test.
1925	Gesell publishes developmental schedules describing the normal developmental attainments of 3- to 30-month-old infants.
1926	Thurstone suggests that Deviation Quotients be used in intelligence tests rather than the MA/CA ratio.
1935	Doll publishes the Vineland Social Maturity Scale.
1937	Terman and Merrill publish the revised Stanford-Binet.
1938	Bender-Gestalt test introduced.
1939	Wechsler-Bellvue test introduced.
1940	Hathaway and McKinley develop the Minnesota Multiphasic Personality Inventory (MMPI).
1943	Sarbin contrasts clinical versus statistical prediction.
1946	Cronbach describes the problem of response sets in clinical assessment.
1947	Halstead introduces a test battery for neuropsychological assessment.
1948	MacCorquodale and Meehl distinguish between hypothetical constructs and intervening variables.
1949	Wechsler Intelligence Scale for Children introduced.
1954	American Psychological Association publishes standards for psychological tests.
1954	Meehl provides a seminal review of the clinical-statistical prediction issue.
1955	Cronbach and Meehl describe construct validity in clinical measurement.
1968	Behavioral assessment sparked by Mischel and described by Goldfried and Pomeranz.

[a]Up to 1970.

tencies and personality functioning. Although many psychological instruments have developed in response to pressing social needs, such as the Binet-Simon intelligence test that was created to screen and place thousands of children in schools and treatment facilities in France, complex theoretical and statistical advances such as Cronbach and Meehl's (1955) concept of construct validity have also sparked new developments in clinical assessment.

Over the past 75 years, a variety of tests of intelligence (e.g., the Weschler-Bellvue, now the Weschler Adult Intelligence Scale), personality (e.g., the Rorschach and TAT), psychological dysfunctions (e.g., the MMPI), brain functioning (e.g., the Bender-Gestalt), and developmental maturity (e.g., the Gesell schedules and the Vineland Social Maturity Scale) have been created and/or empirically evaluated by clinical psychologists. As clinicians have expanded their knowledge of the principles that guide effective psychological testing, these guidelines have been publicly enunciated (e.g., American Psychological Association, 1952) and adherence to them has been required of all clinical assessors and test developers.

Clinical psychologists pioneered several strategies for assessment as well as constructing specific tests. For instance, objective approaches, in which empirically derived relationships between clients' responses to tests and their psychological functioning were used to guide diagnosis, emerged from clinical psychology. Projective and behavioral strategies were also developed. Projective assessment represents an attempt to discern the subtle unconscious conflicts that are considered paramount by psychoanalytic clinicians, while behavioral assessment focuses on obtaining direct samples of real-life behavior in accord with the behavior therapy orientation in clinical psychology. An additional innovation in assessment strategies was the use of statistical formulas, rather than the intuitive judgements of clinicians, to make diagnoses and predictions based on test results. Extensive research starting with Sarbin (1943; see also Meehl, 1954), has evolved to compare "statistical versus clinical" assessment.

Evolution of Intervention in Clinical Psychology

Clinical psychologists have become involved in five basic types of interventions that have evolved as illustrated by the selected landmarks in Table 1-6. Milieu therapy, behavioral training, individual psychotherapy, group therapy, and social change programs have all evolved significantly, especially since the emergence of clinical psychology.

Milieu therapy, in which a special sociophysical environment is constructed to promote relaxation, supportive relationships, and learning of new skills for more effectively managing life, was pioneered by the reformers of the eighteenth and nineteenth centuries such as Pinel and Todd. Putnam (1906) reported the first description of psychological milieu treatment program in a psychology journal. Milieu therapy waned in popularity for 40 years, due to the advent of exciting alternative interventions and the difficulty of having any positive impact with severely disturbed mental patients. In the late 1940s and early 1950s new economic prosperity and the development of effective tranquilizing drugs encouraged psycholo-

Table 1-6   Clincial Interventions: Landmarks[a]

1793	Pinel unchains the inmates and founds moral treatment in asylums.
1796	Tuke establishes the York Retreat to provide a "refuge" and a humane physical and social environment for lunatics.
1824	Todd founds the Retreat to offer moral management as milieu therapy.
1840	Dix begins a 40-year crusade to establish humane mental hospitals.
1891	Bernheim describes treatment by hypnosis.
1895	Breuer and Freud describe transference in the therapist-client relationship.
1896	Witmer advocates pedagogical treatment in psychology clinics.
1900	Freud describes dream analysis and free association as therapy methods.
1905	Worcester and Pratt initiate group therapy.
1905	Franz begins teaching brain-damaged patients with speech loss to recover their speech skills.
1906	Janet proposes relearning of competing responses as a treatment for impulse problems.
1906	Putnam describes multicomponent milieu therapy.
1907	Prince and Coriat describe examples of therapy based on a reeducation process guided by scientifically derived principles of learning.
1908	DuBois advocates talking therapy to persuade clients to master their psychological symptoms and problems.
1909	Healy and Fernald found the Juvenile Psychopathic Institute, spurring the child guidance movement in the United States.
1913	Jelliffe describes countertransference in therapy.
1919	McDougall uses "sympathetic rapport" to treat shell-shocked soldiers.
1920	Watson and Rayner describe a case of conditioned fears.
1922–1928	Adler and Dreikurs pioneer therapy interviews with entire families.
1928	Anna Freud describes psychoanalytic play therapy with children.
1930	Tulchin advocates therapy as a legitimate function of clinical psychologists.
1932	Moreno introduces the concept of "group therapy."
1934	Allen describes "passive therapy," forerunner of Rogerian therapy.
1938	Levy describes "relationship therapy," forerunner of behavior therapy.
1940	Slavson summarizes his principles for group therapy.
1941	Korzbyski popularizes "semantic therapy."
1942	Rogers formulates "client-centered therapy."
1946	Alexander and French describe brief psychoanalytic therapy based on the "corrective emotional experience."
1948	Lewin, Bradford, Berne, and Lippit introduce T-groups.
1948	Bettleheim and Sylvester popularize "milieu therapy."
1949	Salter describes *Conditioned Reflex Therapy* in book of same name, forerunner of desensitization and assertiveness training.
1950	Dollard and Miller offer a synthesis of psychoanalysis and learning theory.
1951	Perls introduces gestalt therapy.
1952	Eysenck criticizes psychotherapy and therapy research.
1953	Frankl introduces logotherapy, an existential approach to therapy.

Table 1-6   *Continued*

1953	Skinner provides a blueprint for the application of operant conditioning to therapy and social change.
1953	Sullivan describes the "interpersonal" approach to psychotherapy.
1957–1963	Cowen pioneers preventive psychological intervention.
1958	Ackerman describes family therapy.
1958	Wolpe pioneers desensitization; *Psychotherapy by Reciprocal Inhibition*.
1958	Ellis introduces Rational Emotive Therapy.
1963–1970	Masters and Johnson pioneer research on sexual therapy.
1964	Berne introduces his book *Transactional Analysis* (TA).
1964	Beck introduces cognitive therapy for depression.
1964–1969	Fairweather pioneers experimental social innovation.
1968	Ayllon and Azrin introduce *The Token Economy* in book of same name.

[a]Up to 1970.

gists to renew their efforts in milieu therapy with programs such as the therapeutic community and the token economy.

Clinical psychologists, aided by colleagues in educational and experimental psychology such as Thorndike, introduced training methods for individual children (Witmer, 1912) and the adults with brain damage (Franz, 1905) or psychologically based dysfunctions (Prince & Coriat, 1907). Witmer coined the term "pedagogical treatment" in 1896 to describe behavioral training interventions in which the goal was to teach clients new skills and knowledge. Behaviorists such as Watson and Rayner (1920) and Jones (1924) extended such learning-based treatments to help clients with fears and phobias, and during the 1930s such "conditioning" treatments were frequently used to treat children's anxiety. Behaviorally oriented interventions continued to surface occasionally, such as Levy's (1938) relationship therapy in which the therapist models effective responding for the client and Korzbyski's (1941) semantic therapy for teaching clients to think rationally, but it remained for Eysenck's (1952) critique of psychoanalytic therapies and progress in research on the principles of learning by experimental psychologists such as Skinner (1953) and Tolman (1948) to spur the recent emergence of behavioral training. Behavior therapy, introduced by Skinner (1953), Salter (1949), and Wolpe (1958), and cognitive therapy (teaching clients to think more effectively), pioneered by Ellis (1958) and Beck (1964), are now major forces in clinical psychology.

Therapy with individuals, in which clients are aided in reevaluating and restructuring their basic personality styles in order to overcome emotional conflicts, was pioneered by Charcot, Janet, and Bernheim's work on hypnosis, Freud and Breuer's extension of hypnotic techniques in psychoanalysis, and DuBois's (1908) formulation of exhortive therapy. Clinical psychologists who provided service for the counseling of war veterans (such as McDougall), children (such as Allen,

1934) and students (such as Rogers, 1952) pioneered a "nondirective" and supportive approach to therapy that continues as a widely used treatment modality. During and following World War II, clinical psychologists were again needed to treat thousands of distressed veterans (Darley & Wolfe, 1946), and by this time psychologists had achieved acceptance on a permanent basis as therapists. Since 1945, many influential therapies have been developed or extended by clinical psychologists.

Therapy with groups was pioneered by a clinical psychologist (Worcester) and an internist (Pratt), who initiated supportive discussion groups with mental hospital patients in 1905. Adler and Dreikurs relied on a similar rationale of having patients learn from each other when they began to interview entire families in therapy in 1922. In the 1920s, psychoanalysts were also developing group therapy procedures. Then in 1932 Moreno introduced the term "group therapy" after having pioneered the specialized method of "psychodrama," and Slavson became an influential teacher of group therapy based on his work with children and adolescents. However, it was not until the 1940s and 1950s, when T-groups were originated by Lewin and his colleagues and family therapy was systematized by Ackerman, that therapy with groups began to flourish. Since then, both group and family therapy have become major treatment modalities.

Although the roots of social change interventions can be traced to the early mental health reformers, clinical psychologists have begun working in earnest to promote the welfare of organizations, large groups, and communities only in the past 25 years. The economic affluence and political activism of the late 1950s and early 1960s sparked pioneering work in the large-scale prevention of psychological dysfunctions by clinicians such as Cowen and the scientific reform of mental health services by psychologists such as Fairweather. The resultant community psychology movement (Rappaport, 1977) continues as a model for clinical psychologists who apply science and professionalism to bring about social change.

Evolution of Research in Clinical Psychology

Clinical psychologists have always been trained as psychological researchers, in the scientific tradition that began with the founding of psychology laboratories in the 1870s and journals for the publication of psychological research in the 1880s. Table 1-7 traces the evolution of clinical research through a sample of major landmark events. The Binet-Simon intelligence test was perhaps the first scientific product of psychologists that was utilized extensively by clinical psychologists in their professional work. In 1906 Prince founded the *Journal of Abnormal Psychology* to publish clinical research, theory, and case reports. In its first year, the *Journal* presented an experiment by Coriat (1906) with a single client suffering from alcoholic amnesia and an experiment by Jung (1907) with several subjects. Coriat demonstrated that his subject could improve memory recall by concentrating intensely through the use of a "hypnoidal state" that was induced by listening to a watch tick for three to five minutes. Jung's study, and a follow-up by Ricksler and Jung (1907–1908), showed that the galvanic skin response (GSR, a physiological measure of skin conductance due to perspiration) was associated

Table 1-7 Clinical Research: Landmarks[a]

1870s	William James and Wilhelm Wundt: separate founders of the first psychology laboratories.
1887	Hall founds the *American Journal of Psychology* for experimental research in psychology.
1905	Binet and Simon present validity evidence for their intelligence test.
1906	Prince founds the *Journal of Abnormal Psychology* for experimental research, theory, and case reports in clinical psychology.
1906	Franz reports experimental data from monkeys to demonstrate that the brain's frontal lobe controls sensory associations, and that habits that are lost due to brain damage can be relearned.
1907– 1909	Jung presents between-groups experiments to demonstrate that persons with different psychological problems manifest different psycho-physiological responses.
1916	Terman reports updated norms for the Binet-Simon intelligence test.
1925	Gesell reports empirically derived developmental norms for infants.
1937	Mathews reports the first experimental study in the *Journal of Consulting Psychology*.
1939	Wechsler reports validity evidence for his intelligence test for adults.
1940	Hathaway and McKinley report validity evidence for the Minnesota Multiphasic Personality Inventory (MMPI).
1947	Snyder reports an early study of the process of individual therapy.
1947	Peres reports an early study of the process of group therapy.
1948	Hamlin and Albee report one of the first quasi-experimental studies of therapy.
1951	Powers and Witmer report one of the first controlled evaluations of counseling.
1953	Warne et al. report an early controlled study of a psychological intervention.
1954	Rogers and Dymond report one of the first controlled studies of Rogerian therapy.
1960	Fairweather et al. report an early controlled study of milieu therapy.
1966	Paul reports one of the first controlled studies of behavior therapy.
1967	Rogers et al. report one of the first controlled studies of individual therapy with schizophrenic clients.
1968	Langsley et al. report major comparative outcome study of family therapy versus inpatient hospitalization.

[a]Up to 1970.

with emotional distress, and that persons with different psychiatric diagnoses such as paranoia or catatonia show different GSRs to the same stimuli (e.g., a sudden noise, a spoken sentence). Ricksler and Jung set a model for experimental research in clinical psychology with their methodology:

> In our experiments care was taken to have the conditions as nearly equal as possible
> (for each subject). It was found that different positions of the body, leaning for-
> wards or backwards, for example, caused a change in the level of the (physiological
> response). The tambour (measurement equipment) itself can cause changes . . . (as
> can) a movement of the (subject's) hands. (p. 193)

Research on Psychological Assessment and Dysfunctions   Clinical research has focused on the development of assessment instruments and the search for causes and consequences of psychological dysfunctions. For example, Franz (1906) pioneered neuropsychological research by studying the effects of experimentally induced brain damage in animals, and the consequences of naturally occurring brain damage in humans. Mathews (1937), in the first experiment published in the *Journal of Consulting Psychology*, demonstrated that good students (as judged by teachers) showed higher intelligence test scores, better home environments, and more positive self-described personality attributes than poor students. Mathews concluded: "In light of these facts it appears that the school which expects to administer to the needs of the whole child must be alive to the conditions of the home and community . . . " (p. 48), illustrating the practical value of clinical research.

Research on Clinical Interventions   Early research was limited to summaries of the number of successes versus failures, without scientific precautions to assure the accuracy of these results. Snyder (1947) and Peres (1947) reported early quantitative descriptions of the actions of therapists and clients in, respectively, individual and group therapy. Snyder's rating system was used by trained observers in both studies to categorize the responses of client and therapist from audio recordings of actual therapy sessions. Snyder concluded that successful therapy involves the use of encouragement and explanations without many direct prescriptions or questions to elicit positive statements about self from the client. Four cases judged to be successful by clinicians were compared to one case that was viewed as unsuccessful by therapist and client. In contrast, Peres compared clients who judged their therapy to have been successful versus unsuccessful and concluded that effective group therapy hinged on the use of "therapeutic statements" (discussion of problems, explanations) that encouraged clients to clarify their feelings.

Studies that attempted to scientifically demonstrate that clinical interventions cause positive changes in clients were initiated by investigations such as Hamlin and Albee (1948). The researchers assessed the changes in untreated college students on a questionnaire test of personality and on the Rorchach inkblot test over a three-month period and compared these data to the changes on the same measures that Rogers had reported for undergraduate clients after individual "nondirective" counseling. Their results demonstrated that the untreated subjects changed just as much as the counseling clients on the personality questionnaire but not on the Rorschach. Although untreated subjects were not exactly comparable to the treated subjects because they had not requested counseling, this early study illustrates the importance of comparisons with untreated subjects and the use of several kinds of outcome measures when the effects of therapy are being researched.

More extensive scientific studies were reported by Powers and Witmer (1951), Warne, Canter, and Winze (1953), and Rogers and Dymond (1954). Powers and Witmer assessed the effects of a multicomponent intervention on the subsequent criminal behavior, health, socioeconomic status, and family adjustment of 506 5 to 13-year-old boys who had been selected by schools, welfare agencies, churches, and police as either "average" or "difficult." This study, called the Cambridge-Somerville Youth Study because it was set in the densely populated, factory-dominated, lower-middle-class area of eastern Massachusetts, was pioneered by the physician Richard Cabot in 1939 as an attempt to prevent delinquency. Both 3 (Powers & Witmer, 1951) and 30 (McCord, 1978) years after the project's termination, the 253 untreated subjects fared no worse, and in some cases (for instance, their health as adults) better, than the 253 subjects who received the following intervention for an average of 5 years:

> *Counselors assigned to each family visited, on the average, twice a month. They encouraged families to call on the program for assistance. Family problems became the focus of attention for aproximately one third of the treatment group. Over half the boys were tutored in academic subjects; over 100 received medical or psychiatric attention, one fourth were sent to summer camps; and most were brought into contact with the Boy Scouts, the YMCA, and other community programs. The control group, meanwhile, participated only through providing information about themselves. (McCord, 1978, p. 284)*

Participants gave very positive ratings of the program even 30 years later, but it appeared to produce minimal objective benefits.

By 1960, studies that more specifically evaluated psychotherapy, rather than the social counseling offered in the Cambridge-Somerville study, began to report far more positive results (Barron & Leary, 1955; Cartwright, 1957; Mink, 1959; Rogers & Dymond, 1954; Warne et al., 1953). In subsequent years, experimental evaluations of milieu therapy (Fairweather, Simon, Gebhard, Weingarten, Holland, Sanders, Stone & Reahl, 1960), behavior therapy (Paul, 1966), individual psychotherapy with hospitalized persons diagnosed as schizophrenic (Rogers, Gendlin, Kiesler & Truax, 1966), family therapy (Langsley, Pittman, Machotka & Flamenhaft, 1968), and group therapy (Lieberman, Miles & Yalom, 1973) first appeared. Clinical psychologists continue to evolve increasingly sophisticated methods for scientific evaluation of clinical interventions, yielding important information to guide practicing therapists, consultants, and administrators.

Evolution of Clinical Psychology as a Profession

Clinical psychologists have established themselves as professionals while maintaining their commitment to science (Louttit, 1939; Watson, 1949; Witmer, 1912). Psychology became formally established as a scholarly discipline in 1892 with the founding of the American Psychological Association (APA), but after 25 years only 16 of 307 APA members were employed outside of academic settings (Riesman, 1966). Most clinical psychologists were ineligible for APA membership because they either did not have Ph.D.s or had not published research after their doctoral dissertation. Clinical psychologists had to work to achieve parity within psychology before they could contend with psychiatry, but by 1919 they had shown sufficient power in their new American Association of Clinical Psychologists to persuade APA to establish a special Clinical Section (Table 1-8).

1920–1950 In 1921 Cattell founded the Psychological Corporation to market psychological tests and consultation, thus beginning to establish clinical psychology in the business world. However, the APA Clinical Section was having little

Table 1-8 Professional Landmarks in Clinical Psychology[a]

1892	Hall, James, Cattell, Ladd, Jastrow, Fullerton, and Baldwin found the American Psychological Association (APA).
1896	Witmer founds the first psychological clinic.
1912	Witmer founds journal *Psychological Clinics* to represent clinical practitioners.
1917	Hollingworth founds the American Association of Clinical Psychologists.
1919	APA establishes a Clinical Section to represent clinical psychologists.
1921	J. M. Cattell founds the Psychological Corporation.
1935	APA Clinical Section establishes standards for clinical training and practice.
1936	Louttit publishes the first text on clinical psychology.
1937	American Association of Applied Psychologists is founded for clinical psychologists as an alternative to American Psychological Association.
1937	*Journal of Consulting Psychology* is founded.
1944	Clinical psychologists rejoin a reorganized APA.
1945	Thorne founds the *Journal of Clinical Psychology*.
1946	National Institute of Mental Health, United States Public Health Service, and Veterans Administration begin funding clinical training and service.
1946	Virginia becomes the first state to certify clinical psychologists.
1946	APA and American Psychiatric Association create a joint committee to promote cooperation.
1947	APA Committee on Training in Clinical Psychology reports training standards.
1947	American Board of Examiners in Professional Psychology (ABEPP) established to certify professional psychologists.
1949	Boulder APA National Conference endorses a scientist-practitioner training model.
1955	U.S. Mental Health Study Act mandates a national health program and established the Joint Commission on Mental Health (JCMH).
1963	Community Mental Health Centers Act evolves from the JCMH report.
1965	Separate training for professional psychologists first proposed.
1965	Boston Conference on Community Mental Health.
1973	APA National Conference at Vail reaffirms scientist-professional training but also endorses Psy.D. training in clinical psychology.
1974	APA National Conference at Austin establishes standards for community psychology training.

[a]Up to 1975.

luck in gaining acceptance in APA or for clinical psychologists as autonomous assessors or therapists. In an attempt to demonstrate high-quality standards for training and practice, to end any arguments that clinical psychologists had insufficient expertise to conduct therapy or assessment without a psychiatrist's supervision, the Clinical Section established a Ph.D. with at least 600 hours of internship training as the minimum qualifications for clinical psychologists. Two years later, clinical psychologists again split off from APA, in the American Association of Applied Psychologists (AAAP), in a further effort to achieve full professional recognition.

Although AAAP founded the *Journal of Consulting Psychology*, which still stands as the premier journal of clinical research (as the *Journal of Consulting and Clinical Psychology*), it was not until World War II when clinical psychologists served in the armed forces, and thus got the first taste of the excitement of clinical work, that they were induced to change their career directions away from other fields in psychology toward clinical research and practice (Britt & Morgan, 1946). APA once again reorganized to attract clinicians back to the fold, this time merging with AAAP but retaining the AAAP organizational plan that permitted major special interest groups such as clinicians to have full input in all policy decisions (Wolfe, 1946). Perhaps more important, the United States was flooded with emotionally distressed war veterans, to the point that an estimated 4700 new clinical psychologists were needed to provide psychological assessment and therapy in Veterans Administration facilities (Darley & Wolfe, 1946). Congress swiftly passed the 1946 Mental Health Act to establish the National Institute of Mental Health (NIMH), with the intent of training and employing mental health professionals who could *prevent* psychological dysfunctions (Snow & Newton, 1976). Although NIMH was largely controlled by psychiatrists, the professional manpower shortage induced them to provide funds to support clinical psychology training programs and their trainees. The Veterans Administration allocated funds to hire clinical psychologists as professional staff members and as interns, as did the U.S. Public Health Service (USPHS) (which supported hundreds of state mental hospitals).

Clinical psychologists responded by initiating a committee that established detailed standards for clinical training (American Psychological Association, 1947) under the direction of Shakow, and by commissioning a joint committee with the American Psychiatric Association to facilitate cooperation between the professions (Shaffer, 1947). These committees' recommendations led to the establishment of (1) the American Board of Examiners in Professional Psychology (ABEPP),[1] which continues to certify clinical psychologists as "diplomates" (signifying superior expertise) if they demonstrate high quality performance after at least five years of postdoctoral experience, (2) the APA Education and Training Board's Committee on Evaluation, which accredits graduate training programs in clinical psychology as having satisfactorily met all requirements for providing complete and excellent scientific and professional preparation for trainees, and (3) a *scientist-practitioner* model of training that requires trainees to demonstrate expertise in scholarship and research as well as in clinical assessment and intervention. The training model has come to be known as the Boulder model because it was strongly endorsed in a national APA conference at Boulder, Colorado, in 1949 (Raimy, 1950). The scientist-practitioner model was reaffirmed in subsequent national conferences in 1955 (Stanford) and 1958 (Miami) (Roe, Gustad, Moore, Ross, & Sokdak, 1959).

1950–1980   Public concern about a shortage of mental health professionals, particularly to serve disadvantaged populations such as racial minorities, grew

---

[1]The word "Examiners" was dropped from the title in 1968.

steadily in a political climate that saw legal breakthroughs in desegregation and welfare funding (e.g., *Brown* v. *Board of Education*, 1954; Economic Opportunity Act, 1964). In 1955 Congress passed the Mental Health Study Act, which mandated the development of a systematic national mental health treatment program and established the Joint Commission on Mental Illness and Health. The Joint Commission sponsored several surveys to assess the American public's current and future needs in mental health services (e.g., Gurin, Veroff, & Field, 1960), and prepared a final report (Joint Commission on Mental Health and Illness, 1961) that recommended the establishment of a nationwide network of community mental health centers. As a result, Congress passed the Community Mental Health Centers Act in 1963 to fund an anticipated 2000 CMHCs by 1975. Clinical psychologists were thus provided with still more opportunities for professional employment and training, with two significant impacts on the field.

First, it became increasingly apparent that many clinical psychologists were going to work primarily as assessors and therapists in facilities such as CHMCs, VA hospitals, and outpatient clinics. Some clinicians began to question the relevance of research training for such professional positions, and by 1965 an APA committee had tentatively recommended the establishment of separate professional schools for training clinical practitioners (Hoch, Ross, & Winder, 1966). Such training, leading to a Psy.D. (Doctor of Psychology), would involve less research training and more supervised clinical experience than in the scientist-practitioner Ph.D. programs. At present, over a decade later, approximately 25 Psy.D. and Professional Psychology programs have been successfully established but few have received APA accreditation.

Second, many clinical psychologists became concerned within very few years that CMHCs represented only a relocation of the traditional medical treatment and individual therapy approach from mental hospitals to community clinics. In 1965 a conference of psychologists who favored broader-scale intervention to prevent psychological dysfunctions by improving community environments inaugurated a community psychology model for professional psychologists (Bennett, Anderson, Cooper, Hassol, Klein & Rosenblum, 1966). In contrast to *community mental health*, which emphasizes making traditional medical and therapy services more accessible to all people, *community psychology* advocates going beyond traditional mental health services to aid citizens' groups, organizations, and communities to enhance the quality of life provided by their social environments. Despite a statement by APA endorsing the community psychology approach (Smith & Hobbs, 1966), the funding priorities established for CMHCs by the federal government clearly relegated community psychology services such as organizational development or program evaluation consultation to a secondary position (Snow & Newton, 1976). As a result, CMHCs have succeeded in extending individual therapy to a wider range of people, but they have not systematically initiated programs to help community groups enhance their total social environment (Windle, Bass, & Taube, 1974; Chu & Trotter, 1972). Clinical psychologists who have adopted a community psychology model have nevertheless continued to organize and develop innovative training and intervention programs (Iscoe, Bloom, & Spielberger, 1977).

Clinical psychologists face a larger challenge with their growing awareness of the political and economic influences on the public status of psychology (Bevan, 1980; Kaswan, 1981; Kiesler, 1980). Professional psychologists have founded the Association for Advancement of Psychology to provide a lobbying group for legislative impact. The involvement of psychologists in the legislative process, as consultants to legislators (e.g., Deleon, 1977) or direct advocates (Dörken, 1977, 1981), is becoming a critical frontier for the survival and development of the profession and science of clinical psychology.

CLINICAL PSYCHOLOGY: A SCIENTIST-PROFESSIONAL INTEGRATION

Clinical psychology is firmly established as a field within psychology that integrates scientific methods and professional services to develop innovative and effective theoretical, assessment, and intervention models for understanding human functioning and remedying psychological dysfunctions. New frontiers are rapidly emerging. More than ever, clinical practitioners (therapists, assessors, consultants) need expertise in scientific research in order to demonstrate their benefit to clients. Similarly, clinical researchers need to maintain their expertise in the practice of assessment and intervention in order to develop investigations that reflect the complexities of clinical practice and will provide useful information for practitioners.

Some psychologists nevertheless warn that a schism is separating clinical researchers and practitioners. For example, Albee (1970) stated that:

> The truly crippling sources of cognitive dissonance in the professional psychologists, which may ultimately destroy the unity of psychology, are the fundamental differences between the scientist and the professional. . . . Science is open, and its knowledge is public. . . . A freewheeling spirit of incisive mutual and self-criticism, replication, debate, and argument over procedures, fundings, and interpretation of data is ever present. In sharp contrast, a profession must jealously guard its secrets. . . . If the knowledge of the professional, his techniques, and his skills are available to anyone, and could be performed by anyone, a profession would disintegrate. Secrecy and mystery are essential. (pp. 1074–1075, italics in original)

Nevertheless, clinical psychologists have come to value both the rigor and openness of science and the expertise and social concern of professionalism, as is evident in three classic descriptions of a scientific-professional integration that span a 30-year period:

> Ideally, diagnosis (description) and treatment of each individual case may be regarded as a single well-controlled experiment. The treatment may be carefully controlled by utilizing single therapeutic factors, observing and recording results systematically, and checking through use of appropriate quantitative laboratory studies. In addition to the general scientific orientation to the individual case, there are frequent opportunities in clinical practice to conduct actual experiments to determine the validity of diagnosis or the efficacy of treatment. . . . Individual clini-

cians are encouraged to apply experimental and statistical methods in the analysis of case results, and larger scale analyses are made of the experience of the whole clinic over a period of years. (Thorne, 1947, pp. 159–166)

. . . the scientist-professional (is) a person who, on the basis of systematic knowledge about persons obtained primarily in real-life situations, has integrated this knowledge with psychological theory, and has then consistently regarded it with the questioning attitude of the scientist. . . . Thus, what defines the ''scientist-professional'' is the combination of the skilled acquisition of reality-based psychological understanding and the attitude of constant inquiry toward this knowledge. (Shakow, 1976, p. 554)

One of the unique beauties of being a psychotherapist in the 20th century is the opportunity for oscillation between observation and participation, between taking part and standing back, between feeling and thinking, between (controlled) abandonment and study. It is this process of oscillation, the unique human ability to resonate, identify, and therapeutically respond to the themes in the patient's experience (that is essential). . . . It should be possible to encourage research that is both rigorous and relevant to clinical and social issues; it should be possible for the therapist to become immersed in the patient's emotional experience and to reflect critically on the nature of the problem, that is, how, as a therapist, he or she might best proceed to alleviate the problem; it should be possible to be open to one's own humanity and range of emotional experience and as a psychological scientist to bring the methods of science to bear on understanding them. (Strupp, 1976, pp. 563; 570)

The unique contribution of clinical psychology is the application of *both* scientific and professional expertise to the development and provision of human services. The challenge facing clinical psychologists in the next decades and the twenty-first century is to simultaneously advance clinical research, assessment, and intervention in both training and practice.

Give me a firm spot on which to stand, and I will move the earth.

Archimedes

If we work marble, it will perish; if we work upon brass, time will efface it; if we rear temples, they will crumble into dust; but if we work upon immortal minds and instill into them just principles, we are then engraving that upon tablets which no time will efface, but will brighten and brighten to all eternity.

Daniel Webster

The Egyptian pyramids suggest the strength and power of a strong foundation.

2

TRAINING IN CLINICAL PSYCHOLOGY

Graduate education in clinical psychology leads to advanced degrees for students who have demonstrated competence in coursework and in written and oral examinations, attained skills in the professional aspects of clinical practice, and planned, executed and reported original research. Consistent with "the scientist-professional model," the doctoral-level student is trained in scientific methods, clinical techniques, and professional attitudes. As a result, most clinical psychology graduate programs seek to prepare students for a career in science (i.e., teaching and research), or professional service (i.e., assessment and intervention).

Since World War II, as various states developed licensing and certification laws, a doctoral degree, earned after four or five years of graduate training, has typically been set as the educational requirement for clinical psychologists. Well over 100 universities offer Ph.D.'s (Doctor of Philosophy) in clinical psychology, a few offer Psy. D.'s (Doctor of Psychology), and a limited number offer graduate training that culminates with the master's degree (two-year programs). Job opportunities for master's-level psychologists are limited in number, so these programs often encourage their students to enter doctoral programs after completing the master's degree. Our description of graduate education in clinical psychology focuses on doctoral-level training, because doctoral training is more broad and comprehensive, and more widely accepted by employers and licensing boards than master's training.

THE CONTENT OF TRAINING IN CLINICAL PSYCHOLOGY

Our description of graduate clinical training includes an overview of (1) the courses that constitute the *academic content*, (2) the guided *research experience*, and (3) the supervised *clinical experiences*.

47

Academic Content

In conjunction with the American Psychological Association's (1979) proposed guidelines for accreditation, certain courses are required by almost every graduate training program. In addition, most programs offer specialized courses in controversial or innovative topics and in areas that meet the particular needs of their students and the training program's emphasis (e.g., child-clinical, community-clinical).

Graduate training in clinical psychology initially includes a broad range of courses in the general field of psychology that are required of all graduate students in all the subareas of psychology. These courses, often called the *"core curriculum,"* usually include courses concerning the psychology of learning and motivation, the relationship of brain physiology to behavior, the psychology of human development, theories of personality, and the application of statistics and research design to clinical questions.

Participation in a special course called "proseminar" often is required within the core curriculum. The general format of a pro-seminar is a series of lectures by several different members of the faculty. For example, one portion of the proseminar may deal with *learning* in which four different instructors may lecture on such topics as classical conditioning, instrumental conditioning, observational learning, and biofeedback. Usually, only one instructor coordinates the lectures for the proseminar and is responsible for any tests, papers, or other materials used for grading.

The core curriculum is designed to provide the graduate student with a basic understanding of the content of general psychology and to provide the graduate institution with some evidence that the student has mastered the knowledge of psychology in general. The goal here is for the student to acquire solid knowledge of basic psychological science. This training procedure reflects the position that clinical psychologists are trained as psychologists first, with a specialty in the clinical area second.

As the student progresses through graduate training in clinical psychology, he or she will likely elect to take one or more seminars. *Seminars* are small groups of students that engage in advanced study and/or original research under the supervision of a faculty person. The desired outcome is that the student develop a detailed, advanced state of knowledge about specific topics. Seminars are scheduled just like classes, for example once a week for two or three hours. The list of particular topics that may be covered in a seminar is almost endless, including any topic of interest to a faculty member and several students. For example, seminars on "women in psychotherapy," "working with dying patients," or "the assessment of schizophrenia" are likely to be of interest. Often, areas of research that are currently under scrutiny in the literature are topics for seminars. Less often, but equally important, a seminar may be offered to fill what participants see as a gap in the existing training program. When grading criteria for successful completion of a seminar are employed, participation in the discussion and the completion of a graduate-level paper (either research or review) is likely, while tests are included less often.

Another format for advanced study is labeled "Readings and Research." Although much like a seminar in focus and requirements, *readings and research* courses are usually done by a single student with a single professor. The goal here is for the student to acquire skills in reading, synthesizing, and criticizing published research and the skills needed to plan and execute research. The student is required to complete readings in a specific area, and prepares a comprehensive review paper (in a readings course) or must develop specific hypotheses, carry out the necessary procedures, and report the results in written form (in a research course). At times two or more students may be involved on a research project and may sign up concomitantly for readings and research. Criteria for grading, however, are still likely to be based on individual performance. Such open-ended courses enable the student and instructor to develop close working ties not unlike those of an apprenticeship.

Along with coursework in psychology, there are often *language* and *minor* requirements. For the language requirement, where it still exists, students must demonstrate competence in one (sometimes two) language(s). This requirement, historically, was designed to assure that the student could read the published literature that appeared in a foreign language. However, since English is now the international language of science and English translations of foreign language publications are often available, the foreign language requirement is open to question. In many universities computer expertise can be substituted for one language.

In most cases courses in a related field of study such as sociology, statistics, physiology, or pharmacology will serve as a supporting area (minor). These courses are important in providing a broad understanding of each individual client and the social context of clinical work. For example, courses in sociology provide a framework for understanding the cultural impact on troubled clients while pharmacology helps the clinician understand the mechanisms of action of a client's medications. In some cases, the supporting area can be completed within the department of psychology by accumulating a sufficient number of course credits in a subarea (other than clinical) of the discipline. Both the language and minor area requirements vary substantially from one graduate school to another.

Additional Academic Requirements   In addition to the requirement that students complete certain coursework, there are often formal academic requirements such as a major review paper and/or comprehensive examinations.

The major review paper is an exhaustive review and integration of a specific area within the field of clinical psychology (see Table 2-1). For example, a student interested in diagnosis might write a paper reviewing the research methods used to evaluate diagnostic procedures. Another student may wish to review the literature on the accuracy of certain assessment instruments to predict the effectiveness of psychological treatment. In either case, the student would search the literature to locate the relevant writings on the topic, read the material, and review and integrate the findings. It is also important for the student to suggest what should be done to answer some of the questions not yet addressed in the literature.

Table 2-1   Abstracts of Two Sample Review Papers

CONVERSION REACTION: ANACHRONISM OR EVOLUTIONARY FORM?
A REVIEW OF THE NEUROLOGIC, BEHAVIORAL, AND
PSYCHOANALYTIC LITERATURE[a]

Molly Modrall Jones
Santa Fe Indian Hospital, Mental Health Branch, Indian Health Service,
Santa Fe, New Mexico

Conversion reactions such as hypoesthesia or anesthesia, which have appeared in contemporary society, are examined in a survey of the literature. The dynamics from neurophysiologic, behavioristic, and psychoanalytic points of view are considered. The relationship of conversion reactions to hysterical neuroses and the hysterical personality types and the boundaries for inclusion of symptoms are established. Neurologic formulations explore the role of inhibition at an operational level and the correlation between organic brain disease and conversion reaction disorders. Behavioristic and social learning theories deal with the effect of environmental stimulation on conversion reaction symptoms, whereas psychoanalytically oriented theory deals with repression, intrapsychic conflict, condensation, and displacement in producing conversion reaction. The role of culture, not only in expression but in diagnosis, is important to an understanding of the various manifestations of conversion reaction. The variety of subgroup cultural patterns in contemporary American society increases the variety of expressions of intrapsychic conflict or need. Psychological testing decreases the dependence on symptomatic diagnoses, providing information about the cognitive and affective styles that underlie symptoms, be they physical or behavioral.

SEX BIAS IN COUNSELING AND PSYCHOTHERAPY[b]

Mary Lee Smith
Laboratory of Educational Research, University of Colorado

The notion that existing research proves the sex bias inherent in counseling and psychotherapy is pervasive. Almost every subsequent study has taken as a major premise the finding by Broverman, Broverman, Clarkson, Rosenkrantz, and Vogel that clinicians hold different standards of mental health for men and women. In the present research, both the published and unpublished studies of sex bias in either counseling or psychotherapy were closely analyzed and their results integrated using meta-analytic techniques. The overall results from the meta-analysis showed an absence of bias against women or against nonstereotyped roles for women in studies of either counselors or psychotherapists. In published studies there was a small (.25 SD) sex-bias effect, and unpublished studies showed the same magnitude of bias *toward* women and a degree of rigor in research design at least as good as that evident in published studies.

According to many graduate students, the comprehensive examinations ("comps"), also known as preliminary examinations ("prelims"), are the most stressful hurdle in their graduate student experience. Under either title, these exams usually consist of a series of written questions that cover many topics from all areas of psychology. Some universities require an oral preliminary examination as well. In the oral exam the student meets with a committee of faculty members and the committee presents questions to the student to be answered in a discussion format.

It is not uncommon for the graduate program to require that students successfully fulfill "comps" requirements before they are formally admitted as candidates for the Ph.D. Some graduate institutions require that students take the preliminary examinations at one specified time during the year. In many settings the examinations are for one or two full days. At other institutions the preliminary examinations are offered in a staggered fashion. There may be four prelims, for example, that must be taken and passed by the student, but each one may be taken at a different time during the year.

Research Experiences

Ideally all graduate students in clinical psychology participate in ongoing research. An excellent format for the acquisition of research expertise is one in which one or more faculty members work with a team of graduate students, each of whom contribute according to his or her level of skill and experience. For example, a third-year graduate student does not need to spend extensive amounts of time collating data. The experienced student would learn more by contributing at a higher level such as supervising other less experienced members of the research team. A new and somewhat inexperienced student may, in contrast, need to observe research in progress before actively participating. During this observation it is desirable for the new student to have an opportunity to see as many of the different stages of the research project as possible (e.g., the design of the study, the collection and scoring of data, the process of data analysis and interpretation, and the writing of the research report). Also important within the research-team approach is the notion of learning and teaching among the participants. The advanced students are learning from supervisors and other students, but they are also teaching the newer and less-experienced members. Such a team approach attempts to assure that each person both learns and contributes maximally. This sharing of knowledge and skill provides for what may well be the most productive pedagogical system for graduate education.

Formal Research Requirements   The major research requirement encountered in graduate schools of clinical psychology is the *doctoral dissertation*. A clinical psychology doctoral dissertation is an extended research project that is written in scholarly fashion and intended to provide the student with an opportunity to contribute new information to the field of clinical psychology.

Dissertations are carefully designed studies that represent a great deal of personal effort on the part of the graduate student. They are original projects; planned, executed, and reported by the doctoral candidate. The development of a dissertation topic is undoubtedly facilitated by prior involvement in research; when the student actively participates in the conduct of research from the outset, the dissertation is not a new or unfamiliar hurdle. Research experiences available throughout graduate school provide the bulk of the training necessary to complete successfully the dissertation requirement.

At colleges or universities that offer a master's degree, or those that offer the student the option of discontinuing their graduate education and accepting a master's degree, graduate students are usually required to conduct a master's thesis. The master's thesis, an original research contribution carried out by the student, is like the doctoral dissertation though typically less extensive. Again, if the student has been involved in a research team and if the members of the team have been educating each other, the thesis is an exciting task, not just a requirement. In many instances, students feel great pride and pleasure in the fact that this time, whether it be the master's thesis or the doctoral dissertation, they are the central figure in the study—they have designed and conducted the study and will write the research report.

Clinical Experiences

The graduate student in clinical psychology can expect to be an active participant in many clinical activities. As in research participation, clinical experiences are designed for involvement in advancing stages. For example, students often begin by observing clinical interviews. This provides opportunities for witnessing clinicians in action, and for discussing cases with practicing clinicians. Next, the student may be given the responsibility for conducting an interview, thereby gaining some first hand experience in a clinical role. Students develop assessment skills by first observing the administration of various psychological tests and then having the opportunity to administer and interpret the tests under supervised conditions. Gradual exposure to the roles of therapist or consultant proceed in a similar fashion: the student is likely to first be a cotherapist or coconsultant with a practicing clinician "sitting in", then to conduct a therapy or consultation session while being observed, and finally to provide therapy or consultation under gradually less direct supervision.

With this experience completed, students undertake more involved tasks such as conducting a psychological assessment and writing a comprehensive and integrated psychological report or initiating and completing a therapy case. Additionally, experienced students may later be called on to aid in the supervision of novice trainees.

Formal Clinical Requirements   There are a number of interrelated formal clinical requirements that the clinical graduate student will encounter: practicum placements, case conferences, clinical supervision, and internship.

Practicum placements   Practica (the plural of practicum) are brief training experiences in a variety of different clinical settings in the community. Practicum assignments often begin with assessment experiences and progress to therapy experiences, and they change location each semester (or quarter, depending on the university schedule). One semester the student may be placed at a Veterans Administration Hospital psychology service where he or she might perform psychological assessments, seeking to better understand and aid former service men and women who are having problems in adjustment. During another semester's practicum the trainee may be placed at the university's counseling center where clinical experiences would be with college students or community residents with a variety of adjustment problems. Still another practicum may be at a community mental health clinic. In this case, the opportunities to work with community groups, families, and couples would be increased.

Initially, different practicum experiences provide the student with an exposure to the many available roles for clinical psychologists. Later in training, as the student further specializes, practicum experiences should be tied to the particular career goals of the student. For example, a student interested in child-clinical psychology might spend advanced practica at centers for disturbed children such as child guidance clinics, adolescent residential schools, and children's psychiatric hospitals. Similarly, clinical trainees who are planning careers with a family therapy orientation would actively seek family therapy practicum placements. Supervised practica provide assessment, therapy, and consultation experiences, and each experience results in a written evaluation of the student's performance by the practicum supervisor.

Case conferences   In nearly every field setting that students in training may find themselves, there will most likely be a weekly *case conference*. These meetings provide the professional staff with an opportunity to discuss particular cases or topics that are of relevance to their current clinical work. For the most part, case conferences concentrate on matters of assessment and/or therapy, but conferences may also focus on ethical or professional issues as well. For example, a member of the clinical staff and a student might present a case where the client's diagnosis is in question. Copies of the assessment data (e.g., test scores, clinician's observations) are distributed to the case conference participants and the question of diagnosis is put before the group. In other instances, the conference may focus on providing suggestions for how best to provide therapy for the client under study.

Although the student typically takes a turn in presenting a case, all students and staff alike are active participants from the audience in every case conference. Case conferences of high quality are open and stimulating meetings with many opportunities for everyone to share ideas and observations (Highlight 2-1). However, case conferences can also fail, as Meehl's (1973) paper, "Why I do not attend case conferences," illustrates. Essentially, Meehl advocates a lesser emphasis on verbal discussion and a serious effort to incorporate more scientific standards into case conferences. Rather than discussing whether or not a client is "extremely anxious," for example, Meehl prefers concise analysis based on scientific interpretations of psychological test data and practical recommendations for the optimal therapeutic intervention based on research findings from studies of the treatment of similar clients.

In some instances individual participants in the case conference may be appointed to help keep the case conferences flowing and stimulating. Case conferences can get bogged down when a few people take over or when one individual digresses on a tangential point, so the role of an appointed coordinator, or "process monitor," is to outline the purpose of the conference and to facilitate constructive group discussion of the central issues. Often the position of process monitor is rotated so that every participant understands and is receptive to the efforts of the current leader.

Highlight 2-1   Case Conference on Termination: An Example of the Ante-Up System

One of the issues to be resolved in all therapy cases has to do with when therapy will be terminated. In some instances, clients do not feel capable of stopping therapy, yet termination is just what the therapist has prescribed! At other times, when the therapist sees a real need for continued treatment, the client terminates against the therapist's advice. How can these termination issues be dealt with? What are some methods for effective termination?

A case conference is an excellent setting for discussion of termination issues. Using the ante-up system, many people can have the opportunity to speak and to share their expertise. The ante-up format is simple—if you wish to be recognized by the conference coordinator and speak to the group you must be prepared to "ante-up" your personal case-related solution. For example, a videotape of a termination session may be played for the case conference group, and at the point where the therapist and client have a conflict the tape would be stopped. Each potential speaker, whether they want to give feedback to the therapist on tape or comment to the group at large, must first "ante-up" by stating exactly what they would do if they were in the taped situation, and why.

Via the ante-up system, a large number of individuals will get both the chance to make comments and the opportunity to say exactly what they would do in the specific case. The experienced clinicians serve as models for those in training by providing actual responses that could be useful in a variety of difficult instances. For example, what would be the professionally appropriate behavior when a client expresses affection for the therapist and therefore does not wish to terminate? How should a therapist respond to a client who makes a suicidal gesture primarily to influence the therapist to continue therapy? What responsibilities does the therapist have for a patient who leaves a voluntary hospital service against professional advice? Rather than leaving the novice therapist to blunder through several initial cases before acquiring a repertoire of skills, the videotaped case illustrates a particular termination problem, and the case conference participants offer suggestions on how to deal with the specific example. The ante-up system prevents repetitious comments from the same person and also guarantees that each comment has an applied focus rather than being a pedantic demonstration.

Clinical supervision   Supervision of student's work as psychological assessors, therapists, and consultants is an integral part of clinical training. The novice clinician must not only acquire many sophisticated skills, but also overcome the anxiety and lack of self-assurance that is associated with the performance of a new task in full view of others. In supervision, the student is given feedback about the strong and weak spots during the sessions with clients. For example, a student-therapist's comments during therapy sessions may be excessively forceful suggestions that the client should improve *now*. The tendency on the part of novice therapists to rush the process of change in their clients would be pointed out by the supervisor and discussed with suggestions for a more effective style.

Novice clinicians may also be trapped or manipulated by clients: for instance, a client may digress from a key problem and manage to keep the focus of the therapy session on a less-provoking topic. The supervisor would direct the student's attention to this and also to the client's verbal and nonverbal behaviors that were a part of the diversion. Again, alternative actions for the clinician can be discussed, enabling the trainee to handle this situation more flexibly and effectively in the future.

Supervision is sometimes conducted in a small group, during which a single supervisor provides feedback to several trainees (typically 2 to 4) about the progress of a particular therapy session, a case, or several cases. Supervision is facilitated by an audio or videotape of the session, since the group can thus observe both the student and the client in action. Therapy supervision is usually provided by members of the faculty of the graduate clinical program and by the psychologists and other human service professionals who are functioning in local community agencies.

Internship   The internship is an intensive clinical experience. According to the APA criteria for acreditation of clinical programs, the internship is an essential component of doctoral training. It is scheduled at or near the end of the student's graduate training and it provides the trainee with the opportunity to grow personally and professionally while integrating academic course content and clinical skills. Trainees are also given the opportunity, with supervision, to take responsibility for major professional functions. More than 40 years ago, clinicians were endorsing the value of practical experiences such as the internship (Hildreth, 1937; Shakow 1938).

> *What are the aims of the psychological internship? Underlying all of its aims is the fundamental principle that the knowledge essential to the practice of psychology cannot be obtained solely from books, lectures, or any other devices which merely provide information* about *people. Rather, experience* with *people is held to acquire a proper perspective and the ability to apply the scientific facts which he has accumulated. (Shakow 1938, APA Committee Report)*

Internships in clinical psychology require a full-time experience for one year, or in some cases two years of halftime experience. Professional-level performance is required on assessment, intervention, and (in some cases) research assignments. The student often has the option to rotate through two or three different settings within the internship facility and thus select different professional duties for specialization. The internship is usually taken at independent clinical training centers, although some students choose to do their internships at an on-campus clinical facility. Internship agencies are evaluated by the American Psychological Association (APA) and the list of APA approved internships is published each December in the *American Psychologist*. In 1979 there were 153 fully approved and 14 provisionally approved internships. Four internship locations were listed as on probation. In addition to those evaluated by APA, there are many other agencies that provide quality internship experiences.

The decision to take an internship on campus or away is usually up to each individual student. Staying at the university maintains continuity of training and research involvement. But the internship is also an excellent opportunity for the student to strike out on his or her own and begin to function more like an independent professional. When real-world issues such as finance or family ties do not interfere, the student may experience more individual growth and more professional development at an internship facility away from the university.

Methods of Clinical Training   At this point you may be curious as to exactly how the assessment and intervention skills of the professional clinician are taught to the trainee. Modeling, rehearsal and feedback, and direct instructions are three of the most frequently used training methods and there has been a good deal of research concerning the efficacy of these methods (Ford, 1979; Matarazzo, 1971; 1978).

Modeling involves direct demonstrations of skills or behaviors—"seeing it done before your very eyes," as it were. For example, if the clinical skill being taught were that of asking open-ended questions during initial therapy sessions, trainees might be shown how to do this via a live "role-play demonstration by their teacher, by watching such a demonstration on videotape, by watching a real therapy session from behind a one-way window, by listening to it on audiotape, or by reading several written examples of it. Trainees might be shown both good and bad examples, and given cues to look for to be able to identify, for example, a good open-ended question from a poor one. Modeling is a very important part of training when trainees are just beginning to learn new skills, because "a picture can be worth a thousand words."

Rehearsal and feedback are often used once the skill has been demonstrated. An essential next step in the learning process is to "try out" the new skill and to learn by trial and error (or better yet, by trial and success). The old saying that "practice makes perfect" is trite but true. Trainees are typically given many opportunities to rehearse the skills that they are acquiring, often through role-play simulations. For example, one trainee can take the role of "client" while another acts as the "therapist." Rehearsal can also be accomplished by conducting single intake interviews with clients who are applying for help at a clinic, by "sitting in" as a therapeutic aide or cotherapist with a more experienced clinician, or even by taking the responsibility for conducting a full-fledged therapy case with supervision. The key to this training method is not just the opportunity to "get your feet wet" (although this is important), but the constructive feedback that is provided during or after the practice session.

Effective feedback has several characteristics: it clearly points out exactly what the trainee did correctly[1] and what he or she did incorrectly or failed to do. For example, "Your first question was an excellent open-ended one, but your next question was closed-ended because the client had no choice except to say 'yes' or 'no.'" It also involves sincere but not exaggerated praise for correct behaviors and constructive suggestions for how to improve the incorrect or omitted behaviors. Good feedback is also as immediate as is possible. For example, colored

[1]"Correct" and "incorrect" are used as shorthand ways of expressing the idea that some behaviors are judged to be "on target" and others to be "less than optimal." Even in the most flexible and open training program, such value judgments are inescapable. The terms are *not* meant to imply, however, that there are universally "good" or "bad" behaviors for clinical psychologists, because the opinions on what is correct versus incorrect can vary.

lights can be used as visual signals telling the trainee whether he or she is on or off target as the interview is actually ongoing. Or feedback can be provided in conjunction with an audio or videotape playback of the practice session so the trainee and trainer can see exactly what they are talking about. Feedback should first be provided by a trained supervisor, but gradually the trainees themselves can become involved in providing feedback (Ford, 1979).

All clinical training programs utilize *direct instructions* as a method for teaching clinical skills, and some rely on written and spoken instructions as the major training method. Instructions are different from modeling in that they involve verbal directions (i.e., listing what to do, in words) rather than showing by example, and from feedback in that they describe future behaviors rather than evaluating current or past behaviors. Prepared handouts, lectures, and textbooks are the major vehicles for direct instructions.

Research evaluations   More than 100 studies have been done to test training methods (cf. Ford, 1977; 1979). It is important to note that many of these researchers have failed to live up to some of the guidelines for scientific rigor, and that the results from this large research literature therefore must be considered somewhat *tentative* at present. It is the task of the next generation of researchers to conduct better-designed studies to develop clinical training methods further. Still, the data offer some reasonably consistent evidence that *modeling is effective* in helping clinical trainees acquire new skills and that *rehearsal with feedback* is equally effective in aiding trainees to improve on skills that they have begun to acquire. The combination of modeling plus rehearsal and feedback offers a powerful one-two punch that appears superior to either method used alone. *Instructions* fare less well when evaluated as a training method, having been shown to be less effective than either modeling or feedback. However, instructions do facilitate modeling and/or feedback, suggesting that all three would make an excellent training package.

Integrated Clinical Training Strategies   Microcounseling, Interpersonal Process Recall, and Integrated Didactic-Experiential Training are three examples of training procedures that employ a carefully tailored sequence of training methods in an effort to systematically develop the trainee's clinical skills.

Microcounseling   Ivey and his colleagues (1971) developed Microcounseling as a systematic sequence of training methods. Trainees focus on learning one, or at most two or three, well-defined therapy skills through participating in the following sequence of learning experiences: (1) videotaping a five-minute role-play therapy session, (2) reading a manual that describes the skills to be learned, (3) viewing model therapists who demonstrate correct and incorrect examples, (4) viewing their own videotape, receiving very specific feedback from an experienced trainer, and rating their own performance, (5) role playing a therapy session with the trainer, to get modeling, practice, and feedback, and (6) videotaping a second role-play therapy session, to evaluate how much they have learned. Microcounseling has been found to be superior to lectures or nonspecific supervision for teaching moderately complex therapy skills and equally or more effective than Integrated Didactic-Experimental Training (Ford, 1979).

Interpersonal Process Recall   Kagan and his colleagues (1967; 1973) developed Interpersonal Process Recall as another way to integrate the major training methods in a systematic sequential program. While similar to Microcounseling in many ways, Interpersonal Process Recall adds new dimensions through (1) the provision of feedback to trainees from a therapy client, (2) having trainees rate the proficiency of model therapists who are viewed on videotape, and (3) providing several opportunities to rehearse interviewing skills with a real client. Trainees receive modeling, opportunities for rehearsing clearly defined skills, and specific performance feedback similar to that provided in Microcounseling. They are also able to watch as their own clients view a videotape of their therapy sessions and describe what they were thinking and feeling and what they liked and disliked about the therapist's (trainee's) actions. Other trainees conduct these "recall sessions" with a trainer as cotherapist and on their own. Interpersonal Process Recall has been shown to be more effective than "traditional" supervision which involved only general discussion of cases (Ford, 1979).

Integrated Didactic-Experiential Training   Truax and Carkhuff (1967) originally developed Integrated Didactic-Experiential Training in order to train the specific skills of "client-centered" therapists (Rogers, 1951). The training methods are very similar to those in Microcounseling and Interpersonal Process Recall. A systematic sequence of instructions, modeling, practice in evaluating the model's proficiency, and several role play rehearsals (with self-ratings and specific feedback from an experienced trainer) are provided. In addition, the supervisors strive to model the facilitative conditions and to provide a supportive learning milieu throughout training. Also, trainees participate in what is labeled "quasigroup therapy"; this is a group experience in which trainees attempt to facilitate one another's development of therapeutic abilities, and not a personal growth therapy experience per se (hence the word "quasi"). Integrated Didactic-Experiential Training has been extensively researched, showing it to be more effective than lectures, "traditional" supervision, or "experiential" training alone (Ford, 1979).

An Example of a Typical Program

Many of the Ph.D. training programs in clinical psychology are five-year programs, and a few are four-year programs. For the full-time Ph.D. student who continues to matriculate as outlined, most programs take four years to complete the academic, research, and practica requirements and an additional year for the internship (Highlight 2-2).

Highlight 2-2   Master's-Level Clinical Psychologists

Thousands of psychologists across the world have completed their formal education at the master's level. A minority of graduate training programs in clinical psychology offer only an MA (Master of Arts) or MS (Master of Science) degree, and some Ph.D. clinical programs allow or request trainees to stop with only an MA or MS. The master's-level psychologist has usually received two years of graduate training. Clinical psychologists have been concerned that master's-level training is not sufficient to produce competent scientist-professionals (Albee, 1977a).

Master's-level clinical psychologists face several advantages and disadvantages compared to Ph.D. clinical psychologists. MA or MS psychologists are not eligible to be licensed as independent providers of psychological services in most states, so they cannot conduct clinical work unless they are directly supervised by a Ph.D. or M.D. licensed clinician. However, master's-level psychologists can do special kinds of counseling that are not deemed exclusively "psychological" in some states: for example, in California, hundreds of MA and MS psychologists are certified as "marriage, family, and child therapists" each year, qualifying them to do therapy without supervision from a licensed clinician.

Master's-level psychologists usually take jobs that pay less than comparable positions for Ph.D. clinical psychologists. For example, in a survey of 300 mental health and human service agencies in Illinois, Dimond, Havens, Rathnow, and Colliver (1977) found the average beginning salary for MA or MS personnel to be $11,000 and the average maximum salary to be $17,000. In contrast, Ph.D. clinicians' salaries usually began at about $13,000 (in universities) to $17,000 (in hospitals and clinics), and may rise as high as $25–30,000 or more. The lower pay scale may prove to be advantageous for some MA or MS psychologists in the current tight economic situation: employers may seek the lower-paid MA or MS rather than pay a Ph.D.'s salary. (Note that these data, published in 1977, were probably collected around 1975. Actual salaries have changed to keep pace with inflation.)

Master's-level psychologists spend most of their professional time doing therapy (56%) or psychological testing (15%), according to Dimond et al. (1977). They report devoting time to consultation (10%) and inservice training (8%), research (5%), and administration (4%). Compared to Ph.D. clinical psychologists (Garfield & Kurtz, 1976a), MA or MS psychologists do more therapy, testing, and consultation but less research, administration, and teaching.

The American Psychological Association does not admit MA or MS psychologists as full members (unless the degree was earned prior to the decision to limit membership to Ph.D.s). Thus, although job prospects appear good for master's-level psychologists according to the Dimond et al. (1977) survey—nearly 90% of the agencies surveyed projected an increased or stable demand for MA or MS psychologists over the next five years—they are not eligible for recognition as independent professionals by the major organization of psychologists. Many master's-level psychologists are undoubtedly highly skilled and effective as therapists and testers, by virtue of many years of experience and good (although brief, unless post-MA/MS continuing education is obtained) training, but their status as scientist-professionals remains in doubt.

The first year entails basic training in content areas such as the material covered by courses in the core curriculum. It is not uncommon for all beginning psychology graduate students, not just the clinical students, to take numerous core courses together. In addition to these general psychology courses, clinical students are often required to begin involvement in assessment and interviewing. Also, research involvement is begun during this period with the student being directed by a professor and working with a research team.

In the second year clinical students will find both required coursework and some electives, mixed in with practica and thesis (master's level) requirements. Recall that not all universities require a Masters thesis, so this component may not appear in all descriptions of graduate programs. Students will continue developing assessment, therapy, research and consultation skills through both course content and practical experiences. Efforts toward completion of requirements such as the major review paper or the comprehensive examinations are typically begun during this year.

In five-year programs the third year is designed for additional coursework and advanced seminars, completing the minor and/or language requirements, and gaining additional experiential training. In four-year training programs, the third year is often specified for the doctoral dissertation.

The fourth year of a five-year program can be focused on either the dissertation or the internship. Depending upon this choice, the completion of the remaining requirement takes a final year (Highlight 2-3).

Highlight 2-3   Training in Clinical Psychology in Other Countries

The discipline of clinical psychology and the functions that clinical psychologists perform are remarkably alike in the United States, Canada, Great Britain, Europe, Africa, Asia, and throughout the world. Clinical psychologists worldwide are people whose daily working life concerns the understanding and resolution of problems of human behavior. Though the exact roles and responsibilities of clinical psychologists around the globe are variable, clinicians contribute to decisions about the diagnosis, treatment, management, placement, and guidance of clients with problems in living.

The training that is required to be a clinical psychologist differs from country to country. From a survey of 23 countries, Fichter and Wittchen (1980) reported finding a great deal of variation in type and length of training required to become a clinical psychologist. "Psychology" can be pursued as an academic course of study in all 23 countries, but the possibilities of specializing in "clinical psychology" varied widely. The requirement of an internship also varied (see table).

Table for Highlight 2-3   University Training in Clinical Psychology by Country

Country	Duration (years)[a]	Title	Formally Defined Specialization	Internship[b]
Australia	5	M.A., M.Sc., M.Ps.	Specialization possible	No
	7–8	Doctorate		
Austria	6	Doctorate	[c]	No

Table for Highlight 2-3 *Continued*

Country	Duration (years)[a]	Title	Formally Defined Specialization	Internship[b]
Belgium	4–5	License in psychology	Specialization without leading to special title	1 year[d]
	8–10	Doctorate		
Canada	4 + 2	M.A.	Specialization possible	Approximately 1 year
	4 + 2 + 3	Doctorate		
Czechoslovakia	4	Promov. Psych.	No	No
	5	Ph.Dr.		
	7	C.Sc.		
Denmark	5 ½	Cand. Psych.	Specialization without leading to special title	No
	8	Mag. Arts.		
France	5	Maitrise	Almost exclusively for psychodiagnostics (no specific title)	No
	6–7	Doctorate		
East Germany	5	Dipl.-Psych.	Specialization in clinical psychology possible	No
	c	Doctorate		
West Germany	5	Dipl.-Psych.	Specialization without leading to special title	No
	8	Doctorate		
Great Britain	3 + 2	M.Phil., M.Sc.	Special exam for title[e]	
	3 + 3	Dipl. Clin. Psy. (B.P.S.)		
	3 + 2 + 3	Doctorate		
Greece	4	Major in psychology	No	No
	c	Doctorate		
Iceland	No	g	No	No
Italy	4	Laurea in Psychology (M.A.)	Some specialization possible (without special title)	No
Luxembourg	No	No	No	No
The Netherlands	6	Doctorate	Specialization in clinical psychology possible	Approximately 1 year

Table for Highlight 2-3 *Continued*

Country	Duration (years)[a]	Title	Formally Defined Specialization	Internship[b]
New Zealand	3 + 2	M.A.	Specialization during postgraduate training	1 year
Norway	6½	Cand. Psychol.	No	2 years[h]
Poland	7½	Doctorate	Specialization possible	No
Portugal	5	M.A.	Specialization possible	No
Soviet Union	5	Dipl. Psych.	Certain specialization possible	No
	c	Doctorate		
Sweden	5	Grad. Psychol.	No	1 year
Canton of Basel, Switzerland	4 / 5	Lic. Phil. Doctorate	Specialization possible	c
United States	4 + 2	M.A., M.Sc.	Specialization during postgraduate training or doctoral course of study	At least 1 year
	4 + 5	Doctorate		

[a]Counted from high school graduation on.

[b]Practical work of short duration not included.

[c]No information available.

[d]At Louvain University only.

[e]The Dipl.Clin.Psy. is merely specialization in clinical psychology for the M.Phil. or M.Sc.

[f]The Dipl.Clin.Psy. involves three years in practice.

[g]A masters program is planned; there has been a Dipl.Clin.Psy. program, similar to that in Great Britain since 1978.

[h]This is from a total of five years of postgraduate training as a specialist in clinical psychology.

Note: M.Sc. = MS, Master of Science.

From M. M. Fichter and H. Wittchen, Clinical psychology and psychotherapy: A survey of the present state of professionalization in 23 countries. *American Psychologist*, 1980, *35*, 16–25. Copyright 1980 by the American Psychological Association. Reprinted by permission.

According to *Careers in Psychology*, a publication of the British Psychological Society (1977), it takes five to eight years of higher education to qualify as a clinical psychologist in Great Britain. There are two requirements, (1) an initial degree in psychology (e.g., undergraduate degree), followed by (2) postgraduate professional training (e.g., graduate school). There are two types of postgraduate training: either (1) two years postgraduate training at a university or teaching hospital, or (2) three years inservice training as a "probationer." Academic training often emphasizes research, with less practical experience than the inservice training, and is more likely to lead to employment at a university. The inservice experience, much like an extended internship, places greater emphasis on the provision of clinical services. Training in clinical psychology in Scotland is the same as in England in all respects.

However, the training in Italy, for example, is different. Following elementary, junior, and senior high school, the student is required to get a degree in philosophy (four years) or medicine (six years) and then a specialization in psychology (three years). In the early 1970s an alternative training sequence was made available at institutions in Padua and Rome. Here, students could earn their four-year degree in psychology. During the first two years the student must pass 10 fundamental examinations covering general psychology and a test of English comprehension. The last two years provide specialization in one of three branches: applicative, experimental, or didactic. Psychological testing and intervention are emphasized in the applicative branch, research is the focus of the experimental branch, and the teaching of psychology is stressed in the didactic branch. A thesis is required in all three branches.

As Fichter and Wittchen pointed out (1980), the training of clinical psychologists in socialist countries of Eastern Europe is quite different from the United States, for example. In the Soviet Union, schools of psychology have developed independently of Western tendencies (e.g., psychoanalytic schools are almost completely ignored). There are about 250 clinical psychologists in the entire country, hardly any of whom practice psychotherapy. This is probably the result of the Soviet Union's restricting psychotherapeutic treatment almost exclusively to physicians. In Czechoslovakia, one can take some courses in clinical psychology; however, there is no formal specialized training leading to a special title. At present, Fichter and Wittchen (1980) note that four-year university courses in psychology permit one to carry out psychotherapeutic treatment. However, as in other socialist countries, clinical psychologists practicing psychotherapy are employed by the state health service: there are no private practitioners.

TRAINING PHILOSOPHIES IN CLINICAL PSYCHOLOGY

Training in clinical psychology has been guided by varying philosophies. In 1945, Shakow observed and described four emphases that he labeled dynamic, diagnostic, diagnostic-therapeutic, and experimental. The *dynamic* approach focused primarily on the study of individual cases, with a special interest in the individual's motivations and personality. The second approach focused on *diagnosis*: the use of psychological test data to shed light on clients' adjustment and maladjustment with a view toward making recommendations for therapy that would be carried out by others. The *diagnostic-therapeutic* approach reflected an interest in diagnostic testing but with a special interest in the therapeutic implications of test results. This approach differs from the dynamic in that it places more emphasis on the test data and it is different from the diagnostic approach since it emphasizes the clinician's role in gathering diagnostic information and in providing therapeutic interventions. The fourth emphasis, the *experimental* approach, did not stress therapy, but rather was concerned with the establishment of scientific laws about the psychology of deviancy.

Perhaps the most notable distinction among training programs today, a distinction that was seen also in Shakow's (1945) models, is the relative emphasis placed on scientific and/or professional experience. Training varies along a continuum from almost total emphasis on the scientific to near total focus on the professional. Our discussion considers today's approaches to training under the headings of *scientist, professional,* and *scientist-professional.*

Emphasis on the Scientist

Within the scientific focus of clinical training we can identify two somewhat independent emphases: the study of the effects of certain conditions on the development of psychological dysfunctions (experimental psychopathology) and the study of the factors involved in the development of personality (personality research). In both cases training would include an abundance of coursework in such areas as the proper way to design and evaluate research projects, the cognitive, behavioral, and emotional symptoms that characterize various abnormal behavior patterns, and the theories of personality and psychological dysfunction. The purpose of such a training emphasis is to prepare the student for a career in research.

Experimental Psychopathology   Training in experimental psychopathology typically involves learning conceptualizations and methods for researching the causes and/or characteristics of different types of psychological dysfunction. For example, clinical psychologists investigate the possible causes of mental retardation, test certain proposed explanations of depression, and study the factors leading to excessive anxiety.

A topic that has been of interest within experimental psychopathology is the study of neurosis. Neurosis is the category of disorders characterized by unrealistic anxiety. Because we cannot ethically create neuroses in humans, researchers have instead created conditions that produce "anxiety" in animals and studied the resulting maladaptive behavior. The experimental procedures introduced by Russian physiologists (Pavlov and others) that have been used to study "experimental neurosis" involve forcing an animal to make increasingly difficult discriminations until it can no longer differentiate between two similar stimuli. For instance, dogs have been taught to make a response to indicate a recognition of the difference between a circle and an ellipse. Gradually, the stimuli were made more alike, thus making the discrimination progressively more difficult. The result was a breakdown in the dog's ability to make the discrimination, resulting in a disturbance in the dog's normal behavior pattern. Some of the more noticeable changes included howling, biting, attempting to get free, and in some cases, falling asleep. Gantt conducted additional research (1944; 1971) using rats, Masserman (1943) using cats, and Liddell (1944) using sheep, and recent research has focused on a neurological analysis of the experimental neurosis phenomena (Thomas & DeWald, 1977).

The learned helplessness model of depression is another product of the experimental psychopathology focus. First, it is important it recognize that depression is a serious problem for many people: it involves emotional states of sadness, worthlessness, and guilt, as well as negative perceptions of the self, future, and world, and withdrawal from other people and a loss of appetite and sleep. The learned helplessness model is an initial attempt to define some of the causes of this multifaceted dysfunction (see also Gurber & Seligman, 1980).

The original experiments on learned helplessness used dogs as subjects to delineate the factors involved in their learning to make avoidance responses—responses that allow a subject to prevent a noxious situation. In a typical experiment two groups of dogs receive different experiences prior to their exposure to the avoidance task. One group initially receives a series of inescapable shocks while the other group receives either no shocks or escapable shocks. When the individual dogs from both groups were later put in a situation where they could run to escape shock, the dogs that had previously experienced the inescapable shock did not learn the avoidance responses whereas the other dogs soon learned to run to avoid the shock. The early exposure to the inescapable shock dramatically affected the ability of the dogs to learn the new response. These dogs appeared to have learned to behave in a "helpless" fashion.

In further research with humans, Seligman and his colleagues have reported some similarities between these helpless animals and depressed humans (see Seligman, 1975). The helplessness model has been reformulated in line with more recent data and the specifics of the reformulation are discussed in Chapter 5.

Personality Research. This scientific aspect of clinical training focuses on the study of various characteristics of people, how these characteristics are integrated within each person, how best to measure these characteristics, and how these personality characteristics are related to actual behavior. Topical concerns for personality research might include the nature/nurture controversy, the question of the existence of traits, and attempts to identify the important characteristics of personality that can be used to predict future behavior.

The "nature/nurture" controversy can be restated as the genetic/environment issue. Consider introversion: is a person's reserved, cautious, and nonsocial style a genetic given? Is introversion the result of the biological contributions of two parents? Can breeding practices alter a person's level of introversion? Or, on the other hand, should we accept the viewpoint that the environment provides the experiences that "make the person" an introvert, regardless of genetic or biological differences? Can an introverted personality be the sole result of the social and psychological environments produced by two parents? To the extent that the content of investigation deals with personality, untangling the nature/nurture issue is an integral part of training in personality research.

In the attempt to predict future behavior, psychologists have measured certain distinctive personality characteristics, called "traits," and used these assessments of personality predispositions to make bets on future behavior. For example, a researcher might develop a personality test to measure introversion and test to see if subjects' scores on this test can predict whether or not they will behave in ways characteristic of introversion (e.g., not seeking out others for social events).

Emphasis on the Professional

A focus on professional (practitioner) training can be found among both the very traditional and the very contemporary approaches to training in clinical psychology. The professional training philosophy is one in which experiential training in the conduct of therapy, assessment, and other professional practices is stressed. Advanced courses in research methodology and the requirement of extensive research work by students are seen as secondary in importance.

The first training philosophy to emphasize primarily professional training in clinical psychology was spurred by psychoanalysis. In the study of psychoanalytic therapy it is often required that the therapist-in-training gain extensive experience in the analytic study of others as well as undergoing a personal analysis. Psychological research, in the scientific sense that we know it, is almost entirely absent. Descriptive discussions and nonquantitative case-studies provide the basic support for the psychoanalytic methods. Some contemporary training programs from a variety of theoretical backgrounds (e.g., behavioral, cognitive, dynamic) have retained the emphasis on experiential training of therapy skills.

The assessment and diagnostic function of the professional clinician is highlighted in other professional training programs. Extensive supervised experience in the use of psychological tests for diagnosis takes on paramount importance. Two issues are focal in such training. First, how can the practicing clinician best differentiate the various types of psychological dysfunctions? What types of tests, measurements, or observations are the most useful in diagnosis? Second, how can the assessment data from various sources best be integrated to help understand the person? Often, a theoretical model is adopted to help organize and integrate the assessment data. Because the emphasis is on the role of the clinician as a professional assessor, the scientific skills necessary for researching the accuracy of the psychological tests and observations would be down-played in relation to the clinical skills needed to make interpretations of test data.

A very contemporary training practice (it is still new and developing) that has underscored professional training is embodied by "*professional schools*" of psychology. "Professional schools" are institutions that are administered by practicing professional psychologists and that award a degree for advanced training that emphasizes professional experiences.

There are two somewhat different types of "professional schools." One is associated with an institution of higher learning, while the other is not. The California School of Professional Psychology[2] is an early example of the latter, a so-called "freestanding" school. (Highlight 2-4)

The graduate program in Clinical Psychology in the University of Illinois at Urbana-Champaign has offered both the traditional Doctor of Philosophy (Ph.D.) degree and a recently introduced Doctor of Psychology (Psy.D.) degree, both of which have been approved by the American Psychological Association.[3]

---

[2]The California School of Professional Psychology in Los Angeles is one of the few to receive APA accreditation.

[3]Rutgers University, for example, also offers both types of graduate training with APA approval.

Highlight 2-4   Positive and Negative Perspectives on "Professional Schools"

POSITIVE

A number of psychologists have taken supportive positions in regard to professional training. For instance Adler (1972) saw professional training in clinical psychology as desirable because the existing training models neglected the manpower needs of society. Research interests were placed over clinical interests and were given greater support in training, yet the mental health field needed more practicing clinical psychologists and fewer researchers. Adler also criticized the type of research that was encouraged by those responsible for training clinical psychologists, stating that it lacked relevance for clinical practice. Professional schools as a source of graduate training have been described as a solution to these concerns (see also Stricker, 1975).

Dörken and Cummings (1977) discussed the development of the California School of Professional Psychology (CSPP) as an example of professional training in action. These authors then went on to point to the employment and licensing records of CSPP graduates as evidence of their having competed successfully in the market place.

NEGATIVE

Perry (1979) detailed some of the reasons why clinical psychology does not need "alternative training models." Perry cited evidence that the scientist-practitioner model is eminently successful and widely accepted. One alternative, the freestanding professional schools, was criticized.

There are . . . an increasing number of professional schools awarding the doctorate in psychology or "primarily psychology" that are independent of any university and are primarily dependent on student tuition and part-time faculty. I am informed of at least 24 such schools in California alone. The number of such free-standing schools labeled psychology and their attendent large number of graduates labeled psychologists are, I believe, a cause for great concern. The concern is not over the numbers per se but over the implications for the type and quality of academic and professional training that seems to me to be inherent in such numbers and in the isolation from university strengths and standards.

Ericksen (1966) said, "Insofar as professional psychology becomes pinched off from scientific psychology it will be taking one clear backward step toward becoming a second-class service technology" (Ericksen, 1966, p. 953). This step has been taken by those free-standing, tuition-dependent schools that have little or no contact with the other substantive content and research areas in university departments. I believe that the backward step has also been taken by those free-standing, tuition-dependent schools that have explicitly or implicitly rejected research. Isolation

from the breadth and depth of a unviersity environment with its diversi-
fied pursuit of quality would alone warrant concern, but there is more.

The cost alone of truly professional education must dictate what would
seem to be major disadvantages of any given free-standing, tuition-de-
pendent school. Can any school primarily limited to the tuiition and fees
of its students offer the quality and breadth of training required for any
doctoral or professional program having substantial public or endowed
support? I am concerned that psychology is the only profession attempt-
ing such an ambitious undertaking which, at the very least, must damage
our hard-earned credibility.

One characteristic shared by the free-standing, tuition-dependent
schools with which I am familiar is an extremely large number of students
relative to paid faculty. I know of no school that publishes the number of
full-time paid faculty, but even very conservative estimates suggest stu-
dent-faculty ratios several orders of magnitude higher than in accredited
programs. Current and proposed accrediting standards give great empha-
sis to a close working relationship between faculty and students, but there
are no specific minimum ratios established yet. It is difficult to imagine a
close working relationship if there are too many students for the size of
the faculty or if the faculty do not have a sufficient time commitment to
the training program.

A common assumption regarding professional schools is that "profes-
sional training is different from academic training in that it trades some
scientific or theoretical training for more practical and professional train-
ing" (Valfer, 1979, p. 17). The assumption that students in professional
schools receive more clinical training is questionable at best but even less
credible with the student-faculty ratios of the tuition-dependent schools.

The implication is made that large numbers of graduates from the free-
standing professional schools result because the dissertation either is not
required or is more "practical," or shorter. It is true for accredited PhD
programs that the dissertation of whatever type is a serious undertaking
on which it is difficult to impose strict time constraints. It is not true that
significantly more graduates could be produced if research standards were
reduced or even eliminated, since research training is concurrent with clin-
ical training in the Boulder model. In clinical training alone, it is difficult
to set strict time constraints because students vary in the time required to
reach various levels of competency.

Does the free-standing, tuition-dependent professional school offer any
advantage to psychology or to society to offset what appear to be over-
whelming weaknesses? Incredibly, its advocates argue that its huge num-
bers of graduates are a necessary response to societal needs unmet by
accredited programs. Thus, a major weakness apparently dictated by eco-
nomics (school, not public, economics) is transformed into public altru-
ism. With similar logic, the ever increasing number of graduates is then
used by some as the primary argument for changing accreditation stand-
ards. The argument is illogical but persuasive to the naive in that the

presumed public demand can ostensibly be met without any apparent training cost to the public.

There is a certain minimum cost required to produce a clinical psychologist, regardless of individual wishes or actual national needs. For the moment, let us suppose that we were given a national mandate and whatever resources necessary to produce the best that professional psychology could offer. Such a mandate would be analogous to that given to the space effort in terms of constraints. In response to impatient queries about why we couldn't go faster toward placing an American on the moon, Werner Von Braun discussed the problem of producing a baby. To paraphrase him, if a baby requires nine months gestation there is no way that the simultaneous impregnation of nine women can yield a baby in one month. The analogy refers to time only, but given the mandate, would psychology's response really be the creation of free-standing professional schools with very high student-faculty ratios? Less than the minimum cost in time, money, and effort might very well produce individuals with societal value, but these individuals should not be confused or equated with PhD graduates in clinical psychology who have received strong clinical and strong research training (Perry, 1979, pp. 607–608).

From N.W. Perry, Why clinical psychology does not need alternative training models. *American Psychologist*, 1979, *34*, 603–611. Copyright 1979 by the American Psychological Association. Reprinted by permission.

The requirements of these two programs are presented in Table 2-2. Note, however, that the University of Illinois Psy.D. program discontinued the admitting of new students in 1981. The major distinctions between the requirements of the programs reflect different degrees of importance placed on research training and professional training. For example, while an inspection of Table 2-2 reveals many similar requirements, the students who are working toward the Ph.D. are required to carry out an experimental master's thesis and doctoral dissertation whereas the Psy.D. students must write a master's and doctoral-level report. The Psy.D. reports are not experimental studies, but are reports on the current status of various psychological practices. Indeed, there has been discussion of the value of the experimental dissertation as a requirement for a clinical psychologist (e.g., Stricker, 1973): While some see it as providing a basic experience to guarantee the student's understanding of the limits and merits of research, others stress the lack of relevance to actual clinical practice.

Table 2-2 Requirements of the Graduate Program in Clinical Psychology at the University of Illinois-Urbana Champaign for the Ph.D. and Psy.D. Degrees

Doctor of Philosophy (Ph.D.)	Doctor of Psychology (Psy.D.)
1. At least 24 graduate units	1. 24–28 graduate units
2. Satisfactory completion of "qualifying" examinations	2. Satisfactory completion of "qualifying" examinations
3. A master's thesis	3. A master's level report

Table 2-2 *Continued*

Doctor of Philosophy (Ph.D.)	Doctor of Psychology (Psy.D.)
4. At least two year-long (part-time) practicum training experiences	4. At least five year-long (part-time) practicum training experiences
5. Advanced courses and seminars in areas of specialization and supporting area[a]	5. Preliminary and final examinations administered by a dean's committee[a]
6. Completion of Ph.D. dissertation	6. An advanced report on a topic in clinical practice (*not* a dissertation)
7. Satisfactory performance on a preliminary and final oral examination (re: dissertation)	7. Satisfactory performance on a preliminary and final oral examination (re: doctoral report)
8. Some teaching experience	8. Some teaching experience
9. One-year internship (recommended)	9. One-year internship (required)

Taken from the 1978 Clinical Psychology Programs Brochure, Department of Psychology, University of Illinois at Urbana-Champaign and the Graduate Programs Catalogue.
[a]specifically from the Graduate Programs Catalogue.

Clinical (practicum) experiences are required of candidates for both degrees, but the Psy.D. candidate spends a greater proportion of time in these efforts. Also, while an internship is recommended for the University of Illinois' Ph.D. students (it is required by almost all other Ph.D. programs), it is required of their Psy.D. candidates.

The program requirements at the University of Illinois illustrate the Ph.D.-Psy.D. distinctions. However, these distinctions are not hard fact and many Ph.D. programs are a meld of both "types" of requirements and such a "dual" emphasis is evident in the scientist-practitioner model of clinical training.

The growth and development of the professional schools, while they have a short history, have been seen as necessary to help fill the increasing need for clinical services. Many students interested in clinical psychology have expressed a desire for professional training per se, and many others are not able to gain admission to already existing traditional graduate programs. Moreover, many clinical psychology graduate students did not wish to do an experimental doctoral dissertation. Thus, there were demonstrable needs and student concerns that helped advance the development of professional schools. However, necessities such as selecting only the most qualified students, providing only quality professional training, and ensuring an adequate degree of understanding of the scientific methods are difficult problems that continue to confront all professional schools.

Emphasis on the Scientist-Practitioner

The majority of graduate programs in clinical psychology, and the training program that we described in this chapter, follow the scientist-practitioner model. Within such programs there is indeed variation in the amount and quality of training in both research and practitioner skills, but the basic assumption is that an adequate doctoral program in clinical psychology must provide graduate students with training in *both* scientific research and supervised professional practice.

As evident from the history of clinical psychology, there have been numerous conferences held to examine the various training models. Although alternative approaches were considered at these conferences,

> the basic scientist-practitioner model was reaffirmed at all of the major national conferences convened to study graduate education in psychology. (APA criteria for Accreditation of Doctoral Training, p. 1, 1979)

These conferences included Boulder in 1949 (Raimy, 1950), Miami in 1958 (Roe, Gustad, Moore, Ross & Skodak, 1959), Chicago in 1965 (Hoch, Ross, & Winder, 1966), and Vail in 1973 (Korman, 1976). At Vail, for the first time, the practitioner model (professional model) was endorsed. This endorsement was accompanied by a "reaffirmation of a committment to comprehensive psychological science as the substantive and methodological root of any education or training enterprise in the field of psychology and by reaffirmation of the value of the more traditional scientist and scientist-practitioner training programs" (APA Criteria, p. 2, 1979). Apparently, the scientist-professional model of clinical training has been sufficiently reaffirmed to allow one to predict that it is here to stay.

For a moment, recall the training philosophies that emphasized research, and recall also those that sought to provide practitioner experience. The scientific-professional or the scientist-practitioner, if you wish, is essentially a combination of these. The practitioner aspects of *assessment* and *therapy* are taught, and experience is provided. The scientific aspects of research methods, critical evaluation, and hypothesis testing are also taught didactically and experientially. Moreover, the scientist-practitioner training integrates the two. That is, assessment skills are developed in conjunction with the research methods to evaluate the accuracy of the assessment. Similarly, carefully supervised therapy and consultation experiences are conducted within a framework that allows for an evaluation of the effectiveness of the clinical interventions. The scientist-practitioner does not stop with the acquisition of assessment and therapy experience, but goes on to ask and attempt to answer questions regarding the utility and efficacy of the methods in use. (Highlight 2-5)

Highlight 2-5   Training Background of Related Helping Professions

In addition to clinical psychologists, mental health professionals such as psychiatrists, psychiatric social workers, and psychiatric nurses contribute to the care of the maladjusted. Although each of these professions share a common goal for their disturbed clients, there are differences in their respective background training.

Psychiatrists, for example, are physicians, having earned the M.D. degree. They are trained first as practitioners of medicine (e.g., neurology) with coursework in the medical sciences (e.g., anatomy, physiology) and later receive same psychiatric training through a residency. The psychiatric residency usually provides supervision for ongoing clinical cases, but, like basic medical education, it lacks the broad study of human behavior and basic research (Kiesler, 1977). A psychiatrist's first expertise is in medicine.

Psychiatric social workers typically emerge from undergraduate backgrounds in sociology and are often trained at the graduate level through supervised fieldwork. That is, in addition to academic coursework, they gain "hands on" expereince working in social welfare programs and agencies. Typically, the psychiatric social worker holds a master's degree (M.S.W., Master of Social Work), awarded after two years of training.

Psychiatric nurses are nurses first, with a special interest in patients with mental problems. Nurses training provides an education relevant for nursing duties, but is not as focused on a broad study of applied human psychology as might be desirable. This fact is underscored when one realizes that it is the psychiatric nurse who spends more time with patients (hospitalized patients) than the other professionals.

It would be unfair to attempt to pair any one mental health profession with any one "school of thought." Instead, each of the professions has a sampling of those with expertise in behavioral, biological, cognitive-behavioral, psychodynamic, humanistic, and other perspectives. Similarly, it would be inaccurate to limit any profession to any specific mental health function. Instead, professionals from each of the above backgrounds are likely to engage in various roles in the treatment of disturbed persons. It may be fair, however, to note the special training and expertise of clinical psychologists in research and diagnosis, of psychiatrists and psychiatric nurses in, respectively, prescribing and managing medications, and of psychiatric social workers in dealing with the social welfare systems and issues.

Can One Person be a Scientist and a Therapist Too?   This question is relevant when one is discussing the potential merits of the scientist-practitioner model. If the scientist is the prototypical intelligent, logical, and objective individual (i.e., the storybook characteristics of the scientist, Mahoney, 1976), can he or she also be the prototype of the therapist—warm, empathic, and understanding (e.g., Rogers, 1957)?

The question has not yet been adequately answered, but a glimpse of the answer is suggested in a large-scale study reported in a book by Sloane, Staples, Cristal, Yorkston, and Whipple (1975). In this study, which compared two types of therapy, psychoanalysis and behavior therapy, 60 patients were seen by one of three behavior therapists or one of three psychoanalysts. Several important findings regarding the effects of the different treatments are reported in both the book and articles by these authors (cf. Sloane, Staples, Cristol, Yorkston, & Whipple, 1976; Staples, Sloane, Whipple, Cristol, Yorkston, 1976); but our present interest is in certain qualities of both the behavior therapists and the psyshoanalysts that were monitored. These qualities included therapist self-congruence (genuineness), accurate empathy (understanding of client's feelings), depth of interpersonal contact (ability to grasp the client's deepest needs and feelings), and unconditional positive regard (warmth and caring). If one were to believe that an individual clinician cannot be both a scientist and a clinician, then one would expect that behavior therapists, those often said to be more scientifically oriented and scientifically trained of the two groups of therapists, would turn up short on the qualities often associated with therapeutic expertise. The outcome was quite the opposite. Behavior therapists showed a significantly higher level of interpersonal contact and a significantly higher level of therapists self-congruence, than the psychoanalysts. Both groups showed an equal degree of warmth and unconditional positive regard. Thus, although these data are only suggestive, the more scientifically oriented therapists were also seen as possessing those qualities often associated with therapeutic expertise.

A study by Fischer, Paveya, Kickertz, Hubbard, and Grayston (1975) resulted in a different outcome, yet one that also supports the idea that one person can be a scientist and therapist. Three types of therapists self-identified as psychoanalytic, behavioristic, or humanistic were compared on measures of empathy, warmth, and genuineness. While it is quite likely that the behaviorally oriented therapists were more scientifically oriented than either the humanists or the psychoanalysts, the three groups were found *not* to differ on the measured variables. Note, however, that the scientific expertise of the various therapists was not measured and the results must again be considered only tentative.

From both an historic and a contemporary viewpoint, the scientist-professional model has a wide-ranging influence on clinical psychologists. Research on the development and utility of psychological tests, the methods and effectiveness of therapy, and the uses and results of consultation are only a select sample of the application of scientist-practitioner skills. Indeed, the studies reported in this text convey the efforts of numerous scientist-practitioners—and it is through these efforts that our field has progressed in both its data base and social acceptance.

ADMISSION TO GRADUATE TRAINING

There are a number of investigations and comparisons that are worthwhile prior to submitting an application to a program of graduate study in clinical psychology. The most important consideration is, of course, whether the program will provide learning opportunities in the areas in which the applicant is most interested. Understandably, the average applicant does not know *exactly* what will be the focus of his or her entire educational experience and professional career. Indeed, some students may purposely wish to be exposed to a variety of topics such that they can then selectively develop individual interests. Even if the applicant is uncertain as to specific goals, decisions to apply to certain programs can be made based on more general issues such as the training philosophy of the university. Careful reading of each university's graduate brochure should indicate the philosophy of the program. Other important considerations include the following: Does the program offer the type of training (e.g., assessment, therapy, research) that the applicant most prefers? Is the program APA approved? Is financial assistance available? (The recent withdrawal of training support funds by the National Institute of Mental Health will likely result in a drastic reduction in the number of programs offering support.) Does the applicant meet the basic admission requirements? What are the financial costs?

The American Psychological Association publishes a book entitled *Graduate Study in Psychology* in which all programs in the United States and Canada are listed along with some valuable descriptive information. This book is a must for the student who anticipates applying to graduate school in clinical psychology, or, for that matter, any other area of psychology. All the programs in clinical psychology, including those that have received APA approval for their doctoral training, are listed in this publication. The list of APA-approved doctoral programs also appears in Table 2-3.

Table 2-3 Current APA-Approved Doctoral Programs in Clinical Psychology

The Committee on Accreditation has approved the doctoral training programs in clinical psychology that are conducted by the following institutions. In these institutions, the approved programs are directed by the department of psychology unless otherwise indicated. Programs that have not requested evaluation and programs that have been evaluated but not approved are not included in the list. Readers desiring information on training approaches, philosophies, and of specific programs are encouraged to write directly to the departments in which the programs are offered. The criteria used in evaluating these programs for APA approval can be obtained from the Educational Affairs Office of the American Psychological Association.

Inclusion of an institution in this list indicates approval of doctoral programs in clinical psychology only. Inclusion or noninclusion carries no implications for other graduate programs in psychology or for programs of graduate education in other disciplines.

The institutions in the following list have been reported to the U.S. Public Health Service, to the Veterans Administration, and to the Surgeon General's Office, Department of the Army, as conducting, at the present time, approved programs of doctoral training in the areas indicated.

FULLY APPROVED PROGRAMS: CLINICAL PSYCHOLOGY

Adelphi University, Institute of Advanced Psychological Studies

Alabama, University of (University)

American University

Arizona State University

Arizona, University of (Tucson)

Arkansas, University of

Boston University

Bowling Green State University

Brigham Young University

California, University of (Berkeley)

California, University of (Los Angeles)

Case Western Reserve University

Catholic University of America

Cincinnati, University of

City University of New York (City College)

Clark University

Colorado, University of

Connecticut, University of

Delaware, University of

Denver, University of

Denver, University of, School of Professional Psychology (Psy.D.)

DePaul University

Duke University

Emory University

Florida State University

Florida, University of, Department of Clinical Psychology

Fordham University

Table 2-3 *Continued*

Fuller Theological Seminary, Graduate School of Psychology
George Washington University
Georgia State University
Georgia, University of
Hahnemann Medical College, Department of Mental Health Sciences (Psy. D.)
Hawaii, University of
Houston, University of
Illinois, University of (Chicago Circle)
Illinois, University of (Urbana)
Illinois, University of (Urbana) (Psy. D.)[a]
Indiana University (Bloomington)
Iowa, University of
Kansas, University of
Kent State University
Kentucky, University of
Long Island University
Louisiana State University
Louisville, University of
Loyola University (Chicago)
Maine, University of
Manitoba, University of
Maryland, University of (College Park)
Massachusetts, University of
McGill University
Memphis State University
Miami, University of (Florida)
Miami University (Ohio)
Michigan State University
Michigan, University of
Minnesota, University of
Mississippi, University of
Missouri, University of (Columbia)
Missouri, University of (St. Louis)
Montana, University of
Nebraska, University of (Lincoln)
Nevada, University of (Reno)
New Mexico, University of
New York University
North Carolina, University of (Chapel Hill)
North Dakota, University of
North Texas State University
Northern Illinois University

Northwestern University Medical School, Department of Psychiatry and Behavioral Science, Division of Clinical Psychology
Ohio University
Oklahoma State University
Oregon, University of
Pennsylvania State University (University Park)
Pennsylvania, University of
Pittsburgh, University of
Purdue University, Department of Psychological Sciences
Rhode Island, University of
Rochester, University of
Rutgers—The State University of New Jersey, Graduate School of Arts and Sciences (New Brunswick)
St. Louis University
South Carolina, University of
South Dakota, University of
South Florida, University of
Southern California, University of
Southern Illinois University (Carbondale)
Southern Mississippi, University of
State University of New York (Albany)
State University of New York (Buffalo)
State University of New York (Stony Brook)
Syracuse University
Teachers College, Columbia University
Temple University
Tennessee, University of
Texas Tech University
Texas, University of (Austin)
Toledo, University of
Utah, University of
Vanderbilt University
Vermont, University of
Virginia Commonwealth University
Virginia Polytechnic Institute and State University
Washington State University
Washington, University of (Seattle)
Washington University (St. Louis)

Table 2-3 *Continued*

Waterloo, University of	Wyoming, University of
Wayne State University	Yale University
West Virginia University	Yeshiva University
Wisconsin, University of (Madison)	

From the American Psychological Association, APA-approved doctoral programs in clinical, counseling, and school psychology: 1980. *American Psychologist*, 1980, *35*, 1116–1118. Copyright 1980 by the American Psychological Association. Reprinted by permission.
ᵃNew students are not being admitted to this program.

Students in their junior or senior year of undergraduate education or other interested individuals usually begin inquiring about graduate education by writing to universities that offer programs of interest. For example, each year the University of Minnesota responds to approximately 6000 initial inquiries and subsequently processes some 400–500 completed applications. Also, there are a great number of applications that are incomplete and are therefore not considered.

Application Requirements

It is from a careful reading of the materials sent out by each psychology department that the interested student will learn just exactly what is required of the applicant. There are, however, several almost standard application requirements. For instance, the applicant is required to provide scores on standardized tests, an undergraduate transcript, letters of recommendation, and a statement of personal interests and motivations. Also a description of either or both research experience and applied experience is usually requested on applications. Based on these data, the faculties of each of the graduate programs select their students.

Scores on Standardized Tests   Applicants are almost always required to provide the graduate program with a number of test scores, including the Graduate Record Examination (GRE) (both the general mathematics and English portions and the specific psychology specialty) and the Miller Analogies Test (MAT). These tests are offered at various times during the year, but scheduling is done well in advance. Interested students should plan several months ahead in order to take the tests and have the scores sent to the institutions to which you have applied. Inquire at your present or local college's department of psychology for how to apply for the GRE and MAT tests.

Undergraduate Transcript   The student's undergraduate transcript, including the total grade point average (GPA) for the applicant's college career and the grade point average for the courses in psychology, is required. Calculating your GPA is simple if you are from a university that has a four-point system (i.e., A = 4.0, B = 3.0, C = 2.0, D = 1.0). However, if your school does not use such a point system then you may need to recalculate your GPA for the application form. Acceptable grade point averages are often listed in each department's graduate brochure, as well as in the APA *Graduate Study in Psychology* publication. Not only the overall GPA, but also the range and quality of courses taken will affect admission decisions.

Letters of Recommendation   In addition to the academic performance criteria, graduate programs request that the applicant either provide the names of three or four people who can be contacted for personal reference or more likely, that three or four letters of recommendation be sent directly to the graduate program. In either case, it is up to the applicant to ensure that the required number of references are in the file. In most instances, professors with whom you have studied or worked are the best sources of letters of recommendation. Professors of psychology, specifically those within clinical psychology, would be highly desirable individuals for letters of recommendation.

Personal Statement   Application forms typically call for a personal statement from the applicant indicating the applicant's interests within clinical psychology, motivations for the plan of intended study, and long-range career goals. Not only does this essay requirement give the evaluating committee an insight into the applicants' projected future but it also provides a sample of the applicants' writing skills.

Research Experience   Since a good portion of the education in graduate school is related to research, either evaluating research outcomes or conducting actual research, an applicant who has already had research experience is at an advantage. Being a part of a research project while completing the undergraduate curriculum also provides an excellent opportunity to establish close ties with a professor so that he or she can write a meaningful letter of recommendation. A professor who has worked with a student can better describe the candidate's qualities, list the actual experiences that the student has had, and provide for the reader of the letter of recommendation a clearer picture of the student's genuine interests. Also, it is not uncommon for an advanced undergraduate student to begin research investigations on topics of their own interest.

Applied Experience   Many undergraduates seek and gain applied experience in preparation for their application to graduate clinical training programs. For instance, you might enroll in a course that includes a practicum where you work in a hospital, a school, or a community mental health center. Or, you might receive training as a crisis hot-line worker, a dormitory resident assistant or a precounselor. Alternatively, you might take a year off and work at a job in a psychiatric or medical hospital. All of these experiences are valuable for you, and provide evidence of your commitment to serving people.

Ratios of Applicants to Positions

Graduate education in the field of clinical psychology is extremely popular and competitive. At present, there is clearly an overabundance of qualified applicants and an absence of space in the training programs. For example, one valuable piece of information available in the APA book is the ratio of the number of applicants to the number of students accepted at each training program. While there are variations in the availability of graduate positions depending on the particular institution (prestigious universities have higher requirements than do less well-known institutions), an overall summary indicates that a great many more students apply (perhaps 25 to 30 times as many) as are admitted. The interested reader should check the current ratio data for each particular university.

The applicant should thus be forewarned that making an application does not guarantee acceptance. Selecting a graduate program is apt to be disappointing since the chances are that you may not be accepted. The suggested approach to graduate application entails the judicious selection of programs from the top, middle, and bottom of your list. Apply to several schools, but do not go overboard. More specifically, this method involves applying to three of the top choices, five or six middle choices, and another two or three that are less desirable but most likely to view your application favorably.

There is a great deal of material that is required for a complete application to even one program, and there are many important deadlines. For both reasons, the interested student should begin to make inquiries about a year ahead of time —in the fall of one year for possible admission in the fall of the next year. Because of the requirements of the applications themselves, some people say that it may be accurate to state that if you can make it through the persistence tasks of applying to the program, you stand a good chance of making it through the program itself.

When one examines these ratios and makes a comparison to the ratios that were reported some 10 or even 5 years ago, an important trend emerges. What appears to be happening is that more and more qualified students are seeking admission to programs in clinical psychology. Some of this increase in the number of applications is, however, due to students' increasing awareness of the difficulty of getting into graduate clinical psychology and their resulting tendency to apply to more schools. Thus, the ratios of applicants to admissions reported by each school gets worse and worse because, in addition to more interested students, each student generates more applications than used to be the case. Also, the financial aid provided by agencies such as the National Institutes of Health is decreasing, forcing many programs to accept fewer students.

Some new training programs have developed, but there is still dramatic evidence that many qualified students cannot find places in graduate programs. It is currently the case that the rejection rate from clinical psychology training programs is higher than that of other professions such as medicine, law, or dentistry. The popularity of the field has definitely increased the competitiveness. As a result, each candidate should examine his or her credentials and interests carefully before undertaking what might be a frustrating experience.

CAREER DECISIONS

Setting out to become a clinical psychologist can be an exciting enterprise. There are a variety of professional roles to choose from and a continually growing body of information by which to be stimulated. But why should you choose a career in clinical psychology? Should you be motivated to cure all your patients? To create a new therapy? To spend your life in a laboratory? To go into private practice? To do research in a medical school? To consult with community organizations?

Indeed, the variety of motivations that spark careers in clinical psychology is as diverse as the individuals in the profession. Similarly, there is room within the profession for people with different interests and goals—with one exception. It is not a good idea to choose a career in clinical psychology in an attempt to understand or solve your own personal problems. Graduate education in clinical psychology is not the same as personal therapy, although some clinical training programs do encourage their students to undergo personal therapy as part of their training (Highlight 2-6). The motivation for study in clinical psychology that is most likely to be satisfied is a desire to develop greater understanding of people through both scientific and clinical methods and to apply this understanding in the process of providing diagnostic and intervention services.

Highlight 2-6   Personal Therapy in Clinical Training

The majority of clinical programs neither prescribe nor proscribe personal therapy as a part of clinical psychology training. To oversimplify somewhat, an argument for this position was, and still is, that therapists who delve into the complex workings of other persons' minds and beings must be fully aware of their own sensitive spots, hangups, and basic needs. Otherwise, these therapists might act dangerously on their own unresolved (and often unconscious) issues and problems, rather than helping their clients to grow and mature therapeutically. Although it is usually accepted that most people are not always fully aware of their most basic needs and motives, requiring personal therapy has become a minority viewpoint in clinical training programs for several reasons:

1. Many approaches to therapy do not hold the view that therapy *must* (or even *does*) involve intensive psychodynamic self-exploration—for instance, behavior therapy or cognitive-behavior therapy. These therapeutic approaches (discussed in greater detail in Chapter 13) have had a major impact on clinical psychology, often because they are viewed as more scientifically testable, more efficient, and less limited to upper-middle-class white clients than, for example, psychoanalysis. While some training programs in clinical psychology hold psychoanalytic orientations, many now subscribe to more eclectic orientations.
2. The utility of personal therapy in clinical training has never been scientifically demonstrated. Although personal therapy may seem intuitively laudable, clinical psychologists demand scientific evidence before they will accept unequivocally any method or theory, and the scientific evidence on the question is almost nil at present.
3. Personal therapy is time consuming and expensive. Graduate students have many responsibilities, so personal therapy is often given a low priority simply for lack of time or funds.
4. Given the wide range of current therapies, who is to say which therapy a graduate student should undergo? Should they be desensitized, cognitively restructured, psychoanalyzed, nondirectively counseled, or what? (Each of these different types of therapy is discussed in Chapters 12 and 13.) There is some merit to the idea that a therapist should personally ex-

perience the type of therapy that he or she will provide so that he or she will know what the client is going through, but that is a different goal than the original rationale for personal therapy (and could be accomplished less expensively via role playing).

The issue is far from resolved, but is certainly one that merits systematic empirical evaluation. The only data that we have at present are from a survey conducted by Garfield and Kurtz (1976b), in which they asked several hundred clinical psychologists about their views on personal therapy in clinical training. Garfield and Kurtz found that 63% of these clinical psychologists had undergone personal therapy, a finding that is consistent with earlier surveys that showed that many clinicians had undertaken personal therapy. Not surprisingly, those respondents who had experienced personal therapy were very strongly in favor of it as a valuable aspect of clinical training, while those who had not undergone therapy viewed it as unimportant or even detrimental. There was also a significant tendency for fewer psychologists employed in university settings (i.e., 57%) to have undergone personal therapy than those in private practice (i.e., 70%) or at outpatient clinics (77%). Whether personal therapy will result in more effective therapists or diagnosticians or researchers or consultants remains to be answered by controlled research.

However, a diversity of interests can be accomodated by clinical training programs. Each individual clinician-in-training has brought with him or her many years of experience in a variety of life events and scholarly pursuits. In many cases what you bring to your institute of graduate education determines how you will develop and where your career will turn. Undergraduate specialties in areas other than psychology may be very valuable in bringing new perspectives into the field. Students who have had experience in a variety of settings and with a variety of different types of people can also contribute unique qualities.

PROFESSIONAL DEVELOPMENT

It is of course important to remember that most career decisions are not completely final and binding. Many persons become clinical psychologists after having concentrated in another area for a large part of their undergraduate years or after having tried out a job in education or business or the physical sciences. Many master's-level clinical psychologists return to graduate school to complete the Ph.D. requirements. What is important is an awareness of the choices and of the responsibilities involved in each choice, so that an "informed" decision about your career is possible.

The final stage in becoming a clinical psychologist, after having earned the Ph.D. involves finding a job, establishing yourself in that position, and fulfilling the requirements for independent professional practice. There are many unwritten challenges that engender both excitement and anxiety for the new Ph.D. as he or she enters professional life as a clinical psychologist.

The job-finding game can be both distressing and exhilarating. With the extremely limited number of academic job openings and the equally discouraging state of affairs in publicly supported institutions, the present conditions might best be considered distressing. Nevertheless, the first step in the job hunt is to identify position openings that fit your qualifications and special areas of experience and expertise and that appeal to your interests. Several resources are available to the job hunter: personal contacts from past field experiences; personal contacts of one's major professor(s) in graduate school; announcements in the monthly newsletter of the American Psychological Association, the APA *Monitor*, and in a monthly employment bulletin published by APA; announcements sent to training programs by prospective employers; and placement services offered at many professional conventions. The arduous remainder of the "hunt" involves sending copies of your resume, providing work samples, attending personal interviews, and enduring the waiting and uncertainty (and usually far more rejections than job offers). For the prospective job seeker in clinical psychology, we recommend a humorous, yet frank and informative paper by Perlman (1976) that describes in detail the phases of, and keys to success in, "the hunt." Woods (1976) has also edited a very useful volume entitled *Career Opportunities for Psychologists* that offers several excellent guides to innovative careers and practical recommendations for how to acquire them.

Getting a job is a major accomplishment, but several further challenges await the clinical psychologist. Aside from the obvious need to fulfill the obligations of the position, licensing and tenure are two formal requirements of importance. (Highlight 2-7) In order to practice therapy or assessment independently of the supervision of another licensed clinical psychologist, one must become *licensed* as a professional psychologist. The major criteria for licensing were described in Chapter 1.

Highlight 2-7   Continuing Education for Psychologists?

As evident across the country, practicing professionals are becoming required to maintain a program of continuing education. Will this be a requirement for psychologists?

According to *The New York Times* (1979), the number of states mandating continuing education for any one profession changes each year. Seven states (California, Colorado, Iowa, New Mexico, South Dakota, Washington, West Virginia) required continuing education in 1979 and another six had passed enabling legislation (Maryland, Michigan, Minnesota, Oregon, Utah, Vermont).

The responsibility for deciding to require continuing education is typically left to professional societies and in many cases it is the professional groups at the state level that are taking action. Whether or not more states will require such ongoing training is hard to predict—two opposing forces exist at present: (1) consumers are concerned and want to be assured of competent care and continuing education is seen as a possible solution, but (2) professionals are often against additional red tape such as the kind that results from programs requiring continuing education.

Tenure is an important achievement in a university, college, or medical school setting. Tenure is granted on a highly competitive basis to the clinical psychologist (as to all academicians) contingent on three basic criteria:

1. Demonstration of quality in teaching (e.g., high ratings by students and/or colleagues on course evaluations).
2. Demonstrations of quality and productivity in research (e.g., number and quality of published scholarly papers; acquisition of a research grant).
3. Demonstration of quality of service to the institution (e.g., participation on departmental or university committees or task forces) and community.

The exact weighting given to each of these areas varies from program to program, although research is usually considered to be of primary importance. The academician is usually evaluated for tenure, first by the department in which he or she teaches and then by the representatives of the college or university, between the third and seventh year of his or her position. Tenure basically provides an assurance that the person can continue to hold the position as long as desired, barring unusual circumstances (e.g., criminal conviction, the closing of the department or institution).

A final professional hurdle, which comes along much further into one's career and which is voluntary in nature, is *board certification*. A psychologist can choose to be reviewed by the American Board of Professional Psychology (ABPP) in order to be certified as a "diplomate." The examination involves both the submission of protocols from actual clinical cases that the candidate has conducted and an oral examination by five ABPP diplomates to determine the candidate's competence in the areas of theory, research, and ethical issues. A minority of clinical psychologists, approximately 2000 as of 1977, have taken and passed the ABPP examination.

As is true with the development of each individual over his or her lifetime, the process of "becoming" a clinical psychologist is a continuing one that does not necessarily end upon receiving a Ph.D. or licensure, or tenure, or board certification. There are always new challenges to be met and new territory to be explored if the clinical psychologist chooses to do so: developing new areas of research; moving from a position that is oriented to direct service to one geared more for teaching and research, or vice versa; or training new clinicians who bring new energy and interests to the field. Although it is often easier to get into one groove (or rut, depending on how it is viewed), continued development is a very real option for the clinical psychologist.

Truth is established by investigation and delay;
falsehood prospers by presipitancy

Tacitus

Thoughts are but dreams till their effects be tried.

Shakespeare

3

RESEARCH METHODS

Despite some decline in research training, clinical psychologists remain among the best prepared of all mental health professionals to evaluate assessment instruments, intervention methods, and community or hospital programs. This expertise is bolstered by the possession of an advanced knowledge of research methods combined with professional experience. Indeed, research methodology, in the broad sense, is the *sine qua non* of clinical psychology as a science.

Clinical psychologists, whether functioning as research scientists or professional assessors, therapists or consultants, attempt to make use of the methods of scientific evaluation. Practicing clinicians can evaluate the effects of their treatments just as research clinicians evaluate elaborate experiments. A variety of research methods are utilized by clinical psychologists in their efforts to assure that the services that they deliver are of high quality.

GOALS OF CLINICAL RESEARCH

Research in clinical psychology is studious inquiry designed for the advancement of our knowledge of human functioning. The purpose of such research is to apply scientific methods to the gathering of the data necessary to corroborate or reject our tentative theories (i.e., our hypotheses) about how people think, feel, and behave. In addition to this general all-encompassing goal, well-designed clinical research also has more specific *second-level goals* that give collective direction and purpose to subareas of the research efforts in clinical psychology.

Clinicians involved in psychological assessment want to be able to describe people accurately and make predictions about their future behavior, so their second-level goal is to identify *what sample of data, gathered in what setting, and with what subject and assessor, produces what information?* For example, the psychologist who studies the validity of various personality tests is working toward the same second-level assessment goal as the psychologist who develops a system for the observation of behavior. Each of these clinical psychologists will gather different data samples. One assessor administers a 45-item true-false test designed to predict aggression and relies on the subject's test score as the predictor. Another assessor selects 6 behaviors, defines them, counts their frequency, and relies on these observational totals as the predictor. These assessors have different theoretical views and perhaps even different uses for the data. However, they share the second-level goal of attempting to develop accurate and meaningful approaches to gathering information about how people function psychologically.

Clinical psychologists involved in clinical intervention research are, as a second-level goal, trying to identify *what intervention, in what settings, and with what client and change-agent produces what effects*? (Kiesler, 1966; Paul, 1969). A question as encompassing as this requires the accumulation and the synthesis of many different types of information. Thus, a clinician who is researching the effectiveness of a treatment for obesity is providing information for this second-level goal just as the clinical researcher who is evaluating the effects of a new approach to consultation. These examples deal with different interventions, with different types of clients, and with different measures of the interventions' effects (loss of weight versus increase in staff morale), and yet both researches contribute to the same second-level goal.

The second-level goals involve several components (e.g., different clients and clinicians, different measures of research outcome) because clinical psychologists recognize that research is rarely a black-and-white or good-versus-bad endeavor. The critical goal is *not* to identify the single "best" assessment or intervention method, or the single "true" theory of human functioning. Instead, clinical psychologists seek to determine when, and for whom, and for what specific purposes, different assessments, interventions, and theories are most effective in advancing our understanding of human functioning and our ability to help people live full lives.

THE SCIENTIFIC METHOD

Clinical psychologists utilize the methods of science to guide their research. Science refers to the systematic collection and evaluation of data. The scientific method requires that research be *empirical, precise,* and *repeatable.* Empirical means that the researcher gathers data through observation. For precision, the researcher must clearly define (1) the phenomena that are being observed, and (2) exactly how these observations will be conducted. Repeatability requires that scientists document their procedures so that other scientists can check to see that the findings can be reproduced. Although the scientific method did not originate within clinical psychology, clinical psychologists have adopted this method for the study of human behavior. However, because of both the complexity of human behavior and the demanding rules of science, clinical research is not always perfect in meeting the ideal of the scientific method. Instead, research in clinical psychology strives to achieve these ideals as best as possible.

Generating Ideas

At the beginning of every psychological research project is an idea. Research ideas typically arise from an interest in solving a clinical problem or testing some aspect of a particular psychological theory. They can come from personal experiences, group discussions, or issues raised in the research literature. For example, a person who worked at a summer camp for children might have seen the majority of campers enjoying themselves but also saw a few of the children being very aggressive. This person may have wondered what causes children to use abusive language and to act aggressively? After some thought, he or she may have speculated that frustration might lead to aggression. Such a question requires germination, and a potentially useful research question can be developed if it is nurtured through the reading of relevant theory and research, consultation with colleagues and other experienced researchers, and personal reflection.

Reviewing Past Research

As one of the first steps in the scientific method, the researcher who has an idea should find out what information already exists about the particular topic. An excellent source of such information is the numerous psychology journals and similar periodicals that are published several times each year. These are available at university libraries and are subscribed to by many clinical psychologists. (A list of a number of the journals of importance to clinical psychologists is presented in the Appendix at the end of the chapter.) Due to the vast array of publications available, the researcher will often need to search through many different journals. Often, the best place to begin is *Psychological Abstracts*. Issued monthly, this resource tool lists and organizes abstracts of most of the articles recently published in psychology journals. The abstracts (i.e., brief summaries of the published article) are listed under 16 major classification categories (e.g., Personality, Treatment, and Prevention), with some categories having subsections. The user of the *Psychological Abstracts* may peruse all the listings within a specific category or may simply look up the topic of interest in the subject index. For instance, someone interested in the topic of aggression might find a dozen or so abstracts listed under "aggressive behavior." Several additional topics might also be listed—"see also animal aggression, attack, conflict, violence." The researcher can then read the abstracts and, if interested, proceed to check the original article. *Biological Abstracts* and *Index Medicus* are other resource tools that frequently contain information sources relevant to clinical psychology.

Computer search systems, available in many libraries, are valuable time saving aids in locating the sources of information. Although they go by a variety of names, these systems all work on the same basic principle. The researcher feeds into a computer certain "key" descriptive terms. These are determined by the researcher after having checked a publication that lists the possible "key" terms. For example, searching the topic of aggression may require the use of key terms such as "aggressive behavior," "violence," and "acting out," in addition to "aggression." The computer then prints out a list of all the sources of information about a particular subject (see sample in Table 3-1). As useful as computer search systems can be, the researcher should keep in mind that they do vary as to the completeness of the search. The completeness depends on the correspondence of the key words used by the searcher and the author of the published work, on the number of years for which information is programmed, and on the range of journals and books that are included in the computer.

Table 3-1   A Sample Printout from a Computer Search of the Recent Literature on
Aggression and Frustration

..SEARCH
BRS – SEARCH MODE – ENTER QUERY
     12__: AGGRESSION AND FRUSTRATION
     14__: ..PRINT 13 BIBL/DOC = 1 – 5
       1
AN   05985 61–3.
AU   BHATIA–KIRAN.   GOLIN–SANFORD.
TI   ROLE OF LOCUS OF CONTROL IN FRUSTRATION-PRODUCED AGGRESSION.
SO   JOURNAL OF CONSULTING & CLINICAL PSYCHOLOGY. APR 78 VOL 46(2) 364–365.

      2
AN   03406 61–2.
AU   ROBARCHEK–CLAYTON–A.
TI   FRUSTRATION, AGGRESSION, AND THE NONVIOLENT SEMAI.
SO   AMERICAN ETHNOLOGIST. NOV 77 VOL 4(4) 762–779.

      3
AN   07545 60-4.
AU   STOLOROW-ROBERT-D. HARRISON-ADRIENNE-M.
TI   THE CONTRIBUTION OF NARCISSISTIC VULNERABILITY TO
       FRUSTRATION-AGGRESSION: A THEORY AND PARTIAL RESEARCH MODEL.
SO   PSYCHOANALYSIS & CONTEMPORARY SCIENCE. VOL 75 4 145-158.

      4
AN   05029 60-3.
AU   FOSS-LINDA. FOUTS-GREGORY.
TI   EFFECTS OF FRUSTRATION AND CATHARTIC OPPORTUNITY ON AGGRESSION.
SO   PSYCHOLOGICAL REPORTS. AUG 77 VOL 41(1) 319-326.

      5
AN   09174 58-5.
AU   TAYLOR-STUART-P. SCHMUTTE-GREGORY-T. LEONARD-KENNETH-E.
TI   PHYSICAL AGGRESSION AS A FUNCTION OF ALCOHOL AND FRUSTRATION.
SO   BULLETIN OF THE PSYCHONOMIC SOCIETY. MAR 77 VOL 9(3) 217-218.

     END OF DOCUMENTS

From Bibliographic Retrieval Services. Reprinted by permission.
Note: AU = author(s), TI = title, and SO = source.

Determining the Variables

One of the most important aspects of psychological research is the concept of a
variable. A *variable* is any aspect of a person, group, or setting, that is measured
for the purposes of the study in question. Age may be a variable since age is a
measurable aspect of a person. Age, however, is not a variable in every study involving human beings—only in those in which age is measured and its effects considered. There are three types of variables: independent, dependent, and relevant.

   Independent variables are those variables that are manipulated by the researcher in order to investigate the effects on an outcome (*dependent variable*). For instance, if a therapist is interested in the effect of intensity of background noise on

clients' ratings of satisfaction with therapy, the independent variable is the background noise. Simultaneously, the researcher would record clients' ratings of satisfaction with therapy (the dependent variable) to determine the effects of the background noise.

The researcher tries to control for all *relevant variables* so that any observed changes in the dependent variable can be attributed to the independent variable. Relevant variables are all those variables (other than the independent and dependent variables) that can potentially affect the manipulation of the independent variable or the measurement of the dependent variable. The effects of relevant variables are unwanted because they make it impossible to know what effects the independent variable alone has on the dependent variable(s).

Types of Relevant Variables   There are three general categories of relevant variables (D'Amato, 1970): attributes of the subjects, called *person* variables; aspects of the situation, called *setting* variables; and the order of the events experienced by the subjects, called *sequence* variables.

Person variables have to do with characteristics of the subjects themselves, such as intelligence, age, sex, marital status, severity of psychopathology, type of psychopathology, and so forth. A clinical researcher comparing two groups of subjects can most accurately determine the effects of the independent variable when subjects in both groups are comparable on these person variables. For example, in studies of the psychology of sex roles it would be necessary to consider the age and intelligence of the subjects because people's concepts of sex roles are likely to be affected by both the generation during which they were raised and their "brightness" (cf. Worell, 1978).

Setting variables have to do with aspects of the environment (or situation) in which data are collected. In the case of an evaluation of the effectiveness of a therapy (referred to as "therapy outcome research"), such variables as the appearance of the therapist's office, when the therapy is conducted (mornings, evenings, on weekends), and the types of therapy tasks are all setting variables.

For example, the effects of office decor as a setting variable was examined by Bloom, Weigel, and Trautt (1977). Male and female subjects were exposed to stereotypic representations of a "traditional" therapy office or a "humanistic" therapy office. The traditional office contained a desk between the therapist's and client's chairs, a file cabinet, professional texts and manuals, four diplomas on the wall, and some additional furniture. The "humanistic" office had the desk against the wall with the therapist's and client's chairs separated by an end table and lamp. On the end table was a box of facial tissue, a modern sculpture, and an ashtray. Instead of diplomas, the "humanistic" office had posters hung on the wall. Half of the subjects were told that the office was occupied by a female psychologist while the other half were told that it was occupied by a male psychologist. The subjects were seated in the client's chair and asked to form an impression of the hypothetical therapist.

The decor of the office was found to significantly affect subjects' impressions of therapist credibility (perception of competence, likelihood of recommending the therapist to a friend). Both male and female subjects consistently rated a female therapist in the traditional office as more credible than a female therapist in the humanistic office. On the other hand, a male therapist was rated as more credible in the humanistic office. Thus, the setting variable (decor) and a person variable (therapist gender) had an important interaction effect. This finding suggests that when studies of the effects of therapy make comparisons of different types of therapy, the decor of the offices used in the studies and the therapist's gender should be comparable. If the offices or the therapists differ, some of the effects that might be attributed to the type of therapy may in fact be the result of these relevant variables.

Factors such as subject fatigue, where repeated participation may tire the subject, or practice, where repeated participation may improve performance, are examples of clinically meaningful *sequence* variables. Sequence variables arise whenever the subjects are seen on two or more occasions. For instance, a researcher may be interested in the effects of an educational program to improve children's knowledge of emotions. The children would be tested for their ability to recognize emotions before and after the educational program and perhaps again six months later to assess how much the children had retained. The children's performance may have improved at each testing period but it is possible that the improvement occurred only because the children learned to recognize the emotions from the repeated presentations of the test and not the educational program.

In a later section of this chapter we consider the various methods for controlling relevant variables so that researchers can clearly evaluate the effects of independent variables on dependent variables.

Developing a Hypothesis

A hypothesis is an idea that has been well formulated in order to be tested using scientific methods. Thus, a hypothesis is an idea subject to verification. Once the researcher has an idea and has reviewed past research, then the procedures used to test it must be determined. Hypotheses must be clearly stated in a fashion that permits an objective test of their correctness.

For clinical psychology it is also important to consider *applied-clinical* hypotheses. Such hypotheses are ones that have the scientific rigor of sound research methodology while also generating information that clinicians can use to better understand and aid people. For example, studies of the effectiveness of various psychological therapies, investigations into the etiology of psychological dysfunctions, and the utility of various psychological tests to make accurate diagnoses, are all of extreme importance in clinical psychology.

The idea, simply stated, that "children who are frustrated will display aggression" is not as it stands sufficiently well formulated to be a hypothesis for scientific investigation. First, the concepts of "frustration" and "aggression" must be operationalized and then the expected relationship between these concepts must be specified.

Operational Definitions   A central issue in the development of a testable hypothesis is the operational definition of each concept to be studied. Operational definitions are used to reduce the ambiguity in concepts used in science. An operational definition is one that defines a concept entirely by the operations used in measuring it.

In our example of frustration leading to aggression, frustration is defined as an obstacle or interference with need satisfaction and aggression is defined as a behavior whose goal is the injury of persons or objects (e.g., Dollard, Doob, Miller, Mowrer, & Sears, 1939). In theoretical terms then, the researcher might hypothesize that children seek to cause injury when they are blocked from doing something that they either want to do or are in the process of doing (see Figure 3-1). Attempting to solve problems that are actually impossible may be adopted as an even more focused operational definition of frustration because it operationalizes the class of situations where there is an obstacle to need satisfaction. Similarly, agression could be operationalized as the amount of verbally abusive language directed to the person who presents the obstacle. McClelland and Apicella (1945) studied the consequences of frustration by inducing failure in a laboratory situation by presenting subjects with ostensibly soluble (actually they were insoluble) tasks and by reprimanding the subjects during their efforts to solve the task (their operationalization of frustration). The subjects' verbal reactions were recorded, with the operationalization of aggression including verbal reactions of anger. Their hypothesis was that increased frustration would cause increased aggression.

The results indicated that while aggression was related to the induced frustration, other responses to frustration were also observed, such as withdrawal. Thus, these operationalizations of the concepts of frustration and aggression allowed for a test that not only lent some clear support to the hypothesis, but also provided new knowledge with which the hypothesis could be modified and refined.

Level	Frustration ⟶	Aggression
Theoretical	Obstacle to fulfillment or satisfaction	Attempts to injure or abuse the environment or people
Operational	Insoluble puzzles	Use of directed verbally abusive language

Figure 3-1 Theoretical and Operational Levels of the Frustration-Aggression Hypothesis

The Null Hypothesis The design and procedures of research used to test hypotheses vary greatly. Nevertheless, in all cases the type and direction of the hypothesized relationship must be stated. Researchers use the *null hypothesis* in order to specify the exact hypothesized relationships among the variables being investigated. The null hypothesis states that *no* relationship exists. In our example of frustration and agression, the null hypothesis states that "If I frustrate these subjects with impossible tasks, they will aggress *no more* than other subjects who were not frustrated." The null hypothesis predicts *no* differences. Researchers establish the null hypothesis as a kind of devil's advocate position contrary to their true hypothesis, so that by rejecting the null hypothesis they can lend support to their true hypothesis.

The null hypothesis would be rejected and the hypothesis that frustration leads to aggression would be supported only if the more frustrated subjects behave more aggressively. If both groups of subjects behave in an equally aggressive manner then the data fail to reject the null hypothesis. Statistical analyses, discussed in greater detail in a later section of this chapter, are employed to determine if the null hypothesis should be rejected (supporting the researcher's hypothesis) or fail to be rejected.

Selecting a Research Strategy

The clinical psychologist employs a wide range of research strategies. A *strategy* is a plan of action, and the next step in research is to select the strategy that will provide the data to test the hypothesis. Each strategy is flexible and may be used in different ways, thus keeping open many avenues of approach to the solution of clinical problems. The choice of a particular strategy will depend on the hypothesis to be tested. There are three general research strategies: observational (the basic component of all research), correlational, and experimental.

Observational Strategies   Observation has played an important historic role in clinical psychology. For example, Kraepelin proposed one of the early systems of diagnostic classification based on his observations of patients, and Freud's observations of his clients fostered the development of his psychoanalytic principles of therapy. However, these forerunners have been criticized because their observations were not collected systematically. For example, Kraepelin's observations of patients were general and not necessarily representative of all patients or the entire range of patient behavior. Freud too has been criticized since his system was based on observations that were restricted to a select sample of patients. Observations should therefore be gathered so that they represent the phenomena of interest. Three important observational strategies are description, ratings, and time sampling.

Description   Description, as an observational strategy, refers to the observing of behavior and the recording of the observations in a narrative style. For instance, an observer may spend three hours inside a mental hospital observing the patients' behavior and subsequently writing a narrative description of the activities and interactions that took place.

Descriptive observations are subject to certain weaknesses. For example, the degree to which the description contains specific examples will vary from one observer to another. Also, the narrative quality of descriptions has the potential for the observer to be describing his or her "interpretation" of what happened rather than what actually occurred. The lack of structure imposed on descriptive observations also results in a large body of data that will later require additional efforts to attain some form of quantification. While an accurate "description" of behavior is desired, clinical psychologists often prefer more systematic ways of achieving this.

Ratings   When observational data are collected via ratings, the observer has a predetermined set of items and uses these items to categorize the behavior of the person being observed at some point along a continuum. These preselected items compose the rating scale. In this strategy the observer watches the subject(s) over a period of time and then makes ratings on the rating scale. For example, if a clinician is interested in a certain child's aggressive behavior, he or she might observe the child in the classroom, at play, or at home and then rate the child (e.g., from 1 to 5) in terms of the extent to which the child displayed fighting, stealing, verbally aggressive behavior, etc. (see Table 3-2).

Table 3-2 A Portion of a Sample Rating Scale for Obtaining Ratings of a Child's Aggression

Child's Name		Rater		Date	
	Not at All		**Sometimes**		**Often or always**
Fighting	1	2	3	4	5
Stealing	1	2	3	4	5
Verbally aggressive	1	2	3	4	5

Rating scales have been criticized because they entail the items chosen by the scale developer and therefore reflect his or her biases. For instance, the rating scale in Table 3.2 omits items reflecting more prosocial behavior such as cooperative play or studying. Nevertheless, the collection of observational data in the form of ratings is very practical because such data are already quantified and therefore more easily subjected to statistical analysis.

Time sampling   Time sampling is a technique for improving the accuracy of observations by standardizing them. Prior to the actual observation, the specific behaviors that are to be observed are identified. Each of these "targeted" behaviors is then carefully defined, including specific examples. During the observation, the researcher fixes his or her attention on the targeted behaviors for a specified period of time and then records their frequency in a standardized, systematic fashion.

For example, the observer interested in aggression might define two target behaviors, physical aggression and verbal aggression: "Physical aggression—engaging in physical contact with the intent to harm or injure a person or object." "Verbal aggression—the uses of language with the intent to harm or ridicule another person." Specific examples of each might include: "Physical aggression—hitting, kicking, throwing objects (not included would be playful tapping on another's arm)"; "verbal aggression—name calling, accusing, derogatory comments (not included would be playful nicknames)." Having the "target" behaviors specified, the observer would then watch the behavior of the subject(s) for a predetermined interval (e.g., 15 seconds) and then immediately record the incidences of these behaviors.

Time sampling has several advantages over other observational strategies. First, it helps to guarantee that what is recorded by one observer is as similar as possible to what would have been recorded if another observer were used. This is accomplished by the specific definition and the systematic timing of the observations. Second, the observations can be scheduled so as to gather a sample of data that is representative of the subject's(s') typical behavior. Finally, like ratings, time sampling produces data that are already quantified and readily entered into statistical analyses.

The major shortcoming of time sampling is that it does not readily allow for qualitative differences in the observed behavior. For example, in the time sampling of verbal aggressive behavior, two observers may record the occurrence of two verbal aggressive incidents within the specified period, but the fact that one was louder and longer than the other would go unnoted. This shortcoming can be corrected by having observers also record the intensity and/or duration of each incident. Such procedures do, however, require extensive training of observers.

Correlational Strategies   A correlation is a measure of the extent to which two (or more) variables are related. For example, is there a relationship between IQ and school performance? Correlations are calculated to determine if a relationship exists and the degree of the relationship. First, pairs of observations must be obtained on a group of subjects. Sample data are presented in Table 3-3. Second, the correlation coefficient (r) is calculated. The resulting correlation coefficients can range from $+1.0$ to -1.0, with the sign and size of the correlation providing an index of the direction and degree of the relationship.

The higher the absolute value of the correlation, the stronger the relationship between the variables. A correlation of either $+1.0$ or -1.0 indicates a perfect relationship—the child with the highest IQ would have the highest school performance score, the child with the second highest IQ the second highest school performance score, and so on down to the child with the lowest IQ having the poorest school performance ($r = +1.0$, see Figure 3-2).

Table 3-3   Pairs of Observations for Determining the Correlation Between IQ and School Performance

Child	IQ	School Performance Score (Academic Achievement)
1	110	92
2	101	75
3	96	81
4	117	94
5	130	95
6	136	97
7	99	81
8	115	86
9	112	97
10	100	79
11	107	79
12	107	93
13	120	79
14	112	81
15	104	92

   A correlation of -1.0 is equally strong but would indicate that the child with the highest IQ had the lowest school performance score, the child with the second highest IQ the second lowest school performance score and so on (Figure 3-2). A moderate correlation, such as that resulting from the data in Table 3-3 ($r = .58$), indicates that the two variables are related but that the relationship is not perfect (Figure 3-2). A correlation of 0.0 indicates that the two variables are not related (Figure 3-2). The child with the highest IQ may score high, medium, or low on school performance and the same would be true for the child with the lowest IQ. Thus, there would be no recognizable relationship between the two variables. In actual practice, as in our data in Table 3-3, correlation coefficients usually indicate degrees of relationship somewhere between the extremes. A "moderate" correlation might be between $\pm.30$ and $.60$, a "high" correlation between $\pm.60$ and $.99$.

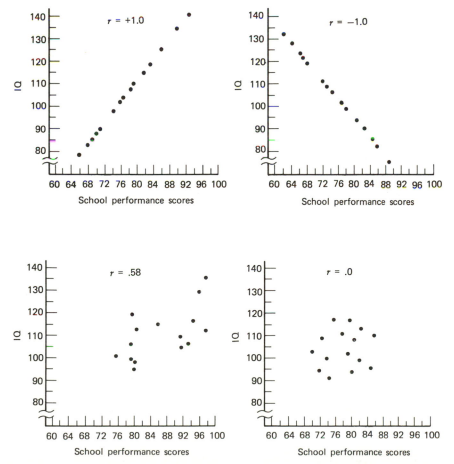

Figure 3-2 Scatter diagrams illustrating perfect correlations (positive and negative), a moderate correlation, and a zero correlation between IQ and school performance scores.

Once a meaningful correlation has been established between two variables, a clinician can make reasonably sound predictions about a person's relative standing on a measure of one variable given knowledge of the person's score on a measure of the related variable. For example, knowing that IQ and school performance are often correlated about $+.50$ to $+.60$, one can predict with reasonable assurance that a person with a high IQ will do better in school than a person with a low IQ. It is of course only possible to make exact predictions from IQ to school performance (or from any variable x to variable y) when $r = 1.0$. At lesser values we need to examine the scatter plot to decide on the range of school performances, given a specific IQ (and vice versa).

However, there are limitations to the correlational strategy. First, correlations only indicate general relationships. As mentioned, unless a perfect correlation is obtained, some people will not show the same relationship between the two variables. For example, some people with high IQs may not do particularly well in school. As a result, researchers do not place total confidence in predictions that are based solely on correlations.

Second, a correlation does *not* inform us that either variable caused the other one. Consider the fact that in the northern United States there exists a positive correlation between the amount of ice cream sold and the number of burglaries that occur in a given year. Does the sale of ice cream *cause* the burglaries? Highly unlikely. Instead, it is more reasonable to think of a third variable such as the weather as influencing both. As warm weather predominates, ice cream sales rise and, at the same time, criminals are more likely to be outdoors than they are during cold weather, so burglaries are more feasible. But even though the weather seems to be a more reasonable explanation, we cannot say that the weather causes burglary either, only that it is related.

There is also a moderate negative correlation between the number of therapy appointments missed by clients and their level of improvement at termination. This relationship does not prove that a lack of attendance at therapy causes restricted improvement. For example, clients who are dissatisfied with therapy ("resistant") may miss many sessions and also improve only slightly. Attendance and improvement may be highly negatively correlated, but "resistance" may be the cause of both.

Correlations are important because they inform us of the interrelatedness of variables, and when meaningful correlations exist, allow for reasonable predictions. However, extensive additional inquiry is required before one can establish cause-and-effect relationships.

Factor analysis   Factor analysis is a method derived from correlational research for examining the interrelationships of a number of variables at the same time. The factor analytic process makes use of the matrix of all the possible correlations of the particular variables under study. A small number of new, hypothetical variables are constructed statistically, each of which is a central "factor." Each factor accounts for the effects of many of the original variables, thus condensing the data from many variables into a more easily understood pattern of a few basic factors.

Table 3-4   An Illustration of a Factor Analytic Solution

Hypothetical Intercorrelations of Eight Anxiety Test Items

Anxiety Items	1	2	3	4	5	6	7	8
1. My palms are sweaty.	[a]1.00	.90	.92	.91	.41	.06	.25	.20
2. My heart beats fast.		1.00	.90	.94	.31	−.18	.28	−.21
3. I have difficulty swallowing.			1.00	.91	.28	.28	.31	.15
4. I feel sick to my stomach.				1.00	.32	.18	−.06	.17
5. My feelings get hurt easily.					1.00	.51	.47	.53
6. I have trouble making up my mind.						1.00	.62	.68
7. I worry about things.							1.00	.71
8. My mind seems to wander.								1.00

[a]The correlations of 1.00 (maximum correlations) are the correlations of the score on that test item with itself.

Anxiety Items	Factor Loadings for a Two-Factor Solution	
	Factor A	Factor B
1. My palms are sweaty.	.87	.21
2. My heart beats fast.	.86	.03
3. I have difficulty swallowing.	.85	.31
4. I feel sick to my stomach.	.87	.29
5. My feelings get hurt easily.	.32	.52
6. I have trouble making up my mind.	.05	.64
7. I worry about things.	.13	.57
8. My mind seems to wander.	.07	.62

As an example of how a factor analysis identifies "factors" from within a correlation matrix, consider the data presented in Table 3-4. These data are the hypothetical correlations of the responses of 250 students to eight items from a test that measures anxiety. Subjects were asked to respond to each item by indicating how often the statement would be true for them from "0" for not at all to "4" for almost always.

The computational procedures involved in factor analysis[1] produce *factor loadings* for each original variable, and these loadings inform the researcher of the degree to which the item contributed to (loaded on) each factor. Each loading is a correlation between one of the original variables and of the new factors.

Items 1, 2, 3, and 4 were found to load substantially on Factor A, while these items did not load highly on Factor B. These test items were highly correlated with each aother (see double-line triangle) and can be said to be measuring a similar aspect of anxiety. After examining the factor loadings and the content of the items that load highly, the researcher produces a label for the factor. In the case of Factor A, those items that load highly are concerned with the various physiological aspects of anxiety and the researcher may choose to label this "physiological anxiety."

[1]For further details about the procedures of factor analysis see Comrey (1973) and Gorsuch (1974).

The intercorrelations of items 5, 6, 7, and 8 (enclosed by single line triangle) are moderately high. While these items did not load meaningfully on Factor A, they did load substantially on Factor B. In this case, the items are concerned with worry, indecision, and sensitivity. An appropriate label for this factor might be "cognitive anxiety."

As an example of factor analysis, Mirels (1970) demonstrated that a personality test that was thought to measure only one personality dimension—locus of control—in fact measured two distinct dimensions. The locus-of-control construct (Rotter, 1966) refers to individuals' beliefs that they have personal control over the rewarding events in their lives (an internal locus of control) versus the belief that luck, fate, chance, or powerful others control the outcome of events (an external locus of control). Mirels (1970) used factor analysis to identify a group of items within the test that reflected a specific "political" locus of control and another subset that assessed the more general locus of control orientation. Based on the internal-external distinction, "internal" subjects should be more likely than "external" subjects to be political activists. However, Abramowitz (1973) reported that while scores on the overall locus of control scale did not predict activism, scores on the "political" factor identified by Mirels (1970) were predictive.

Experimental Strategies   The experimental approach to research differs from correlational strategies in that the researcher directly exerts an influence on (manipulates) one or more variable(s), rather than measuring the natural occurring relationship of variables. Recall that the manipulated variable is the independent variable. Experiments involve the study of the effects that different amounts (levels) of the independent variable have on the dependent variable(s) when the relevant variables are controlled. Several variations are available in the experimental approach: (1) between groups and within groups research designs, (2) direct manipulation and manipulation by selection, and (3) simple versus factorial research designs.

Between- and within-groups designs   A simple experimental study may have two separate groups of subjects that each receive a different level of the independent variable. This strategy employs a between-groups comparison. In a within-groups design, each subject is exposed to all the levels of the independent variable.

As an example of a between-groups design, consider a study of frustration and aggression. One group of subjects could have an obstacle placed in the way of their need satisfaction, such as impossible tasks to solve. Another group of similar subjects could be frustrated less intensely by having a few soluble problems among the impossible ones. Samples of the subjects' aggressive behavior following their efforts to solve the problems could be the dependent variable. The researcher could then examine the differences in aggression *between the groups* by comparing the amount of aggression displayed by members of one group to the amount of aggression displayed by members of the second group.

In such a design it would also be desirable to have a *control group.* A control group consists of subjects that receive all aspects of the study *except* the independent variable to be evaluated. In our example, the control group subjects could be given *soluble* problems to work on (thus experiencing little or no frustration) and their aggression afterwards would also be measured. The researcher would then compare the amounts of aggression displayed by members of the three groups: high frustration, moderate frustration, and no frustration. If the degree of aggression observed was highest in the first group, moderate in the second, and lowest in the third, the experiment would support the hypothesis that frustration causes aggression.

In a within-groups design, the same subjects are assessed at different times and their scores at these different times are compared. For example, if one wanted to investigate the amount of *change* in aggression that results from high levels of frustration then measures of aggression would be taken both before and after the frustrating experience. Here, the amount of aggression seen within the same subjects before and after frustration would be compared.

One group of subjects:	Assess aggression at time 1	→	Frustrate subjects	→	Assess aggression at time 2

Manipulation of the independent variable   There are two types of manipulation: direct clinical manipulation and manipulation by selection. Direct manipulation is achieved when the levels of the independent variable are created by the experimenter. For instance, in our between groups example of the study of the effects of frustration the researcher exposed groups of subjects to different amounts of frustration. In this case, the amount of frustration was directly manipulated.

In contrast, manipulation by selection is done when the levels of the independent variable are naturally created and the researcher selects people who already fit each level. For example, if age were the independent variable and two levels were defined as "adult" and "child," the researcher would select a group of adults and a group of children and compare these two groups on the dependent variable. This approach is really a combination of the correlational and experimental strategies because the experimenter is using age as the independent variable even though it is not being altered from its natural pattern. As such, it is subject to the same limitations as a pure correlation (i.e., no causative conclusions can be drawn).

Simple versus factorial designs   As in the examples of the within- and between-groups design, simple experimental research designs involve the manipulation of only one independent variable. Factorial experimental designs are used when the researcher is interested in the simultaneous effects of two or more independent variables. That is, since behavior may be the result of multiple determinants, it could be important to simultaneously manipulate several possible causes within one research project. In factorial designs the researcher can examine the effects of each of the independent variables separately as well as their interaction. An *interaction* occurs when the results of the manipulation of an independent variable produces results that are different for different levels of other independent variables. An important aspect of the factorial design is the identification of meaningful interactions.

Table 3-5   An Illustration of a Factorial Design

Level of Hypnotic Susceptibility		Type of Treatment	
		A_1 Acupuncture	A_2 No acupuncture
B_1	High		
B_2	Low		

A and B are separate independent variables, each with two levels. Thus, this would be called a 2 by 2 factorial design.

A = Different levels of the acupuncture independent variable

    A_1 = acupuncture; A_2 = no acupuncture (control group)

B = Different levels of the hypnotic susceptibility independent variable

    B_1 = high susceptibility; B_2 = low susceptibility

The scores on the dependent variables are entered into the cell that is appropriate for each of the four different types of subjects. These dependent variables, pain threshold scores in this instance, are then subjected to statistical analyses to determine if the scores for the subjects in different cells differ significantly.

When there are additional levels of the independent variables the factorial design can become 3 by 2, 3 by 3, etc. In each case, the number indicates the levels of that independent variable. For instance, in a 3 by 4 factorial design there are 2 independent variables, the first has 3 levels and the second has 4 levels.

For example, Knox and Shum (1977) examined the effects of two independent variables, acupuncture versus no treatment, and high versus low hypnotic susceptibility (see Table 3-5). The assignment of subjects to either the acupuncture or no-treatment group was directly manipulated by the experimenter whereas the high/low hypnotic susceptibility variable was manipulated by selection. The two independent variables were used simultaneously in a factorial design to create four groups of subjects: high-susceptible subjects receiving acupuncture, low-susceptible subjects receiving acupuncture, high-susceptible subjects given no treatment, and low-susceptible subjects given no treatment. The dependent variable was the amount of pain reported by subjects while performing a cold-pressor task. The cold-pressor task requires that subjects immerse a hand and forearm in a tank of circulating ice water. During one-minute immersion, the subjects report pain intensity every five seconds. The accupuncture analgesia was induced via two needles, one inserted 3 centimeters between the thumb and forefinger of the experimental arm and the other approximately 4 centimeters into the experimental forearm. Low-voltage pulses were delivered at a rate of four or five per second by a battery-operated apparatus. Does acupuncture work—can it eliminate or reduce pain? Is acupuncture related to hypnotic susceptibility?

Knox and Shum (1977) addressed these questions and their results indicated that acupuncture and hypnotic susceptibility *interact* significantly, with only high-susceptible subjects being responsive to the acupuncture treatment. That is, the effects of acupuncture (versus no acupuncture) were not the same for high and low hypnotic suggestible subjects. Only the highly hypnotically susceptible subjects benefit significantly from acupunture. This significant interaction suggests that hypnotic suggestibility is an important aspect of the responsiveness to acupuncture treatment (see Highlight 3-1).

Highlight 3-1   Researching the Interaction of People and Clinical Treatments

Although a fundamental goal of science has been to discover and confirm *general laws*, that is, principles that hold true for all persons and situations, psychology has had to face the fact that there are as many differences between people as there are similarities among them.

As Vale and Vale (1969) have expressed it:

Psychologists must now consider whether we can reasonably continue the practice of building general behavioral laws without incorporating into the structure of these laws information derived from the differences in the organisms to which the laws are to pertain. If organisms are meaningfully different, they may be expected to react differentially to the same treatment, and the search for general, invariant relationships between environmental treatments and behavioral responses may be foredoomed. The psychologist's task then is to somehow use individual differences data for nomothetic purposes. (p. 1094)

Since people are different in many ways, such as personality characteristics or home environments, you may well wonder how any general law could apply to all. Fortunately, although every person is in some ways unique, we all share similar attributes and experiences with at least some other persons. For instance, not all men are alike, but all men do share a common gender. Similarly, people who score above average on intelligence tests are seldom alike in all ways, but the above-average score is one thing they all share. If we can find independent variables that divide people into meaningful groups, perhaps we can find laws that hold true for at least the members of each group. This means that we must look for ways in which person variables interact with treatment variables.

Studying the interaction of people and treatments illustrates the successful cooperation of "correlationists" and "experimentalists" within clinical psychology. When Cronbach addressed the convention of the American Psychological Association in 1957, he spoke of the two methodological disciplines— the experimental and the correlational—into which psychological inquiry seemed to divide itself. In the experimental method, the researcher changes conditions in order to observe their consequences. In the correlational, the researcher seeks to observe and organize conditions as they exist in the world. The experimenter tries to establish the general rules and is annoyed by differences among individual subjects. It is these individual differences, however, that are the major interest of the correlationist who is, in turn, less concerned with treatment differences.

In 1957, Cronbach was calling for a united discipline that would study both the differences among people and the effects of treatment variables. Eighteen years later, again addressing the American Psychological Association, Cronbach (1975) acknowledged that most areas of psychological investigation had taken to the study of the interaction between treatments and individual differences, thus merging the two research approaches rather than creating a divisive split among psychologists.

Table 3-6   An Illustration of a 2 by 3 Mixed Factorial Design

Between Subjects	Within Subjects		
	Pretreatment	Posttreatment	Follow-Up
Treatment A			
Treatment B			

Factorial designs can also accommodate both within-groups and between-groups manipulations. For example, the repeated measurements that are often a part of the evaluation of clinical intervention require that the same subjects be assessed before treatment, after treatment, and often at a later follow-up period (within groups). The researchers may also be interested in comparing two treatments each given to a separate group (between groups). Such a *mixed factorial* would be described as a 2 by 3 design with two treatment groups and three measurement periods (see Table 3-6).

Controlling Relevant Variables

In experimental research, the controlling of relevant variables is essential to assure that only the independent variables cause the differences in the dependent variables. The procedures that are often employed to control for relevant variables include matching, randomization, counterbalancing, randomized blocks, and single- and double-blind controls.

Matching   Researchers sometimes attempt to assure that the subjects in all groups are comparable by defining the important ways that subjects could differ from one another and then putting an equal number of subjects of each type in each group. Matching would control, for example, the sex of subjects by having an equal number of both male and female subjects in each group. If there are to be 24 subjects in each of the two groups then having 12 males and 12 females in each would control for subject sex. Such a matching procedure also allows the researcher to examine the data separately for men and women to determine if there were differences between the two sexes.

Although matching creates equivalent groups, it may not always be a perfect solution. For example, if the social classes of schizophrenic (a category of severely disturbed persons) and nonschizophrenic subjects are being compared, the researcher might reason that level of education is a relevant variable to be controlled and therefore match the groups on this variable. However, the schizophrenic group is generally less likely to have had extended schooling than the nonschizophrenic group. When only the most highly educated schizophrenic subjects and the least educated nonschizophrenic subjects are chosen, the matching procedure may produce atypical people from each group (see Figure 3-3). In such an event, other control strategies are available.

Randomization   When a researcher assigns subjects to the experimental and control groups purely on a chance basis, such as the flip of a coin, the toss of a die, or use of a table of random numbers, this is called randomization. Not only

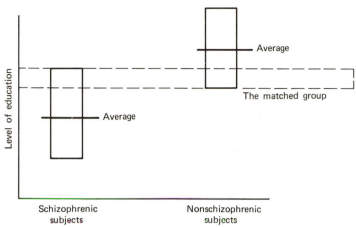

Figure 3-3   Creating matched groups can result in atypical subject samples. The matched sample of subjects is not typical of either group.

can randomization be used in assigning subjects to groups, it can also be used to settle such issues as the order in which subjects will be scheduled to participate in the study.

Random assignment will create well-matched groups in general, just as coin tosses eventually end up half heads and half tails after many tosses. However, when there are only a few tosses, say 20, it is not always the case that 10 will be heads and 10 tails. On some rare occasions you may have 18 and 2! Similarly, the use of randomization cannot guarantee that the groups will not differ on some important variable when there are a small number of subjects. When randomization is utilized, it is wise to check the groups that are formed to rule out any major initial differences between them.

Counterbalancing   When different aspects of an experiment are presented to subjects sequentially, it is important to consider the order of presentation. For example, a researcher may require subjects to complete several tests designed to measure sexuality and anxiety. If all the subjects first complete the questionnaire on sexuality and then the one on anxiety, they may report much more anxiety than if the order were reversed.

When an independent variable has several components that are presented to subjects sequentially, the order of presentation must again be considered. For example, a therapy procedure might involve three components: an educational film, group discussion, and individual counseling meetings with a therapist. The order in which these components are presented might make a difference in their effectiveness, so the researcher could *counterbalance* the presentation order by having some subjects receive them in one order (e.g., film, discussion, counseling), while other subjects receive them in a different order (e.g., counseling, film, discussion), and so forth until there is a group of subjects for every possible order of presentation. Then, the effects of different orders can be treated as an independent variable and examined by comparing the groups on the dependent variable.

Table 3-7 A Balanced Square

First sequence	A	B	D	C
Second sequence	B	C	A	D
Third sequence	C	D	B	A
Fourth sequence	D	A	C	B

This can require a large number of groups, so in many cases researchers use an approximation that is called a balanced square (Table 3-7). In a balanced square, each test or treatment component (A, B, C, D) occurs at each position in the sequence, and each component precedes and follows each other component an equal number of times. Thus, fewer groups are required, and the effects of presentation order are controlled.

Randomized Blocks   Matching and randomization are combined in the randomized-blocks procedure. The randomized-blocks method allows the researcher to make random assignments of subjects to conditions and also provides for an approximate matching of the groups on relevant subject characteristics. Consider the following example from a study of the treatment of social anxiety. Forty-two subjects will participate, 14 in each of three groups (two treatment groups and a control group). The subjects are suffering from high levels of social anxiety but the severity differs from person to person. In order to make all three groups comparable before treatment on the dependent variable, a measure of social anxiety, the researcher rank orders their scores on this measure from highest to lowest (see Table 3-8). Next, the scores are divided into blocks of three—the first block would be the three highest-scoring subjects, the second block, the next three subjects, and so on. Then, one of the three subjects from each block would be randomly assigned to one of the three groups. The result of randomized blocking is that subjects were assigned randomly and they are not likely to differ on an important variable (i.e., the initial degree of problem severity).

Single- and Double-Blind Controls   If subjects are aware that they are receiving a special treatment, they may expect to change, and this expectancy may alone cause changes (Wilkins, 1977). Therefore, subjects are sometimes not told what treatment they are receiving, producing a "single-blind" control. For example, if the independent variable is a drug that is designed to reduce children's hyperactive behavior, some subjects may be given the drug and other subjects may be given sugar pills, but neither group of subjects is told which they have received. The sugar pill is called a *placebo*, because it has no active physical effects but still may produce change because subjects receiving it may believe they are receiving a real treatment and thus change simply because they believe they should. Psychologists often use similar placebo controls (O'Leary & Borkovec, 1978), such as simulated treatment groups that are not believed to provide any specific therapy but that may lead subjects to believe that they are receiving a worthwhile treatment.

Table 3-8 Use of Randomized Blocks Procedure to Assign Subjects to Conditions

	Pretreatment Social Anxiety Scores		Conditions		
			Treatment A	**Treatment B**	**Control**
	98	86	97	98	97
First	97	86	93	94	94
block	97	86	90	91	92
	94	86	89	89	89
Second	94	86	89	89	89
block	93	85	88	88	88
	92	85	87	86	88
	91	85	86	86	86
	90	85	86	86	85
	89	85	85	85	85
	89	85	85	85	84
	89	84	84	83	81
	89	84	79	79	80
	89	83	72	76	77
	89	81			
	88	80	Total 1210	1215	1215
	88	79	Average 86.4	86.7	86.7
	88	79			
	88	77			
	87	76			
	86	72			

Initial (pretreatment) social anxiety scores are ranked, blocked, and then randomly assigned. The result is three groups not differing on the initial severity of social anxiety.

A double-blind control goes one step further, also keeping the person who actually administers the treatment to the subjects, such as a therapist or teacher, uninformed as to which subject is receiving which treatment. If the treatment agent expects subjects receiving one particular treatment to change more than those receiving other treatments, this expectation can lead him or her to behave more optimistically with those subjects and thus to bring about more change in them. However, in many clinical experiments the treatment agent cannot help but know which subjects receive each treatment; in this case it is especially important that any persons who are involved in measuring the dependent variables (for instance, clinicians who administer personality tests or observe and evaluate the subjects) be kept unaware of subjects' treatment assignments. As a general rule, anyone involved in an experiment or the measurement of the dependent variable(s) should be given the least possible amount of information that might cause them to change their expectations or behavior (see Highlight 3-2).

Sampling Subjects

Once a research design with appropriate control procedures has been formulated, the researcher must select the people who will actually participate as subjects. This requires that the relevant *population* and *sample* be defined.

Highlight 3-2   Control Groups in Therapy Research

The importance of appropriate control groups can be illustrated through the use of hypothetical experiments on the effects of one type of psychological therapy. In our study suppose we wish to examine the effects of a treatment procedure called systematic desensitization (Wolpe, 1969) on the interpersonal anxiety of middle-aged adults. For the sake of clarity, we will study subjects who are extremely fearful of interacting with other adults. Our dependent variable will be the subjects' anxiety level during an interpersonal interaction. If we were to systematically desensitize 10 subjects and then have them interact with a group of adults, would we be able to fully evaluate the therapy? The answer is No. First, we would need to have assessed the subjects' initial level of interpersonal anxiety. This procedure allows the researcher to compare anxiety after treatment to anxiety before treatment. Unfortunately, even if the treated subjects reported being less anxious after treatment than before, the researcher would not be certain that this improvement was due to the therapy per se. For instance, the subjects could have shown improvement simply as a result of having completed the assessment measures on two different occasions—the decreased fearfulness may be simply the result of the repeated exposure to the assessments. Additionally, the improvement may be the result of experiences that occurred outside of treatment, the passage of time, or subject maturation. For instance, subjects may have grown less fearful because of seeing a movie about their fears or having had a long talk with a friend.

In order to eliminate these unwanted rival hypotheses, the researcher designs control groups against which the effects of the treatment can be compared. The control groups that would be necessary for our example would include an exposure control, a placebo/discussion control, and a waiting-list control. The exposure control group would consist of subjects who were asked to complete the assessment measures on several occasions, corresponding to the amount of exposure of the treated subjects. The availability of these scores allows the researcher to control for the effects of simple exposure to the dependent variables (the assessments).

Subjects who are assigned to a placebo/discussion control group will receive exposure to the assessment measures and might participate in discussions of the problematic topic "interpersonal anxiety." These subjects would not receive the specific desensitization treatment, so any changes in their anxiety can be inferred to be due to such relevant variables as involvement and expectations of changing due to this involvement.

The waiting-list control subjects do not receive treatment until after the treatment group is completed, but nevertheless are evaluated for changes in their anxiety. This shows us how much change occurs due to time and maturation. These subjects will also be aware that treatment is forthcoming, which may produce relief and optimism that could lower their anxiety.

The anxiety of the subjects in our control groups would be compared to the behaviors of the subjects that received treatment. If the statistical tests indicate significant differences in the hypothesized direction (i.e., treatment group changing more than any control group), then the researcher can be reasonably sure that treatment was responsible for the observed changes.

Often, clinical researchers are interested in the relative effectiveness of two or more different types of therapy. Research along these lines must also employ control groups to insure that the different treatments actually cause meaningful change, in addition to showing their efficacy relative to one another. Controls are also necessary to show that each treatment is presented to the clients with equal enthusiasm, and are provided by therapists with comparable skills in the therapies being evaluated. Moreover, the different treatments should be equally "believable" to all the clients.

The subject population is the total group of people to whom the researcher wishes to apply the findings of the study. If the investigation is an attempt to test a hypothesis that is believed to hold true for all people, then the subject population is "humanity." More limited populations are often studied in clinical research, such as the population of juvenile delinquents or the population of outpatient clients at a mental health clinic. Experienced researchers recommend that every investigator carefully select their target population so that only the people for whom the hypothesis could really be expected to hold true are included (Vale & Vale, 1969).

The subject sample is that group of people who are actually involved in the study. Most research projects cannot involve every person in the relevant population, so a *representative* sample must be selected. A sample is representative to the extent that the people in the sample do not differ from the total population on important variables such as age, sex, social status, marital status, motivation to participate in the research, or scores on the dependent variables. Just as researchers strive to create comparable experimental and control groups, so too must they attempt to create a subject sample that is comparable to the overall population. For instance, if the population is all registered students in a university, the researcher could randomly select every one-hundredth person from the registration files and then compare this sample with the overall population to make sure that the sample is not markedly different on relevant variables.

These sampling precautions are necessary to guarantee that the research findings are *externally valid*, that is, that they hold true for the people in the target population and not merely for a select subgroup. Often researchers are unable to achieve a completely representative sample, for instance in a study where participants were the special subgroup of hospital patients who were willing to volunteer to take the psychological tests. In this case, the researcher must clearly note how the sample differed from the total population when reporting the study's results. The findings are no less true, but they can only be assumed to hold true for the special subgroup who participated, and not for all hospitalized patients in general. As is true for the sampling of subjects, the situations studied and the stimulus-persons employed in research should also be representative (Brunswick, 1947; Maher, 1978).

Conducting the Research Study

The nuts and bolts of actually measuring the dependent variables, and when an experimental investigation is being undertaken, administering the independent variables to subjects, pose several practical issues. Coordination and standardization are the two central considerations.

Coordination involves planning and organization. To avoid mistakes and confusion, advance preparation is essential. A detailed schedule should be formulated to describe exactly who does what tasks at what times and in what places (see Table 3-9). Relevant responsibilities range from preparing publicity to recruit subjects, to conducting the actual sessions, to training all research personnel, to actually administering and scoring the measures that assess the dependent variables. Frequent communication among members of the research team is important if problems are to be discovered and rectified.

Table 3-9   A Project Schedule for a Study of the Effects of an Assertiveness Training Program

Date(s)	Principal Investigator	Research Team	Trainers
Aug. 17	News release to media	Prepare and compile assessment measures and training materials	Review and finalize training materials and procedures
Aug. 21– Sept. 11	Telephone screening and scheduling of interviews	Mail screening measures and program description to applicants	
	Train research assistants to score questionnaires and videotapes	Training in data scoring	
Sept. 11– Sept. 29	Screening/pretest interviews	Distribute and collect pretreatment measures	
	Supervise data scoring	Data scoring and keypunching	
Oct. 2– Nov. 10	Supervise treatment groups	Audiotape treatment sessions and prepare tape segments for analyses	Conduct treatment: T1—Mon. 9–12; Mon. 1–4; Fri. 9–12
		Distribute and compile dependent measures	T2—Mon., Tues., Wed. 9:30–12:30
		Prepare refreshments	
		Child care during sessions	

Table 3-9 *Continued*

Date(s)	Principal Investigator	Research Team	Trainers
Nov. 13– Nov. 22	Coordinate posttreatment data collection and scoring	Distribute and collect outcome measures in posttreatment interview	
	Begin to compile pretreatment data	Data scoring and keypunching	
Feb. 1–9	Coordinate follow-up data collection and scoring	Distribute and collect outcome measures in follow-up interview	
Feb. 12– Mar. 15	Conducting training with wait-list group. Analyze data. Begin to write up research reports.		

The *standardization* issue involves precautions to insure that every subject is interacted with in exactly the same way, except where an independent variable dictates differential treatment. Thus, each subject should be provided with the same environmental setting, the same instructions, and the same courteous but businesslike personal contact by the same research personnel, as is every other subject.

The experimenter tries to set the tone for the research by being serious, organized, and direct, but the aura of the psychological experiment and experimenter sometimes creates a "demand" for the subjects to behave in certain ways (Orne, 1962; Rosenthal, 1966). These effects of the experimental situation or the experimenter can be called "demand characteristics." For example, a meticulous and fastidious man in a white laboratory coat may, due to these personal characteristics, create a demand for the subjects to behave in a rigid overcontrolled fashion. In a similar vein, a very disorganized, hurried, and sloppy experimenter may create a situation where a subject behaves in a forced, incomplete, and perhaps even inaccurate manner. It is important for researchers to design studies that minimize and/or measure the effects of demand characteristics: the behavior of the subject is thereby more likely to reflect the effect of the actual independent variables.

Analyzing the Results

Once the measures of dependent variables have been collected, the researcher must systematically examine them to determine whether or not the data are sufficient to reject the null hypothesis. Several types of statistical analyses are utilized for this purpose. The key ingredients include the following concepts: the distribution of scores on the dependent variables, descriptive statistics, inferential statistics, and restrictions on inferences about individual subjects.

Score Distributions   The *distribution* of scores on the dependent variables refers to the pattern of scores that subjects in the sample actually obtained on these measures. For example, a hypothetical distribution of scores on a questionnaire measuring anxiety is depicted in Figure 3-4. The distribution is shaped like a bell, thus approximating the *normal distribution*—the pattern of scores that would emerge if very large numbers of subjects were tested. A majority of statistical analyses are based on the assumption that the total population's distribution of scores is normal, with most people scoring near the average and progressively fewer people achieving scores at increasingly high or low levels. Thus, the researcher checks to determine that the sampling distribution did not deviate severely from the normal pattern. In our example, the distribution is slightly different from the normal distribution but not sufficiently to rule out the use of more advanced analyses.

Descriptive Statistics   Descriptive statistics are numerical measures that enable a researcher to describe important aspects of the sampling distribution. These include three measures of *central tendency*: the mean, the average of the scores

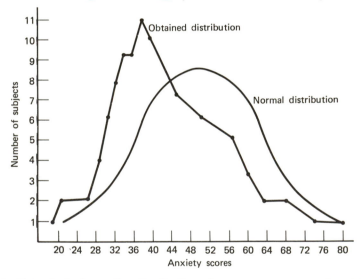

Figure 3-4   Hypothetical sampling distribution of scores on a measure of anxiety

				Anxiety Scores					
Subject	Score	Subject	Score	Subject	Score	Subject	Score
		24	34	48	49	72	40
1	37	25	40	49	56	73	49
2	32	26	38	50	60	74	49
3	56	27	80	51	46	75	56
4	63	28	21	52	40	76	30
5	60	29	34	53	38	77	32
6	20	30	32	54	37	78	34
7	74	31	30	55	37	79	32
8	68	32	56	56	28	80	38

Figure 3-4 *Continued*   Anxiety Scores

Subject	Score	Subject	Score	Subject	Score	Subject	Score
9	21	33	46	57	40	81	38
10	36	34	49	58	28	82	36
11	36	35	56	59	36	83	37
12	38	36	40	60	36	84	37
13	40	37	40	61	34	85	36
14	46	38	36	62	37	86	30
15	34	39	36	63	32	87	32
16	40	40	37	64	46	88	56
17	68	41	40	65	46	89	37
18	38	42	38	66	49		
19	38	43	60	67	38		
20	30	44	46	68	38		
21	49	45	34	69	40		
22	46	46	38	70	34		
23	63	47	37	71	34		

(41.45 in our example); the mode, the most frequently occurring score (38 in our example); and the median, the score that half of the subjects score above and half score below (38 in our example). Two descriptive statistics characterize the amount of *variability* in the scores: the standard deviation, a measure of the average variation of the individual scores from the group mean (SD = 11.38 in our example); and the range, the highest and lowest scores (20–80 in our example). When a researcher employs the standard deviation and the mean, it becomes possible to calculate statistics that indicate whether a correlation or the manipulation of an independent variable are meaningful.

Inferential Statistics   The statistics that are used for judgments of the meaningfulness of the data are called inferential statistics because they enable the researcher to infer whether or not the null hypothesis can be rejected.

Recall that the null hypothesis states that there are no meaningful differences between groups: that the population means for the two groups are the same and that any observed difference between sample means is merely the product of sampling error.

In correlational research, the most frequently used inferential statistic is a test that provides a comparison of the obtained correlation with the correlation of .00 that would be expected if the null hypothesis were true. For example, if the researcher who collected the anxiety data in Figure 3-4 also assessed the hostility of the same subjects, and obtained a + .19 correlation, two steps would be necessary to calculate if this correlation is indeed meaningful. First, the researcher must determine how many *degrees of freedom* exist in the research design: this is the amount of variability that can be expected in the dependent variable, and is equal to the number of subjects minus one, or 88, in our example. Second, the researcher must determine how certain he or she wishes to be that the correlation is truly different from .00. Most researchers set a cautious limit and accept findings as meaningful only if there are fewer than 5 chances in 100 that the correlation is not significantly different from .00. This limit is called the probability (or *p*) value.

Though p values are arbitrary, depending on the degree of confidence one wishes to have, the most frequently used p value is .05 (5 chances in 100 that the results are not meaningful when we say that they are). The researcher would consult a statistical table that lists the minimum correlation that must be obtained to be meaningful with the given degrees of freedom and p value. When the obtained correlation is greater than the minimum value, the correlation is said to be *statistically significant* (the .19 correlation in our example is not sufficient to be considered significant).

Inferential statistics are also used in experimental studies. For example, if a researcher compared 10 subjects who received Therapy A for anxiety and 10 matched subjects who received Therapy B on their anxiety scores at the end of therapy a t test could be used. Consider the data in Table 3-10. The mean scores and the standard deviations would be used to compute a numerical value indicating the extent to which the two groups differed on the dependent variable. When the t value has been calculated, the researcher consults a statistical table that tells how high a t is necessary (given the degrees of freedom, 19, and the p value, .05) for the groups to be considered *significantly* different. In our example the t is greater than that required and the results would be considered statistically significant.[2] The experimenter rejects the null hypothesis that the two groups came from populations with the same mean and accepts the experimental hypothesis that Therapy A exerted an effect greater than Therapy B.

Additional inferential statistics are available to aid researchers to determine whether they can reject the null hypothesis with more complicated research designs such as the factorial designs (e.g., the F test). However, the basic principles remain the same: the researcher calculates a numerical value and compares it to the minimum numerical value that is required if the data are significantly supportive of the researcher's original hypothesis beyond a level that would be expected by chance alone. Statistical signficance depends on the sampling distribution, the number of subjects, the variability in the subjects' scores, and the p value that is used.

Restrictions on inferences   Even when the statistical analysis indicates a significant finding, this does not imply that the hypothesis is true for every single subject, nor for every person in the population. Statistical tests provide an estimation of the probability that the null hypothesis can be rejected for the *group*, but not

Table 3-10   Posttreatment Scores on an Anxiety Measure for Two Therapy Groups

Therapy Groups	Statistic	Posttherapy Anxiety Scores
Therapy A	Mean	32.4
	Standard deviation	7.6
Therapy B	Mean	48.4
	Standard deviation	8.7

[2]Recall that in an actual comparison of the effects of two therapies it would be important to assess the subjects both before and after treatment and to include certain control groups (see Highlight 3-2).

for each individual subject. For this reason, it is always a good idea to closely examine each individual's scores before concluding that that single person has responded according to the research hypothesis. Similarly, findings from research studies can only be used as initial guidelines when clinicians are making predictions about individual clients. Even if most people fit a hypothesized pattern, we cannot be certain in each individual case.

Reporting Research Results

A scientist's research project is not complete until the results have been disseminated, that is, described in a written or oral report that is made available to other scientists and the public. Research findings are most often disseminated by being published in scholarly journals such as the *Journal of Consulting and Clinical Psychology* or the *Journal of Abnormal Psychology* (see appendix at the end of the chapter for a list of such journals). Psychologists also present papers at professional conventions such as the annual meeting of the American Psychological Association. Research may be reported in books as well.

It is essential that research reports be concise yet clear in reflecting the importance of the study and the care that has been taken to follow the methodological guidelines that we have described. The American Psychological Association (1974) published a *Publication Manual* that provides an excellent description of exactly how to write an acceptable research paper.

Developing Programmatic Research

Individual studies produce useful information, but it is the research program that has the greatest potential for advancing knowledge in the field of clinical psychology. A research program consists of a series of studies designed to answer related questions. Each study, building on the ones before, generates new hypotheses as well as immediately useful findings.

Programmatic research requires that the researching clinician be skilled in a variety of research methods. No one method can answer all questions, whereas a variety of methods in a systematic sequence can address the diversity of issues that arise.[3]

Designing Meaningful Research

Designing meaningful research can be both exciting and humbling. The researcher may be energized by his or her idea and its potential ramifications for society and yet be troubled by the difficulties of measurement, sampling, and the problems of time, effort, and cost. Research in clinics, hospitals, and other mental health centers is often difficult due to the limited time available after the requirements of the clinical job have been met. However, academic clinical psychologists are usually allotted time for research and collaboration between practicing clinicians and academic research psychologists can result in meaningful research contributions (Highlight 3-3).

---

[3]The interested reader is referred to Brendon Maher's special issue of the *Journal of Consulting and Clinical Psychology* (Volume 46, No. 4, 1978) that was devoted entirely to the topic of methodology in clinical research.

Highlight 3-3   Do Basic Research Assumptions Restrict Our Findings?

Scholars from several branches of psychology have criticized the experimental research strategy as a method for understanding human functioning. Specifically, these critics object to the implicit assumptions that, they claim, underlie the experimental method. They maintain that these assumptions create a situation where any research using the experimental method serves only to confirm the basic assumptions with which the research began. The situation is described as a self-fulfilling prophecy: You can't find what you refuse to look for, and all you can ever find is that which you believed in advance that you would find!

Argyris (1968, 1975), Gadlin and Ingle (1975), and Wachtel (1973) have all independently presented this criticism. Each attempts to provide a social-psychological analysis of the experimental method in order to identify the biases inherent in experimental strategies. They conclude that the experimental method is based on three assumptions:

1. The experimenter unilaterally controls the research environment and thus dictates the subjects' responses. That is, each subject's participation in an experiment is usually orchestrated by the experimenter. The location of the research, the specific tasks that subjects are required to perform, and the sequence of events that take place are not the choice of the subject.
2. Subjects are allowed only a limited number of responses, all of which are prescribed in advance by the experimenter. For example, when a researcher uses a questionnaire to assess subjects' emotional levels, subjects must indicate their emotions by responding to the items on the questionnaire. Subjects are given no choice about how to express their emotions but must simply answer the questions.
3. Subjects always act on the basis of rational hedonism, that is, to maximize their immediate gains and minimize their immediate risks or losses. Here, experimental research is criticized because researchers too often assume that subjects will behave rationally. The options for unlikely behavior are limited.

The result of these assumptions is the creation of a situation, according to the critics, that is not applicable to real life:

1. The subject is not allowed to select the situation in which he or she is interacting, whereas in our daily lives one of our most important actions is to *choose* where and with whom we will be.
2. The subject is not allowed to influence the experimenter so as to change the situation, whereas in most social interactions all participants have an impact on one another.
3. The subject cannot choose a preferred type of response, whereas in most real-life situations choosing *how* to respond, independent of the content of the response, is a crucial action.

4. The subject is not allowed to reevaluate his or her relationship with the experimenter, whereas in most daily interactions we are able to change "the rules of the game." For example, if we do not like a friend's behavior, we often can register a protest and ask for a change.

5. Rather than assessing the patterns of interrelated behaviors that, in fact, make up our lives, experiments measure restricted numbers of distinct behaviors separately.

Kruglanski (1976) and Mischel (1973a) have defended the experimental strategy against these criticisms. Kruglanski (1976) views the experimental method as a neutral tool. Although it can be used with artificiality, it can also be used to create a sophisticated sample of real-life social interactions. He maintains that the only assumptions underlying the experimental method are the premises that the conditions of peoples' lives affect their functioning and that the influence of a particular condition can best be understood by controlling the other conditions and systematically manipulating the condition of interest. Kruglanski argues that, in fact, situations in real life *do* constrain the range of allowable responses, that they *are* to a certain extent selected for us by external forces, and that they usually involve certain rules that can*not* be easily altered.

Mischel (1973a) maintains that researchers are indeed examining realistic interactions between the person and the situation in their investigations, because they are increasingly conducting studies in naturalistic settings where the full range of responses can occur and be measured. He suggests that it is not the experimental method itself but the ingenuity and sophistication of the researcher that dictates whether or not the research will be unbiased.

The issue is far from resolved. Note, however, that both the critics and advocates of the experimental method agree that is is possible to construct experiments in such a way that the results are artificial and invalid. Trivial responses can be measured, artificially powerful conditions can be created, or untested assumptions about subjects can be quietly built into experimental methods. For instance, until the past decade the interactive effects of gender and treatment interventions on human functioning were seldom examined. It was simply assumed that men and women would be equivalently affected by any independent variable. Today, most researchers realize that the client's gender can and often does interact with the type of treatment that is provided, and therefore examine the effects of treatments separately for male subjects and for female subjects. In spite of these difficulties, the experimental method can be a valuable tool, and the thoughtful and innovative experimenter can avoid the pitfalls and use this strategy to produce meaningful research.

Internal validity refers to the scientific accuracy of a study. According to Campbell and Stanley (1963) experiments are internally valid when the outcome can be attributed confidently to the independent variable that was manipulated. Internal validity is essential to draw valid conclusions. *External validity* refers to the degree to which research findings can be generalized to situations, persons, or locations beyond those employed in the study. Clinically meaningful research must attain sufficient scientific merit in terms of internal validity and sufficient utility in terms of external validity.

ETHICAL ISSUES IN RESEARCH

Individuals who participate as subjects in psychological research have certain rights, and it is the researcher's responsibility to protect these rights. The American Psychological Association has published a *Casebook on Ethical Standards of Psychologists* (1974), and a statement of the *Ethical Principles in the Conduct of Research with Human Participants* (1973), to stipulate the experimenters' ethical responsibilities to subjects, to employers, and to the broader public. The *Casebook* provides excellent examples of real ethical dilemmas confronting experimenters, and suggestions for the application of the *Principles* (see Highlight 3-4)

Highlight 3-4   An Excerpt from *Ethical Principles in the Conduct of Research with Human Participants*[4]

To illustrate the ethical guidelines that the American Psychological Association (1973) has provided, the following excerpt on "informed consent" has been selected (pp. 27–29).

Section 3-4.   Obtaining Informed Consent to Participate (Including Issues of Concealment and Deception)

The psychologist's ethical obligation to involve people as research participants only if they give their informed consent rests on well-established traditions of research ethics and on strong rational grounds. The individual's human right of free choice requires that the decision to participate be made in the light of adequate and accurate information. The fairness of the implied agreement between investigator and the research participant (Section 6, pp. 52–58) also rests upon the latter's informed consent.

Ethical problems arise because the requirements of effective psychological research often conflict with the simple fulfillment of this obligation to obtain informed consent. The relevant information may be too technical for the person to evaluate. In most tests of quantitative hypotheses, for example, the theory is beyond the research participant's comprehension. In the field of psychophysiology, the processes being studied may be completely unfamiliar to the participant. In many cases, the degree of discomfort or embarrassment to be experienced that would be relevant to the decision to participate may not be fully ascertainable prior to the conduct of the research. Certain classes of people (e.g., children, the mentally retarded, psychotics) may be incapable of responsible decision. By far the most common reason for limiting information, however, is that if the individual were to be fully informed about the purpose and procedures of the research and of the experiences to be anticipated, valid data could not be obtained. Methodological requirements of the research may demand that the participants remain unaware of the fact that they are being studied or of the hypotheses under investi-

---

[4]From the American Psychological Association, *Ethical principles in the conduct of research with human participants.* Washington, D.C.: American Psychological Association, 1973, Copyright 1973 by the American Psychological Association. Reprinted by permission.

gation. Incomplete information or misinformation may have to be provided to elicit the behavior of a naive individual, or to create a psychological reality under conditions that permit valid inference.

These research requirements present the investigator with frequent ethical dilemmas. Under what circumstances, if any, is it acceptable to bypass, delay, or compromise acting on the obligation to give the person full information about the research and obtaining on this basis the required consent or refusal to participate? About what aspects of the research must information be provided? The issues that are involved here are closely entwined with ones subsequently examined in Section 5, Assuring Freedom from Coercion to Participate. They also touch upon considerations relating to the responsibility of the investigator to provide clarifying information at the end of a study (Section 8-9, pp. 75–87). This section provides a discussion of issues that center on the informed *component of ''informed consent''; the* consent *component appears in Section 5. Since deception, when it is employed in research, intrinsically compromises the information upon which consent is gained, it is considered here. It is to be noted, however, that, in addition, deception involves bad faith and thus raises a second and more serious ethical concern. For this reason, a separate principle is devoted to deception (Principle 4) rather than treating it entirely within the context of informed consent.*

The range of problems arising in this broad category is suggested by the following incidents, selected from among the many submitted.

Incidents

1. While the operational details of the experiment that affected him were explained to the subject, the basic purpose of the study was misrepresented by telling him that it was a test of the speed of the visual system, when it was actually a test of long-term memory. Telling the actual purpose of the experiment might have effected the subject's behavior and made the results difficult to generalize. In any case, the subject who was willing to take part for the stated purpose would probably be as willing to take part for the actual one.

2. One of my doctoral students did an experiment designed to determine some correlates of the ''cheating threshold'' in college students. A test was administered, all test papers were collected and then photographed and returned. The students did not know that the papers had been photographed, and it was then made rather easy to change answers on the exam so as to improve the score.

3. Research on techniques for reducing racial and religious hostilities required participation of highly prejudiced subjects. The operational procedures were made clear to the subjects before they were asked to consent to participate, but neither before nor after the experiment was it disclosed to them that the research was sponsored by an antiprejudice group or that the research was explicitly designed to study techniques for affecting racial attitudes.

Principles

From the introductory statement of the problem, and from the incidents just presented, it is clear that the ethical idea of obtaining fully informed consent cannot be realized in much research without a serious risk that the results of the research will be deceptive or misleading. In addition, technical aspects of the research may exceed the limits of what participants can comprehend. Principles 3 and 4 are statements that may provide helpful guidelines to ethical behavior for

> the investigator who must cope with the complex problems of informed consent and deception.
>
> *Principle 3. Ethical practice requires the investigator to inform the participant of all features of the research that reasonably might be expected to influence willingness to participate, and to explain all other aspects of the research about which the participant inquires. Failure to make full disclosure gives added emphasis to the investigator's responsibility to protect the welfare and dignity of the research participant.*
>
> *Principle 4. Openness and honesty are essential characteristics of the relationship between investigator and research participant. When the methodological requirements of a study necessitate concealment or deception, the investigator is required to ensure the participant's understanding of the reasons for this action and to restore the quality of the relationship with the investigator.*
>
> As evident, psychologists believe that research subjects should be informed about their role sufficiently to permit a decision about participation.

in each case (see also Korchin & Cowan, 1982). Four aspects of this protection include informed consent, confidentiality, debriefing, and deception.

Informed Consent

Clinical psychologists, their scientific colleagues, and the government all endorse the principle that before subjects are allowed to participate in research, they must be informed about the experience that they are likely to have. Informed consent is designed to protect human subjects in research by guaranteeing that privacy, safety, and freedom are not infringed upon (see Highlight 3–5).

Highlight 3-5   A Sample Informed Consent Form

CERTIFICATE OF INFORMED CONSENT

Description of the Project and Your Involvement

The Person Perception Project is a research study that has been designed to find out how persons such as yourself react to the people that they meet in everyday situations, and to see if these reactions play a role in determining how they behave and feel towards those persons.

You will be asked to <u>read</u> written descriptions of several imaginary interactions, to <u>imagine</u> that you are one of the two persons involved in those interactions, and then to give <u>written answers</u> to questions about your reactions to those interactions. You will also be asked to fill out short questionnaires which ask you about your personal reactions to a variety of ideas and situations.

<u>All</u> of your answers will be kept strictly confidential; in fact, we do not want you to put your name on any of the answer sheets so that they will remain completely anonymous.

There are no "right" or "wrong" answers to any of the questions that you will be answering. What is important is that you answer openly and honestly by telling us what you really feel is true for you. We will <u>not</u> be evaluating any one person's answers as an individual; what we are looking for is how a large number of persons such as yourself react to these situations and questions.

If you have any questions, please feel free to ask.

You are free to withdraw from this study at any time, if you wish.

We hope that you will find participating in the study exceedingly interesting and enjoyable.

<u>Your Consent</u>

Please read and sign the following statement if you wish to participate in the Person Perception Project.

The project in which I am about to participate has been explained to me and all of my questions have been answered satisfactorily. I voluntarily agree to participate in this project. I understand that I can withdraw from the project at any time and that I can decline to participate in any of it or decline to answer any questions without prejudice to me.

_____   _____
Name (Print)   Date

_____
Signature

Confidentiality

An important aspect of subjects' rights is the confidentiality of all personal information and of their behaviors during the study. Subjects' responses to tests or tasks are not open to the public. The current practice to guarantee confidentiality is to assign each subject a number and to use the number, and not the subject's name, as identification. The data are open to the public, but this is done without identifying the specific subjects. Finally, subjects have the right to withdraw from an experiment at any time if they feel the need, without prejudice.

Deception

Deception involves misleading or withholding information from subjects. For example, in a study of conformity (Asch, 1956), the subject might be exposed to four lines that appear to be of equal length. Seven subjects may be seated in a row and each asked to state whether the lines are the same length or different lengths. If the first six subjects say they are different, even though they appear the same, will the seventh subject conform? In this example, the first six subjects are experimental confederates who are aware of the purposes of the study and who are playing the role of subject when they are actually a part of the research.

Several difficulties may arise when using deception. Practical complications such as subjects guessing the deception, and methodological problems such as difficulty in providing subjects with a plausible fake reason for their participation while they are being deceived, have been identified. Still more important, psychologists are concerned that subjects may leave the experiment feeling shocked or disillusioned. Therefore, researchers who use deception are required to be extremely careful in obtaining informed consent and providing full debriefing. Some researchers have advocated having subjects fully informed and asking them to role play—that is, to pretend that they were not informed and act accordingly (Seeman, 1969). No simple answer exists for this issue, but psychologists permit deception only when the study is arranged to protect all rights of every subject, including an explicit detailed debriefing.

Debriefing

Debriefing, clarifying the reasons and methods of the research, is an important aspect of psychological research because subjects have the right to know why and how their behavior has been studied. Consider the following study as an example of debriefing. The researchers (Kendall, Finch, & Montgomery, 1978) were interested in the characteristics of people who experience "vicarious anxiety," a state of emotional upset resulting from observing another person in discomfort. Consider for a moment what it is like when you are at a performance of a play and the star has been replaced by an unprepared understudy. If you have been in such a situation you know that there are large differences in the behaviors of the ticket holders. Some will get up out of their chairs, go to the box office and demand a refund, while others will stay in their seats and work themselves into an anxious sweat! What are the relevant personality differences associated with the different ways people handle the situation?

Kendall et al. presented a guest lecturer to a class of undergraduate psychology students. The students had already completed several personality tests and the guest speaker was really an experimental confederate. The speaker began to talk and soon behaved anxiously, fumbling into troubles with stuttering, repeating phrases, dropping papers, spilling coffee, etc. Just as the speaker was trying to locate a slide projector to show some slides a confederate announced that it appeared that it hadn't been delivered. At this point, the speaker distributed a sample questionnaire (a measure of current level of anxiety) and asked the students in the audience to complete it. The scores on the anxiety measure, in comparison to scores taken during a previous nonstressful condition, were indications of the anxiety aroused in the audience by the anxious speaker. Briefly, the results indicated that the students who scored high on a measure of empathy (Hogan, 1969) reported increased anxiety due to the anxious speaker. Low-empathic subjects did not become anxious for the speaker. For our current discussion, the debriefing used by Kendall et al. (1978) is particularly important.

Since the personality measures had been completed prior to the guest speaker's performing the anxiety manipulation, most of the data were scored before the class met. For example, subjects were divided according to their empathy scores into high- and low-empathy groups prior to the class meeting. As soon as the subjects had experienced the anxious guest speaker and had completed the measure of anxiety, the study was complete and the experimenters provided debriefing.

The debriefing entailed a full explanation of the study, its purposes, hypotheses, expected outcomes, and implications. All questions were answered and subjects were given ample time to discuss their feelings with the researcher. During the debriefing the subjects were also told that a summary of the findings would be presented at the end of the class. Before further debriefing, the speaker gave his talk in a normal nonanxious fashion. During this time, the experimenter scored the anxiety measure that had just been completed and tabulated some summary data. Following the actual talk, the experimenter then presented a summary of the results to the class. Thus, the students were debriefed as to the purposes of the study, the performance aspects of the anxiety manipulation, and some of the actual results of the study. In this manner, the debriefing was also educational.

Since the researchers were interested in vicarious emotionality, an uncomfortable state for the subjects, the researchers took the additional precaution of having a clinical psychologist available to talk with any subjects who felt adversely affected by their experience in the study. No subjects did actually react adversely, but the precaution was nevertheless essential.

APPENDIX

A representative sample of journals relevant to clinical psychology

American Journal of Community Psychology

American Journal of Orthopsychiatry

American Journal of Psychiatry

American Psychologist

Archives of General Psychiatry

Behavior Genetics

Behaviour Research and Therapy

Behavior Therapy

Behavioral Assessment

Biofeedback and Self-Regulation

The Clinical Psychologist

Cognitive Therapy and Research

Educational and Psychological Measurement

Family Process

Journal of Abnormal Child Psychology

Journal of Abnormal Psychology

Journal of Applied Behavior Analysis

Journal of Autism and Childhood Schizophrenia

Journal of Behavior Therapy and Experimental Psychiatry

Journal of Child Psychology and Psychiatry

Journal of Clinical Psychology

Journal of Community Psychology

Journal of Consulting and Clinical Psychology

Journal of Counseling Psychology

Journal of Experimental and Clinical Hypnosis

Journal of Marital & Family Therapy

Journal of Personality

Journal of Personality Assessment

Journal of Personality and Social Psychology

Professional Psychology

Psychological Bulletin

Psychotherapy: Theory, Research, and Practice

Review of Educational Research

Schizophrenia Bulletin

Big Julie by Fernand Leger, 1945.

II

CONCEPTUAL FRAMEWORKS IN CLINICAL PSYCHOLOGY

Painting by Erhard Jacoby.

No man is an island, entire of itself;
Every man is a piece of the continent, a part of the main;
If a clod be washed away by the sea, Europe is the less,
As well as if a promontory were,
As well as if a manor of thy friends or of thine own were;
Any man's death diminishes me, because I am involved in mankind;
And therefore never send to know for whom the bell tolls;
It tolls for thee.

John Donne

Read not to contradict and confute, nor to believe and
take for granted, nor to find talk and discourse,
but to weigh and consider.

Francis Bacon

4

CONCEPTUALIZATIONS OF HUMAN FUNCTIONING AND SOCIAL ENVIRONMENTS

First and foremost, clinical psychologists work with people. Therefore, clinicians need a set of guiding principles concerning the nature of human functioning and the impact of social environments. Theoretical conceptualizations of (1) *personality*, (2) *development and adaptation*, and (3) *social groups and communities* offer frameworks that can help clinical psychologists to utilize the many diverse bits of information about their clients in the development of integrated and effective understandings of, and interventions for, each client. Each type of conceptualization is discussed in this chapter.

Theoretical principles and frameworks provide clinicians with basic *assumptions* about how people and their environments interact and a practical number of *categories* in which data about people can be placed and organized. The assumptions ("postulates," "axioms," "principles") provide a basis for predicting what people are likely to do in the future, thus enabling the clinical psychologist to correctly anticipate clients' needs, problems, and capabilities. The categories ("personality types or traits," "developmental stages," "situational variables") enable clinicians to pinpoint the focal themes and key aspects of peoples' actions, thoughts, feelings, and life contexts in an accurate and efficient manner.

With their conceptual assumptions and categories, clinical psychologists can develop hypotheses ("educated guesses") about how best to understand and aid each unique client. Such hypotheses tend to be most accurate and useful when they (1) are supported by prior research and (2) are carefully evaluated by the clinician to assure their applicability to the particular client. Conceptual schemes can be "blinders," narrowing the clinician's range of vision so that useful hypotheses are ignored. However, when clinical psychologists frequently evaluate, revise, and expand their conceptual assumptions and categories, they are able to efficiently and therapeutically translate large quantities of information about a client into effective interventions for the client's benefit. Clinicians attempt to avoid the pitfall of jumping to hasty or prejudiced conclusions about clients—a tendency that has been well documented as a part of the human condition (Asch,

1946; Bem, 1972; Kahnemon & Tversky, 1973; Meehl, 1960; Soskin, 1959; Wyatt & Campbell, 1950)—by rechecking the validity of their assumptions and categories on a regular basis. A healthy skepticism and a focus on theories that are not only elegant and empirically validated but also meaningful (Koch, 1981) are also essential.

Clinical psychologists cannot use every part of every available theoretical framework. Instead, they must integrate the diverse perspectives into a personal/professional conceptualization that abstracts the fundamentals of the many existing theories and permits them to provide effective services to clients. Some clinical psychologists adhere solely to one theory, but the majority take an "eclectic" approach by combining bits from several theories into their own guiding principles for clinical assessment and intervention.

PERSONALITY

Theories of personality offer clinicians conceptualizations for understanding each unique person, as well as a vocabulary for communicating this understanding to the client and to other professionals. Personality theories also provide criteria with which clinicians can (1) judge the effectiveness of a person's overall functioning, (2) pinpoint dysfunctions, (3) formulate specific goals for research or intervention, and (4) identify a person's assets and positive capabilities.

All people formulate implicit conceptualizations to make sense of the personalities of significant persons in their lives (Kelly, 1955). This is done by identifying recurrent behavior patterns and classifying these by means of trait labels such as "shy" or "imaginative." Clinical psychologists go beyond such social labeling by attempting to explain the *causes* of these consistencies in human functioning. Three major types of personality theory have evolved in this effort: psychodynamic, self-actualization, and social learning.

Psychodynamic Theories

Psychodynamic theories emphasize internal psychological structures that are assumed to guide each person. These structures cannot be observed directly like a bodily organ, but are inferred to exist based on recurrent patterns of behavior. Although it is acknowledged that people experience important interactions with their external environments, the resolution of inner strife among the psychological structures is considered paramount for an effective and happy life.

Freud: Psychoanalysis Freud (1904; 1923; 1938) postulated three competing psychological structures within each person. The *id* represents instinctual needs and drives for sexual and aggressive gratification, operating on a "pleasure principle" ("I can have whatever I want right now!") that is based on the "primary processes" of fantasy and imagination rather than logic and fact. In contrast, the *ego*, although emerging originally from the id as the person strives to meet the challenges posed by the external environment, is attuned to a "reality principle" ("I have to strike a realistic balance between what I want and what I can really have") that is based on conscious reasoning. The *superego* evolves after id and ego to represent the internalized values and ideas of society as transmitted by the person's parents, often taking a rigid and moralistic approach to life ("I ought to be a better person!").

Freud believed that psychological functioning hinged on an ego strong enough to temper the demands of id and superego while coping with the stresses of social life. Psychological dysfunctions are seen as arising when life traumas render the ego incapable of handling certain problematic situations. This occurs when problems arise that, due to stressful experiences or deficient learning in childhood, the adult ego lacks the skills or strength to handle. The person experiences anxiety in such crises, and the ego temporarily "goes underground" to an unconscious stockpile of "defense mechanisms" (Table 4-1) that reduce anxiety but never fully resolve the crisis. Defense mechanisms are seen as causing more problems than they solve, because by protecting the ego from anxiety they prevent the ego from ever overcoming the deficiencies that are the basic source of that anxiety. For Freud, effective personal functioning hinged on attaining sufficient awareness of the demands of id and superego and sufficient resolution of the ego's longstanding weaknesses to permit the ego to orchestrate a lasting balance between id, superego, and external environment.

Table 4-1   Sample Defense Mechanisms

Repression	The central defense mechanism for Freud, repression is a totally unconscious blocking of threatening ideas or feelings from ever entering consciousness. It can be contrasted with suppression, which is not a Freudian defense mechanism because it involves a *conscious* attempt not to think about anxiety-evoking ideas or feelings (e.g., via distraction).
Denial	Denial is the unconscious act of not admitting that a threatening idea or feeling might apply to oneself. Rather than totally voiding the anxiety-evoking stimulus, denial involves admitting that it exists but not admitting that it is personally relevant.
Projection	When anxiety, guilt, or other threatening emotions are blamed on, or attributed to, another person(s), projection has occurred. Blame is transferred to others rather than taken on oneself.
Reaction Formation	Reaction formation is the unconscious expression of attitudes or feelings that are the opposite of the person's true stance. Unacceptable motives are translated into palatable opposites to avoid anxiety.
Regression	Regression is a strategic, altogether unconscious, retreat to a safer time from past life, a reenactment of childish thinking or behaving in order to reduce adult stresses.
Intellectualization	When a person intellectualizes, or rationalizes, a logical and socially acceptable explanation is constructed for otherwise painful situations, thoughts, or feelings. The rationalization is superficial and self-defeating but temporarily soothing.

Jung: Psychic Individuation   Jung (1917; 1933) described individuation as the crux of effective human functioning. A person is seen as individuated to the extent that he or she recognizes, differentiates, and then integrates several internal psychological processes in a harmonious fashion.

The *collective unconscious* is the central coordinator that evolves from every person's inherited archetypes. Archetypes are the central principles and wisdoms that have developed as mankind has acquired increasing ability to live fully. For example, the distinctive qualities of masculinity ("animus"), feminity ("anima"), motherliness, love, or god are thought to be archetypes that all persons share. The *personal unconscious* reflects the unacceptable impulses and experiences that each person develops when life's challenges are unresolved, whereas the *shadow* are the feelings and attributes that the person recognizes consciously but attempts to hide. *Personna* reflects the person's social roles, while *anima/animus* are, respectively, the man's and the woman's other-sex qualities. Finally, *ego* is the source of conscious rational planning and decision making.

In contrast to Freud, Jung believed that ego is not the best executive for creating an individuated person. Rather, a blend of all these internal sources is believed to come about when all are recognized and accepted, and this total "self" is viewed as the basis for effective personality.

Adler: Overcoming Inferiority   Adler (1927) proposed that, contrary to Freud, the central human impulse is not sexuality or aggressiveness but rather a drive to overcome inferiority and achieve superiority. The phrase "inferiority complex" comes from Adler's theory that every person instinctively feels inferior and must undergo a three-stage process to achieve effective human functioning.

First, inferiority feelings must be *compensated* for, through satisfying and secure relationships, community participation, a productive career, and the courage to meet life's challenges. Second, the person must *strive* for superiority by developing a life-style that enables him or her to seek out new experiences and challenges that serve as the basis for fuller relationships and endeavors. Finally, the person can *create* a complete self by dispensing with "guiding fictions" (self-protective beliefs such as, "You can't lose if you don't try") and developing a firm but realistic self-confidence that enables him or her to constantly test the validity of his or her beliefs and ways of dealing with other persons. Adler believed that it is through relationships with peers, rather than parents, that people achieve more effective functioning.

Horney: Integrating the Real and Ideal Self   Horney (1950) focused on the dilemmas that can result from a gap between who a person *is* ("real self") and who that person *wishes to be* ("ideal self"). For Horney, effective human functioning requires that the person achieve an integration of the real and ideal selves, in that the real self is accepted and the ideal self serves as a helpful guide for continued growth and improvement. If people divorce themselves from their real selves and frantically pursue an unrealistic ideal self, this is viewed as an "alienation from self." This self-defeating "search for glory" can take three forms: a rigid demand for perfection, an unrealistic ambition for supremacy, or a need for vindictive triumph.

In contrast, the effective person is seen as accepting the real self despite flaws and foibles, and attempting to gradually achieve ideal goals through a balance of three basic ways of relating with other persons: moving *toward* them (such as creating friendships), *against* them (such as competing for a job), and *away from* them (such as enjoying a walk by oneself). Horney thus postulated that effective human functioning is achieved through balanced patterns of interaction with other persons that enable the person to achieve an internal balance between the real and ideal selves.

Self-Actualization Theories

Once a person has transcended basic conflicts and satisfied basic needs, the door is open for honest self-evaluation and an expansion of emotional, cognitive, and behavioral capabilities. Several theorists have focused on the ideal characteristics of such "self-actualizing" persons. Where psychodynamic theories emphasize internal psychological conflicts, self-actualization theories examine people's strivings for enhancement of positive aspects of themselves.

Maslow: Toward Self-Actualization   Maslow (1968) stated that people must satisfy four types of basic needs: first, *physiological* (such as hunger or fatigue), then *psychological* (such as security or calmness), then *relationship* (such as intimacy or acceptance), and finally *self-esteem* (such as self-respect). Only when these needs are fulfilled can a person pursue self-actualization. Self-actualizing persons are not necessarily happier, wealthier, or more popular than the average person, but Maslow believed that they are more curious, caring, tolerant, spontaneous, and accepting of themselves and others than most people. They are bonded with only a few special persons, rather than casually involved with many people, and they appear to be exceptionally creative, self-directed, independent, and ethical. "Self-actualizers" are able to transcend the limits of tradition and social norms to develop their own personal values and goals. They are seen as especially open to new and intense experiences, while still genuinely appreciating even the most common events. Finally, self-actualizers are viewed as accurate in their perception of themselves and others, able to solve problems effectively, and able to distinguish between means and ends so as to be maximally effective without compromising their fundamental values.

For Maslow, self-actualization is not a fixed endpoint but an ongoing process of "being" in which the person appreciates and integrates all aspects of psychological and social life. No person is ever entirely self-actualized, but the challenge is to develop an honest, tolerant, caring, and growth-oriented approach to life.

Allport: Mature Goal-Seeking   Maturity, according to Allport (1961), is an ongoing quest for self-enhancing personal goals in all areas of life. In Allport's view, this requires that a person take the initiative in constructive, innovative, and self-consistent attempts to resolve problems and achieve new accomplishments but to do so in a warm and caring manner that is the basis for meaningful relationships. Maturity hinges on the development of a *sense* of emotional security, an *ability* to perceive one's self and the world accurately, *skills* for all the tasks of living, and a basic *orientation* of learning from all life experiences. Allport also stressed the importance of a unifying philosophy of life, that is, a clearly articulated and well-tested system of consistent values for purposeful living. Such a personal creed need not be complicated or technical, but an integrated statement about "how life should be lived" is seen as essential for personal satisfaction and growth and enhancing interpersonal relationships.

Rogers: Toward Authenticity   To be authentic is to engage in the process of living in a way that reflects caring for and awareness of one's self and other persons, spontaneity and openness to new experiences, self-direction and responsibility, and a realistic balance between the contingencies of reality and the ideals to which the person aspires (Rogers, 1961).

Authentic people are seen as honest and forward looking; they share of themselves and others without compromising their own needs or those of the other persons, and without using the disguises and deceptions of social appropriateness. In their attitudes toward themselves and others, and in their relationships, authentic people express empathic understanding, unconditional positive regard, and complete genuineness. Rogers believes that this willingness to be "real," in combination with a basic faith in the goodness of all people, is essential for effective human functioning.

Social Learning Theories

Social learning theories focus on the ways that people learn life skills through their behavioral and cognitive interactions with the external environment. Effective human functioning is seen as resulting from matchups between people and their environments that facilitate this learning process. The focus is on the person *in situ* (in his or her life context), rather than only on characteristics of people's inner conflicts or strivings.

Rotter: Expectancies as Guides for Living   Rotter's (1954; 1972) social learning theory posits that people handle life's challenges by developing expectancies. *Expectancies* are subjective predictions about the consequences of different courses of action. Two types of expectancies are viewed as crucial. The *probable outcomes* of an action are the consequences that the person has learned to expect from each of the potential responses to a situation. The *subjective value* of each outcome is the person's evaluation of the importance, and "goodness-badness," of each potential outcome. For example, Rotter would hypothesize that an adult's decision to drink alcohol will hinge on that person's expectations about the probable outcomes (e.g., pleasant intoxication, social acceptance by other drinkers, long-term risk of alcoholism) and each outcome's subjective value (e.g., good but insignificant, very positive, very negative).

Rotter also hypothesized that people are guided by *generalized expectancies*. These are rules for understanding and dealing with the world that are seen as developing as a result of many consistent learning experiences. Rotter (1966) postulated a central generalized expectancy, "locus of control," which involves the

belief that one is either controlled by external forces such as luck or powerful politicians (external locus of control) or that one is the master of one's own destiny
(internal).

Each new life experience both contributes to the development (or change) of
these specific and generalized experiences, and is responded to based on prior expectancies. Effective living requires expectancies which guide the person toward
rewards and away from punishments.

Bandura: Reciprocal Social Learning   Bandura (1969; 1977a; 1978) views effective personal functioning as the product of continuous reciprocal interactions
among (1) learning experiences provided by the social environment, (2) the cognitive processes through which the person understands these experiences and plans
reactions to them, and (3) the behaviors that the person uses to cope with, and
also to alter, the environment. All three facets of social living—environment,
cognition, and behavior—must be considered in a complete description of human
functioning.

Bandura highlighted the importance of learning through observation—modeling—in addition to the direct rewards and punishments that had been emphasized
in earlier learning theories of personality. Although direct learning is viewed as
more powerful, observational learning is a safer and more versatile means of acquiring cognitive and behavioral skills because it takes place from a distance.

Bandura (1977b) also furthered Rotter's analyses of expectancies, distinguishing between *outcome expectancies* ("This is what will happen if I take that action") and *efficacy expectancies* ("I am/am not a skillful/capable person"). A
person may thus believe that the future holds the promise of many rewards but
yet feel depressed because these payoffs are seen as coming due to luck and despite a lack of personal skill. These expectancies mediate between the person's environment and his or her behavior, sometimes leading to responses that appear
incongruous in light of the objective situation. For example, the person just described is likely to show behavioral signs of depression such as fatigue, giving up
goal-directed efforts, and irritating requests for reassurance, despite what seems
on the surface to be a paradise of rewards and pleasures.

Mischel: Skills for Effective Psychological Functioning   Mischel (1968; 1973b;
1979) proposed a set of cognitive and behavioral skills that he believes underlie effective human functioning. According to Mischel, each new situation requires
new tactics for action, but certain behavioral skills and cognitive strategies are always necessary to enable the person to select the optimal course of action. *Competencies* are the specific skills that are required by different situations, while *self-
regulatory systems and plans* are the underlying skills that enable the person to
autonomously set goals, select specific behaviors, and regulate these plans and actions. For example, skill in evaluating one's past actions, and either rewarding
oneself for success or developing new tactics for the future, is central to personal
happiness and effective interaction with other persons. Thus, Mischel emphasizes
an analysis of people's skills for handling the challenges of their environments,
rather than a focus on internal conflicts or strivings for self-improvement.

Need for Multiple Conceptualization

What then are the benchmarks of effective human functioning? Psychodynamic theories suggest that an inner balance and harmony is essential, with a secondary emphasis on the person's competency to achieve and maintain intimate, self-enhancing, productive, and growing relationships. Self-actualization theories focus on openness to all experiences, authenticity, spontaneity, constructive reevaluation of one's beliefs, and acceptance of self and others. Social learning theories stress a facilitative social environment from which the person can learn cognitive and behavioral skills for self-regulation. All of these attributes, orientations, and skills are likely to contribute to a full life for most persons, and as such they all offer important building blocks for comprehensive clinical conceptualizations.

DEVELOPMENT AND ADAPTATION

We all encounter a series of challenges during our lives requiring the development of new skills, beliefs, values, and self-confidence so that we can fulfill our potentials for satisfaction, achievement, and self-esteem. A variety of *adaptation processes*, including physiological, cognitive, behavioral, and emotional, are necessary as the person confronts problematic life situations. After discussing these processes, our attention turns to the *developmental challenges* that people face from infancy to adulthood and older age.

Processes of Adaptation

People are frequently faced with life experiences that require new responses. Without such diversity and novelty, life would be unexciting and growth would be impossible. However, the process of formulating, executing, and evaluating new responses to problematic situations is indeed demanding. Four types of adaptation processes are necessary: physiological, cognitive, behavioral, and emotional.

Physiological Processes   Restoration, preparation, and arousal are three basic physiological processes of adaptation. When the body is deprived of physical essentials such as oxygen, fluids, or nutrients, or when the level of bodily elements such as salt, neural transmitters, or red blood cells exceeds normal capacities, restoration of a sufficient but not excessive quantity is essential.

If restoration is not possible, or in instances when external stresses threaten the existing balance, the physiological processes of arousal and preparation are activated. Selye (1956) described this as the first stage of a "general activation syndrome," labeling it as *activation*. The person reacts with heightened alertness and vigilance due to a generalized increase in bodily arousal and a special increase in chemical (hormones) and muscular (contractions) preparation in the body areas that are most stressed. If restoration continues to be impossible, a second stage, *resistance*, begins, in which the individual essentially turns off the alarm systems and gears up for a prolonged defense against stress. This process requires a decrease in the initial arousal and a defocusing on the stressor in order to minimize the pain and damage that is inflicted. Should the stresses continue unabated for a long time, the third adaptation stage of *exhaustion* will set in. At this point, the person's physical resources have given out, and physical illness or psychological dysfunction are likely to result. For example, the person will be unusually prone to infectious illness and to serious psychological problems such as depression or psychosis.

A variety of physiological dysfunctions that are treated by clinical psychologists are hypothesized to be, at least in part, due to lengthy contact with stressors that elicit the general activation syndrome. For instance, essential hypertension (chronic high blood pressure), migraine headaches (chronic contraction of the frontalis and occipitalis muscles in the forehead and neck), and stomach ulcers (perforations of the stomach lining) are all thought to be exacerbated by prolonged excessive stress.

One portion of the brain, the diencephalon, has been tentatively identified as the coordinator of the physiological processes of restoration, preparation, and arousal (Akiskal & McKinney, 1975; Leukel, 1976). Within the diencephalon, an area called the hypothalamus appears to play a role in the increase and decrease of bodily arousal, the regulation of body hormones, the activation and satiation of fluid and food consumption, and the control of extreme rage and fear behavior (Leukel, 1976). The diencephalon responds to signals from the body, and then issues reciprocal signals to deal with needed physiological adaptations. Clinical problems involving these adaptations, for instance psychological depression, have been hypothesized to result, in part, from problems in the diencephalon's functioning (Akiskal & McKinney, 1975). However, all areas in the brain have an impact on psychological functioning, so clinicians devote special attention to developing conceptualizations of brain functioning.

Neuropsychological functioning   The study of the structure, function, and dysfunctions of the brain (neuropsychology) has demonstrated that the brain is composed of between 10 and 18 billion neurons, which are arranged in three hierarchical structures: the hindbrain, midbrain, and forebrain (Figure 4-1).

Special functions such as speech, cognition, sensory perception, and coordination and production of voluntary motor acts are controlled by the outer edges of the forebrain area called the cerebrum—the cerebral cortex. This brain area is the focus for neuropsychological assessment, the assessment of disorders of the brain that cause impairments of psychological functioning.

The cerebral cortex is organized along two spatial planes, consisting of a left hemisphere and a right hemisphere ("lateral organization"), and an anterior (front) and posterior (rear) section ("longitudinal organization") (see Figure 4-2). The left hemisphere appears to be responsible for logical thinking and language use, while the right hemisphere controls nonverbal, spatial, and sensory processes that are involved in such activities as driving a car, writing and drawing, and making "intuitive" hunches. The two hemispheres are, however, in constant

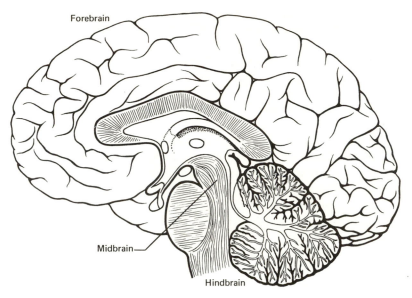

Forebrain

Midbrain

Hindbrain

Figure 4-1 Representation of the brain's sections.

communication so that both verbal and nonverbal aspects of an activity can be accomplished in harmony. As Gazzaniga (1975) summarizes:

> *Most clinical data suggest that the brain is not a homogeneous system with every part equally involved in every function . . . (However,) various cerebral functions which are managed in discrete areas interact with other cerebral sites . . . (so that) . . . a variety of spheres of influence in the brain, some with functions that overlap with those of others, are all interacting in a dynamic way to produce a final integral behavioral response. (pp. 573–575)*

Similarly, each cortical hemisphere can be divided into four sections, called lobes, which are located in the anterior (i.e., the frontal lobe) and posterior (i.e., the parietal, temporal, and occipital lobes) areas of each cortex (Figure 4-2). The frontal lobe is responsible for the planning and executing of motor acts, while the parietal, temporal, and occipital lobes specialize in, respectively, spatial and kinesthetic, auditory, and visual perception. The cortical areas lying in between the four lobes have the all-important task of integrating and coordinating the disjoint sensory and motor inputs and outputs from each lobe. Without these "association areas" we would be flooded with what would seem like overwhelming numbers of random and meaningless sensations. For example, kinesthetic/vestibular association areas bordering the parietal lobe organize feedback from all areas in the body to make balanced action possible, while the visual association areas at the edges of the occipital lobe enable us to comprehend visual stimuli as whole figures.

In addition to overseeing the basic physiological adaptations of restoration, preparation, and arousal, the brain thus coordinates more complex behavioral and cognitive adaptations that are manifested in such acts as speech, logical de-

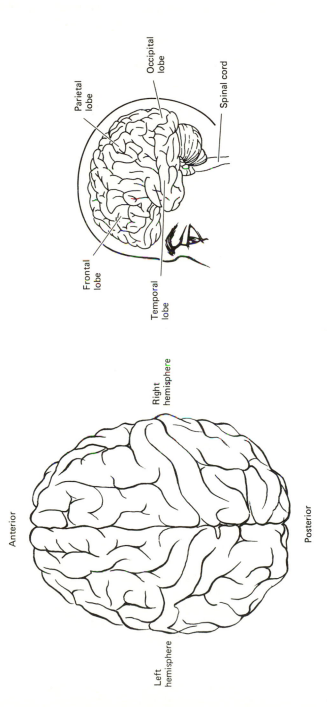

Parietal lobe

Occipital lobe

Spinal cord

Frontal lobe

Temporal lobe

Right hemisphere

Anterior

Posterior

Left hemisphere

Figure 4-2 Representation of the sections of the cerebral cortex.

cision making, and perception. When such functions are disordered in a client, the clinician uses the methods of neuropsychological assessment to determine whether or not physical damage in the brain is a cause.

Cognitive Processes   Thought plays a major role in human functioning. The inputs from our bodies and our environments to which we must adapt are filtered through cognitive translators and censors. By thinking we can also modify our physiological, behavioral, and emotional reactions to such inputs, thus facilitating successful adaptations. *Memory* and *decision making* are of direct relevance for clinical psychologists because they are required for purposeful action. Memory and decision making are actually interrelated components in a four-step process that is required for cognitive adaptation.

First, the person must *screen* out inputs from the body and the environment that are not relevant to the current situation, and then *detect* inputs that are crucial to an effective adaptation (Erdelyi, 1974). This screening and detection process is, due to the large volume of information that people must handle, often done outside the person's awareness. Thus, clinicians often find that their clients are failing to attend to inputs that are crucial for effective responding, and these clients are typically unaware of the "blinders" that they seem to be wearing.

Second, a rapid *search-and-comparison* process takes place in which the new inputs are used as cues to activate the person's long-term memory, in search of a strategy for handling the present situation (Schneider & Shiffrin, 1977). Long-term memory is like a data bank in a computer that houses massive amounts of information awaiting the appropriate signals to retrieve it for current use. If an input is "close friend experiencing emotional trauma," and you have learned an effective strategy for handling this situation in the past, then this action plan can be activated smoothly and quickly by retrieving it from your long-term memory. The search-and-comparison process enables people to act swiftly in a complicated but coordinated fashion. The integrated action plans stored in long-term memory, however, require frequent revision or they soon become outdated.

When an appropriate action strategy cannot be located in long-term memory, the third step is a more effortful and time-consuming *search-and-rehearsal* process (Schneider & Shiffrin, 1977). This "controlled" search is done in a step-by-step fashion, guided by the person's conscious attention, where automatic search occurs in a swift and total sweep that does not require conscious awareness. Items from long-term memory are selected and, one by one, compared to the new inputs. If there are many inputs requiring processing, if many items in long-term memory may be relevant in dealing with the inputs, or if the person is being bombarded with many inputs at a fast rate of simultaneous occurrence, the search process is more difficult, more prone to error, and slower (Atkinson & Shiffrin, 1968). Clinical psychologists often help their clients deal with information overload by encouraging them to deal with one issue at a time with a focus on only the very most important inputs and time reserved for periods of rest and relaxation.

Once an action strategy has been formulated through the controlled search process, it must be quickly transferred to long-term memory or else it will be forgotten in the flood of new inputs (Atkinson & Shiffrin, 1968). The key to such storage in long-term memory is rehearsal, that is, the active and repeated mental utilization of the information. Ideally, the action strategy will be organized into a concise and coherent package and then indexed with a meaningful label, much as books are bound and then filed with a call number in the library. Mnemonic devices, such as a picture or a simple story that represent all of the components of the action strategy, are excellent means for indexing and filing away information in readily retrievable fashions in long-term memory. For example, Lewinsohn, Danaher, and Kikel (1977) aided clients who suffered memory deficits due to brain damage to recall important information by teaching them to systematically use mnemonic devices.

Fourth, the person must *evaluate* and *modify* (if necessary) the selected action strategy. Changes in the person, such as new personal goals or values, or variations in the environment, such as the differing requirements of a lecture versus seminar class, require adjustment in action strategies. Psychological dysfunctions often are caused, at least in part, by deficient cognitive evaluation. For example, marital discord may result when spouses lack the skill or willingness required to give and receive useful feedback so as to modify their relationship in areas such as sex, expression of feelings, finances, or relationships with friends and relatives.

Several special aspects of cognitive adaptation merit further attention, including personal constructs, problem solving, and intelligence.

Personal constructs   When people organize inputs to facilitate action strategies and effective memory storage, they do so using what Kelly (1955) calls "personal constructs." Personal constructs are basic assumptions about how to categorize new inputs and about the value that should be assigned to inputs in different categories. Examples of personal constructs include traits, expectancies (Rotter, 1954), or life scripts (Berne, 1970). Personal constructs are each person's beliefs about how the world works, how to describe himself or herself, and how to describe other persons.

Personal constructs (or "schemas") are like eyeglasses in that they help us to focus our attention most clearly on important new inputs, but they can induce a form of tunnel vision. For example, several studies have shown that people tend to adopt personal constructs based on first impressions in many situations, and that these beliefs and categorizations are often retained even in the face of disconfirming evidence (Asch, 1946; Soskin, 1959).

Clinicians often find that a central ingredient in effective intervention is aiding clients to reexamine their self-defeating beliefs to help them develop more realistic and self-enhancing personal constructs. For example, people with low esteem tend to ignore or forget positive information about themselves (Mischel, Ebbesen, & Zeiss, 1973; Phares, Ritchie, & Davis, 1968), as well as being more open to accept negative inputs about themselves (Bramel, 1962). Therapy that aims at aiding such clients to acquire a new sense of personal power and worth can alleviate this problematic vicious cycle (Johnson & Matross, 1977).

Problem solving   Cognitive adaptation is especially important in situations where there are several alternative actions that can be taken and the optimal response is not readily apparent. D'Zurilla and Goldfried (1971) describe a five-stage process that research suggests is ideal for handling such problematic situations.

1.	*Orientation:*	First become aware that a new response is needed.
2.	*Problem definition:*	Assess all relevant inputs and formulate specific operational goals.
3.	*Generating alternatives:*	Brainstorm (engage in a freewheeling, noncritical, and innovative search for action strategies).
4.	*Decision making:*	Estimate the value and likelihood of success of the most plausible response possibilities, then weigh each response's costs and benefits, and finally select the optimal one.
5.	*Evaluation:*	Monitor the outcomes produced by the selected response and modify it to increase benefits or reduce costs.

For instance, if a person seeks to behave more assertively, he or she must first recognize a need for improved assertiveness and make a commitment to hold off on any attempts until he or she has planned effective action strategies (Hollandsworth, 1977). Constructive goals must then be developed and stated in specific terms. Brainstorming can then be undertaken to create a list of possible assertion strategies. For instance, a disquieted wife with a concern for independence might consider yelling at her husband, expressing her priorities to her husband in a clear, nonjudgmental and serious manner, joining an assertion training group at the local university or counseling center, or seeking a job. The costs and benefits of each response possibility can next be weighed (e.g., yelling has a strong impact but is likely to lead to counterattacks), and the best elements in each possible response can be combined to form an even better action strategy. For instance, the woman in our example might decide to first join an assertion training group to learn how to most effectively express her priorities and find a satisfying job. Finally, the selected response must be evaluated and improved until the person's goals are accomplished. The wife might have to consider returning to school, for example, before deciding whether or not to take on a new job. Thus, systematic problem solving enables people to control their lives in even highly problematic situations. Clinicians often utilize problem solving as a model for assessment and intervention (Urban & Ford, 1971), as well as teaching clients problem-solving skills (D'Zurilla & Nezu, 1982; Urbain & Kendall, 1980).

Intelligence   Wechsler (1958) defined intelligence as "the aggregate or global capacity of the individual to act purposively, to think rationally, and to deal effectively with his environment." Controversy existed as to whether a single general ability underlies most of all intelligence (Spearman, 1904) or intelligence is comprised of several distinct specific abilities (Thorndike, Lay, & Dean, 1909). Contemporary clinical psychologists have been most strongly influenced by Wechsler's (1958; Matarazzo, 1972) intermediate view that intelligence is a global *competence* for handling life's challenges that derives from the integration of cognitive and behavioral capabilities.

Piaget (1954), Cattell (1957), and Guilford (1959) among others have offered integrated conceptualizations of the capabilities involved in intelligence. Piaget viewed intelligence as an ongoing process of cognitive adaptation to the environment that hinges on two central skills. *Accommodation* involved creating changes in one's own beliefs and ways of thinking so as to more successfully adjust to the environment, while *assimilation* involves the direct incorporation of new beliefs or thought processes from models in the environment. For Piaget, intelligence is the process of refining the cognitive skills that enable people to adjust to, and profit from, their environments.

Cattell (1957) described intelligence as involving two factors. *Fluid* intelligence is the component that enables people to perceive relationships and thus organize their views of the world in a coordinated fashion that facilitates effective action. It is viewed as independent of education and experience, while *crystallized* intelligence is conceptualized as the specific result of each individual's unique educational and cultural experiences (e.g., vocabulary or arithmetic skills). Factor analytic research supports Cattell's model (Horn, 1968), although it has not been proven that "fluid" abilities are unlearned as Cattell postulated. In fact, a central goal in most clinical interventions is to *teach* clients more effective ways to cognitively coordinate their perceptions and action.

Guilford (1959) developed a tridimensional model that describes not only the skills (*operations*), but also the *contents* and *products* that are believed to comprise intelligence (Figure 4-3). Intelligence is seen as a multifaceted set of abilities with which the person cognitively utilizes figures, symbols, words, and actions in order to create new thoughts, behaviors, and environments. The operations include skills for comparing, analyzing, creating, remembering, and cognitively organizing ideas. Although not widely utilized by practicing clinicians (Matarazzo, 1972), Guilford's model provides a comprehensive orientation for assessment of intellectual skills and functions.

Intelligence is a construct with many implications for clinical psychology. As more is learned about the skills that enable people to make effective cognitive adaptations, clinicians will be increasingly able to develop assessments and interventions that translate an understanding of human intelligence into services for enhancing clients' lives and capabilities.

Emotional Processes   Everyone has feelings. Positive emotions are a clear signal that we are functioning effectively, and distressing emotions are a central element in the problematic experiences that clients seek to resolve in therapy. Emotions involve variations in (1) physiological arousal (e.g., increased heart rate), (2) cognitive labeling (e.g., "I feel scared!"), and (3) behavioral responses (e.g., crying or smiling), but how these three response systems are integrated to provide a total emotional experience remains a controversy. In many cases the specific responses that we might expect to co-occur in a given emotion do *not* consistently co-occur (e.g., Ax, 1953). Sometimes we feel happy, yet physiologically we may be experiencing disturbing levels of arousal and behaviorally we may be acting "indifferent" or even "scared." Clinical psychologists must be prepared to deal with such incongruities in emotional responses, especially when their clients are experiencing disruptively intense feelings.

Researchers and theorists have proposed several conceptualizations of the basic dimensions of emotion (Table 4-2). Recent research by Russell (1978) supports a modified scheme in which two bipolar emotional dimensions are central (i.e., pleasant-unpleasant; arousal level), and three basic cognitive beliefs about the antecedents and consequences of the emotion modify the experience (i.e., belief in

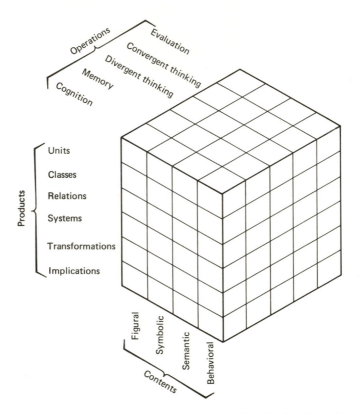

Figure 4-3 Guilford's 120 different "cells" of the intellect. Each cell consists of a unique combination of the three dimensions: contents, operations, and products. (From J. P. Guilford, Three faces of intellect. *Ameican Psychologist*, 1959, *14*, 469-479. Copyright 1959 by the American Psychological Association. Reprinted by permission.)

one's personal power and potency, perceived depth of the emotion, belief in one's ability to control one's life). Thus emotion derives in part from cognition but transcends these origins to form an integrated "total" response.

Several factors may contribute to an emotion. *Evolutionary* theorists, beginning more than 100 years ago (Darwin, 1872), posit that emotions are inborn responses that help to orient and motivate the individual as well as serving as a communication that motivates significant others (Izard, 1977). *Peripheralist* theories view arousal in the outer regions of the body as the cue that activates emotions (James, 1890), while *centralist* theories argue that the same bodily arousal may be experienced as many different emotions (Maranõn, 1924) and that emotions are produced by activation of the brain (Cannon, 1929; Papez, 1937). *Cognitive* theorists posit that emotions occur when bodily or brain arousal are cognitively labeled, based on past learning experiences—for example, "I know from the past that when I'm feeling these sensations I'm probably depressed"—and the current environmental context—for example, "I feel aroused, I can't think of anything I ate or drank that could be causing this, and everyone else here looks happy, so I must be feeling happy" (Mandler, 1975; Schachter, 1971).

Table 4-2 Dimensions of Human Emotion

Schlosberg (1954)	Bush (1973)	Averill (1975)	Russell (1978)	Examples
Pleasant-unpleasant	Pleasant-unpleasant	Evaluation (positive-negative)	Pleasant-unpleasant	Happy-sad Pride-shame
Activation	Activation	Activation	Arousal	Fear level Anger level
Attention-Rejection				Anger-fear Joy-depression
	Potency/Aggressiveness	Uncontrol	Potency belief	Anger-fear Disgust-grief
		Depth of experience	Depth of experience	Shallow-involved sadness Intense-superficial fear
			Internal-external control	Sadness-despair Love-apathy

Thus, emotions may arise as signals to the person and his or her significant others that good or bad events require an adaptation, and as after-the-fact cognitive explanations for unusual levels of physiological or behavioral arousal. Clinicians can teach their clients to use their emotions as aids in evaluating their current psychological and environmental situation, and as signals that new adaptations may be necessary to maintain or restore positive functioning.

Behavioral Processes People often adapt to change by modifying their behavior. Three behavioral processes have been postulated: association, reinforcement, and modeling. Pavlov's (1927) classical conditioning theory and Guthrie's (1952) contiguity theory propose that response alterations occur because the person *associates* a particular environmental condition with the new response pattern. In contrast, Thorndike's (1932) connectionism and Skinner's (1938) operant conditioning hold that behavior changes only when there is a positive or negative payoff (*reinforcement*). Bandura's (1969) observational learning theory suggests that exposure to the demonstration of new behavior also induces behavior change (*modeling*).

Clinical psychologists utilize all three principles of behavioral adaptation. In assessment, attention is paid to the *antecedents* that regularly occur before a problematic behavior, in an attempt to understand the associations that may be signalling the client to behave in that maladaptive fashion. For example, if a child manifests aggressive behavior, the clinician could search for behavior of the parents that might be eliciting these aggressive responses. Therapy could involve aiding both the child to use more prosocial actions and the parents to change their behavioral signals and modeling.

The role played by the *consequences* that regularly follow problematic behaviors is also emphasized in clinical work. Consequences are essentially payoffs, and they influence behavior in five ways. *Positive reinforcement* occurs when a response's consequences lead the behaver to repeat that action in similar future situations. *Punishment* occurs when a response's consequences lead the behaver to *cease* the action in similar future situations. *Extinction* is a process whereby the behaver temporarily repeats a response but then stops it altogether because the response produces neither positive nor negative consequences. *Negative reinforcement* occurs when the consequences of an action are the withdrawal of a current or imminent aversive event, leading the person to repeat the response in similar future situations. Finally, *response cost* occurs when the individual is penalized as a consequence of a response by the withdrawal of a positive payoff, thus inducing him or her to cease that action.

In clinical assessment, an attempt is made to ascertain whether the consequences that the client regularly accrues as a result of problematic behaviors are leading to the continuation of that response pattern due to positive or negative reinforcement. Clinicians also search for punishment, response cost, or extinction contingencies that might be discouraging their clients from engaging in more self-enhancing behaviors. Intervention often focuses on changing the consequences received by the client so that positive behaviors are maintained by positive reinforcement and problematic behaviors are discouraged through response cost, extinction, or punishment. Particular care is required when punishment (Johnston, 1978), negative reinforcement (Barlow, 1973), or response cost (Kazdin, 1972) are utilized in clinical interventions, because of the danger of harming or disillusioning clients when negative consequences are involved. For example, when aversive or punishment techniques are used to help clients stop smoking, taking addictive drugs, or engaging in abnormal sexual activities, the client is usually given full control of the administration of the aversive consequences (e.g., brief and sharp, but not harmful, electric shocks).

Consequences rarely follow every action in a single pattern. Most often, consequences occur after some occurrences of a response but not after others, in an *intermittent* pattern (Ferster & Skinner, 1957). Intermittent consequences tend to produce behavior that is quite persistent even when the consequences are no longer provided (extinction). When clients manifest problematic behaviors in the absence of apparent reinforcement, clinicians are alert to the possibility that these behaviors have been previously maintained by intermittent reinforcement. For instance, Klinger (1975) describes the adaptation process that often occurs when an intermittent reinforcer becomes unavailable (e.g., death of a spouse, loss of a job). First, the person is likely to accelerate efforts to regain the reinforcer (Wortman & Brehm, 1975). Then, a period of "resignation" sets in and the person becomes immersed in feelings of sadness that can lead to serious depression. The key to avoiding depression appears to be the development of an involvement with new reinforcers, thus making it possible to gracefully disengage from the lost reinforcer. For this reason, therapy for depression often focuses on helping the client to establish new enjoyments and satisfactions (e.g., Lewinsohn, Biglan, & Zeiss, 1976).

When teaching clients or students new behavioral adaptations, clinical psychologists utilize the principle of *shaping by successive approximations* (Skinner, 1953). Rather than requiring the learner to produce an entire new response pattern, the target response is divided into several interim steps beginning with an act that is currently within the learner's repertoire. As the learner masters each step, reinforcement is shifted so that it is provided only as a consequence of performance of the next step. For example, in teaching a retarded child to speak, the first step—or "approximation"—might be to praise the child for simply making audible noises when spoken to. Once this first approximation is occurring reliably, the learner is guided toward and reinforced for a gradual refinement such as vocalizing legitimate vowel sounds one at a time. Once this second approximation is mastered, a third step is taken, and then a fourth, and so on. The two keys to successful shaping are (1) selecting approximations that are close enough together so that each step is not too large for the learner, and (2) consistently reinforcing only the current approximations without slipping up by either going back to a prior one (unless too big a step has been attempted, and regrouping is necessary) or moving on too quickly to a new one.

Developmental Challenges

Life calls on all of us to reach just a bit higher and take another step forward, frequently providing challenges that require the development of new skills, beliefs, or feelings. Psychologists have identified a series of developmental tasks that confront people as they move through life from infancy to older age. Clinical psychologists are often sought for aid when people experience psychological distress during difficult developmental transitions. Therefore, a coherent conceptualization of the skills and adaptations normally required at different life stages is essential for clinical practice—the perspective of life-span development (Baltes, Reese, & Lipsett, 1980; Lerner & Ryff, 1978).

Infancy   From birth to approximately two years the infant has a lot to learn. A variety of interactions with the environment (Bijou, 1975), combined with inborn maturational forces (Kagan, 1971), enable the infant to deal with six basic issues: exploration, emotion, gratification, imitation, personal causation, and self-control.

The environment is a rich and varied source of information and stimulation, and it is through active *exploration* that the infant learns to use this resource. Infants' visual abilities develop as they follow slow-moving objects, and as they gradually acquire a preference for staring at people rather than inanimate designs (Haith, 1976; Krantz, 1958) and for perceiving and appreciating whole figures rather than their isolated parts (Kagan, 1971). By age four months, infants are developing a variety of motor exploratory actions—such as mouthing, patting, turning, shaking, and "bringing together" or "letting go"—which they gradually coordinate with visual exploring. Through such exploration, infants begin to understand the structure and processes of their environment, how to differentiate objects from one another, how to get what they want from the environment, and how to differentiate themselves from other people and things. Future cognitive and behavioral skills, a sense of identity, and relationships with others, all begin here.

From birth, people show signs of experiencing *emotions,* and Izard (1977) hypothesizes that most emotions develop through automatic maturation processes in the first two years of life. Across several cultures, facial signs of emotion evolve in the following approximate sequence: interest and joy are present at birth; anger appears at about four to five months; fear, primarily of unfamiliar persons, emerges at about eight months; surprise, disgust, contempt, guilt, and shame appear in the second year. The exact time points for the emergence of emotion expressions are, as with all developmental mileposts, variable for different infants. However, significant delays in the development of emotion expressions could foreshadow difficulties with that or related emotions later in life, and a lack of knowledge on the part of parents concerning the natural evolution of emotions might also create dysfunctional parent-child interactions.

Freud (1905) postulated that the basic goal for infants is the *gratification* of needs for food, warmth, and contact, while Erikson (1950) believes that the more fundamental task underlying these attempts is the development of a basic sense of trust in other persons and the world—a feeling of "I'm safe" that may serve as the basis for many future relationships and accomplishments. Although there is no definitive evidence that such early beliefs persist into later life, the unsuccessful child may be learning enduring behavioral styles (e.g., dependency, suspiciousness) and cognitive schemas ("I can't trust people I love to take care of my needs") that will be problematic as he or she grows. Consistently successful attempts at gratification can, however, establish a basic sense of trust in self and others that will be an asset throughout life.

At the end of the first year, most infants have begun to *imitate* familiar sound patterns, and in the next few months they begin to imitate novel sounds and to modify their imitations so as to create new words (Uzgiris & Hunt, 1975). Infants thus are developing the capability to profit from modeling which will accelerate their learning throughout life.

Toward the end of the first year, infants also begin to demonstrate a repertoire of skills for making things happen, thus evolving the capability for *personal causation*. The act of grasping or the use of vocalizations to influence parents or move objects are rudimentary forms. By 10 to 13 months most infants are able to move their entire bodies in pursuit of an object, as well as to use handles as supports, to retrieve objects by pulling on attached handles or strings, or to return objects to an adult who has made them move in interesting ways (as if to say, "Do it again"). In the second year, infants can use sticks to move objects, thus demonstrating the concept of "tool," and can activate mechanical objects independently. Erikson (1950) described the task at this age as one of developing autonomy, the skills and self-confidence necessary to achieve one's goals independently. Failure to accomplish this task is seen as leaving the person with an underlying sense of doubt, shame, and inferiority that may haunt him or her for years to come.

Object-relations theorists (e.g., Ferenzi, 1938; Winnicott, 1972) and attachment theorists (e.g., Bowlby, 1977) view infancy as crucial for the development of a central faith in self and other persons that is postulated to underlie positive trust, self-efficacy, and capacity for play. A biologically imprinted drive to develop an emotional attachment to an adult caretaker is hypothesized to have developed as a survival mechanism in human evolution. If the caretaker is able to be sufficiently responsive to the infant's needs, these theorists believe that a lifelong sense of relatedness and self-esteem results for the child. If not, it is hypothesized that angry, fearful, and ambivalent feelings develop about oneself and significant others, such that future relationships are marred by fear of abandonment and rejection, self-doubt, hostility, and mistrust. Many conflicted adult relationships could result at least in part from these carried-over resentments and distresses, but the understanding and acceptance of such attachment/separation dilemmas can be facilitated through clinical interventions that provide nurturance and redirection.

By the second year, most infants are undergoing the needed but sometimes frustrating experience of toilet training. Freud (1905) speculated that excessively harsh or restrictive training would produce a person who was obsessed with being proper and orderly while excessive permissiveness would result in a lack of self-discipline and responsibility. The permanence of such outcomes has not been empirically established, but this is clearly the infant's crucial first crisis of *self-control*. Clinical psychologists have developed effective teaching methods that parents can use in order to make toilet training a profitable learning experience in self-determination rather than the source of self-doubt or harsh parent-child conflict (Azrin, Sneede, & Foxx, 1974).

Childhood   The optimal environment for an infant, given the nature of the special developmental challenges, seems to be one that is stimulating, rewarding, predictable, responsive, and clear in its expectations and requirements. The issues of infancy continue on into childhood and throughout life, with the addition of new challenges requiring new skills and learning experiences. The world opens up dramatically from ages 2 to 11, requiring the development of skills for independent initiatives and self-determined accomplishments.

From approximately 2 to 6 years, most children are given increasing opportunity to make their own choices and to take the *initiative* in achieving goals (Erikson, 1950). Play is the primary vehicle through which children can test their competencies and develop new ways for starting, coordinating, and following through with interactions with the social and physical environment. In this period, children often engage in parallel play (Millar, 1968) in which they play side by side without consistently sharing games or ideas with one another. At these ages, children are also developing a strong attachment to their other-sex parent which, though it may provoke anxiety [the Oedipal and Electral complexes postulated by Freud (1905)], sparks an interest in interpersonal involvement. From active social play, children learn to take care of their own feelings (Winnicott, 1971), to overcome egocentrism in their thinking (Piaget, 1954), to develop empathy for other persons (Shantz, 1975), and to initiate a variety of self-enhancing social roles (Erikson, 1950).

As children enter school and become involved in more independent social relationships and more demanding tasks of learning and producing, the emphasis shifts toward carrying through and successfully *accomplishing* the activities that were initiated in earlier years. A difficult balance between compliance with adult rules and assertion of independent competency must be struck or the child may be left with a sense of either guilt or inferiority (Erikson, 1950). Industrious work in school and truly social play (Millar, 1968) offer a testing ground for children to compare themselves with peers in order to gain a stronger sense of self and self-worth. Children develop the cognitive capability for systematic logical thinking during this period, enabling them to make independent plans and decisions and to begin to appreciate the variety in people and things. According to Piaget (1954), children are not yet able to think in completely abstract terms, and thus they must rely on "things as they are" rather than cognitively created concepts.

Adolescence   Adolescence is often depicted as a stormy period of life. A radical shift is undertaken from a life dictated largely by the rules of authority figures to an appreciation of proactive (anticipatory and self-directed) thought and action. The development task is the establishment of an identity (Erikson, 1950; Levinson, 1977: Lowenthal, Turner, & Chiriboga, 1975). Every individual must develop an integrated set of skills and expectations concerning three basic life areas: peer-group role, sex role, career role. The person's chosen roles must be congruent with the expectations of significant others and with a personal view of how the world works and what kind of a person he or she seeks to be. The roles must also be congruent with one another, or else the adolescent is likely to feel like a hollow role player rather than an integrated individual.

The peer group tends to be the major environmental force during adolescence, sometimes causing conflict when peer-group norms run counter to adult regulations. Psychologically, Freud (1905) saw the quest for identity as caused by a renewal in sexual interest during puberty. In contrast, Piaget (1954) theorized that the development of capabilities for conceptual thinking provides the major impetus by opening up a world of new ideas, possibilities, and fantasies. The adolescent is no longer restricted by what can be directly and immediately perceived but can now envision new worlds and new selves that must be evaluated and either chosen as models or discarded. Moral issues and responsibilities confront the adolescent, and the only certainty appears to be either what other people agree on or what the adolescent has the courage to assert as a personal value (Kohlberg, 1973).

Adolescence is a time of searching. Self-directed experiences are of the essence, because the control of other persons (unless accepted voluntarily) is antithetical to the adolescent's search for self-determination. The support and caring of adults such as parents, teachers, or therapists is still important for the times when the adolescent's experiments with social, sexual, or academic experiences backfire, but adults help more as consultants rather than as controllers. Families or schools that experience conflict due to the stresses of adolescence can benefit from an understanding of the importance of constructive rebellion and the inevitability of peer-group pressures as adolescents resolve social, cognitive, and moral challenges. Careful clinical assessment and intervention can thus assist the adolescent, the family, and the school to work in harmony during this period.

Adulthood   Some conceptions of human development abruptly stop at adolescence, leading Sheehy (1976) to question, "Is there life after youth?" In the past 25 years, psychologists have devoted increasing attention to the "predictable crises" that occur in adulthood. Clinicians need this information so that the difficulties that clients may encounter in their adult transitions will not be mistaken for signs of serious, longstanding, or "abnormal" psychological dysfunction (Levinson, 1977; Lowenthal et al., 1975).

Erikson (1950) described the overriding task of midlife (ages 30 to 49) as the development of a sense of *generativity*. That is, adults try to formulate and carry out individualized and self-determined life plans that reflect their own needs and values as well as the interests of significant others. Adults have to answer this question: "What do *I* want for and of myself, given my *own* personal assessment of who I am, what my limitations are, and how I wish to develop relationships with other people?" No final answers exist, but it is the process of self-appraisal and values clarification that is essential to real satisfaction, growth, and happiness in adulthood.

The first self-evaluation often comes around age 30. Until then, most people are absorbed in achieving success in their careers and relationships. Suddenly they realize that they are no longer youths, but rather full-fledged adults with responsibilities for family, career, and their own values. The young adult has typically established competency in one or more social roles, and now feels freer to contemplate new directions within these roles.

Somewhere between the late thirties and the mid-fifties, many adults pause from their work of establishing a stable, secure, and satisfying home to face a second life upheaval. Levinson (1977) terms this the "midlife transition," that creates an "authenticity crisis" (Sheehy, 1976). Up to this time, most adults have stayed within the basic framework that they inherited from their families of origin and their peer groups, at most trying to broaden the options within these limits. For example, the woman who went to college but then gave up a career to be a housewife, the man who joins the family business, or the person who manages to be spouse, parent, and worker but who has opted for a career and marriage that are socially approved, all feel the midlife crisis most keenly. When the children leave for school, when job security is attained and advancement becomes less possible, and when there are more years "behind" than "ahead," most adults are caught (unaware) in the throes of this second identity crisis. A search for a personal identity that transcends the past and current expectations of other persons ensues: "What's it all been about? What will I have to look back on when I retire? Who do I want to be in the final analysis?"

Adulthood involves longer periods of stability and security than previous life periods for most people, but nevertheless requires the confrontation of both practical and philosophical questions about one's fundamental identity and life pursuits. Adult developmental challenges can evoke distressing emotional reactions such as anxiety, depression, anger, or confusion, while also provoking sometimes radical shifts in behavior and lifestyle. Clinicians can most effectively serve their clients by maintaining an awareness of the normal tasks of adulthood and a distinction between deeprooted psychological dysfunction versus situational adjustment reactions. At the same time, clinical psychologists themselves must resolve these personal issues in their own lives.

Older Age   Due to physiological, social, and political changes, persons over 60 must confront several developmental challenges (Fozard & Popkin, 1978; MacDonald, 1973; Schaie & Schaie, 1977). Perhaps the most pervasive task is the development of a mature perspective on death (Kubler-Ross, 1973). A twofold challenge is inevitable: (1) fully accepting one's life and oneself despite the inevitable imperfections and disappointments, (2) fully acknowledging one's mortality. There is no substitute for having lived a full and varied life, but there can also be real satisfaction in coming to terms with one's past and setting realistic goals in light of an honest self-appraisal. There is honor and integrity in simply having the courage to accept mortality and imperfection.

Life after 60 is not, however, a somber process of resignation. An honest confrontation of one's life can be a source of renewed energy and inner peace. There are usually many good years to be lived, although the older person must make adjustments to inevitable decrements in some perceptual, cognitive, and motor abilities. For instance, although ill health is *not* automatic, visual acuity in dim or glaring light, memory, and motor speed and strength do decline. A socially derived change is the increase in leisure time that is afforded to, and too often imposed on, older persons. Family responsibilities and career options inevitably decrease, but older persons who maintain a psychological outlook of extroversion and active interest can and do continue to grow in their careers, relationships, and recreational pursuits. Grief must often be dealt with when special people, such as spouses, partners, or friends, die and new relationships are important to provide continued interpersonal support.

The years after 60 bring the challenges of an ultimate self-confrontation, adjustment to the socially imposed restrictions and natural physiological declines of older age, and a renewal through the integrity of self-acceptance and a fundamental self-reliance. Clinical psychologists can help such persons, through counseling and consultation, to create environments that aid in this process, as alternatives to settings such as are too often found in nursing homes and hospitals that may inadvertently intensify feelings of despair, isolation, and degradation by creating impersonal and limited milieus.

Need for a Developmental Perspective

The human organism is constantly changing and the processes of adaptation and development play central roles in this change. Clinical assessments, interventions, and research must recognize each client's developmental level and consider the issues pertinent to each developmental level. Such a developmental perspective gives the clinician an enhanced ability to empathize with and provide aid to each client across the lifespan.

SOCIAL GROUPS AND COMMUNITIES

Social scientists have demonstrated that social groups and communities can provide milieus that either facilitate or disrupt effective human functioning. Studies of the impact of different cultures convincingly demonstrate the impact of social forces. For example, the Harvard University Comparative Study of Values in Five Cultures (Parsons & Shils, 1952) identified significant differences among Navaho, Zuni, Mormon, Texan, and Spanish-American cultures in such diverse areas as child raising, decision making, courtship and marriage, and economic exchanges, even though these groups inhabit a similar geographical area. Similarly, Whorf (1956) has shown how the different language patterns of different cultures both reflect and determine how people in each culture perceive and respond to their environment. For example, Eskimos have more than 10 different words to describe "snowflakes," thus enabling fine discriminations that are essential in their unique milieu.

Within a culture, differences in the physical, social, economic, political, and familial environments of different groups or communities may also influence human functioning. Whyte's (1943) classic study of *Street Corner Society* demonstrates how the norms (rules of conduct) of a community affect behavior patterns in such domains as dating and sex, gang activities, occupational aspirations and choices, and decision making. Hollingshead and Redlich (1958) conducted a classic study on *Social Class and Mental Illness* in which they identified a relationship between the prevalence of "mental illness" and socioeconomic status. A much higher proportion of people from the poorest and least-educated social class were classified as "mentally ill" compared to persons from all higher social classes.

Even within problematic social settings, small groups of persons inevitably spring up to provide a base of personal support in otherwise impersonal environments (Shils, 1957). For example. Selznick (1948) described the importance of informal support groups in bureaucratic organizations such as big-business or government, Gans (1962) noted how such groups can create a sense of community even in crowded cities, and Goffman (1960) stressed the value of peer support groups in mental hospitals. Clinicians have also identified the family as a key source of personal and interpersonal security and growth (Ackerman, 1958; Minuchin, 1974). Without such support groups, people can be left destitute of essential psychological resources. Thus, social groups and communities are important factors for consideration in clinical assessment, intervention, and research.

Dimensions of Social Environments

Social groups and communities can be described as composed of six basic *components*: physical, spatial, and architectural elements, and distributions of persons, roles, and resources. These parts are organized into a coherent system through a social *structure* that involves a belief system and varying degrees of diversity, flexibility, and intimacy. Three key *processes* are required to preserve and propel this social structure: maintenance, change, and control functions.

Physical, Spatial, and Architectural Elements   The geophysical variables that influence human functioning include ambient temperature, noise, climate, sunlight, and terrain (Esser, 1974). Similarly, spatial factors have impacts, including personal space (Hayduk, 1978; Sommer, 1969), territoriality (Edney, 1974; Hall, 1966), and crowding (Worchel & Teddie, 1976). (See Highlight 4-1.) For example, both laboratory (Baron & Bell, 1975) and naturalistic (Baron & Ransberger, 1978)

Highlight 4-1   Crowding, Noise, and Controllability

A decade ago, Glass and Singer (1972) demonstrated that the stresses of urban life may have lasting negative effects on city dwellers even when they have escaped these "urban stresses." Two of the most noxious characteristics of a high-density environment such as a major metropolis are crowding and noise. Research on both of these environmental "pollutants" is beginning to point to a common underlying feature that may be at the root of many of the ill effects they can produce.

Crowding is a multifaceted spatial phenomenon that depends on the population density (i.e., number of persons per unit of space) and numerosity (i.e., the number of persons with whom each person is in social or perceptual contact) (Stokols, 1972; Worchel & Teddlie, 1976). A recent study by Baum, Aiello, and Calesnick (1978) sheds further light on this issue, demonstrating that environments that force people into unsolicited close contact with one another produce initially positive but long-term negative consequences. When college students living on either crowded or uncrowded dormitory corridors were asked to participate in an experimental game that assessed their attempts to assert personal control, the students from the crowded dorms evidenced *more* effort early in the school year. However, when the game was repeated with comparable students later in the year, the crowded students showed *less* effort to assert personal control than the uncrowded students. Baum et al. (1978) posited that the key feature of the crowded setting was the lack of controllability for its residents. Thus, they hypothesized that crowding forces people to make contact with one another and essentially renders them helpless to control this flood of unsolicited contact. They believe that, at first, people react by increasing their attempts to control the situation; but, the crowded environment defeats their attempts and they gradually give up on asserting any personal control. Perhaps, then, a central aspect of crowding is its limitation of each person's control of his or her life.

Research on the effects of noise suggest a similar hypothesis (Broadbent, 1978; Poulton, 1978). Experimental studies indicate that noise can have several negative impacts, including serving as a distraction, interfering with the person's perception of external communication and inner speech, producing both increases and decreases in arousal that cause further interference, and forcing the person to use coping techniques that are inappropriate when the noise is gone. These effects are particularly debilitating when the noise cannot be controlled by the person, and appear to produce a similar kind of reactance-helplessness response as does crowding!

In sum, the research on the effects of unpleasant environmental conditions seems to be converging on *controllability* as a central factor. Consider your own experience: Do you find that you can tolerate aversive situations longer and more comfortably when you feel that you have some control over the unpleasant surroundings? We would guess that, in most cases, your answer is, "If I have to be subjected to a noxious situation, at least let me have some control over it!"

research suggest that increases in a milieu's temperature leads people to experience unpleasant feelings and to act aggressively, although temperatures above 85 to 90 °F appear to be sufficiently stifling to inhibit violent outbursts. Similarly, the establishment of appropriate social distance, based on the spatial boundaries that each individual maintains through aggressive or avoidant reactions is a skill that can affect psychological well-being and interpersonal relationships (Sommer, 1969). Clinicians can teach clients to maintain more self-enhancing personal spaces, as well as adjusting client-therapist distance in therapy to suit the client's psychological needs and the changing tasks of intervention.

Architectural arrangements can bring people together or keep them apart, facilitate or impede social interaction, enhance or detract from learning and motivation, and even cause or diminish conflict, prejudice, and psychological distortions. For example, Spivack (1967) described how long, unchanging, and well-polished corridors of a large mental hospital can result in visual and auditory distortions that can be disturbing. Lieberson (1961) similarly demonstrated that ethnic groups that are isolated from other cultural groups and the mainstream society by their residential segregation tend to be less successful in entering and attaining success in their communities.

Distributions of Persons, Roles, and Resources   An environment is shaped by the types of persons that inhabit it (Sells, 1963) and the behaviors they produce (Barker, 1963), the roles they can or must fulfill, and the resources available to them (Iscoe, 1974). Barker (1968) for example, distinguished between environments that are *undermanned* (a shortage of persons for the necessary tasks in the milieu) versus *overmanned* (a surplus of persons compared to the number required by current tasks in the milieu). Research studies in diverse settings have shown that undermanned settings have distinct advantages (Wicker & Kirmeyer, 1976). These benefits include greater tolerance and acceptance of marginal or even deviant persons (such as nonconformists, older persons, or lawbreakers), greater effort to support the setting and greater participation in a variety of tasks and roles that are more involving and rewarding for all participants, a greater emphasis on what a person can "do" than what a person "is," and a greater tolerance for diversity. Many clients may suffer in part because they are caught on the fringe of overmanned life settings where they become mere faces in the crowd.

A *role* is "a socially defined or collective expectation" (Bensman & Rosenberg, 1967, p. 136) that evolves to assure that each citizen will contribute to maintenance of the social system. Some roles are universal, while others are luxuries: for example, the leader role is required in all groups and communities, while the role of psychotherapist has more often emerged in affluent societies. Some roles are exclusive, that is, restricted to certain special people, while other roles can be filled by most any person. In clinical assessment and intervention, an awareness of the roles that are available to clients, the problematic conflicts that may occur within each role or between several competing roles, and the specific responsibilities and rewards built into each role, is invaluable. Problems in living often arise when roles are thrust on unqualified persons, when taking a role places the person in conflict, or when desirable roles are "closed out." Furthermore, groups and communities experience troubles that cause stress for their members when essential roles are not defined, defined in vague or conflicting terms, left unfilled, or filled by unqualified people.

Social *resources* include services such as schools, hospitals, and government; facilities such as recreational areas, libraries, and housing; and influence levers such as money, knowledge, or access to facilities and services. The greater a person's or group's resources, the greater their ability to attain their goals and the greater their impact on other persons or groups (Parsons, 1963; Tedeschi & Bonoma, 1972). French and Raven (1959) identified five "bases of social power": *reward power* is derived from controlling rewards; *coercive power* is based on control of punishments; *legitimate power* derives from the possession of social positions or roles that have traditional prerogatives and privileges; *referent power* is based on possession of characteristics that enhance modeling, such as attractiveness, comparable values, and similarity; *expert power* is based on knowledge, skills, or public recognition as an expert. Power can cause problems when restricted to a few persons or groups, when insufficient for the goal being pursued, or when it is wielded without sufficient knowledge or skill. Clinicians seek to increase their clients' resources, both psychologically and environmentally, while recognizing that they hold special power in the client-therapist relationship that must be balanced by responsible concern for the client's welfare (Hare-Mustin, Maracek, Kaplan, & Liss-Levinson, 1979).

Power and resources can be a psychological reality even when not an observable actuality. Research in social psychology has demonstrated that the most satisfying and effective relationships are characterized by the belief by all participants that they are receiving a fair payoff from the relationship compared to the amount of resources that they are investing in the relationship (Walster, Walster, & Berscheid, 1978). Such a social system is termed *equitable.* Equity is based on the participants' psychological evaluation of their inputs and outputs and can be achieved even in milieus with few real resources as long as everyone involved concurs that the system and their relationships are "fair."

Belief Systems   Social groups and communities create belief systems, including beliefs concerning "what to do and think" (values) and "how to do it" (norms). These designations of, respectively, "good and bad" and "right and wrong," serve both to guide participants in their roles and to *post hoc* justify the system's basic rules of thought and conduct. Another label for a social system's belief system is "culture," which has been defined in many ways:

> Culture is . . . that complex whole which includes knowledge, belief, art, morals, law, custom, and any other capabilities and habits acquired by man as a member of society. (Tylor, 1872, p. 1)

> Culture . . . refers to the distinctive way of life of a group of people, their complete "design for living" . . . the instrument whereby the individual adjusts to his total setting and gains the means for creative expression (Kluckhohn, 1967, pp. 74–75).

Shared beliefs enable people to plan actions cooperatively with one another without sacrificing each individual's unique qualities and needs (Wallace, 1970). A group or community's belief system provides its members with fundamental certainty about life's basic transactions, as well as a set of priorities that describe the aspirations, skills, actions, and relationships that can be expected to provide the optimal payoff in that social system.

No belief system works perfectly in guaranteeing individual rights as well as the survival and prosperity of the group or community. Even the most totalitarian culture cannot wipe out individual differences, and even the most humanitarian culture will produce conflicts between individuals' needs and desires and the total system's norms and values. Often "subcultures" or "contracultures" (Yinger, 1960) are retained by new members in a group or developed by discontented members, so as to preserve beliefs or behavior patterns that are at odds with the "mainstream." Clinical psychologists recognize the importance of each culture's or subculture's belief systems when setting or evaluating assessment, intervention, or research goals, as well as emphasizing that the most basic responsibility of every belief system is to provide groups or community members with a sense of identity (Mead, 1932) and the right to be different (Kittrie, 1971).

Diversity, Flexibility, and Intimacy   Groups and communities vary in the extent to which they foster or discourage diversity: Are all members or groups expected to look, act, think, and feel in an identical fashion? Although a moderate amount of uniformity may increase a system's efficiency, excessive emphasis on conformity often produces dysfunctions in both the social system and its participants. For example, a mental health clinic that permits only one theoretical viewpoint is likely to be unable to fully meet the diverse needs of its community (e.g., Graziano, 1969). Diversity may lead to arguments and disagreements among members, but research suggests that organizations that encourage heterogeneity and open expression of views are likely to experience fewer *major* destructive conflicts (Corwin, 1969). Greater diversity also means that community or group members have a wider range of models for growth and development (Iscoe, 1974).

Diversity can be facilitated by change in the group or community's members through turnover. Although adding new members to an organization is positively correlated with tension and conflict (Corwin, 1969), Kelly (1969) demonstrated that a high school with a high turnover rate (42%), compared to a matched school with less turnover (10%), showed greater degrees of social interaction, openness to newcomers, communication across social status levels, and diversity in dress and friendships. Large organizations are often criticized for resisting "new blood" and encouraging employees to become "bureaucratic virtuosos" (Merton, 1949) who are stagnant and ineffective "company people." Groups, families, and communities that encourage new members to bring in new ideas and practices are most likely to continue evolving in ways that promote the welfare of all participants.

Diversity can also be instituted in a group or community through rules, policies, and norms that encourage flexible reevaluation and constructive innovation in the system. Consistency and organization are important in every milieu's values and procedures such that efficiency and stability are guaranteed, but rigid and narrow constraints can lead participants to value precision and "appropriateness" more than the quality of the final products or the efficacy of the system in meeting its overall goals (Burns & Stalker, 1961; Thompson, 1969; Weber, 1947). Organizations that are extremely formal, impersonal, and standardized (bureaucracies) (Weber, 1947) tend to be less successful in meeting the needs and desires of their members than systems that have flexible decision-making and communication policies and procedures (Pheysey, Payne, & Pugh, 1971). Groups and communities that are flexible in their attempts to promote growth and prosperity for both individual people and the entire system tend to generate involvement by members, and this in turn fosters a commitment to support and defend the system (Porter & Lawler, 1965; Sarason, 1972).

Flexibility and diversity are restricted when one central "power elite" (Mills, 1956) controls power and communication in the group, family, or community. In contrast, a diversified and balanced plurality of separate interest groups and communication channels enables a greater number of participants to be meaningfully involved in the system (Riesman, 1953). Centralized power impedes the innovations that enable a group to survive and prosper as illustrated by Aiken's (1969) finding that communities with less centralized power structures were more likely to implement federally funded innovations in public housing, urban renewal, wars on poverty, or model cities programs. Centralized communication channels, where most or all messages are funneled through a central switchboard or translator, tend to be effective only if the system's tasks are limited to simple collation of information (Shaw, 1971). When the group or community must solve complex problems, centralized communication channels tend to become overloaded with messages to the point that clear communication and effective decision making are impossible (Gilchrist, Shaw, & Walker, 1954). As consultants, clinical psychologists help organizations and communities to develop systematic and efficient procedures for involving as many members as possible in decision making and communication. For instance, a community might be aided in establishing a citizens' advisory board that is composed of several action committees that (1) assess community needs in areas such as education or recreation, and (2) propose appropriate legislation to the city council and mayor.

Norms and values that encourage interpersonal involvement, and facilities and services that provide participants with both privacy and opportunities to join together, facilitate intimacy as well as flexibility and diversity. A moderate degree of intimate involvement with other people appears important for psychological well-being (Moos, 1974, 1975; Olson, Sprenkle & Russell, 1979). Too much intimacy can be frightening and overwhelming, while too little intimacy leads to isolation and despair.

Maintenance Processes   Groups and communities are like living organisms in that they must constantly work to maintain a balance among their internal elements and a balance between themselves and the other social systems with which they have contact (Highlight 4-2). In order to attain such homeostatic (health promoting) internal and external equilibria, four regulatory processes are required.

Highlight 4-2   Maintenance Processes in the Family

Families create rules that define what actions are required, permitted, or prohibited for its members. These rules are usually unstated, but they can be inferred by observing the family's repeated patterns of interactions (Jackson,

1965). For example, if a family's interactions repeatedly involved one person expressing a need and others replying with criticism or indifference, we might infer that the family rule is "Family members are not allowed to openly express their feelings or requests" (see Table). Dysfunctional families tend to manifest rules that call for secretive, aggressive or avoidant, and self-defeating interactions, and to maintain these policies excessively, inconsistently, and/or harshly (Fisher, 1977). For example, one family member may be singled out as the "scapegoat" and alternately praised or severely punished for certain actions (Ackerman, 1958; Zuk, 1967).

In addition to the formal structure created by age generations (children, parents/spouses, grandparents), families create informal structures when their members join together to form coalitions (Minuchin, 1974). Dysfunctional families are often characterized by *intergenerational* coalitions that are based on *conflict*. For example, a mother and son may form a coalition by constantly fighting about the son's appearance or schoolwork. Although mother and son are angry with one another, they form a coalition because they are so involved with each other that neither has the time or energy to maintain meaningful relationships with other family members. This can create a barrier between mother and father, especially if they disagree about how to handle their son. Such a family is likely to be splintered by structural imbalance.

Communication also contributes significantly to family success or strife. *Validation*, *clarity*, and *congruence* are central dimensions of communication. Communication is validating if it includes an acknowledgement of the ideas, beliefs, requests, and feelings of the listener. Dysfunctional families tend to communicate resentment and anxiety through demands, threats, denouncements, criticisms, and irrelevant messages, rather than the acceptance and caring that are conveyed by validating interactions (Doane, 1978).

Table for Highlight 4-2   Family Rules

Family rules are really abstractions from repeated patterns of behavior—only rarely are such rules actually spoken by family members, and often they are vigorously denied. However, family members regularly behave *as if* they were following a rule. Here are examples of family rules that will cause problems for a family, along with alterations that provide for more positive interactions.

Family Rules	Positive Alteration
Feelings cannot be expressed or else I will be rejected and I will break down.	Feelings can be expressed without causing people to be rejected or to go crazy, if they are expressed clearly and with "I" statements.
Everyone must be, act, and feel the same.	Family members are always going to be different, and such differences can be the glue that connects them to each other.
Children come first: parents live only to serve the children.	Everybody counts, and each person has unique and legitimate needs.
Nothing ever gets finished in this family.	Whatever we start is important enough to be completely finished.
One member speaks for everyone.	Every person speaks for him/herself.

Table for Highlight 4-2 *Continued*

If something goes wrong, panic (or blow-up, or put the screws to someone)!	If something goes wrong, new ways of handling the situation are needed and can be found.

Similarly, functional families show greater clarity in their communications than do disturbed families (Doane, 1978). Clear messages are specific statements that are phrased in a manner, and with a vocabulary, that is comprehensible to the listener. Where a member of a functional family might say, "Please stop talking while I'm working," the same idea might be expressed vaguely or evasively in a troubled family: "Will there ever be quiet?" or "I'm haunted by noises!"

Congruent communications convey consistent messages on all verbal and nonverbal channels. Incongruent messages, as for example when a person says "I'm perfectly happy" in a tone of voice that suggests anger or despair, are confusing and distressing. Perhaps the best documented form of incongruent communication in families is the *double bind* (Bateson, Jackson, Haley, & Weakland, 1956). A double-bind message is one which simultaneously tells the listener, "Do this" *and* "Do *not* do this," as well as implicitly requiring that the listener *not* ask for clarification or directly acknowledge the hopelessness of the situation. Tentative empirical evidence suggests that dysfunctional families utilize more double-bind communication than functional families (Doane, 1978).

Families work together, intentionally or not, to create a distinctive family environment. Maintenance processes can produce a milieu that is chaotic, cramped, constricted, or warlike, or an environment that is supportive, secure, and growth promoting. Through therapy or consultation, clinicians can offer an important service by helping families develop more facilitative maintenance processes.

Feedback is communication that enables people to learn from one another. Feedback is usually most effective if it is immediate, nonevaluative, or positive in tone, encouraging rather than demanding, specific, complete, backed up by social authority, and geared to meet the needs of the participants. For example, a consultant might say, "I have observed that employee suggestions have been converted into policy changes only one time this year, in contrast to five times a year ago, and despite 73 specific suggestions that were submitted. I think that some positive readjustments might be worth considering since your goal is to be responsive to employees." This feedback is more likely to have an effective impact than if phrased as, "You have been grossly negligent in responding to employee needs and goals." Feedback also tends to have the most complete and constructive influence if it is delivered via a medium that is salient for the recipient. For instance, brief memos followed by more extensive meetings might best suit a harried executive, while a videotape containing sample therapy sessions with a supervisor's comments is extremely valuable in clinical training.

Feedback is often transmitted by *nonverbal* channels such as facial expression, gestures, posture, or vocal tone and fluency (Harper, Wiens, & Matarazzo, 1978; Mehrabian, 1971). However, nonverbal messages are often very difficult to interpret, especially when they contradict one another. Clinicians cautiously use nonverbal cues to provide clients with feedback, as well as teaching clients to more effectively use such signals.

Rule enforcement is accomplished by policies that differentiate acceptable from "deviant" actions, and through regulations that creat different levels of social status. Rules concerning *deviance* help the members of a community or group know what to do and what not to do, as well as specifying the consequences that must be paid by persons who violate these norms (Erickson, 1962). However, trouble results when not only the action, but also the person performing it, is considered deviant (Ryan, 1971; Ullman & Krasner, 1975). Rules concerning *social status* define people's prerogatives in society (Davis & Moore, 1945). While most societies create social strata (e.g., upper versus lower socioeconomic status) to ensure that crucial jobs are filled by the most capable persons, lower-class people may be harmed or unjustly ignored unless they are given access to social resources such as education and therapy.

Tension reduction processes enable groups and communities to smooth over problems temporarily without fundamentally altering the system to correct problems (Coser, 1957). Perhaps the most basic tension reduction method is *cooptation*: "the process of absorbing new elements into the leadership or policy-determining structure of an organization as a means of averting threats to its stability or existence" (Selznick, 1948, p. 32). Cooptation is a subtle form of "buying off" troublesome groups or persons by giving them greater power or resources but not allowing them to change the basic system. Other short-term tension reduction operations include denial of problems, refusal of responsibility for remedying problems, blaming failures on external sources, or exaggerating the system's successes in order to disguise problems (Zander, 1977).

Finally, *socialization* is the educational process by which a social system imprints its norms and values upon its memebers (Benedict, 1938; Bensam & Rosenberg, 1967). People learn to value some things and shy away from others, to communicate and think in certain ways, and to observe a variety of rules through the socialization provided by parents, teachers, peers, co-workers, and media such as television. Breakdowns in socialization may occur when the socialization agent is absent or inadequate, or when contradictive norms and values are taught by different agents or at different ages or times. In such cases, clinical psychologists can help to restore the socialization process through assessment and therapy or consultation.

Change Processes   Groups and communities cannot afford to simply maintain themselves as they are: unless the system can change it will become stagnant and obsolete. Systems that survive and flourish encourage adaptive change where dysfunctional ones resist change. For example, a psychological clinic that uses only the treatment methods that were developed before 1950 would be more effective if it incorporated newer therapeutic strategies as well. Attempts to anticipate new inputs and stresses are also more effective than after-the-fact reactions. For example, if a community plans an expansion and relocation of a medical center that is rapidly becoming outdated, this is likely to be more timely and better designed than belated attempts to provide better services in an old hospital that has already become overwhelmed.

Change occurs primarily through conflict or innovation. *Conflict* forces members of a group or community to examine the system more carefully, thus setting the stage for new improvements (Coser, 1957). Conflict may occur due to many different incompatabilities. When conflict centers on clashes of values, this is more difficult to resolve than conflict concerning how to achieve a shared value. When conducting therapy or consultation, clinicians often focus on helping clients redefine what may initially seem like conflicts over values to negotiable issues. For example, when parents and teenagers clash, both parties typically believe that it is important for the teenager to grow into a healthy independent adult . . . a shared value. The basic difference may center on how much leeway to currently allow the teenager, and a clinician can help the family stop arguing and begin listening to one another's views.

While conflict can lead to harsh actions that can destroy a group or its members, *innovation* provides a more constructive mechanism for change. Innovation involves systematic and carefully tested attempts to create new social structures or processes through social problem solving (Wallace, 1970; Zaltman et al., 1973). Innovations are often resisted even though they might produce significant gains, because the system's constituents perceive the change to be risky, costly, or only a negligible improvement. Resistance may take many forms: passive inaction, withholding of participation, rejection on grounds of scientific or theoretical disagreement, rejection because of lack of formal approval, sabotage, or cooptation of the innovator or the innovation (Highlight 4-3). For example, clients in group therapy may resist honest confrontation by talking about superficial positive topics, pretending to be perfectly happy, focusing all blame on one particular member (the "scapegoat"), or simply failing to attend meetings. Innovations tend to be adopted, however, when the innovator has assessed the causes and products of past innovation attempts that have succeeded *or* failed, so as to create a new program that meets the needs of the group or community and its major powerbrokers without threatening their security and strength (Sarason, 1972).

Highlight 4-3   The Vicissitudes of Innovation

Graziano (1969) presented an illustration of the clash between innovative change and homeostatic maintenance in the mental health field. Beginning with the request of a small group of parents for effective treatment services for autistic children, nearly a decade passed before adequate funding was procured for a program that did in fact meet the parents' needs. For six years, the lay group negotiated with and later collaborated with an existing psychoanalytically oriented child clinic to attempt to provide treatment services. At the end of this time, the laypersons withdrew their participation because adequate treatment was not being offered and the clinic professionals had rejected any plans for altering their services.

The lay group then linked up with a psychologist who attempted to help them get support for an alternative treatment program and the use of indigenous paraprofessionals. The proposed project was rejected by a local university's high-level administrators on the grounds that it would be too controversial—primarily because it was not supported by the existing child clinic and the community's mental health professionals. The lay group and their consultant nevertheless set up a treatment program, determined to get financial support from governmental or fundraising agencies in the community or the state.

For three more years, the lay group was stalled and delayed by a fundraising agency that was controlled by an informal consortium of local businessmen (and which funded the existing child clinic) and flatly turned down by the state Department of Mental Health. The delays were based on such reasoning as lack of a written proposal, lack of real ongoing services, ongoing services were too new to be evaluated, the services must be evaluated by the very mental health professionals who were running the competing clinic, the services only "duplicated" those of the existing clinic, and, finally, the program was "uncooperative" because it refused to divulge confidential information about its clients and their parents. Only when the new program was already receiving substantial state funding—based on a reevaluation by the Department of Mental Health and highly positive findings—and when it was fractionated by a controversy over the treatment of minority-group children, did the agency provide real funding. In fact, the psychologist and his professional staff finally chose to establish yet another program, which was the only child clinic that was able to maintain a program for autistic children in the end, when a minority in the lay group refused to allow poverty-level children to be treated in their newly funded clinic.

Graziano draws several valuable conclusions from this experience. First, innovations in a community are likely to be staunchly resisted by the existing community, because such power structures are:

> . . . primarily concerned with justifying and maintaining themselves, while they pay scant attention to the scope of mental health services and even less to the objective evaluation of quality or effectiveness. They maintain their own self-interest which clearly conflicts with humanitarian ideals, science, and social progress. (p. 15)

When the goals of a social system focus on perpetuating itself, this is the result of a concentration of power in the hands of a relatively few persons "at the top." Why? Because these powerbrokers then have too much to lose if change threatens their control, and all other members of the system are sufficiently deprived of real remuneration for their services that they tend to become either apathetic or intensely loyal to the existing system in a fashion akin to Festinger's (1957) cognitive dissonance formulation. The resistance to real change is amplified by the fact that the power brokers and their existing programs band together:

Thus the active mental health field in this city was made up of parallel bu-reaucracies, that is, various social agencies which, by virtue of their "ex-pertise," had been granted legitimate social power by the community in the area of mental health. Despite the essential autonomy of the bureau-cratic structures, they closely cooperated in several major ways which tended toward mutual support and perpetuation of the existing bureau-cratic structures. This cooperation occurred through (a) normal and clear-ly legitimate professional channels, such as reciprocal referrals of clients; (b) tacit uncritical acceptance of agency "territories" and functions; (c) interagency "sharing" of upper-level decision-making personnel; (d) tem-porary variable-composition coalitions which briefly intensified agency power in order to deal with specific issues. (p. 14)

The community power structure can block innovative change through out-right rejection, threats, delay, requests for more data, setting up evaluations so that poor results are inevitable, or even by publicly proclaiming support while building in safeguards such as controlling committees or restrictive regulations that ensure that existing power and communication channels retain control and nothing really changes.

When a community commits itself to the vastly expensive reality of a men-tal health center, and then refers *control of the center back to the existing power structure, it has created "innovation without change." The major result might be to enrich and vastly reinforce the old power structure, thus making it vastly more capable of further entrenching itself, and success-fully resisting change for many more years. (p. 17, author's italics)*

The people who lose most in the end are the very members of the social sys-tem for whom the system is purportedly working. In this case, these persons are the clients who sorely need, and often cannot afford, treatment:

The power-structure clinics tend to limit their services to white middle-class children with mild to moderate disturbances, that is, to those chil-dren with the best chances of improving even when left alone; those chil-dren whose parents would be most cooperative in keeping appointments, being on time, accepting the structure, and, of course, paying the fees; those children who do not present the vexing and, to the middle-class clinician, alien *problems of lower-class minority groups. Certainly a clinic is much "safer," much "quieter," more neatly run, when it limits itself to the most cooperative clientele, and, we might suggest, when it selectively creates a pool of cooperative clients . . . In this process, we suspect the client might too often be exploited rather than helped. (pp. 15–16, author's italics)*

Innovation does not come easily in social systems.

Control Processes   Maintenance and change are not completely incompatible, because effective homeostatic regulation can provide the stability that makes possible successful innovation, and innovation can enhance a system's maintenance capabilities. However, maintenance is based on reducing deviancy and stabilizing social stratification, while change often amplifies deviancy and threatens existing political differentiations. Every group or community therefore needs mechanisms to strike a *balance* between change and maintenance: these are control processes, which include decision making and leadership functions.

Decision making is the control process responsible for adding, deleting, or modifying structures or processes so as to increase a system's ability to achieve its goals. Researchers such as Corwin (1969), Shaw (1971), and Whyte and Lippitt (1960) delineated four approaches to decision making. *Democratic* decisions are based on the principle of majority rule, and usually result in moderate productivity, high creativity, cohesiveness, and satisfaction, and low rates of conflict in the system. *Autocratic* decisions are determined by a single person or controlling group, resulting in high productivity, but low creativity, cohesiveness, and satisfaction and frequent conflict in the system. *Laissez-faire* decisions occur when each individual makes his or her own independent choice, typically leading to low productivity and cohesiveness and moderate creativity, satisfaction, and rates of conflict in the system. Finally, *consensual* decisions are made with unanimous support from all participants, and although difficult to negotiate, most often produce maximal productivity, creativity, cohesiveness, and satisfaction in the system with minimal conflict. Clinical psychologists frequently teach clients strategies for consensual decision making, both in therapy and in consultation, because this approach enables people to work cooperatively toward realizing self-determined goals.

Leadership is necessary to guide the process of making and implementing decisions. Bales (1958) and Fiedler (1967) have distinguished between two basic leaderships styles. *Task specialists* focus on rational problem solving with an emphasis on efficiency and organization but without empathy for people's needs or feelings. *Social-emotional specialists*, in contrast, focus on facilitating interpersonal relationships and system policies that recognize and care for the needs and feelings of individual members. Fiedler (1967) has demonstrated that task specialists are most effective when the group situation is either extremely favorable or dangerous, while social-emotional specialists are optimal in moderately favorable situations. Task specialists are, however, always less well liked and less able to create a cohesive group than social-emotional specialists. Clinical psychologists utilize both leadership styles in their professional work, to assure that both "the job gets done" and "the people get their strokes."

Decisions are often made not by either a leader or the entire group, but rather by *coalitions*. Coalitions take place when two or more persons can maximize their gains by working together. Research suggests that coalitions are most often formed by people who either share a common ideology or who can successfully bargain with each other so that, despite having competing goals, they all get more by working together than they would on their own (Murnighan, 1978). Thus, a clinician might form a coalition with a hospital administrator despite sharing different views on the methods for delivering mental health services, if together they have enough "clout" to establish a new clinic that bolsters the administrator's prestige and provides the psychologist with a base for improving the mental health services in that community. Such a coalition can be an effective political maneuver, but the clinician does also risk cooptation. Coalitions often play a major role in clinical assessment and intervention as well, as for instance in approaches to family therapy that emphasize restructuring troublesome coalitions in distressed families (Minuchin, 1974).

Need for an Understanding of Groups and Communities

Clinical psychologists deal with a variety of social systems whenever they do research, assessment, or intervention. Even if the focus is on working with an individual person, the groups and communities that influence that client are important targets for assessment and intervention. Clients' family, school, work, peer-group, or community environments can serve as powerful resources in clinical intervention, and clinicians are also often called on to consult to groups or communities that seek help with innovation or the resolution of conflict. As researchers or administrators, clinicians require complete and sensitive awareness of the norms and values of local community, professional organizations, state and federal governments, and the facility in which they work, as well. For instance, in order to acquire a government grant for research or development of a clinical program, the clinical psychologist's proposal must meet both local community and university needs as well as conforming to the standards and priorities established by governmental funding agencies. Careful attention to all relevant dimensions of group or community social systems can thus greatly facilitate all phases of clinical work.

The Grey Hills by Georgia O'Keeffe, 1942.

*It is a meloncholy of mine own, compounded of many simples,
extracted from many objects, and indeed the sundry contemplation
of my travels, which, by often rumination, wraps me in a most
melancholy sadness.*

Shakespeare

5

PERSPECTIVES ON PSYCHOLOGICAL DYSFUNCTIONS

The study of psychological dysfunctions is the study of problems in living and, quite simply, includes the study of those behavior patterns that are labeled as "abnormal" in our society. Effective or "normal" human functioning is, in part, an absence of dysfunctional patterns of action, cognition, and emotion (Jahoda, 1958; Sarbin, 1969; Smith, 1961). An understanding of psychological dysfunctions is therefore essential whenever clinicians seek to help clients regain effective functioning.

In this chapter we consider several methods for defining psychological dysfunctions and different theoretical models for describing and explaining psychological dysfunctions. We also describe systems for classifying psychological dysfunctions, including the most often used diagnostic classification system, DSM III. Diagnostic classification is not without controversy and several opposing positions are described and evaluated. Several additional dimensions of psychological dysfunctions are described and psychological depression is discussed as an example of the diversity of these dimensions and explanatory models.

PERSPECTIVES ON DEFINITION: POTENTIAL CRITERIA

Many different criteria exist for defining abnormality, resulting in a variety of often discrepant definitions. This variability can be frustrating to clinicians and clients, since any given behavior may be classified as "normal" in one instance, but "abnormal" in others, depending on the definition that is applied.

The *criteria* that are used in definitions of "abnormality" are specific standards or rules with which judgments can be made for purposes of assessment, research, and treatment. For example, a definition of "abnormality" as "socially unacceptable behavior" uses one criterion, (e.g., the collective judgment of a person's social groups). When a researcher clearly specifies the criteria used to define a particular dysfunction being studied, it is possible for other researchers to conduct studies with equivalent subject samples. Similarly, before a practicing clini-

165

cian prescribes a treatment that is appropriate for a certain type of psychological dysfunction, it is essential that clear assessment criteria be used to determine what *is* the client's specific problem. Accurate delineation of the actual criteria used to define the subject groups is essential for replicating and extending research findings, as well as for encouraging on-target clinical intervention.

Scott (1958) listed the following criteria that have traditionally been used by *researchers* to define psychopathology: social maladjustment, formal diagnosis, presence in a mental hospital, subjective unhappiness, and scores outside the normal range on objective psychological inventories. The researcher can define groups of subjects based on the presence/absence of some or all of the above criteria. However, not all of these potentially defining criteria are equally useful. Some are too broad and all encompassing. For example, subjects in a mental hospital could be defined as psychologically dysfunctional although some of them might be classified as "normal" on psychological tests or in subjective happiness. Clinical researchers and assessors usually attempt to use several criteria that, together, enable accurate, consistent, and meaningful classification of people and behaviors as functional or dysfunctional. Several definitions of abnormal behavior have evolved, including the legal, cultural, statistical, personal, and professional perspectives.

Legal Definition

The term "insane" is a legal concept often used with reference to individuals who are judged by a court of law to be sufficiently incompetent to require commitment to an institution for psychological treatment or the appointment of a guardian. *Incompetency* refers to a judgment made regarding whether or not the individual has sufficient insight or capacity to make responsible decisions. If a person is judged incompetent, then he or she will lose the right, for example, to make contracts, vote, drive, and adopt children. Society has instituted this process of judgment and restriction of rights to protect the "insane" individual from squandering all material possessions or being cheated by swindlers, and to protect other citizens from negligence or violence by the "insane" person.

Commitment to an institution, either voluntary or involuntary, is usually the result of the individual's being judged to be sufficiently "insane" to be a danger to himself or to others, or to be incapable of adjusting to life in the community. Thus, both dangerousness and competency are involved in the legal definition of insanity. However, opinion rather than pure fact is involved in all aspects of determining legal insanity, and professionals such as clinical psychologists are called on to assist in making insanity judgments. Though "insanity" carries legal meaning, it is based on global and relatively imprecise criteria.

Cultural Criteria

The cultural criteria for defining abnormality are based on the standard behaviors that are approved by the majority of people or the people who possess the majority of power in a given culture or society. "Abnormal" behaviors are those that deviate from those standards. There is usually no one "standard," for society tolerates many variations of behavior within a culture and rejects only extremes. Moreover, the accepted "standard behaviors" can vary from culture to culture with the result that behavior that is aceptable in one culture may be considered abnormal in other cultures. Similarly, within a single culture a given behavior may go from being abnormal to normal or vice versa as social standards change. Homosexuality is a good, although perhaps overused, example of a contemporary redefinition of what is and what is not psychologically dysfunctional. In ancient Greece homosexuality was an acceptable life-style. In contemporary western society, however, homosexuality has often carried with it the implication that the individual is disturbed. Yet, recent cultural trends have evolved toward greater acceptance of homosexuality and the gay life-style. Presently, there are efforts by certain social groups to either reclassify homosexuality as abnormal or, from the opposing camp, to fully remove the negative connotations of a homosexual life-style.[1] Nevertheless, cultures do not change quickly and most of the behaviors that are classified as "abnormal" have been so designated for a very long time and in a variety of cultures.

Statistical Criteria

The incidence rate of all behavior can be determined and "distributions" for each behavior can be derived. Numerical norms, based on statistical procedures, can then be derived from the rates of behaviors. The mathematical calculations would tell us what most people do; the most frequent (modal), most central (median) or average (mean) behavior. In the statistical model, these measures of central tendency define normality. Behavior that differs significantly from the population's mode, median, or mean is considered abnormal. In Figure 5-1 you can see that 95% of the people have an IQ between 70 and 130. An individual who scores below 70 is one of only 2.5% of the population, and the person's IQ is thus statistically "abnormal."

From this statistical perspective, IQs over 130 are "abnormal," which would suggest that being too "smart" is dysfunctional. The statistical approach to defining abnormality and deviance has a shortcoming—extremes are not always dysfunctional. For instance, winning the World Cup Championship in rugby is rare—indeed, only one team earns that honor each year. Is winning abnormal? Statistically, yes, but it is certainly not dysfunctional in any ordinary sense.

The statistical criterion is precise because it is quantitive. However, labeling behavior as "abnormal" because it occurs rarely does not help the clinician assess or treat the causes and consequences of dysfunctional behavior. Clinical assessment and intervention require more information as to the causes, consequences, and exact nature of psychological dysfunctions. Nevertheless, the use of statistical procedures to select subjects with extreme scores on various psychological measures (e.g., measures of anxiety or depression) does provide clinical researchers with an exact and replicable standard.

---

[1]For a recent discussion of clinical psychology and homosexuality, the reader is referred to Davison (1976), Bieber (1976), Halleck (1976), Sturgis and Adams (1978), and Davison (1978).

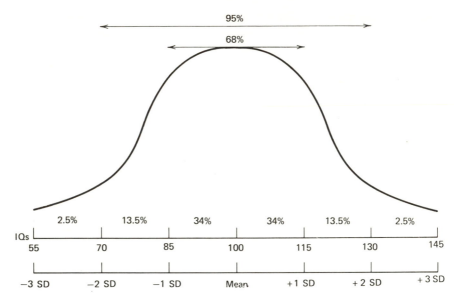

Figure 5-1 A normal distribution illustrating the relative frequencies of scores within standard deviations from the mean. Though this example uses IQ scores the same distribution could be established for depression scores, anxiety scores, etc.

Epidemiologists, in an effort to establish a criterion for statistical deviancy, have offered 10% as a numerical cutoff (Shepherd, Oppenheim, & Mitchell, 1971). According to this statistical criterion a behavior would be considered deviant if it is evident in 10% or less of the general population. Interestingly, the Shepherd et al. (1971) study of childhood psychological dysfunction found, surprisingly, that many behaviors generally regarded as "abnormal" were highly prevalent in all kinds of children. At least with children, it may be that the "unusual" behavior is not so unusual at all and is rather an aspect of normal development (see also MacFarlane, Allen, & Honzig, 1954).

Personal Criteria

When an individual seeks the assistance of a mental health professional the individual can be said to be self-defined as suffering psychologically. The accuracy of this criterion varies depending on certain characteristics of the person in question. First, the person must be aware of the mental health professional whose help can be sought. A very troubled but *uninformed* person who does not know about mental health professionals may still be exhibiting dysfunctional behavior, thought, or affect. Second, some people may evaluate their mental status by comparison to others in their environment and incorrectly conclude that they do or do not need psychological aid. For instance, the behavior of a manic individual may be labeled abnormal by many criteria but that person may say "Hey, I'm doing real fine." Third, a person may be psychologically distressed but still reluctant to seek treatment, perhaps due to a fear of being socially ostracized and stigmatized as "crazy." As a result, though the personal criterion is often used as a defining characteristic for clinical research and treatment, it is potentially inaccurate.

Professional Criteria

In relation to the other criteria of psychological dysfunction that we have discussed, the professional criteria are both the most basic and the most multifaceted. Professional criteria are the most basic because there is a professional judgment of a sort in almost all other criteria. The complex nature of the professional decision is evident in the fact that each professional must consider all aspects of the individual's behavior pattern—the legal, sociocultural, statistical, and personal—before defining it as psychopathological. Clinical psychologists are trained to develop and utilize the psychological tests and professional skills necessary to integrate these diverse sources of information and produce judgments about the presence of psychologically dysfunctional behavior. To facilitate professional judgments concerning psychological dysfunctions, mental health researchers and practitioners have developed several sophisticated models to describe and explain people's problems in living.

MODELS OF PSYCHOLOGICAL DYSFUNCTION

How do clinicians conceptualize psychological dysfunction? What representations are used to organize and symbolize an understanding of abnormal behavior? Several tentative theoretical structures, or "models," are employed to describe and explain psychological dysfunction.

A *model* is a conceptual analogue. Models have an "as if" quality that facilitates our thinking about certain sets of events. For example, the computer can be used as a model of the brain because the brain can be described as functioning as if it were a computer. Ideally, models serve to assist the clinician by (1) identifying the variables or events that are worthy of further study or inquiry, (2) providing a context into which information can be integrated, and (3) fostering the accurate specification of the relationships between variables and events.

There are, however, a few potential difficulties with the use of "models." First, it is possible to overgeneralize beyond the domain of the model. For instance, once we know that certain behaviors can be explained by a certain theoretical model we may be tempted to use the model to explain "all" behavior. Second, faithful adherence to a specific model may result in "professional blinders" that restrict the advancement of scientific understanding. For example, a learning theorist may look for the current reinforcements that are maintaining a certain troublesome behavior and, unwittingly, miss other aspects of the behavior that may be equally or more important. Finally, models are, by the nature of their "as-if" quality, incomplete and tentative. Models merely serve as tentative guides for thinking that must be continuously modified. With these cautions in mind, conceptual models can be used as worthwhile frameworks for the advanced study of psychological dysfunctions.

Although there are numerous models of psychological dysfunction that have
been proposed (see Maser & Seligman, 1977; Millon, 1973; Sahakian, 1970)—including the cultural model, the systems model, the existential model, the genetic
model, the humanistic model, the learning model, the medical model, the moral
model, the psychodynamic model, and others—a discussion of the four major
models will represent the majority of perspectives. These are the *medical, psychodynamic, learning,* and *systems* models.

The Medical Model

The medical model of psychological dysfuntion has also been called the disease
model or the organic model. According to this conceptualization, abnormal behavior is linked to physical ailments—the symptoms of psychopathology are seen
as the result of biological/biochemical maladies. Many psychiatrists, as a result
of their being trained as physicians, endorse the medical model, although several
contemporary psychiatrists align themselves with more of a social learning perspective. Before discussing the strengths and weaknesses of this approach, let us
consider how it developed.

Prior to the medical model of abnormal behavior, primitive concepts such as
demonology were often invoked to explain socially unacceptable behavior. Although demonic possession was not widely held, early writers who espoused the
medical model (e.g., Griesinger, 1845; Kraepelin, 1883) further eliminated demonology as an explanation of psychological dysfunction and expounded on the
relationship between brain function and human behavior. The discovery that
syphilis was the basis of *general paresis* (syphilitic infection of the cerebral cortex)
and that such a physical disease caused gross psychological impairment and deterioration was both an impetus to the medical model and strong evidence against
demonic possession.

Syphilis was originally viewed as an example of demon possession, but physicians then implicated the "spirochete" as the cause of general paresis. When a
test to determine the presence of syphilis in the blood was developed (Wasserman,
1905) and later researchers found the spirochete in the brains of deceased paretic
patients, the causal link appeared complete. The successful use of penicillin as a
treatment was used to substantiate the appropriateness of the medical model in
this instance. Extrapolating from this case, the medical model generally suggests
that other psychological dysfunctions are also the result of an inherited or acquired physiological disorder.

Szasz (1976), a psychiatrist, and others from a variety of disciplines (e.g., Albee, 1971; Grinker, 1969; Zubin, 1972b) have discussed and criticized the medical
model for its reliance on paresis as its prototype. While syphilis was identified as
the cause of progressive deterioration of the brain and resultant disorganization
of behavior, this did not demonstrate that the majority of other psychological
dysfunctions are physiologically caused. However, supporters of the medical
model often assert that although a direct relationship between physiological pathology and abnormal behavior has not yet been found, such a relationship exists
and will some day be discovered. Growing evidence of linkages between brain

functioning and psychological dysfunctions such as depression and chronic schiz-ophrenia (e.g., Gottesman & Shields, 1972; Kallman, 1953; Kety, 1959; Rosen-thal, 1970) offer support for the medical view. However, research demonstrating psychological and interpersonal factors in both psychological *and* physiological dysfunctions (e.g., cancer, heart disease) clearly indicate that a purely medical ex-planation is insufficient in most cases.

There are additional problems with a totally medical model of psychological dysfunctions. Notably, along with the causal assumptions of the medical model comes emphasis on remedial physical/medical treatment. Pills, electroconvulsive shock, psychosurgery, and megavitamins are all medical methods of treatment. Although certain medications may be, for example, of value for certain disor-ders, many clients need to restructure relationships, explore feelings, or acquire skills instead of, or in addition to, simply ingesting pills.

As Buss (1966) pointed out, there are actually several illness or disease models; traumatic, infectious, and systemic. *Traumatic* disease is the result of an external agent, such as a poisoning or fracture. An *infectious* disease results when a micro-organism affects the body through a particular organism. According to Buss, in-fectious and traumatic diseases do not provide the best concepts for understand-ing abnormal behavior as symptoms of illness. Buss considers *systemic* disease, where an organ or system of organs breaks down, as the optimal illness perspec-tive since an organ may break down due to a hereditary predisposition or as the result of extreme environmental stress.

The main point to be remembered is that the value of the medical model de-pends on the psychological dysfunction that is under study. In some instances it has a place and contributes substantially. In other cases the medical model either does not fit or is not sufficient alone. It is also important to recognize that biolog-ical causes do not necessarily imply biological treatments, or vice versa.

The Psychodynamic Model

The psychodynamic model of psychological dysfunctions developed mainly from the writings of Freud (e.g., Freud, 1920; see also Hall & Lindzey, 1978) and others who followed in his tradition (e.g., Cameron, 1963; Fenichel, 1945; Freud, 1946; Holzman, 1970). There are several basic assumptions in the psycho-dynamic model: unconscious processes are thought to play a central role in deter-mining behavior; three psychological agencies, id, ego, and superego, are said to interact whenever a psychological conflict must be resolved; adult functioning is determined by the effectiveness of the resolution of conflicts at the various psy-chosexual stages of development; and psychological conflict leads to anxiety, which the ego attempts to reduce by employing unconscious defense mechanisms.

The notion of unconscious processes as determinants of behavior is based on a division of human experience into three types. Conscious experience is that which is within a person's current awareness. Preconscious material includes all the thoughts, ideas, and memories that are available to the person but are not cur-rently in consciousness. The unconscious holds all the memories, fears, impulses, and hopes that are seldom if ever available to the person. This material is thought to be psychologically painful, and thus not easily brought into consciousness. Instead it remains hidden, like a concealed festering wound within the person causing inexplicable pain and aberrant behavior whenever it is touched by psychological conflict.

Freud's psychoanalytic perspective emphasizes three psychological structures: id, ego, and superego. The demands of these structures are often conflictual and it is the ineffective resolution of such conflict that is implicated by the psychodynamic theorists as the prime source of psychological dysfunctions. For instance, an individual who is not capable of controlling excessive id impulses would likely find himself or herself in conflict with society's rules. Or an individual may lead an extremely rigid and uneventful life responding to the superego's fear of some potential harm that will occur if the pleasure sought by the id is experienced. The model is "dynamic" because it focuses on the constant interplay of inner thoughts and feelings as expressed by the id, ego, and superego.

In contrast to the medical model, dynamic models place less causal emphasis on physiological causes of psychological dysfunctions and a greater importance on the person's experiences in infancy and early childhood and their effects on the current interaction between ego, id, and superego. Traumatic experiences that exceed the infant ego's capacity for coping are thought to be repressed in the unconscious as painful psychological wounds. This predisposes the person to experiencing anxiety in similar adult situations, even if the ego should now be able to cope with the trauma. Instead of handling the resultant anxiety effectively, the individual is said to resort to childlike "defense mechanisms" such as denial or projection, because the pain caused by the unhealed wound interferes with rational problem solving and action.

Critics have suggested a number of weaknesses in the psychodynamic conceptualization of psychological dysfunctions. Among these is the general lack of success of the psychodynamic model to withstand the rigorous standards of science. This criticism has two parts: First, the theoretical formulation is said to be stated in a fashion that is difficult to verify empirically—most of the theory concerns nonobservable events and psychic structures, and hidden conflict between id, ego, and superego. Second, when empirical tests of the theory are attempted the data are often interpreted as failing to support the theory. Also limiting the psychodynamic model is the fact that Freud's material for the development of the model came from individual cases and his experience as the therapist. Moreover, the clients who Freud saw were a very restricted sample, clearly lacking in the diversity of psychological dysfunction we recognize today.

On the positive side, the psychodynamic model offers a rich theory that considers subtle psychological phenomena, such as the unconscious. The model integrates normal personality development with the development of psychological dysfunctions and it focuses on the uniqueness of the intricate operations within people's personalities.

The Learning Model

The learning model views psychological dysfunctions as the result of faulty social learning (Ullmann & Krasner, 1975). Physiological factors are seen as of secondary importance in most cases, although never so trivial as to be ignored. According to this model, there is nothing inherently abnormal about the process of learning when a person experiences psychological distress. Indeed, only the responses that are learned are considered to cause the person sufficient problems in living to warrant change. Abnormal behavior is seen as learned in the same basic way as normal behavior, only the environmental conditions were such that the former resulted and not the latter.

The stage was set for the development of the learning model by Watson who, in 1913, criticized the introspective method and turned psychology toward the study of behavior. Dollard and Miller (1950) aided the development of the learning model by reexamining traditionally psychodynamic principles from a learning perspective. Developments in classical conditioning (Pavlov, 1927), operant conditioning (Skinner, 1953; 1972), and observational learning (Bandura, 1969) also played central roles in the advancing of the learning model.

Relative to other models, the learning model concentrates on behavior itself rather than the internal conflict processes or the physiological factors affecting behavior. Through a reliance on actual behavior, the learning model enables the use of the scientific method with fewer assumptions than other models (Goldfried & Kent, 1972). The learning model also holds that the same principles of learning that led to the development of maladaptive behavior are useful in modifying behavior. The scientific and treatment oriented aspects of the learning model are its strengths.

The potential drawbacks of the learning model are related to its lack of willingness to recognize the mediational quality of human cognitive processing and the predisposing quality of biological factors in the learning or unlearning of maladaptive behavior. This hesitancy appears to be passing (Mahoney, 1974; Meichenbaum, 1977), and a less pristine learning model, including the role of genetic "preparedness" (Seligman, 1971) and biological predispositions (Eysenck, 1967) appears to be in the offing.

The Systems Model

Systems theorists apply concepts from the physical (e.g., biology), information processing (e.g., computers), and social (e.g., anthropology) sciences to conceptualize human interactions, whether adaptive or dysfunctional, as components in a social system (Bateson, 1972; Miller, 1979; Watzlawick, 1978). Social networks such as families or peer groups are seen as evolving static and repetitive patterns of interaction in order to maintain a balance ("equilibrium") that maximizes the network's chance of survival. Any change, whether from within or outside the network, and whether constructive (e.g., a life-enhancing innovation) or destructive (e.g., a revolutionary coup), threatens the "homeostatic" (literally, fixed health) equilibrium (Speer, 1970). Networks are thought to have monitoring mechanisms which function like informal sergeants-at-arms to signal the presence of any deviations from the established patterns. These monitors provide "feedback," much like a thermostat's electronic signal to a furnace when the temperature rises or drops beyond allowed limits. Participants in the network must then neutralize the change by expelling its source from the system (e.g., ostracizing a deviant individual) or reshaping its source within the system (e.g., influencing the deviant individual to conform).

According to the systems model, psychological dysfunctions result in two cases: (1) when people must think, feel, or behave in psychologically or physically harmful or painful ways in order to fit their social networks and (2) when people attempt to change their roles or interactions in their social networks without sufficient power or skill to overcome or work around the network's inertial forces. As an example of the first instance, Bateson, Jackson, Haley, and Weakland (1956) hypothesized that persons who are diagnosed as "schizophrenic" have developed aberrant patterns of thought and behavior because their families create a "double bind" system. A double bind occurs when a person is punished no matter what he or she does—"damned if you do, and damned if you don't"—and the individual is prohibited from even acknowledging that this "crazy-making" system is in effect. A patient who has failed in attempts to gain recognition as an autonomous adult from his or her family might have developed schizophrenic-like thinking due to a "double bind."

Systems theory downplays the role of physiological, internal psychological, or individual learning factors while emphasizing the role of complex patterns of interpersonal interactions in psychological dysfunctions. The person's total social context, rather than isolated physiological, psychological, or learning events or mechanisms, is seen as defining deviance and causing psychological dysfunctions. Systems-oriented clinical psychologists attempt to incorporate physiological, psychodynamic (e.g., Framo, 1976), and learning (e.g., Gurman & Knudson, 1978) factors into their model, arguing that these are the building blocks for human social systems but that a broader view of the total network is necessary to fully explain why one person experiences psychological dysfunctions and other persons with similar psychological and physiological makeups and learned behaviors do not. Research evaluations of the systems model as yet offer only tentative support (Doane, 1978) although applications of systems theory to therapy with families is gaining both research and clinical endorsement (Gurman & Kniskern, 1978).

Closing Caveat

The medical model emphasizes organic, physical, and biological sources of dysfunctions, while the psychodynamic model stresses "unconscious" processes, the learning model highlights the central role of environmental stimuli, responses, and reinforcement in the acquisition of abnormal behavior, and the systems model focuses on homeostatic regulatory processes in social networks. It is important to realize that no one model can fully explain all psychological dysfunctions. Certain dysfunctions are primarily the result of brain lesions or disease and in such cases the medical model can be said to "fit" the data. Yet even in these cases, psychodynamic conflicts or faulty learning can contribute significantly to the resultant psychological dysfunction. For example, a cancer patient's psychological and behavioral readiness to cope with the prospect of pain and death is critically important to his or her adjustment. In still other cases it may be useful to consider the homeostatic forces in the person's social systems.

Rigid adherence to any single model of psychological dysfunction is likely to limit the clinician. As one investigates the etiology, remediation, and prevention of psychological disorders, each model serves as a valuable source of hypotheses. Models that produce testable propositions are particularly worthwhile because they can be examined empirically and improved and modified accordingly. The effectiveness of any model is unrelated to the polemical talents of its proponents but is a function of the knowledge and insights it helps to generate and of its integrative and predictive value (Garmezy, 1971).

DIAGNOSTIC CLASSIFICATION OF DYSFUNCTIONAL BEHAVIOR

Unlike the science of personality description where classification encompasses all normal variations in behavior, diagnostic classification requires a categorization of only those behavior patterns that are considered maladaptive, dysfunctional, or abnormal.

Diagnosis means "to distinguish between," "to make a scientific discrimination of any kind." Diagnostic classifications of psychological dysfunctions employ assessment data to make a determination of the proper diagnostic category to describe a client's maladaptive behavior. Many clinical psychologists are involved on a daily basis in making diagnoses, although some other clinicians prefer to use the assessment data to help understand and treat the client without assigning a diagnostic label.

Several systems for the classification of abnormal behavior have been outlined over the years. The American Psychiatric Association's Committee on Statistics formulated a classification of mental disorders as early as 1917. In 1952, largely as a result of the psychiatric casualties of World War II, the diagnostic system was revised and a diagnostic and statistical manual (DSM) of "mental disorders" was published. In an effort to work toward an international classification system, the DSM was again revised in 1968. The 1968 version, DSM II, incorporated some of the suggestions of the World Health Organization's International Classification of Diseases (ICD) and the result was the most widely used classification system in history.

Currently, a third revision of the diagnostic and statistical manual (DSM III, 1980) has replaced DSM II. Efforts again have been directed toward an international system. The ICD-9 (Ninth Edition, 1978) has been modified for use in the United States and the developers of DSM III worked to ensure that, as far as possible, DSM III would be compatible with ICD-9.

In clinical psychology today, two systems of classification receive the majority of attention: DSM III, and behavioral classification, an approach to diagnosis that emphasizes the identification of the environmental conditions that evoke or maintain the problem behaviors.

DSM III

DSM III is the national psychiatric classification system[2] for the mental disorders in the United States. The general outline of the DSM III is provided in Table 5-1. The text of the DSM III contains information about each of the specific disorders including a list of the essential features that must be present for a diagnosis to be made, a mention of related features that are usually but not always present, and a record of information about the disorder. This record provides information concerning the usual age when the disorder begins (onset), the likely events to be seen as the disorder progresses (course), factors that are often involved in the development of the disorder (predisposing factors), disabilities that may result from the disorder (impairments and complications), the rate of the disorder (prevalence), the degree to which the disorder has genetic qualities (familial and sex patterns), and factors that are important in differentiating one disorder from another (differential diagnosis).

Table 5-1   DSM-III Classification: Axes I and II Categories and Codes

All official DSM-III codes and terms are included in ICD-9-CM. However, in order to differentiate those DSM-III categories that use the same ICD-9-CM codes, unofficial non-ICD-9-CM codes are provided in parentheses for use when greater specificity is necessary.

The long dashes indicate the need for a fifth-digit subtype or other qualifying term.

DISORDERS USUALLY FIRST EVIDENT IN INFANCY, CHILDHOOD OR ADOLESCENCE

Mental Retardation
(Code in Fifth digit: 1 = with other behavioral symptoms [requiring attention or treatment and that are not part of another disorder], 0 = without other behavioral symptoms.)
317.0 (x) Mild mental retardation,_____
318.0 (x) Moderate mental retardation, _____
318.1 (x) Severe mental retardation, _____
318.2 (x) Profound mental retardation, _____

319.0 (x) Unspecified mental retardation, _____

Attention Deficit Disorder
314.01   with hyperactivity
314.00   without hyperactivity
314.80   residual type

Conduct Disorder
312.00   undersocialized, aggressive
312.10   undersocialized, nonaggressive
312.23   socialized, aggressive
312.21   socialized, nonaggressive
312.90   atypical

Anxiety Disorders of Childhood or Adolescence
309.21   Separation anxiety disorder
313.21   Avoidant disorder of childhood or adolescence
313.00   Overanxious disorder

Other Disorders of Infancy, Childhood or Adolescence
313.89   Reactive attachment disorder of infancy
313.22   Schizoid disorder of childhood or adolescence
313.23   Elective mutism
313.81   Oppositional disorder

[2]Note that the DSM III is largely a product of the American Psychiatric Association, with only limited and consultative input from the American Psychological Association.

Table 5-1   *Continued*

313.82   Identity disorder

Eating Disorders
307.10   Anorexia nervosa
307.51   Bulimia
307.52   Pica
307.53   Rumination disorder of infancy
307.50   Atypical eating disorder

Stereotyped Movement Disorder
307.21   Transient tic disorder
307.22   Chronic motor tic disorder
307.23   Tourette's disorder
307.20   Atypical tic disorder
307.30   Atypical stereotyped movement
          disorder

Other Disorders with Physical Manifestations
307.00   Stuttering
307.60   Functional enuresis
307.70   Functional encopresis
307.46   Sleepwalking disorder
307.46   Sleep terror disorder (307.49)

Pervasive Developmental Disorders
Code in fifth digit: 0 = full syndrome
present, 1 = residual state.
299.0x   Infantile autism, _____
299.9x   Childhood onset pervasive
          developmental disorder, _____
299.8x   Atypical, _____

Specific Developmental Disorders
Note: These are coded on Axis II.
315.00   Developmental reading
          disorder
315.10   Developmental arithmetic
          disorder
315.31   Developmental language
          disorder
315.39   Developmental articulation
          disorder
315.50   Mixed specific
          developmental disorder
315.90   Atypical specific
          developmental disorder

ORGANIC MENTAL DISORDERS

*Section 1. Organic mental disorders whose
etiology or pathophysiological process is
listed below (taken from the mental disorders section of ICD-9-CM).*
    *Dementias Arising in the Senium and
Presenium*
          Primary degenerative dementia, senile
          onset,
290.30   with delirium
290.20   with delusions
290.21   with depression
290.00   uncomplicated
Code in fifth digit:
1 = with delirium, 2 = with delusions, 3 =
with depression, 0 = uncomplicated.
290.1x   Primary degenerative dementia,
          presenile onset, _____
290.4x   Multi-infarct dementia, _____

Substance-Induced
    Alcohol
303.00   intoxication
291.40   idiosyncratic intoxication
291.80   withdrawal
291.00   withdrawal delirium
291.30   hallucinosis
291.10   amnestic disorder
Code severity of dementia in fifth digit:
1 = mild, 2 = moderate, 3 = severe, 0 =
unspecified.
291.2x   Dementia associated with
          alcoholism, _____
          Barbiturate or similarly acting
          sedative or hypnotic
305.40   intoxication (327.00)
292.00   withdrawal (327.01)
292.00   withdrawal delirium (327.02)
292.83   amnestic disorder (327.04)
    Opioid
305.50   intoxication (327.10)
292.00   withdrawal (327.11) Cocaine
305.60   intoxication (327.20)
          Amphetamine or similarly acting
          sympathomimetic
305.70   intoxication (327.30)

Table 5-1 *Continued*

292.81   delirium (327.32)
292.11   delusional disorder (327.35)
292.00   withdrawal (327.31)
         Phencyclidine (PCP) or similarly act-
         ing arylcyclohexylamine
305.90   intoxication (327.40)
292.81   delirium (327.42)
292.90   mixed organic mental disorder
         (327.49)
         Hallucinogen
305.30   hallucinosis (327.56)
292.11   delusional disorder (327.55)
292.84   affective disorder (327.57)
         Cannabis
305.20   intoxication (327.60)
292.11   delusional disorder (327.65)
         Tobacco
292.00   withdrawal (327.71)
         Caffeine
305.90   intoxication (327.80)
         Other or unspecified substance
305.90   intoxication (327.90)
292.00   withdrawal (327.91)
292.81   delirium (327.92)
292.82   dementia (327.93)
292.83   amnestic disorder (327.94)
292.11   delusional disorder (327.95)
292.12   hallucinosis (327.96)
292.84   affective disorder (327.97)
292.89   personality disorder (327.98)
292.90   atypical or mixed organic mental
         disorder (327.99)

*Section 2. Organic brain syndromes whose
etiology or pathophysiological process is
either noted as an additional diagnosis
from outside the mental disorders sections
of ICD-9-CM or is unknown*
293.00   Delirium
294.10   Dementia
294.00   Amnestic syndrome
293.81   Organic delusional syndrome
293.82   Organic hallucinosis
293.83   Organic affective syndrome
310.10   Organic personality syndrome
294.80   Atypical or mixed organic brain
         syndrome

SUBSTANCE USE DISORDERS

Code in fifth digit: 1 = continuous, 2 =
episodic, 3 = in remission, 0 = unspecified.

305.0x   Alcohol abuse, _____
303.9x   Alcohol dependence
         (Alcoholism), _____
305.4x   Barbiturate or similarly acting
         sedative or hypnotic abuse,
304.1x   Barbiturate or similarly acting
         sedative or hypnotic depend-
         ence, _____
305.5x   Opioid abuse, _____
304.0x   Opioid dependence, _____
305.6x   Cocaine abuse, _____
305.7x   Amphetamine or similarly acting
         sympathomimetic abuse, _____
304.4x   Amphetamine or similarly acting
         sympathomimetic depend-
         ence, _____
305.9x   Phencyclidine PCP or similarly
         acting arylcyclohexylamine
         abuse, _____ (328.4x)
305.3x   Hallucinogen abuse, _____
305.2x   Cannabis abuse, _____
304.3x   Cannabis dependence, _____
305.1x   Tobacco dependence, _____
305.9x   Other, mixed or unspecified
         substance abuse, _____
304.6x   Other specified substance
         dependence, _____
304.9x   Unspecified substance
         dependence, _____
304.7x   Dependence on combination of
         opioid and other non-alcoholic
         substance, _____
304.8x   Dependence on combination of
         substances, excluding opioids and
         alcohol, _____

SCHIZOPHRENIC DISORDERS

Code in fifth digit: 1 = subchronic, 2 =
chronic, 3 = subchronic with acute exacer-
bation, 4 = chronic with acute exacerba-
tion, 5 = in remission, 0 = unspecified.

Table 5-1 *Continued*

Schizophrenia,

295.1x   disorganized, _____
295.2x   catatonic, _____
295.3x   paranoid, _____
295.9x   undifferentiated, _____
295.6x   residual, _____

PARANOID DISORDERS

297.10   Paranoia
297.30   Shared paranoid disorder
298.30   Acute paranoid disorder
297.90   Atypical paranoid disorder

PSYCHOTIC DISORDERS NOT ELSEWHERE CLASSIFIED

295.40   Schizophreniform disorder
298.80   Brief reactive psychosis
295.70   Schizoaffective disorder
298.90   Atypical psychosis

NEUROTIC DISORDERS

These are included in Affective, Anxiety, Somatoform, Dissociative, and Psychosexual Disorders. In order to facilitate the identification of the categories that in DSM-II were grouped together in the class of Neuroses, the DSM-II terms are included separately in parentheses after the corresponding categories. These DSM-II terms are included in ICD-9-CM and therefore are acceptable as alternatives to the recommended DSM-III terms that precede them.

AFFECTIVE DISORDERS

Major Affective Disorders
Code major depressive episode in fifth digit: 6 = in remission, 4 = with psychotic features (the unofficial non-ICD-9-CM fifth digit 7 may be used instead to indicate that the psychotic features are mood-incongruent), 3 = with melancholia, 2 = without melancholia, 0 = unspecified.

Code manic episode in fifth digit: 6 = in remission, 4 = with psychotic features (the unofficial non-ICD-9-CM fifth digit 7 may be used instead to indicate that the psychotic features are mood-incongruent), 2 = without psychotic features, 0 = unspecified.

Bipolar disorder
296.6x   mixed, _____
296.4x   manic, _____
296.5x   depressed, _____
Major depression
296.2x   single episode, _____
296.3x   recurrent, _____

Other Specific Affective Disorders
301.13   Cyclothymic disorder
300.40   Dysthymic disorder (or Depressive neurosis)

Atypical Affective Disorders
296.70   Atypical bipolar disorder
296.82   Atypical depression

ANXIETY DISORDERS

Phobic disorders (or Phobic neuroses)
300.21   Agoraphobia with panic attacks
300.22   Agoraphobia without panic attacks
300.23   Social phobia
300.29   Simple phobia
Anxiety states (or Anxiety neuroses)
300.01   Panic disorder
300.02   Generalized anxiety disorder
300.30   Obsessive compulsive disorder (or Obsessive compulsive neurosis)
Post-traumatic stress disorder
308.30   acute
309.81   chronic or delayed
300.00   Atypical anxiety disorder

SOMATOFORM DISORDERS

300.81   Somatization disorder
300.11   Conversion disorder (or Hysterical neurosis, conversion type)
307.80   Psychogenic pain disorder

Table 5-1   *Continued*

300.70	Hypochondriasis (or Hypochondriacal neurosis)
300.70	Atypical somatoform disorder (300.71)

DISSOCIATIVE DISORDERS (OR HYSTERICAL NEUROSES, DISSOCIATIVE TYPE)

300.12	Psychogenic amnesia
300.13	Psychogenic fugue
300.14	Multiple personality
300.60	Depersonalization disorder (or Depersonalization neurosis)
300.15	Atypical dissociative disorder

PSYCHOSEXUAL DISORDERS

Gender Identity Disorders
Indicate sexual history in the fifth digit of Transsexualism code: 1 = asexual, 2 = homosexual, 3 = heterosexual, 0 = unspecified.

302.5x	Transsexualism, _____
302.60	Gender identity disorder of childhood
302.85	Atypical gender identity disorder

Paraphilias

302.81	Fetishism
302.30	Transvestism
302.10	Zoophilia
302.20	Pedophilia
302.40	Exhibitionism
302.82	Voyeurism
302.83	Sexual masochism
302.84	Sexual sadism
302.90	Atypical paraphilia

Psychosexual Dysfunctions

302.71	Inhibited sexual desire
302.72	Inhibited sexual excitement
302.73	Inhibited female orgasm
302.74	Inhibited male orgasm
302.75	Premature ejaculation
302.76	Functional dyspareunia

306.51	Functional vaginismus
302.70	Atypical psychosexual dysfunction

Other Psychosexual Disorders

302.00	Ego-dystonic homosexuality
302.89	Psychosexual disorder not elsewhere classified

FACTITIOUS DISORDERS

300.16	Factitious disorder with psychological symptoms
301.51	Chronic factitious disorder with physical symptoms
300.19	Atypical factitious disorder with physical symptoms

DISORDERS OF IMPULSE CONTROL NOT ELSEWHERE CLASSIFIED

312.31	Pathological gambling
312.32	Kleptomania
312.33	Pyromania
312.34	Intermittent explosive disorder
312.35	Isolated explosive disorder
312.39	Atypical impulse control disorder

ADJUSTMENT DISORDER

309.00	with depressed mood
309.24	with anxious mood
309.28	with mixed emotional features
309.30	with disturbance of conduct
309.40	with mixed disturbance of emotions and conduct
309.23	with work (or academic) inhibition
309.83	with withdrawal
309.90	with atypical features

PSYCHOLOGICAL FACTORS AFFECTING PHYSICAL CONDITION

Specify physical condition on Axis III.

316.00	Psychological factors affecting physical condition

Table 5-1 *Continued*

PERSONALITY DISORDERS

Note: These are coded on Axis II.

301.00	Paranoid
301.20	Schizoid
301.22	Schizotypal
301.50	Histrionic
301.81	Narcissistic
301.70	Antisocial
301.83	Borderline
301.82	Avoidant
301.60	Dependent
301.40	Compulsive
301.84	Passive-Aggressive
301.89	Atypical, mixed or other personality disorder

V CODES FOR CONDITIONS NOT ATTRIBUTABLE TO A MENTAL DISORDER THAT ARE A FOCUS OF ATTENTION OR TREATMENT

V65.20	Malingering
V62.89	Borderline intellectual functioning (V62.88)
V71.01	Adult antisocial behavior
V71.02	Childhood or adolescent antisocial behavior
V62.30	Academic problem
V62.20	Occupational problem
V62.82	Uncomplicated bereavement
V15.81	Noncompliance with medical treatment
V62.89	Phase of life problem or other life circumstance problem
V61.10	Marital problem
V61.20	Parent-child problem
V61.80	Other specified family circumstances
V62.81	Other interpersonal problem

ADDITIONAL CODES

300.90	Unspecified mental disorder (nonpsychotic)
V71.09	No diagnosis or condition on Axis I
799.90	Diagnosis or condition deferred on Axis I

V71.09	No diagnosis on Axis II
799.90	Diagnosis deferred on Axis II

From the American Psychiatric Association, *Diagnostic and statistical manual of mental disorders (3rd ed.): DSM III.* Washington D.C., American Psychiatric Association, 1980. Copyright 1980, American Psychiatric Association. Reprinted by permission.

Diagnoses in DSM III are made according to a "multiaxial" procedure, signifying that there are multiple (in this case, five) dimensions or axes on which diagnostic judgments must be made. The first and second axes of the system comprise all the mental disorders within the system. The first axis is for those psychiatric syndromes and other conditions thought to be major disorders, such as the organic mental disorders and the schizophrenic disorders. Axis II is reserved for less serious impairments as reflected in the category Personality Disorders (e.g., Psychosexual Disorders) in adults or Specific Developmental Disorders (e.g., eating disorders) in children. These two axes were outlined in Table 5-1.

Axis III allows the clinician to indicate any *nonmental* medical dysfunctions (e.g., diabetes) that are relevant. Axis IV requires the clinician's rating of severity of one or more psychosocial stressors that have contributed to the client's current disorder. Using Axis IV the clinician rates the severity from "no apparent psychosocial stressor" (i.e., 1) to "catastrophic" (i.e., 7—multiple family deaths, concentration camp experiences, or a devastating natural disaster). A "moderate" rating (i.e., 4) reflects moderate stressors such as a change to a different line of work, death of a close friend, pregnancy, or a child leaving home.

The fifth and final axis is used by the clinician to indicate the highest level of *adaptive* functioning that the client has exhibited (for at least a few months) during the last year. A code of 1 is used for "superior" and indicates unusually effective functioning in a wide range of activities and relationships. At the other extreme, "grossly impaired" functioning is coded by a "7" and indicates that the patient was unable to function in almost all areas. "Fair" adaptive functioning, a scale code of 4, designates an adequate general functioning but with some impairment in at least one area.

Will these new axes result in an increase in the amount of time necessary for diagnostic purposes? Will the additional information prove valuable? Two specific axes of the multiaxial system appear to be definite improvements, Axis 4 indicating environmental factors and Axis 5 indicating the client's personal, positive resources. The rating of environmental stress (Axis 4) and the rating of the patient's highest level of adaptive functioning (Axis 5) should be quite useful in both determining appropriate treatment and in making prognostic predictions. The truth of this prediction will be determined by future research.

An important potential improvement in the third edition of DSM is in the efforts to provide *specific* and *operational* diagnostic criteria. The DSM III has attempted to provide a series of *diagnostic criteria* for each of the specific disorders. These criteria are designed to include the behaviors, thoughts, and mood states that define each of the disorders and the intensity and duration that is required for a diagnosis. For example, in a conversion disorder the predominant disturbance is a loss or alteration of physical functioning suggesting a physical disorder but which is actually a direct expression of a psychological conflict or need. DSM III criteria for a diagnosis of "conversion disorder" are as follows:

A. The predominant disturbance is a loss or alteration of physical functioning suggesting a physical disorder.
B. Psychological factors are judged to be etiologically involved in the symptom, as evidenced by one of the following:
    1. There is a temporal relationship between an environmental stimulus that is apparently related to a psychological conflict or need and the initiation or exacerbation of the symptom.
    2. The symptom enables the individual to avoid some activity that is noxious to him or her.
    3. The symptom enables the individual to get support from the environment that otherwise might not be forthcoming.
C. It has been determined that the symptom is *not* under voluntary control.
D. The symptom cannot, after appropriate investigation, be explained by a known physical disorder or pathophysiological mechanism.

E. The symptom is not limited to pain or to a disturbance in sexual functioning.
F. Not due to Somatization Disorder or Schizophrenia. (DSM III, 1980, p. 247).

These criteria, and those for each of the other disorders, are intended to improve diagnostic reliability and, subsequently, to advance clinical research studies.

It may be surprising to the reader that specific diagnostic criteria have not always been provided. Research has indicated that earlier versions of DSM had several problems related to the unreliability that resulted from a lack of specific criteria for diagnosis (e.g., Beck, Ward, Mendelson, Mock, & Erbaugh, 1962; Zigler & Phillips, 1961). In the Beck et al. (1962) study, for example, the lack of reliability was attributed to inconsistencies on the part of the patient (5%), inconsistencies on the part of the diagnostician (32.5%), and inconsistencies of the diagnostic system (62.5%). Importantly, it was the view of the diagnosticians that 62.5% of the disagreements were the result of unclear criteria (Ward, Beck, Mendelson, Mock, & Erbaugh, 1962). The provision of more specific diagnostic criteria in DSM III could improve diagnostic reliabilities, but this outcome remains to be demonstrated by the actual use of DSM III in clinical practice and research.

Another positive step concerns the strategy that has been adopted for the national study and implementation of the DSM III system. Clinicians and diagnosticians at mental health institutions will use the system as part of a *field trial* and provide feedback about its strengths, errors, inconsistencies, and needed additions. The feedback will be incorporated into improvements in the system. Thus, the final DSM III should have profited from extensive field testing prior to its implementation on a national scale.

On the other hand, the system is elaborate and more complicated than the former DSM II. Busy therapists and assessors may find DSM III's complexity burdensome, and they may find it difficult to adjust to the new system. Even if some or all practitioners do try to learn the new system, they may find it difficult to use without errors because it is novel and detailed. Some practitioners may accept some changes and others may accept others, resulting in profesionals essentially using many different systems. Extensive training in the use of the system and gradual implementation of its requirements will likely be helpful.

Another drawback, DSM III has included just about *everything* as a mental disorder. *Mental* disorders are designed as a subset of *medical* disorders, although psychological dysfuntions are often not best described under a medical umbrella. According to Schacht and Nathan (1977), "of the more than 230 problem behaviors included in DSM III, more than half are certainly or almost certainly *not* attributable to known or presumed organic causes." (p. 10, italics added). For example, Developmental Arithmetic Disorder is included within DSM III. Does this mean that a child who cannot add has a psychiatric mental disorder? According to the system the answer would be "yes." While this inclusiveness was probably motivated by a sincere interest in helping children overcome developmental disabilities, it produces a problematic side effect (Highlight 5-1). With the definition of such a category as a medical disorder comes an increased tendency for laypersons and professionals to expect that psychiatrists are the best providers of services for its prevention or treatment. In fact, clinical,

school, or counseling psychologists, educators, guidance counselors, or other
nonmedical professionals may be better prepared to handle such cases.

Highlight 5-1   "Never Mind the Psychologists; is It Good for the Children?"

As evident in the title, Garmezy (1978) goes beyond evaluating the impact of
DSM III on psychologists and directs his critical attention to the section of
DSM III on *Disorders Usually Arising In Childhood or Adolescence* and its re-
lation to the well-being of America's children.

   In the all-encompassing list of children's "mental disorders" (see DSM III,
p. 176–177), are such categories as "Reading Disorder," "Language Disorder," and "Arithmetic Disorder." While psychological and emotional factors may contribute to difficulties in these intellectual/academic skills, labeling
them as psychiatric disorders implies that they are caused by organic dysfunctions such as brain lesions. The role that more straightforward factors such as
poor educational environments or deficiency in directly trainable skills may
have is greatly downplayed, although these issues could be directly handled
without medical diagnosis or treatment.

   For example, Garmezy examined the category of Reading Disorder and
found it ill defined and its causes unspecified. Furthermore, varied approaches
to intervention were recommended with no clue as to what tack to take with
different specific clients. Considering the number of children that are markedly deficient in reading in America (i.e., 10%), it is difficult to conceive of med-
ically diagnosing and treating so many children. Importantly, reading disorders are primarily treated in an educational-remedial fashion, an approach
to amelioration that is not the expertise of psychiatry. Garmezy quotes Spitzer,
Sheehy, & Endicott (1977) from the guiding principles of the DSM III:

> *Because the DSM III classification is intended for the entire profession, and be-
> cause our current knowledge about mental disorder is so limited, the Task Force
> has chosen to be inclusive rather than exclusive. In practice, this means that when-
> ever a clinical condition can be described with clarity and relative distinctness, it is
> considered for inclusion. If there is general agreement among clinicians, who
> would be expected to encounter the condition, that there are a significant number
> of patients who have it and that its identification is important in their clinical
> work, it is included in the classification. (p. 3)*

   Garmezy goes on to criticize the DSM III because, instead of a scientifically
oriented classification, "we have a potpourri of categories, the truly psychiatric disorders presented with greater precision and clarity while others that are
beyond the province of psychiatry are described in a vague and indeterminate
manner" (Garmezy, 1978, p. 6)

   The final upshot is that, although in many instances children's disorders are
beyond the province of psychiatry, they will receive psychiatric labels. While
labeling theory may not explain all the causes of serious psychological dysfunctions it does tell us that many children will be subject to the victimization

of the label (Ullmann & Krasner, 1975). In the recent past, a U.S. vice-presidential candidate was eliminated from consideration because of an earlier bout with depression. Should every child who has a reading problem be given a psychiatric label that may haunt his or her future? Garmezy thinks not, and we agree.

Schacht and Nathan (1977) view the multiaxial system as providing professionals with more thorough knowledge for planning clinical interventions, but they also note that the system does *not* include an additional axis for coding *responses to treatment.* They suggest that such an axis would allow for large-scale research evaluation of therapy and that the value of such an axis merits serious consideration. In conclusion, according to Schacht and Nathan (1977), "the DSM III is both a major advance and a document that leaves much to be desired" (p. 1017).

Criteria For Evaluating Classification Systems

A set of criteria are needed to evaluate the methods of diagnostic classification. Such criteria would allow researchers to conduct studies that would educate us about the strengths and weaknesses of classification systems.

Blashfield and Draguns (1976) have provided four criteria for the evaluation of psychiatric classification. These criteria are *reliability, coverage, descriptive validity,* and *predictive validity.* The primary criterion, reliability, is essential for all classification systems since it is a prerequisite to the other criteria. The reliability of diagnostic classification refers to the ability of independent diagnosticians to classify the same cases in the same ways. For example, a system is reliable to the extent that any two psychologists both give the same patient the same diagnosis. To the extent that diagnostic categories are clearly defined, independent diagnosticians are more likely to produce an identical diagnostic classification.

"*Coverage* refers to the applicability of a classification to the domain of patients for which it was intended" (Blashfield & Draguns, 1976, p. 144). A valuable classification system has categories relevant to all people seeking help, so that every individual can be classified and best helped. However, an offshoot of complete coverage is that there are likely to be "wastebasket" categories for those dysfunctions that do not fit the criteria of other categories. For example, under the heading "Disorders of Impulse Control," DSM III has a category "other impulse control disorders." This "other" category is set aside for impulse disorders that do not "fit" exactly into the specific categories. As you might suspect, a complete system is likely to be more reliable because it avoids the uncertainty that occurs when some persons just do not "fit." However, wastebasket categories do little to help the clinician in formulating a treatment intervention.

When a classification system achieves homogeneity in terms of behaviors, symptoms, personality characteristics, or other criteria, then it is said to have *descriptive validity.* However, homogeneity is a relative term—achieving homogeneity in one set of characteristics or symptoms may not produce homogeneity in a second set. Nevertheless, determining whether or not a classification system has

descriptive validity entails an analysis to determine that the descriptions of dysfunctions within any one category are similar to one another but different from
those of other categories.

Blashfield and Draguns' fourth criterion is *predictive validity,* which requires
that the classification system accurately predict the effectiveness of different
treatments for each of the classification categories. Correspondingly, the optimal
intervention for each patient in each category should be accurately predicted.
Much like the criterion of descriptive validity, predictive validity also requires homogeneity of subject groups.

Applying the Blashfield & Draguns (1976) criteria to the DSM III might lead to
the following conclusions. The reliability is likely to be better than DSM II since
there are more specific criteria for each diagnostic category, but reliability research will be needed to determine if this is the case. Preliminary data on the reliability of DSM III, gathered as part of the field trials, indicates that there have
been some improvements: the reliabilities for most of the classes of adult disorders is generally higher than that previously achieved. The reliabilities were calculated using two mental health professionals' diagnostic judgments and applying
the kappa statistic (see Spitzer, Forman, & Nee, 1979). Coverage is good, since
the system covers all psychopathology, but there are several wastebasket categories that may reduce reliability and the "all-encompassing" quality has led to serious criticism. Descriptive validity, although subject to different opinions, can be
considered adequate. Most importantly, however, predictive validity is as yet unknown and the relationship between most DSM III categories and treatment recommendations is unclear. Much additional research is thus required to evaluate
DSM III.

Behavioral Diagnosis

An alternative to DSM III diagnostic classification, behavioral diagnosis stresses
the importance of locating specific environmental and behavioral dysfunctions
and translating them into a form that will allow for direct treatment (Kanfer &
Phillips, 1970). With this approach, the clinical psychologist (1) identifies specific
problem behaviors, (2) determines the environmental conditions maintaining
them, and (3) plans changes in the environment that should replace problem behaviors with adaptive ones (Mischel, 1968; Peterson, 1968).

Kanfer and Saslow's (1965, 1969) system of behavioral diagnosis is representative. As these authors point out, their system:

> is not intended to lead to assignment of the patient to diagnostic categories. It
> should serve as a basis for making decisions about specific therapeutic interven-
> tions, regardless of the presenting problem. (Kanfer & Saslow, 1969, p. 430)

With behavioral diagnosis the clinician classifies clients' behaviors as either (1)
excesses—behaviors that are problematic as a result of their excessive frequency,
intensity, duration, or setting, (2) deficits—problematic behaviors that are too in-
frequent, inadequate in intensity, short in duration, or fail to appear in settings
when the behaviors would be appropriate, or (3) assets—nonproblematic behaviors. Then, the environmental conditions contributing to the problem behaviors

are assessed through an analysis of antecedent events, consequent events, contingency relationships, and the biological condition of the client. For example, Jeff S. is a child (seen in a community mental health facility) whose behavior problem is primarily one of acting out and aggression. A clinical psychologist working with Jeff and his family notes that his parents lack interest in Jeff's activities and this seems to evoke aggression in Jeff. When Jeff acts out, however, the parents focus on him and, although briefly, pay attention to him. These consequent events are part of the environmental factors that maintain the acting out. An important contingency relationship in this example is that the child is not given attention unless he acts out: parental attention is provided contingent on acting out. In keeping with the treatment orientation of the behavioral approach, these antecedents, consequents, and contingencies would be subject to alteration in order to modify Jeff's acting-out behavior.

Many clinicians have adopted this behaviorally oriented approach to classification, but DSM III diagnoses often remain a requirement. That is, institutional case records, insurance coverage forms, and even some professional journals require a "diagnosis": the chart isn't complete, the insurance company won't pay and the article won't be published unless the DSM III diagnoses are reported.

Controversy Concerning The Classification Of Psychological Dysfunctions

"Should people be pigeonholed?" "Diagnoses do not lead to better treatment, so why bother?" "Psychiatric labels are self-fulfilling." "Diagnoses are too unreliable to be of any merit." Each of these statements represents one of the several tactics used to attack the classification of psychological dysfunctions.

The self-fulfilling and self-defeating quality of diagnostic labels has been emphasized by Szasz (1976). He argues that there is no evidence that the diagnostic label of schizophrenia, his prime example, helps clinicians to understand or truly serve people with problems in living. Rather, Szasz argues that the diagnosis implies that the person is "diseased," and leads therefore to stigmatizing rather than aiding troubled people.

Rosenhan (1973) reported a study that is often cited as demonstrating that psychiatric diagnoses lead to self-fulfilling prophecies. In this study pseudopatients (average persons who acted in such a way as to get diagnosed and admitted to a psychiatric hospital) were found to be treated differently when in a psychiatric hospital than when outside, although they behaved in their normal fashion once admitted to the hospital. Also, the pseudopatients were not identified by psychiatrists as having faked their disorder. The difference that Rosenhan (1973) highlights is that the subjects were labeled patients when in the hospital and were not so labeled outside the hospital. The depersonalizing treatment they received in the hospital was attributed to their having been labeled "patient" in that setting.

Note, however, that the Rosenhan study has been criticized for having numerous flaws. Spitzer (1975), for example, pointed out that while Rosenhan's question is important (the utility of psychiatric diagnoses), the attempt to study it by testing whether or not the "sanity" of pseudopatients in a mental hospital could be discovered was inappropriate. That pseudopatients are not detected by professional hospital staff is not relevant to the utility of the diagnoses. Millon (1975) noted methodological flaws that rendered the Rosenhan study "improperly controlled." For instance, the pseudopatients were confederates of the experimenter and they were fully aware of (and favored) the hypothesis being studied. Such a potential bias is likely to effect the outcome of the study. Apparently, there are questions as to exactly what the Rosenhan study contributes.

In the controversy over classification, as in any controversy, there are two sides, each with a well-prepared and supported position. Consider the following statements. "Diagnostic labels are shorthanded methods to increase the ease of professional communication." "Research that requires that subjects be assigned to different groups requires that we have meaningful standard ways to classify our subjects' psychological dysfunctions." These comments highlight two of the main reasons for having diagnostic systems: (1) communication and (2) prediction.

When a clinician is informed that a client has been diagnosed as having a conversion disorder, for example, much information is concisely communicated. Assuming that the diagnosis was accurate, the clinician now knows that the client's major disturbance is a loss or alteration of physical functioning suggesting a physical disorder but that the problem is psychological. The diagnosis is used by the trained clinician as a professionally meaningful shorthand to communicate about clients.

Prediction, the ability to make reasonable declarations about future events, is enhanced by the accumulation of research evidence. Maher (1970) has argued for the utility of classification by pointing out that research on the causes of, or intervention for, psychological dysfunctions cannot begin until reasonably good definitions of the pattern of behaviors thought to reflect the disorders have been established. Without classification, it is impossible to group subjects for comparisons. Indeed, Shakow (1968) contends that all scientific study requires classification.

Meehl (1959) also argued for the value of the classification of psychological dysfunctions, as illustrated in the following quotation:

> there is a sufficient amount of etiological and prognostic homogeneity among patients belonging to a given diagnostic group, so that the assignment of a patient to this group has probability implications which it is clinically unsound to ignore. (p. 103).

Basically, Meehl is pointing out that use of diagnostic classifications provides valuable information for making predictions about what factors may have been involved in developing the disorder, what will be the course of the disorder, what is the prognosis, and what treatments are likely to work best.

Although still unsolved, a great deal of the psychological literature has dealt with the numerous issues pertaining to diagnosis and the classification of psychological dysfunctions (see Katz, Cole, & Barton, 1968). Should research on classification be abandoned? No. The scientific efforts devoted to classification are young, as clinical psychology is itself a young profession. The practicing clinician will, without a doubt, make a greater contribution to clients and mental health colleagues if he or she works to improve classification rather than trying to abandon it totally.

DIMENSIONS OF PSYCHOLOGICAL DYSFUNCTION

A perusal of the categories of psychological dysfunction presented in Table 5-1 reveals the breadth and complexity of abnormal behavior. Indeed, entire courses in abnormal psychology are necessary to describe the behavior patterns and discuss the causes of each of the psychological disorders. There are, however, several dimensions or distinctions within the broad field of abnormal behavior that are central to effective clinical service.

The Neurotic-Psychotic Distinction

The major categories of psychological dysfunction are *neuroses* and *psychoses.* An individual manifesting behaviors that would be categorized as typically neurotic suffers from excessive anxiety and handicapped interpersonal relations, but continues to function in daily routines. In contrast, persons behaving in ways labeled psychotic usually show severe personality disorganization, a loss of contact with reality, perceptual, cognitive and emotional distortions, (e.g., hallucinations, delusions), and a marked impairment of personal and social functioning.

Richard G. is a 26-year-old employee of a large department store chain. He does his job well and has been retained by the firm through several cutbacks. However, basic feelings of inadequacy and a sense of everpresent anxiety result from Richard's inaccurate evaluations of everyday problems as threatening. He fails to cope with these daily problems and, instead, resorts to defensive and avoidant tactics. Small errors at the register bring on massive anxiety, and Richard staunchly defends his innocence even before examining the problem. By failing to adjust to these small problems he also fails to develop close relationships and blocks his own personal growth. There are several specific types of neurotic behavior patterns but Richard's general neurotic style is evident when he avoids situations that induce feelings of inadequacy and clings rigidly to his defensive and avoidant style.

Howard A. is a 32-year-old white male who once worked in a nonprofessional capacity at a state agricultural board. His diagnosis, paranoid schizophrenia, indicates a form of psychosis. Howard's history shows a more than typical degree of suspiciousness and he had, on different occasions, reported that he thought he was being watched and followed. Recently, Howard had been at home for several weeks due to a work-related injury. During this time he watched construction workers rebuild a broken water pipe in front of his house. The construction staff were young men with long hair who spent long hours (even into early evening) working to weld the pipes back in place. Howard believed that these workers were putting electrons (welding sparks) into his water to try to gain control over him. Howard ordered distilled water from a nearby store and refused to use the internal plumbing. One day when a young man with long hair delivered his distilled water Howard became convinced that now even the "store bought" water was "electroned," and eventually he went to a local mental health facility describing his predicament. Clearly, Howard's dysfunctional thoughts and behaviors are more disturbed than Richard's for he is preoccupied with delusional thinking that markedly affects his ability to function.

The neurotic-psychotic distinction has important implications for several facets of clinical psychology. In assessment, the utility of some psychological tests has been studied by examining their diagnostic accuracy in differentiating persons exhibiting neurotic versus psychotic behaviors. Major differences in the effectiveness of psychological (and medical) treatments have been found for persons whose dysfunctions are considered neurotic versus psychotic. For example, therapies where the client and therapist collaborate to teach the client new skills are more likely to be effective with neurotic depression, whereas more intensive inpatient care and perhaps medication is often desirable for psychotic depression. Evidence has also been developed from clinical research to suggest that neurotic and psychotic dysfunctions differ in their causes and courses. Based upon this knowledge, clinicians who have accurately distinguished between neurotic and psychotic level disturbances can make more specific statements about the likelihood of improvement and the long-range effects of the disorder.

Organic-Functional Psychoses

Within the psychotic category of psychological disorders there is an important distinction between *organic* psychoses, which are seen as primarily the result of an underlying physical malady, and *functional* psychoses where no underlying physical disturbance can be identified. Organic psychoses are linked to brain tissue pathology that may have resulted from genetic defects, infection, ingested chemicals, or traumatic accidents. For example, alcoholic psychoses are caused primarily by tissue damage resulting from a "poisoning" due to excessive alcohol consumption. In contrast, with functional disorders such as schizophrenia, disturbances of thought, mood, and action, and related misinterpretations of reality, are of psychological rather than organic origin. (See Highlight 5-2).

The Process-Reactive Dimension

The differentiation of process versus reactive dysfunctions is another subclassification used primarily in the area of schizophrenia. It is unique in that it is based on clients' premorbid (prior to the disorder) adjustment rather than their current behavior problems. Schizophrenics who display poor premorbid social adequacy, or whose disorders show insidious onset, and the absence of a precipitating factor are classified as *process*. The individual whose dysfuntion is classified as *reactive*, on the other hand, has achieved a reasonable level of premorbid social functioning, and suffers from a disorder that has a sudden onset and a specific precipitating factor (Garmezy, 1970).

The variables that go into the determination of premorbid social competence include the subject's age, intellectual level, education, occupation, employment history, and marital status. Phillips (1953) organized these variables into an em-

Highlight 5-2   Schizotaxia, Schizotypy, and Schizophrenia

Meehl (1962) has proposed an integrative theory to explain the causes of schizophrenia that includes genetic, neural, and social learning factors.

Meehl begins by asking, what single piece of information would a clinician most want to have in order to be sure that a client diagnosed schizophrenic truly warranted that diagnosis. Would it be socioeconomic status? The child-rearing practices of the mother? Although these factors have been linked to schizophrenia, Meehl would place his bet on knowing if the individual had a schizophrenic identical twin.

The evidence to date on the causes of schizophrenia does support the position that if one identical twin is diagnosed as schizophrenic, his or her twin very probably will also manifest schizophrenic behaviors. Thus, genetic factors appear to contribute to the development of schizophrenia. As Meehl suggests, however, there are other psychological-environmental factors that are also implicated in the etiology of schizophrenia. How do these pieces of data fit together?

First, there is a component of the disorder that Meehl suggests is genetically inherited. This component is a "neural integrative defect" called *schizotaxia*, due to impaired transmission of nerve impulses. Second, an individual's social learning history then determines whether schizotaxia will produce *schizotypy*. Schizotypy is a personality organization that is characterized by four personality traits: cognitive slippage (thinking distortions), anhedonia (inability to experience pleasure), ambivalence, and interpersonal aversiveness. Meehl postulates that these traits are learned as the person grows. Finally, if social learning experiences are unfavorable, schizotypy can evolve into the total personality disorganization characterizing *schizophrenia*. These unfavorable conditions include all those psychological factors thought to be associated with the learning of maladaptive behavior. By way of summary, Meehl (1962) states:

> I hypothesize that the statistical relation between schizotaxia, schizotypy, and schizophrenia is class inclusion: All schizotaxics become, on all actually existing social learning regimes, schizotypic in personality organization; but most of these remain compensated. A minority, disadvantaged by other (largely polygenically determined) constitutional weaknesses, and put on a bad regime by schizophrenogenic mothers (most of whom are themselves schizotypes) are thereby potentiated into clinical schizophrenia. What makes schizotaxia etiologically specific is its role as a necessary condition. I postulate that a nonschizotaxic individual, whatever his other genetic makeup and whatever his learning history, would at most develop a character disorder or a psychoneurosis; but he would not become a schizotype and therefore could never manifest its decompensated form, schizophrenia.[3] (p. 832)

[3]Certain maternal rearing styles have been said to be involved in the development of schizophrenia. Mothers who display this pattern are referred to as "schizophrenogenic." However, the research literature on schizophrenogenic mothers is not unequivocal (see Jacob, 1975).

pirically derived Scale of Premorbid Adjustment and Harris (1975) has developed a short form of the Phillips scale. In addition, Ullmann and Giovannoni (1964) have developed a measure of the process-reactive continuum that follows a self-report format.

Research on process-reactive schizophrenia has led to some interesting distinctions (see Table 5-2, from Kantor, Wallner, & Winder, 1953). Although the process-reactive destination is based on premorbid adjustment, research by Zigler and Phillips (1960, 1962) has demonstrated that process and reactive schizophrenics do show some different types of symptoms. These researchers categorized the symptoms of patients as either (1) self-depreciation and turning against the self (e.g., suicide ideas and attempts, depression, bodily complaints), (2) self-indulgence and turning against others (e.g., maniacal outbursts, perversions, assaults), or (3) avoidance of others (e.g., withdrawal, bizarre ideas, unsubstantiated suspicions). A global analysis of the symptom picture of process and reactive schizophrenia indicated that the persons manifesting reactive schizophrenia evidenced more "turning against the self" symptoms than did clients exhibiting process schizophrenia. In contrast, the process schizophrenics, those with poor premorbid social competence, had symptomatology best classsified as either "avoidance of others" or "self-indulgence and turning against others."

The applicability of these findings was broadened when Zigler and Phillips (1962) studied the role of the process-reactive distinction and symptomatology in different types of persons including both those who were and were not diagnosed as manifesting schizophrenia. Again, the hypothesis that a person's process-reactive status would be related to symptomatology was supported. That is, even among individuals whose disorders were not considered schizophrenic, superior premorbid adjustments (reactive cases) were related to turning against self symptoms whereas poorer premorbid adjustments (process cases) were related to avoidance or turning against others.

The distinction between process and reactive disorders was initially described more as a dichotomy than as a continuum. For example, in the early writings of Bleuler (1930) process and reactive schizophrenia were considered distinct phenomena with different causes. The speculation at that time was that process schizophrenia was determined chiefly by an organic etiology whereas reactive schizophrenia was primarily due to psychological causes (see also Brackbill, 1956; Langfeldt, 1937). Representative of research suggesting this dichotomy are the results of a study by Gottesman and Shields (1972). These researchers examined the premorbid data and the rate of agreement in a diagnosis of schizophrenia in monozygotic and dizygotic twins. Recall that monozygotic twins have the same genetic makeup whereas dizygotic twins develop from different fertilized eggs. If process schizophrenia is more organic than reactive schizophrenia, then there should be a relationship between premorbid adjustment and the degree to which twins are *both* considered schizophrenic. The data indicated that when the target schizophrenic twin had a poor premorbid adjustment the other twin was more likely to be seen as schizophrenic. Essentially, these findings suggest a greater genetic in-

Table 5-2 Differentiating Process and Reactive Schizophrenia

Process Schizophrenia	Reactive Schizophrenia
Birth to Fifth Year	
1. Early psychological trauma	1. Good psychological history
2. Physical illness, severe or long	2. Good physical health
3. Odd member of family	3. Normal member of family
Fifth Year to Adolescence	
1. Difficulties at school	1. Well adjusted at school
2. Family troubles paralleled with sudden changes in patient's behavior	2. Domestic troubles unaccompanied by behavior disruptions. Patient "had what it took."
3. Introverted behavior trends and interests	3. Extroverted behavior trends and interests
4. History of breakdown of social, physical, mental functioning	4. History of adequate social, physical, mental functioning
5. Pathological siblings	5. Normal siblings
6. Overprotective or rejecting mother, "Momism"	6. Normal protective, accepting mother
7. Rejecting father	7. Accepting father
Adolescence to Adulthood	
1. Lack of heterosexuality	1. Heterosexual behavior
2. Insidious, gradual onset of psychosis without pertinent stress	2. Sudden onset of psychosis; stress present and pertinent; later onset
3. Physical aggression	3. Verbal aggression
4. Poor response to treatment	4. Good response to treatment
5. Lengthy stay in hospital	5. Short course in hospital
Adulthood	
1. Massive paranoia	1. Minor paranoid trends
2. Little capacity for alcohol	2. Much capacity for alcohol
3. No manic-depressive component	3. Presence of manic-depressive component
4. Failure under adversity	4. Success despite adversity
5. Discrepancy between ability and achievement	5. Harmony between ability and achievementment
6. Awareness of change in self	6. No sensation of change
7. Somatic delusions	7. Absence of somatic delusions
8. Clash between culture and environment	8. Harmony between culture and environment
9. Loss of decency (nudity, public masturbation, etc.)	9. Retention of decency

From R.E. Kantor, J.M. Wallner, and C.L. Winder, Process and reactive schizophrenia. *Journal of Consulting Psychology*, 1953, *17*, 157–162. Copyright 1953 by the American Psychological Association. Reprinted by permission.

volvement in process than reactive schizophrenia.

A note of caution is in order, however, since there have been telling criticisms of the process-reactive dimension. Higgins (1969), for instance, cites several studies that have failed to replicate earlier findings and others where strong relationships have been reduced. Several possible explanations, such as methodological shortcoming of some of the studies, may account for the differing outcomes and Higgins does see the process-reactive distinction as worthy of additional research since it is valuable in reducing the heterogeneity within the schizophrenic disorders (see Garmezy, 1970).

Continuity-Discontinuity Hypotheses

Continuity-discontinuity hypotheses concern whether psychological disturbances all fall on a single continuum or not. There are two such hypotheses. The first concerns the progression of psychological dysfunctions and suggests that severe disorders result from progressive deterioration of milder problems, rather than from entirely different causal factors. The second hypothesis concerns lifelong development and raises the possibility that adult psychological dysfunctions are extensions of similar problems in childhood, suggesting that children with specific psychological dysfunctions grow into adults with the same or similar problems.

Continuity-Discontinuity From Mild To Severe Psychological Dysfunctions   Continuity theories propose that psychological dysfunctions lie on *one* continuum with an individual's specific location on the continuum being determined by severity. That is, if a person suffers from a neurotic disorder, and if this should become more severe, it would lead eventually to a psychotic disorder (see Figure 5-2). The *discontinuity* position, in contrast, states that mild and severe psychological dysfunctions are distinct, that is, qualitatively different. Disorders at different levels of severity are hypothesized to stem from different causes and to follow markedly divergent courses (see Figure 5-2).

The psychodynamic model is an example of a continuity model. In this psychodynamic framework, intrapsychic conflicts cause the neuroses and psychoses. These conflicts are said to take their toll at various points in the psychosexual stages of development. Well-functioning persons are thought to be not strongly fixated at a childhood stage of development, whereas persons suffering from neurotic and psychotic disorders are viewed as hampered by such a fixated conflict. Neurotic disorders are due to a fixation at later stages of development, while psychotic disorders are thought to be caused by fixations at early ages. Thus there is a continuum of stage fixation that is said to correspond to a single continuum from normal to psychotic.

The learning model blends the continuity and discontinuity positions. Clinical psychologists of a learning orientation see the development of psychological dysfunction as due to the acquisition of abnormal behavior patterns. In the initial stages of development, deviance may be less serious than after the dysfunction has been ingrained. The majority of the psychological dysfunctions as well as normal behaviors are seen as the result of learning. Thus, there is one explanation

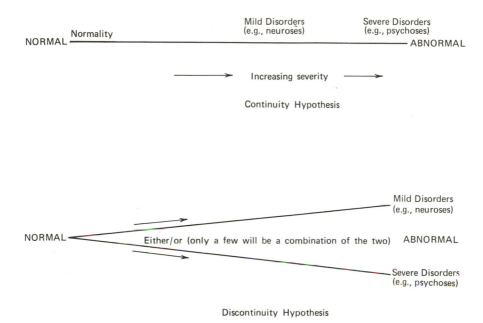

Figure 5-2   Diagrams illustrating continuity and discontinuity hypotheses. Adapted from A. H. Buss, *Psychopathology*. New York: Wiley, 1966. Copyright 1966. Reprinted by permission of John Wiley & Sons, Inc.

for both normal and abnormal behavior. However, the learning model suggests that persons learn their *specific* psychological dysfunction as a result of the consequences of their behavior. Thus it can be argued that learning positions are discontinuous, because a person learns the inappropriate behaviors of the neurotic pattern *or* those of the psychotic pattern.

A more clear-cut example of the discontinuity hypotheses is the medical model. Given the medical model's emphasis on the diseases that lead to mental disorders, such theories support the position that each mental disorder results from a different, discontinuous, underlying disease. Each "mental illness" is viewed as having a distinct cause and course, such that a milder dysfunction like a phobia will not degenerate directly into a more severe disorder such as paranoia (unless the original fear was just masking a "true" paranoid disorder).

At present there is equivocal evidence to support or refute both continuity and discontinuity positions. The critical question that requires scientific study is whether certain dysfunctions (e.g., neuroses) are prerequisites to more severe problems (e.g., psychoses). Both models have, however, received some support from current research data. For example, there are some clients that show both neurotic and psychotic symptoms. Recently, this has been labeled borderline schizophrenia (Singer, 1976). Does this finding support either of the models? Buss (1966) argues that the continuity theorist would say yes: some of the neurotics that have broken down and become psychotic still show their neurotic symptoms, and therefore this supports a continuity model. The discontinuity theorist replies that cases where neurotics are said to show psychotic symptoms is simply a misclassification (Buss, 1966). No definite conclusions can yet be drawn.

A related research question is whether neurotic and psychotic disorders are empirically distinct phenomena when assessed through psychological tests. For example, although the results of factor analytic methods of studying this question indicate that neuroticism and psychoticism are independent factors (Eysenck, 1955; 1961), there have been some concerns expressed about the validity of the psychoticism measure (Eysenck's P scale).[4]

Continuity–Discontinuity and Life-Span Development.

This continuity-discontinuity question pertains to the type of psychological disturbance (if any) that is observed in adults who were diagnosed as dysfunctional as children. Is there continuity within clients between child/adolescent dysfunctions and adult dysfunctions? (see also Brim & Kagan, 1980).

Robins (1966) selected the files of 526 patients who had received psychiatric treatment in their childhood and also selected a group of nonclinic children. The nonclinic and clinic children were matched for age, sex, race, IQ, and location of residence during childhood. These groups were then studied some 30 years later, with the author successfully locating 88% of the clinic cases and 98% of the controls.

Among the striking results, there were 26 adults diagnosed schizophrenic from among the clinic sample and only two from the controls. Regarding freedom from psychological dysfunction, 52% of the controls were so categorized while only 20% of the target cases were considered without disorder. Robins then conducted further analyses on the childhood/adolescent experiences of the subjects who were found to have been diagnosed schizophrenic as adults (called preschizophrenics). The preschizophrenics were compared to (1) nonclinic controls, (2) former patients who were free of disorder as adults, and (3) former patients who were diagnosed as suffering from a variety of psychopathologies other than schizophrenia. The results were not entirely clearcut in that, although the families of the preschizophrenics were found to be globally more dysfunctional, there were no particular relationships of family patterns to subsequent schizophrenia. However, mothers who were considered psychotic had a higher incidence of children who were labeled psychotic. Overall, Robins' results suggest a possible, but by no means automatic link between childhood disorders and subsequent dysfunctions in adulthood.

One classic speculation about the continuity of psychological dysfunction is that the shy, inhibited, withdrawn, seclusive child is more prone to develop adult schizophrenia than other children. Robins (1966) addressed this notion, finding that none of these variables predict the children's later adjustment. Morris, Sowker, and Burruss (1954) also reported this result. In fact, none of the preschizophrenics in Robins' report were described as shy or withdrawn and only a small percent were thought to be seclusive. However, evidence was presented to suggest that the preschizophrenics were *antisocial* children. In more than half of the pre-

---

[4]The interested reader is referred to the concerns expressed by Bishop (1977) and Block (1977a; 1977b) as well as the reply by Eysenck and Eysenck (1977).

schizophrenic cases, the records indicated running away from home, theft, incorrigibility, and poor school performance. In general, the more disturbed the antisocial behavior of the children the poorer the adult adjustment. Other authors have also reported that severely aggressive children often develop schizophrenia as adults (Fleming & Ricks, 1970; Waring & Ricks, 1965).

Shea (1972) analyzed the adult adjustment of children who had been either "externalizers" or "internalizers" of conflict. This distinction, proposed by Achenbach (1966), separates (1) symptoms pertaining to control and inhibition of impulses—internalization of conflict—and (2) symptoms that result in conflict between the behavior of the child and the reactions they bring about in others—externalization of conflict. Thus, Shea was interested in the adult adjustment of children who had been seen for "acting out" problems (externalizing) versus inhibition, depression, and anxiety (internalizing).

Shea was able to compare 85 internalizers, 81 externalizers, and an equal number of controls. Subjects were matched for sex, age, socioeconomic status, intelligence, "intactness" of family, and location of residence. Subjects were then interviewed by examiners who were unaware of the subjects' psychiatric status as adolescents.

A selective summary of Shea's data includes the following results. Fathers of externalizers had more problems with alcoholism while fathers of internalizers had more physical disorders. Mothers of externalizers showed a greater incidence of psychological disorder, and both parents of externalizers evidenced greater marital conflict, compared to internalizers. Externalizers had a more traumatic childhood than internalizers, with poorer peer relationships and more school problems. In adulthood, externalizers were more likely to be diagnosed as having personality/behavior disorders while internalizers were diagnosed more often as having a neurotic disorder or psychophysiological disorder. This latter finding suggests continuity in that acting-out children had personality/behavior disorders as adults and internalizing children had more "turning against self" disorders as adults. In general, Shea's analyses, like Robins' (1966), indicate that children whose antisocial behavior brings them to the attention of mental health professionals are vulnerable to adult psychopathology.

There are some methodological shortcomings to retrospective studies like those discussed above (see also Garmezy, 1974), but they are fairly consistent in highlighting the predictability of adult dysfunctions for children with externalizing, acting-out problems. Why this continuity occurs is an issue left unanswered by these studies—it may be due to deficiencies in the persons that persist through adulthood, to the stigma that is likely to be attached to such intrusive and disruptive externalizers, or a combination of both and perhaps other factors.

DEPRESSION: AN ILLUSTRATION OF MODELS AND DIMENSIONS

As a reading of the DSM III categories indicates, there are many types of psychological dysfunctions. To further illustrate the models used to conceptualize these disorders, and to provide examples of various dimensions that have been proposed to further subdivide the disorders, we take a closer look at one frequently occurring psychological problem—depression. Several models that have been advanced to explain psychological depression are presented, along with related research and a discussion of several of the dimensions of depression that have been suggested.

A Variety Of Models

Of the models that have been proposed to foster an understanding of the phenomena of depression, the psychodynamic models, biochemical/biological models, and psychological/learning models are the dominant conceptualizations (Blaney, 1977). Within the psychological learning models we will discuss Beck's (1967; 1974) cognitive theory of depression, Lewinsohn's (1974a; 1974b) theory of the importance of low rates of response-contingent reinforcement, and Seligman's (1974; 1975) learned helplessness model.

Psychodynamic models rely heavily on intrapsychic conflicts as the explanation of depression (Abraham, 1911; Freud, 1917; Rado, 1928). Depressed persons are said to suffer from "anger turned inward"—that is, from punishing themselves emotionally as a substitute for expressing anger openly toward other persons. Dependency needs, another key factor, are said to result from traumas that occur during early childhood. An individual receiving insufficient gratification as a child is seen as developing feelings of being unworthy of love as an adult. These dispositions are said to combine with personal loss, such as death of a loved one or recurrent criticism, to produce depression (Jacobsen, 1971; Mendelson, 1974).

Although research directly evaluating the dynamic model is almost nonexistent, studies of depressed individuals have indicated poorer self-concepts than other psychiatric groups (e.g., Flippo & Lewinsohn, 1971). The role of anger in depression has also received some support (e.g., Schless, Mendels, Kipperman, & Cochrave, 1974). In addition, children have been reported to show reactions of depression following extended maternal separation (Bowlby, 1969; Spitz, 1949) as have infant monkeys (e.g., Suomi, Harlow, & Domek, 1970). In general, certain personality characteristics have been associated with depression and certain stresses have been shown to result in depression, but such evidence only indirectly supports the psychodynamic model.

Among biochemical hypotheses regarding depression, Schildkraut (Schildkraut, 1965; Schildkraut & Kety, 1967) has reviewed the evidence concerning the hypothesis that biochemical changes in catecholamine metabolism are related to mood changes. The basis for this position is that drugs that increase the catecholamines (i.e., norepinephrine) have been found to stimulate excitement while those that reduce catecholamines result in inactivity. Schildkraut concludes that depressives are relatively deficient of catecholamines. However, a catecholamine deficiency has never been proven to be the sole cause of psychological depression, and such a biochemical abnormality may result from depression rather than being the cause. Recent reviewers have proposed that biochemical causes combine with psychological factors to produce depression (Akiskal & McKinney, 1973; 1975).

Genetic studies offer an additional biological model to conceptualize depressive disorders (see Mendels, 1970). Here, the tendency for a person to develop a depressive disorder is seen as an hereditary characteristic, much like eye color. The degree to which people with similar genetic makeup (family members, twins) develop similar depressive conditions (when the environments are not identical) describes the genetic component of the disorder. Although supportive studies have been reported (Winokur, Clayton & Reich, 1969) the format of the transmission of a genetic component to depression is not yet clear (see also Beck, 1967).

Beck's theoretical position (1967; 1974), a cognitive learning model, describes a depressive "cognitive set" as the central aspect of depression. This depressive cognitive set is thought to have three parts—a negative view of the self, the world, and the future. For the depressed individual, the self-concept is low, the world is offensive, and the future is bleak. When certain events happen to most people they do not get depressed, but when these same events are seen through a depressive cognitive set, they are seen as evidence of their personal lack of value. Thus, it is the person's cognitive appraisal of the event that is causing the resulting depression. Experimental work by several researchers (e.g., Averill, 1969; Strickland, Hale, & Anderson, 1975; Velton, 1968) have demonstrated that the affective state of a subject can be influenced by the content of the cognitions that are given attention by the subject. For instance, subjects who read "I have too many bad things in life" showed reduced performance latencies on a work association task (Velton, 1968). These studies lend credence to Beck's cognitive theory. Again, however, research does not demonstrate that the proposed explanation, a negative cognitive set, actually causes or maintains all serious clinical depression.

The behavioral notions of Lewinsohn (1974a; 1974b) emphasize the depressing effect that a low rate of response-contingent positive reinforcement has on an individual. Depression is said to follow when a person performs behaviors that rarely lead to positive consequences. Reduced activity results from the low rate of reward, and this subsequently reduces the amount of positive reinforcement even further. This low rate of reinforcement can occur for several reasons: the person may find few events to be reinforcing, may not get involved in events that would be reinforcing, or may not perform the actions necessary to earn reinforcement (Ferster, 1973). Recent research has produced results that are inconsistent: sometimes supporting the theory but not ruling out other theoretical views (Lewinsohn & Graf, 1973; Lewinsohn & Libet, 1972), sometimes partially supportive (Coyne, 1976; Padfield, 1976; Wener & Rehm, 1975), and sometimes not supportive (e.g., Hammen & Glass, 1975). Here again, the proposed factor—a low rate of response-contingent positive reinforcement—appears linked to aspects of depression, but its role as a key cause has not been documented.

The helplessness model suggests that depression is the result of prior experience with uncontrollable aversive conditions (Overmier & Seligman, 1967; Seligman, 1975). Accordingly, the "helpless" individual is said to have learned that responses and their outcomes are independent, and thus that goal-directed actions are useless. More recently, this model has been reformulated with a specific emphasis on the attributional style of the psychologically depressed individual (Abramson, Seligman & Teasdale, 1978), thus linking it with Beck's cognitive model. "Helplessness" experiences are said to teach the person that he or she cannot control life and produces an apathetic, depressed style of life. Research generally supportive of the helplessness model includes studies by Miller and Seligman (1975) who reported depressed mood following performance on uncontrollable tasks, and Klein and Seligman (1976) who were able to improve depressive mood states by exposing subjects to solvable problems. However, other researchers have found that the uncontrollability manipulation used to produce depressive mood also produced hostility and anxiety (Gatchel, Paulua, & Maples, 1975), and Willis and Blaney (1978) were *unable* to replicate several of the important helplessness findings. Gotlib and Asarnow (1979), also questioned the helplessness notion based on their findings of an absence of both response initiation and anagram learning deficits that the helplessness model would predict (see also Comments by Rohsenow, 1980, and Gotlib and Asarnow, 1980). More extensive critical reviews by Depue and Monroe (1978a) and Blaney (1977) suggest that additional research is needed to determine the merits of the helplessness model of depression, although Costello (1978) has gone so far as to caution against further research due to the conceptual and methodological problems such as the appropriateness of inducing helplessness in unsuspecting subjects.

The variety of models that are offered as explanations of depression serve to illustrate the multifaceted nature of this pervasive psychological dysfunction. The fact that no one model has proven superior to all others should not be discouraging. Our understanding of the causes and treatment of psychological disorders benefits from cumulative data gathered from distinct perspectives and employing a diversity of paradigms. Moreover, therapeutic strategies for preventing or alleviating depression have been developed by proponents of each of the theoretical models, advancing our knowledge of how to best help people suffering from this disorder.

A Variety Of Dimensions

Clinicians utilize *dimensions* in order to attempt to place people who all suffer a psychological dysfunction into more homogeneous (and therefore more readily described and aided) groups. The process-reactive dimension is an example of a dimension used to subdivide persons diagnosed as schizophrenic. Several other dimensions have been proposed to advance our understanding of the different possible causes and types of psychological depression.

One distinction that has been proposed for subclassifying depression deals with the presence or absence of a previous history of psychological dysfunction. This distinction used the terms *primary* and *secondary* depression. Primary depression is used to designate those clients who do not have a history of other psychological dysfunctions, whereas secondary depression describes clients who have had other disorders (Robins & Guze, 1972; Winokur, 1972; 1973).

A second dimension distinguishes between *reactive* and *endogenous* depression. This distinction pertains to the presence or absence of a clear precipitating cause of the depressive episode, such as death of a spouse, demotion, divorce, or other life stresses. Endogenous depression, where no precipitating life events are apparent, is often hypothesized to be caused by biochemical or biological factors. The reactive type of depression is, in contrast, said to be primarily the result of acute life stresses (Beck, 1967; Heron, 1965; Mendels & Cochrane, 1968).

Yet another distinction is between *neurotic* and *psychotic* depression. Depression is diagnosed as neurotic when it is a part of a pattern of apprehension, nervousness, and avoidance. When psychotic symptoms such as delusions, hallucinations, debilitating deterioration and withdrawal are observed, then the depression is classified as psychotic. Some times however, the neurotic-psychotic distinction is undermined when diagnoses are based more on the presence or absence of a precipitating event—the reactive-endogenous dimensions.

There is also a distinction between *bipolar* and *unipolar* depression. Consistent with the DSM III, different diagnoses are made depending upon the presence or absence of manic episodes with intermittent depression. If the client suffers from manic states that are somewhat cyclically intermingled with depressive episodes then the person is considered a bipolar depressive. When there are no indications of former manic states, the person is considered unipolar (see Depue & Monroe, 1978a, 1978b). This distinction may prove to be of major importance in that studies of various medications, studies of the varying role of genetics (Becker, 1974), and studies of the utility of cognitive therapy appear to be meaningfully affected by separation of unipolar and bipolar depressives.

Perhaps you are wondering how one sorts out all of this information or integrates all of these dimensions? Actually, there are no absolute answers. The clinical psychologist must be knowledgeable about the distinctions, such as within the depressive disorder, and must be prepared to make accurate diagnoses and to provide appropriate treatment, but there are no simple answers. The idea to remember is that each dimension seeks to subdivide the disorder into meaningfully homogeneous units that allow for more precise interventions.

Tide No. 1 by David Simpson

III

CLINICAL PSYCHOLOGICAL ASSESSMENT

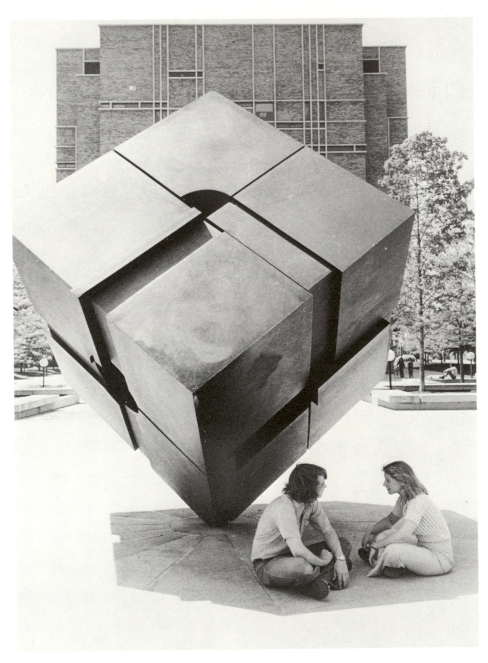

To see a world in a grain of sand
and a Heaven in a wild flower,
Hold infinity in the palm of your hand,
And eternity in an hour.

William Blake

6

ASSESSMENT: PROFESSIONAL AND SCIENTIFIC CONCERNS

Clinical *assessment* is the process of gathering information about a client or subject to gain a better understanding of the person. Within this process, the clinician selects the assessment method, conducts the assessment, examines and interprets the resulting information, summarizes the relevant conclusions (if appropriate) for the client, and communicates the results to other professionals. In all assessments the clinician seeks to gain the specific information about the person that will most facilitate decision making. For example, a married couple might seek a clinical psychologist for an assessment of their relationship problems and of their individual psychological characteristics that contribute to these dilemmas. Or, a schoolteacher might recognize some behavior problems in a student and request that the student see a psychologist for an assessment of the child's problems and for recommendations on how best to work with the child.

How does the clinical psychologist conduct an assessment? What type of information is looked for, and how is it sought? In this and our next four chapters we deal with these questions and others that are related to the clinician's role as a psychological assessor. This chapter also provides an overview of the professional and the scientific concerns that are relevant to the assessment process and highlights some of the classic and contemporary issues in assessment that face the clinician.

REASONS FOR ASSESSMENT

The information that is gathered in clinical assessments contributes to decisions in a variety of areas such as *screening and diagnosis, evaluations of interventions,* and *research*. Several of these purposes are often simultaneously accomplished. In all instances, as emphasized by Korchin (1976), clinical assessments are necessary for making informed decisions.

Screening and Diagnosis

The screening function of assessment involves the selecting and grouping of people, and uses the clinician's ability to develop assessment methods, to gather data, and make sophisticated judgments. For example, screening assessments are often conducted to facilitate the selection of the proper clients for specific intervention programs. Assessments may be used to select clients who would be most appropriate for a new treatment program that is being established in settings such as hospital wards. Certain tests of personality may be administered to the applicants and those who, based on the tests, appear likely to benefit the most are selected. In another instance, where some clients might be detrimentally affected by some types of therapy experiences (e.g., a confrontation group), clinical assessments could be used for screening out therapy candidates. Testing the abilities of candidates for training as pilots, the trustworthiness of nominated industrial officials, and the reading level of children prior to a remedial reading program, are still more examples where clinical assessments provide valuable information to assist in making screening decisions.

Knowledge gained from a clinical assessment is also used to further sort and group people by enabling the determination of an accurate *diagnosis*. A diagnosis identifies the client's specific problem(s) and is intended to efficiently communicate information to other professionals so that informed decisions can be made about how best to serve each client. For example, having diagnosed an inpatient client as depressed and suicidal provides information to aid in subsequent professional decisions about discharge from the hospital, types of treatment, and recommendations for joining social support groups. As we saw in Chapter 5, however, diagnosis is not without criticism.

Clinical assessments are also central in the legal determination of sanity. Separating those defendants who are legally judged to be insane from those who are considered sane can have severe ramifications (e.g., jail, commitment, freedom). The final decision on sanity, for legal purposes, is made by a court of law. However, judges rely on clinical assessments in making such decisions.

In each of the above instances, the assessor analyzes the situation for which individuals are being screened, noting the elements or components most likely to be critical. A detailed analysis of the task(s) that participants will be asked and expected to do is undertaken, leading to the selection and/or development of assessment methods that will provide information useful for screening.

Evaluation of Clinical Interventions

Without assessment, clinicians would not be able to evaluate the effects of clinical interventions. Data can be gathered through assessment to determine the client's strengths, weaknesses, and the severity of psychological problems before, during, and after intervention, permitting a clear evaluation of the changes occurring during and after intervention. For example, a client who is transiently distressed due to divorce may begin therapy with psychological testing indicating a high level of depression and anxiety. Repeated assessments during and after therapy enable the therapist to judge the client's improvement in these areas and to adjust the therapy interventions accordingly.

When a clinician functions as a consultant to large organizations such as hospitals, schools, prisons, or businesses, the clinical intervention is provided at the level of an entire program, affecting many people at once rather than one individual client. Assessments are again required, with preconsultation and postconsultation measurements used to evaluate the intervention program.

Research

Essential to all research efforts is an accurate and thorough assessment of the variables that are under investigation. In research, assessments are included to allow for the testing of specific hypotheses about both normal behavior and psychological dysfunctions and are designed to provide new information that will increase our understanding of human functioning. For example, the effects of pornography on the incidence of rape or the morality of a community cannot be determined unless we can accurately assess all of the variables in question. Research is also used to evaluate the strengths and weaknesses of existing assessment instruments and to develop new methods of assessment that may be used in the future.

One other reason for clinical assessment is to provide individuals with information about themselves. Although not common, persons who have not been involved in screening, therapy, or consultation may simply seek to discover how they are put together psychologically. These individuals may want to use the assessment information, and advice of the clinician, to help make their own personal decisions.

TARGETS FOR ASSESSMENT

When the clinician is called on to conduct a psychological assessment, there are a host of possible targets. The clinician can focus on the individual's *dysfunctions*, highlighting the abnormalities or deficits in the person's thoughts, emotions, or actions. In other cases, the focus can be on the client's *strengths*, with outstanding abilities, skills, or sensitivities being targeted for evaluation. Still other evaluations specifically request the clinical psychologist to evaluate and describe the *personality* of the subject. The clinician may call on tests, observations, and interviews to help unravel the subject's needs, motivations, defenses, and characteristic behavior patterns.

Clinical psychologists also assess the strengths and weaknesses of the client's social environments and the effects that the environment has on the client's thinking, feeling, and behavior. These assessments are considered *functional analyses* in that the clinician is interested in evaluating the changes in behavior that result from specific alterations in the client's life situation. For example, how is a client's eating behavior affected by rearranging his or her daily schedule? In most assessments the clinical psychologist focuses on a broad scope of targets ranging from assets to deficits and from determinants of stable behavior to determinants of behavioral change.

METHODS OF ASSESSMENT

How does the clinician gather the information that will be needed for making informed decisions? The answer is that the clinical psychologist uses any one, or a combination of several, of a variety of assessment methods that include interviews, structured written tests, unstructured tests, and behavioral assessments. What follows is a detailed discussion of the interview and a brief description of the other assessment methods. Subsequent chapters deal with these latter methods in more detail.

The Interview

Diverse professionals rely on the interview method of assessment. Though the interview is sometimes the sole method of assessment employed by the clinician, it is more often used along with several of the other methods. The goals of interviews vary depending on the context. For example, a client may be interviewed for pretherapy assessment, evaluation of vocational functioning, for legal determination of sanity, and for decisions regarding discharge from mental health facilities. Importantly, since many of the other tests and/or observations are taken during an interview, the interview can be said to be the basic context for almost all assessments.

Sullivan (1954) describes the interview as:

a situation of primarily vocal *communication in a* two-group, *more or less* voluntarily integrated, *on a progressively unfolding* expert-client *basis for the purpose of elucidating* characteristic patterns of living *of the subject person, the patient or client, which patterns he experiences as particularly troublesome or especially valuable, and in the revealing of which he expects to derive* benefit. *(p. 4, 1954 Author's Italics)*

The interview is *not* a cross-examination. Instead, it is a process during which the interviewer must be aware of the client's voice intonations, rate of speech, and the sensitivity of being asked questions and stared at directly in the eyes. The interview is primarily vocal, but the interviewer must remain aware of nonverbal messages as well (e.g., posture, gestures, facial expressions). In a comfortable interview the two people involved will freely exchange communications. Sullivan suggests that the interviewer not be overly concerned with the client's initial willingness or unwillingness to divulge information but focus instead on adapting to this initial attitude and working toward a more comfortable interchange. The expert-client aspect of the interview highlights the client's expectation that the interviewer will deal sensitively with the information that is discussed and will not use the information to enhance personal satisfaction at the expense of the client. The essential goal of the interview is to gain an understanding of the client's characteristic patterns of living. This requires answers to several questions. What is the client like as a person? Are there noteworthly symptoms? What does the client think about and how does the client explain the events of life? How is the client seen by others and what do the client's friends and relatives think of him or her? How would one describe the client's interpersonal context? What are the client's predominant moods and emotions, and when and how do they change? How does the client cope with failure and success?

Sullivan goes on to state that the interview should occur in such a fashion that the client perceives some potential benefit from the experience. If the interviewer notices that the client does not feel this way, the interviewer should set the stage for the client to learn something of personal importance from the interview. An excerpt from a sample interview is provided in Highlight 6-1.

Highlight 6-1   Transcript of an Assessment Interview

This sample illustrates an initial interview that might occur at a university psychological clinic.

Interview Dialogue	Comments
INTERVIEWER (I): Beautiful day isn't it?	Initial nonstressful conversation can help to reduce some of the client's anxiety.
CLIENT (C): Yeah. (Sighs) Not that nice.	Note the nonverbal sign of gloomy feelings.
I: Could you tell me why you decided to come to our clinic today.	Interviewer highlights significance of client's choice to come to the clinic at this particular time.
C: Well, I'm having real difficulties in school	
I: Am I correct in assuming that you came on your own.	Interviewer checks to see if client has been referred or is under pressure.
C: Yes.	
I: O.K. I'd like to briefly explain what I hope we can accomplish in the next hour, to give you a clear idea of what to expect and how this interview can be of help to you.	Interviewer provides basic goals and guidelines to reduce the client's uncertainty and to promote positive expectations.
This hour is a chance for us to talk openly about you as a person and the concerns that have brought you here. I'll ask questions to help us explore all the important areas for you, but I'll rely on you to fill me in as completely as you can. Of course, everything we talk about will be completely confidential, so you can talk freely. At the end, we'll discuss what steps to take next so that your needs can be fully taken care of.	General orientation to the roles and responsibilities of client and interviewer. Emphasis on teamwork between client and interviewer.
Maybe we could start by talking about how you decided to come to the clinic at this particular point in your life.	Open ended question, but with a focus on "why *now*?"

C: Well, I'm afraid I'll flunk out of the university if I don't get over feeling anxious about tests (begins to clasp hands nervously and blushes while looking at the ground, some light laughter also).

Nonverbal cues reflecting anxiety.

I: I notice that you seem to be worried. Troubles at school can really be painful.

Gentle acknowledgement of client's nonverbal cues and distress.

C: Especially when your parents are pressuring you to get into law school.

An important tie-in: the family plays a role as well as school problems.

I: Are you feeling that kind of pressure?

An open-ended encouragement to continue.

C: My parents just won't let up (voice is tight and cracks).

I: Mmhmm.

Brief encouragement to continue.

C: What can I do?

I: If you had your way, what would you choose to do?

Interviewer emphasizes the client's capability and responsibility, for resolving problems.

C: I can't have my way. My parents won't let me.

I: Your parents have a powerful and hurtful impact on you, I hear you very clearly. I'm just wondering what you'd do if you could magically have control of your own future?

Acknowledges client's belief, but challenges the hopelessness. Facilitates exploration of alternatives.

C: Well, I guess I'd change my major to theatre, that's where my real interests and talents are.

I: How are you stopping yourself from doing that now?

Focus on the client's responsibility.

C: I'm not. It's my parents.

I: Your parents certainly make it hard, but I wonder if you aren't concerned that bad things will happen if you change your major. What *would* happen, do you think?

Exploring the client's fears.

C: Well, I'd enjoy school, finally. But my parents might stop paying my tuition. And, they'd be mean as hell.

I: I'd like to explore that, but first, let's get a picture of what it's like to be in your family. Could you describe your family, and how you fit it?

Holds off on specific issues, to get a general background.

(10 minutes later)

I: Could you tell me about your experi-   Exploring school issues.
ence in school as you've grown up—
how have you been doing academically over the years? And how have you
handled your feelings about tests until
now?

(10 minutes later)

I: Tell me about your relationships with   Exploring social relationships.
friends, including both casual and
close friends of both sexes.

(10 minutes later)

I: Well, you've given an excellent sketch   Relying on client to fill in gaps.
of several important areas in your
life. Have we missed some important
sides of you or your situation?

C: I don't know if it's relevant, but I'm   Another important life concern.
concerned about how much I've been
drinking lately.

I: Why don't you tell me more about it.

(10 minutes later)

I: We may not have covered everything,   Acknowledges that more information
but I'd like to use our remaining time   may still be needed, but makes sure to
to summarize my understanding of   provide a summary and a discussion of
you and your situation, and then to   the client's alternatives.
have us both discuss what you might
do next.

Important throughout the interview, although it is especially so in the initial segment, is the establishment of *rapport* with the client. Rapport refers to a positive and warm relationship based on the shared interests of the parties involved. The interviewer can set the stage for the client to feel free to communicate openly by insuring confidentiality and privacy. Moreover, the clinician's manner can indicate a sincere interest and concern for the client's problems. Refraining from voicing disapproval or in any way judging the client's responses also leads to an open interview.

Several specific approaches to interviewing have evolved, including the mental status interview, the social-clinical interview, the "fractionated interview," and structured interviews.

The Mental Status Interview   Mental status examinations are used extensively in the field of psychiatry and psychology as a means of gathering material on patients' current functioning. The mental status examination includes a description of the person's appearance, general behavior, motor activity, alertness, mood, stream and content of thought, orientation in time/place/person, memory, concentration, abstract thinking, judgment, dreams, insight, and values. According to Detre and Kupfer (1975), most of the information essential for assessing the patient's mental status can be gathered through direct conversation with the client and observation of the client's behavior during the interview (see Table 6-1). For example, the client's orientation in time, place, and person can be acquired by asking the client three questions: What's your name? What's today's date? Where are you right now? If the subject answers these questions correctly, then the person can be said to be oriented.

The client's verbal abilities and the freedom with which the client speaks are also noted. Client interview responses can vary from those that are spontaneous and genuine to those that are evasive and noncommital. The mental status examiner also pays attention to the client's predominant ideas during the interview. Asking the client to "subtract by 7's backward from 100," to compare "how a house and a barn are alike," and to "describe what you would do if you were alone in a house and the window curtains caught fire," are methods used by the mental status examiner to evaluate, respectively, memory and attention, comprehension, and judgment.

Observations during the mental status interview provide information about the client's physical appearance, emotional state, and style of relating. The interviewer observes and records the client's apparent state of health, manner of dress, and care of appearance. The client's emotional state can be gleaned from facial expressions and from both the direct and indirect statements made by the client. For instance, a client's stating "I'm no good to anyone" indicates a more depressive mood than "I had a bad day today." The range and the appropriateness of emotions expressed by the client during the interview are noted, as are the client's attitudes and feelings toward others (as seen in the manner in which the client relates

Table 6-1   Sample Items from a Brief Mental Status Questionnaire[a]

1. Where are you now? (What place is this? What is the name of this place? What kind of place is this?) _____

   _____

2. Where is it? (Address? Location?) _____

   _____

3. What is today's date? Day _____Month _____Year _____(day is correct if + or − one day)

4. How old are you? _____

5. When were you born? Month_____ Year_____

6. Who is the president of the United States? _____

7. Who was president before him? _____

[a]See Kahn, Goldfarb, Pollack, and Peck (1960). The interested reader is also referred to Spitzer, Fleiss, Burdock, and Hardesty (1964) and Spitzer, Fleiss, Endicott, and Cohen (1967) for more detailed descriptions of more elaborate mental status schedules.

to the interviewer). Thus, the interactions that constitute the interview can be seen as a sample of the client's typical manner of relating to people. A client may reach out for help in a pleasing fashion or may remain distant and "cool." Some clients may be congenial and warm or apathetic and indifferent, while others may be ingratiating or seductive. Although these are only a few examples, they illustrate the modes of relating that the examiner may observe during the interpersonal exchanges.

Social-Clinical Interview   Peterson (1968) proposed an approach to the interview that takes a broader scope by identifying both specific problems and their determinants. In the social-clinical interview, the clinician tries to determine the nature and severity of the problem(s) as defined by the client. The clinician asks questions like "What is the problem as you see it," "How serious is the problem for you," or "How often does the problem occur and in what circumstances?"

The social-clinical interview also seeks to provide the clinician with an understanding of the determinants of the problem(s). The clinician asks "What conditions intensify the problem," and "What conditions alleviate it?" The clinician may also want to inquire about the client's perception of what caused the problem—"What was going on the first time it happened," and what were its consequences—"What happened after that," and "How did it make you feel?" Also, the client has probably thought a lot about the problem and may have tried to alleviate it independently. Knowledge of the different strategies that the client has used in attempts to modify the problem provides the clinician with valuable information about the client's coping skills and about interventions that duplicate unsuccessful past actions and that therefore probably will not be effective. Peterson (1968) recommends that the clinical interviewer try to discover some leads for further inquiry by asking "What else do you think I should know about you in order to help you with this problem?"

The Fractionated Interview   The technique of the clinical interview varies substantially depending on the interviewer's theoretical and personal style. One interview style, the fractionated interview described by Storrow (1967), divides the alloted interview period into sections of time that focus on the opening gambit, the preliminary survey, following up leads, filling in gaps, and explanations and recommendations.

The *opening gambit* involves the typical introductory comments made between people and an inquiry about the reasons for the person's coming in: "I'd like to talk with you about what's on your mind and why you are here today." Some information about the reason for the appointment is probably at hand, but it is important here to get the client's reasons for coming. The opening gambit usually takes about 10% of the interview.

During the *preliminary survey* the interviewer listens, and simply lets the client tell his or her story. The interviewer should exercise good listening skills: provide minimal encouragements—"Mmhmm", validation statements—"That makes sense to me," and brief clarifications or summaries (see Table 6-2). This survey takes about 20% of the interview.

Table 6-2 Storrow's Tactical Summary: "How to keep the communication channels open and how to get the facts"

Although the following lists overlap somewhat, each set of tactics is thought to be effective for the purpose stated. Tactics first on the list convey little information while those at the bottom convey a great deal. Storrow (1967) suggests that low-information tactics are likely to increase both reliability and validity of the data obtained. These are therefore to be used more often. If they are inappropriate or ineffective, then tactics providing the client with high information can be employed.

Tactics for Keeping the Channels Open	Tactics for Getting the Facts
Attentive silence	Attentive silence
Nonverbal expressions of interest	Nonverbal expressions of interest
Encouraging comments	Encouraging comments
Clarifications	Repetitions of the patient's last few words, with a questioning inflection
Summaries	
Leaving unproductive topics	Questions based on something the patient has said
Introducing new topics	Clarifications
Discussing the usefulness of the interview with the patient	Summaries
Focusing attention on communication Labeling the trouble	Confrontations
Questions and answers about the trouble	Questions introducing new topics
	Leading questions suggesting expected answers
Terminating the interview when the patient is not receptive and resuming it when the patient is receptive	

The interviewer then spends about 30% of the time *following up leads:* "Could you tell me more about this?" For any of a number of reasons (e.g., low verbal ability, defensiveness), the client may not provide as complete a description as would be desired. The interviewer therefore helps elicit additional information in a nonjudgmental fashion.

New topics are introduced during the next 20 to 30% of the interview, and, as is often necessary, topics may be rescanned to pick up on things that might have been missed. The interviewer tries to *fill in any gaps* in the information that has been presented. As important information about the client becomes increasingly clear, the interviewer begins to test some hypotheses in more detail. When the interviewer thinks that a touchy topic has been sidestepped, it may be worthwhile to again bring it up. Inexperienced interviewers may avoid sensitive topics and inadvertently communicate that such topics can be or should be left alone (Siegman, 1977). However, a more direct approach often proves revealing and even reassuring.

Storrow's last 10 to 20% of the fractionated interview is spent providing the client with a preliminary description of the interviewer's perceptions, with a summary of the interviewer's plans and recommendations, and with the establishment of a plan for future contact.

Structured Interviews   To achieve greater standardization of interview procedures researchers have developed *structured* interviews. A structured interview requires that the interviewer ask a series of predetermined questions, using standard
wording and asking the questions in the same order each time.

There are several different structured interviews, but the Schedule for Affective
Disorders and Schizophrenia (SADS) and its Lifetime version (SADS-L) (developed by Spitzer and Endicott, 1978) are illustrative.

In both versions of the SADS, the interviewer first explains that the interview
will focus on the client's difficulties and that the same questions are asked of ev-
erybody who is interviewed. Then, the interviewer obtains basic demographic information such as age, marital status, and occupational history.

In using the SADS-structured interview, the clinical psychologist seeks to acquire background information about the client, an overview of the psychiatric
disturbance, and descriptions of specific episodes of severe disturbance, and to
then match the interview data with criteria for diagnosing different disorders.
The structured interview procedures provide both the questions to be asked of the
client and the choices or response categories for the interviewer to endorse for the
client. The following is an example related to the gathering of background information.[1]

How far did you get in school?
(Did you have any special training)?

0 No information
1 Completed graduate school (M.A.,
  M.S., M.E., M.B.A., M.D., Ph.D., L.L.B.)
2 4-year college graduate
3 1 to 3 years college, business, or trade
  school
4 High school graduate
5 10 to 11 years of school (part high
  school)
6 7 to 9 years of school
7 Under 7 years of school

The questions that are asked in relation to an overview of the psychiatric disturbance are like the following:

How old were you when you first saw
someone for _____?
(Client's presenting problem.)
Did you ever go to a doctor for your
nerves?

_____Age at first outpatient care
      (Leave blank if never.)
0 No information
1 No contact
2 Consultation or brief period of treatment
3 Continuous treatment for at least 6
  months or several brief periods
4 Continuous treatment lasting several
  years or numerous brief periods

[1]From R. L. Spitzer and J. Endicott, *The schedule for affective disorders and schizophrenia—Lifetime version (SADS-L)* (3rd ed.). New York: New York State Psychiatric Institute, Biometrics Research, 1979. Copyright 1979 by Spitzer and Endicott; reproduced by permission.

These items are only a very small sample of the SADS-L interview questions, but they illustrate the structured aspects of the interview: the questions are spelled out, and possible answers are provided to make data recording easy for the interviewer.

The structured quality of the interview continues throughout. The following sequence is part of the interview that is designed to determine if the "episode" of disturbance was part of a manic syndrome. Here, an episode is defined as a relatively discrete period of impaired psychological functioning that can be clearly distinguished from prior and subsequent functioning.

Criteria for Episodes of Manic Syndrome (there are 3 criteria)

1. Has had one or more distinct periods lasting at least one week (or any duration if hospitalized) when the predominant mood was either elevated (i.e., unusually good, cheerful, high, expansive) *or* irritable (i.e., easily annoyed). (Do not include if apparently due to alcohol or drug use. Note: This is frequently falsely rated as positive when the subject is merely describing feeling very good in contrast to periods of depression.)

   Did you ever have a period that lasted at least a week (or when you were hospitalized), when you felt extremely good or high —clearly different from your normal self? Did friends or your family think this was more than just feeling good? What about periods when you felt very irritable or easily annoyed?

   0 No information or not sure.
   1 Never had a period lasting at least one week (or was hospitalized) when the predominant mood was either elevated or irritable
   2 Never had a period when predominant mood was elevated, but had at least one period when he was irritable
   3 Had at least one period when predominant mood was elevated (with or without irritability)

2. Had at least two symptoms associated with the most severe period of euphoric or irritable mood (inquire for all symptoms). (Do not include if apparently due to alcohol or drug use.)

	DURING THE MOST SEVERE PERIOD		
	No Info	No	Yes
During the most severe period . . .	X	1	2
. . . were you more active than usual—either socially, at work, at home, sexually, or physically restless?			
. . . were you more talkative than usual or felt a pressure to keep on talking?	X	1	2
. . . did your thoughts race or did you talk so fast that it was difficult for people to follow what you were saying?	X	1	2
. . . did you feel you were very important, had special powers, plans, talents, or abilities (grandiosity).	X	1	2

. . . did you need less sleep than usual?	X	1	2
. . . did you have trouble concentrating on what was going on because your attention kept jumping to unimportant things around you distractibility?	X	1	2
. . . did you do anything foolish that could have gotten you into trouble—like buying things, business investments, sexual indiscretions, reckless driving?	X	1	2

Number of definite symptoms = _____. If euphoric, criterion = 2, if irritable only, criterion = 3.

If criterion II is not met, skip to Episodes of Major Depressive Syndrome.

3. Symptoms were so severe that meaningful conversation was impossible, there was serious impairment in functioning, or he was hospitalized.

    0 No information
    1 No
    2 Yes

    Were you hospitalized?
    Were you so excited that it was almost impossible to hold a conversation with you?
    Did it cause troubles with people, with your family, with your work, or other usual activities?

    _____ Number (Note minimum number rather than a range or a question mark, 99 if too numerous or ill defined to count.)

Total number (minimum) or episodes of Manic Syndrome, (separated from each other by at least two months).

    How many episodes like this have you had?
    If unable to give exact number: Would you say that you have had at least _____ different episodes like that?

The SADS-L provides similar interview material for the classification of a variety of psychological dysfunctions, such as the affective disorders and schizophrenia. The structured interview is an effort to improve the clinical utility and reliability of diagnostic classification that results from interview procedures, by making the client's responses easily scored in a standard numerical fashion.

Not surprisingly, in our age of computers, interview procedures have been computerized to create the ultimate structured interview. Griest, Klein, and Van Cura (1973) developed a system where subjects sit at a computer terminal with a small TV screen and a typewriter. The TV screen helps to describe the client's tasks and the client uses the typewriter to respond to the questions. Note that while the computerized system is direct and saves professional time, a portion of the subjects did not like the impersonal machine, the multiple-choice questions, or the length of the interview. Even if the subjects enjoy the computer interview, a clinician would be necessary to observe the client's nonverbal communications such as body movements and tone of voice (see Mahl, 1968).

General Considerations   The exact procedures of an interview differ from clinician to clinician, depending on the purpose of the interview. Nevertheless, there are several topics of concern to all interviewers.

The interview and client anxiety   It is not uncommon for clinicians to conduct interviews that purposefully do *not* make the client anxious. These clinicians try to relax the client and establish a comfortable setting for the therapist-client interaction to take place. On the other hand, some clinical psychologists will try to engender anxiety in the client in hope of getting an accurate picture of the client in a stress condition.

Sullivan (1954), for example, suggests that the interviewer at times attempt to gain information that provokes anxiety for the client. This "anxiety focused" style is not intended to break down the client's defenses, but rather to keep the client on the edge of anxiety—the critical line between anxiety that is indicative of crucial life issues for the client and anxiety that is potentially debilitating. With caution, the client's responses during an anxiety-evoking period in an interview can be more gently explored in later interviews.

Still other psychologists may not try to either remove or induce anxiety but will simply keep their eyes and ears open for signs of anxiety and use signs of tension to further their diagnostic impressions. For example, questions about sexuality may make the client anxious. The interviewer should neither avoid nor dwell on these stressful questions, but recognize their anxiety-arousing quality. It is important to keep in mind that the desired outcome of a clinical interview is to gather as much useful information as possible while respecting the client's rights and feelings. This goal is achieved by being flexible but task oriented and by recording accurately the information that the client provides.

The interview and record keeping   At the conclusion of a 50- or 60-minute interview the clinician will have gathered a large quantity of information. How are these data recorded and/or reported? In nearly all cases, the data are recorded on paper or taped (audiotape or videotape).

Handwritten reports can be recorded as the information is collected during the interview or, based on recollection, after the interview is over. Summarizing an entire interview after it is over, however, leaves many opportunities for the interviewer to forget, distort, or fail to highlight certain points. Recording necessary data during the interview is often recommended, as it is usually not disturbing to the client. With practice, the interviewer learns a smooth pattern of inquiry and record keeping that clients find perfectly natural.

When a closer look at certain details of the interview is desired (e.g., tone of voice, hesitancies, nonverbal gestures), as may be the case when teaching students how to interview, audiotape or videotape can be very helpful. In most cases, audiotape serves the purpose well. Since subjects must provide informed consent for the recording of an interview, it is not acceptable to use hidden microphones or cameras. There is little need for this, for very few subjects are upset by the presence of a microphone (Roberts & Renzaglia, 1965).

Record keeping is much less a problem in structured, or even semistructured interviews where specific responses can be easily marked on an answer sheet. In general, it is desirable to have a format for record keeping that the interviewer can take into the interview and use to write down the information.

The interview and scientific cautions   The scientific and methodological problems associated with the interview center on the weakness of using the client's self-report as evidence of actual behavior (Kanfer & Phillips, 1970). During the interview the client describes former events, experiences, or emotional states, but these descriptions are not independent of the behavior of the interviewer, of the person's history of being interviewed, of the client's biases or desire to appear socially acceptable, or of what takes place during the current interview. It has been repeatedly demonstrated (see Matarazzo & Wiens, 1972) that changes in the verbal behavior of the interviewer have an effect on characteristics of the interviewee's speech. For example, Kanfer, Phillips, Matarazzo, and Saslow (1960) examined the effects of different interviewer speech styles—neutral versus interpretive. In one portion of the interviews with student nurses, the interviewer would maintain a neutral, nonjudgmental, open ended, and nondirective interview style. In the other portion of the interview (counterbalanced for control) the interviewer would make interpretive comments. The results indicated a meaningful drop in the interviewee's mean duration of utterance under the interpretive condition. These findings suggest that interpretations during an interview have the effect of reducing the length of the interviewee's responses. An interviewer seeks to gather as much information as possible, so interpretations should be kept to a minimum.

In studies of the accuracy of interview data (if a client says he is 42 years old, is he actually 42 years old?) it has been reported that subjects' reports can vary substantially from the actual facts (Maccoby & Maccoby, 1954). Interview subjects can also be inaccurate in describing their typical behavior or their motivations for certain actions. When the interview topic is personal (e.g., sexuality), subject accuracy may be even more seriously questioned. These concerns highlight the fallible nature of the interview. However, as pointed out by Wiens (1976), this weakness does not mean that the interview method should be discarded. Instead, like other measurement procedures, the interview has unique advantages that make it an important component of assessment. Even if the client is inaccurate, the ways that this inaccuracy occurs is important information in its own right, often suggesting cognitive factors in the client's dysfunctions.

Structured Tests

An often-used method of clinical assessment in addition to the interview, structured tests require subjects to respond to questions that are unambiguous and uniform in meaning, and to respond to the questions in a fashion that is somewhat restricted. For example, a structured written test might ask subjects to read a series of sentences, such as "I like mechanics magazines," and to answer either true or false (i.e., the Minnesota Multiphasic Personality Inventory; see Table 6-3).

Table 6-3 Sample Items from the MMPI—A Structured Psychological Test

Subjects answer true or false		
1. I like mechanics magazines	T	F
2. I have a good appetite	T	F
3. I wake up fresh and rested most mornings	T	F
4. I think I would like the work of a librarian	T	F
5. I am easily awakened by noise	T	F

From S. R. Hathaway and J. C. McKinley, *Manual for the Minnesota Multiphasic Personality Inventory.* New York: Psychological Corporation, 1943. Reproduced by permission, copyright 1943, renewed 1970 by the University of Minnesota. Published by the Psychological Corporation. All rights reserved.

In other structured tests the subjects may be asked to read a series of alternative answers and choose one of the alternatives, or to read a descriptive statement— "I am self-confident"—and rate themselves on a continuum (e.g., from "very much" to "not at all"). Some of the popular structured tests that are discussed in greater detail in subsequent chapters include the Minnesota Multiphasic Personality Inventory (MMPI), the California Psychological Inventory (CPI), the Locus of Control scale, and the State-Trait Anxiety Inventory (STAI). Structured written tests are often referred to as self-report measures since the subjects read the questions and then report the answers themselves.

Not all structured tests are written. Many tests of intelligence used by clinical psychologists, for example, are structured, but they require both verbal responses and actual behavioral performance rather than written self-reports. Both the Wechsler intelligence scales and the Stanford-Binet test are examples because they ask respondents to engage in such actions as arranging pieces of puzzle in a pattern or solving arithmetic problems.

Structured tests are developed with a special focus on the understandability and representativeness of the actual test items. Scoring is usually based on a simple arithmetic addition of all responses into a total sum. Interpretation is also usually based primarily upon total scores, rather than subjective analysis. Also, careful *standardization* and representative *norms* are required.

Standardization   To be useful, most assessment instruments are designed to be administered to subjects in a standard fashion. Standardized testing procedures help to reduce the effects of unwanted extraneous factors such as differences in the way two examiners phrase a question. This increases the likelihood of attaining accurate and valid data.

All aspects of the assessment can be standardized. The test-giving procedures should be consistent from one subject to the next. Allowing one subject more time to complete a task than another subject, for example, would prevent any meaningful comparison of their performances. Test instructions should be identical to ensure, as best as possible, that subjects equally understand what is required of them. Often, test instructions are printed directly on the assessment instrument. Of course, the test items themselves should be the same. The scoring and interpretation of assessment instruments can also be standardized, with reference manuals providing specific scoring procedures and interpretive information. Finally, the examiner's attitude and interpersonal style should be uniform. The clinician as assessor, just like the clinician as researcher, must be cautious to not bias the data. Hurried and impatient examiners will rush subjects, unfriendly examiners restrict them, while patient and friendly, but businesslike, assessors will acquire more accurate and less biased data.

Norms   A norm is a set of scores obtained from a group of people who have taken the test. Interpretations of test performance are often *norm referenced*: that is, an interpretation of a particular subject's score is made in comparison with the scores of the normative group. In order for this comparison to be meaningful, the normative group should be representative of the population from which the subject comes. The American Psychological Association (1974) considers it essential that test developers publish norms obtained from a sample that represents as accurately as possible the relevant population.

In the area of intellectual assessment, for example, an individual's score is compared with the scores of hundreds of other similar people who took the test earlier. The normative group often consists of males and females of all ages, races, and socioeconomic and geographic backgrounds. Thus, terms like "average," "superior," and "inferior" are used to describe the person's score in relation to the norms.

Unstructured Tests

Instead of presenting the subject with questions that require a choice from an array of specific responses, the clinician may choose to give the subject greater freedom in responding by approaching the subject with *unstructured* test stimuli. For example, an unstructured test might present a subject with a picture and ask the subject to tell a story about the picture, such as for the Thematic Apperception Test (TAT). (A TAT-like picture appears in Figure 8.2.) Or the clinician might show the subject an inkblot and ask the subject to describe what it looks like. The Rorschach Inkblot test is an example of this type of unstructured test (see Figure 8-1).

Unstructured tests are less concerned with the test items than structured tests and more concerned with how the subjct responds to the ambiguous material. As a result, scoring and analysis require greater efforts—the clinician must often interpret the meaning of the clients' responses rather than compare them to norms. Unstructured tests are less likely to be thoroughly standardized, although test items and some scoring procedures may take on some qualities of standardization. Unstructured tests actually have some structure (instructions are provided), but they allow more flexibility in subject's responses by not providing ready-made answers.

Behavioral Assessments

Behavioral approaches to assessment seek to acquire direct samples of the behavior under investigation. Instead of employing tests to gain an understanding of personality traits or psychodynamics, behavioral approaches are designed to describe the person's patterns of real-life behavior and the effects of the environment on these patterns. For instance, if a person is afraid of heights, a behavioral measure might involve the number of stories climbed on a fire escape. This approach does not explicate the person's mental or emotional processes, but it does provide specific behavioral data about fear of heights that can be related to treatment and treatment evaluation. It will, for example, be important to know if the person really can go up to high places after completing therapy for the acrophobia.

Consider a client who reports an inability to assert himself or herself in interpersonal discussions. The clinician might select three or four colleagues and, along with the client, form a small group. The client's actual interactions can be observed and evaluated for their degree of assertiveness in this group situation. Does the client express opinions and feelings? Is he or she trembling or flushed? These questions can be answered in this behavioral assessment.

One defining characteristic of many behavioral assessments is the observation of the behavior in the natural setting in which it occurs ("naturalistic observation"). Typically, a limited number of significant behaviors are targeted for assessment. These behaviors are then clearly defined, an observer is taught to record the incidence of the behaviors, and, finally, the observer goes into the actual environment and observes the behavior of interest (see Table 6-4). Though the assessment provides the clinician with a sample of actual behavior, not all client problems are easily assessed in so direct a fashion (e.g., feelings of inadequacy, irrational beliefs).

THE PSYCHOLOGICAL REPORT

Each of the methods of assessment contributes to an understanding of the client. In actual practice, a complete assessment involves multiple methods. For example, a clinician might interview a client, administer several structured and unstructured tests, and then observe the client's behavior. When conducting an assessment to provide a psychological evaluation, a "battery" of assessment tests is often employed. One often-used battery includes an interview, select structured tests (e.g., MMPI; WAIS), select unstructured tests (e.g., Rorschach inkblots; Draw-a-Person; TAT), and observations of behavior. The results of the various assessments are organized, integrated, and communicated in the psychological report.

Why are psychological reports undertaken? In many instances psychological reports result from another professional's request for information about a client or potential client. What types of questions might be asked? Referral questions that are likely to appear, for instance, in a Veterans Administration Hospital might read something like the following: "Evaluate for possible brain damage." "Is Mr._____a good candidate for the Ward C program?" Would you please give us your diagnostic impressions of Ms._____." The psychological report communicates the results of psychological assessments designed to answer such referral questions.

Table 6-4   A Sample Behavioral Assessment System

	Code Definitions for Child Behaviors		
Behaviors	**Coding Symbols**	**Definition of Code**	**Example Behavior**
Attends	C ⊙ S; C P	C gives full-faced attention to some task S prescribes. Task is defined as any behavior S requires of C (e.g., listening, writing, etc.).	S lectures; C listens attentively. S asks C to work quietly at desk; C gives full-faced attention to desk materials
Nonattends	C ∅ S; C P	C does not give full-faced attention to some tasks S prescribes	S lectures; C looks out window or sleeps. C plays with fingers rather than working with materials prescribed by S.
Calls out	C ′ S; C P	C inappropriately verbalizes or makes some noise. Inappropriateness is defined by S's rules regarding speaking out.	S lectures; C yells out, makes a loud noise. S requires hand recognition; C calls out without raising hand.
Negative verbal interaction	C × S or C × P	An aggressive verbal interaction with the intention of hurting or harming. Must observe facial expression and gestures to determine aggressiveness.	C curses at P, or name calls. C curses staff member. Facial expression indicates harm is intended.
Negative physical interaction	C ✳ S or C ✳ P	An aggressive physical interaction with the intention of hurting or harming. Must observe facial expression, gestures, and body stance to detemine aggressiveness.	C hits P: a fight ensues. C pushes S into a corner. Facial expression indicates intention to harm.
Inappropriate verbal interaction	C × S; C × P	C talks to P when S has specified that talking is inappropriate. Interaction is nonaggressive.	S lectures; C and P carry on a conversation. No aggressive intent is observed.

From W. R. Nay, Comprehensive behavioral treatment in a training school for delinquents. In K. S. Calhoun, H. E. Adams, & K. M. Mitchell (Eds.), *Innovative treatment methods in psychopathology*. New York: Wiley, 1974. Copyright 1974 by John Wiley & Sons, Inc. Reprinted by permission of John Wiley & Sons, Inc.

Note. C = Child, S = Staff, P = Peer. If C, S, or P is underlined, this indicates the initiator of the behavior.

General Format

Psychological reports vary in form, style, and length, in each instance reflecting the purpose of the evaluation. Nevertheless, the report, in addition to being used in decisions concerning the referral question, will be filed in the client's records and read by those professionals who will interact with the client in the future. Therefore, most reports cover certain basic areas in a somewhat consistent format (Table 6-5). When writing the report it is useful to label each of the sections for the reader.

Table 6-5   Suggested Format for Psychological Reports

Identifying Data
> Name, Age, Date of birth, Address, Telephone number, Place of assessment, Date of assessment, and Examiner's name.

Referral Question
> What questions were asked? Why was the person referred for assessment? Who was the referral agent?

Social/Family History and Current Context
> Background information regarding family relationships, health, occupation, and social systems should be included, especially when relevant to the referral question. The degree of detail necessary in this section depends on whether or not another person will be taking a history. In many cases another mental health professional (e.g., social worker) will gather a complete background history and this portion of the report need only highlight key events.

Behavioral Observations
> Reports of the client's verbal and nonverbal behavior during the assessments, as well as before and after performing the specific tasks, are provided. Was the subject overly medicated? hyperactive? How did the subject feel about being tested? The client's physical appearance and physical abilities (e.g., gait, vision, hearing) are noted. Interactions with significant others, if persons such as family or friends were present during the assessment, are also described.

Tests Administered
> The examiner provides a list of all the tests that were administered.

Test Results
> Describes the results of the different tests and presents an integration of these results. The report includes a discussion of the client's characteristic behavior patterns, defenses, interpersonal relations, life-style, and self-concepts, as can be determined from the tests. A statement describing the current subjective distress of the client is also provided.

Conclusions
> Based on the information provided above, answer the question at hand: reach a diagnostic formulation, make treatment recommendations, provide prognostic impressions. Also, provide a summary of the person's coping styles, needs, conflicts, social environment, skills, and deficiencies.

Summary
> Briefly review the key points of the report. Others may only read this section, so it is desirable to touch on all salient concerns here.

Writing Style

To facilitate communication, the language used in the report should be clear and concise. Throughout, the report is written in narrative style and in understandable English rather than professional jargon (Palmer, 1970; Sargent, 1951; Tallent, 1976). Consider the following brief example: "This patient is extremely defensive. . . ." Written in understandable English, this statement would become "This patient tries to avoid recognition of his own feelings, since they threaten his security by making him appear irrational and unstable" (Klopfer, 1960, p. 60). Similarly, "This patient has great need for affiliation" could become "This patient would very much like to have friends" (p. 61).

Reports should be case focused (Tallent, 1976). That is, the psychological report should focus on the individual case, not limited to a certain theory, to a certain psychological test, or to a stereotyped image of clients in general. (Highlight 6-2) Use of the client's name in the report is therefore desirable (e.g., Mr. Jones feels . . . Mr. Jones is the type of person who . . .).

Highlight 6-2   Characteristic Stereotyped (Nonindividualized) Psychological Reports

A number of criticisms have been directed at psychological reports: they are filed away in the client's records and not read, they do not help with planning or evaluating treatment (Mintz, 1968), they "psychologize" excessively, and others. Some criticisms pertain to the way the report is written (Tallent, 1976).

AUNT FANNY DESCRIPTION

The "Aunt Fanny Report" (Tallent, 1958) describes the client in such a fashion that the reader of the report would be likely to think, "this is true of anybody's Aunt Fanny." The characteristics attributed to the client are so general that they would be true of almost anyone. For instance, "the client is sometimes immature" or "this subject is anxious about examinations." The weakness of the Aunt Fanny report is that it fails to identify the unique characteristics of the client.

BARNUM REPORTS

Like the Aunt Fanny report, the Barnum report (Meehl, 1956) is general; it is a mixture of stereotypes, evasion, and, in order to gain acceptance, a dash of flattery (Tallent, 1976). It is a description of personality that has a few mildly negative generalities that are hidden among neutral and flattering comments that apply to almost anyone.

TRADEMARKED REPORT

This report overemphasizes the psychologist's personal concerns, conflicts, interests, or shortcomings at the expense of accuracy. It is as if the psychologist sees the same issues in different cases because he or she is confessing his or her own problems with the clients. Repeatedly, for example, Dr. Y describes his cases as compensating for inferiority and struggling with authority.

PROSECUTING ATTORNEY BRIEF

The "prosecuting attorney" report is saturated with negative characteristics to the exclusion of positive ones. It reflects a "maladjustment bias" on the part of the report writer. For instance, a 42-year-old male client is described as aggressive and hostile in relation to authority, untrustworthy and manipulative in interpersonal situations, and lacking an understanding of both children and employees. Nothing is said about the fact that these characteristics have not always been observed, nor about the fact that the client actually participates in many family activities. The report reads like an exposé (see Rosen, 1973).

MADISON AVENUE REPORT

The material provided in the Madison Avenue report is slanted toward the preferences of the reader. That is, the report is written to please the individual who referred the case. For example, such a report written to a school counselor who firmly believes that a "problem" student's intelligence is inferior might overemphasize the youth's poorer scores on intelligence tests while ignoring stronger scores.

Integrating Assessment Data

The report writer would also benefit from the reminder—"integrate." Simply listing adjectives that describe the client or observations of the client's actions is less valuable than pulling the data together into a cohesive characterization that tells the reader the answer to the referral question and to the questions, "What type of person is this?" and "How can this person best be aided?" When certain data do not readily fit into the proposed integration, the reader should be so informed. Although these recommendations pertain in all instances, the actual length of the report, level of language used, and specificity of information that is provided will be determined by the report writer in relation to the primary reader of the report.

Coordinating and integrating all the information that results from the interview, structured and unstructured tests, and behavioral observation requires quite an effort. To this the clinician adds the data from other professional evaluations, social histories, and any prior treatments. Every bit of information does not have to be reported, but the report should not omit anything that may be important—even if it does not pertain directly to the referral question. Reading over the information several times is not uncommon for the clinician who is integrating diverse data.

A useful approach to the integration of assessment data requires three steps. First, the examiner scores all the tests and makes a list of the questions to be addressed. Typically, this includes the referral question and some statements pertaining to the client's current functional, perceptual and motor abilities, intelligence, mood, ability to cope, personal assets, and current environmental stresses and resources.

Second, the examiner takes each assessment instrument and makes a summary statement pertinent to each of the questions. As yet, no effort is made to find consistencies across tests—each test is used separately.

Third, the examiner returns to the summary statements from each test and begins to integrate the material according to the outline of the report. Special emphasis should be paid to congruencies, discrepancies, deviant behavior, and typical behavior (Sundberg, Tyler, & Taplin, 1973). *Congruencies* are common features of the person that emerge from different assessment methods. When evidence of detrimental levels of anxiety appears on structured and unstructured tests, in the interview, and in behavioral observations, the clinician is more confident in providing a diagnosis. *Discrepancies* are dissimilarities across assessment methods. The clinician might have to question why the client shows severe anxiety during the interview and behavioral observations but not on the tests. Is it the presence of another person that elicits the anxiety?

In every instance, *deviant behavior* is of interest. Behavior that is atypical for clients of a certain age, uncommon responses to certain tests, or instances that are exceptional under any circumstances are all noteworthy. Typical behavior is also important because the person's characteristic pattern of behavior provides the best overall picture in most cases.

In the final report, the reader should be presented with a clear and concise statement of the examiner's professional opinion in relation to the referral question and other relevant concerns. The examiner should state the degree of confidence he or she has in the recommendations, and when something is uncertain it should be so stated.

SCIENTIFIC CONCERNS OF ASSESSMENT

The basic scientific concepts that underlie assessment are reliability and validity. *Reliability* is the degree to which a test or a series of observations are stable, dependable, and self-consistent. There are different kinds of reliability: (1) temporal stability, (2) interscorer (interrater) reliability, and (3) internal consistency. *Validity* refers to the degree to which a psychological measure, be it a test, an observed behavior, or an interview report, actually measures what it purports to measure. However, there are actually many validity questions. A central concern is whether users can confidently assume that the test thoroughly measures the particular phenomenon of interest, and *only* that phenomenon (APA Standards, 1974). According to the APA test standards, there are three major types of validity: (1) content, (2) criterion related, and (3) construct. Thorough development of a test involves research documentation of all types of reliability and validity.

The principles of reliability and validity are illustrated in the use of a yardstick to measure a desk top. The yardstick is a highly reliable instrument if (1) each time it is used it produces the same measurement of length, (2) any portion of the yardstick can be used interchangeably, and (3) it yields consistently similar results when different persons serve as measurers. But reliable results may still not be valid results. The inch markings of the yardstick may be poorly calibrated such that measurements do not give the true distances. The measurement would only be valid if the yardstick had accurate calibrations (e.g., if what is marked on the yardstick as "1 inch" is in fact a true inch).

Reliability

Temporal Stability   Temporal stability refers to the computation of test-retest reliability. When the same test is administered at two different times, the degree to which the scores from the first administration are correlated with scores from the second testing is the retest reliability. The correlation indicates the consistency of the test over time. This is not a simple problem, as we can only conclude that a low retest correlation is due to poor test stability when (1) we have independent evidence that the variable being measured has not changed over the time period in question, or (2) we have committed ourselves to a definition of the variable being measured that excludes significant changes over time. For example, if we accept a definition of intelligence that precludes changes in IQ within a week, then a test of intelligence that shows marked changes in one week is assumed to be unstable.

Interscorer Reliability   Interscorer reliability involves an evaluation of the ability of two or more independent scorers or raters to agree on their scoring or rating. Interscorer reliability is a very different issue than retest reliability. Interscorer reliability can be detrimentally affected by poor definitions of the scoring or observing categories, inadequate training of the scorers or observers, or unmotivated or incompetent scorers or observers. In general, the more subjective and less objective the rating or observations, the lower the interscorer reliability.

Internal Consistency   Internal consistency can be established by intercorrelating the items of the test using split-half (or odd-item/even-item) correlations. For example, a test can be split into two halves, and the total score determined by summing the first half of the items of the test is correlated with the total score of the second half of the items. Internal consistency is an independent issue from temporal stability or interscorer agreement. Moreover, whether or not one needs internal consistency depends upon what is being measured. If the behavior being measured is multidetermined then a test that taps each of the separate determinants may be more predictive than a test with a purer level of internal consistency. Two more statistically sophisticated methods for assessing internal consistency are the Kuder-Richardson formula 20 (Kuder & Richardson, 1937) and Cronbach's alpha (Cronbach, 1951) for true-false tests and rating scales, respectively.

Validity

Evaluating the validity of a psychological measurement instrument is often a continuous process requiring a variety of methods. Each method provides additional data to help answer the question, "What can be inferred about what is being measured by the test?"

Content Validity   A psychological test can be said to have demonstrated content validity to the extent that it taps a representative sample of the universe of behaviors relevant to the psychological variable being measured. If a clinical assessment instrument is said to measure anxiety, then one wants to know if it covers the full range of contents that are associated with anxiety (e.g., physiological responses, affective tension, avoidance behaviors, cognitive apprehension). Face validity, a somewhat related notion, refers to the apparent value of individual test items. That is, if a specific question in the test seems *prima facie* to refer to the psychological variable in question (e.g., anxiety), then it is regarded as having face validity. For example, an item such as "Do you frequently feel apprehensive?" would have face validity for a test of anxiety. According to the APA standards for psychological tests, evidence of content validity is required when one wishes to estimate how an individual performs across the universe of situations that the test is intended to measure.

Criterion-Related Validity   When a clinician wishes to use a test score to infer an individual's standing on some other variable, called the criterion, the test must have criterion-related validity. There are two types of criterion-related validity: predictive validity and concurrent validity. According to the APA test standards, predictive validity indicates the extent to which an individual's future behavior on the criterion can be predicted from knowledge of current test performance. Concurrent validity indicates the extent to which test scores may be used to estimate an individual's current standing on a criterion. Evident here is a distinction based on time: predictive validity involves an interval during which something may happen, while concurrent validity reflects performance in the present moment. In either fashion, criterion-related validity is essential and other forms of validity cannot serve as acceptable substitutes. If a test is to be clinically used in making statements about behavior, such as predicting response to treatment, the test must have been shown to possess criterion-related validity. Criterion validities are calculated as correlation coefficients.

Construct Validity   A construct is a concept that is "constructed," based on scientific knowledge, to explain and organize certain aspects of existing knowledge. Examples of clinical constructs are intelligence, anxiety, or ego development. A psychological measurement instrument is said to have construct validity only when the accumulation of a number of studies are integrated and judged to be indicative of the underlying theoretical concept or construct.

The APA test standards suggest that an investigator interested in construct validity begin by formulating hypotheses about the characteristics of those persons who would have high scores on the test and those who might have low scores. These hypotheses can be tested through research, and if supportive evidence is found, the investigator can begin to conclude that the theory about what the test measures is essentially correct (Cronbach & Meehl, 1955).

Further analysis of the ability of a psychological instrument to measure the construct in question can follow the *multitrait-multimethod* approach of Campbell and Fiske (1959). These authors proposed that there are two types of information that are important in the evaluation of the validity of a psychological instrument: convergent validity and discriminant validity. *Convergent validity* refers to the degree to which different instruments yield similar results, and it includes both concurrent and predictive validity. In contrast, *discriminant* validity

Table 6-6   Multitrait-Multimethod Matrix

Traits	Methods			
	Self-report		Physiological	
	Anxiety	Depression	Anxiety	Depression
Anxiety (self-report)	1			
Depression (self-report)	2	1		
Anxiety (physiological)	3	4	1	
Depression (physiological)	4	3	2	1

The upper half of the diagonal of a correlation matrix contains the same information as does the lower half of the matrix.

refers to the degree to which the construct that is being measured is distinct from other constructs. Consider the clinician's assessment of anxiety. If the anxiety inventory produces results that are similar to those produced by other anxiety tests, then there is evidence of convergence. If, however, the anxiety scale and a measure of depression were to result in similar findings, then the anxiety scale would be said to lack discriminant validity. In order for the measure to achieve discriminant validation, it would have to produce results that could not be obtained by measures of other constructs.

In the multitrait-multimethod process, the clinician measures several different *constructs* (e.g., anxiety and depression) by several *assessment methods* (e.g., subject self-report, physiological measures). Intercorrelations of the various scores are presented in a table like the one in Table 6-6. The correlations that would appear in the squares numbered 1 are an index of the test-retest reliability of the measures. That is, each trait is measured on two occasions and the scores are correlated. Squares numbered 2 are the correlations between different traits measured by the same method, while squares numbered 4 are correlations between different traits measured by different methods. These correlations are discriminant validity coefficients. Finally, the correlations that would appear in squares numbered 3 are the *validity* coefficients, representing the degree to which two methods of assessing the same trait are correlated. For purposes of validation, the researcher would hope to find high validity coefficients and low discriminant validity coefficients.

Clinical Utility

One can examine the utility of an assessment instrument by determining its "hit rate." *Hit rate* refers to the accuracy of the clinician's prediction based upon the test for each individual assessed. Consider a woman who is tested to determine if she is pregnant. For our discussion, let us say that she is truly pregnant. This fact would place our subject in the group of "positive" cases. Now, if the test says that the woman is pregnant we have a *valid* positive because the prediction has been confirmed. If the test incorrectly indicated that our subject is not pregnant (when in fact she is) then we would refer to this outcome as a *false* negative because of the prediction of a "negative" condition (not pregnant). Later, another woman comes for testing and she is actually not pregnant. If the test were to indicate nonpregnancy that would be true negative, whereas if the test said that she is pregnant (when in fact she is not) this is a false positive (see Figure 6-1).

Test utility requires high levels of both true positives and true negatives. False positives and false negatives decrease a test's clinical utility, although the effects of these two types of errors can be markedly different. For instance, informing a woman that she is pregnant when she really is not may lead her to experience unnecessary anxiety and friction in her relationships, and she may take expensive and inconvenient, but needless, precautions to protect the imagined fetus. In contrast, telling a woman that she is not pregnant when she really is may lead her to neglect to see a physician, to continue smoking, drinking, or taking tranquilizers (possibly harming the fetus), and to be psychologically and financially shocked when the truth becomes clear.

An instrument's hit rate is affected by the *base rate* of the phenomenon being measured in the sample of people who are being assessed (Meehl & Rosen, 1955). For example, the base rates for a diagnosis of schizophrenia are, respectively, as low as 1% and as high as 50% for the general public versus clients at a mental health facility. Using the same test to predict who will and will not be diagnosed schizophrenic, false positives are far more likely in the general public sample, where 99 chances out of 100 are that a person does not warrant the diagnosis of schizophrenic, than in the clinic sample (assuming the test was validated on samples from the same population). The safest guess, and also least damaging to the individuals being assessed in most cases, is that a person from the general public does *not* warrant a diagnosis of schizophrenia *regardless of what the test says*. The test would have to identify the 1-in-a-100 exception, and *only* that person, as schizophrenic in order to be clinically safe and useful. Thus, the cost of using this test to identify persons requiring help for schizophrenia is difficult to justify in this case.

ASSESSMENT DATA

	Cases predicted positive	Cases predicted negative
Positive cases	Valid positives	False negatives
ACTUAL CONDITION		
Negative cases	False positives	Valid negatives

Figure 6-1   Possible outcomes of prediction (diagnosis).

However, false positives are far less likely in the clinic sample. Here, false negatives are a greater risk compared to the public sample because so many people at the clinic truly warrant a schizophrenic diagnosis. Nevertheless, the test is likely to have greater utility overall with the clinic sample because it is only a 50-50 guess about who will be diagnosed schizophrenic where it was 99-to-1 that the diagnosis would not apply in the general population. Thus, if the test can correctly identify 43 of the 50 people who warrant a diagnosis of schizophrenia and 43 of the 50 people who are truly nonschizophrenic, it is 86% accurate overall (with only 7% rates for false positives or false negatives), and this is much better than a 50-50 guess. The cost of testing clients appears warranted in this case.

Not all tests are as accurate in identifying valid positives as they are with valid negatives. An 86% accuracy could have resulted from perfect diagnoses of nonschizophrenics (50 out of 50) but misdiagnoses in identifying the actual cases (only 36 of 50). As in the example of diagnosing pregnancy, one must consider the effects of false positives and false negatives when evaluating test accuracy. It is far more important, for example, that a test reduce the rate of false positives if we are using the test to select public officials who will be honest and ethical in their jobs.

In sum, a determination of the utility of a test cannot be made without knowledge of the base rate, the proportion of false negatives and false positives, and the possible effects of making wrong positive and wrong negative decisions. The cost of testing (including the harm caused by false negatives and positives) must be weighed in relation to whatever gains in predictive accuracy the test data provide above guesses based on base rates to determine whether testing is truly useful.

SPECIAL ISSUES

In nearly every case, assessment concerns both the scientist and the professional. Tests are often developed and studied by scientific clinicians, but their value is determined, in part, by their utility for practicing clinicians. A balance between scientific rigor and clinical utility is often difficult to achieve, but both perspectives are vital to quality assessment. Several specific issues illustrate the importance and difficulty of achieving such a balance.

Clinical Versus Statistical Prediction

Most psychological testing is done for the purpose of making some sort of a prediction about human behavior. For example, clinicians working in industry may be called on to predict how well several job applicants will handle the job if they are hired. Or, therapists may seek to predict the likelihood that a client will attempt suicide. A controversy that has been a central theme for much research has centered on the relative superiority of clinical versus statistical methods for making predictions about behavior.

By the term clinical, we mean procedures for the arrangement of assessment data without the aid of numerical calculations. That is, the clinician uses "intuition," which is really a carefully reasoned judgment based on his or her prior experience with clients and relevant research to make determinations about future behavior. A decision based on clinical intuition is often difficult to explain in words because it is often based on many subtle factors. For example, a particular facial expression at a particular point in an interview may be intuitively used as a sign of a certain psychological dysfunction because the clinician has found this to yield accurate predictions with similar past clients.

In contrast, the statistical method, called the actuarial method by some, is the straightforward application of numerical calculations, based on past research, to the prediction of behavior. For example, consider the actuarial tables employed by insurance companies. These actuarial tables describe characteristics of the insured person such as age, sex, and marital status, and the actual number of accidents that persons with different characteristics have had. Younger adults (20 to 25), for instance, tend to have more accidents than older adults (40 to 60). Females, even between 20 and 25 years of age, have fewer accidents than males. Also, married drivers have fewer accidents than unmarried or divorced drivers. Use of the actuarial table to make predictions about the "quality of risk" of an insured person involves creating a numerical formula based on combination of such variables as age, sex, and marital status. In clinical psychology, actuarial prediction might numerically combine test scores, biographical data, and ratings from observations of specific behaviors to predict diagnosis, prognosis, or socially important life events or behavior patterns.

In a most influential book entitled *Clinical Versus Statistical Prediction*, Meehl (1954) summarized numerous studies comparing these two approaches. An early study by Sarbin (1943) compared the accuracy of two methods of prediction of academic success: clerks using a mathematical combination of test scores and high school rank (statistical method) and counselors using these and other data from interviews and biographical histories without the formula (clinical method). The results indicated that counselors were no better than clerks using the formula in making predictions, even though the counselors had more data and clinical training to (hopefully) improve their accuracy.

Similar results were reported by Goldberg (1965) who compared the ability of 29 clinicians (13 Ph.D.'s and 16 predoctoral trainees) against 65 different test indicants that were scored by computer to diagnose psychosis or neurosis. The assessment test was the MMPI. Comparing the clinician's judgments versus the computer's numerical judgments for 591 patients who had already been officially diagnosed as either neurotic or psychotic, an interesting pattern emerged. The average Ph.D. was found to have correctly classified 66% of the cases, as did the average trainee (66%). There were, however, at least 14 formulas that exceeded the hit rate of the clinicians, with the average of these being 69% (range = 66 to 74%). Thus, statistical prediction was found to be more effective than clinical prediction in this study.

Meehl tallied "box scores" of how many studies showed statistical prediction better than, equal to, or worse than clinical prediction (see Table 6-7). Meehl's overall conclusion paralleled that of Sarbin and Goldberg. That is, the statistical predictions were equal to or better than those made by the clinician with only one exception. Other reviews (Cronbach, 1956; Gough, 1962; Meehl, 1965) have drawn similar conclusions.

Table 6-7 Meehl's "Box Scores" of Studies Comparing Clinical and Statistical Prediction

Source	No. of Studies	Prediction Domain	"Box Score"		
			Stat >clin	Stat = clin	Stat <clin
Meehl (1954)	16–20	Success in academic or military training; recidivism and parole violation; recovery from psychosis	11	8	1
Meehl (1957)	27	Success in academic or military training; recidivism and parole violation; recovery from psychosis; personality description; outcome of psychotherapy	17	10	0
Meehl (1965)	51	Success in academic or military training; recidivism and parole violation; recovery from psychosis; personality description; outcome of psychotherapy; response to shock treatment; formal psychiatric nosology; job success and satisfaction; medical (nonpsychiatric) diagnosis	33	17	1

From J.S. Wiggins, *Personality and prediction: Principles of personality assessment.* Copyright 1973, Addison-Wesley Publishing Company, Inc., Chapter 5, page 184, Table 5.1, "Box Scores." Reprinted with permission.

Taking a different tack, Sawyer's (1966) review also supported actuarial approaches. Sawyer asked a dual question: are statistical or clinical predictions better, *and* are statistical or clinical procedures differentially important in making the predictions? Sawyer considered interviews and unsystematic observations as clinical measurement, while test scores and biographical facts were seen as statistical measurement. In addition to concluding that the statistical method of combining data was superior to the clinical method, Sawyer pointed out that data gathered by clinical measurement added importantly to the assessment process. That is, statistical predictions were again considered superior, but both clinical and statistical measurements made important contributions to the predictions.

A Rejoinder   Perhaps the most successful of those who countered the arguments for the superiority of statistical predictions, Holt (e.g., 1970, 1978) provides rejoinders. First, Holt has pointed out that most of the comparisons between clinical and statistical methods were not fair to the clinical method. To understand this concern, consider Holt's three types of prediction.

Type I. Pure Actuarial: *Only objective data are used to predict a clearcut criterion by means of statistical processes. The role of judgment is held to a minimum. . .* (Holt, 1978, p. 25)

Type II. Naive Clinical: *The data used are primarily qualitative with no attempt at objectification; their processing is entirely a clinical and intuitive matter, and there is no prior study of criterion or of the possible relation of the predictive data to it. (Holt, 1978, p. 25)*

Type III. Sophisticated Clinical: *Qualitative data from such sources as interviews, life histories, and projective techniques are used as well as objective facts and scores, but as much as possible of objectivity, organization, and scientific method are introduced into the planning, the gathering of data, and their analysis. . . . Quantification and statistics are used wherever helpful, but the clinician himself is retained as one of the prime instruments, with an effort to make him as reliable and valid a data-processor as possible; and he makes the final organization of the data to yield a set of predictions tailored to each individual case. (Holt, 1978, p. 25).*

When Holt (1978) reexamined the studies reviewed by Meehl (1954) and Cronbach (1956), he noted that most were comparisons of Type I with Type II and, therefore, it was not surprising that statistical predictions were more efficient.

Holt's criticisms of the more recent Sawyer (1966) review are also noteworthy.

1. The statistical formula in one-third of the studies was not cross-validated (applied and tested on a new sample). This detail is important since the formula's ability is almost uniformly reduced when applied to a new sample.
2. The criterion that is predicted is inadequate. According to Holt, only 12 of the 45 studies reviewed by Sawyer were concerned with criteria related to clinical psychology.
3. Like the problem of nonclinical criteria, Holt points out that many of the professional judgments were not always made by clinicians. Psychologists or psychiatrists were the clinical predictors in only 22 of the 45 studies.
4. Some of the studies reviewed had too few subjects to permit definitive conclusions.
5. In six of the studies, clinicians were only shown quantitative data. Holt argues that the clinician would fare better when possessing both quantitative and qualitative information.

Based upon these criticisms, Holt concludes that the evidence cannot favor the statistical over the clinical approach. Moreover, the specific predictions of individual clinicians were rarely reported, and as a result we have no way of knowing how well the best of the clinicians did.

The main outcome of the clinical versus statistical controversy has been the realization that the clinician can benefit from statistical analyses and prediction equations in making decisions about diagnosis and treatment. Unfortunately, while even those clinicians who argue that personalities cannot be understood without the subjective processes of the clinician (e.g., Holt, 1971) recognize the impressive "track record" of the actuarial method, actuarial tables are not yet available for clinicians to use in most areas of human behavior and psychological dysfunctions. However, practicing clinicians can begin to keep records of assessment data and their eventual accuracy, so as to take the initiative in developing tabular data and equations that are useful in their particular setting.

Reactivity and Unobtrusiveness

Where the clinical versus statistical question relates primarily to psychological tests, the issues of reactivity and unobtrusiveness refer more to behavioral observations. *Reactivity* has two meanings for our discussion. First, reactivity has to do with the changes in behaviors of individuals who are being observed that are due to the presence of the observer. In this sense, we are referring to the unwanted changes in behavior that produce a distortion of the actual behavior. A child who has been cheating on exams may decide not to cheat simply because the observer is in the room. The resulting observational record is therefore not an accurate estimate of the child's actual cheating behavior, but more a consequence of the observer's presence.

Second, reactivity refers to the changes in behavior that result when individuals monitor their own behavior. For example, select a behavior of your own that you know you occasionally do such as scratching your head, smoking cigarettes, or saying "ya know." If you were to begin a program of self-monitoring, you would probably change the frequency of that behavior because you have become more aware of it as a result of observing and recording it.

In some instances reactivity is undesirable. This condition occurs when there is a distortion that reduces the validity of the observations or when there is an increase in undesirable behavior. For example, in an experimental school classroom, observers record the behavior of the children, and the effects of different classroom management procedures are evaluated. If the children in the classroom are reacting to the observers, then the researcher does not have an accurate indication of the occurrences of the behaviors being observed. Alternately, a client who is trying to discontinue smoking cigarettes may be asked to monitor the number of urges that he or she has for a cigarette. Due to a heightened awareness, the number of urges may be found to increase (an undesirable effect).

However, reactivity can have positive effects in other cases. In a study by Johnson and White (1971) college students were assigned to one of three groups. One group was instructed to self-monitor their study activities, a second self-monitored dating activities, and the third group were given no instructions to self-monitor. The results indicated that the weekly grades of the students who monitored their own study activities were superior to the control group that did not self-monitor. Also, the mean weekly grades of the group that self-monitored dating fell below the mean of the other two groups. Self-monitoring of dating behaviors did not have the positive effects on grades that self-monitoring of studying did. These findings suggest that when an individual self-monitors relevant behaviors there may be a facilitative effect. These findings also suggest that as a reader of this book enrolled in a course in clinical psychology, you might begin to monitor your own study habits!

Usually we wish to obtain assessment data that are, to the best of our knowledge, not affected by reactivity. Webb, Campbell, Schwartz, and Sechrest (1966) suggest several procedures that come very close to providing nonreactive or "unobtrusive" data.

Natural erosion methods are one such approach. For example, a committee was formed to set up a psychological exhibit at Chicago's Museum of Science and

Industry. According to Webb et al. (1966), the committee learned that the vinyl tiles around the exhibit containing live, hatching chicks had to be replaced every six weeks or so; tiles in other areas of the museum went for years without replacement. Comparisons of the rates at which floor tiles around different museum exhibits require replacement can give a rough ordering of the popularity of certain types of exhibits. An example of psychological measurement by erosion might include a family's stock of foods in the cupboard (controlling for new purchases) if this is used to indicate how often family members eat dinner foods at home (an indirect measure of family involvement and support).

Physical accretion (remnants of past behavior) is a second unobtrusive measure. Consider a dentist, Dr. Henry, who is interested in reducing his patients' anxiety in the waiting room by playing soft music. He may have his secretary schedule appointments for his clients on a random basis and then have the radio play soft music on one day and not on the next. Barring uneven numbers of cigarette smokers on each day (controlled by randomization), Dr. Henry could examine the ashtrays and compare the number of cigarette butts that accumulated on days with versus days without the soft music. Assuming that people smoke more when anxious, the accumulation of cigarette butts could provide a valuable source of unobtrusive data concerning anxiety.

The ongoing records of society, our *archives*, are also sources of unobtrusive information. Records of marriages, divorces, births, deaths, and purchases can be used. Some researchers have even used high school yearbooks as sources of information about people (cf. Barthell & Holmes, 1968). A fact that is often cited about the blackout in New York is that there were a disproportionate number of births nine months after the time of the blackout. This archival information tells us something about prior behavior. However, archival information is not always perfect, since illegitimate births and suicide deaths are sometimes recorded differently to protect certain individuals (a reactivity problem).

Finally, Webb et al. (1966) suggest that certain *"hardware"* methods such as audio and/or video tape recording, infrared photography, or photo electric cells be used to unobtrusively gather data. For example, Hess and Polt (1960) measured pupil dilation from a film as an assessment of interest level, and related it to stimulus materials—a baby, a mother holding a child, a partially nude woman, a partially nude male, and a landscape. There were differences in pupil size between males and females and clear differences in pupil size in response to the different stimuli.

Although nonreactive assessment offers a means of gaining accurate data, we must consider the rights of the public (e.g., privacy, informed consent). Wilson and Donnerstein (1976) discussed the ethical aspects of nonreactive research. These authors examined the general public's reactions to nonreactive research methods used in social psychology by presenting interviewees with short descriptions of eight different studies that had employed nonreactive assessments. The subjects then responded to questions such as "If you discovered that you had been a subject in this experiment would you feel that you had been harassed or annoyed?" or "Do you feel that such an experiment is unethical or immoral?" Although the majority of subjects did not react negatively to the research methods, in some cases substantial minorities were upset. For example, a study by

Zimbardo (1969) provoked few negative responses. In this study automobiles parked on the street were made to look abandoned while experimenters hid in nearby buildings and filmed people who had contact with the cars. In contrast, more than half of the subjects expressed feelings of harassment to a study by Schaps (1972) in which a female visited a crowded shoe store and, while wearing a shoe with a broken heel, rejects whatever the salesman shows her. Unknown to the salesman, a confederate takes notes on the salesman's behavior.

Unquestionably, nonreactive assessment would be unacceptable by contemporary standards of ethical research unless certain precautions are taken. Before using nonreactive (or reactive) methods it is the responsibility of researchers to consider the ethical aspects of these methods of assessment.

Who Is the Client?

Since individuals are often referred for psychological assessments by persons such as their parents, institutions such as courts or their place of employment, or other mental health professionals, the clinician is placed in a precarious position. Who is the client? Is the person who is being assessed the client, or is the client the source of the referral? These problems present some rather challenging ethical issues for psychological assessment (see also Monahan, 1980).

Consider for a moment an 11-year-old child who is brought to the attention of a clinician as a behavior problem in school and at home. The clinician is asked by the parents to assess the child and diagnose the child's problem. After conducting interviews with the child and the parents and observing other interactions between the child and the parents, a consistent pattern is noticed. Each time the child starts to speak, the father cuts the child off and finishes the sentence. Then the mother shouts at her husband and bitterly chastises him for being domineering. The pattern is consistent, and the child appears frustrated. Furthermore, the child is constantly exposed to aggressive adult models who strike out when they are upset. Now, back to our original question—is the child the client or are the parents? In this case, the child may benefit from therapy in which he or she can learn effective ways for coping with the parents and his or her feelings, but it also appears that therapy will be incomplete if the parents are not helped in changing their destructive interactions. Clinical assessments must be directed by accuracy and utility, but one must be cautious in identifying the targeted client!

It is important to remember that the person(s) or institution(s) who control the payoffs for the clinician (e.g., salary, fees, recommendations) may have the greatest influence on the clinician's actions (Stolz, 1978). Thus, unless precautions are taken to increase the influence of less powerful people or groups and to guard against unthinking biases by clinicians, it is inevitable that the goals, and sometimes even the methods, pursued by the clinical assessor will be determined primarily by the controlling person(s) or institution(s). Parents and their children, psychiatric hospitals and their patients, prisons and their inmates, business organizations and their employees, and teachers and their students—in all these cases, the first element in each pair has the greatest impact on the clinician's professional survival and advancement, and therefore the major leverage when assessment goals and methods are planned.

Yet the clinician has an ethical responsibility to incorporate the goals and needs of *all* participants, including the less powerful ones. How can this be done without sacrificing career rewards? In correctional and treatment institutions, an attempted solution has been to establish advisory boards to represent the interests of the patient or inmate. This strategy is only effective, however, if the advisory board (1) truly represents the wishes of the patients or inmates (e.g., by basing their policies on the directly expressed desires of patients or inmates), (2) has power to influence prison policies, and (3) has a tangible influence on the clinician's career rewards (e.g., input into hiring and promotion decisions). A more immediate, although less systematic, solution is for each clinical assessor to solicit the goals of all participants before beginning the assessment and to establish a contract that is acceptable to all parties. For example, the clinician may agree to provide the prison with a mental status report and a recommendation about the best educational programs for an inmate only as long as the inmate is free to accept or decline participation in these interventions without prejudice. There are *no* surefire answers to this issue, but the principle of integrating the interests of all parties into the assessment and intervention plan offers a good starting guideline.

The Scientist-Professional Model and Assessment

A closing caveat concerning the potential divergence of scientifically and professionally oriented clinical psychologists is in order. The field of clinical psychology has offered both research-based and clinically derived contributions to theory and practice in psychological assessment. Unfortunately, practicing clinicians often place confidence in psychological tests that have not been scientifically proven effective. To complicate matters, research clinicians often dismiss the assessment enterprise as inaccurate and invalid. Thus, a gap sometimes exists between research and practicing clinicians. The immediate imperative is for the practicing clinical psychologist to recognize the necessity of continually validating the assessment instruments and procedures and for the research clinician to continually develop and improve practical and meaningful assessment instruments.

Can the clinical assessor wear both hats, as researcher and assessor, simultaneously? In many cases the answer is "Yes!" An example of an integrated scientist-professional assessment is provided by Dougherty (1976). Using 11 predictor variables from several assessment measures (e.g., MMPI, Personal Orientation Inventory), patients and therapists from a university counseling center were divided into three homogeneous groups. The predictive validity of the assessment measures was then evaluated separately for each group, with the criterion being therapists' evaluations of patient gains in therapy. The combination of assessment measures that best predicted therapy outcome for each therapist-client group was then used to predict which client-therapist dyads in the next academic year would show positive or negative results. As hypothesized, certain combinations of client types and therapist types produced optimal outcomes, while other client-therapist matchings yielded consistently poor outcomes. The importance of this study is, as the author states, *not* the specific combination of assessment measures that were used in this particualr study. With therapists and clients of different types and in new settings, the optimal assessment measures would probably change. Instead "what is generalizable is the methodological paradigm" (p. 896): that is, intervention can be scientifically improved by rigorously using assessment data to optimally match clients and therapists in a clinical setting. Thus, fruitful scientific-professional assessment models are available.

Measure your mind's height by the shade it casts!

Robert Browning

This photograph of Einstein's study, just after his death, lets you begin to wonder what might be on the blackboard.

7

ASSESSMENT OF
INTELLECTUAL FUNCTIONING

The assessment of intellectual capabilities and/or deficits was one of the original tasks undertaken by psychologists, and, indeed, the history of psychology is laced with instances where intellectual assessment played an important role in the development and advancement of the discipline. Sir Francis Galton, for example, provided one of the earliest studies of intelligence in his investigation of the hereditary quality of genius (Galton, 1869). Note that Galton included in the term "genius" many kinds of achievement that we would not normally regard as related to measured intelligence (e.g., preachers, wrestlers, musicians).

Related to this research, Galton created the concept of correlation. Perhaps one of the major breakthroughs for psychology, the correlational strategy remains a widely used method in clinical research. Galton also emphasized a statistical concept of intelligence. That is, Galton talked about gifted individuals as being "one in each million." Currently, descriptions of intellectual ability rely on a similar statistical concept of intelligence.

Intellectual assessment was perhaps the first scientist-professional controversy within clinical psychology. Academic theoreticians and researchers were interested in the structure of the intellect, or the mind, and in being able to outline its different components. To develop this type of understanding required advanced measurement and statistical procedures and large numbers of subjects. One such theory-oriented university scientist, Spearman, proposed that only one general factor was needed to account for basic intellectual ability (Spearman, 1904). Related to his research, he originated the procedures for factor analysis. The factor analytic procedures allowed Spearman to examine a large matrix of the correlations between measures of various intellectual abilities. Although Spearman reported evidence to support his "general factor" theory, other researchers, such as Thorndike, did not find support for a general factor of intelligence and these scientists debated.

On the other hand, practicing psychologists were interested in using standardized tests to make more individualized practical decisions in schools and hos-

243

pitals. Binet, a forerunner in this effort, left a position at the Sorbonne in France and went to work at an institution for the retarded where he planned to help a colleague, Simon, put into practice the assessment of intelligence as a method for making decisions about mental retardation (see Binet & Simon, 1905). It was the combining of the intellectual efforts of both practicing and academic psychologists that resulted in scientifically meaningful and practically useful instruments for assessing intelligence.

Intelligence is a construct, and as such it cannot be observed. However, through our assessment instruments we can measure intelligent behavior. As a result we have learned a great deal about human mental capabilities, but as we shall see in this chapter, exact answers to some specific questions continue to elude creative inquiries.

DEFINITION OF INTELLIGENCE

A we begin to contemplate the measurement of intelligence, we must first understand the meaning of the concept of intelligence. Unfortunately, a variety of definitions of intelligence have been proposed and psychologists have not unanimously supported any one of them. The most widely accepted definition of intelligence is likely that proposed by Wechsler (author of the major tests of intelligence)—*"Intelligence is the aggregate or global capacity of the individual to act purposively, to think rationally, and to deal effectively with his environment"* (Wechsler, 1958) (p. 7). More recently, Wechsler (1980) described intelligence as a matter of relative position—how a person does on a performance task in relation to his peers. Thus, both absolute ability and capability relative to other persons must be considered when intelligence is assessed.

SOURCES OF INTELLIGENCE: GENETICS, ENVIRONMENT, AND GENETICS AND ENVIRONMENT

In the not too distant past, the nature-nurture controversy was thought to have become a question of solely historical importance. However, psychological interest in the controversy reemerged in the early 1970s and took on special meaning as scientists began to evaluate the federally funded programs that had been designed to improve the intellectual level of deprived youngsters. In a controversial article, Jensen (1969) questioned, "How much can we boost the IQ?" and many social scientists responded. The controversial interpretation of the article suggested that remedial programs would be ineffective since genetics accounted for an individual's IQ (Highlight 7-1).

The genetic position holds that the best predictor of a child's intelligence is the IQ of the parents of the child, independent of who rears the child. Some evidence in support of the relationship of intelligence and heredity was published by Erlenmeyer-Kimling and Jarvik (1963) and is reproduced in Figure 7-1.[1] This review includes 52 independent studies of the correlations of relatives tested for intellectual

---

[1](See also the more current and expanded summary reported in *Science* by Bouchard & McGue, 1981).

Highlight 7-1   Controversy Surrounding Sources of Intelligence

The controversial nature of the Jensen (1969) article is evident in the fact that it has been cut out of the journal in which it first appeared in many of the university and public libraries around the country. For example, an attempt to acquire a copy of the article through an interlibrary loan service in the state of Virginia was unsuccessful. Going out of state via a second interlibrary loan service was also unsuccessful (mostly mid-Atlantic states). Finally, a similar search in a northern California community also revealed that the article had been cut out of the journal in many of the libraries. Attempting to find a copy of the paper is indeed difficult, and the interested reader might pursue either an interlibrary loan system or a copy of the paper as it was read into the *Congressional Record*.

An additional reason for labeling the article as controversial relates to the preface of the book, *Intelligence: Genetic and environmental influences*. In the preface Cancro (1971) mentions the apprehensions, fears, and threats that surrounded the conference from which the book emerged. In fact, there was a bomb threat directly related to the conference on intelligence. A great deal of emotional vigor has been associated with the antigenetic point of view.

The progenetic camp has also been maintained with great emotional vigor. In fact, one major proponent of the genetic position, the late British psychologist Sir Cyril Burt, has been said to have gone so far as to have faked his data. For instance, Burt published data on the correlation between IQs of dizygotic twins and monozygotic twins reared together and reared apart (a total of 156 pairs). Subsequent twin data, reporting different numbers of twins, presented identical correlations. In a nutshell, although the sizes of Burt's samples changed, many of his reported correlations, some 20 in all, did not. They were identical to three decimal places (Hearnshaw, 1979)! Also, Burt refers to two colleagues, Mrs. Conway and Ms. Howard, yet no one has any evidence that either person existed.

---

abilities, involving over 30,000 pairings from eight countries in four continents, obtained over a period of more than two generations. As can be seen in Figure 7-1, there is an emerging consistency—a clear relationship between genetic similarity and intelligence. As noted in Highlight 7-2, behavior geneticists make effective use of the study of twins to investigate the sources of intelligence.

Taking the genetic (nature) viewpoint one step further, one may speculate that since the heredity-intelligence relationship does exist, special effort to remediate "slow" children might be unsuccessful. After all, the genetic given sets the limits for the development of capabilities such that prescribing special training would not be worthwhile. Only a minority of professionals hold such pessimistic attitudes.

In marked contrast, the environmental (nurture) position holds that environmental conditions can override heredity in determining intellectual capacities. One environmental view was promoted by a strict behaviorist, Watson (1925)— "Give me a dozen healthy infants, well formed, and my own specialized world to

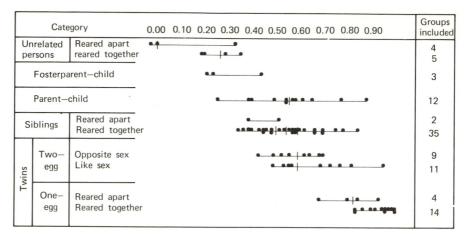

Category		0.00 0.10 0.20 0.30 0.40 0.50 0.60 0.70 0.80 0.90	Groups included
Unrelated persons	Reared apart		4
	reared together		5
Fosterparent–child			3
Parent–child			12
Siblings	Reared apart		2
	Reared together		35
Twins — Two–egg	Opposite sex		9
	Like sex		11
Twins — One–egg	Reared apart		4
	Reared together		14

Figure 7-1 Correlations between IQs of paired individuals of genetic relations ranging from none to complete. From L. Erlenmeyer-Kimling and L. P. Jarvik, Genetics and intelligence: A review. *Science*, 1963, *142*, 1477–1479. Copyright 1963 by the American Association for the Advancement of Science. Reprinted by permission.

bring them up in, and I'll guarantee to take any one at random and train him to become any type of specialist I might select—doctor, lawyer, etc.'' (p. 82). Denouncing the inheritance of capabilities, talents, or abilities, Watson contended that our intellectual behavior, like our other behavior, is a *learned* pattern of responding.

Hightlight 7-2   The Twin-Study Methodology

In an analysis of the genetic components of behavior, the study of identical twins (monozygotic) and fraternal twins (dizygotic) can be very illuminating. Monozygotic (MZ) twins are the result of one fertilized egg that has split, and both children then have the same identical endowment. Dizygotic (DZ) twins are the product of two separate, genetically different eggs. The comparison of MZ and DZ twins is an important methodology of the behavioral geneticists who study the inheritance of certain behavior.

Concordance is a term used to designate the degree of similarity of two twins with respect to a given trait. When twins are studied (e.g., intellectual level), the concordance of DZ and MZ pairs can be compared. Evidence for a genetic contribution to the trait is seen in the higher concordance between sets of MZ twins than DZ twins. That is, if one member of an MZ twin pair is, for example, retarded, then the likelihood that the other twin is also retarded is greater than for members of a DZ twin pair.

These methods can also be refined comparing twin pairs that were reared together in the same family setting and environment with other twins who were reared apart from each other. Some elements of the environmental influences can be teased apart using just such methodology.

There are, however, a few potential kinks in the twin-study methods. First, twins are more likely to be born early in gestation and to be born to younger mothers. Both early birth and early mothering are themselves known variables of importance that affect the children's development. Second, it is sometimes thought that the environment that is created for identical twins may be more similar than that for fraternal twins simply because of the physical similarity of the youngsters. Loehlin and Nichols (1976) report that "identical pairs are subjected to environments that are in many respects more similar than those of fraternal twins" (p. 89). However, note that while Loehlin and Nichols (1976) reported a relationship between the similarity of twins' environments and the similarity of their abilities, other researchers have presented evidence that the twin environment does not affect cognitive abilities (Vandenberg & Wilson, 1979). Moreover, Shields (in press) reports correlations of intelligence within twins that is striking for both twins from similar environments (.87) and twins from dissimilar environments (.84). As a result, the validity of this criticism of the twin method remains in question.

Twins: Identical (a) and fraternal (same sex (b) and opposite sex (c)).

a

b

c

A behavioral analysis of intelligence would examine the individual's intellectual history in search for cases where cognitive activities had been shaped and subsequently maintained by reinforcement. The individual's responses to the test items that contribute to the IQ score are seen as a function of the individual's *environmental* opportunities.

The extreme differences of opinions expressed by geneticists and environmentalists are currently not rigidly adhered to. Genetic effects are not seen as inevitable. Some characteristics that are genetically related still require available and acceptable environments. Also, there is no single IQ gene. Nor is there any single environment—we must certainly make a distinction between biological, social, and psychological environments. For instance, the biological environment that the unborn being experienced *in utero* may have been valuable in terms of potential intellectual development. The genetic/environment discussion can no longer be considered an either-or question: the genetic endowment can only express itself in an environment, and an environment cannot supersede certain genetic constraints.

Researchers who study intelligence from the perspective of behavior genetics provide a useful model for understanding intelligence. Their focus is on identifying the genotypes that correspond to certain behavioral phenotypes. *Genotype* re-

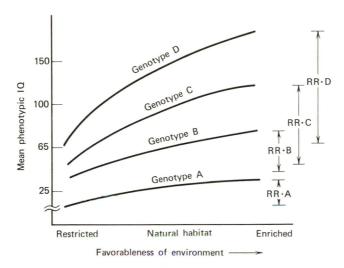

Figure 7-2   Scheme of Gottesman's reaction-range (RR*) model. From I. I. Gottesman, Genetic aspects of intelligent behavior. In N. Ellis (Ed.), *The handbook of mental deficiency: Psychological theory and research.* Copyright 1963 by McGraw-Hill Book Company. Used with the permission of McGraw-Hill Book Company.

fers to the individual's total complement of genetic factors (seen or unseen), whereas *phenotype* refers to the observable characteristics of the individual that result from the interaction of genotype and environment. A conceptualization that is useful to explain the simultaneous contribution of genotype and environment to variations in phenotype is Gottesman's *reaction range* model (1963, 1972, 1974). The reaction-range model first assumes that any observed variability in intelligence must be attributed to some combination of genetic and environmental variances. However, different genotypes can have different degrees of responsiveness (or environmental sensitivity) and thus be differentially affected by the environment. The reaction-range concept is illustrated in Figure 7-2. According to Gottesman (1972), the best way to conceptualize the contribution of heredity to intelligence is to think of heredity as fixing a reaction range. That is, the genotype determines "an indefinite but nonetheless circumscribed assortment of phenotypes" (p.34). This model also indicates that the intellectual differences between those who are high and low on genetic endowment will be minimized in poor environments, whereas, in stimulating and enriched environments, the differences among those with varying genetic endowments is maximized. In all cases, a favorable environment aids the person to achieve his or her fullest potential, but genetic inheritance sets limits on people's ultimate possibilities.

Clinical Implications

In regard to remedial education, one can ask "What is the best policy given the hereditary involvement in IQ?" Clearly, clinical interventions and/or remedial programs should be pursued. As the reaction-range concept illustrates, when you enrich the environment you can improve the IQ score, although the range of potential improvement is restricted by the genetic endowment. For example, consider the data reported by Bloom (1969) concerning the IQ scores of Jewish children reared at home *or* in a kibbutz. Jewish children of European origin were found to have a mean IQ of 105 when reared at home, but an average of 115 when reared in a kibbutz (22 hours a day for four or more years). Also, Middle Eastern Jewish children had a mean IQ of 85 when reared at home, but an average of 115 under the kibbutz system. The groups of children were matched according to their parents' educational and occupational level as well as the kibbutz in which they were reared. The results of Bloom's study are quite interesting—different groups of Jewish people evidenced the genetic influences on intelligence, but the effects of the kibbutz on both groups supports the effectiveness of environmental interventions.

A second important implication of the genetic and environmental involvement in intelligence pertains to individual testing. Data have been reported showing the existence of racial differences in IQ (e.g., Kennedy, Van de Reit, & White, 1963) and it is often stated, for example, that blacks as a group score some 10 to 15 points lower than whites as a group (Shuey, 1966). What is often overlooked, however, is that there is an enormous overlap in the distributions of these scores and that knowledge of the subject's race is *not* alone a useful predictor of intelligence in an individual case. It is therefore essential, for both scientific and ethical reasons, that a subject be carefully tested rather than assuming an *a priori* IQ.

ASSESSING ADULT INTELLIGENCE

Asking the solution to a problem that requires specific mental abilities, examining a sample of handwriting, or even requiring the construction of a model from certain building materials may all be construed as examples of intellectual assessment. But, each such procedure provides only one small and restricted sample of behavior. What is needed is a methodology that requires similar sorts of intellectual activities but samples from a wide range of possible behaviors. In addition, each person's scores on these activities must be compared to the results of a representative sample of other individuals to establish their position relative to this normative group. These measures should be reliable and valid, and as culturally unbiased as possible. The majority of psychological tests designed to measure adult intellectual functioning have been developed in just this fashion. The most widely accepted tests in this area include the Stanford-Binet Intelligence Scale, and the Wechsler Adult Intelligence Scale.

Stanford-Binet Intelligence Scale

The original instrument for the measurement of intelligence was the Binet-Simon scale (Binet & Simon, 1905). This preliminary test consisted of 30 questions that ranged from least to most difficult and that measured sensory and perceptual abilities as well as verbal skills. Several revisions appeared in the following decade. The major revision, undertaken in America by Terman (1916) at Stanford University, became known as the Stanford-Binet. The 1916 revision was based on data that provided normative standards of intellectual performance for average Americans from age 3 to 16. The tests were arranged by age levels, beginning with the youngest ages and moving through to the adult level, and items on each test were placed in order of ascending difficulty. The basic assessment methodology was to administer the test items, score them, and make a comparison of the subject's scores to the standards for a large group of normal subjects of the same age. The final result was a score representing the subject's relative level of performance.

The 1916 revision was pioneering in its efforts to obtain a representative sample of the American population, to specify detailed instructions for test administration, and to provide specific criteria for the scoring of each test. A subsequent revision in 1937 resulted in two alternate forms of 129 items each. As with the earlier tests, age comparisons were again employed, and the goal was to employ a variety of measures that together could be considered "intelligence." In 1960, an additional revision returned to a single form of the test combining the items that were most highly correlated with meaningful criteria from each of the two previous forms. The performance of 4498 subjects (aged 2½ to 18) from six states constituted the sample. Although this standardization group did not attempt to achieve representative sampling, it was used to help make changes in some items and in the order of item presentation.

The 1960 Stanford-Binet (Terman & Merrill, 1960) includes a number of tests that are grouped into age levels extending from age 2 to superior adult (see sample items in Table 7-1).

Table 7-1   Sample Items from The Stanford-Binet Intelligence Scale

The six samples below are only examples. They were selected from various age levels (the early years through average adult) of the Stanford-Binet to illustrate the types of tasks that are required. Note: "S" is an abbreviation for "subject."

PICTURE VOCABULARY (this example is from Year IV)

Material: Eighteen 2 in. × 4 in. cards with pictures of common objects.

Procedure: Show the cards one at a time. Say, "What's this? What do you call it?"

Score: 14 plus.

PICTORIAL IDENTIFICATION (this example is from Year IV)

Material: Card with pictures of objects.

Procedure: Show the card and say: "Show me what . . ." or "Which one . . ." or "Show me the one that . . ."

(a) ". . . we cook on."

Score: 3 plus (out of 6 items) Naming the object is not sufficient. The child must point to it on the card.

OPPOSITE ANALOGIES II (this example is from Year VI)

Procedure: Say:

(a) "A table is made of wood; a window of . . ."

Score: 3 plus (out of 4 items)

Table 7-1 *Continued*

REPEATING 6 DIGITS (this example is from Year X)

Procedure: Say, "I am going to say some numbers and when I am through I want you to say them just the way I do. Listen carefully, and get them just right." Pronounce the digits distinctly and with perfectly uniform emphasis at the rate of one per second.

(a) 4-7-3-8-5-9

Score: 1 plus. The series must be repeated in correct order without error after a single reading.

MEMORY FOR DESIGNS I (this example is from Year XI)

Material: Card with two designs.

Procedure: With the card in your hand, but before showing the designs, say, "This card has two drawings on it. I am going to show them to you for 10 seconds, then I will take the card away and let you draw from memory what you have seen. Be sure to look at both drawings carefully." Then show the card 10 seconds, holding it at right angles to the child's line of vision and with the designs in the position given in the plate. At the end of approximately 4 seconds say, quietly, "Look at both." Have S reproduce the designs immediately, and note which is the top of his drawing.

Score: 1 ½ plus.

VOCABULARY (this example is from Year XIV)

Procedure: Say, "I want to find out how many words you know. Listen, and when I say a word, you tell me what it means. What is an orange?" Vary the form of the question to avoid a stilted manner of presentation, e.g., "What does . . . mean?" "Tell me what a . . . is," or give just the word without any further question. If S hesitates, urge him to try by saying, "Just tell me in our own words; say it any way you please. All I want to know is whether you know what a . . . is." Or "You know what a . . . is! Tell me, what is a . . . ?" Give S the vocabulary card containing the word list and let him look at each word as you read it. If the subject's meaning is not clear, that is, if his response can't be scored plus or minus without further explanation, say, "Tell me what you mean," or "Tell me more about it." Continue until six consecutive words have been failed.

Score: 17 plus.

Adapted from L.M. Terman and M.A. Merrill, *Stanford-Binet Intelligence Scale, Form L-M*. Copyright 1960, 1972 Houghton Mifflin Company. Used with permission from Riverside Publishing Company.

The Stanford-Binet test items require a variety of skills on the part of each subject. For example, the items classified at the level of an average 3-year-old include naming objects that are presented pictorially, stringing beads, and using a pencil to draw. At the 10-year-old level, the subject is asked to give the meaning of words, to count objects, to name as many words as possible in one minute, and to repeat numbers presented by the examiner. The average adult level requires, among other tasks, vocabulary, arithmetic reasoning, understanding differences, and describing the meaning of proverbs. Because many adults show limited interest in some of the Stanford-Binet tasks, and because many adults surpass the highest ceiling age, the test is more often used with children and adolescents than adults.

Test Administration   Each subject is asked to begin with test items that the examiner judges, based on the subject's age and general mental status, to be just below the subject's actual capabilities. If the subject answers all items at this age level correctly, he or she proceeds on to items at each higher age level until reaching a level where he or she cannot correctly answer any items (ceiling age). If the subject does not correctly answer all items at the initial age level, the subject is asked to attempt the items at the next younger age level, and this continues until the subject answers all items at one age level correctly (basal age). The subject's scores are translated into an "intelligence quotient" (IQ), on a scale with a mean of 100 and a standard deviation of 16 (see Highlight 7-3).

Highlight 7-3   Psychometric Intelligence: The IQ

The concept of *mental age* (MA) was introduced in the original measure of intelligence (Binet-Simon Scales) and remained a part of intellectual assessment practices for many years. Mental age notions categorize test items according to age: for example, the 8-year level contains the items that the majority of 8-year-olds in a normative sample could complete. Each subject is given an opportunity to complete as many test items as possible, and the test score reflects the highest age level that the subject successfully completed, plus partial credit for test items passed at higher levels.

For example, suppose you have just finished testing a boy who is 8 years 0 months old. The child successfully completed all the Year IV items, thus receiving a basal age of 4 years 0 months. At Year X, the child did not pass any of the tests and thus 10 years 0 months is his ceiling age. On the tests for the years between 4 and 10 your subject received partial credit totalling 22 months. Calculation of the subject's mental age combines the basal age 4-0 with the additional credit 22 months (1 year 10 months) resulting in a mental age of 5 years 10 months.

However, the mental age unit is not constant across different ages. That is, basic intellectual abilities appear to increase more rapidly up to a certain age and then seem to reach a plateau, but the notion of MA does not adjust to this effectively. For example, there appears to be more intellectual growth from age 4 to 10 than from 40 to 46, despite the fact that six years have elapsed in both cases! As a result, the mental age unit shrinks with increasing chronological age. For example, if a boy continues to function at the same level of deficit relative to his peers at age 12 as he did at age 5, and if he scored 1 year retarded at age 5 (mental age of 4), he would score 3 years retarded at age 12 (mental age of 9). In order for there to be uniformity in the meaning of the test scores regardless of the subject's chronological age, the intelligence quotient (ratio IQ) was introduced (Stern, 1912).

The ratio IQ, unlike the MA, was interpreted to be integrated similarly for all ages. IQ that is independent of the age of the subject is calculated as follows:

$$IQ = 100 \times \frac{MA \text{ (subject's attained score)}}{CA \text{ (score expected for subject's chronological age)}}$$

Using this formula, average or normal intellectual performance turns out to be an IQ of 100. For instance, a 12-year-old girl whose MA is also 12 would receive an IQ of 100.

A problem emerges, however, since the variability in performance among mental ages increases with increasing chronological age. That is, the range of scores typically obtained by young subjects is restricted in comparison to the broader range of scores that can be obtained by adults. As a result of this discrepancy in standard deviation for different aged subjects the same ratio IQ (e.g., 125) might indicate superior performance for a 10-year-old but only above average performance for a 30-year-old.

The solution is to calculate the IQ in terms of deviation quotients. *Deviation quotients* are like standard scores in that they employ the same standard deviation at each age level. Thus, a deviation IQ of 115 will be the same distance above the mean for subjects at all age levels. Deviation IQs are currently employed by most tests of intelligence, including the Stanford-Binet and the Wechsler scales. The resulting IQs are thus meaningfully comparable across different ages.

The IQ represents the composite score on a variety of subtests that have been transformed to allow meaningful interpretation at various ages. The IQ is not a score that is fixed and unmodifiable, nor is it the result of a "brain count." Instead, an individual's standing in terms of intellectual abilities relative to same age peers is communicated by the IQ score.

Reliability and Validity   Because of the numerous revisions of the Stanford-Binet, reliabilities can be cited for each of the various forms of the test. For example, when two separate forms were available (Form L, Form M, 1937 revision), reliability could be calculated using alternate forms. Reliabilities calculated in this manner, as well as in test-retest situations, evidenced reliabilities averaging approximately .90 (e.g., McNemar, 1942). Similarly high reliabilities are reported for the 1960 revision of the Stanford-Binet.

Criterion-related validities for the Stanford-Binet often involve correlating the test scores with measures of school achievement. For example, Churchill and Smith (1974) gave a large sample of children in grades 1 and 3 the Stanford-Binet and standardized tests of basic academic skills (achievement tests). The resulting correlations ranged from .33 to .79 with an approximate average of .54. Although these positive correlations support the validity of the Stanford-Binet, some portion of these relationships may be due to the similarity of the Stanford-Binet and the achievement tests in format.

Wechsler Adult Intelligence Scale (WAIS)

The WAIS (Wechsler, 1955), probably the most widely used and accepted test of intelligence for adults, consists of 11 subtests.[2] Six subtests are combined to form a scale measuring *Verbal* skills, while the remaining five subtests form a scale measuring *Performance* skills. Verbal and Performance scale scores are combined to calculate a Full Scale IQ.

Verbal Subtests   The WAIS verbal subtests include Information, Comprehension, Arithmetic, Similarities, Digit Span, and Vocabulary (see examples in Table 7-2).

Information   Twenty-nine questions are presented to test subjects' general knowledge. Although the answers to these items require memorized factual information, they are not restricted by specialized fields taught in formal schooling. Instead, the items assess the information people have gleaned from daily living in

Table 7-2   Paraphrased WAIS-like Questions from the Verbal Subtests

General Information
1. How many wings does a bird have?
2. How many nickels make a dime?
3. What is steam made of?
4. What is pepper?

General Comprehension
1. What should you do if you see a man forget his hat when he leaves his seat in a restaurant?
2. Why do some people save sales receipts?
3. Why is copper often used in electrical wires?

Arithmetic
1. Sue had two pieces of candy and Joe gave her four more. How many pieces of candy did Sue have altogether?
2. Three children divided 18 pennies equally among themselves. How many pennies did each child receive?
3. If two pencils cost 15¢, what will be the cost of a dozen pencils?

Similarities
1. In what way are a lion and a tiger alike?
2. In what way are a saw and a hammer alike?
3. In what way are an hour and a week alike?
4. In what way are a circle and a triangle alike?

Vocabulary
1. This test consists simply of asking, "What is a _____ ?" or "What does _____ mean?" The words cover a wide range of difficulty or familiarity.

Adapted by permission from the Wechsler Intelligence Scale for Adults. Copyright 1947, 1955 by The Psychological Corporation. All rights reserved.

[2] A revised form of the WAIS, the WAIS-R, became available in August 1981.

their familial and cultural environments. Responses are scored "1" for a correct answer and "0" for an incorrect answer.

Comprehension   The subject's level of practical judgment and common sense is measured with 14 items. These questions ask the subject to explain what should be done under certain circumstances, why certain social conventions are followed, and the meaning of various sayings or proverbs. This subtest assesses social judgment, the ability to apply past information in everyday situations, and a capacity for insight or abstraction. A certain amount of "reality testing" is a part of the Comprehension subtest: the subject's concept of the world, of society and of self are checked against some relatively objective standards. More than the recall of facts is required: the comprehension questions assess the subject's ability to make active and sensible use of these facts. Item responses are scored "2," "1," or "0," based on the scorer's judgment of full, partial, or no credit for the answer.

Arithmetic   This subtest evaluates the subject's ability to solve elementary school-level arithmetic problems. Since the problems do not go beyond this level, this subtest is more a measure of concentration and attention span than arithmetic ability alone. The 14 problems (scored "1" or "0") are presented orally, and the subject cannot use paper and pencil. This subtest is timed, and, in some cases, extra points are awarded for rapid correct responses.

Similarities   Each subject is required to describe how several pairs of things are alike. The subject's memory, comprehension, abstract reasoning, and capacity for associative thinking and conceptual judgments are tapped with this subtest. There are 13 items scored "2," "1," or "0."

Digit span   Subjects are instructed by the examiner, "I am going to say some numbers, listen carefully, and when I am through say them right after me" (Wechsler, 1955). A series of lists (3 to 9 digits per list) is presented orally. The subject is required to reproduce the first series of lists as given, and to repeat each list in the second series in a backward order. Relaxed and attentive subjects perform better on this test than do easily distractible, anxious, or nonattending subjects. The 17 subtest trials assess attention, short-term memory, and immediate auditory recall (scored "1" or "0").

Vocabulary   Forty words of increasing difficulty are presented to the subject orally and on a printed word list. This subtest measures the subject's range of ideas, thought content, and the relative richness of his or her cognitive processes and environment (scored "2," "1," or "0" for most items). Vocabulary subtest scores are most highly correlated with complete WAIS scores and therefore this subtest is said to be the best indicator of general intellectual functioning. The subject's score is primarily dependent on his or her wealth of educational experiences, and test performance is not thought to be affected by the subject's psychological disorders or current turmoil.

Performance Subtests   The Performance subtests of the WAIS are as follows: Digit Symbols, Picture Completion, Block Design, Picture Arrangement, and Object Assembly (see examples in Table 7-3).

Table 7-3   WAIS-like Questions from the Performance Subtests

Performance tasks involve the use of blocks, cut-out figures, paper and pencil puzzles, etc. The WAIS-like items in the diagram are from the Digit Symbol subtest.

WAIS Digit Symbol Test

1	2	3	4	5	6
√	↵	II	∂	/	◇

SAMPLE

2	1	4	6	3	5	2	1	3	4	2	1	3	1	2	3

Adapted by permission from the Wechsler Intelligence Scale for Adults. Copyright 1947, 1955 by The Psychological Corporation. All rights reserved.

These are simulated items.

Digit symbol   This performance subtest contains nine numbers that are paired with nine symbols. The subject is presented with this "answer key" and a sheet with a series of numbers (see Table 7-3). The task is to fill in as many of the symbols that correspond to the numbers as possible during a 90-second trial interval. Quality task performance requires a coordination of visual and motor capacities and psychomotor speed and thus measures visual-motor dexterity and fine-motor coordination. Digit symbol can also be used to indicate a subject's degree of persistence in sticking to an unattractive task.

Picture completion   Each of 21 pictures has an important component that is missing and the subject must identify the missing component. This is a test of visual discrimination, concentration, and reasoning in which the subject's ability to differentiate essential from nonessential details is assessed. One point is awarded for each correct response provided within a 20-second time limit.

Block design   Blocks that are red, white, or both red and white on various sides, are presented to the subject along with a design printed on cards. The subject's task is to arrange the blocks to make them look like a picture. The task is initially modeled for the subject using a practice design. There are 10 actual test designs of increasing difficulty. The subject is timed and bonus points are available for rapid and correct responding. Block design performance reflects nonverbal reasoning, performance speed, and visual motor coordination.

Picture arrangement   There are eight sets of cards in this performance subtest, each of which contains pictures that the subject must put into proper sequence to tell a story. This subtest primarily measures the subject's ability to employ accurate visual perception, to have foresight and planning, and to a lesser extent, to interpret social situations. The subtest is timed, and bonuses are available for varying degrees of speedy and accurate performance.

Object assembly   Four different objects that have been dissembled into pieces are presented one at a time to the subject. Subjects are instructed to "put this together as quickly as you can." Although this is another test of visual-motor coordination, the subject plays a more active role than in the Picture Arrangement subscale by producing something from the almost unrecognizable parts. Visual analysis, simple assembly skills, and the ability to deal with part-whole relationships are measured with this subtest. Points are awarded for correct arrangement of parts and for rapid assembly.

Standardization Sample   The standardization of the WAIS was accomplished according to the 1950 U. S. Census. Specifically, the test norms were based on subjects from each of seven age groups with an equal number of males and females from four different geographic regions. Cases were also selected to achieve an urban/rural balance, a white/nonwhite balance, and a representative sampling of occupations and educational levels.

Test Administration and Scoring   Individual administrations of the WAIS should follow a standard procedure: the same procedures that were followed during the collection of the normative data. As reviewers of the procedural, situational, and interpersonal variables in individual intelligence testing have emphasized (Sattler & Theye, 1967), valid results from the WAIS require standard test-administration procedures. For example, an examiner who gives praise contigently for correct answers, as compared to a friendly but noncontingently rewarding examiner, produces an inflation of the subject's score (Edlund, 1974). Much like the requirement for replication of an experiment, standard administration is vital. Adherence to the testing procedures is especially important for the clinician since departures from standard procedures are more likely to affect specialized groups than normal groups (Sattler & Theye, 1967).

Prior to test administration, the examiner should be well acquainted with test materials and procedures. Test materials should be conveniently arranged on a surface appropriate as a working area for both the subject and the examiner. Moreover, time should be spent talking with the subject to establish rapport before beginning the test. Testing should then be done in an unhurried manner and the examiner should make an effort to elicit the subject's cooperation and to maintain motivation. Comments by the examiner such as, "I hope you find this interesting," or "Here is something different for you to try," are acceptable. However, direct feedback about test performance is not acceptable (i.e., informing the subject "that's right" or "that's correct") (Wechsler, 1955). The examiner always reads the instructions and test questions directly from the manual in order to ensure standard wording.

Items in each of the subscales are arranged in order of increasing difficulty, and after a predetermined number of consecutive errors the examiner discontinues questioning from one subtest and moves on to the next one. The actual number of consecutive errors varies from one subtest to another, but the examiner has these discontinuance rules at hand during testing. This procedure is designed to prevent a subject who is performing poorly from experiencing an excessive amount of frustration.

The scoring of the various test items is completed according to criteria provided in the manual so as to minimize subjectivity. In instances where objective scores are not as readily available (e.g., in the Vocabulary subtest), numerous sample answers for each score category are provided. The subject's subtest scores are then converted into scale scores. This is accomplished by computing the subject's exact age to the nearest month, selecting the scaled-scores table for that age in the rear of the manual, and identifying the correct scale score for the subject's raw score. These scale scores put the various subtest performances into a consistent framework and allow the examiner to make comparisons between different subtests. Scale scores are then plotted on the WAIS answer sheet in the form of a "profile." The WAIS profile (Figure 7-3) provides a pictorial representation of the subject's relative standing on each of the subtests in comparison to the normative data.

Reliability and Validity   Reliability coefficients for the WAIS are high, ranging from .90 to .97 for the Full Scale IQs and from .84 to .96 for the Verbal and Performance scales (Matarazzo, 1972). These results were obtained using a variety of

TABLE OF SCALED SCORE EQUIVALENTS												
	RAW SCORE											
Scaled Score	Information	Comprehension	Arithmetic	Similarities	Digit Span	Vocabulary	Digit Symbol	Picture Completion	Block Design	Picture Arrangement	Object Assembly	Scaled Score
19	29	27–28		26	17	78–80	87–90					19
18	28	26		25		76–77	83–86	21			36	44	18
17	27	25	18	24		74–75	79–82		48	35	43	17
16	26	24	17	23	16	71–73	76–78	20	47	34	42	16
15	25	23	16	22	15	67–70	72–75		46	33	41	15
14	23–24	22	15	21	14	63–66	69–71	19	44–45	32	40	14
13	21–22	21	14	19–20		59–62	66–68	18	42–43	30–31	38–39	13
12	19–20	20	13	17–18	13	54–58	62–65	17	39–41	28–29	36–37	12
11	17–18	19	12	15–16	12	47–53	58–61	15–16	35–38	26–27	34–35	11
10	15–16	17–18	11	13–14	11	40–46	52–57	14	31–34	23–25	31–33	10
9	13–14	15–16	10	11–12	10	32–39	47–51	12–13	28–30	20–22	28–30	9
8	11–12	14	9	9–10		26–31	41–46	10–11	25–27	18–19	25–27	8
7	9–10	12–13	7–8	7–8	9	22–25	35–40	8–9	21–24	15–17	22–24	7
6	7–8	10–11	6	5–6	8	18–21	29–34	6–7	17–20	12–14	19–21	6
5	5–6	8–9	5	4		14–17	23–26	5	13–16	9–11	15–18	5
4	4	6–7	4	3	7	11–13	18–22	4	10–12	8	11–14	4
3	3	5	3	2		10	15–17	3	6–9	7	8–10	3
2	2	4	2	1	6	9	13–14	2	3–5	6	5–7	2
1	1	3	1		4–5	8	12	1	2	5	3–4	1
0	0	0–2	0	0	0–3	0–7	0–11	0	0–1	0–4	0–2	0

Figure 7-3   Ms. A's WAIS profile. This particular subject is a 33-year-old female piano teacher, who had completed two years of college. Reproduced from the Wechsler Intelligence Scale for Adults, copyright 1947, 1955 by The Psychological Corporation. All rights reserved.

methods, leaving little question that the WAIS is a reliable instrument. However, the reliabilities of the individual subtests are consistently lower than those of the overall scale, probably due to the small number of items that constitute some of the individual subtests. Caution must therefore be exercised when making judgments based on single subtests (Highlight 7-4).

Using various methods, the consensus of research supports the validity of the WAIS. For example, Conry and Plant (1965) found the WAIS IQ scores of 335 college freshmen to be predictive of the criterion of college grade-point average (correlated .43) and predictive of academic rank in high school (correlated .62). Similarly, according to Matarazzo's (1972) summary of thousands of studies, the average correlation between IQ and academic grades is .50. Such a correlation, however, accounts for only 25% of the common variance.

IQ scores have also been found to be useful predictors of success in job training and on-the-job proficiency (Ghiselli, 1973). In fact, IQ scores are consistently better predictors than measures of more specific abilities that were relevant to the occupational criteria. These results are evident in Table 7-4, where the correlation coefficients between intelligence and training and proficiency data (first two col-

---

Highlight 7-4   Factor Analyses of the Wechsler Tests

Wechsler has produced tests of intelligence for adults, children, and preschoolers. When a researcher conducts a factor analysis of one of the Wechsler tests, the goal is to examine the interrelationships of the subtests. Cohen has factor analyzed both an earlier version of the WAIS (the Wechsler-Bellvue) (1952a; 1952b) and the WAIS itself (1957a; 1957b). The first factor to emerge involves the Vocabulary, Comprehension, Similarities, and Information subtests. Since these tasks share a focus on the ability to verbally comprehend, this factor was labeled *Verbal Comprehension*. A second factor included Object Assembly, Block Design, Picture Completion, and Picture Arrangement. This factor was labeled *Perceptual Organization*, because each subtest required nonverbal perceptual analysis. Digit Span and Arithmetic subtests contributed to a lesser factor labeled *Memory* or *Freedom from Distractibility*. The consistency of this factor structure is evident in the similarity of results from factor analyses of both normal and disturbed groups (e.g., Berger, Bernstein, Klein, Cohen, & Lucas, 1964; Sprague & Quay, 1966; Zimmerman, Whitmyre & Fields, 1970).

Similarly, factor analyses of the Wechsler Intelligence Scale for Children (WISC) and its revised form (WISC-R), as well as factor analyses of the Wechsler Preschool and Primary Scale of Intelligence (WPPSI), have reported *Verbal Comprehension* and *Perceptual Organization* factors, and a less stable factor *Freedom from Distractibility* (Finch, Kendall, Entin, Montgomery, & Schwartz, 1979; Hagen & Kaufman, 1975; Kaufman, 1975; Wallbrown, Blaha, & Wherry, 1973).

In general, the observed consistency in the factor structure of the Wechsler tests and the contents of the two major factors lend support to Wechsler's (1955) original guideline that the subtests are best grouped into Verbal (Verbal Comprehension) and Performance (Perceptual Ability) categories.

umns) are higher than the correlation coefficients between specific abilities and training and performance data (last six columns) for nearly all occupational areas. Practical skills involved in IQ tests are more central to job performance than any single specific ability.

The correlations between IQ and other types of behavior are not always as strong. The validity of the WAIS is most evident in research that uses the IQ to predict intellectually relevant behaviors such as scholastic performance, rate of school attrition, and social and personal adaptation.

Interpretation of Test Results   The WAIS manual provides the normative information that allows for an interpretation of the individual's intellectual functioning in relation to other Americans of the same age. To do this, the subtest scale scores are directly added together to produce a Verbal Score that is then converted to a Verbal IQ and a Performance Score that is converted to a Performance IQ. The Verbal and Performance Scores are summed and this total score is then converted into a Full Scale IQ using tables provided in the test manual. The examiner can then determine the subject's overall standing by consulting the table of intelligence classification (see Table 7-5).

The Full Scale IQ is useful for intellectual classification, yet the clinician is also interested in the individual's relative strengths and weaknesses as evident in the scores on the various subtests. These scores are usually examined within the WAIS profile. For example, a female piano teacher who took the WAIS received a Full Scale IQ of 115, with a Verbal IQ of 117 and a Performance IQ of 112. Overall, this subject fell in the High Average range of intelligence. When we look at the profile in Figure 7-3, we see that this subject's subscale scores varied a moderate amount, ranging from 17 to 9. This is a statistically significant amount of variability, which leads the examiner to further explore the subtest scores.

Ms. A appears above average on practical judgment or common sense (Comprehension) and Vocabulary. In contrast, Arithmetic and Digit Symbol as well as Digit Span and Block Design were Ms. A's weaknesses. It has been argued that the timed tests on which Ms. A did poorly are the same tests that are the most sensitive to anxiety and that when they are disproportionately low the subject's anxiety may have been interfering with task performance. In this case, Ms. A did poorly on Digit Span and several timed tests and the notion of interfering anxiety appears to be a worthwhile hypothesis for the further inquiry of the clinical psychologist. Interestingly, the anxiety that we hypothesize to be interfering with Ms. A's performance is more likely to be situational in nature ("state anxiety") than a generalized trait of Ms. A's ("trait anxiety"), according to recent research (e.g., Hodges & Spielberger, 1966).

Analyses of scatter in WAIS subtests   Scatter analyses examine the variation among the individual's subtests with the hypothesis that the larger variation ("scatter") results from pathological rather than normal conditions. Scatter is sometimes seen in the WAIS profile of normal individuals, but it is more likely that the performance of a schizophrenic subject will show excessive variability (Korchin, 1976). This scatter can be either intertest or intratest. *Intertest scatter* is the variability between a subject's subtest scores, while *intratest scatter* is the pattern of successes and failures within a particular subtest. Extreme scatter of either

Table 7-4 Mean Validity Coefficients for Various Aptitude Areas for Training and Proficiency Criteria in Various Occupational Areas for Studies Between 1920 and 1971. The Number of Studies Averaged Ranges from 100 to 10,000.

| | Aptitude Area | | | | | | | |
| | Intelligence | | Spatial and Mechanical | | Perceptual Accuracy | | Motor Abilities | |
Occupational Area	Training	Proficiency	Training	Proficiency	Training	Proficiency	Training	Proficiency
Managers	.29	.29	.28	.22	.23	.25	.02	.14
Clerical	.46	.30	.34	.17	.40	.29	.14	.16
Sales clerks	—	-.06	—	.14	—	-.02	—	.09
Salespeople	—	.34	—	.20	—	.23	—	.16
Protective occup.	.65	.23	.35	.18	.30	.21	—	.14
Service occup.	.42	.26	.31	.13	.25	.10	.21	.15
Vehicle operator	.21	.15	.31	.20	.09	.17	.31	.25
Trades and crafts	.41	.25	.41	.23	.35	.24	.20	.19
Industrial workers	.38	.20	.40	.20	.20	.20	.28	.22

Adapted from E.E. Ghiselli, The validity of aptitude tests in personnel selection. *Personnel Psychology*, 1973, 26, 461–477. Copyright *Personnel Psychology*, 1973. Also adapted from T. Bouchard, *Differential psychology*. New York: Wiley, in preparation. Reprinted by permission. These data are summarized over numerous studies and they include a variety of different tests of intelligence.

Table 7-5   Categories of Intellectual Functioning

IQ	Classification	Percent Included
130 and above	Very superior	2.2
120–129	Superior	6.7
110–119	High average (bright)	16.1
90–109	Average	50.0
80–89	Low average (dull)	16.1
70–79	Borderline	6.7
69 and below	Mentally deficient	2.2

From D. Wechsler, *Wechsler Intelligence Scale for Children—Revised Manual*. New York: The Psychological Corporation, 1974. Reproduced by permission. Copyright 1974 by The Psychological Corporation, New York, New York. All rights reserved.

type can be indicative of psychological problems, but it is important to recognize that the scatter may also be the result of factors associated with the subject's sociocultural background or actual differences in the subject's abilities or personality.

Although clinicians have expended much research energy, there does not appear to be specific, clinically diagnostic meaning associated with patterns of subtest scatter. In a series of reviews by Guertin and his colleagues (Guertin, Ladd, Frank, Robin, & Heister, 1966; Guertin, Rabin, Frank, & Ladd, 1962), these researchers stated that:

> *Measures of intersubtest scatter frequently distinguish groups of delinquents, schizophrenics, and organics from normals; however, the diagnostic value of this "sign" alone is negligible since it is clearly not unique to any one diagnostic group or sufficiently discriminative to be reliable in the individual case (p. 16, 1962).*

They again stated in 1966 that:

> *Evidence continues to accumulate indicating that subtest patterns differentiate between diagnostic groups, but these patterns alone are not diagnostic because they are not unique (p. 402).*

Some of the possible reasons for the ineffectiveness of diagnostic interpretations based on the WAIS profile include the insufficiently high reliabilities of the subtests themselves (differences between scores on two tests of moderate reliability may be due to the unreliability of the tests rather than due to the subject), the naturally occurring rate of statistically significant subtest differences in the general (normal) population, and the fact that the profile may be the result of educational, cultural, and employment factors rather than of any type of specific psychological dysfunction. Also, pattern analyis assumes that the variance for each subtest is homogeneous (each subtest contributes equally to the total test) and that within each subtest all items are arranged in order of increasing difficulty—two assumptions that are not entirely met by the WAIS.

Sociopathy Those persons diagnosed as "sociopaths," "psychopaths," or "personality disorders" characteristically have difficulty with the law, profit little from experience or punishment, frequently violate social norms, and have difficulty developing close relationships. Such persons consistently score higher on performance subtests than on verbal subtests. There is, however, an important qualification—although *group* means for sociopaths do evidence a performance-greater-than-verbal differential, this is not always true in each individual case. Therefore, knowledge that a person's Performance IQ is greater than their Verbal IQ is not sufficient for a diagnosis of sociopathy nor would a person who had been independently diagnosed as sociopathic necessarily have a Performance greater than Verbal IQ.

Clinical interpretation of WAIS subtests Aside from providing a quantitative index of general intellectual functioning, and in addition to providing the different scores on the subtests, the intelligence test can also be used to elicit material for the clinician to interpret. Such interpretations, although their validity remains undetermined, involve drawing inferences from certain responses, and making use of that special process of "clinical intuition."

What special meaning might there be, for example, in the following response to an item from the Comprehension subtest: Examiner: "What does the saying 'One swallow doesn't make a summer' mean?" Subject: "One beer doesn't mean its summertime." The saying actually refers to jumping to conclusions: generalizing from seeing one summer bird (a swallow) to the conclusion that it is therefore summer. The subject in the example reacted to "swallow" in terms of his or her beer consumption. Such a response could be interpreted to indicate that the subject spends a good bit of time drinking beer (and may be further suggestive of problems with alcohol) or, that he has a quick sense of humor.

An item from the information subtest might ask: "Who are Woodward and Bernstein?" A subject's response, might be, for example: "Weren't they the communist spies who tried to destroy our country by creating Nixon's involvement in the Watergate affair? Yeah, they're the ones who did it." Consider also a different subject's response to the examiner's query, "How far is it from San Francisco to New York?" The reply: "I'd fly and not worry about how far, let someone else worry about how far, all I want to do is get there." In both of these examples the subject's attempt to provide anwers to information questions also reveals potential clues to his or her personality. Paranoia may be an accurate interpretation of the first response, and certainly there is evidence of a certain amount of righteousness being conveyed. The second response communicates a rather uncaring attitude and a desire to achieve an end without concern for the means used to reach the end. This type of response hints that the subject is manipulative of others and not interpersonally genuine. These interpretations go beyond scoring the test items to determine an IQ, and a subject's response to any of the items on an intelligence test may be seen as revealing something about him or her as a person. Caution must be used to further check such interpretations with additional assessment data.

Indications of severe psychological dysfunction can also be obtained from responses to the WAIS. The examiner asks a vocabulary item, "What does the word 'pattern' mean?'' The subject replies: "The pattern of my life is an integrated connection, a pattern that cannot be copied but one that is like all others because we all breathe.'' This response to a straightforward vocabulary question is suggestive of a thought disorder. That is, the subject has responded to "pattern'' as if it were a reference to himself. Typically, the word "pattern'' does not elicit a self-reference, and excessive unsolicited self-referencing is suggestive of a thought disorder. The response is also bizarre and overelaborated. Diagnoses are not based on such limited samples of behavior, but this type of response illustrates a schizophrenic type of thinking.

Performance subtests can likewise provide material for clinical interpretation. For example, after the testing is completed, the examiner may bring back one set of the picture arrangement cards and place them in the order that the subject decided was the proper order "to tell a story.'' The examiner might then ask the subject to describe the story in some detail, telling about what is going on in each part of the story. The resulting transcript, much like a projective test response, can then be interpreted by the examiner (Rapaport, Gill, & Schafer, 1945; Wechsler, 1958). For example, pictures from the picture arrangement subtest had been put in the following order by the subject: a picture of a man in jail was placed first, a picture of the man before a judge second, and a picture of the man being caught stealing last. The examiner asked the subject to describe the story in the pictures and the subject replied "a con came up for probation, got out but got caught again.'' The story offers an expectancy of repetitive crime (that pardon leads to recidivism) and an absence of a sense of rehabilitation. The correct series has the picture of the theft first, the judge second, and the jail scene third, and communicates a more morally acceptable story of a criminal who is caught, convicted, and sent to prison.

Short Forms of the WAIS   As early as 1962, Satz and Mogel proposed an abbreviated form of the WAIS for clinical use, and soon after that Pauker (1963) suggested a split-half abbreviated form of the WAIS. Other suggested short forms include selected subtests or selected items from different subtests used together. Early research regarding the ability of short forms to estimate the Full Scale scores relied mostly on an examination of the short form-Full Scale correlations (e.g., Doppelt, 1956). More recently, Resnik and Entin (1977) proposed three criteria for evaluating short forms of intelligence tests:

1.   Correlations between the short form and standard form should be significant.
2.   *t* tests between the mean short form and standard form IQ's should be *non*significant.
3.   The percentage of changes in IQ classification should not be so great as to preclude the effective use of the short form [subjects placed in a classification category (see Table 7-5) based on the complete test usually should be placed in the same category based on a short form]. Inaccurate classification would dramatically reduce the practical utility of the test.

Using these criteria, Finch, Thornton, and Montgomery (1974) and Edinger and Norwood (1975) evaluated the relative efficacy of various WAIS short forms.

These authors used hospitalized psychiatric patients and clinic outpatients, respectively. In both studies, the correlations between the short-form and complete-form IQs were high (i.e., *r*s in the .80 to .95 range), but most mean scores were significantly different and the rate of IQ *mis*classifications relatively high. Although the Satz-Mogel (1962) short form satisfactorily met all three criteria with black inpatients (Finch et al., 1974), and the Pauker (1963) form had a reasonably low misclassification rate with male outpatients (Edinger & Norwood, 1975), the safest conclusion regarding short forms of the WAIS is that none of the short forms consistently met all three criteria. Short forms essentially reduce the observations from which the clinician can derive hypotheses. Moreover, it has been pointed out that any new short version of subtests or items raises issues of reliability, validity, and score standardization, none of which can be assumed to be the same as the complete version of the test (Tellegen & Briggs, 1967).

An additional approach, using multivariant profile analysis, was used by Geobel and Satz (1975) to examine the profile similarity of the standard WAIS and the Satz and Mogel (1962) short form. These authors report that the WAIS profiles of the standard and short-form scales were similar. Since this research utilized psychiatric and brain-injured subjects, an extension and validation with normal subjects appears necessary before extensive use of the short form is recommended.

In the final analysis, one must be concerned with the question "Does the time and money that is saved by using a short form warrant the risk of misclassification?" When a clinician is using the WAIS to provide an initial screening, for example, to identify persons whose IQs are sufficiently high to require that they be excluded from a program designed for "remedial training," short forms may suffice. However, when one wants to use the test results for more detailed assessment and diagnosis, the use of short forms cannot at this time be recommended.

ASSESSING INTELLIGENCE IN CHILDREN

As in the case of adults, there are many tests that are designed to assess a child's mental abilities. In spite of the large number of such tests, both the Wechsler Intelligence Scale for Children-Revised and perhaps to a lesser degree, the Stanford-Binet Intelligence Scale are the most often used and most widely accepted measures of intelligence in children.

Wechsler Intelligence Scale for Children-Revised (WISC-R)

The WISC-R, published in 1974, is a revision of the 1949 WISC. The revision includes a change in the ages that are appropriate for the scale. The WISC was designed for children between 5 years, 0 months, and 0 days to 15 years, 11 months, and 30 days; however, the new WISC-R covers ages 6 years, 0 months, 0 days to 16 years, 11 months, and 30 days.

In order to achieve the revision and update of the already well-established WISC, comments and criticisms from the research and professional experiences of psychologists were solicited. In response to these concerns came new test items, materials, and instructions. In addition, all the proposed changes had to be tried out and evaluated prior to the adopting of the revisions.

Test Standardization   The WISC-R was standardized on 2200 white and nonwhite American children who were considered representative of the entire U. S. population as indicated by the 1970 census. Two hundred children in each of 11 age groups were utilized. There were major efforts to also take into account such variables as sex, race, geographic region, occupation of the head of household, and urban-rural residence. Each of the age levels included representative proportions of girls and boys, whites and nonwhite, and persons whose families were from four geographic regions and five different occupational groups. Finally, based on the total sample, a balance of urban and rural residences was obtained.

Subtests   The 12 subtests of the WISC-R are the same as those of the original WISC. These include Information, Similarities, Arithmetic, Vocabulary, Comprehension, and Digit Span as the Verbal portion of the test. Picture Completion, Picture Arrangement, Block Design, Object Assembly, Coding, and Mazes serve as the Performance portion of the test. Two subtests, Digit Span (Verbal) and Mazes (Performance), are optional, and most administrators of the WISC-R include only the 10 major subtests. In general, these subtests are structurally very similar to those of the WAIS, with the content of the material being age appropriate for children.

The mazes subtest, not included in the WAIS, is a supplemental performance task in which the child is shown a maze from a booklet and told, "This is a maze. You are to start here (point to the start) and find your way out here (point to the exit) without crossing any lines. Try your best not to go into any blind alleys— that is, stay out of roads that are blocked." The examiner checks to see if the child understands, informs the child not to lift the pencil until finished, and instructs the child to begin. Scoring of the maze subtest is basically an error count. Errors are defined as instances where the child enters a blind alley, and an entrance is defined as a crossing of the imaginary line across the mouth of the blind alley. This subtest includes nine mazes that are performed within varying time limits.

Test Administration   As with the WAIS, the intention of the WISC-R is to assess the child's performance under a *fixed set of conditions* (Wechsler, 1974), requiring that each individual examiner precisely follow the instructions in the manual. Careful adherence to the testing instructions, however, should not supplant the examiner's relationship with the child. The examiner should talk with the child, put the child at ease, and maintain the child's interest and effort toward doing well. Rapport is important, especially so with young subjects. It is also important to have the testing materials organized and to have mastered the details of administration in advance. The procedural rules are similar to those for the WAIS.

The 12 subtests are administered in a standard order. Although the test author grants permission to reorder the subtests to meet the needs of a particular child, Sattler (1974) strongly urges that since standardization was conducted with the standard order, test administration should follow that order. Since some of the Performance tests have been thought to help maintain interest in the testing materials, Wechsler decided to alternate the two different types of subtests to maintain rapport.

There are also instructions for the starting, discontinuing and, when necessary, timing of each of the subtests. Since the items within each subtest are ordered from the easiest to the most difficult, the examiner starts at different points in the sequence depending on the child's age and estimated abilities. If the test began at a level too difficult for the child, the examiner would present the earlier items in reverse sequence.

Scoring   The WISC-R manual provides directions for scoring each subtest. In cases where all the possible specific answers are not presented, scoring criteria are outlined, such that scoring of the WISC-R requires minimal subjective interpretation (Wechsler, 1974). For example, when scoring answers, Wechsler (1974) indicates that "only the *content* of the response—not the elegance of the child's expression—be evaluated. *A child's score on a Verbal item should never be penalized because of improper grammar or poor pronunciation"* (p. 61).

The scores for each subtest are tallied and recorded on the front page of the answer form. Subtest scores are converted to scale scores using a table in the WISC-R manual that takes into account the child's age in years, months, and days. From the obtained scaled scores, the Verbal score, Performance score, and Full Scale score are obtained by summing the five major Verbal subtests, the five major Performance subtests, and all 10 subtest scores, respectively (see Figure 7-4).

Reliability and Validity   The results of a variety of assessments of the reliability and validity of the WISC-R are reported in the manual (Weschler, 1974) and summarized by Sattler (1974). It is safe to conclude that the WISC-R is a highly reliable (the majority of the coefficients being > .90) and very valid instrument (concurrent validities with other tests of children's intelligence averaging around .90). Moreover, Sattler (1974) has concluded that the predictive validity of the WISC is favorable. For example, Dudek, Lester, Goldberg, and Dyer (1969) tested 100 children using, among other instruments, the WISC and reported correlations averaging about .50 between the WISC IQ and both teacher's assigned grades and achievement test scores (see Table 7-6). A .50 correlation accounts for 25% of the common variance.

In an earlier summary of a decade of research, Littell (1960) reported that many independent investigators have found predictive validity coefficients between WISC scores and achievement tests/academic criteria averaging approximately .60. In light of the similarities between the WISC and WISC-R, it appears that the WISC-R will be as reliable and valid an instrument as the WISC and that it will find a place within the assessment battery of most clinical psychologists working with children. Additional research using the WISC-R is necessary to confirm these expectations.

Interpretation   Like the WAIS, the WISC-R manual provides normative information to allow an analysis of the subject's intellectual functioning in relation to children of the same age. The WISC-R is also a popular instrument for use in the

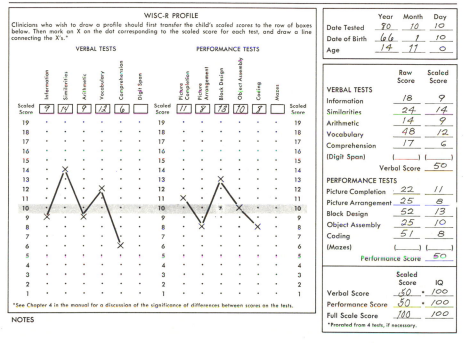

Figure 7-4 (Reproduced from the Wechsler Intelligence scale for Children-Revised, copyright 1971, 1974 by The Psychological Corporation. All rights reserved.)

determination of mental retardation. However, the WISC-R manual provides IQs only as low as 46, and this could have been a hindrance in identifying profoundly retarded subjects. This potential weakness was corrected by Ogden (1975) when he reported extrapolated IQs for the WISC-R that extended beyond those reported in the manual.

When classification of the child's level of retardation is the goal of the assessment, the examiner can check the information provided by the American Association of Mental Deficiency (see Table 7-7). For example, a school-aged child receiving a WISC-R IQ of 59 would be considered *mildly* retarded (see Table 7-7) and might be expected to achieve sixth-grade level performance by the late teens (see Table 7-8). A school-aged child earning a WISC-R IQ of 29 would be considered *severely* retarded, would not be expected to learn academic skills but could profit from habit training.

The more complicated question of the etiology of the retardation—psychosocial deprivation versus brain dysfunction—requires additional analysis. This question may be particularly important in terms of the type of program that is de-

Table 7-6 Correlations of the WISC at Kindergarten and Grades 1 and 2 with Teachers' Grades and Achievement Scores for Grades 1 and 2

Grade	Teachers' Grades		Achievement Test	
	I	II	I	II
K	.42	.40	.49	.53
1	.54	.53	.61	.62
2	—	.51	—	.65

Reprinted with permission of authors and publisher from S.Z. Dudek, E. P. Lester, J.S. Goldberg, and G.B. Dyer. Relationship of Piaget measures to standard intelligence and motor scales. *Perceptual and Motor Skills*, 1969, *28*, 351–362, Table 7.

Note: Dash indicates no correlation reported.

signed for the child. Here, the clinician should carefully examine the child's family history, prior level of functioning, and performance on other tests designed more specifically to test for brain damage. As noted in a review of the use of the WISC with mental retardates (Baumeister, 1964), attempts at achieving additional diagnostic information from the WISC beyond the classification of the level of retardation may be futile. It is likely that such cautions are relevant to the WISC-R.

Scatter analyses of the WISC-R   Scatter analyses have produced mixed results (Sattler, 1974). Generally speaking, significant differences between subtests can provide hypotheses, but the clinician would require additional support from other sources before considering these confirmed. For example, although a poor performance on only the arithmetic subtest may suggest a learning disability, further testing would be desired. Ogdon (1967) has emphasized that it is necessary to consider the extent to which an entire host of variables—age, sex, race, socioeconomic status, education, special training, family background, and others—have affected the child's performance on one or more subtests. For example, a family environment where all members displayed a fear of arithmetic-type problems may have led to the child's poor performance in that one area.

Juvenile delinquency   In research with delinquents using the WISC, there has been a great deal of support for a Verbal-Performance discrepancy (Smith, 1969; Wiens, Matarazzo & Gaver, 1959). Juvenile delinquents consistently show a Performance Scale IQ significantly higher than a Verbal Scale IQ. Kendall and Little (1977) examined WISC-R data and reported higher Performance than Verbal IQs in a representative sample of juvenile offenders. However, Sattler (1974) pointed out that the discrepancy that occurs in groups of delinquents cannot necessarily be used as a diagnostic sign for individual children. The same Performance > Verbal discrepancy may be the outcome of any number of learning difficulties that result, in part, in a lowered Verbal functioning. For example, a socioeconomically deprived background may effect the child's verbal abilities.

Learning disabilities   Unlike juvenile delinquents, who can be identified by incidents with the court and, in many cases, placement under the supervision and

Table 7-7 AAMD Standard Deviation (SD) Ranges According to Measured Intelligence Levels

Word Description of the Level of Retardation	Range in Standard Deviations	Corresponding Range in IQ Scores	
		WISC (50 = 15)	Stanford-Binet (50 = 16)
Borderline	−1.01 to −2.00	70–84	68–83
Mild	−2.01 to −3.00	55–69	52–67
Moderate	−3.01 to −4.00	40–54	36–51
Severe	−4.01 to −5.00	25–39	20–35
Profound	Below −5.00	Under 25	Under 20

From R.F. Heber, A manual on terminology and classification in mental retardation. *American Journal of Mental Deficiency*, 1961, 64, Monograph Supplement. Copyright 1961 by the American Association on Mental Deficiency. Reprinted with permission. 50 = Mean, 15/16 = Standard Deviation.

Table 7-8 Levels of adaptive behavior paralleling the classification of measured intelligence

Level	Preschool Age 0–5 Maturation and Development	School Age 6–21 Training and Education	Adult 21 Social and Vocational Adequacy
Mild	Can develop social and communication skills, minimal retardation in sensorimotor areas; rarely distinguished from normal until later age	Can learn academic skills to approximately 6th grade level by late teens. Cannot learn general high school subjects. Needs special education, particularly at secondary school age levels.	Capable of social and vocational adequacy with proper education and training. Frequently needs supervision and guidance when under serious social or economic stress.
Moderate	Can talk or learn to communicate; poor social awareness; fair motor development; may profit from self-help; can be managed with moderate supervision	Can learn functional academic skills to approximately 4th grade level by late teens if given special education	Capable of self-maintenance in unskilled or semiskilled occupations; needs supervision and guidance when under mild social or economic stress
Severe	Poor motor development, speech is minimal; generally unable to profit from training in self-help; little or no communication skills	Can talk or learn to communicate; can be trained in elemental health habits; cannot learn functional academic skills; profits from systematic habit training	Can contribute partially to self-support under complete supervision; can develop self-protection skills to a minimal useful level in controlled environment
Profound	Gross retardation; minimal capacity for functioning in sensorimotor areas; needs nursing care	Some motor development present; cannot profit from training in self-help; needs total care	Some motor and speech development; totally incapable of self-maintenance; needs complete care and supervision

Adapted from W. Sloane and J. Birch, A rationale for degrees of retardation, *American Journal of Mental Deficiency*, 1955, *60*, 258–264. Copyright 1955 American Association on Mental Deficiency. Adapted by permission.

care of the state, children with "learning disabilities" are difficult to pinpoint accurately. Learning disability means too many things to too many different writers. For example, studies have defined "learning disability" using criteria such as neurological difficulties or failure in certain school subjects. In one study that compared children with known neurological difficulty, those with suspected neurological difficulty, and those without any neurological difficulties (Boshes & Myklebust, 1964), there were no significant differences between the groups on the WISC or WISC subtest scores. When performances on the WISC of underachievers (perhaps learning disabled) are examined, they tend to show better scores on the Performance than on the Verbal subtests (cf. Jenkin, Spivack, Levine, & Savage, 1964). Thus, different definitions of learning disability have led to different findings with the WISC. More precise definitions of specific deficiencies in skills required for successful school performance, rather than these inexact attempts at defining a single "learning disability," are necessary before the WISC can be effectively used in the diagnosis and treatment of learning disabilities.

Emotional disturbance   Studies using the WISC in an attempt to identify subtests that differentiate emotionally disturbed children from other groups of children have not been successful (Sattler, 1974). The overall level of intelligence of the children has also not been an indication of emotional disturbance. For example, the mean Full Scale IQ of one sample of emotionally disturbed children who were psychiatric inpatients was 113—13 points above average for the standardization sample (Finch, Childress, Wilkins, & Kendall, 1974)! Thus, children who are troubled by emotional disturbances are not necessarily below average in intelligence; they may be *above* average in some cases.

It would appear from this brief review that the different childhood disorders, excluding mental retardation, do not show characteristic patterns on the WISC/WISC-R. This suggests that many of the childhood disorders can occcur within a wide range of intellectual abilities. Clearly, while intelligence tests provide a valid index of the child's mental abilities and are quite useful for diagnostic categorization in the area of mental retardation, they would not be considered as sufficient information for diagnostic categorization in other areas.

Case illustration   Ralph J. is a 13-year-old, male, seventh-grade child who was referred for intellectual testing because his teacher and parents had conferred and agreed that he was not meeting their expectations in school. Ralph's WISC-R profile is presented in Figure 7-4. As we can see, Ralph obtained a Verbal IQ of 100, a Performance IQ of 100, and a Full Scale IQ of 100.

Ralph achieved scale scores of 12 or greater on Similarities and Block Design subtests, indicating that his reasoning abilities in both the verbal and performance modes are quite good. Similarly, his vocabulary score indicates more than adequate mastery of the spoken language. In contrast, the Comprehension score is quite low suggesting a lack of common sense and a disinterest in daily concerns. The low Picture Arrangement score would suggest a lack of social awareness as well as poor foresight and planning. The Coding score was also low indicating poor hand-eye coordination and a limited degree of perseverance.

The results of testing with a full battery of psychological instruments would be needed for a complete analysis. From an overview of the WISC-R on page 267, however, it appears that Ralph has the necessary intellectual abilities to perform at an average level, but that social awareness, common sense, and hand-eye coordination are areas of weakness. Essentially, Ralph appears to be capable of better school performance but his social deficits and poor coordination have interfered with his early socialization and he apparently does not want to be involved any further at this time. In fact, Ralph is quite overweight, has few friends, and is not involved in sports or activities.

Short Forms of the WISC-R   Among the alternatives to administering the entire WISC-R is the selective administration of a WISC-R short form. The results of short-form research using the WISC are summarized by Sattler (1974) when he states that "short forms are practical, save time, and can serve as screening devices. However, coupled with these advantages are many disadvantages." These disadvantages include the loss of the complete set of scores needed for producing the intellectual profile, and an IQ that is less stable than that obtained from the complete test. Also as evidenced in studies with emotionally disturbed children (Finch et al., 1974) and retarded children (Finch, Ollendick, & Ginn, 1973), misclassification of intellectual capacity occurs 50% of the time and more. The misclassification in these WISC studies and in others using the WISC-R (Kendall & Little, 1977) occurs even though the short form IQs correlate highly with the IQs from the complete test. The general consensus is that the short forms are *not* acceptable substitutes for the full WISC-R when one is concerned with accurate diagnostic classification.

Additional Tests of Child Intelligence

The WISC-R is the instrument of choice in evaluating a child's intellectual capacities. Nevertheless, there are other instruments that may also be useful in special cases.

Peabody Picture Vocabulary Test (PPVT)   The PPVT was developed by Dunn in 1959 and expanded in 1965. The test was standardized on 4012 individuals from the Nashville, Tennessee, area. The PPVT was designed to evaluate children between the ages of 2½ and 18 years by measuring receptive knowledge of vocabulary.

There are 150 picture plates in the PPVT, and each plate has four pictures. The child's task is to point to the picture that best demonstrates the meaning of the word said by the examiner. The PPVT task is untimed, and there are two parallel test forms available. Scores can be converted into mental ages or deviation IQs.

The PPVT is somewhat limited since it measures the extensiveness of vocabulary but does not acquire an assessment for performance tasks. In general, the test is easy to administer and score and is appealing to the child, but it should only be used as a screening device and not in making important decisions about intellectual classification (cf. Kendall & Little, 1977).

Leiter International Performance Scale   While the PPVT focused on the child's vocabulary, the Leiter emphasizes the assessment of performance. Thus, the Leiter can be conducted with children who are language handicapped. There

are only a minimum of instructions for the Leiter, and they may be given in pan-
tomime.

The test materials consist of a series of printed pictures presented on a display
frame. The child's task is to insert wooden blocks into the frame and match the
series on the printed pictures. For example, a series of small, medium, and large
circles presented on the display frame would have to be matched by placing the
small, medium, and large *squares* in the proper place. The test items are arranged
by year levels, and each level begins with an easy task.

The reliability of Leiter IQs has been questioned, the test has been said to ignore totally the verbal abilities component of intellectual functioning, and the
difficulty of items at different levels is said to be uneven (Werner, 1965). Nevertheless, the Leiter is useful in examining the functioning of children who do not
have sufficient language abilities for the WISC-R or the Stanford-Binet. As an
example, consider the autistic child who is severely delayed in language. The
Leiter is particularly suited for this type of child due to the lack of emphasis on
verbal skills. Evaluating the autistic child's intellectual ability with the Leiter can
be very valuable to the clinical psychologist in making appropriate prognostic
statements about the child's potential for acquiring some form of functional
speech. The child with the higher Leiter score would be more likely to be successful in a program for developing speech skills.

ASSESSING INTELLIGENCE OF PRESCHOOL CHILDREN

Psychologists agree that the preschool years are a very important period in each
person's life for the development of intellectual skills and personality characteristics. This time is primarily a time of learning and adjusting to a new and complex
world. Several measures have been developed to assess cognitive and social development in preschoolers and infants. Among the frequently utilized tests are the
Gesell Developmental Schedules (Gesell and Associates, 1949), the Bayley (1965)
Motor and Mental Development Scales, the Cattell (1947) Infant Intelligence
Scale, the Boyd (1974) Developmental Progress Scale, the Vineland Social Maturity Scale (Doll, 1965) and the Uzgiris-Hunt (1975) Ordinal Scales of Psychological
Development. In addition to these tests, the Stanford-Binet is used with
preschoolers as is the Wechsler test developed for preschool children.

Wechsler Preschool and Primary Scale of Intelligence

Wechsler (1967) designed and developed the Wechsler Preschool and Primary
Scale of Intelligence (WPPSI) (along with the Psychological Corporation) as a
test that tapped the age-appropriate intellectual abilities of 4- to 6½-year-olds.
Using a stratified sampling technique and the 1960 U. S. Census, 1200 cases were
selected as the standardization sample. This sample satisfied the requirements of
balancing four major geographic regions, urban-rural areas, white and nonwhite
children, and father's occupation.

Since the WPPSI is very akin to both the WAIS and the WISC-R, we will go into less detail here in our description of the test. Among those subtests similar to
the WISC-R, the WPPSI modifications involved the addition of easier items, the

removal of more difficult ones, and some changes in the method of administration.

Several WPPSI subtests, however, are not present on the WISC-R. One of these, Animal House, requires the child to associate a sign with a symbol (e.g., place the chicken in the correct color house—according to an answer key). This subtest can be considered a substitute for the Coding subtests of the WAIS and WISC-R. The Geometric Design subtest of the WPPSI requires the child to correctly reproduce geometric figures. It measures perceptual ability and visual-motor organization. Finally, the Sentences subtest instructs the child to repeat sentences just as they are said by the examiner. This subtest measures similar abilities as the Digit Span of the WAIS and WISC-R, but is a supplemental subtest that is not often given.

Most WPPSI administration procedures very much resemble those of the WAIS and WISC-R. However, certain changes are permitted due to the age of the subject. For example, if the child appears to be tired, the examination may be discontinued and a second appointment made to complete the testing. In some cases the examiner may want to conduct the test in the child's home to achieve a less disquieting environment than a hospital or clinic. Also, establishing rapport with a young child is of special importance, as is maintaining the child's interest in the tasks.

The administration of the tasks follows a standard order that alternates Verbal and Performance subtests. Scoring is mostly objective, but there are a few places where examiner judgments may be required. Sometimes the child may respond with an answer that may have additional meaning beyond the WPPSI scoring. Responses to stimuli other than the test material itself may also be valuable sources of hypotheses about the child. For example, threats of physical aggression toward the examiner or the task materials may suggest the hypothesis that aggression is a problem in the child's home environment. High degrees of need for achievement may be indicated by a child who continues to try and solve a task beyond the time when a correct solution would earn test credit. Isolated instances should not be overinterpreted; however, consistent indications of a certain type of behavior may prove worthwhile if noted for later verification.

Intellectual classification according to the WPPSI is somewhat less reliable and less valid than with the WISC-R or WAIS. Children's scores at these young age levels tend to show fluctuations (hence lowering reliability) and are less predictive of future behavior. Although Wechsler (1967) interprets the scores as indicative of the child's mental endowment relative to other same-aged children, WPPSI scores can only be used as a tentative indicator of a child's stable intellectual potential due to the likelihood that current developmental or environmental factors may obscure the child's true capabilities.

Research on the WPPSI   WPPSI research has centered on three areas: reliability of specific scoring criteria for certain subtests, comparisons of matched black and white children, and development of a short form (although the test author himself suggested that the test not be abbreviated).

In studying the scoring criteria of the Geometric Designs subtest, Sattler (1976) examined the level of agreement between graduate students and between school psychologists who had each scored 50 designs from 26 available protocols. The reported outcome consisted of unanimous agreement on only 11 out of 50 for graduate students and 7 out of 50 for the school psychologists. These results suggest that caution should be exercised when scoring this WPPSI subtest and that some adjustments may need to be made in the scoring criteria provided in the manual. Although the majority of the WPPSI subtests (like the WAIS and WISC-R subtests) are scored based on objective standards, the Geometric Designs subtest is not and must be scored cautiously.

In Kaufman's study of the performance of matched black and white students on the WPPSI (1973), the white children were found to score significantly higher on Verbal and Full Scale IQs, and at lower age levels, on the Performance IQ as well. These findings are consistent with the general finding (often using WAIS or WISC results) that blacks score, on the average, 10 IQ points lower than whites matched on a number of relevant variables (Shuey, 1966).

Kaufman (1972) proposed a short form of the WPPSI consisting of Comprehension, Arithmetic, Block Design, and Picture Completion subtests. These subtest scores are totaled, multiplied by 1.63, and added to 34.7 to produce the estimated Full Scale IQ. Although correlation coefficients are high (.92 to .94) and low errors of estimate (within 5 to 6 points of the Full Scale score) were reported, Woo-Sam and Zimmerman (1973) found Kaufman's short form to be inaccurate for predictions of individual scores. Again, as with the WAIS and the WISC-R short form studies, there is evidence that consistently undermines the search for viable abbreviated measures of intelligence.

Case Illustration The following is a case of a child with developmental immaturity.[3] The WPPSI subtest scores are as follows:

Verbal Scale	Performance Scale
Information = 8	Animal House = 5
Vocabulary = 13	Picture Completion = 6
Arithmetic = 10	Mazes = 8
Similarities = 7	Geometric Design = 7
Comprehension = 9	Block Design = 9

Psychological Evaluation

Name: Debbie Adams   Date of examination: June 12, 1972
Date of birth: November 25, 1966   Date of report: June 15, 1972
Chronological age: 5-6   Grade: Kindergarten
Test administered: Wechsler Preschool and Primary Scale of Intelligence (WPPSI)

Debbie is an attractive youngster, of average height and weight for her age. While a speech impediment was evident, her speech was understandable. She exhibited some awkwardness in motor coordination. Her walking gait was uneven,

[3]Adapted from Sattler (1974) (pp. 398–400) with the author's permission. The examiner was Jane Jones.

and she had some difficulty in turning the pages of a test booklet. At times she was restless during the testing. However, she was cooperative and attempted to answer the questions and do the tasks asked of her.

The WPPSI results were as follows: Verbal Scale IQ of 96, Performance Scale IQ of 80, and Full Scale IQ of 87 ± 6. Her IQ is in the Dull Normal classification and falls at the 20th percentile rank of children of her age in the normative group, which was roughly representative of the U. S. population. The chances that the range of scores from 81 to 93 includes her true IQ are about 85 out of 100. The good rapport that existed between Debbie and the examiner and the child's ability to follow directions and to attempt to respond to the items suggest that the present results are valid.

Debbie's performance skills are not as well developed as are her verbal skills. The 16-point difference between her scores on the verbal and performance parts of the scale suggest that visual-motor ability, perceptual ability, ability to attend to perceptual details, and persistence are at a level of development that is below normal. In contrast, not only do her verbal skills show more variability than her performance skills, but also the overall level of verbal development is within the normal range. Her outstanding strength was her word knowledge. She was able to define words at a level that was higher than normal and above the average of her verbal scaled scores. Thus, for examle, she gave satisfactory definitions to such words as "fur," "join," and "diamond." Arithmetic skills appear to be at an average level and above the level of the average of her verbal scaled scores.

Debbie's answers were usually short, precise, and direct. Her failures were manifested both by incorrect answers and by her saying "No" when she did not know an answer. She seemed to experience more difficulty on the Similarities subtest questions than on most other verbal subtests. Instead of giving analogies, she would repeat part of the question in her answer or give associations. For example, to the question, "You ride in a train and you also ride in a - -," she said, "choo-choo." This one verbal subtest, more than any of the other verbal subtests, reflected her difficulty in grasping concepts and suggested some immaturity in reasoning. She also at first refused to complete the Animal House subtest, but with encouragement and support finally proceeded with the task.

What appears to be Debbie's principal handicap is a gap between visual-motor skills and verbal skills, in favor of the latter. In school situations she will not likely be perceived as being extremely slow because of her average verbal skills. However, she will need encouragement and attention, because she may tend to remove herself from difficult situations by inattention or by simply refusing to try. Her parents should be helped to accept her present level of development and not place unrealistic demands on her. Special programs to improve her muscle coordination and speech are recommended.

BEHAVIORAL OBSERVATIONS DURING INTELLIGENCE TESTING

As we have seen, use of the measures of intelligence to acquire information about capabilities requires careful administration of the test according to the test manual instructions. These standardized procedures allow the examiner to make the necessary comparisons with other test responders and to draw conclusions about the subject's "relative intellectual abilities."

Although standardization is essential in intellectual testing, the examiner should also be observant of the subject's individual *behavioral differences*. The intelligence test administrator creates the situation in which the examinee performs, but each subject will emit any number of behaviors that may provide important clues to that person's intellectual functioning in addition to the responses that are formally scored as part of the test.

The most important behavioral observations to be recorded during intellectual assessment are those that repeatedly "stand out" in either a positive or a negative fashion. For example, after completion of the Block Design or Object Assembly subtests, the examiner should be observing to see if the subject assists the examiner in organizing the test materials and/or replacing them in their appropriate cases. Such behavior may be indicative of a cooperative behavioral style. Similarly, the subject who damages or destroys the test materials is displaying defiant behavior that may be a source of problems in other situations.

Evidence of more severe psychological dysfunctions may also be shown in the subject's behavior during testing. For example, when asked what does the word "airborne" mean, the subject immediately rose from his chair and began to recite a poem he had written while in the 53rd Airborne of the USAF. Both the tangential association to the word and the rather impulsive recitation are suggestive of distress. Excessive looking around the room, continuous movement while seated, or the total absence of conversation are just a few examples of other types of observable behavior that should not go unnoticed.

Although the behaviors to be observed may vary from person to person, there are certain things that the examiner should always observe. The subject's handedness . . . did the subject use just one hand? Which one? Did the subject use both hands? Were they used alternately? Similar general questions include: How did the subject walk? Was there a steady or an irregular gait? Did the subject wear glasses? A hearing aid? Is there evidence that glasses or a hearing aid may be needed? Did the subject give up quickly on certain tests, or was persistence observed even on difficult ones? We have drawn some material relevant to behavioral observations from the Stanford-Binet Intelligence Scale. One page of the Stanford-Binet test booklet is reproduced in Figure 7-5. This summary sheet provides the examiner with several categories of behavior to observe so as to facilitate the examiner's integrating and reporting of the test results.

ISSUES IN ASSESSING INTELLIGENCE

The development and standardization of measures of intelligence offer evidence of the compatibility of scientific and professional efforts. Although the quality and quantity of effort that has gone into this undertaking by both clinical practitioners and researchers are outstanding, several controversial issues merit special attention. Indeed, Jensen (1980) has written over 700 pages on bias in mental testing.

Intelligence Tests and the Disadvantaged

One of the major sources of current concern regarding intelligence testing has to do with the "fairness" or "unfairness" of such procedures with disadvantaged individuals. This dilemma has both scientific aspects: Is there research evidence that tests discriminate against disadvantaged persons? practitioner aspects: Can clinicians use the intelligence measures ethically with disadvantaged clients? Moreover, there are ethical concerns about the use of intelligence tests that have resulted in a "moratorium" on testing called for by the representatives of minority groups (Baxter, 1969). Are these tests fair? What data are relevant to such a discussion?

First, we must attempt an answer to the question,"Who are the disadvantaged?" Most conceptions of "disadvantaged" are relative; that is, someone (or some group) is disadvantaged in relation to someone else. So, relatively speaking, the disadvantaged are those who are handicapped in leading a productive life in their society. This group may include low-income families, very rural families, females, older adults, ethnic minorities, nonwhite races, and, in some cases, members of bilingual families.

Next we need to know what is meant by "intelligence." Although no single definition of intelligence is uniformly agreed on, we might rely on Wechsler's definition (see p. 242) or on the definition that has been provided by a special committee of the American Psychological Association (Cleary, Humphreys, Kendrick, & Wesman, 1975): intelligence is viewed as the repertoire of acquired knowledge, ability, learning sets, or generalized tendencies of an intellectual nature available at a given moment.

Factors Affecting Test Performance
Overall Rating of Conditions

Optimal	Good	Average	Detrimental	Seriously detrimental

Attention
(a) Absorbed by task . . . . Easily distracted

Reactions During Test Performance
(a) Normal activity level. . . . . Hyperactive or depressed
(b) Initiates activity . . . . Waits to be told
(c) Quick to respond . . . . Urging needed

Emotional Independence
(a) Socially confident . . . . Shy, reserved, reticent
(b) Realistically self-confident. . . . . Distrusts own ability or overconfident
(c) Comfortable in adult company. . . . . Ill-at-ease
(d) Assured . . . . Anxious about success

Problem Solving Behavior
(a) Persistent . . . . Gives up easily or can't give up
(b) Reacts to failure realistically . . . . Withdrawing, hostile, or denying
(c) Eager to continue . . . . Seeks to terminate
(d) Challenged by hard tasks . . . . Prefers only easy tasks

Independence of Examiner Support
(a) Needs minimum of commendation . . . . Needs constant praise
                                                                  and encouragement

Was it hard to establish a positive relationship with this person? _____

From L. M. Terman and M. A. Merrill, *Stanford-Binet Intelligence Scale, Form L-M*, copyright 1960, 1972 Houghton Mifflin Company, used with permission from Riverside Publishing Company.

Figure 7-5   Relevant behaviors to observe during testing.

Now we must consider three sources of potential test unfairness: the actual test questions, the interpreters of the test results, and the predictions made by the test results. In constructing an intelligence test, it is important to gather a variety of test questions each of which contributes meaningfully to the overall assessment of intellectual functioning. After all, it is the total of the individual questions that is used to make relevant predictions. One issue here is whether or not members of the "disadvantaged" groups are a part of the original standardization of the test items. A central problem for the WISC was that it was standardized on white children, but the WISC-R standardization sample included minority members. What if a child were asked "What does the word castle mean?" and the child responded "a place to buy hamburgers," then the awareness of White Castle hamburger stands within the poorer sections of the inner city suggests that this is, in some respects, an "intelligent" answer. Nevertheless, the inclusion of minorities within the standardization sample of the WISC-R is a strong point, but this does not guarantee that all of its questions are truly fair.

The test items can also be "unfair" if they do not measure what is thought to be intelligence. Here, we must determine that the questions come from the universe of questions that are relevant to the construct of intelligence. Recall the subtests of the Wechsler scales and draw a conclusion for yourself. Note that there are some who contend that the questions are a reflection of the white middle class and do not tap the knowledge of information relevant to other classes or groups of people. Williams (1972) developed the Black Intelligence Test of Culture Homogeneity (BITCH) specifically to examine the knowledge of information that was black-culture specific. Unfortunately, there is a limited amount of published data on this test. Only one known study, by Matarazzo and Wiens (1977) examined the BITCH and the WAIS as measures of intelligence. This project was done in the context of studying police applicants and reported that there was a lack of concurrent validity—leaving the question, what does the BITCH measure? Also reported in this study was that all the black subjects scored highly and with little spread in the test scores. Finally, Matarazzo and Wiens (1977) reported that there is still an absence of predictive validity data on the BITCH. Without such data, there is no way to know if knowledge of slang or street vocabulary, as measured by the BITCH, is predictive of relevant intelligent behavior (e.g., vocational or academic achievement).

The second source of unfairness lies in the interpretation of test results. The interpreter can be unfair in two ways: in interpreting the IQ as an indication of innate ability that cannot be altered, and in abusing the test results to promote unjustified conclusions. In both cases the unfairness is due to the *interpreter* and *not* the *test* itself. Indeed, the person could misuse any assessment instrument to seek to achieve the same result.

Third, a test is unfair to members of a group, such as the disadvantaged, if their scores on the test predict poorer performance on a criterion than do scores by another group when, in fact, the two groups do not actually differ in performance on the criterion. The results of numerous studies suggest that intelligence tests, in general, have demonstrated equal predictive abilities for the various groups. For example, Cleary et al. (1975) present evidence that confirms the hypothesis that low IQ scores predict poor school performance, regardless of race. Thus, one is likely to conclude from our analyses of test questions, "fair" interpretations, and equality of predictions, that we can perhaps dismiss claims of test unfairness. This conclusion, however, is not shared by all (see Bernal, 1975; Jackson, 1975).

Schmidt and Hunter (1974), while they would probably agree with the arguments presented above, presented evidence that the tests may be unfair to minority groups when fairness is defined in a different way. This definition of fairness, proposed by Thorndike (1971), states that a test is fair if for any given criterion of success, the test selects the same proportion of minority applicants that would have been selected using the criterion itself. Attempts to apply this definition are also not without problems. For example, if a "proportion of applicants" is determined by a criterion and then this proportion is applied to the predictor test, some minority members may be chosen with predictor scores lower than those of majority members simply to complete the proportion requirement. Schmidt and Hunter (1974) go on to say that use of this approach would make certain majority applicants be rejected in favor of minority applicants with lower statistical probabilities of success—a condition sometimes called reverse discrimination.

Lest we leave the issue unresolved, there are some suggestions that can be useful to deal with the question of testing and the disadvantaged. First, tests that are culture free may be beneficial. Second, abusers of the test data can be reprimanded. Third, and perhaps most important, if the disadvantaged do score lower on intelligence tests then we should not argue the differences but rather take notice and seek to (1) help the persons learn the skills that they lack, and (2) attempt to identify the other special skills that they possess.

Culture Fair Tests of Intelligence

Let us reexamine a crucial question: Are intelligence tests merely assessing skills specific to the white middle-class culture? Can we eliminate biases by examining intelligence with tests that are *culture free*? The separate efforts of Raven (1938) and Cattell (1949) have resulted in two different examples of tests that are purported to be culture free.

Raven's Progressive Matrices tests the relationships among abstract figures. This is accomplished by providing a design with a missing part and requiring the subject to choose from the alternatives the insert that would correctly complete the pattern. The test consists of 60 of these items (see Table 7-9). The Progressive Matrices have received moderate research interest. The reliabilities are moderate (.70 to .90 range) and concurrent validity (correlations with other tests of intelligence between .40 and .75) are fair (Anastasi, 1968). However, predictions of academic performance from the Matrices are less accurate than from the usual tests of intelligence.

Cattell's Culture Free Intelligence Test is a paper-and-pencil instrument available for subjects at three age levels, with alternate test forms at each level. Each level consists of four tests: series, classification, matrices, and conditions (see Table 7-10). In the series test the subject is shown a series of figures and instructed to select the next in sequence from an assortment of choices. The classification test asks the subject to identify which member of a group does not belong. The matrices portion of the test provides several line drawings and requires the subject to select the one that completes the pattern. In the conditions test, the subject is required to select the response alternative that contains figures that meet the same conditions as a standard.

The reliabilities for the Culture Fair Intelligence Test are only moderately high (i.e., .50 to .70), and there are inadequate data on the validity of the test (Anastasi, 1968). In addition, when the test was administered in a number of countries, the performance of subjects from cultures different from ours was considerably lower than the norms, suggesting that the tests may not be culture free. In general, this measure of intelligence has received very little professional use among clinical psychologists.

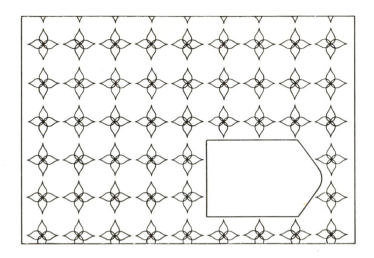

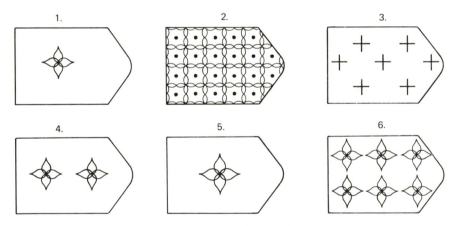

Table 7-9   Sample item from Raven's Progressive Matrices

From J. C. Raven, *Progressive matrices: A perceptual test of intelligence, 1938, Individual form.*
London: H. K. Lewis, 1938. Reprinted by permission of J. C. Raven Ltd. and A. P. Watt Ltd.

Both the Progressive Matrices and the Culture Fair Intelligence Test were spurred by the desire to remove white middle-class value judgments from the measures of intelligence. The motives are applauded, as are the resulting tests, but the less than adequate predictions that result from the test scores leave much to be desired. Perhaps intelligence tests should not be culture free! After all, we are trying to predict behavior that exists in a particular culture and that is affected by that culture.

Reifying the IQ

The IQ is an intelligence quotient that results from mathematical manipulations of the individual's correct answers on a variety of tests of specific abilities. The IQ score indicates how the individual performed in relation to other people of the

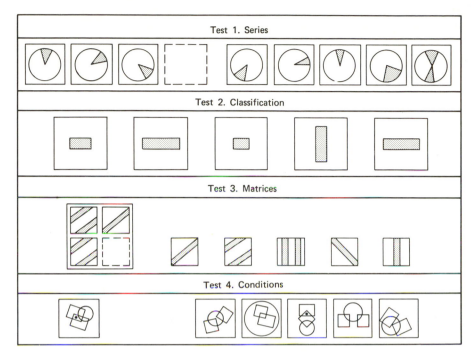

Table 7-10 Sample items from Cattell's Culture Fair Intelligence Test

From R. B. Cattell, *Culture Fair Intelligence Test, Scale 2, Form A* Copyright 1949, 1960, by the Institute for Personality and Ability Testing, Inc. All rights reserved. Reproduced by permission of the copyright owner.

same age. An unfortunate misconception is that the IQ is often seen as an index of inflexible innate abilities. This reification, or transformation of a concept into a concrete thing, misleads the general public to interpret IQ scores as fixed and unchangeable.

Reification can be avoided. To achieve this, the results of intelligence tests will have to be viewed as additional data to aid in the understanding of the person rather than as scores for simple categorization. Also, if and when subjects are informed of their IQs, they should be told from the outset that there are standard errors of measurement (plus or minus ≈ 5 points is typical for the Wechsler scales) and that their current IQ reflects only their current level of functioning. Since IQs are relatively consistent over time, subjects should, however, not be misled into thinking about pursuits that are far beyond their abilities.

Intelligence And Aging: Do The Data Demonstrate A Decline?

Wechsler (1955) expected that most individuals' performance on intelligence tests will show a decline with age. "Mental deterioration," in contrast, is seen when a person's decline in IQ shows a loss of ability greater than the amount of decline that may be expected for others of the same age.

The data that are considered to suggest an age-related decline in intelligence are of the cross-sectional variety. That is, a number of different samples of individuals at different ages were tested, and a single mean for each group was determined. At each older age level, lower average IQ scores were found. What are needed to answer the question at hand, however, are data on the *same* individuals reexamined at different fixed ages as they grow older. Such a longitudinal project takes a very long time—a lifetime to be sure!

In order to examine methodologically sound data and in order to conduct the evaluation within reasonable time limits, Schaie and Strather (1968) utilized a design that contained the elements of both the cross-sectional and longitudinal approaches. These researchers used a stratified sample of 25 men and 25 women at five-year-age intervals from ages 20 to 70 (500 subjects). The initial data constituted a cross-sectional sample. However, the researchers retested 302 of the original subjects and thus achieved a longitudinal component within the study. The results indicated that while the cross-sectional portions of the data suggested the "decline," the more rigorous longitudinal data analysis did *not* show intellectual decline with age.

Although the methods of Schaie and Strather (1968) are commendable, it should be noted that only 302 of the original individuals were retested. Were these "select" subjects? Were these the most intellectually capable and/or most biologically healthy? If these questions are answered affirmatively one can argue, as Matarazzo has (1972), that "attrition of the least able" may be a sufficient explanation for the apparent lack of decline in the upper age groups.

Horn and Donaldson (1976) suggested, among other more scientific comments, that the human ability for wishful thinking may be in part responsible for the need to disprove the decline of intellectual functioning, and they contend that our current knowledge is insufficient to say for certain whether or not there is an important age-related decrement in intelligence. More recently, Baltes and Schaie (1976) asserted that it is too soon for a total rejection of "intellectual decline." Hopefully, a carefully conducted long-term longitudinal analysis—with a minimum attrition of the least able—will be reported and will provide the information that is needed on this important psychological topic.

. . . the character which shapes our conduct is a definite and durable "something", and therefore it is reasonable to measure it.

Sir Francis Galton

8

ASSESSMENT OF PERSONALITY

Have you ever noticed that when you ask a question about someone the reply often includes, although sometimes quite brief, some description of the individual's personality? For example, "Did you take the course with Professor Smith?" "Yeah, he's the young guy who's such a stickler for details." Although being concerned about detail is only a small portion of a personality description, when we talk about people we are usually describing something about their personality.

The colloquial use of descriptive adjectives suffices as a brief verbal portrait of the person in question, but the psychological characterization of that individual's personality requires much more. When a psychological assessment of personality is undertaken, a great deal of time and effort is involved and a number of issues must be considered.

In personality assessment, the dominant methods employed by clinicians are unstructured and structured tests. Unstructured tests are derived largely from theories of personality and are considered *projective methods* of personality assessment. Projective tests involve the use of ambiguous test stimuli, leaving the test materials ill defined so that the client will project him or her self onto the material and disclose his or her personality. Structured tests are concerned with clients' responses to specific test items and rely more on empirical analysis of the data and less on specific personality theories for interpretation. These are termed *objective methods* of personality assessment. Structured and unstructured interviews and naturalistic observations (Chapter 10) are also important methods of assessment that are used for personality appraisal, however, the two major approaches to the appraisal of individual personality are the projective and objective methods of assessment.

PROJECTIVE ASSESSMENT

The projective method of personality assessment has developed from the theoretical perspective that espouses psychodynamic characteristics as the core of personality (such as psychoanalytic theory). Therefore, the basic method involves providing the subject with novel, ambiguous, and almost contentless forms to which to respond along with a minimum of structure or instruction. Theoretically, the examiner assumes that if all the testing materials contain only a minimum of content then the subject's responses are solely a function of the subject's personality. Stated another way, the more opportunity the subject has to respond freely and idiosyncratically, the more personal and meaningful will be the responses. Based on the psychodynamic view of personality, projectives are seen as instruments that are sensitive to unconscious aspects of behavior. Defense mechanisms and latent tendencies are inferred from the unstructured fantasy data that are produced in a context where there are no right or wrong answers.

Lindzey's definition (1961) encompasses all the vital characteristics of the projective techniques.

> *A projective technique is an instrument that is considered especially sensitive to covert or unconscious aspects of behavior, it permits or encourages a wide variety of subject responses, is highly multidimensional, and it evokes unusually rich or profuse response data with a minimum of subject awareness concerning the purpose of the test. Further, it is very often true that the stimulus material presented by the projective test is ambiguous, interpreters depend upon wholistic analysis, the test evokes fantasy responses, and there are no correct or incorrect responses to the test. (p. 45)*

There are numerous psychological tests that fall into the projective category. These tests vary, for example, in the way that they are administered, their purpose, and the type of response that they elicit. They may be designed to produce a comprehensive picture of the person or to describe only one aspect of personality. Lindzey (1961) categorized projective tests according to the type of response that is elicited: (1) association, (2) construction, (3) completion, (4) choice or ordering, and (5) expression.

According to Lindzey (1961), *association* techniques require the subject to associate and respond to a stimulus presented by the examiner. Both the Rorschach inkblot test and word association tests would be of the associative variety of projective tests. *Construction* tests require the subject to construct or create a story or a picture. In comparison to the association techniques, construction methods require more complex cognitive activity. The Thematic Apperception Test and Blacky Pictures Test would be construction tests. When an incomplete stimulus is presented and the subject is required to complete it, the test would be of the *completion* category. Examples include sentence-completion and picture-frustration tests. When the subject is asked to choose from a number of alternatives, the test would be a *choice or ordering* projective technique. The Szondi test is one such assessment method that requires the subject to repeatedly select a most- and a least-liked photograph. The repeated choosing allows the examiner to order the selected pictures and make subsequent analyses. Another test of this variety is the picture arrangement test. Finally, *expressive* projective measures require the subject to create a production, like the construction method, but here the subject plays an active role in determining what is to be constructed, and both the creation and the manner of creating are analyzed along with the content of the creation. Play, drawing and painting, and psychodrama would be considered expressive projective measures.

Rorschach Inkblots

The Rorschach inkblots are clearly a classic example of the associative projective technique. These 10 cards (half are achromatic and half have color) were developed by a Swiss psychiatrist, Hermann Rorschach, in 1921. Although it is difficult to determine exactly why Rorschach became interested in inkblots, Exner and Clark (1978) noted that during the late nineteenth and early twentieth centuries inkblots were used in a familiar parlor game Blotto. Since that time, the Rorschach inkblots have enjoyed periods of being the most popular of the projective tests of personality and, despite a deceleration of the teaching of the Rorschach in clinical psychology graduate programs (Biederman & Cerbus, 1971), the test remains widely used.

Administration   The administration of the inkblots usually follows a standard order, the examiner and subject sitting side by side, one card at a time, and with instructions something like the following:

> This is a personality test and it will help us understand your areas of strength and weakness and give us an overall picture of your personality functioning. I have 10 cards which I'll show you one at a time. On each card is a inkblot—that's a pattern made by an artist with ink put on half a page of paper and folded in half so that when you open the page you have a symmetrical pattern. It is important to remember that these are not pictures or drawings of anything specific, they're simply abstract patterns that may remind you of things. Also, there are no right or wrong answers. I just want you to look at each card and honestly tell me what the card reminds you of, looks like, or suggests or brings to mind. People see all kinds of things; tell me what you see.[1]

The instructions are not standardized and there exists marked variability in the administration of the Rorschach (Jackson & Wahl, 1966). Nevertheless, test administration consists of two parts: free association and inquiry. During the free-association period, the subject responds by describing what the inkblots "look like" or "suggest," and the examiner records verbatim what the subject says in response to the inkblot stimuli. This includes comments, questions, and exclamations, as well as all of the subject's perceptions. The examiner also times the subject's latency to respond to each of the inkblots and notes and records the subject's mannerisms and gestures. The inquiry begins after the subject has free associated to each of the inkblots. The inkblots are again presented to the subject to assess what factors contributed to the subject's perception (see Figure 8-1).

Scoring and Interpretation   Subjects' responses to the Rorschach inkblots can be said to represent projective material—the cards are ambiguous and they elicit the client's personal responses to the stimuli. The projective quality notwithstanding, objective scoring systems have been developed and applied to the inkblot responses (e.g., Beck, 1944; 1945; 1952; Exner, 1974; Exner & Clark, 1978;

---

[1]James A. Moses, Jr., of the Palo Alto Veterans Administration Medical Center provided us with his instructions as a sample of what a subject is usually told. Importantly, these instructions are taken from Jim's daily work—he did not sit down and draft, clarify, dress up, and perfect a description of his instructions. This is how it might happen in an actual clinical setting.

Figure 8-1   A Rorschach-like inkblot.

Klopfer, Ainsworth, Klopfer, & Holt, 1954; Klopfer & Davidson, 1962; Rapaport, Gill, & Schafer, 1968). The scoring systems include ascertaining the *location* of the subject's perception, categorizing the *content* of the perception, and recording the *determinants* of the subject's response. The clinician acquires this information during the inquiry, where the subject is asked what exactly was seen, where on the card was the percept, and what made it look like that. Exner, Weiner, and Schuyler (1976) provided sample instructions:

> *Now I want to go back through the cards again. I won't take very long. I'll read what you told me you saw and then I want you to help me to see it as you did. In other words, I want to know where you saw it, and what there is there that makes it look like that, so that I can see it just like you did. Understand?*

Location is scored first. The subject indicates the area of the blot that contained the response. Location is either the entire blot or some portion of it. In scoring location the examiner identifies whether the subject's response referred to the whole inkblot (W), average detail (D), small detail (Dd), rare detail (Dr), or white space (S). Different psychological meaning is given to responses that use varying amounts of the inkblot. For example, a response that successfully integrates the entire inkblot has been said to indicate a better organizational ability than responses that do not include the entire blot, whereas excessive reliance on detail suggests that the subject might "miss the forest for the trees."

From the subject's answers during the inquiry, the examiner identifies whether form (F), color (C, or C^1 for achromatic color), shading (c, K), or movement (HM, FM, m) was the determinant of the perception. Form is further classified as either good (F+), indicating that the form of the percept on the inkblot matches the form in reality (e.g., the blot is actually shaped like a "bat"), or as poor (F−), indicating an unclear correspondence between the subject's perception and the inkblot. Color is scored as the determinant when the subject indicates that the percept was based upon the color of the blot. For instance, the subject stated "It looks like blood because it is red." Often, both form and color are the determinants. Depending upon which factor dominates, either FC or CF is scored. For instance, if the subject had stated "It looks like blood because it's red and it's like a drop" it would be scored CF. Shading scores include surface or texture (c), such as a subject's perception of a crack being determined by how the blot is shaded, and three-dimensional depth or vista (K), such as the perception of a view from the top of a mountain. Movement consists of human movement (HM), animal movement (FM), and inanimate movement (m). Seeing two people dancing would be a human movement response. Individuals whose Rorschach responses evidence a lot of movement are said to be intellectually bright, imaginative, and sometimes tending to be more introverted than extroverted. In contrast, animals moving might be more likely perceived by a more immature person.

The content of the subject's responses is scored simply by indicating the class of the object that was seen. These scores are typically no more than an abbreviation of the class or category of the response. For instance, having seen "lots of underwater animals" would be classified as animal (An) content. "A garden of flowers" would be Bt for botany, and "male genitals" would be classified as sexual (Sex) content. The examiner also categorizes the subject's responses as either popular (P) or original (O). Whether a response is popular or not is determined solely by the frequency with which it occurs.

Recently, Wainer, Hurt, and Aiken (1976) undertook a study of the categorization of Rorschach responses. These authors provided a new look at the Rorschach using an advanced mathematical analysis (multidimensional scaling). The Rorschach cards were presented in pairs on slides to samples of normals from two universities and to psychiatric patients with a variety of diagnoses from a state hospital. The results indicated that subjects' responses could be characterized along two dimensions, one of color and one of form. This finding was replicated in a second study, and, taken together, the Wainer et al. study suggests that color and form are the principal characteristics that underlie a subject's perception of the inkblots.

Interpretation of the Rorschach is a more difficult task than either administration or scoring. The examiner must review all the subject's responses, score the test responses, calculate certain ratios of one type of response to another (e.g., ratio of movement to color responses), and begin to develop an understanding of the person. There is no single formula for diagnosis or personality appraisal, and most Rorschach interpreters prefer to downplay statistical approaches and emphasize clinical methods. Also, no single response is sufficient to tell us anything meaningful about the person. Interpretation emphasizes a wholistic, integrative analysis of all the data with the result being a comprehensive description of the subject's needs, drives, defense mechanisms, and personality organization. Thus, although scoring adds a quantitative flavor to the Rorschach test, there is still a large portion of the interpretation process that lies in the subjective realm and depends on the experience, skill, and theoretical orientation of the examiner (see Highlight 8-1).

Research Status   No one statement can do justice to the research status of the Rorschach test. So many studies (thousands) of different varieties and with conflicting results supplant any clearcut statements. Perhaps the most accurate conclusion is one which states that the status of the Rorschach depends on who is asked the question. Proponents of the inkblot method refer to its clinical utility and criticize the quality and relevance of the research, while critics point to the

Highlight 8-1   Caution—The Illusory Correlation

One of the most vexing problems facing the interpreter of projective test data is the potential interference of "illusory correlations." The notion of an illusory correlation concerns the phenomenon that people report associations between projective test responses and clinical disorders even when such associations are not supported by validational analyses (Chapman, 1967; Chapman & Chapman, 1967; 1969).

It has been proposed that illusory correlations are the result of semantic or "face valid" associations. For instance, a subject's reported perception when presented with an inkblot is "gun." "Gun" is semantically associated with aggressive and violent behavior and the person is therefore assumed to be aggressive and violent. This is an illusory correlation since the percept in question may not necessarily be related to behavioral aggression.

Consider the Chapmans' experiments in which they used the Rorschach test. First, note that two responses had been found to separate male homosexuals from male heterosexuals: seeing monsters on Card IV and a part animal/part human figure on Card V. Percepts that "on their face" might appear to be distinctive, such as feminine clothing, humans with uncertain sex, and male genitalia, were not found to be valid signs—they did not differentiate between the homosexual and heterosexual persons. In the first part of the Chapmans' research they report that practicing clinicians identified certain Rorschach responses as characteristic of homosexuals—but they were the face-valid signs and not the signs that would actually differentiate the groups.

In a second phase of the study, laypersons rated the relatedness of the signs to the presence of homosexuality. The invalid signs were rated as having a moderately strong relationship whereas the valid (but not obvious) signs showed only a very slight relationship.

The next phase of the study involved laypersons who were asked to respond to a series of Rorschach cards. The materials contained either homosexual symptoms or neutral symptoms written adjacent to Rorschach responses that were either valid, invalid (but with some face validity), or neutral (fillers). The materials were designed such that there was no relationship between any symptoms and the responses to the Rorschach. The illusory correlation again appeared. Subjects reported that the *invalid* responses (those with face validity) were associated with the homosexual symptoms whereas the valid and filler responses were not.

In yet another variation on the theme, the Chapmans varied the degree of a relationship between the valid Rorschach responses and the symptoms of homosexuality that were presented to their subjects (i.e., 50%, 67%, 83%, and 100%). These results indicated that the subjects failed to recognize the valid relationships: increasing degrees of a relationship were not perceived by the subjects.

What happens when one is taught—specifically warned—to be on guard against illusory correlation? Kurtz and Garfield (1978) reported that despite

> their attempts to modify the occurrence of illusory correlation through train-
> ing, it was not possible to reduce illusory correlation. We close with a rephras-
> ing of the title of this highlight: illusory correlation—caution!

same research data as evidence for the need to move on to new alternative personality assessment procedures. A closer look at these issues should provide a valuable example of one type of scientific question that clinical psychologists have researched.

Reliability   When the variety of procedures to assess reliability is applied to the
responses to Rorschach stimuli, the results indicate that there are problems. The
current evidence documents that there is much to be desired before reliability can
be claimed for the Rorschach (Zubin, Eron, & Schumer, 1965). Test-retest, split-
half, and interrater/intertester reliability have all been evaluated. In these cases
the data have not been encouraging. For example, Henry and Rotter (1956) demonstrated that subjects will change their way of responding in different situations.
One group of college students was administered the Rorschach with standard instructions—people see different things, tell me what you see, there are no right or
wrong answers; a second group was given the regular instructions and also told
that the test had been used in mental hospitals to study emotional disturbance but
that it was presently being used for a college survey. There were no other differences between the groups. Nevertheless, the outcome was a marked difference in
the two groups' average number of responses, 16 for the experimental group as
compared to 23 for the controls, and the number of popular or stereotyped responses, 12% in the experimental and 4% in the controls. These findings meant
that subjects in the experimental group were more cautious, less imaginative, and
generally less free in responding than were the controls. A slight variation in instructions altered subjects' response style; an alteration that would be likely to
lead to different personality appraisals.

   As alluded to above, some proponents of the Rorschach method do not see the
research data in the same way. Instead, the appropriateness of the research methods are criticized and the less-than-supportive results are discounted. For example, how can the Rorschach be expected to have split-half reliability since it is
argued that each card has a different theme, eliciting different responses? Also,
the test captures a large picture, a description, a dynamic analysis, and there is no
way to put parts of this whole picture into little categories that can be researched.
Furthermore, even if the scores are not reliable, the overall interpretation would
not be affected. These are examples of the arguments put forth to attempt to reduce the consistently negative research evidence to the level of inappropriate and
inconsequential data.

Validity   When the variety of methods to evaluate test validity are applied to the
Rorschach, the results are, at best, equivocal (Goldfried, Stricker, & Weiner,
1972; Zubin et al., 1965). Validity in terms of differentiating normal and abnormal groups, describing a relationship (specific hypotheses from the Rorschach) to

actual behavior, interpreting specific perceptions in certain ways, and generating ratings of adjustment has been at best weakly demonstrated for the Rorschach.

An Alternate Inkblot Test

With the problems of the Rorschach inkblot test clearly before us, it is worth noting that an alternate inkblot test has been developed. The Holtzman Inkblot Test (Holtzman, Thorpe, Swartz, & Herron, 1961) was designed to provide a more objective, quantitative, reliable, and standardized procedure to the use of inkblots to measure personality. The Holtzman Inkblot Test (HIT) has 45 inkblots to which subjects provide one response to each and there are two equivalent alternate forms of the test. Unlike the Rorschach, the HIT administration requires that the free-association period be followed directly by the inquiry for each card and the HIT is more time consuming to administer and score.

The research on the HIT has been reviewed (Gamble, 1972) yielding equivocal conclusions. For example, although there have been numerous studies, no clear conclusion can be drawn as to whether the HIT is better than the Rorschach. Other reviewers draw diverging conclusions: Exner (1976) considers it an appealing approach while Zubin (1972a) expresses disappointment. Apparently, additional research is required.

Thematic Apperception Test

The Thematic Apperception Test (TAT) is a projective test which, like the Rorschach and other inkblot tests, requires the subject to respond freely to somewhat ambiguous materials. The TAT was designed by Murray (1943) and colleagues to measure the "needs" that were important factors in his theory of personality. A series of drawings (one is blank) portraying people in various situations was selected (see Figure 8-2). Usually fewer than 15 or 20 cards are used. Unlike the Rorschach, the TAT is a projective test of the construction variety: the subject is asked to construct a story about each picture, telling what led up to the scene, what is presently going on, and what will happen in the future. In addition, the subject is asked to include the thoughts and feelings of the characters in the story. The examiner records the story as nearly verbatim as possible and intervenes only minimally after the initial introduction.

Unlike the Rorschach inkblot test, the TAT does not have a widely used global objective scoring system. However, Murray (1943) did recommend scoring the TAT by identifying the story's hero figure, the "needs" of the hero (forces emanating from the hero), and the "presses" or environmental forces pushing on the hero. Both needs and presses would then be rated on a 1 to 5 scale according to intensity, frequency, and duration.

Other quantitative scoring systems include Dana (1959), Eron (1950), and McClelland, Atkinson, Clark, and Lowell (1953). McClelland et al., (1953), developed a scoring system for studying one particular need—the need for achievement. A normative approach was proposed by Eron (1950) whereby the emotional tone and outcome of each story was evaluated using rating scales. In various

Take a look at this picture. Now tell a story about it. How does your personality affect what you include in your story? How does your environment affect the story? How does your history of good and bad experiences in a similar situation affect what story you will tell?

Figure 8-2 A TAT-like picture. The Flying Codonas by John Stewart Curry, 1932. Collection of Whitney Museum of American Art, New York.

specific research projects the TAT has been scored to measure needs for food (Atkinson & McClelland, 1948), sex (Clark, 1952), and power (Veroff, 1957). Also, in a research vein, group administration has been suggested as being as useful as the individual procedure (Lindzey & Heinemann, 1955).

Clinical interpretation of the TAT, however, usually follows a more qualitative approach such as those discussed by Bellak (1947), Henry (1947), and Piotrowski (1950). In these approaches, the examiner relies heavily on an interpretation of the action in the story, the hero's conflicts and needs, and the dynamic structure of the story content. Though the TAT's validity is equivocal with respect to diagnosis (Murstein, 1963), it has been a widely accepted projective test of personality with its main clinical use being a technique for gaining hypotheses concerning the client's primary motivations. Rather than applying one of the scoring procedures, most practicing clinicians prefer to employ a qualitative analysis of the content of the TAT stories. The TAT is very much like the Rorschach in this sense since the test taps unconscious processes by allowing the subject to project him- or herself onto the ambiguous material. Specifically, for the TAT, the projective hypothesis is that the experiences felt by the hero of the story are the projected tendencies from within the storyteller.

Sentence Completion

The completion method of projective assessment is another approach to collecting data from somewhat ambiguous stimuli. In the sentence completion method, the subject is given a list of sentence stems that are used to elicit certain kinds of information. Within this standard format, different sentence stems can be used for different purposes. For example, some sentence stems that might be used to assess the parents of an emotionally disturbed child might be:

1. When my child misbehaves I _____.
2. My child _____.
3. My child makes me _____.
4. A mother's responsibility is to _____.

The most noted sentence completion test is perhaps the Rotter Incomplete Sentence Blank (Rotter & Rafferty, 1950). This form, used with college students, contains 40 stems, an elaborate system for scoring responses, and normative data. However, the majority of sentence completion tests used in clinical work do not use scoring systems or norms, but instead rely on a qualitative interpretation of content. In the case of our sample sentence blanks above, the clinician may interpret subjects' responses with an interest in identifying attitudes toward the child, conflicts within the family, and/or the personal strengths and weaknesses of the parent respondent. Unfortunately, such idiosyncratic instruments are not psychometrically sound.

Picture Arrangement Test

An example of the choice or ordering type of projective test is the Tomkins-Horn Picture Arrangement Test (Tomkins, 1957). The subject is asked to order three different but related figure drawings and to say what is going on in the series of pictures. There are 25 such tasks. The picture arrangement test has a volume of records of normal and disturbed subjects' responses and an objective scoring system to be applied in the analysis. Nevertheless, the clinician's use of this test for personality assessment often relies on subject's verbal responses. Picture arrangement is also a subtest of the Wechsler Adult Intelligence Scale and in this capacity has been researched as a component of intellectual functioning.

Draw-A-Person

An expressive projective procedure for personality assessment is to simply require the subject to "draw a person" (Machover, 1949). The use of this method for clinical purposes was developed following Goodenough's (1926) demonstration that children's drawings of a man could be used to produce an estimate of intelligence.

The examiner tells the subject that artistic ability is of no concern and that he or she should draw the person however he or she wishes. A sharp pencil and several sheets of 8 1/2 by 11 inch blank white paper are provided. After the subject has drawn one person, the examiner may then ask the subject to draw another person only this time of the opposite sex of the first figure drawn. Other variations of the projective drawing technique include asking the subject to draw a family doing something (Kinetic Family Drawing) or having the subject draw a house, a tree, and a person (HTP) (Buck, 1948).

Drawings are usually interpreted in terms of the formal characteristics of the figures, such as the thickness of lines, size, and placement of the drawing on the page and symmetry, as well as any important characteristics of the content. For example, a drawing made with hard, solid lines, an absence of erasures, and encompassing the entire page may be used to infer that the subject was a dominant, self-assured, or perhaps arrogant individual.

Perhaps since they do not require verbal behavior, projective drawings are often used by those who are interested in assessing the personality dynamics of children. An example of a child's drawing is presented in Figure 8-3.

Although Machover (1949) and Hammer (1958) brought the projective drawing technique clearly in view of those interested in clinical and personality assessment, and it remains an often-used procedure, research evidence suggests that projective drawings do not fulfill the scientific requirements of acceptable assessment methods. In two reviews of the empirical literature evaluating human figure drawings, Swensen (1957, 1968) concluded that human figure drawings are doubtful as measures of personality and that reliabilities are too low for making meaningful clinical judgments. Similarly, Roback (1968), while also criticizing the quality of the research, concluded that most studies of human figure drawings fail to support the interpretations that were suggested by Machover (1949).

Evaluations of the human figure drawing technique conducted by Adler (1970, 1971) add still more negative findings to the relatively convincing archives. In Adler's studies, along with a lack of scoring reliability and an inability to differentiate diagnostic categories, it was found that the figure drawings represented one factor that measured a dimension of cognitive maturity. Based on this, inferences about psychological dysfunctions are likely to be in error since primitive drawings are more than likely due to cognitive immaturity.

The Rorschach, TAT, Sentence Completion, Picture Arrangement, and Draw-A-Person tests are a representative sample of the projective techniques, but they are not an exhaustive list. There are others, although they are typically not a part of the standard personality assessment.

Issues in Projective Personality Assessment

Even though projective tests continue as a part of the psychological assessment armamentarium of many practicing clinicians, and even though the techniques elicit the theoretically desired free-response material, numerous negative research findings have resulted in a generally less than enthusiastic attitude toward projective tests. One major weakness of the projective tests is that they are often interpreted qualitatively rather than in relation to normative data. In the absence of adequate norms, the clinician falls back on "general clinical experience" to interpret the test. Certainly, as humans, we are all susceptible to selective, if not inac-

The child was asked to draw his family doing something.

Child's Name: Frank
Child's Age: 8 years 7 months
Reason for referral: Frank suddenly failed to attend school and became rigid about wanting to stay and work on the farm at home. Lack of interest in typically fun activities and loss of sleep were also reported.

Frank stated that his family was sitting down to dinner and that he was sitting on the tractor.

Frank's father had passed away approximately four months prior to the assessment. This drawing may be interpreted as Frank's conflict over fears of having to accept adult responsibility at an early age. Frank sees himself, as the oldest son, as having to accept all the responsibilities of the farm and family care. Since this was not specifically stated by the mother, Frank had either assumed this himself or heard it from someone else.

Figure 8-3 An example of a child's drawing.

curate, recall of such clinical experience. Thus, interpretations from projective tests may reflect the personal beliefs and biases of the interpreter as well as the actual personality or behavior of the person being tested.

Research results have cumulatively suggested that the reliability of projective tests is low and that their validity is at best tenuous (see Mischel, 1968). On certain occasions, it is argued, the reliability of projective tests can be improved. For example, if the examiners have extensive experience, similar training, and shared theoretical beliefs, projective tests will yield reliable data. The theme of this reasoning is that if the clinician is "properly trained" the tests will be reliable. Research that compares the accuracy of individuals varying in clinical training and in clinical experience often indicates quite the contrary—no clear advantage for the trained or experienced test interpreters.

The validity of projective tests can be said to be equally tenuous when one considers, for example, Anastasi's (1968) summary of numerous studies in which subjects' responses to projective material were found to be very susceptible to temporary states such as food or sleep deprivation, frustration, or anxiety (and thus not valid measures of an enduring trait). When the basic foundations of assessment, reliability, and validity, are questioned, the utility of the projective testing method becomes dubious. Nevertheless, clinicians who employ the projective assessment methods continue to report satisfaction. Perhaps, as Exner (1976) suggested, the current "healthier" atmosphere in psychology will allow for further studies of projective assessment that are less biased and more creative.

Projectives and Treatment

One purpose for carrying out a psychological assessment, and often seen as the most important one, is to assist the clinician in the forthcoming intervention. It has been noted that the link between assessment and treatment varies as a function of the type of assessment that is carried out and that projective assessment does not make a direct assessment-treatment hookup. Instead, projectives have been criticized for providing only a global personality description that does not specify the causal and maintaining variables that can be directly changed in treatment (Mischel, 1968).

One way in which Rorschach test responses have been used in a more "treatment-oriented" fashion is where they have been employed as prognostic indicators in an attempt to identify clients who will benefit from psychotherapy. The Rorschach Prognostic Rating Scale (RPRS) (Kirkner, Wisham, & Giedt, 1953; Mindess, 1953) combines weighted Human, Animal, and Inanimate Movement, Shading, Color, and Form Level scores and sets out to predict therapy outcome. Although research evaluating the Rorschach test has tapered off dramatically in recent years, the RPRS successfully predicted patient response to a wide range of treatment approaches.

A New Twist: Using Projectives to Assess "Impact"

In a fashion different from the traditional use of projective tests to assess intrapsychic personality characteristics, research has developed around the Rorschach and TAT as instruments to assess "interpersonal impact" (Singer, 1976). Here, the shift is away from testing primarily to diagnose, and toward the use of testing to try to predict the subject's effect or impact upon others. To do this, the stimulus cards are presented to family members both individually and in groups. Data analysis consists of interpreting the joint transactions of the group members discussing the stimulus cards, rather than the responses of one person taking the test by him- or herself. Through this use of projective measures the researchers can conceptualize aspects of the impacts of the family members on the cognitive and affective expression and relationship styles of the other family members. The findings of this line of research have shed some light on our understanding of the communication styles of disturbed (schizophrenic) families (see also Bauman & Roman, 1964; Levy & Eppstein, 1964; Loveland, Singer, & Wynne, 1963).

OBJECTIVE ASSESSMENT

The objective approach to personality assessment is an enterprise that seeks to scientifically describe the characteristics or traits of an individual or group of individuals as a means of predicting behavior. This approach to acquiring assessment data seeks the same basic outcome as the projective method—to predict future behavior—but the ways in which the data are collected are markedly different. In a learning module on objective personality assessment, Butcher (1971) lists three essential projective/objective differences. First, projectives are more interested in intrapsychic dynamics while objective assessments seek a trait description—a description of the person's usual or characteristic style. Second, projective tests are vague or ambiguous and there is freedom to respond, whereas objective tests are well-defined stimuli that require limited answers (e.g., true or false). Third, the content of the projective test response is typically interpreted for each person without reference to norms. An objective test score on the other hand, although partially reflecting the test items themselves, compares the subject's item responses to the responses of many other test takers. For this reason, standardization is vital in objective assessment whereas it is less so with projectives. Objective assessment, in summary, is a structured, scientific, nonsubjective approach to the description of an individual.

Minnesota Multiphasic Personality Inventory

Characteristic of the objective method of assessment is the Minnesota Multiphasic Personality Inventory (MMPI) developed by Hathaway and McKinley (1942). The MMPI consists of 550 test items to which the subject responds with either "True" or "False," (or "Cannot Say"). The test items were selected from a wide variety of sources, they are stated in the first person, and they are written for ease of reading. The items are also worded in various ways such that a "Yes" response is not always associated with disturbed behavior. Sample MMPI items are presented in Table 6-3.

Test administration simply requires that the subject be given the MMPI test booklet (also available in different formats and in different languages) and asked to read each item carefully and mark the answer on an answer sheet. Once completed, scoring templates are used to tally the total for each of 4 validity scales and 10 clinical scales. The scale means are then converted to T scores and plotted on a summary sheet to produce an MMPI profile. The T score is a standardized score that allows for comparisons of elevations and low points across the different MMPI scales. A *T* score of 50 is average for general population subjects. Typically, based on the normal distribution of these *T* scores, 68.7 of test takers will get *T* scores between 40 and 60. No special clinical meaning is attached to scores in this average range. Only 16% score greater (or lower) than *T*-score 60, and *T* scores greater than 70 occur in about 2% of normals. Such high scores are rare and indicate that the subject deviates from average in certain ways. Clinical meaning is usually attached to such deviant scores.

Consistent with the standards of the objective method of assessment, the clinical scales of the MMPI were devised by comparing the responses of known psychiatric groups with those of normative groups. Items were included in a particular scale *only* if they "significantly" differentiated between the normal and the clinical or criterion group. Although this criterion group was usually less than 50 patients, these subjects were all very much alike in terms of their clinical picture.

MMPI Scales   The basic MMPI scales are listed in Table 8-1. The first four scales are the validity scales: *?* (cannot say), *L* (Lie scale), *F* (Fake Bad Scale), and *K* (Subtle Defensiveness). Before the clinician interprets the MMPI, he or she checks the validity scales to see that the subject did not present him- or herself in an evasive, careless, or defensive fashion. The *?* scale is the total number of items that the subject indicated he or she did not answer either "True" or "False." If this scale score is very high it may indicate that the subject was being intentionally vague and evasive. The *L* scale is composed of items that are almost universally answered "*True*." A high *L* score would suggest that the subject is attempting to falsify the responses and appear in a more socially desirable, virtuous light. The *F* scale also informs the test interpreter of the validity of the MMPI responses. A reasonable *F*-scale score is considered to be an indication that the subject's responses were thought out rationally and that the subject was not "faking bad" (trying to appear more disturbed by claiming excessive symptoms). In contrast, an elevated *F*-scale score indicates careless or confused responding, a faking bad approach, or, in some cases, randomly responding to the test items. The last validity scale is the *K* scale. This scale was an additional scale that was added to increase the validity of the clinical scales. *K* is said to be an indication of subtle defensiveness and the *K*-scale score is used with other scales (clinical) as a correction factor. The validity scales tell the interpreting psychologist something about the person who is responding to the test, but, more importantly, these scales are vital indicants that tell us the validity of the other clinical scales.

A subject who responds in such a fashion as to acquire a high score on *Hs* is described as the type of person who presents numerous physical problems, appears preoccupied with self, and is overly complaining. High *Hs* scores also suggest a cynical, defeatist quality of the subject. The second clinical scale, *D*, indicates the degree to which the subject would be described by words nearer the end of the following list: euphoric, jovial, cheerful, sober, solemn, dejected, disconsolate, despondent, hopeless (Buss & Gerjuoy, 1957). Thus high scorers on the *D* scale would be depressed, pessimistic, and perhaps suicidal, whereas low scorers are probably cheerful, optimistic, and self-confident. The *Hy* scale is elevated in cases where the subject is a naive, dependent, yet very sociable type. The high *Hy*

Table 8-1 Basic MMPI Scales

Validity Scales	?	Cannot say
	L	Lie Scale
	F	Fake Bad Scale
	K	Subtle Defensiveness
Clinical Scales	Hs	Hypochondriasis (1)
	D	Depression (2)
	Hy	Hysteria (3)
	Pd	Psychopathic Deviant (4)
	Mf	Masculinity-Femininity (5)
	Pa	Paranoia (6)
	Pt	Psychasthenia (7)
	Sc	Schizophrenia (8)
	Ma	Mania (9)
	Si	Social Introversion (0)

These basic MMPI scales are referred to by either the letters that are a shortened version of the scale name, or by the number that appears to the right in parentheses.

subject also expresses a variety of physical complaints, reacting to stress and avoiding responsibility by developing physical disorders. These vague physical complaints are usually the result of psychological problems and not physical ones. An individual who would be described as antisocial, rebellious, unsocialized, and untrustworthy would show an elevation on the *Pd* scale. More severely psychopathic individuals are usually in trouble with authority figures (often legally) and in discord with their family or spouse. *Mf* items are designed to differentiate men and women (based on traditional roles).

Pa elevations reflect an overly sensitive, suspicious person who is shrewd and guarded. High scorers on *Pt* are highly anxious, obsessional people who think in a ruminative fashion, behave phobically, and are generally rigid and self-critical. The seriously disturbed patient who has poor contact with reality, bizarre sense experiences (hallucinations), and strange thoughts (perhaps delusions), will have an elevated *Sc*-scale score. Slightly elevated *Sc* scores indicate a shy, withdrawn individual who may behave in an idiosyncratic style. *Ma* reflects the degree to which an individual is described on a continuum from outgoing, sociable, and optimistic, to excessively energetic, disoriented, and confused. Finally, *Si* represents an introversion-extroversion dimension. High socially introverted individuals are shy, withdrawn, modest, and inhibited while low socially introverted (i.e., extroverted) individuals are more socially confident, outgoing, spontaneous and spirited.

Additional MMPI Scales   Though there are several hundred additional MMPI scales (see Dahlstrom, Welsh, & Dahlstrom, 1972) the following is a select list of those that are often used by practicing clinical psychologists. Barron (1953) reports on the development of the *Es* (Ego Strength) scale composed of 68 items from the MMPI. This scale was developed by selecting from the total MMPI those items that significantly correlated with ratings of improvement in psychotherapy. Thus, the scale is designed to assess adaptability, personal resourceful-ness, or, if you prefer, ego strength, and to predict whether or not therapy will be effective for the patient.

A second example of an additional MMPI scale is MacAndrew's Alcoholism Scale (1965). This scale consists of 51 items and has been found to accurately dis-criminate between alcoholic and nonalcoholic psychiatric patients. Moreover, Hoffman, Loper, and Kammeier (1974) reported that the MacAndrew scale is ef-fective in picking out prealcoholics who later become alcoholic.

Two other examples of additional MMPI scales are Welsh's (1956) *A* (Anxiety) and *R* (Repression) scales. The *A* scale is composed of 39 items that measure the thinking, emotional, and energy aspects of anxiety. Those individuals who score high on the *A* scale are anxious, uncomfortable, lethargic, shy, and hesitant. In contrast to the unhappy, maladjusted person with high *A*, the person with a low *A* score is comfortable, nonanxious, expressive, colorful, and self-confident. It has been pointed out that the high *A* subject is often highly motivated for psycho-therapy.

The *R* scale contains 40 items and measures the degree to which the individual is outgoing, emotional, and spontaneous. Low *R* scorers would be characterized as outspoken, outgoing, enthusiastic, and emotional while high *R* scorers are for-mal, conventional, submissive, and, in general, live a cautious life-style.

Finally, a Control (*Cn*) Scale (Coudra, 1953) was developed to aid in the identi-fication of patients who were in sufficient control to be treated as outpatients rather than having to be hospitalized.

The MMPI Profile The final product of the MMPI is a personality profile that contains the relative elevations on each of the different basic scales. There is also a place for plotting some of the additional scales that may have been of interest to the particular test user. An interpretation of the subject's personality is deter-mined by examining the scale elevations, and, in addition to single scale eleva-tions, much attention has been placed on the use of profile or pattern analysis for interpretation of the MMPI (e.g., Gilberstadt & Duker, 1965; Graham, 1977; Marks & Seeman, 1963). What is frequently done in this type of analysis is a fo-cusing on the two or three highest scales. Different patterns represent different types of individuals, and the pattern interpretations are usually more important than those of the individual scales (Figure 8-4).

Illustratively, we will look at five patterns (code types) that are found to be use-ful: the 4-9, 2-7, 8-9, 1-2-3, and 2-4-7 (these numbers correspond to the scales of the MMPI—see Table 8-1). These patterns were selected as examples, as were the additional MMPI scales, based on their supporting data and their utility to the practicing diagnostic clinicians we contacted.

The 4-9 profile is characterized by the *Pd* (4) and the *Ma* (9) scales being greater than *T* score 70 while no other scales scores are above *T* score 70. This profile or pattern is considered indicative of an "antisocial personality." Complaints in-clude drinking, hostility, and work and home conflicts. These individuals are also considered to have an inability to experience anxiety or stress. Instead, problems are someone else's fault! Why worry? Although this is descriptive of an adult, many adolescents also show 4-9 profiles, but fortunately many are no longer 4-9s

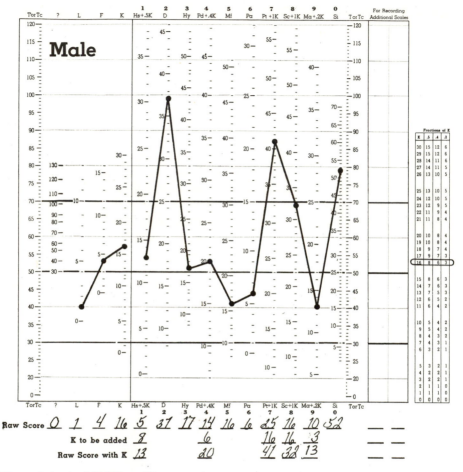

Figure 8-4 An MMPI profile—scored, coded, and plotted. (The MMPI profile sheet is reproduced from the *Minnesota Multiphasic Personality Inventory*, copyright 1948, by The Psychological Corporation. All rights reserved.)

Take a look at this profile and try to think about what type of person would have produced it. Use the individual scales, combined scales, and your knowledge in general to try and best describe this person.

PSYCHOLOGICAL REPORT: MMPI

Name: Johnson, David
Age: Forty
Sex: Male
Marital Status: Married
Date of Testing: 7/31/80

Background Information: Mr. Johnson's presenting complaint is "Anxiety attacks, nervousness." He has had several hospitalizations of unspecified length or number for anxiety and depression. Mr. Johnson has been married for 14 years, has three children aged 7 to 12, and reports needing no help with his marriage. Until June 1977, Mr. Johnson was employed as a field supervisor on construction sites. Since that time, however, he has been employed only sporadically. He reports that his lack of employment has been due to his psychiatric condition. Presently, Mr. Johnson reports never drinking alcohol, although he was considered a heavy drinker three years ago. Presently, he is being prescribed Thorazine, Sinequan, and Cogentin. He reports using no other drugs regularly.

Reason for Referral: Mr. Johnson was referred for psychological testing in order to further evaluate his psychiatric status that will have a bearing on his upcoming review for increased compensation from the Veterans Administration.

Behavioral Observations: Mr. Johnson came to testing neatly dressed and groomed. It was evident at times that he had dryness of the mouth, which is probably due to his medication. Mr. Johnson reported that he was feeling nervous on the day of testing. However, he reported that this anxiety was no better and no worse than usual. He was pleasant and cooperative throughout testing, and rapport was easily established. Testing conditions were adequate and there is no reason to suspect invalidity of any of the tests. Mr. Johnson's test-taking attitude on the MMPI appears to reveal some defensiveness, although the profile appears valid. Individuals with this MMPI code type (see Figure 8-4) tend to display a distress syndrome (anxious, tense, high strung, and dysphoric). They worry excessively, tend to anticipate problems before they occur, and overreact to minor stresses. They may have somatic symptoms, including vague complaints of fatigue, tiredness, and exhaustion. Although these persons may not report feeling especially depressed, they may show symptoms of clinical depression, including weight loss, slow personal tempo, slowed speech, and retarded thought processes. They are extremely pessimistic about the likelihood of overcoming their problems and brood and ruminate about their problems much of the time.

Individuals with this MMPI profile have a strong need for achievement and for recognition for their accomplishments. They tend to feel guilty when they fall short of their goals. They tend to be rather indecisive, and they harbor feelings of inadequacy, insecurity, and inferiority. They are intrapunitive, blaming themselves for all their problems. These individuals are rigid in their thinking and problem solving, and they are meticulous and perfectionistic in daily activities. They also may be excessively religious and extremely moralistic.

Persons with this profile tend to be rather docile and passive-dependent in their relationships with other people. In fact, they often find it difficult to be even appropriately assertive. They have the capacity for forming deep, emotional ties, and in times of stress, they become clinging and dependent. They are not aggressive or belligerent and they tend to elicit nurturant and helping behavior from other people.

Mr. Johnson appears to be a socially introverted and withdrawn person. In interactions with other people, he can be expected to demonstrate considerable insecurity and lack of social skills, especially with women. He may have learned to expect a considerable amount of depression as an integral part of himself, which may detract from the motivation and capacity to change. He does not appear to be at risk for problems with chemical dependency.

Summary Impressions: Mr. Johnson may be described as anxious, ruminative, indecisive, and depressed. His main difficulties involve social anxiety and maladjustment in addition to anxiety over achievement and dependency issues. The therapeutic task for Mr. Johnson appears to be enabling him to lower his expectations of himself and increase his self-confidence. However, because his depression appears to be long and somewhat characterological in nature, he is accepting of his present state and not highly motivated to change.

after time passes (i.e., they "grow up"). In contrast, the adult 4-9 is considered difficult to treat, and many persons with such a profile remain unchanged after hospitalization, therapy, or prison.

A 2-7 profile (*D* and *Pt* greater than *T* score 70) indicates a person very much different from the 4-9 profile. The 2-7 profile subject is depressed and anxious. High strung, nervous, and jittery are adjectives used to describe the 2-7 individual. Behavioral signs can include slow rate of speech, trembling, and sweating. Sleep difficulties are often noted as well. "Reactive depression" is sometimes used to describe their symptoms of nervousness and gloominess. The characteristics of the 4-9 person are characteristics that are not seen in the 2-7 individual. That is, problems with authority, argumentative behavior, and an absence of anxiety are not likely observed in the subject producing a 2-7 MMPI profile.

The 8-9 MMPI profile (Marks & Seeman, 1963) is when both scales 8 and 9 are above *T* score 70, and scale *F* greater than *L* and *K*. Seventy percent of the patients of this type are psychotic, often schizophrenic. In other instances, this code type may be considered an indication of the excited phase of manic-depressive psychosis. Descriptions of persons with an 8-9 profile code type include excessive activity, disorganization, distractibility, low frustration tolerance, and an absence of personal and often interpersonal insight. These individuals can be said to be unpredictable, disoriented, and irritable. Clients with 8-9 profiles are very difficult to work with in psychotherapy since they have difficulty focusing and have difficulty coming to grips with personal issues.

Gilberstadt and Duker's (1965) rules for the 1-2-3 code type include scales 1, 2, and 3 over *T* score 70, scale 1 > scale 2 > scale 3, no other scales over *T* score 70, *L* < *T* score 65, *F* < *T* score 85, and *K* < *T* score 70. Individuals whose MMPI profile corresponds to these rules are said to lack aggressive or sexual drive but to be relatively stable at work and in marriage. The important aspect of the 1-2-3 profile is the subject's presentation of somatic symptoms. These people are often depressed and anxious, but they express their difficulties in somatic terminology. Therefore, they often present complaints of pain, nausea, headaches, nervousness, and fatigue.

Our last example of an MMPI pattern includes three scales elevated over T score 70: 2 (*D*), 4 (*Pd*), and 7 (*Pt*). This profile indicates someone with the anxiety depression of a 2-7 but with some of the lack of impulse control of the 4. Briefly, then, this type of person would be a tearful, anxious individual who is likely to be argumentative.

These three examples of MMPI profile "code types" do not exhaust the list. There are many others. However, these should communicate how profiles are interpreted and how code types consist of contributions for the various separate scales.

Computer Scoring   Some researchers have contended that "human error" can be removed from the assessment by computerizing the psychological interpretation. For example, Fowler (1969) has developed such a computerized system, and the computerized MMPI interpretations are available through a professional service. Basically, once the subject has responded to the MMPI items on an answer sheet, the answers are turned into computer cards, scored by the computer, and subsequently interpreted. The computer selects interpretive statements appropriate for the respondent by using preprogrammed criteria based on the scale score elevations. The computer then prints out the MMPI profile and interpretation.

Butcher (1971) lists some of the advantages of the computer-based interpretations over those performed by human clinical psychologists: the computer can handle more complex prediction equations, the computer stores all previous cases in its memory, the computer is almost perfectly reliable, and the computer reduces the professional time required for the assessment task. Nevertheless, there are several different computerized analyses available (see Butcher & Owen, 1978) and such systems are not always favored over the clinician's personal MMPI interpretation (see reviews by Butcher in Buros, 1978).

MMPI Short Forms   While the MMPI has proven to be a valuable assessment tool, its length may be prohibitive for some research and practical applications. For instance, completion of the MMPI takes from 50 minutes to two hours. In an attempt to solve the problem, several researchers have developed short forms of the MMPI (Faschingbauer, 1974; Hugo, 1971; Kincannon, 1968; Overall & Gomez-Mont, 1974). Evaluations of the MMPI short forms have considered correlations with the entire MMPI, *t* tests between the means of the separate MMPI scales, and agreement of the long and short forms in the MMPI profile peaks. Although evaluations using a single short form (e.g., Edinger, Kendall, Hooke, & Bogan, 1976; Hoffman & Butcher, 1975) generally report significant correlations between the long and short forms, there are significantly different mean scale scores and poor profile-peak correspondence. These differences severely limit the utility of the short forms. Hoffman and Butcher (1975) have also shown the inability of the MMPI short forms to produce accurate predictions of the MMPI code types. Taken together, research findings demonstrate the apparent limits on the clinical use of the MMPI short forms.

Whether or not a short form of an established measurement instrument can be clinically useful is an example of an applied-clinical research question generated directly from clinical assessment. Practicing clinicians have a problem—at times, the MMPI is too long. Researchers seek to answer the applied problem—can an equally effective short form be devised? The researchers set out to directly answer an applied question. Such efforts are an example of the opportunities to achieve a scientist-practitioner fusion.

An Evaluation   The mere quantity of researchers evaluating numerous aspects of the MMPI is overwhelming. Summarizing such a quantity of information is not without weakness but a generally acceptable consensus is that the MMPI has been sufficiently demonstrated to be a valuable tool in the screening of patients and the assigning of psychiatric diagnosis to warrant continued use. In many respects, the MMPI remains a standard of psychological assessment.

But for those clinicians who prefer a more behavioral perspective, for those whose services entail more therapy than assessment, and for those whose jobs do not require them to provide psychiatric diagnoses, the MMPI may not be entirely helpful. For instance, a clinician who is working to modify a client's fears may not find the MMPI useful beyond the initial description. Nevertheless, the MMPI continues to be a valuable and widely used assessment instrument.

California Psychological Inventory

The California Psychological Inventory (CPI) is a 480-item test that contains 18 scales (Gough, 1957). Although the CPI is like the MMPI in format and, indeed, shares 178 virtually identical items, it is particularly different in its lack of symptom-oriented test items. Most of the content of the CPI consists of reporting typical behavior patterns and customary feelings, opinions, and attitudes about social ethics and family matters (Megargee, 1972). The CPI was intended primarily for use with nondisturbed, "normal," subjects and it addresses personality characteristics more than diagnostic description. Thus, as an objective measure used in assessment, the CPI would be most useful to gain an understanding of the subject as a person and less useful in making a diagnosis.

Gough has organized the 18 scales of the CPI into four groups (classes) presented in Table 8-2. Fifteen of these 18 scales are considered measures of various personality traits, and 3 scales (i.e., *Wb*, *Gi*, and *Cm*) are considered validity scales. The validity scales, however, also say something about the individual's behavior, thus serving a dual purpose.

Interpreting the CPI consists of examining the height of individual scale scores, the relative elevations among the different homogeneous groups of scales, and the heights of the four classes of scales as described in Table 8-2. Finally, the clinician integrates the CPI data in an overall portrait of the person. Gough and many others have carried out numerous investigations to provide empirical evidence of test score correlates, but Gough recommends (see Megargee, 1972) that the final interpretation emphasize the clinician's subjective analysis.

16PF

The Sixteen Personality Factor questionnaire (Cattell, Eber, & Tatsuoka, 1970) yields 16 scores for 16 relatively independent dimensions such as dominance, in-

Table 8-2   CPI Basic Scales in the Four Scale Classes

Class I	Measures poise, ascendancy, self-assurance and interpersonal adequacy	
	Do	Dominance
	Cs	Capacity for Status
	Sy	Sociability
	Sp	Social Presence
	Sa	Self-Acceptance
	Wb	Sense of Well-Being
Class II	Measures maturity, responsibility, socialization, and interpersonal values	
	Re	Responsibility
	So	Socialization
	Sc	Self-Control
	To	Tolerance
	Gi	Good Impression
	Cm	Communality
Class III	Measures achievement potential and intellectual efficiency	
	Ac	Achievement via Conformance
	Ai	Achievement via Independence
	Ie	Intellectual Efficiency
Class IV	Measures intellectual and interest modes	
	Py	Psychology Mindedness
	Fx	Flexibility
	Fe	Femininity

telligence, radicalism, will control, and emotional stability. The scales of the 16PF were developed via extensive factor analytic research. Initially, Cattell and his colleagues factor analyzed numerous descriptive adjectives and reduced the mass of "descriptors" down to the 16 dimensions measured by the test. Subsequently, Cattell's efforts have focused on examining the cross-cultural stability and profile-prediction validity of the 16PF.

Although the test is a good example of a factor analytically derived personality instrument, there is a noted absence of any validity scales or other methods to examine subject distortion or faking. Furthermore, although Cattell's test has evidenced theoretical and psychometric advances, there is as yet insufficient external validation within practical assessment situations (Rorer, 1972).

Other Personality Inventories

Several additional personality inventories are in relatively wide use. Eysenck developed the Eysenck Personality Inventory (EPI) as a test that assesses the dimensions of neuroticism and introversion-extraversion (Eysenck & Eysenck, 1968). Neuroticism refers to the group of personality disorders characterized by anxiety, while introversion-extraversion refers to the differences between inward turning, timid, quiet, and nonadventurous persons and outgoing, funloving, friendly, and adventure-seeking people. More recently, the scale has been revised, now the EPQ (Eysenck Personality Questionnaire), and includes a measure of psychoticism

(Eysenck & Eysenck, 1976). The EPQ is a 90-item, yes-no questionnaire. The Junior EPQ contains 81 items and is for children aged 7 to 15.

The Edwards Personal Preference Schedule (EPPS; Edwards, 1953) uses a forced-choice format. In this format, subjects are presented with pairs of items and asked to select the one statement which is more characteristic of what they are like. Edwards used this format to control for social desirability. Social desirability is the tendency for people to try to appear as best as possible when presenting themselves—we do not typically choose to describe ourselves in undesirable terms. In order to control the social desirability of test items, Edwards first had individuals rate each item for its levels of social desirability. Then, when constructing the test, the items that were paired for the forced choice were of comparable social desirability. The EPPS consists of 225 forced-choice items and yields scores on 15 personality dimensions.

Samples of Specific Objective Personality Research Instruments

Within the assessment of personality, the instruments that are used to measure specific personality characteristics play a vital role. It is through the use of scientifically developed assessment instruments that we can empirically examine our theories of personality and human functioning (see Highlight 8-2). There are, however, literally thousands of scales, inventories, and tests that are used to assess various aspects of personality, and it would take several volumes to properly cover the diversity of available measurement instruments. The *Mental Measurements Yearbook* is a useful source, a "consumers guide," for selecting psychological tests. The following four instruments represent only a sample of some of the types of inventories, the types of scores that they provide, and the content of the related research.

Locus of Control   One of the most often used personality measures in recent times is Rotter's (1966) measure of a generalized expectancy for internal versus external control of reinforcement. His 29-item, forced-choice test (6 items are fillers and are not scored) measures whether an individual perceives both positive and negative event outcomes as being contingent on his or her own behavior—internally controlled—or as being the result of luck, fate, or powerful others—externally controlled. A considerable number of research studies have demonstrated a relationship between the generalized expectancy called locus of control and numerous other behaviors (see Phares, 1976). There is also available a scale to assess locus of control in children (Nowicki & Strickland, 1973).

Empathy   The degree to which an individual can intellectually or imaginatively understand another person's condition or state of mind can be measured using Hogan's (1969) Empathy Scale. The importance of the concept of empathy is evident in its role in research in both moral development and as a characteristic of psychotherapists. That is, more mature individuals, in terms of their abilities to be fair and kind to others, and more effective psychotherapists tend to be persons with strong empathic abilities. Hogan's scale is a 64-item, self-report measure.

Highlight 8-2   Implicit Personality Theories

Although the scientific study of personality is only a few decades old, it has always been, and will always be, important for people to understand themselves and others around them. In a sense, everyone is a personality psychologist, for each one of us has definite ideas about how people are put together, and each one of us acts on those ideas every day.

Academic psychologists have a keen interest in these "folk" personality ideas. In the last 20 or so years a great deal of attention has been paid to so-called "implicit personality theories," which are ideas that people have concerning how various personality traits are related to each other. For example, the belief that people who are very "sociable" also tend to be "poised" (or that fat people are jolly) would be an example of an implicit personality theory.

The technique of factor analysis has been most useful in the study of the implicit structure underlying peer ratings. Tupes and Christal (1961) conducted several factor-analytic studies of peer ratings. They used a set of 35 bipolar ratings scales constructed by Cattell (1957) from an initial list of 4504 trait names compiled by Allport and Odbert (1936), a list that represented all of the trait names that appeared in *Webster's New International Dictionary, Unabridged*. Although Tupes and Christal varied such factors as the level of education of the raters and the length of acquaintance between raters and ratees, they consistently found the same five-factor solution. That is, various personality descriptions are consistently grouped into the following categories: extroversion, agreeableness, conscientiousness, emotional stability, and culture (refined, artistic).

Indeed, a factor-analytic study by Passini and Norman (1966) shows that this same factor structure emerges even when the raters and ratees don't know each other at all. Passini and Norman asked their raters to rate one another on the Cattell scales, even though they had been in the same room for *less than 15 minutes* and had not had a chance to talk to each other. Again, a five-factor structure emerged that was virtually identical to that found by Tupes and Christal.

These studies show a seemingly universal structure that underlies ratings of others. For example, it seems that if one is rated as being very "good-natured," one will also be rated as being very "gentle" and highly "cooperative," and apparently this will be true for almost any rater-ratee pair, regardless of such factors as length of acquaintance.

Self-Concept   One measure of an individual's self-concept is the Tennessee Self-Concept Scale (Fitts, 1964). This scale provides both specific scores across many subareas as well as an overall score and a self-concept profile. The five self-concept areas that are measured include physical self, moral-ethical self, personal self, family self, and social self. In addition, a self-acceptance score and variability score are available from this measure. The test contains 100 items, 90 of which are directly concerned with measuring self-concept and 10 of which (lie items) are used to check subject faking.

Psychological Androgyny   The study of masculinity and feminity as characteristics of personality was redirected by Bem (1974) when she introduced a new sex-role inventory that measures masculinity, feminity, and androgyny. The Bem sex-role inventory asks persons to indicate on a seven-point scale how well each of 60 masculine, feminine, and neutral personality characteristics are accurately descriptive of themselves. Unlike previous measures that conceptualized masculinity and feminity as opposite ends of a single continuum, this inventory treats masculinity and feminity as two independent dimensions and thereby makes it possible to characterize subjects as masculine, feminine, or androgynous. With the current emergence of new and different sex roles for both men and women, this inventory should spur meaningful research on psychological androgyny—the ability to have both masculine and feminine characteristics in the sense of displaying both types of behaviors (e.g., both assertive and yielding) depending upon the situation.

Other Samples of Objective Instruments for Assessing Psychological Dysfunctions

The assessment of personality and the measurement of psychological dysfunctions are, in some instances, very much related (e.g., MMPI). However, not all personality tests provide information concerning the subject's problems, and consequently a number of inventories have been designed specifically to assess psychopathology.

Psychological Screening Inventory (PSI)   Lanyon (1970) developed the Psychological Screening Inventory (a 130-item, true-false self-report inventory) in order to provide a brief test for use in routine screening situations in social service, mental health settings. The PSI takes only 10 to 20 minutes to complete. Thus, this brief screening device can be very practical and useful in mental health-related settings where time and psychological skills may be at a premium.

The PSI contains five scales that assess the client in terms of his or her similarity to psychiatric patients (Alienation), and to incarcerated prisoners (Social Nonconformity), and by assessing the personality factor of anxiety or perceived maladjustment (Discomfort), the factor of extraversion or undercontrol (Expression), and a general test-taking attitude (Defensiveness). In distinguishing the PSI from some of the other instruments discussed thus far, it is important to remember that it is a brief inventory yet it maintains practical utility and that it focuses on screening potential mental health patients.

Inpatient Multidimensional Psychiatric Scale   The Inpatient Multidimensional Psychiatric Scale (IMPS) was developed by Lorr, Klett, McNair, and Lasky (1962) to identify the dimensions of psychosis. Due to the need for an objective, standardized assessment instrument that could be used to assess the *changes* that take place in psychiatric patients, the IMPS has been used as a measure of the current functioning of the patients both before and after an intervention. The IMPS consists of 75 items rated for intensity, frequency, or presence by trained interviewers or observers at the conclusion of a 30- to 45-minute interview. The IMPS can be scored for some second-order factors: Excitement versus Retardation, Schizophrenic Disorganization, and Cognitive or Thinking Distortion.

The Corresponding Development of Theory and Objective Measurement: The Case of Anxiety

Clinical psychologists have developed a variety of theories to explain the causes and manifestations of anxiety, and a corresponding diversity of instruments to assess anxiety. We will focus on three such measures in order to illustrate how our theories and their empirical bases are enhanced as the assessment methods develop, and vice-versa.

Psychological theories of anxiety can, as can many psychological concepts, be traced to Freud's writings. His concept of anxiety (Freud, 1938) entailed an unpleasant state, similar to nervousness, that is a signal that the person's ego is unable to cope with the present psychological conflicts. Freud's analysis generated a great deal of heat, but little light, until psychologists began to develop systematic ways to measure anxiety.

By operationalizing the concept of anxiety, Taylor (1953) played a major role in the enhancement of the investigation of anxiety. The Taylor Manifest Anxiety Scale (TMAS) is a 52-item inventory measuring anxiety as a drive, with the assumption that individuals differing in their level of anxiety also differ in their drive or motivational state. Questions on the TMAS are taken from the MMPI, based on Taylor's validational research.

More recently, however, researchers have drawn a distinction between anxiety "states" and anxiety "traits" (Cattell & Scheier, 1958). This distinction has dramatically altered research. States are viewed as transitory conditions, while traits are more permanent personality predispositions to respond in certain ways. Advancing from the state-trait distinction, Spielberger, Gorsuch, and Lushene (1970) developed two coordinated 20-item inventories that assess anxiety as a state and as a trait (i.e., the State-Trait Anxiety Inventory; STAI). The instructions for the A-state portion of the STAI request that the subjects give the answer that seems to best describe their *present feelings*. In contrast, the A-trait portion of the STAI seeks to elicit a description of how the subject *generally* feels (see Table 8-3). The theoretical expansion of the concept of anxiety, from a general notion of drive to a more specific view of states, has spurred some important clinical research (Spielberger, 1972).

Results of research using the STAI have supported the state-trait distinction (cf. Kendall, Finch, Auerbach, Hooke, & Mikulka, 1976; Spielberger, Auerbach, Wadsworth, Dunn, & Taulbee, 1973). Specifically, the state portion of the inventory shows changes due to stress (e.g., an examination), while the trait portion remains relatively unchanged. In addition, factor analytic studies have supported the state-trait distinction of the STAI with state and trait items loading on sepa-

Table 8-3   Sample State-Trait Anxiety Inventory Items

State Anxiety

DIRECTIONS: A number of statements which people have used to describe themselves are given below. Read each statement and then blacken in the appropriate circle to the right of the statement to indicate how you *feel* right now, that is, *at this moment*. There are no right or wrong answers. Do not spend too much time on any one statement but give the answer which seems to describe your present feelings best.

	Not at All	Somewhat	Moderately So	Very Much So
1. I feel calm.................	①	②	③	④
2. I feel secure	①	②	③	④
3. I am tense..................	①	②	③	④

Trait Anxiety

DIRECTIONS: A number of statements which people have used to describe themselves are given below. Read each statement and then blacken in the appropriate circle to the right of the statement to indicate how you *generally* feel. There are no right or wrong answers. Do not spend too much time on any one statement but give the answer which seems to describe how you generally feel.

	Almost Never	Sometimes	Often	Almost Always
21. I feel pleasant	①	②	③	④
22. I tire quickly.................	①	②	③	④
23. I feel like crying	①	②	③	④
24. I wish I could be as happy as others seem to be....................	①	②	③	④
25. I am losing out on things because I can't make up my mind soon enough	①	②	③	④

rate factors (e.g., Kendall et al., 1976). Thus, state and trait anxiety appear to be distinct psychological phenomena.

Further research using inventories to assess anxiety states and traits have demonstrated that the *situation* that elicits the anxiety is a vital source of information that requires systematic inclusion within anxiety assessment inventories. While indirectly maintaining the state-trait distinction, Endler and Okada (1975) developed an anxiety measure with emphasis on measuring situational variance (i.e., The S-R Inventory of General Trait Anxiousness, S-R GTA). In the S-R GTA, which is the current form of earlier tests by Endler and his colleagues (1962), the anxiety trait is considered multifaceted—with each facet corresponding to a situation that elicits anxiety. In responding to the S-R GTA, subjects provide their reactions to general situations (see Table 8-4). The same 15 items are answered by all subjects for each situation. The items describe various types of anxiety responses (e.g., cognitive, physiological). This test can thus examine, beyond a subject's general tendency toward anxiety, their trait level of anxiety for each type of anxiety-arousing situation.

The S-R GTA itself does not measure anxiety states, but other measures such as the state anxiety portion of the STAI can be used in conjunction with the multidimensional trait measures of the S-R GTA. However, a situation-specific trait-state test for the measurement of affective responses such as anxiety was recently developed by Zuckerman (1977). This scale contains 20 situations to which sub-

Table 8-4 Samples from the S-R Inventory of General Trait Anxiousness: A trait anxiety measure that includes the situation

This inventory represents a means of studying peoples reactions to and attitudes towards various types of *General* situations. On the following pages are represented five general kinds of situations which most people have encountered. For each of these general kinds of situations certain common types of personal reactions and feelings are listed. Indicate the degree to which you would show these reactions and feelings in the situations presented at the top of each page by circling the appropriate number.

"YOU ARE IN SITUATIONS WHERE YOU ARE ABOUT TO OR MAY ENCOUNTER PHYSICAL DANGER" (We are primarily interested in your reactions in *General* to those situations that involve dealing with *potentially dangerous things or objects.*)

Circle one of the five alternatives for each of the following 15 items.

Seek experiences like this	1 Very much	2	3	4	5 Not at all
Feel upset	1 Very much	2	3	4	5 Not at all
Perspire	1 Very much	2	3	4	5 Not at all
Feel relaxed	1 Very much	2	3	4	5 Not at all

Table 8-4 *Continued*

"YOU ARE IN SITUATIONS WHERE YOU ARE BEING EVALUATED BY OTHER PEOPLE" (We are primarily interested in your reactions in *General* to those situations where you are being *evaluated* or *observed* by other people. This includes situations at work, school, in sports, social situations, etc.)

Circle one of the five alternatives for each of the following 15 items.

Seek experiences like this	1	2	3	4	5
	Very much				Not at all
Feel upset	1	2	3	4	5
	Very much				Not at all
Perspire	1	2	3	4	5
	Very much				Not at all
Feel relaxed	1	2	3	4	5
	Very much				Not at all

From N. S. Endler and M. Okada, A multidimensional measure of trait anxiety: The S-R Inventory of General Trait Anxiousness. *Journal of Consulting and Clinical Psychology*, 1975, *43*, 319–329. Reproduced with permission of Norman S. Endler.

jects describe their reactions within a variety of emotional or affective responses. Thus, the Zuckerman Inventory of Personal Reactions (ZIPERS) can be used to assess a variety of emotions while maintaining both the state-trait distinction and situational specificity.

Theoretically, the inclusion of situations in the assessment of traits should allow for more accurate prediction. Anxiety may be experienced in different ways and to different degrees depending on the situation and on the person involved. To paraphrase Endler (1975), when we research the effects of personality traits and threatening situations on subjects' state anxiety, it is essential that the measure of trait anxiety be specific and congruent with the threatening situation.

A recent study (Kendall, 1978) compared the global (situations not specified) trait measure of the STAI with two of the situational trait measures of the S-R GTA in predicting the anxiety arousal of college students in two situations. The two situations were (1) an evaluation threat (i.e., working on an extremely difficult task said to be an intelligence indicator) and (2) a physical danger threat (i.e., observing a car-crash film just prior to driving home). The measures of trait anxiety were acquired well before the stressful situations were presented. The state anxiety measures were taken just following the subject's participation in each situation. The results of this study indicated that state anxiety reactions could be predicted from the situation-specific trait measures but not from the overall, nonsituational measure. These results confirm the utility of situational trait measures as predictors of state anxiety arousal when the situation of the trait measure is congruent with the actual threatening situation.

In our tracing of the development of personality inventories that measure anxiety and the corresponding theoretical advances, we have highlighted the psychologist's attempts to predict behavior in a given situation from measures taken prior to that experience. Are there personality traits that appear in all types of situations? Are situations the determinant of behavior? What appears to be emerging from the research along these lines is that traits, when measured with some situational specificity, have the power to predict behavioral arousal in a similar situation. How specific does the situational trait have to be? Can certain situations, since they are similar, be classed together and used to develop a situational trait measure that predicts for a variety of related situations? These questions and others like them are the current focus of clinical research on anxiety and other personality variables.

Impact via Objective Assessment

The reader will recall that we considered the measurement of interpersonal impact as "a new twist" for the projective method of assessment. Now, using objective assessment procedures, we will examine another method for assessing impact. Kiesler and his colleagues (Perkins, Kiesler, Anchin, Chirico, Kyle, & Federman, 1979) developed the Impact Message Inventory (IMI) to measure an individual's "impact" on another during ongoing communication. The IMI is a 90-item, paper-and-pencil objective personality instrument. The actual inventory consists of 6 items per each of 15 interpersonal styles. Within these 90 items, there are three subscales of impact messages (direct feelings, action tendencies, and evoking messages), with 30 items assessing each subscale. The IMI yields objective data regarding an individual's interpersonal impact.

Interest in a psychological phenomenon such as "interpersonal impact" does not guarantee that different researchers will use the same assessment methods. Quite the contrary, impact has served to demonstrate that one topic can be assessed in several ways. The researcher strives to develop the most reliable and valid instrument, but the methods may differ as a function of the interests and biases of the researchers.

Issues in Objective Personality Assessment

The advances of the objective approach to personality assessment notwithstanding, there remain many unsolved issues. Two issues worthy of consideration are the problem of response sets and the determination of the goal of the assessment.

It has been suggested that the response set or response bias of the subject is a drawback for the objective measurement of personality. Jackson and Messick (1958) report research demonstrating that subjects tend to answer items on objective tests (subject's answering "yes" or "no," for example) based more on their tendencies to be either generally resistant or generally acquiescent (i.e., their *set*, or basic response tendency, to cooperate or not) than on other features of their personality. Edwards (1957) argued that the subject's desire to appear acceptable and socially desirable seriously affected test item responses. Each subject's response set or response style has thus been said to interfere with the accuracy of objective assessment. However, Block (1965) presented compelling evidence to contradict the "response set" account of objective test responses. His research utilized objective personality tests that controlled for the social desirability and resisting/acquiescing sets. With the response set eliminated, the different test scores were found to be valid indicators of individual subject differences. The taking into account of and controlling for response sets (e.g., remove social desirability) has become an important concern for those devising objective measures for personality assessment.

The second issue pertaining to objective assessment is its goal—the accurate description of the subject's personality characteristics or traits. While such a description is designed to predict future behavior and has been clinically useful, there is the unfortunate absence of a direct link to treatment. Shouldn't the assessment answer the question, "What treatment would be best for this person?" But does it? In some cases the answer is yes, in others, no. Researchers have examined pretreatment and posttreatment MMPI profiles and other objective personality measures in order to help design individualized treatment programs, but are the findings being applied systematically? The answer is primarily No. However, clinical researchers are increasingly attempting to use objective personality tests to predict what clients will benefit most from different interventions, so the future holds promise.

ON THE FUTURE OF PERSONALITY ASSESSMENT: CONFLICTING POSITIONS

Although personality assessment is one of the basic functions performed by clinicians in a variety of work settings, there has been some disagreement about the future of personality assessment. A recent article by Mischel (1977b) in *American Psychologist* examines several issues in personality theory and assessment, focusing mainly on what has developed in the area of personality and what we should have learned from these developments. A contrasting position is taken by Hogan, DeSoto, and Solano (1977) in their *American Psychologist* article on tests, traits, and personality research. The following discussion summarizes these articles' positions. An important theoretical position related to personality traits and social situations is discussed in Highlight 8-3.

Highlight 8-3   Are Traits in the Eyes of the Beholder?

The notion of human "personality" is based on the assumption that people have certain stable qualities—called "traits"—that refer to behavior that is consistent at different times and across various situations. Personality assessment has largely consisted of the measurement of various traits. The assumption that people have traits is not unique to psychology. Instead, it seems to be the way that all of us see each other. We all make trait statements of the type "John is introverted" or "Ginny is good-natured" or "Dick is dishonest."

Some researchers have attacked the validity of this trait notion and have argued that the available empirical evidence does not support the trait notion, but rather shows that people act differently in different situations. If this is correct, how can one explain the widespread popularity of the trait concept among psychologists and laymen alike? One suggested answer is provided by

Jones and Nisbett (1971), who argue that there is a strong tendency to explain *our own actions* in terms of situational variables (e.g., "I went to college because my folks wanted me to go") but to explain *the actions of others* in terms of trait dispositions (e.g., "She went to college because she enjoys learning"). Jones and Nisbett feel that this tendency is at least partly due to the fact that we have more information about ourselves and our own behavior than about other people. Thus, they feel that the trait assumption is generally incorrect and is employed only when the lack of information obscures the true (situational) cause of behavior.

A study by Nisbett, Caputo, Legant, and Marecek (1973) provides support for the Jones and Nisbett hypothesis. They asked each subject to write several paragraphs describing (1) why he had chosen his own girlfriend, (2) why he had chosen his college major, (3) why his best male friend had chosen his girlfriend, and (4) why his best friend had chosen his college major. Not all of the results supported the Jones and Nisbett hypothesis, but the general trend did: subjects attributed their own choices more to situational variables than to traits, but used trait explanations more often than situational explanations in describing their best friends' choices.

Other studies have not been as supportive of the Jones and Nisbett hypothesis, suggesting that the phenomenon may not be as pervasive as originally thought. In a recent review of the literature, Monson and Snyder (1977) explained the discrepancies in the data by arguing that Jones and Nisbett were partially right, and partially wrong. Monson and Snyder assert that Jones and Nisbett were right when they argued that our self-explanations are based on more information—and are hence "more correct"—than our explanations of others' behavior; however, they feel that Jones and Nisbett erred when they argued that this "correct" explanation would necessarily be situational rather than in terms of traits. According to Monson and Snyder, sometimes the actor will "correctly" describe his or her behavior in terms of traits, and other times will "correctly" describe it in terms of situational variables.

The final status of the Jones and Nisbett hypothesis—as well as Monson and Snyder's revision—awaits further empirical study, and its fate will have important implications for both personality assessment and clinical practice.

Mischel (1977b) puts little confidence in traits and personality tests, yet Hogan et al. (1977) declare that "personality assessment is an intellectually and scientifically defensible enterprise (p. 255)." Mischel has been an active critic of the field of personality assessment. In a 1968 volume, Mischel argued that traits were less meaningful than the context or situation in which the person was behaving, and that the instruments used in personality assessment had not demonstrated their utility. Hogan and his colleagues have been active researchers with a special interest in the measurement of personality. We present the material in a relatively neutral fashion and hope that you, the reader, will inquire further, discuss the issues, and formulate a personal position.

Skepticism

The issues that were discussed by Mischel include (1) the multiple determinism of behavior, (2) the multiple goals for measurement, (3) the need for *in vivo* investigations, (4) the use of the "subject" as expert and colleague, (5) the analysis of environments, (b) the concepts of "cognitive social learning person variables," (7) the interface of personality and cognition, and (8) the need for a research-based image of the individual.

A variety of variables shape each individual's personality. Situations within the environment are prime examples. However, the way that individuals view and perceive situations will vary according to their own cognitive makeup. According to Mischel, one of the most impressive lessons from the history of personality assessment and research is the need to recognize the multiple determinism of behavior. No single test can explain or describe any person's entire personality, because there are so many determining factors.

Correspondingly, it is essential that clinicians and researchers use the variety of measurement techniques available in order to describe a person fully. Not just any measures can be used: the goals of measurement and the methods of measurement must coincide. Mischel also speculates that much would be gained in the area of personality measurement by focusing on tests that predict change in therapy as well as describing personality factors of general interest: such tests would capture the truly pivotal facets of personality.

Although the reactions of subjects to experimental situations have provided worthwhile data, researchers have recently emphasized that people not only respond *in* situations, but that they also select which situations to enter and which to avoid. Therefore, personality assessment must deal with how people choose real-life situations.

The use of the subject as expert and colleague is a suggestion that grows out of Mischel's noting that our subjects are usually much smarter than researchers often realize. Thus, instead of gathering only the responses to specific questions, we could learn a lot about personality by simply asking the subjects themselves.

Now that personality theorists and researchers have accepted the value of situational variance in predicting behavior it is only a short time before researchers will want to categorize and organize the different situations. Mischel, by noting the difficulties encountered in trait categorizations, recommends that we avoid searching for a taxonomy of situations. Instead, he feels, we must carefully select a limited number of key dimensions of situations to guide research and assessment.

Mischel further suggests that clinicians and researchers focus on a limited number of person variables. The person variables suggested by Mischel are seen as useful ways of conceptualizing how the qualities of the person influence and transform the effects of the environment. The "cognitive social learning person variables" (Mischel, 1973b) include *construction competencies*, which are the individual's abilities to think and behave in certain ways; *expectancies*, the outcomes that individuals associate with behaving in certain ways; *values* of the expected outcomes; and the *self-regulatory systems and plans* that each individual has with him or her at all times and in a variety of situations.

Mischel also suggests that those who study personality also study the developments in the area of cognitive psychology. The recommended interface could examine such interesting problems as how people organize their experiences into meaningful rules that help to guide their behavior.

Finally, Mischel cautions personality assessors against theoretical commitments and biases that may interfere with empirical discovery. The point being made is that the most viable understanding of personality will develop when biases are put aside and research outcomes are integrated.

Cautious Optimism

The skepticism that exists regarding personality assessment is noted by Hogan et al. (1977) and five sources of this skepticism are discussed: (1) the concept of "traits" has been widely criticized, (2) the use of personality assessment tests have been evaluated and considered to be of little value, (3) the interest in experimental research tends to reduce interest in personality variables, (4) labeling theory (and behavior therapy) has suggested that tests are irrelevant for therapy, and (5) personality tests are easily turned into data and this ease has contributed to some thoughtless research. Hogan et al.'s comments on these criticisms lead them to suggest that personality assessment is a viable aspect of personality research.

In considering the criticisms of "traits," Hogan et al. point out that current personality researchers do *not* hold the radical position concerning traits for which they are criticized. For example, personality assessors do not necessarily define traits as enduring psychic structures but instead view them as indications of how people will be described by others who know the subjects very well. Similarly, current personality researchers do *not* think that personality tests measure "traits" as much as they are thought to be objective scores that are helpful in making predictions about the subject's future behavior. Finally, the use of personality tests does not, in and of itself, make the researcher a trait theorist.

Hogan et al.'s reply to the criticism that personality assessment instruments are of little value rests on research that has demonstrated a reasonable degree of utility. One such case (Gough, 1965) rests on data from the Socialization scale of the California Psychological Inventory, and numerous other studies using the MMPI are available. Hogan et al. also describe the results of research suggesting that personality is a relatively stable phenomenon that is more than a concept created by an observer. These authors stress that the study of personality characteristics is a particularly important ingredient in the study of people's psychological functioning.

Labeling theory considers neurotic traits and psychotic symptoms as "labels" that are placed by mental health workers on certain deviant behaviors. The effects of labeling theory have been to reduce the credibility of personality "trait" tests, but Hogan et al. reply by citing some cross-cultural data that demonstrate that disturbed thoughts and behaviors similar to schizophrenia are found in most cultures and that such disturbance is sufficiently distinctive that almost everywhere a name has been created for them. These data do not deal with neurotic behaviors but do seem to suggest that the extreme position of labeling theory (regarding very pathological behavior) is unsubstantiated.

Finally, the fact that personality assessment instruments are often paper-and-pencil tests fosters their use in "quick and dirty," mindless research. It simply does not take a great deal of effort to administer a series of tests and correlate them. But, as Hogan et al. note, personality assessors have not cornered the market on simplistic research; this is a danger for all researchers.

Hogan et al.'s conclusions include three main points: that those who are most pessimistic about personality measurement seem to be those who are least involved in personality assessment research; most of the concerns of test critics do not apply to personality research as it is currently practiced; and all in all, personality assessment continues to offer an important arena for clinical research and practice.

As you undoubtedly recognize, there are differences of opinion in the field of personality assessment. Our interest has been in highlighting the issues, but we strongly suggest that you consult some of the original sources and consider the data in more detail. Many practical decisions must be made by the clinical psychologist and the assessment of personality has often played a role in these decisions. Therefore, one central point that should be kept in mind when considering the future of personality assessment is "practicality": in most cases, psychological testing makes practical sense.

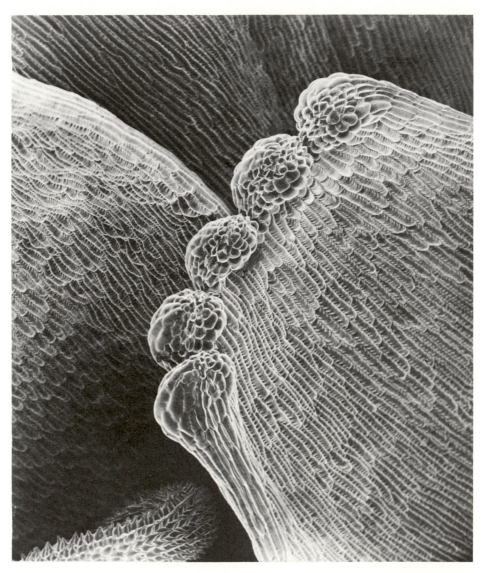

Search well another world; who studies this,
Travels in clouds, seeks manna, where none is.

Henry Vaughan

A photograph of a common dandelion taken with a scanning electron microscope camera.

9

ASSESSMENT OF NEUROPSYCHOLOGICAL FUNCTIONING

Neuropsychological assessment involves the measurement of behavioral signs that reflect healthy or impaired brain functioning. Professionals trained in the methods of *clinical neuropsychology* (the scientific study of relationships between brain anatomy or physiology and behavior in humans) have developed an extensive array of tests for neuropsychological assessment (Golden, 1978; Lezak, 1976; Reitan & Davison, 1974). Some clinical psychologists specialize as clinical neuropsychologists, and many more have become expert in the use of neuropsychological assessment techniques (Lubin, Wallis, & Paine, 1971; Wade & Baker, 1977).

Although the specific methods of neuropsychological assessment vary from practitioner to practitioner, the general process parallels that of personality or intellectual assessment in that the assessor administers, scores, and then integrates the results of several tests for each client. For example, a subject may be asked to tap an index finger as fast as possible, or to copy a geometric figure from memory, or to solve a hypothesis-testing task. The assessor organizes the resultant data, makes comparisons between scores on the various tests, and compares the test scores to normative standards for comparable persons. An educated guess is then made concerning the presence of brain damage, and (if possible) the specific brain locations involved. Should treatment or rehabilitation interventions be carried out, or should the problem appear to be one that grows progressively worse with time, the assessor will reevaluate the client at later time points to assess changes in neuropsychological functioning.

This chapter overviews the activities of clinical psychologists engaged in neuropsychological assessment. First, the focal questions investigated in neuropsychological assessment are discussed. Then, several of the major neuropsychological tests will be described, and procedural guidelines for the use of these tests are considered. Finally, research evidence concerning the reliability and validity of neuropsychological assessment tests are reviewed.

QUESTIONS THAT NEUROPSYCHOLOGICAL ASSESSMENT SEEKS TO ANSWER

Whenever a person's brain is damaged, whether through infection, toxins, trauma, or genetic anomaly, the resultant lesion(s) are likely to produce changes in behavior, thought, and/or emotion. At times this may seem a positive change, as for instance when right hemisphere damage causes increased sociability and relief from anxiety (Lezak, 1976), but almost inevitably negative effects follow. Neuropsychological assessment attempts to pinpoint the presence, and location, of brain damage (see Table 9-1) by answering the following six questions:

Is the Brain Damage Focal or Diffuse?

Generally, if brain damage is limited to fairly specific sites, the resultant cognitive, affective, and behavioral dysfunctions will be specific and limited. However, when brain damage is diffuse rather than focal, the resultant dysfunctions tend to be correspondingly generalized. Sources of diffuse brain damage include oxygen deficits (anoxia), infectious diseases, degenerative diseases, drug abuse, and head injuries (see Table 9-2). Focal brain damage results from more specific trauma, space-displacing lesions such as tumors, localized infections, or vascular disorders. The initial symptoms of focal brain damage, however, often mimic signs of diffuse damage when the trauma is sudden in onset: thus, neuropsychological testing is usually delayed for several days after injury or surgery to try to assure more valid data.

Is the Damage Due to Tissue Removal or Tissue Disease?

Removal of brain tissue, as in a clean bullet wound, usually produces specific and limited behavioral symptoms (except with massive tissue removal, as in lobotomies). Tissue disease (e.g., due to closed-head wounds or infections) more often causes generalized brain damage and behavioral dysfunction, including "distance effects" ("diaschisis"—adverse effects on brain tissue in nonadjacent areas of the brain).

Is the Damage Progressive or Nonprogressive?

The prognosis for continued deterioration versus a static condition is important for the planning of rehabilitation and treatment, as well as for the client's knowledge. Single-incident traumas, such as blows to the head, aneurysms, or stroke tend to have effects that do not grow worse over time. In contrast, diseases, infections, malnutrition, and diffuse brain damage are more likely to cause progressive deterioration. One useful predictive sign is the duration over which the person is unconscious following trauma. The longer the person is unconscious the greater the risk of progressive degeneration and generalized disabilities.

Is the Damage Acute or Chronic?

The most rapid and extensive recovery of impaired behavioral and cognitive functions tends to take place in the first month or two after brain injury. In some

Table 9-1   Neuropsychological Dysfunctions and Their Sources

Behavioral/Cognitive/Affective Dysfunctions	Probable Sources in the Brain[a]
1. Visual Perception	
Blind spots	Rear occipital
Visual agnosia (inability to comprehend or respond to visual stimuli)	Front right occipital, right parieto-occipital
Visual distortions	Front right occipital, right parieto-occipital
Inability to recognize, scan, or organize reading materials	Left occipital
Prosopagnosia (inability to recognize familiar faces)	Right parieto-occipital
Apperceptive visual agnosia (Inability to synthesize seen elements into complete wholes)	Front right occipital, right parieto-occipital
Simultanous visual agnosia (inability to perceive more than one object or point in space at a time)	Front right occipital, right parieto-occipital
Associative visual agnosia (inability to recognize familiar figures despite seeing the parts)	Front right occipital, right parieto-occipital
Contralateral homonymous hemianopia (field cuts):	
(a) Loss of right half of visual field	Left occipital
(b) Loss of left half of visual field	Right occipital
Inferior quadrantanopia (loss of lower half of visual field)	Interior parietal
Superior quadrantanopia (loss of upper half of visual field)	Interior temporal
Disorientation of right and left sides	Left parietal
Visual seizures (flashes of light, luminous or dark spots)	Rear occipital

Table 9-1 *Continued*

Behavioral/Cognitive/Affective Dysfunctions	Probable Sources in the Brain[a]
2. Auditory Perception	
Auditory agnosia (inability to understand and discriminate verbal auditory stimuli, while comprehension of nonverbal stimuli unimpaired)	Upper left temporal (Wernicke's area)
Inability to understand and recognize nonverbal auditory stimuli	Right temporal
Amusia (inability to create or appreciate music due to inability to distinguish tones, tonal patterns, beats, and timbre)	Forward right temporal
3. Kinesthetic, Vestibular, and Tactile Perception	
Astereognosis = tactile agnosia (inability to recognize objects by touch)	Parietal, sensory projection; Fibers from cortex to thalamus
Inability to orient or position oneself in space	Parietal, sensory projection; Fibers from cortex to thalamus
Elevation of pain or vibration threshold	Parietal, sensory projection; Fibers from cortex to thalamus
Position sense (inability to specify the relative positions of body limbs or the direction of passive movements)	Parietal, sensory projection; Fibers from cortex to thalamus
Agraphesthesis (inability to recognize numbers or letters written on finger tips)	Parietal, sensory projection; Fibers from cortex to thalamus
Impaired localization of tactile sensations or two-point discrimination (inability to recognize two tactile stimuli as separate)	Parietal, sensory projection; Fibers from cortex to thalamus
Impaired tactile adaptation (ceases to perceive a continuously applied tactile stimulus when applied faster than normal)	Parietal, sensory projection; Fibers from cortex to thalamus
Finger agnosia (cannot name or identify fingers)	Left parietal
4. Voluntary Motor Coordination and Steadiness	
Apraxia of gait (dysfunctional walking: "*marche a petits pas*"—very small steps, "slipping clutch"—walking movements without moving anywhere)	Frontal

Anosagnosia (hemiplegia—paralysis of left side of body—but S denies this exists)	Right parieto-tempero-occipital
Motor slowing (decreased rate and spontaneity of self-initiated actions)	Frontal
Motor perseveration (inability to make cognitive or behavioral shifts, rigidity)	Frontal
Impaired arm movements	Upper-middle posterior frontal
Impaired leg movement	Upper posterior frontal
Impaired facial movement	Lower posterior frontal
Motor (Jacksonian) seizures (clonic contractions on one side of the body)	Contralateral frontal
Motor (adversive) seizures (turning of the eyes and head to the right or left)	Contralateral frontal or occipito-frontal
Vertiginous seizures (dizziness, loss of balance)	Posterior temporal
Impaired lateral (side-to-side) gaze	Contralateral frontal

5. Voluntary Motor (Constructional) Functioning

Acalculia (Inability to calculate numerically)	
(a) Inability to perceive spatial relationships among numbers	Right parietal
(b) Inability to construct written numbers	Frontal, left parieto-occipital
Apraxia for dressing (cannot dress oneself due to perceptual disorientation)	Right parietal
Constructional apraxia (inability to construct meaningful patterns with objects or tools	Parietal
(a) Disrupted patterning and oversimplification (e.g., cannot construct angles)	Left parietal
(b) Visuospatial disorders (e.g., constructing fragmented wholes, neglect of entire side of a construction)	Right parietal
(c) Disrupted planning for construction	Parietal, frontal
(d) Disrupted comprehension of serial ordering	Parietal
Dysgraphia (impaired writing)	Left parietal or temporal
Ideomotor apraxia (inability to perform a previously well-learned act)	Left parieto-occipital
Ideational apraxia (inability to remember or perform acts except by habit)	Left parieto-occipital

Table 9-1 *Continued*

Behavioral/Cognitive/Affective Dysfunctions	Probable Sources in the Brain[a]
6. *Memory*	
Verbal amnesia	Left temporal or hippocampus
Amnesia for complex spatial, auditory, or visual forms	Right temporal or hippocampus
Inability to use verbal mnemonic memory aids	Left parietal
7. *Language Performance*	
Aphasia due to disrupted sequential ordering of speech (inability to produce coherent speech)	Left parietal
Broca's aphasia (inability to write or speak)	Left frontal (Broca's area)
Reduced speech rate	
Dysarthria (inability to vocalize)	
Hesitations	
Impaired prosody (modulation of tone, loudness, and rate of speech)	
Unusual effort required to speak	
Literal paraphasias (distorts words)	
Agrammatism (omission of grammatical words)	
Dysgraphia (inability to write coherently)	
Wernicke's aphasia (inability to speak coherently)	Upper left temporal (Wernicke's area)
Literal paraphasias	
Verbal paraphasias (use of incorrect words)	
Paragrammatism (incorrect syntax or grammar)	
Anomia (inability to recall names for familiar people or things)	
Word-finding difficulty	
Dysgraphia	
Amnesic aphasia (speech difficulty due to memory)	Middle parietal (angular gyrus)
Hesitations	

Dysfunction	Brain area[a]
Word-finding difficulty	
Anomia	Frontal
8. Conceptual Reasoning	
Dyslexia (inability to read) due to inability to cognitively process word symbols	Frontal
Excessive concreteness and literalness	Frontal
Lack of planning and foresight	Frontal
Cognitive rigidity	Frontal
Confusion and illogical reasoning (e.g., confabulation, clang associations)	Frontal or temporal
Acalculia due to inability to process number concepts	Left parietal
9. Problems of Attention, Concentration, or Alertness	
Visual or auditory inattention (S ignores parts of stimuli or of the perceptual field)	Right parieto-occipital (visual) / Right parieto-temporal (auditory)
Hemisomatagnosia (complete inattention to left side of body and space)	Right parieto-tempero-occipital
Distractability, short attention span, deficient sustained goal-directed activity	Frontal
Orientation in time, perception of time spans	Frontal
Orientation in space	Parietal
10. Emotional/Psychological Balance	
Cognitively based affective disorders (e.g., anxiety, depression)	Left cortex
Deficient reality-testing disorders (e.g., impulsivity, apathy, irresponsibility, excessive euphoria)	Right frontal
Wide mood swings and temper outbursts	Temporal

[a]Brain areas thought to be associated with each dysfunction are listed: frontal = frontal lobe; temporal = temporal lobe; parietal = parietal lobe; occipital = occipital lobe; right = right cortical hemisphere; left = left cortical hemisphere; S = subject or client.

Table 9-2 Brain Dysfunctions Involving Multiple Disabilities

Syndrome	Brain Dysfunctions	Behavioral Dysfunctions
Vascular Diseases (disorders of blood vessels supplying the brain)		
Stroke	Blood supply blocked by cholesterol deposits	Amnesia, apraxia, aphasia, anarthria
Cerebral Embolism	Blood supply blocked by clots	Amnesia, apraxia, aphasia, anarthria
Intracerebral Hemorrhage	Bleeding due to aneurysm (rupture) or complications of other circulatory disorders	Amnesia, apraxia, aphasia, anarthria
Traumatic Syndromes (severe blows to the head)		
Concussion	Temporary dysfunction due to thrusting brain against skull	Disorientation, amnesia, headaches
Contusion	Bruises causing swelling of capillaries in brain	Disorientation, amnesia
Lacerations	Tearing of brain tissue	Disorientation, amnesia, sensory distortions
Hematoma	Ruptured artery or vein causing deposit of blood near outer edge	Disorientation, coma and death if blood not drained
Gerstman's Sydrome	Left parieto-occipital damage	Acalculia, agraphia, left-right spatial disorientation, finger agnosia
Infection		
Meningitis	Infection of brain coverings (meninges)	*Young Children*: fever, drowsiness, vomiting, mental retardation in 20% of cases; *Older Children, Adults*: fever, aches, vomiting, headache, drowsiness, coma
Encephalitis (Acute viral)	Invasion of brain by infectious virus	*Adults*: vomiting, headache, drowsiness, convulsion, stiff neck, coma; *Children*: same plus risk of hyperactivity and mental retardation
Encephalitis (chronic bacterial)	Bacterial infection of brain	Convulsions, dysarthria, muscular incoordination, impaired logical reasoning, mood swings, death if not treated with penicillin

Table 9-2 *Continued*

Syndrome	Brain Dysfunctions	Behavioral Dysfunctions
Encephalitis (purulent)	Pus from other bodily infection enters brain after brain trauma and forms an expanding abcess	Varies depending on brain area affected, death if not treated via draining or antibiotics
Tumors (Neoplasms)	Tissue growth in brain	Depends on area affected

Degenerative Diseases (gradual deterioration of brain cells)

Syndrome	Brain Dysfunctions	Behavioral Dysfunctions
Alzheimer's disease	Diffuse degeneration of cortex	Amnesia, anxiety, agitation, loss of intellectual abilities over time, death
Pick's disease	Frontal lobe degeneration	Amnesia, anxiety, agitation, loss of intellectual abilities over time, death
Parkinson's disease	Basal ganglia degeneration (causes depletion of the body chemical dopamine)	Akinesia: tremors, slowing of movement, muscle rigidity, gradual intellectual impairment
Huntington's chorea	Excessive sensitivity to dopamine due to inheritance of a particular dominant gene, frontal lobe degeneration	Involuntary muscle spasms of face, tongue, extremities; amnesia, gradual intellectual impairment; confused and illogical thinking; death
Dementia ("chronic brain syndrome")	Diffuse bilateral brain degeneration	Disorientation, amnesia, acalculia, impaired conceptual reasoning and concentration, inattention, apathy, impaired social judgment, delusions, aphasia, apraxia, agnosia, hyperactivity

Nutritional Deficiency (deficient nutrients for maintenance of brain cells)

Syndrome	Brain Dysfunctions	Behavioral Dysfunctions
Pellagra	Deficiency of niacin	Phobic behavior, agitation, disorientation, depression, hallucinations
Beriberi	Deficiency of thiamine (Vitamin B)	Fatigue, irritability
Wernicke's disease	Deficiency of thiamine (Vitamin B)	Drowsiness, inability to walk, aphasia
Korsakoff's syndrome	Deficiency of thiamine due to prolonged (2+ weeks) drinking of alcohol and in-	Amnesia due to inability to consolidate, retrieve, or utilize data in short-term

Table 9-2 *Continued*

Syndrome	Brain Dysfunctions	Behavioral Dysfunctions
	sufficient food intake, bilateral lesions of hippocampus in anterior temporal lobe	memory; retrograde amnesia (long-term memory loss); confabulation; deficient integration of sequential data
Toxic syndrome	Noninfectious toxic substances enter brain (e.g., lead, DDT)	Irritability, amnesia, confusion, convulsions, paralysis, coma, death
Oxygen deficit	Deficient oxygen (e.g., birth complications)	Impaired intellectual functioning, hyperactivity possible in children
Epilepsy	Random discharges by hyperexcitable brain cells	Seizures (grand mal, petit mal, motor, focal)

cases, especially with focal brain damage, gradual improvement can continue to take place for years, while in other cases chronic brain dysfunctions produce progressively more widespread and debilitating cognitive and behavioral deterioration. Quite often young adults, aged 30 or less, will regain full functioning, while older adults rarely recover all functions lost due to the damage (Lezak, 1976).

Is the Dysfunction Organic or Functional?

The implications of discriminating between physiologically versus psychologically caused problems are also important. Persons whose brains are not damaged often display behavioral and cognitive dysfunctions that closely parallel the symptoms of brain damage when they are encountering serious psychological difficulties. Misdiagnosis in either direction can have negative effects on the patient's social adjustment and gains from therapy. If brain damage is incorrectly diagnosed, especially diffuse or degenerative disorders, this can lead to the abandonment of psychological therapies and/or the use of inappropriate drug treatments, both of which can seriously worsen the person's disabilities and his/her chances of recovery. There are a few, although tentative, clues that can help the clinician spot neurotic and/or schizophrenic persons who might be misdiagnosed as brain damaged: bland indifference, symbolic meaningfulness of symptoms, variation in symptoms with regular changes in key situational factors, secondary gain—strong reinforcement for ''sick'' behavior, presence of serious external stress in the person's social environment, and symptoms that are unlikely, such as in some conversion reaction syndromes. In contrast, more specific sensory or motor deficits, especially if restricted to one side of the body (i.e., lateralized), suggest that brain damage exists.

Differentiating between chronic schizophrenics and brain-damaged persons is particularly difficult because many of the symptoms of known lesions to the frontal lobes are similar to the signs used to diagnose schizophrenia: confusion, thought disorders, indifference to social norms, poor perceptual and motor tracking, progressive memory loss, perseveration, decreased verbal fluency and productivity, and mood disorders (Lezak, 1976; Reitan, 1976). Similarly, temporal lobe lesions often produce symptoms that are like those that define affective psychoses such as manic-depressive psychosis: wide mood swings, irrationality, temper outbursts, progressive memory loss and decline in logical reasoning, and difficulty in perception of complex visual patterns (Lezak, 1976). Neuropsychological research is now ongoing to develop assessment methods that can differentiate these groups more reliably (Highlight 9-1).

Highlight 9-1   Controlling for Extraneous Effects in Neuropsychological Assessment: Faking and Anxiety

The goal in neuropsychological assessment is to identify and localize brain damage, independent of other psychological problems that may be causing distress. Thus, it is most important that neuropsychological test findings be uncontaminated by factors such as clients' motivation or anxiety. Two recent studies indicate that such extraneous factors can substantially affect neuropsychological test results, although there appear to be ways to spot and remove these contaminating variables.

Heaton, Smith, Lehman, and Vogt (1978) explored the possibility that persons without brain damage could fake test results that mimic those of brain damaged individuals. Sixteen subjects with known recent head injuries (and neurological signs indicating brain damage) were compared with 16 same-age and equally well-educated persons who were definitely not brain damaged but who were instructed to "fake bad responses." Each subject was administered an MMPI, WAIS, and all tests in the Halstead-Reitan Neuropsychological Test Battery by trained examiners who believed all subjects to be patients with potential brain damage. When the scores on the tests were compared for the brain-injured versus normal ("malingerers") subjects, distinctly different profiles emerged on the MMPI and on 10 of the 18 primary neuropsychological test scores, although the two groups did not differ on WAIS subtest scores.

The normals were able to produce neuropsychological test scores in the range usually classified as "brain damaged," but primarily on tests of motor and sensory functioning rather than on tests of cognitive/language abilities. Furthermore, the normals produced significantly higher scores than the brain-injured subjects on one MMPI validity scale (F) and the scales for Hypochondriasis, Hysteria, Paranoia, Psychasthenia, Schizophrenia, and Social Introversion, showing a definite pattern of simulated personality disturbance. Heaton et al. conclude that non-brain-damaged persons *can* produce test scores that might suggest brain damage, but that such "malingerers" can also be spotted based on their inability to fake certain tests and their distinctive MMPI profiles. Clinicians will have to be trained to utilize these diagnostic cues, because Heaton et al. found that 10 neuropsychologists with no special preparation were generally unable to identify the "malingerers" in this study based on the test scores. However, with further research to cross-validate the signs of "malingering," clinical neuropsychologists could be prepared with a practical set of rules for weeding out those whose scores fall in the brain-damaged range and subjects who have good reason to fake bad results, such as defendants in criminal cases or persons seeking injury compensation.

Even with the best of motivations, subjects may experience anxiety that may lead them unintentionally to score in the brain-injured range on neuropsychological tests. King, Hannay, Masek, and Burns (1978) tested 30 male and 30 female right-handed subjects on two tests from the Halstead-Reitan Battery (i.e., finger tapping and form board). Results showed that the cutting points established nearly 30 years ago to distinguish between normal and brain-damaged persons (Reitan, 1955) produced many false positives, while more recent normative data suggested far more accurate cutting points (Kløve, 1974). Furthermore, a measure of trait anxiety correlated significantly and negatively with performance on both tests for women (although not for men). Thus, the cutting points used to classify subjects as having or not having brain damage must be up to date, and even then the effects of an extraneous factor such as anxiety must be accounted for (at least with female subjects). If this finding is cross-validated, it indicates that neuropsychological assessors must consider their subject's level of anxiety before concluding that brain damage is evident.

Is "Minimal Brain Dysfunction" Probable?

A particularly difficult group of persons for clinical psychologists to accurately diagnose are those children who show behavioral and cognitive disorders similar to those that are evidenced by brain damaged children, but for whom neurologists cannot find clear evidence of brain lesions. These children have been variously labelled "minimal brain dysfunction" (MBD), "hyperactive," and "learning disability" (Hallahan & Cruickshank, 1973; Klein & Klein, 1975; Rourke, 1975; Touwen & Kalverboer, 1973). Extensive research has shown that no single dysfunction characterizes MBD children, but rather at least five different groups can be identified: hyperactive, neurotic, psychopathic, schizophrenic, and specific learning disorder (Klein & Klein, 1975). Several types of symptoms may lead to a diagnosis of MBD, including motoric disorders such as excess activity, coordination dysfunctions, short "attention spans" and/or deficient ability to maintain concentration on a task, impulsivity, perceptual organization dysfunctions such as an inability to utilize cues from one sensory modality in reading, poor interpersonal relations such as noncompliance with parents or fighting with peers, and problems in learning certain skills such as arithmetic or writing. Thus, "MBD" subsumes many specific behavior disorders rather than pinpointing a delimited syndrome. Research is ongoing to clarify the role of brain damage versus psychosocial factors in "MBD" children.

Satterfield (1973) reported that MBD children who showed abnormal electroencephalogram (EEG) or neurological examination signs responded significantly better to drug treatment with methylphenidrate than did children labeled MBD but who scored in the normal range on these tests. Detailed neuropsychological assessment is necessary to identify children who evidence real brain dysfunctions, and so that educational and psychological interventions can be tailored to more closely suit the wide range of different specific needs shown by children who are labeled "MBD" (e.g., Tsushima & Towne, 1977).

NEUROPSYCHOLOGICAL ASSESSMENT TESTS

The complete array of neuropsychological assessment tests is so extensive that only selected examples of the more widely used instruments will be described. The sample tests correspond to the first eight types of neuropsychological dysfunctions in Table 9-1. The final categories (Attentional Problems; Emotional Balance) can be indirectly assessed through most any of these tests.

Tests of Visual Perception

Tests of Facial Recognition (Benton & Van Allen, 1973) The subject views several "criterion" pictures of faces, one at a time, and after each must match the criterion with one of six pictures of similar faces. The correct picture is made progressively more difficult to recognize by presenting it first as a front view identical to the criterion picture, then as a three-quarters view, and finally as a front view with very different lighting (see Figure 9-1). A total of 54 pictures are shown to the subject, and a score of 33 or below is considered to indicate impairment in visual perception.

Hidden Figures and Hidden Word Tests (Talland, 1965) Subjects must identify a simple figure that is hidden in a complex figure by tracing it. Similarly, a word that is hidden in a nonsense string of letters must be found in the Hidden Word Test. For example, "hello" might be hidden in a series of letters as follows: "a m h e l l o a n t r e d." These tests are especially sensitive to lesions in Broca's area and Wernicke's area, as well as frontal lobe lesions more generally.

Word or Picture Recognition and Recall (Battersby, Bender, Pollack, & Kahn, 1956) The subject is presented with (1) familiar words that are printed in large bold type (for instance, **NEWSPAPER**), and (2) symmetrical (along the vertical axis) pictures. Subjects must read the words and describe the pictures. This test is particularly useful for identifying homonymous field cuts, for persons with such dysfunctions are likely to report seeing only part of the word (e.g., **PAPER**) or the figure (for example only the right side).

Tests of Auditory Perception

Seashore Rhythm Test (Seashore, Lewis, & Soetvert, 1960) On this subtest of the Seashore Tests of Musical Talent, the subject is asked to discriminate between 30 pairs of rhythmic beats that are sometimes the same and sometimes different.

Speech-Sounds Perception Test (Reitan & Davison, 1974) The subject listens to 60 spoken nonsense words on an audiotape. The nonsense words all have the same "ee" vowel sound in the middle, but vary in the consonants that precede and follow it. For example, "Sea*t*," "Mee*t*," and "*Creep*" are potential stimulus words. The subject must underline the correct word from a list of four possi-

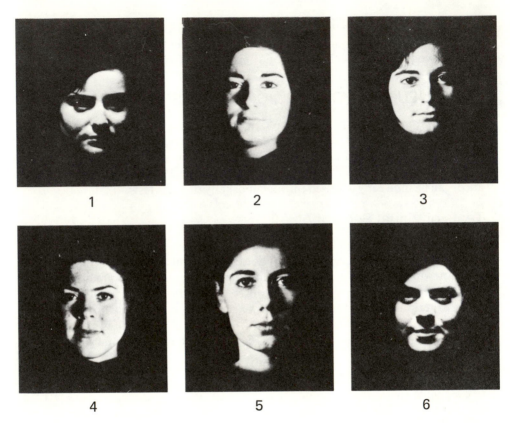

Figure 9-1   Test stimuli from Benton's (1973) Test of Facial Recognition. (Adapted from A. L. Benton and M. W. Van Allen, *Test of facial recognition manual.* University of Iowa Neurosensory Center Publication No. 287. Copyright 1973 by A. L. Benton and M. W. Van Allen. Reprinted by permission.)

ble answers, thus requiring the coordination of visual and linguistic skills with auditory perception.

Tests of Tactile Perception

Sensory Perceptual Examination: Tactile Perception and Finger Recognition (Reitan & Davison, 1974) The examiner sits facing the subject, and (with the subject's eyes closed) gently touches the subject's hands with a cotton ball. This is done first with each hand separately, and then interspersed with trials on which both hands are touched simultaneously. Subsequently, the examiner touches different fingers on each of the patient's hands, and the subject must identify the finger touched. This may be done by assigning each finger a number, "1" through "5," and requires two or three practice runs (with the patient's eyes open) to be sure that the subject is correctly using the number system.

Fingertip Writing (Reitan & Davison, 1974) The examiner traces a series of one-digit numbers on the fingertips of each hand, and the subject (whose eyes are closed) must identify verbally the correct number. A standard series of numbers is used, and the sequence of fingers is also standardized. With children aged 5 through 8 years, "X" and "O" are used rather than numbers.

Tests of Motor Coordination and Steadiness

Finger Oscillation Test (Reitan & Davison, 1974) In this test the subject taps his or her index finger as fast as possible on a telegraph key for 10 seconds. The arm is positioned in a standard fashion on a board with the key, and strapped down so that only the finger will move. This is done first with the subject's preferred hand, and then with the other hand, each time involving five 10-second trials.

Kløve-Matthews Motor Steadiness Battery (Reitan & Davison, 1974) Seven tests of motor coordination and steadiness are involved: (1) Maze Coordination requires the subject to traverse a maze (positioned vertically directly in front of the subject) with an electric stylus. This is done twice with each hand, and the score includes the length of time required and the number of times that the stylus touches a wall of the maze. (2) Vertical Groove Steadiness and (3) Horizontal Groove Steadiness require the subject to move a stylus either up and down or right and left in a 4-millimeter-width groove. Total time and number of contacts with sides are scored. (4) Static Steadiness involves inserting a stylus into a small hole and holding it without bracing the arm for 15 seconds. (5) Resting Steadiness replicates the latter test but allows the subject to brace the arm on the examining table. (6) Grooved Pegboard involves a pegboard with 25 randomly positioned slots to match the shape of the pegs. Total time and number of pegs dropped are scored. (7) Foot Tapping requires the subject to tap each foot as fast as possible on a pedal attached to an electric counter. The right and left feet are alternated, each for five separate trials.

Tests of Sensorimotor Construction Skill

Block Rotation Test (Satz, Fennell, & Reilly, 1970) The subject is shown 44 simple designs constructed from small wooden blocks much like those used on the WAIS Block Design Test. The subject's task is to reconstruct the designs with identical blocks, but each design must be rotated 90 degrees to the left or right (see Figure 9-2).

Tactual Performance Test (Reitan & Davison, 1974) The subject is blindfolded and never sees the test apparatus. Several wooden forms of different shapes are placed into a form board that has one appropriate space for each form. The subject first does this as quickly as possible with the preferred hand, then with the nonpreferred hand, and finally with both hands. Then the board and forms are removed from sight, the blindfold is removed, and the subject is asked to draw a picture of the form board with each space drawn in the correct shape and the correct location on the board. For the latter task, a Memory score is obtained from the number of forms correctly reproduced, and a Localization score is obtained from the number of forms that were placed in approximately the correct location.

Bender-Gestalt Test (Bender, 1938; Hutt, 1969) The subject is instructed to reproduce nine two-dimensional figures on one blank sheet of unlined 8 1/2 by 11 inch paper (see Figure 9-3). The examiner presents each figure one at a time on a card, carefully placing the card in front of the subject so that it is horizontal to the subject and its edges are lined up with the edges of the examining table. Lezak

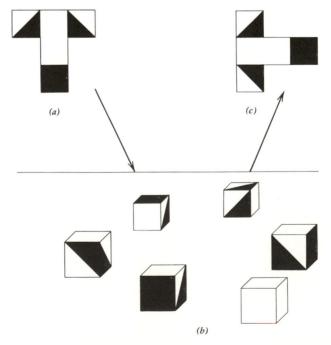

(a)   *(c)*

(b)

Figure 9-2 Example of a block rotation test. (*a*) Test stimulus. (*b*) Blocks. (*c*) Rotated solution.

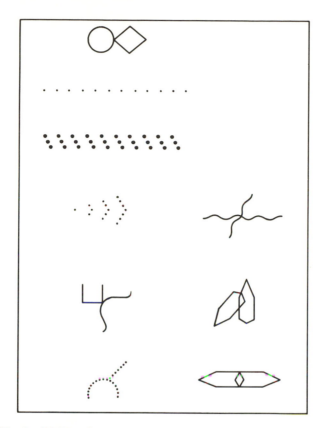

Figure 9-3 Hutt's (1969) adaptation of the nine Bender-Gestalt figures. (From L. Bender, *A visual-motor Gestalt test and its clinical use.* New York: American Orthopsychiatric Association, 1938. Copyright by American Orthopsychiatric Association, 1938. Reprinted by permission. Plate 1, p. 4.)

(1976) suggests the following instructions, to minimize the restrictions on the subject's responses while maintaining a standardized method of examination:

> *I've got nine of these altogether (hold up the pack of cards with the back facing the patient). I'm going to show them to you one at a time and your job is (or "I want you") to copy them as exactly as you can. Here you go. (p. 313)*

The subject is also asked to not turn the sheet of paper on which the figures are copied more than is needed for a comfortable writing angle, so that any rotations of the stimulus figures will be clearly due to misperception or incorrect reproduction rather than to an artifactual rotation of the paper. The test usually takes between 5 to 10 minutes to administer.

The Bender-Gestalt is a widely used test, and several systems for scoring have been developed. These include the Pascal-Suttell (1941) method, which assigns "points" for errors on each separate figure and for seven "layout" variables that involve the entire array, and the Hain (1964) method, which assigns "points" for errors without regard to the frequency with which they occur. More recently,

Hutt (1969) has designed a 17-factor Psychopathology Scale on which each of 17 signs of perceptual-motor problems are rated from 1 to 10 (except Factor 2, which is rated either 1 or 3.25). The scale and its factors are defined with detailed criteria for ratings and can be rated reliably (Hutt, 1969).

Benton Visual Retention Test   (Benton, 1974) Similar to the Bender-Gestalt, this task involves reproducing 10 cards each of which depicts one, two, or three geometric designs. Benton (1974) describes four types of administration procedures, although the most widely used method (Method A) requires that the subject draw the figures on each card immediately after the card has been withdrawn from view (after a 10-second exposure). Scoring is based on both the number of designs drawn correctly and the number of errors. There are six types of errors: omissions, distortions, perseverations, rotations, misplacements (incorrect positioning of the designs), and incorrect size. Benton (1974) has compiled norms for Administration A for persons of different ages and premorbid IQs, and states that if the Error Score is 5 or more above the expected value and/or if the Number Correct Score is 4 or more below the expected value then brain damage is "strongly indicated."

Graham-Kendall Memory-for-Designs Test   (Graham & Kendall, 1960) The subject is shown each of 15 geometric figures one at a time for five seconds and then asked to reproduce each figure immediately after it has been withdrawn from view. The figures vary in complexity from an equilateral triangle to a line with two squared portions in the midsection and a tail at either end. Scoring is based on errors in each figure, using a four-point system: 3 = rotations or reversals, 2 = gross distortion or fragmentation, 1 = two or more errors although the basic design is preserved, 0 = one or fewer errors. Despite the simplicity of the scoring system, Quattlebaum (1968) demonstrated that it correlated very strongly (+.85) with the Hain scoring method for the Bender-Gestalt.

Tests of Memory

Wechsler Memory Scale   (Wechsler, 1945) Short- and long-term verbal and nonverbal memory are assessed in this often-used, seven-part test. Personal and Current Information questions involve items concerning the subject's basic self-awareness (age, name, birthdate) and knowledge of practical current information (such as names of prominent public officials). Orientation items assess the subject's awareness of time and place. Mental Control is assessed by having the subject count backward from 20, recite the alphabet, and count forward by threes from 1 to 40. Logical Memory is tested by having the subject repeat in spoken words all that can be recalled from each of two 50 to 60-word paragraphs that have been slowly read out loud by the examiner. Digit Span is assessed as on the WAIS. Visual Reproduction is measured using two one-figure geometric designs and one two-figure design, each of which is presented for 10 seconds and then immediately drawn from memory by the subject. Finally, the Associate Learning subtest involves three presentations of a 10-item, paired-associates list, half of which involve logical pairings (such as "baby-cries" or "North-South"), and the other half involving random pairings (such as "obey-inch" or "crush-dark").

The order in which the pairs are presented is varied in each presentation and the score is calculated by summing the number of "Hard" pairings that were recalled correctly across all three presentations and one-half the number of "Easy" pairings that were correctly recalled. The scores from all subtests are added to obtain a total raw score, adjusted based on the subject's age, and converted into a Memory Quotient (similar in logic to an Intelligence Quotient) by reference to a table of normative data. More recently, Hulika (1966) has provided separate norms for five age groups between the ages of 15 and 89.

Tests of Verbal/Language Abilities

Aphasia Screening Test (Halstead & Wepman, 1959; Wheeler & Reitan, 1962) The subject is instructed to name common objects, spell simple words, identify individual numbers and letters, write and read brief phrases and sentences, make simple arithmetic calculations, repeat out loud words and phrases that are presented by spoken word, identify body parts, differentiate between right and left, and copy simple shapes. For example, the instructions at one point run as follows:

> I am going to say something that I want you to say after me, so listen carefully: "He shouted the warning." Now you say it. . . . Would you explain what that means? . . . Now I want you to write that sentence on the paper.

Rather than creating a single general score, Wheeler and Reitan (1962) score for presence or absence of individual behavioral indicators of brain damage.

Token Test (Boller & Vignolo, 1966) The subject is asked to perform 62 different brief tasks with a set of 20 wooden "tokens." The tokens are of two shapes (circles and squares), two sizes (small and large), and five colors (red, yellow, blue, green, and white). The examiner describes each task out loud. For example, an early item is: "Touch the small yellow circle." The tasks become progressively more difficult. For instance, a later item states: "Before touching the yellow circle, pick up the red triangle." Scoring is based on the number of tasks performed correctly.

Neurosensory Center Comprehensive Examination for Aphasia (Spreen & Benton, 1969) While aphasia screening tests can identify persons who have language disabilities, more comprehensive test batteries are necessary to precisely pinpoint specific aphasic dysfunction(s) and to permit focused and effective treatment. The Neurosensory Center Examination includes 20 separate subtests, each of which assesses distinct language skills. The subtests are brief (approximately five minutes or less) and require only a few common objects such as pencils, scissors, silverware, and coins, and specially printed cards.

Tests of Conceptual Reasoning Skills

Category Test (Halstead, 1947; Reitan & Davison, 1974) The subject is seated facing a screen on which stimulus figures are projected. The task is to determine which of four figures is "correct" and to record this choice on an answer panel that has four response levers. The examiner tells the subject only that he or she must guess the correct figure but never instructs the subject as to how to choose among the four figures. The subject receives feedback after each choice in the form of a bell for correct answers and a buzzer for incorrect ones. Before the test, the subject is told that the test is divided into seven groups of pictures and that each group has a single *principle* that will enable a correct solution on every item in that group. The subject must determine the principle based only on the feedback received after each trial. The first trial in each group requires a random guess, and thereafter, the subject uses the feedback to formulate and test hypotheses about the underlying principle. Figure 9-4 gives a difficult example of this type of problem.

The "principles" for the first and second groups are usually determined even by persons with serious brain damage, but subsequent tasks become steadily more challenging. In the final group, items from all past groups are repeated, and the

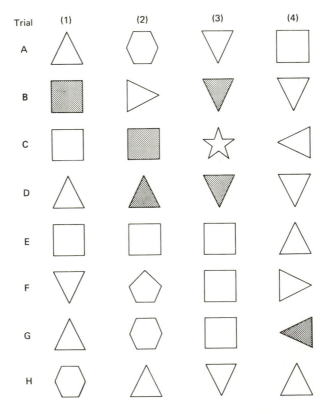

Figure 9-4　Here is a sample of the tasks involved in the Halstead Category Test, similar to items actually used in the test. Can you guess what answer is correct for each row? (It is either 1, 2, 3, or 4.) See if you can figure out the principle that will tell you which figure is correct. (Correct answers are Row A: 2, Row B: 3, Row C: 1, Row D: 4, Row E: 1, Row F: 3, Row G: 2, Row H: 3).

subject has to recall the correct rule for each. Thus, Group 7 serves as a review, as well as a test of the subject's ability to flexibly shift from rule to rule.

(P.S. The principle involved in the example in Figure 9-4 is that the correct answer is determined by the number of items in the test figure that have an odd number of sides.)

Trail Making Test   (Reitan & Davison, 1974) The subject is asked to draw a line connecting a series of circled numbers and/or letters that are scattered over an 8 1/2 by 11 inch paper (Figure 9-5). The test is done in two separate parts. Part A requires the subject to connect 25 numbered circles in numerical order, without lifting the pencil from the paper, as fast as possible. Part B is the same, except that the subject must alternate from number to letter, proceeding in numerical and alphabetical order. Before both tests, a brief practice trial is done to assure that the subject understands and follows instructions. In cases of error, the subject is stopped and quickly instructed to continue from the last correct circle (without stopping the timing). Scoring is done is terms of the total number of seconds required to complete all 25 circles. Reitan (1970) reports that a score of above 92 seconds on Part B enables an 85% accurate classification of adults as brain damaged or not. Similar tests integrating cognitive (problem solving) and visual-motor skills include the Color Form Test and the Progressive Figures Test (Reitan & Davison, 1974).

Comprehensive Neuropsychological Batteries Developed by Halstead and Reitan

Most clinical neuropsychologists use several tests to provide a comprehensive evaluation of each patient's capabilities and deficits. Given the wide range of behavioral, cognitive, and affective dysfunctions that can be caused by brain lesions, no one test would be sufficient to provide all information needed for an accurate diagnosis and an effective treatment program. Although all of the tests described in this chapter are valuable resources for the clinical neuropsychologist,

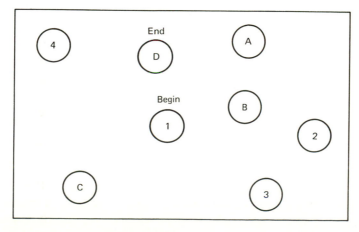

Figure 9-5   Sample Trail Making Test Part B.

the most widely used standard battery of tests is the Halstead-Reitan Neuropsychological Battery (Halstead, 1947; Reitan, 1974, 1976; Reitan & Davison, 1974).

Halstead first described this battery of tests in *Brain and Intelligence* (1947). Although he utilized 27 separate measures, the 10 that he selected to contribute to an overall "impairment index" have been thoroughly researched by Reitan (1970, 1976; Kløve, 1974). Seven of these measures have been shown to singly differentiate brain damaged and non-brain-damaged persons: the Category Test; the Tactual Performance Test (TPT) scores for Time, Memory, and Localization; the Speech-Sounds Perception Test; the Seashore Rhythm Test; and the Finger Oscillation Test (Reitan, 1955). The remaining three measures contribute to an overall impairment index, but are not as well validated as indicators of brain damage: Critical Flicker Frequency, Absolute and Deviation Scores, and Time Sense Test Memory Score. The impairment index is calculated as the proportion of the 10 tests on which the patient achieves a score above the cutting point for identifying brain damage.

Most clinical neuropsychologists use portions of the complete battery, usually including the seven most effective tests, and supplement it with tests that provide important additional information. The Trail Making Test Part B, the Aphasia Screening Examination, the Sensory-Perceptual Examination, the Bender-Gestalt, the Benton Visual Retention Test, and the WAIS are among the most frequently utilized additional neuropsychological measures.

Reitan has extended neuropsychological assessment to children aged 15 or less through the development of the Halstead Neuropsychological Test Battery for Children (ages 9 to 14 years) and the Reitan-Indiana Neuropsychological Test Battery for Children (ages 5 to 8 years). The Halstead Battery included many of the tests from the Halstead-Reitan Battery for Adults with some exceptions and changes. The Reitan-Indiana is a further revision, based on Reitan's observation that children below 9 years require still simpler tests and apparatus adjusted to their smaller body size.

NEUROPSYCHOLOGICAL ASSESSMENT: PROCEDURAL GUIDELINES

When clinical psychologists conduct neuropsychological assessment, they bring together (1) the data on brain functions and dysfunctions and (2) their skills and tools for assessment. Clinicians use several basic guidelines in conducting neuropsychological assessment no matter what specific tests are utilized.

Practical Considerations for Neuropsychological Assessment

Imagine for a moment that you are ready to use several neuropsychological assessment tests to assess a patient's skills and deficits so as to either rule out brain damage as a problem or identify the source and types of brain lesions. Although the tests used by clinical neuropsychologists tend to be relatively straightforward, the fact that they are being administered to a patient who is experiencing psychological distress implies that care be taken to establish rapport and reassure the patient. As in all testing situations, neuropsychological assessment begins with an informal talk with the patient to establish trust and rapport.

Thereafter several precautions are observed in order to assure that a representative sample of the patient's true skills and deficits is obtained. Several recommendations are relevant in this respect. First, never underestimate the importance of being sure than the patient clearly understands all instructions. One way of doing this is to have the patient repeat back your instructions verbatim, especially if the patient seems to not be following them correctly. Second, the patient must be able to see and hear all test instructions and materials. Particularly if the patient is disabled by problems of vision, hearing, attention, or general orientation and reality contact, it is important that the assessor be able to separate out the effects of these dysfunctions from the patient's actual skills or deficits on the tests themselves. Third, the assessor must also take care to set a pace that does not lead the patient to become excessively distracted or fatigued. Pacing can be accomplished both by the speed with which each test is administered and through the use of rest breaks. Finally, the patient's apprehensions and anxieties can be reduced if the assessor communicates support and encouragement as the tests are ongoing, although feedback on the correctness of specific answers is not given except when a part of the standard test administration procedure (e.g., Category Test).

Quantitative Methods of Inferring Brain Damage from Neuropsychological Tests

Reitan (1970) has described four related but different ways in which the clinical psychologist can make predictions about the presence or absence, and location, of brain damage from neuropsychological test results. Ideally, the clinician uses all four approaches in order to formulate a maximally accurate diagnosis and efficacious treatment plan for each patient. These four approaches represent a quantitative/normative orientation to neuropsychological assessment and include (1) level of test performance, (2) specific deficits, (3) test score pattern, and (4) right/ left differences.

Level of Performance   How well does the patient do? Cutoff scores have been established for several neuropsychological tests, based on research showing that most non-brain-damaged persons score above that level and most brain-damaged individuals score below it. Although this method enables the assessor to see whether the patient is responding in a way that suggests a brain dysfunction, no test has ever been developed where *all* brain-damaged persons score below a certain level. Thus, diagnosing a patient on the basis of performance level alone may result in persons being misclassified as either brain damaged or non-brain-damaged. The best way to operationalize this level of performance method is to develop cutoff scores based on *combinations* of tests, rather than with single tests alone. However, even the multiple-test approach has not been found to be more than 75 to 90% accurate in most cases, so substantial numbers of patients may still be misdiagnosed.

Specific Deficits   Does the patient commit certain types of errors that occur almost exclusively among brain-damaged persons? The assessor observes carefully to identify certain cognitive and behavioral deficits that are highly likely to be signs of certain types of brain damage in certain areas of the brain (Table 9-2).

However, as with level of performance standards, the normative research that has established these brain-behavior relationships has not shown that all persons with a particular brain lesion show a particular behavioral or cognitive deficit.

Test Score Pattern   Is there a significant degree of variability in scores on different tests that fits a pattern known to be shown by persons with particular types of brain damage? Several test score patterns have been evaluated as predictors of brain damage. For example, if an individual's IQ is within the normal range, but he or she scores within the abnormal range on half or more of the Halstead-Reitan Battery tests (resulting in an ''Impairment Index'' of .5 or higher), then some form of brain damage is likely. Persons with below-average IQ scores are likely to score within the abnormal range on the neuropsychological tests even though they are not brain damaged, so a high Impairment Index is not a strong predictor of brain damage with such persons (Reitan, 1970) (see Highlight 9-2).

Differences in Performance on Right and Left Sides of Body   Do comparisons of identical motor or sensoriperceptual functions on the two sides of the body, controlling for handedness, show discrepancies that are found far more with brain-damaged than non-brain-damaged persons? Because most motor and sensoriperceptual functions are controlled by the contralateral (opposite side) cortical hemisphere, tests that reveal marked discrepancies between left and right body sides (over and above those that would be expected due to the person's handedness) suggest brain lesions in the brain hemisphere on the side opposite to the deficient body side. For example, if finger-tapping speed with the right hand is no faster than that with the left hand for a right-handed person, or if it is 20% or more slower than with the left hand for a left-handed person, left hemisphere damage is indicated (Reitan, 1970). Similar results have been obtained with tests of grip strength, and recognition of tactile, visual, and auditory stimuli. As with the Verbal IQ-Performance IQ pattern (Highlight 9-2), the evidence for left-sided deficiencies as signs of right hemisphere damage is less consistent. In both cases, as with the other three inference approaches, there is not a perfect correspondence for all patients between body-side deficiency and lateralization of brain damage.

Once again, we must stress that all four methods can and should be used together in interpreting neuropsychological assessment data. Only when several tests and several data interpretation perspectives are skillfully integrated can the inaccuracies of each single test or perspective be overcome to produce a consistent picture of the patient's true brain functioning.

Qualitative Neuropsychological Assessment

Soviet neuropsychologists have adopted a somewhat different approach to neuropsychological assessment (Luria & Majovski, 1977). Their ''qualitative'' strategy involves a hypothesis-testing method applied to the study of one subject at a time. This approach relies on a theory of the human brain's functional organization that has evolved over 40 years of clinical research (Luria, 1966, 1973). The basic premise is that each system within the brain continuously contributes in a unique way to the brain's overall functioning, and that psychological dysfunctions can

Highlight 9-2   Tests of Intellectual Functioning as Predictors of Laterality of Brain Damage

Several research studies have investigated the utility of Verbal IQ (VIQ) and Performance IQ (PIQ) scores as predictors of the lateral location of brain damage (see Lezak, 1976; Matarazzo, 1972) (see figure). The logic underlying such research is that VIQ subscales measure primarily verbal and conceptual skills, while PIQ subscales assess visuospatial capabilities. The former are thought to be governed by the left hemisphere of the cortex, while the latter have been found to be controlled primarily by the right hemisphere of the cortex.

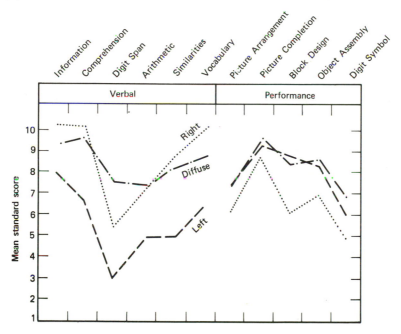

Mean standard scores on Wechsler-Bellvue I subtests for groups with left, right, and diffuse cerebral lesions. (Adapted from R. M. Reitan, Certain differential effects of left and right cerebral lesions in human adults. *Journal of Comparative and Physiological Psychology*, 1955, *48*, 474–477. Copyright 1955 by the American Psychological Association. Reprinted by permission. P. 475.)

Kløve (1959) used electroencephalogram (EEG) data as the criterion for brain damage, classifying persons with abnormal EEGs as brain damaged and those with no abnormal EEG signs as non-brain-damaged. He found that persons with right hemisphere lesions showed significantly higher VIQs than PIQs, while individuals with left-side lesions had significantly higher PIQs than VIQs, and subjects with diffuse brain damage achieved approximately equal VIQ and PIQ scores.

Doehring, Reitan, and Kløve (1961) replicated these findings, using a different criterion for brain damage. Doehring et al. classified subjects as right-side damage if they exhibited homonymous field cuts in their left visual field. Fields and Whitmyre (1969) replicated these results using the WAIS rather than the Wechsler Bellvue (which Kløve and Doehring et al. had used).

Subsequent research by Golden (1977) and Russell, Neuringer and Goldstein (1970) with adults, and by Boll (1974), Reed, Reitan, and Kløve (1965), and Reitan (1974b) with children, has confirmed the validity of the VIQ-PIQ discrepancy for predicting left-hemisphere brain damage. However, the PIQ-VIQ discrepancy was not found to be as consistent or as accurate in predicting right-hemisphere brain damage. This may be due to the fact that, where the VIQ subscales require almost no visuospatial skills, the PIQ subscales such as Picture Completion, Digit Symbol, and Block Design involve conceptual reasoning and problem-solving skills that are often controlled by areas of the left hemisphere. Thus, VIQ may be a "purer" measure of left-brain functions, while PIQ assesses primarily right-brain functions with an intermingling of left-brain processes.

All in all, the VIQ-PIQ discrepancy has strong research support as a predictor of left-hemisphere brain damage. However, PIQ-VIQ discrepancies are apparent in juvenile delinquents and certain culturally deprived groups. Thus, though the PIQ-VIQ discrepancy has meaning for brain-damage versus non-brain-damage comparisons, it is not sufficient by itself to identify brain damage. Moreover, this single sign alone is rarely able to correctly assign more than two-thirds of tested patients to the correct (left or right) diagnostic group. Clinicians cannot safely use *only* the VIQ-PIQ difference in diagnosing individual clients, and will do far better with a battery of several tests that includes an IQ measure.

occur due to a wide variety of problems in different combinations of the brain systems.

In view of this emphasis on multiple causation, the qualitatively oriented assessor rejects the use of group norms and standardized tests, contending that each unique subject's brain dysfunctions must be pinpointed through creative and individualized testing that systematically narrows the range of potential causes until the true dysfunction clearly emerges. Tests are selected to delineate possible areas of damage. Each test is given to the subject building on the data provided by all previous tests, constantly disconfirming hypotheses as to the cause of the dysfunction until only one hypothesis remains unchallenged. Test results are combined and used to create a gestalt rather than considered independently in a simple additive fashion.

> All relevant clinical data are used in formulating a working hypothesis of the patient's presenting problem, in contradistinction to a "blind" approach. It is a "dynamic," that is, flexible, approach, in contrast to the rationale of the Halstead-Reitan Neuropsychological Test Battery. Each patient analysis is a theoretically based dynamic experiment on the behavior effects accrued from a disturbance in the brain (Luria & Majovski, 1977, p. 962).

Although the qualitative approach allows for maximal creativity and individualization, the lack of standardization mitigates against the demonstration of the reliability or validity of its results. It has not been experimentally demonstrated that the qualitative strategy does in fact reliably pinpoint brain dysfunction, because (1) it is not a replicable method, with a standard set of specific tests, but rather a theoretical orientation to neuropsychological assessment, and (2) its results have not been systematically validated against surgical or scanning procedures as the criteria of brain dysfunction.

However, even the most eclectic qualitative assessor does rely on a finite number of tests that are used according to guidelines that are amenable to standardization. Luria and Majovsky (1977) describe a hypothetical assessment sequence that is replicable, although it does involve several branching points where the results of prior tests, rather than some fixed general "how-to" rule, dictate what tests come next.

An Integration of Quantitative and Qualitative Approaches

In actual practice, a rapprochement of the quantitative and qualitative strategies is probably the rule rather than the exception among clinicians who adhere to a scientist-professional model. This is because each approach embodies several distinct scientific and clinical strong points that are *not* mutually exclusive with the other strategy's strengths.

A model for integrating qualitative (QL) and quantitative (QT) assessment is suggested by the way in which researchers have blended the single-subject and between-groups experimental designs. Neuropsychological assessment tests could be evaluated, alone (QT)[1] and in theoretically derived combinations (QL), for reliability and validity through the use of "blind" analyses with representative samples from the populations who will be tested in the future (QT). Once several tests' psychometric *and* clinical utilities have been demonstrated for the identification of brain lesions, then the tests could be used in a creative and individualized fashion (QL) within the limits of the validational research (QT). That is, if a particular patient seems to require the use of a sequence of tests that has never been experimentally validated, the assessor can double check conclusions via additional tests or assessment data (QL), and the new test sequence can be submitted to normative validational research to assure future assessors of its reliability and validity (QT).

Golden, Hammeke, and Purisch (1978), Hammeke, Golden, and Purisch (1978), Purisch, Golden, and Hammeke, (1978) and Lewis, Golden, Moses, Osmon, Purisch, and Hammeke (1979) have in fact developed a standardized test battery based on Luria's QL method. The Luria-Nebraska Battery comprises 269 separate tasks, organized into 11 subtests (motor function, rhythm function, tactile function, visual function, receptive speech, expressive speech, writing functions, reading functions, arithmetical functions, memory function, and intel-

[1]In the following discussion, (QT) refers to a contribution of the quantitative approach, while (QL) denotes that of the qualitative strategy.

lectual processes). Three additional summary scores are calculated: right-hemi-sphere tactile and motor functions, left-hemisphere tactile and motor functions, and pathognomonic signs (i.e., the 34 tasks that best differentiated brain dam-aged from psychiatric patients). The stimulus materials are compact and simple (e.g., a comb, a paper clip, a compass, a quarter, audiotaped rhythms), and the entire test takes only two and one-half hours.

Validation research has demonstrated that the Battery produces a hit rate of 100% for identifying non-brain-damaged medical patients, 86% hit rate for com-parable brain-damaged (as certified by neurological examination) patients, and a 92% overall hit rate. The Battery also significantly differentiates between di-agnosed schizophrenics who had no history of seizures, head injury, or alcohol-ism versus brain-injured patients with an 88% hit rate. Although neurological examinations were not reported to more definitely rule out brain damage in the schizophrenic group, the schizophrenics tended to be moderately chronic (Mean chronicity = 12 years) thus indicating that the Battery is unusually effective in dis-tinguishing between brain-injured and functionally-impaired dysfunctions.

Further research (Lewis et al., 1979) demonstrated that the profile of 14 sum-mary scores was highly effective for the prediction of not only existence, but also localization, of brain lesions. Based on computerized axial tomography scans, surgical findings, and/or angiograms, neurologists pinpointed the lateral (i.e., left versus right hemisphere) and longitudinal (i.e., frontal lobe versus sensori-motor area versus temporal lobe versus parietal-occipital lobes) location of each of 60 patients' brain lesions. Each of the 14 test scores identified significant dif-ferences among patients with lesions in different locations, and each of the eight possible lesion sites yielded a distinctive profile on the Battery's summary scores (Figure 9-6). Thus, the Luria-Nebraska Battery shows evidence of strong clinical utility. Further refinement in this integration of QL and QT approaches to neuro-psychological assessment should continue to enhance clinical psychologists' abil-ities to pinpoint and remediate brain dysfunctions.

RESEARCH ON NEUROPSYCHOLOGICAL ASSESSMENT

Clinical neuropsychology research has been conducted to (1) differentiate brain-damaged from "normal" adults, (2) validate tests that discriminate between brain-damaged adults and non-brain-damaged adults with psychiatric dysfunc-tions, and (3) validate neuropsychological tests for the localization of brain lesions. Each research area is discussed and then a few comparable studies conducted with children are reviewed. Finally, the methodological criteria that determine whether or not we can place confidence in the conclusions from neuro-psychological assessment research are described.

Before discussing the validity research for neuropsychological assessment pro-cedures, it is worth noting that reliability data are only rarely reported for neuro-psychological tests. One exception is a study by Matarazzo, Matarazzo, Wiens, and Gallo (1976) that reported retest correlations for the Halstead Impairment Index. Reliability coefficients were good for subjects who were classified as schiz-ophrenic or brain damaged, ranging from .63 to .83. Although only a .08 retest correlation was obtained for "normal" subjects, all 29 scored in the non-brain-damaged range on both tests, so the index was 100% accurate in this respect. Further attention to retest reliability, and other reliability forms (e.g., internal consistency) is greatly needed because test reliability is important for both clinical and research purposes. For the latter, accurate specification of true brain lesions depends on having tests that yield the same diagnosis if administered twice to the same subject. For the former, unreliable tests can conceal real differences among brain-damaged versus non-brain-damaged groups or between groups with different types or areas of brain damage (Parsons & Prigatano, 1978).

Neuropsychological Test Validity: "Organics" Versus "Normals"

Spreen and Benton (1965) reported that single neuropsychological tests were, on the average, 71% accurate in discriminating brain-damaged and normal persons, based on 65 separate analyses from several studies. Taken together, the investigations that they reviewed showed a median "hit rate" of 75%—thus, it appears that neuropsychological tests are able to pinpoint three of every four persons who have brain lesions. When multiple tests were combined to make the brain-damaged versus normal prediction, the hit rate was raised to 82%.

Filskov and Goldstein (1974) offer impressive evidence of the validity and utility of the Halstead-Reitan Battery, showing it to be equally or more accurate in both identifying and localizing brain damage than the more risky and invasive medical procedures such as angiograms and pneumoencephalograms, or the more expensive medical assessments from computerized axial tomography (CAT) scans, skull X rays, or EEGs. The Halstead-Reitan Battery had a 100% hit rate for diagnosing the specific pathology—for example, trauma, neoplasms, degenerative disease, or arteriosclerotic cerebrovascular disease.

In contrast, Butler, Coursey, and Gatz (1976) and Lyle and Quast (1976) used the Bender-Gestalt in several different ways—the subjects' recall scores, the Hain scoring system, the Pascal-Suttell scoring system, and clinicians' judgments using Bender-Gestalt protocols—and found all approaches to be at best only moderately accurate. Although the low hit rates—ranging from below 50 to 73%—might be due to the use of only mildly brain-damaged subjects and controlling for IQ (which tends to obscure differences between brain-damaged and nonorganic subjects, cf. Heaton, Baade & Johnson, 1978), both studies concluded that the Bender-Gestalt should be used only as a part of a more comprehensive test battery in clinical practice.

Russell, Neuringer, and Goldstein (1970) developed a standard method for combining the results from tests including the Halstead-Reitan Battery, the WAIS, the Trail Making Test, and the Aphasia Screening Test that they call the "neuropsychological key." Combining clinical judgment and normative data, numerical weightings are assigned to the scores for each test, and the resultant diagnosis has been found to be equally as accurate (75%) as a sophisticated statistical analysis called discriminant analysis (Swiercinsky & Warnock, 1977). The neuropsychological key was much more accurate in pinpointing brain damage (87% versus 74%), but very poor in identifying normal subjects correctly; 51% of

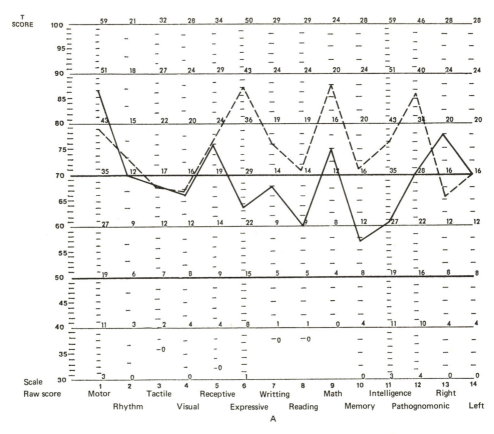

Figure 9-6 Mean performance of the patients diagnosed by the test battery as (A) frontal lobe damage and (B) sensorimotor area damage. The dotted line represents the left hemisphere group and the solid line represents the right hemisphere group on each graph. (Adapted from G. P. Lewis, C. J. Golden, J. A. Moses, Jr., D. C. Oseman, A. D. Russell,

the normal were diagnosed as brain damaged! The statistical procedure is likely to be somewhat less accurate if its cutoff points are used with other patients by clinicians, because it tailors its cutoff points for the particular group of subjects for which it is tested (Parsons & Prigatano, 1978). However, diagnosing a normal person as brain damaged may have profoundly negative effects, so it is clear that the "key" approach requires further development before it can be widely applied.

Neuropsychological Test Validity: "Organics" Versus "Psychiatric Disorders"

Heaton, Baade and Johnson (1978) have reviewed 94 studies in which neuropsychological tests were used to discriminate between persons with brain damage and subjects who were diagnosed as non-brain-damaged but psychiatrically impaired. The most frequently used tests were the Bender-Gestalt, the Graham-Kendall

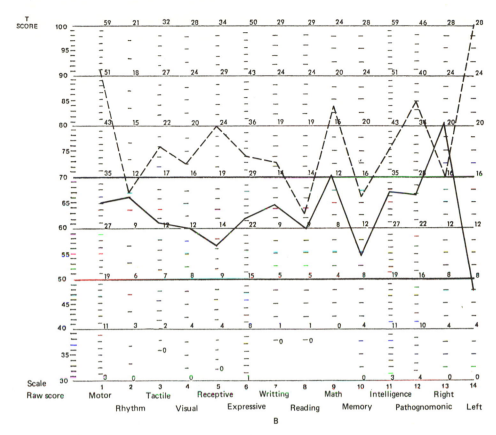

and T. A. Hammeke, Localization of cerebral dysfunctions with a standardized version of Luria's neuropsychological battery. *Journal of Consulting and Clinical Psychology*, 1979, *47*, 1003–1019. Copyright 1979 by the American Psychological Association. Reprinted by permission.)

Memory for Designs, the Benton Visual Retention Test, the Trail Making Test Part B (Trails B), the WAIS, and the Halstead Impairment Index. Across 84 studies that attempted to separate organics from psychiatric disorders, excluding chronic and process schizophrenics, the tests yielded a median 75% hit rate—very comparable to that cited by Spreen and Benton (1965) and recent studies comparing organics and "normals." When psychiatric disorders were grouped as (1) nonpsychotic, (2) mixed psychiatric, (3) affective (such as depression), (4) mixed psychotic, (5) acute or reactive schizophrenics, and (6) mixed schizophrenics (including both acute and chronics), then median hit rates for the tests were, respectively, 82%, 77%, 77%, 70%, 77%, and 69%.

Stack and Phillips' (1970) finding that clinicians could differentiate acute schizophrenics from chronic brain-damaged patients with a 72% hit rate with the Halstead-Reitan Battery adds further replication, as does the recent study by Kiernan and Matthews (1976) in which the Impairment Index, Trails B, and two visuo-motor tests separated brain-damaged from outpatient psychiatric patients with 72 to 84% accuracy. Golden (1977) adds further evidence with the finding that a discriminant analysis using tests from the Halstead-Reitan Battery, the WAIS, Trails B, and the Aphasia Screening Examination correctly identified 100% psychiatric disorders and 94% organics. Several single tests produced 70 + % hit rates, but clearly the full battery is optimal for accurate diagnosis. These findings are especially important because they indicate that, even in the often-ambiguous and complex task of diagnosing brain damage in patients who appear to present only psychological/psychiatric problems, neuropsychological testing can greatly assist the practicing clinician.

However, when neuropsychological tests were used to discriminate between chronic or process schizophrenics and brain-damaged persons, the median hit rate across 34 studies was only 54%. Thus, only about one of every two patients was correctly diagnosed, barely better than would be expected by just random guessing. Chronic and process schizophrenics also score significantly worse on neuropsychological tests than do more acute or reactive schizophrenics or any other psychiatric or normal group (Heaton et al., 1978). Thus, chronic schizophrenics cannot be distinguished from brain-damaged persons, and this may be for any of three possible reasons. The serious motivational and thought disorders characterizing chronic schizophrenics may impair their test performance. This is not a sufficient answer, because acute schizophrenics should theoretically share the same thought disorders, and yet they score in the normal range on neuropsychological tests. The alternative reasons are based on the hypothesis that many chronic schizophrenics are, in fact, brain damaged, due to either adverse effects of long-term medication with psychotropic drugs or to a preexisting brain pathology. The latter possibilities are bolstered by the fact that only 15% of the studies reviewed by Heaton et al. (1978) administered neurological exams to the "psychiatric patients," and even those that did may have failed to eliminate all brain damaged subjects from the "psychiatric" group. Thus both Heaton, et al. and Reitan (1976) strongly suggest that many chronic schizophrenics are, in fact, brain damaged. This hypothesis merits further research.

Two other approaches have been taken to differentiate persons diagnosed as schizophrenics from persons with brain damage. Neither strategy has yet been successful. Watson (1971) developed a "Schizophrenia-Organicity" (Sc-0) scale including the items from the MMPI that discriminated between the two groups. However, Halperin, Neuringer, Davis and Goldstein (1977) found that the Sc-0 scale could not differentiate between schizophrenics who were diagnosed as brain damaged or non-brain-damaged, and concluded that the Sc-0 scale is primarily useful in discriminating between schizophrenics and nonschizophrenics rather than as a neuropsychological test.

The second approach is based on the intriguing idea that brain-damaged and schizophrenic persons may achieve similar test scores by *different methods*. Goldstein and Neuringer (1966) attempted to discriminate between the two groups based on differences in qualitative style on the Trails B test. This study achieved an unusually high hit rate with chronic schizophrenics (77%). This study, although promising, requires further research before clinical application is warranted. Research by Chelune, Heaton, Lehman, and Robinson (1979) indicates that simple examination of the profile pattern on neuropsychological tests does not provide sufficient qualitative information: at best, profile information increased diagnostic hit rates from 68 to 80%. More sophisticated qualitative information appears necessary for accurate separation of brain-injured versus schizophrenic subjects.

Neuropsychological Test Validity: Localization of Brain Damage

Neuropsychological tests will have greater clinical utility if they enable the clinician to determine the brain area that is damaged as well as just indicating that brain lesions exist. Less research has been done in this more sophisticated area. The basic principle underlying such investigations is that verbal-cognitive tasks will suffer most from lesions in the left hemisphere (LH), while tasks requiring nonverbal spatial perception and motor performances will show pronounced deficits when there is damage in the right hemisphere (RH), among right-handed and most left-handed individuals.

Wheeler, Burke, and Reitan (1963) offered encouraging initial evidence, reporting that more than 90% of brain-damaged persons could be correctly diagnosed as LH, RH, or diffuse damage using discriminant analysis with the Halstead-Reitan Battery tests. More recently, Golden (1977) showed that several WAIS and Halstead-Reitan tests were able to correctly classify persons from a mixed psychiatric and brain injured population as LH or RH with 80 + % hit rates. Trails B, Aphasia Screening Exam, Impairment Index, Speech-Sounds Perception Test and the WAIS Arithmetic, Digit Span, and Vocabulary subtests pinpointed LH, while Trails B, Finger Oscillation (left hand), Spatial Relations test, and the WAIS Block Design, Digit Symbol, Picture Arrangement, and Object Assembly subtests accurately identified RH subjects. This finding is consistent with the rule that large VIQ-PIQ discrepancies favoring VIQ are strongly suggestive of RH lesions while LH damage is not as well predicted by a discrepancy favoring PIQ over VIQ (Highlight 9-2).

Neuropsychological Assessment Research with Children

Reed, Reitan, and Kløve (1965) and Boll (1974) have conducted validation studies of the Halstead Battery for Children and the Wechsler-Bellvue IQ Test with 9 to 14-year-old children, and Reitan (1974) has evaluated the Reitan-Indiana Battery and the WISC-R with 5 to 8-year-old children. Reed et al. found that the Wechsler Verbal subtests, the Trail Making Test, and the Speech-Sounds Perception Test were most effective in distinguishing normal from brain-damaged children, although all 27 separate measures used were able to discriminate the two groups at a statistically significant level. Boll replicated this finding, concluding that verbal reasoning and problem solving tests were significantly better at differentiating normals from brain-damaged children than tests of perception, memory, and alertness. Of the 40 tests that Boll used, 37 significantly discriminated the two groups. Unfortunately neither study reported hit rates, so clinical utility still remains to be addressed.

Reitan found that different tests were maximally effective in predicting brain damage for 5 to 8-year-olds than those identified for 9 to 14-year-olds. The WISC-R Full Scale IQ was most effective, with a 90% hit rate. Several tests of visual-motor performance, perception, and alertness, as well as tests of conceptual/verbal skills, yielded hit rates above 75%. These three studies indicate that accurate neuropsychological assessment will be possible with children and youths, pending further clinical cross-validation, but that the two age groups (5 to 8 versus 9 to 14) should be considered separately when predictors are being developed and utilized.

More recently, Selz and Reitan (1979) have developed 37 rules for pinpointing brain damage in 9 to 14-year-olds, and demonstrated that non-brain-injured, learning disability (with no neurological evidence of brain damage) and brain-injured (as verified by neurological examination) children could be distinguished with a 74% overall hit rate using a summary score based on all 37 rules. The rules are derived from all four of Reitan's (1970) approaches to interpreting neuropsychological tests, and applied with neuropsychological tests from the Halstead Battery. The learning-disability group was most difficult to classify correctly, but only 12% of this group was misclassified as brain damaged. The use of research-based algorithms and multiple assessment measures thus appears to offer an approach with clinical utility for distinguishing subjects with damaged and normal functioning.

Methodological Issues: Potential Shortcomings in Neuropsychological Research

As discussed in Chapter 3, clinical research is only as good as its methodology. Intriguing findings may only be chance occurrences unless precautions of reliability and internal and external validity are taken. In considering the research on neuropsychological assessment, we must conclude along with Heaton et al. (1978), Parsons and Prigatano (1978), and Reitan and Davison (1974) that several methodological problems limit the findings of neuropsychological assessment research (see also Filskov & Locklear, 1982) to one general conclusion: a comprehensive test battery administered by an experienced clinician is likely to yield a correct diagnosis of brain damage or no and RH or LH in about 75 to 85% of his or her cases. Several specific precautions, that are *not* always fulfilled by neuropsychological assessment research studies, have been identified for future research:

1. Subjects must be described explicitly in terms of demographic data such as age, education, sex, race, and socioeconomic status. Studies have shown that persons who differ on these characteristics often score significantly differently on neuropsychological tests (Amante, Van Houten, Grieve, Bader, & Margules, 1977; Finlayson, Johnson & Reitan, 1977; Parsons & Prigatano, 1978) and that different methods for combining tests are more or less effective with different groups (Kiernan & Matthews, 1976). When different groups are used in a validation study, it is essential to demonstrate that they are comparable on demographic characteristics. Ideally all subjects will be from relatively homogeneous groups, for example "40 to 50-year-old black men," so that the effects of differences

among subjects within each group will not be large enough to obscure important differences between brain-damaged and non-brain-damaged groups.

2. Subjects must be assigned to brain-damaged, psychiatric disorder, and "normal" groups based on reliable and valid criteria. Because no one method has proved infallible for diagnosing brain damage, studies that classify one group of patients as "brain damaged" must take several precautions or else many of these patients may *not* in fact have brain lesions. Ideally, two skilled neurologists would each make an independent diagnosis based on a thorough neurological exam and results from several medical tests such as the CAT scan. Short of this, Parsons and Prigatano (1978) suggest that the diagnosis be determined by positive signs of brain damage from a neurological exam and at least one independent medical test, and that the neurologist later rerate the exam results on a blind basis for a sample of the patients, to check reliability. Unfortunately, 71% of the studies reviewed by Heaton et al. (1978) failed to state how brain damage was identified or did so on the basis of one psychiatrist's clinical exam—and Heaton et al. cite evidence that psychiatrists' diagnoses are *not* likely to be reliable or valid.

Similarly, it must be clearly determined that the non-brain-damaged subjects really do *not* have brain lesions, especially with chronic schizophrenics. However, this was done in only 15% of the studies reviewed by Heaton et al. (1978), leaving grave doubt as to the true neuropsychological status of the "non-brain-damaged" groups.

3. Subjects must also be clearly described in terms of psychological, physiological, and intellectual characteristics that are likely to affect the ways in which brain damage would show up on neuropsychological tests. Just as demographic characteristics of subjects must be reported and controlled for, several aspects of subjects' psychosocial and physical functioning must be controlled in neuropsychological assessment research: age at which brain damage probably occurred; chronicity of the neurological or psychological disorder; subjects' emotional states; subjects' handedness; and, the size and extent of brain lesions. Subjects who may be comparable in terms of presence or absence of brain damage may nevertheless score signficantly differently on neuropsychological tests if they differ on these characteristics. Although it is important to consider subjects' level of intelligence before brain damage occurred—through the use of prior IQ scores or by estimating from current IQ test performance—Heaton et al. (1978) consider it "inappropriate" for brain-damaged and non-brain-damaged groups to be matched on current IQ because this is likely to obscure real differences between the groups on other neuropsychological tests.

4. A neuropsychological assessment procedure's clinical utility depends on three factors: (1) the true positive rate, that is, the accuracy with which it identifies persons who are truly brain damaged, (2) the true negative rate, that is, the accuracy with which it identifies persons who are truly *not* brain damaged, and (3) its ability to achieve true and false positive hit rates that exceed the base rate for brain damage in the population being studied. Thus the test must be able to accurately identify both brain-damaged and non-brain-damaged persons, and to do so more accurately than would be possible with base-rate (Meehl & Rosen, 1955) predictions. For example, if we know from past research that 30% of the people with psychiatric disorders also have brain lesions—as is suggested by

Heaton et al. (1978)—then we would be correct 70% of the time if we simply guessed that every such person did not have brain damage, and 30% of the time if we guessed that they all had incurred lesions.

Unfortunately, most studies report only combined hit rates rather than separate rates for true positives and negatives, and base rates are rarely available or reported. Satz, Fennell, and Reilly (1970) have demonstrated that certain medical and neuropsychological tests are best for true positives while others are more effective in identifying true negatives. Although they believe that false negatives—misdiagnosing persons who do have brain lesions as "non-brain-damaged"—are more harmful for clients than are false positives—misdiagnosing non-brain-damaged persons as "brain damaged"—it is clear that either type of error can be devastating for a client who is seeking reassurance and effective treatment. Therefore, further research is needed to develop tests that maximize either true positives or negatives, so that clinicians can combine both types of tests and achieve most accurate diagnoses.

5. Validation studies must be replicated before they can be considered definitive. Especially when discriminant analysis techniques are used to combine several test scores, cross-validation investigations are essential to demonstrate that the hit rates can be generalized beyond the specific persons tested in the study.

6. Parsons and Prigatano (1978) cite evidence that different behavioral styles by examiners can lead to different performance levels by brain-damaged persons on neuropsychological tests. They recommend that the test administrator's training, experience, and specific test administration procedures be clearly reported.

Future Research Directions

Despite the promising results and generally high level of sophistication of neuropsychological assessment methods and research, the methodological issues we have discussed suggest that several improvements are warranted in future studies. Parsons and Prigatano (1978) state their opinion that:

> . . . the search for the Holy Grail [i.e., the neuropsychological test(s) that will give a high discrimination of brain-damaged patients from controls or other psychopathological groups in all types of settings, with all socioeconomic levels] is not likely to be as productive as other research approaches. (p. 614)

They recommend the development of specific tests that can pinpoint the site and extent of brain damage in specific groups of subjects, and a greater reliance on single-subject case studies.

Two optimistic directions for future clinical research involve the prediction and facilitation of recovery from debilitating brain lesions. Meier (1974) discusses how brain-damaged persons may regain capabilities that are lost due to brain injury, suggesting that this may occur because brain centers that have essentially been "in shock" may become functional once again or because the brain may actually reorganize itself so that old tasks are handled by different substitute brain centers. Brain-damaged patients could be very much reassured by prognoses that, whether positive or negative, are sufficiently accurate to enable them to make the best adjustment to their dysfunctions. Meier also describes some initial research in which neuropsychological tests have been successfully used to predict neurological recovery one year after acute cerebral infarctions.

Further research is also needed in the parallel area of the rehabilitation of brain damaged persons. Lewinsohn, Danaher, and Kikel (1977) describe promising results in the use of visual imagery as mnemonic aids for brain-damaged persons whose memory capabilities are impaired. They note that research must especially be directed toward the development of treatment procedures that will produce behavioral improvements that will persist after the treatment program has ended.

We conclude with a reminder that clinical psychologists who conduct neuropsychological assessment with real clients do not mechanically rely on test scores and standard cutoff points as the sole basis for diagnosing and pinpointing brain lesions. Instead, they combine these numerical data with their knowledge of the relationships between different brain areas and behavioral capabilities and their past experience with clients, to follow an integrated quantitative/qualitative strategy. Therefore, future neuropsychological assessment research will probably focus on clearly describing and empirically validating the procedures that clinicians actually use, rather than on only demonstrating that test scores can yield high hit rates.

TRIPLE DEAD HEAT FOR "WIN"

THE CARTER HANDICAP
$10,000 added
Time 1:23 2/5 - 7 Furlongs

	win	place	show	jockey
#6 BROWNIE	$2.40	$2.30	$2.30	Eric Guerin
#1 BOSSUET	3.50	3.40	3.70	Jim Stout
#3 WAIT-A-BIT	4.30	3.90	3.90	Gayle L. Smith

The most famous race ever run anywhere in the world was at
Aqueduct Race Track on June 10, 1944.

*General observations drawn from particulars are the jewels of knowledge, comprehending
great store in a little room.*

Locke

Observational assessment seeks to be specific. This photo illustrates, or perhaps exemplifies, specificity in measurement.

10

BEHAVIORAL ASSESSMENT

The behavioral approach to assessment focuses on identification of clients' specific behaviors or environmental systems that may require change. For example, when working with a client who is experiencing debilitating anxiety, the behavioral assessor might inquire: What specific situations result in feelings of anxiety? What behaviors occur when anxiety is felt? Are certain environmental conditions associated with changes in the severity of the anxiety? How does the client currently cope with anxiety? In this chapter we describe the perspective that underlies behavioral assessment and discuss the methods that are utilized in behavioral assessment.

Behavioral assessment has evolved as a model for helping clinicians to formulate and evaluate specific intervention plans for their clients. Behavioral assessment is a *situation-specific* approach, in that specific variations in environmental conditions are carefully examined to determine their influence on clients' functioning. Behavioral assessment can also be seen as a conceptual viewpoint in which the reciprocal influence of people's actions and their environmental contexts is emphasized. Typically, behavioral assessors will seek to identify the relationships between a client's interpersonal and physical environments and the behaviors that reflect the client's problems in living. The assessment is undertaken in order to develop a precise and effective strategy for helping the client to alter his or her environment in ways that will enable him or her to behave more effectively. For example, the clinician may observe the client who is experiencing severe anxiety while the client is in especially anxiety-provoking situations in order to determine what aspects of these situations are most difficult for the client to handle. If it is determined that conversations with angry authority figures are the central source of anxiety, the clinician can then work with the client on ways to cope with such persons and ways to defuse their anger in advance. The clinician is likely to then observe the client once again in these aversive situations, in order to evaluate the success that therapy has had in helping the client deal with his or her anxiety.

Behavioral assessment can be done in many ways, such as through interviewing clients and asking about the specifics of their daily lives, or through actually observing clients as they interact with their friends, families and co-workers. Before discussing the methods used by behavioral assessors, however, it is important to review the theoretical and clinical issues that have spurred the development of behavioral assessment.

Central to behavioral assessment is Skinner's (1953) paradigm of "functional analysis." A functional analysis involves the assessment of events or stimuli that precede (i.e., "antecedents") a target behavior and those that follow it (i.e., "consequences"). When a pattern of certain antecedents and certain consequences is observed to regularly occur with a target behavior, the assessor can infer that the function of these particular antecedents is to set the occasion for the target behavior and the function of these particuar consequences is to reinforce the target behavior. Or, from the viewpoint of the behaver, the function of the target behavior is to bring forth these particular consequences in the context defined by these particular antecedents. A behavioral assessment is incomplete unless all three elements in the functional analysis—antecedents, behavior, consequences—are accurately assessed: only then can the assessor pinpoint (and thus predict) how the subject's behavior changes in line with changes in the environment.

RATIONALE FOR BEHAVIORAL ASSESSMENT

A Theoretical Foundation

From the behavioral perspective, human functioning is seen as the product of the ongoing *interaction* of the *person* and the *situation* (e.g., Bandura, 1978; Mischel, 1977a). People shape their own lives through their behaviors, their thinking and planning, and their emotions. For example, the decision to stop a longstanding habit such as cigarette smoking is an important step toward successfully halting that health hazard. However, people's environments also shape their lives. For example, it is much more difficult to stop smoking when friends or family members create a situation that encourages smoking than when they create an environment that discourages smoking. Thus, people are seen as constantly constructing their own lives and environments, but also as constantly being shaped by the learning experiences that their environments provide for them.

Behavioral assessment is the practical extension of this *interactional* theory of human functioning. When a behavioral assessor is gathering information about a client, the central question is: What specific situations make up this client's psychological, interpersonal, and physical environment, and how does this client attempt to cope with and modify the environment? A variety of research investigations have demonstrated that the *combination* of specific situations and specific people and their responses is the key to positive human functioning (see Highlight 10-1). Although some environmental situations will cause distress and dysfunction no matter how people respond to them (e.g., concentration camps), most situations affect different people in very different ways. For example, novice thera-

Highlight 10-1 The Person × Situation Interaction

People shape their life environments, for example, by choosing where to live or what careers to pursue or by creating roadways and cities. By the same token, the environment shapes people, for example, by offering rewards or penalties for certain actions. Thus, people and their environmental situations can be said to be *interacting reciprocally* (Bandura, 1978). Just as we create the situations that make up our lives, so do those situations determine what kinds of persons we will become.

The research base for the study of this *person × situation interaction* is impressive (Bandura, 1978; Bem & Allen, 1974; Bowers, 1973; Endler & Magnusson, 1976; Mischel, 1973a, 1977a). Investigations of the functioning of laypersons, therapy clients, therapists, teachers, and many others demonstrated that a most accurate prediction of how a given person will feel, think, or behave requires data concerning both (1) what personal characteristics best describe that *person* (e.g., skills, fears, interpersonal style) and (2) the nature of the *situations* which that person will be encountering (e.g., city crowds, final examinations, social parties). It is the particular *combination* of this specific person and that specific situation which is said to be most important in determining what behaviors, feelings, or thoughts are likely to result. In statistical terms, it appears important to have information about both the person *and* the situation, *and* about the interaction (combination) of this person and that situation if psychologists are to fully understand why people experience life's joys and problems as they do.

People interact with situations much like the interaction of two volatile chemicals: just as hydrochloric acid can be created from two innocuous substances, so too can unexpected occurrences happen when people and situations are mixed together. For example, Bowers (1973) summarizes more than 10 studies that consistently show personal characteristics contributing an average of 13% of the variance in people's behavior, while situational factors accounted for an average of 11% of the variance. However, it is the interaction of the person and situation that has the greatest impact, averaging a 21% contribution.

As Mischel (1973a) and Wachtel (1973) noted, some situations are extremely powerful, while others allow or encourage diversity from people. Thus, just as people appear likely to respond in a consistent fashion in areas that are central to their self-images, so too certain kinds of situations are likely to limit people's freedom of choice more than others. The implication is that a complete assessment must obtain data on the nature and relative power of both clients' personal predispositions and their life situations.

pists are often asked to conduct therapy sessions with their supervisor observing them, and this can be either an exciting educational opportunity or a traumatic trial by fire depending on how the trainee sets up the situation. If the trainee takes time to get to know his or her supervisor and to work out an agreement that the observation will be focused on providing constructive feedback to the trainee, there is a far better chance that the situation will be a positive learning experience rather than a grueling and frightening test.

On the other side of the coin, some people seem to get themselves into trouble no matter what they do or where they are, and some kinds of responses are likely to cause distress and dysfunction no matter what the situation. A person who responds to every situation in an attacking and aggressive fashion because he or she believes that people are "out to get" him or her is, for instance, going to experience fear and disappointment in most every life situation. However, here again it is usually the specific *combination* of the particular person and his or her particular responses with the particular situation that determines how well the person will fare. Different people prefer different kinds of situations, and different kinds of responses produce the best outcome in different situations. One client may fare best in a situation where he or she has a clear set of rules to follow, while another client may be better suited by a situation in which he or she sets his or her own rules and guidelines.

Thus, in behavioral assessment, the goal is to determine how each unique client is responding in his or her life situations, and to identify ways in which the client can modify his or her responses *and* environmental contexts so that a new and better combination of responses and situations is achieved. In order to accomplish this goal, precise information is obtained to define the client's life situations and his or her response patterns in those settings.

Behavioral Versus Traditional Assessment

Proponents of the behavioral assessment approach have described several differences in the clinical strategies of behavioral versus traditional assessment (Goldfried & Kent, 1972; see also Ciminero, Calhoun & Adams, 1977; Mash & Terdal, 1976). First, behavioral assessors assert that the *target* of assessment should be information that is directly relevant to the practical question of what goals should be pursued through what clinical interventions for each unique client. Although other approaches to clinical assessment seek to obtain therapeutically relevant information, behavioral assessment focuses on *directly observable* behaviors and environmental features. Although other approaches to assessment often produce elegant and interesting portraits of people (e.g., an MMPI profile or a Rorschach protocol), behavioral assessment emphasizes gathering data that provide the most clear and direct answers to the practical question of what combinations of responses and situations are producing distress for the client and how can these specific responses and situations be changed so as to promote the client's welfare. For example, behavioral assessors would seek to learn how a client couple with marital problems actually interact on a day-to-day basis, rather than how they respond to a personality questionnaire.

A second feature of behavioral assessment is *specificity*. Rather than relying on general personality descriptions or diagnostic labels such as "schizophrenic" or "hyperactive," behavioral assessors document the specific behaviors, thoughts, feelings, and physiological responses that clients produce and the specific makeups of the situations in which these responses occur. The specific data obtained in a behavioral assessment can be used to develop a comprehensive description of the client and his or her responses to life settings, as well as to pinpoint the precise determinants of the client's psychological dysfunctions.

Third, the focus in behavioral assessment is on obtaining a *sample* of the client's actual interactions in real-life settings. In contrast, traditional approaches to assessment are portrayed by behavioral assessors as emphasizing *signs* of the client's underlying personality traits, psychodynamics or general personal capacities. A sample is a piece of the client's actual behavior in daily situations that is directly representative of how the client responds in actual life settings. In contrast, a sign may be far removed from the client's normal life situations and responses (e.g., the only time most people free associate to an inkblot is in a psychologist's office), but is thought to give a truer picture of the client's personality than any sample from real-life situations. The validity of the use of signs in clinical assessment has been called into question by researchers and clinicians, and behavioral assessors rely on samples in order to get the most direct picture of how clients actually handle life's challenges.

Fourth, behavioral and traditional assessors diverge in their strategies for *developing assessment measures*. When an assessment instrument is developed, its originators must select items for it, whether these are multiple-choice questions, inkblots, or real-life interpersonal situations. The items used by many traditional assessment measures have been criticized as deficient because they do not systematically sample the situations and behaviors that are necessary in order to produce a complete understanding of the client (Loevinger, 1957). Behavioral assessors attempt to overcome this problem by empirically identifying the responses and situations that are crucial to clients' welfare, and then including samples of all relevant responses and situations in their assessment instruments.

Fifth, the assessment *procedure* differs in behavioral versus traditional assessment, in that behavioral assessors seek to gather assessment information not only before and after but also during clinical intervention. The traditional approach to assessment has been to collect information about clients only on an informal basis during therapy. In contrast, behavioral assessment measures are usually designed to be administered several times during therapy so as to provide a more exact assessment of the client's progress and changing needs throughout the intervention. Here again, the behavioral approach represents an attempt to provide specific, accurate, and practically-useful information about the client's real-life functioning in order to facilitate effective clinical intervention.

Behavioral and traditional assessment approaches both offer special advantages and disadvantages, and many clinicians use tools and techniques from both models in order to get a balanced and thorough understanding of each unique client. However, both the theoretical and clinical rationales for behavioral assessment represent an important innovation in clinical psychology.

REPRESENTATIVE BEHAVIORAL ASSESSMENT METHODS

Five major methods of behavioral assessment have been developed: naturalistic observation, self-monitoring, situation-specific self-report by the client, analogue observation, and observations and ratings by significant others.

Naturalistic Observation

One means of assessing the functioning of a client or research participant is to observe directly that person in the settings and interactions that the client actually experiences. Such *in situ* (in the natural setting) observations can also provide the psychologist with data concerning the situations and their impact on people. Such observation is called "naturalistic" because it involves watching the person's behavior in the "natural environment"—the settings that are actually a part of the person's life. Naturalistic observation, therefore, has the advantage of providing a *direct sample* of the relevant behavior or situational factors for that particular person.

All clinical assessment seeks to provide accurate descriptions of people as they truly are, and the ultimate criterion for the estimation of a person's functioning is what that person does in real-life interactions and relationships. However, lest you conclude that naturalistic observation is an infallible assessment method, it should be pointed out that different observers may draw different conclusions from identical observations, and, thus, naturalistic observations cannot be considered the one and only "measure of a man." Hence, clinical psychologists emphasize a reliance on multiple assessment measures from multiple sources and not just on naturalistic observation alone.

Development of Naturalistic Observation Measures   Observations of behavior that are taken *in situ* are recorded via coding systems. A coding system is a predetermined strategy for defining each behavior and for observing and recording the frequency of these behavioral categories. For example, the assessment of behavior in a classroom might involve the observation of reading, off-task, and talking behaviors. Each of these behavioral categories would be specifically defined so that observers could accurately tell when they do or do not occur.

Since the specific behaviors to be assessed may vary from one client to another, or from one research project to another, the clinical psychologist who employs behavioral assessments must be prepared to develop new behavior categories for different purposes. Although certain settings are sufficiently typical that somewhat standard observational codes have evolved, the development, revision and/or adaptation of coding systems is an important function of a behavioral assessor. The following steps illustrate this process.

Step 1.   The clinical psychologist must first compile a *preliminary pool of categories* for observation (Patterson, 1977). What exactly is to be observed? What behaviors and what aspects of the situation merit attention? The chosen targets for observation should be *relevant* and *comprehensive*. Only behaviors that are meaningful in terms of the clinician's and client's basic goals or the researcher's basic hypotheses should be included, because the greater the number of categories the greater the likelihood that the observer will be overloaded and, therefore, inaccurate. However, every issue and concept of interest should be fully presented or else the observations will paint an incomplete picture. For example, if the primary target is "interpersonal interactions," then the relevant behavioral categories might include "initiates conversations," "maintains conversations," and "maintains eye contact," among others. Categories that are not likely to be relevant might include "studying," "consuming alcohol," "driving," or "running," although such categories might be necessary in other cases.

Several sources should be utilized in formulating the initial observational categories. These sources include past clinical experience, research, theory, case studies, interviews with experienced persons, and, especially, informal "pilot" observations of representative persons in the target situation. Barker (1968) developed a straightforward yet innovative method for pilot observations: "stream of behavior" observations are gathered by having observers simply describe the flow of events in phrases and sentences, either in writing or by speaking into a tape recorder.

Step 2. Each behavioral or situational category must be *operationally defined.* This means that *specific* and *directly observable* behaviors or setting characteristics must be provided to define each category. A definition for an observational category is "operational" when the precise operations that signal its appearance are explicitly stated such that any two observers can agree when it has or has not occurred. This task is not easy when complex human interactions are being observed, and extensive practice trials should be conducted with a code to identify the special cases, exceptions, and ambiguous occurrences that are almost always found. Table 10-1 illustrates some of the pitfalls and requirements of effective operational definitions.

Step 3. Concurrently with the formulation of operational definitions, the people who will serve as *observers* must be selected. Highly experienced mental health professionals offer an excellent pool of expert observers, but this is very costly and runs the risk that the professionals might bias their observations with their theoretical assumptions. Often, research assistants or clinical aides are recruited instead. Another source of observers is the group with whom the target person regularly interacts: parents, spouse, friends, teachers, co-workers, etc. Such persons are not usually trained as extensively as research assistants or clinical aides and, thus, are often called on to make only a limited number of observations. Also, the client can be called on as an observer of his or her own behavior and environment, although this is a special case that will be discussed separately in the upcoming section on self-monitoring. In general, observers must be selected so as to balance cost with the quality and comprehensiveness of the data they provide, and the type and number of observational categories must be geared to the special strengths and weaknesses of the particular persons who are chosen.

Step 4. A *unit of analysis* must be chosen. This concerns the length of time and type and number of responses that will be used in the actual observational recording.

Dollard and Auld (1959) distinguish between three types of units of analysis: the *scoring unit*, the *contextual unit*, and the *summarizing unit*. The scoring unit is the segment of time or behavior that is to be rated or categorized. For example, a scoring unit could be each spoken word, each complete utterance, every three

Table 10-1   Sample Operational Definitions for Observational Measures

Category	Operational Definition	Incomplete Operational Definition
Command	Audible statement of an action that must be performed; must include the words "must," "will," "have to," "insist," "command," "demand," "no choice," or "order."	A forceful statement of an action to be taken.
Self-disclosure	Describes *own personal* experiences, feelings or attitudes. Must be something that has actually been done, felt, or believed, not something which the client is simply advised to emulate on principle or the experience of others. Does not include objective or professional experiences, feelings, beliefs.	Says something about himself/herself.
Negative affect	States *own* negative emotion or mood. Key words: sad, angry, hate, depressed, envious, fear, guilt, resentful, shock, confused, anxious, "blah," disgust, spiteful, furious, aggravated, dismal, gloomy, upset. Does *not* include statements of belief that begin with "I feel."	Expresses an unpleasant feeling. Seems distressed.
Insult	States a description of a person or a person's actions or significant others that explicitly connotes some negative quality, including stupidity, insensitivity, failure, craziness, physical deficiency, physical abnormality, ugliness or dirtiness. Includes rhetorical questions.	States a putdown.

minutes or every 30 seconds. The contextual unit is the segment of time or behavior that an observer examines in order to rate each scoring unit. For example, a contextual unit might be an entire therapy session, a complete exchange between father, mother, and son, or 10 minutes during the class study period. Finally, the summarizing unit is the grouping of scoring units about which conclusions will be drawn. Here, for example, the unit might be a two-week baseline, three representative interactions, or the first and second halves of a semester. There is no single unit of analysis that is best for all purposes; and, therefore, the clinical psychologist defines scoring, contextual and summarizing units differently for each specific purpose.

Research on the effects of using time segments of different lengths for the scoring unit has generally shown that different segment lengths result in similar total scores for the behaviors being observed. However, time segments can unwittingly affect the results when the behaviors being observed occur for extended periods of time or when behavior varies significantly at different time points (e.g., a parent may behave harshly in response to misbehavior, but later in the evening behave very warmly). As a consequence, the results can be very different because different patterns of behaviors may appear when segments of varying length are used (e.g., Kiesler, Mathieu, & Klein, 1964; Mintz & Luborsky, 1971). Thus, thought must be given to the issue of selecting a scoring unit such that the phenomena being observed are "preserved" as they are categorized by observers.

The same caution applies with regard to the contextual unit, as illustrated by an exchange between Rappaport and Chinsky (1972) and Truax (1972) concerning the issue of the rating of "accurate empathy" from the behavior of therapists. Empathy is one of the central concepts in psychotherapy discussed by Rogers (1957): it is the act of accurately experiencing and reflecting back to the client the client's emotions. Empathy is a very complex collection of behaviors and rating it often requires extensive inference by observers. Nevertheless, with extensive training, observers can rate empathy with precision—so well, in fact, that ratings based on only observing the *therapist's* behavior turn out to be virtually as efficient as those made when the context was both *therapist and client* behaviors. Rappaport and Chinsky (1972) point out that this is all fine and well, except that empathy is theoretically defined as an accurate appraisal from the client's viewpoint, and if raters never see or hear the client, then how can they possibly know whether or not the therapist is accurate? Truax (1972) replies that the important thing in empathy is for the therapist to express a genuine and in-depth understanding of the client's feelings, and that this hinges only on the therapist's behavior. Both viewpoints have merit: certain forms of behavior seem to have a reliable impact regardless of the particular situation; but, on the other hand, many behaviors are difficult to understand without the complete interpersonal interaction as the context. This interchange illustrates that the clinical psychologist should be sure to choose a context that enables observers to have a perspective that will make their observations meaningful.

Context also includes prior observations. That is, once a scoring unit is observed, it is now a part of the context for all subsequent scoring units for that observer. When an observer rates a single individual or group on several consecutive occasions, even if spaced over substantial time intervals, the observer is likely to recall the previous observations and this may produce bias (Rappaport & Chinsky, 1972). Although the data concerning this problem are not conclusive (Cicchetti & Ryan, 1976), it is important for observers to be cautioned to base their observations on only what they currently see and hear and not on any previous observations or on their expectations. In contrast, it also appears that observers become more accurate when they observe the same person(s) or setting(s) repeated times, so the clinical psychologist must balance the possible biasing effect of repeated observations with the value that practice and familiarity can have on accuracy (Frick & Semmel, 1978).

One way to make it more difficult for observers to use their past observations as biases is to assign each observer to observe several persons and/or settings, with no person or setting being observed a second (or third. . .) time until all other persons and settings have been observed at least once. For example, Observer A might be asked to observe each of five classrooms five times each, but he or she would observe each classroom once before returning to any classroom for a second or third observation.

The summarizing unit must also be carefully defined so as to be of sufficient duration to permit all relevant patterns of behavior and stimuli to emerge stably (Baer, Wolf, & Risley, 1968). For example, Patterson (1974) has found that a two-week summarizing unit is necessary to produce a representative picture of interactions of aggressive boys and their families. When shorter time periods are used, the observers may by chance see the family at times that are better or worse than "usual," and, thus, lead to false conclusions. There is no definite time length or number of interactions that will always be optimal as a summarizing unit. However, it is essential to select a length that has been empirically established as long enough to show consistent repeated patterns of behavior. For example, the psychologist might conduct pilot observations for two weeks so as to determine that the target behaviors do change from hour to hour but not from day to day. This would be strong empirical evidence for using a summarizing unit that is at least as long as a day, so that the assessment provides the most accurate information.

Step 5. Once the appropriate units of analysis have been determined, the *specific form* that the observer's ratings will take must be decided. Several forms may be utilized. Ratings of the *intensity* of a behavior are illustrated by a scale from 0 to 10 which might be used to rate how much warmth a person's behavior conveys. Alternately, the *duration* of behavior can be recorded. For example, the number of minutes during which conversation occurs. *Frequency counts* involve a tabulation of the exact number of times that a behavior occurred. Finally, ratings of *occurrence-nonoccurrence* involve the straightforward recording of whether or not a behavior occurred, regardless of how long, frequently, or intensely. Intensity, duration, and frequency measures are *ordinal* data, while *occurrence-nonoccurrence* is a type of *nominal* information. Ordinal information is on a numerical scale such that the higher the number the more (intense, lengthy, or frequent) that behavior can be said to have been manifested. In contrast, "nominal" means that each separate rating tells us only if the behavior was observed or not, and not how much, how often or how long. Ordinal information is more complex than nominal data, thus requiring more extensive training for observers and more detailed operational definitions. Many important behavioral phenomena are best described as ordinal data, so the extra work is often warranted. Here again, the clinical psychologist must determine the optimal form for each behavior based on the nature of the phenomenon and the questions that need to be answered. For example, ordinal data in the form of frequency counts do not work well when a behavior occurs very rarely (e.g., explosive outbursts). Here, duration or intensity information might provide meaningful data.

Step 6. Having developed the basic framework, the clinical psychologist must next decide on a specific *procedure* for observation (Kent & Foster, 1977). One method, participant observation, involves having the observers placed right in the very settings that they are observing: sitting in the back of a classroom, for example. Other methods include *one-way mirrors, videotape,* and/or *audiotape* recordings, and *written transcripts.*

As you might imagine, each medium has several advantages and limitations. Participant observation allows the observer to have a full and direct appreciation of the context of the behavior but may result in data that are, in part, the result of the observer's very presence. The one-way mirror reduces the obtrusiveness of the observer while still allowing for direct and complete observation. Videotape is useful in that each tape can be played and replayed in any order and at any time desired; thus, the behaviors are never lost as they are when observers must produce their observations immediately as the situation unfolds. Videotapes are, however, limited by the fidelity of the recording and the playback equipment, by the skills of the camera operator, and by the scope and precision of the camera. Audiotape is more economical than videotape, but all visual information is lost. Finally, written transcripts minimize the chance that target persons' words will be misheard or forgotten by the observer, but they omit all visual and vocal cues. Also, transcripts must be done with great care or else the mistakes of the transcribers can result in inaccurate data.

Step 7. A *scoring format* must be selected. Observers can, for instance, write in or check off the behavioral categories on a written record sheet (Table 10-2). Computer microtechnology can be applied, for example, with portable data recording instruments such as the keyboard model illustrated in Figure 10-1 (Sykes, 1977). Observers alternately can time durations with stopwatches or with event recorders that automatically record the time whenever a switch corresponding to a behavior is pressed. Observers can also keep frequency counts on wrist or hand counters such as those used by golfers or shoppers. Whatever the form, one goal is to minimize the amount of time and effort required by observers in making their recordings, so that they can focus their attention on observation. Additionally, when observers must make ratings in a scoring unit that is defined as a certain time period, it is important to signal the observer when each period begins and ends. Otherwise, inaccurate ratings are likely to occur when different observers start and end at different times. To remedy this, researchers have used such devices as a "bug-in-the-ear" (an earphone) that "beeps" when a time interval endpoint is reached.

Step 8. Observers must be *trained* so that their ratings are accurate. Observers must first be familiarized with the observational code, and using a written manual with detailed operational definitions and multiple examples for each category is advisable. Next, videotaped examples are useful to provide observers with clear

Figure 10-1 A keyboard model portable data recording instrument. (Reproduced by permission of Electro/General Corporation, Minneapolis, Minn.)

and specific instances of the behaviors to be observed and cues that show them exactly when each behavior category has occurred. Once the observers have seen some examples, they can begin to practice observing. Such rehearsal is first done with brief and unambiguous interactions that exemplify one or two categories at most, and for which a *criterion* has been established (Frick & Semmel, 1978). A "criterion" is a standard rating that has been agreed upon by at least two highly experienced observers as the "true" observation, and which can thus be used by observers to check the accuracy of their ratings. Once observers are reliably accurate in these easier ratings, they can be graduated to observing samples of behavior that are more akin to the complex, confusing, and ambiguous situations that will be observed for the actual data collection (Frick & Semmel, 1978; Kent & Foster, 1977).

Once the observers are accurate in their ratings of real-life situations, then they may begin the actual observation process. Cautiously, Kent and Foster (1977) recommend that observers be overtrained before beginning real ratings, by simply continuing practice observations for several sessions even after they are found to be reliable. They also recommend that training should not stop once the observers have begun real observations.

Table 10-2 A Sample Coding Sheet on which Observers Can Record Their Observations

Behavior	Frequency of Occurrence (each "✔" = 1 occurrence)	
	10:30–11:00 A.M.	2:30–3:00 P.M.
Fighting	✔ ✔	✔ ✔ ✔ ✔
Noncompliance		✔ ✔ ✔
Interruptions		✔ ✔
On-task questions	✔ ✔	✔
Raises hand to answer a question	✔ ✔ ✔ ✔	

Observer: Dean F.   Student being observed: Chris B.

Date: November 30, 1981

Step 9. As observers prepare to engage in real observations, the clinical psychologist must set an *observation schedule.* It might be tempting to just have observers select a time and place that is most convenient, but certain methodological points should be considered. For instance, the same observers should not always observe at the same time and in the same place. Observers should be assigned to gather data at various times and in various settings so that no one observer will collect all of the data for any given client or setting or time period.

The steps that are required to develop a system of naturalistic observation are time consuming. As a result, it is sometimes difficult to use these procedures with individual clients. Nevertheless, several behavioral observation systems have been developed and utilized in both clinical research and practice. These more standard systems require less initial investment than newly created ones, and can be adjusted for various uses.

Sample Observational Measures Somewhat standard observational measures are available for use in several settings, including homes, classrooms, inpatient mental hospitals, and outpatient psychotherapy sessions. We will describe some sample codes for each setting. While these observational codes have been useful in clinical research, the clinical practitioner might need to scale down and individualize these codes to best fit the needs and issues of each client and the available resources.

Home observation The family is an important support system for adults and agent of socialization for children, and most people spend a great deal of time in their homes. Many problems in living can be traced, at least in part, to the client's pattern of family interactions. For this reason, both the researcher and the practitioner will often find home observations to be a useful source of data. Such observations may focus on the interactions of husband and wife, parent and child, or sibling and sibling.

Patterson (1977) and his colleagues have developed the Behavior Coding System (BCS) over several years of a clinical research project that has focused on in-

terventions for aggressive and noncompliant boys (Patterson, 1974). The BCS
(Table 10-3) contains 28 separate categories that the observer records as having
occurred or not every six seconds. The home observers sit at the periphery of the
family's dining room just before and during the family dinner hour. Observers
may talk informally with the family before or after the observations, and doing
so may help the family accept the observer's presence more readily, but they are
specifically forbidden to interact with the family while making observations. The
observer focuses on one person at a time for five consecutive minutes and then
switches to another person, observing each member for two five-minute samples
in each observation session. Observational assessments have been gathered before, during, and at several intervals after the treatment program. Each time, observations are conducted for 10 to 15 days, one session per day. Thus, the scoring
unit is six seconds and the contextual unit is one to two hours per day over several
days in the late afternoon. For research analyses, Patterson (1974) summarizes
the scores for each family member over the entire 10- to 15-day period.

Mash, Terdal, and Anderson (1973) have developed a code for rating parent-
child interactions that they call the "Response-Class Matrix." The categories for
this measure parallel Patterson's (1977), but the summarizing procedure focuses
more explicitly on *interactions* than on the separate actions of parent and child.
Observers record an observation every 10 seconds, but rather than observing one
person at a time, both parent and child behaviors are recorded by placing a single
mark in one of the cells of a matrix (see Table 10-4). Thus, for example, if the
predominant interaction in a 10 second period was "child hits younger brother,
mother slaps child," the appropriate recording would be a mark in the cell across
from "Negative" for the child and under "Negative" for the mother (Cell 26).

Table 10-3   Sample Categories From Patterson's Behavior Coding System

Categories	Definition[a]
Verbal	
CM (command)	An immediate and clearly stated request or command
CR (cry)	A person cries
Nonverbal	
DS (destructiveness)	The person destroys, damages, or attempts to damage, any nonhuman object
IG (ignore)	When Person A has directed behavior at person B and Person B appears to have recognized that the behavior was directed at him, but does not respond in an active fashion
Verbal or Nonverbal	
AP (approval)	A clear gestural or verbal indication of poisitive interest or involvement
CO (compliance)	A person immediately does what is asked of him.

[a]These definitions are summaries; more complete operational definitions were used by observers.
(Adapted from G. R. Patterson, Naturalistic observation in clinical assessment. *Journal of Ab-
normal Child Psychology*, 1977, 5, 307-322. Copyright 1977 by Plenum Publishing Corporation.
Reprinted by Permission.)

Table 10-4 The Response-Class Matrix

Child's Antecedent	Parent's Consequent						
	Command	Command Question	Question	Praise	Negative	Interaction	No Response
Compliance	1 11	2 111	3 1111	4	5 11	6	7 卌
Competing	8 11	9	10 111	11 11	12 卌	13	14 111
Play	15	16 卌	17 11	18 111	19 11	20	21 111
Negative	22 1	23 111	24 111	25 1	26	27 11	28 卌
Interaction	29 11	30	31 11	32 111	33 11	34 111	35 11
No response	36 1111	37 卌	38 1	39 11	40 111	41	42 1

Adapted from E. J. Mash, L. Terdal, and K. Anderson, The response-class matrix: A procedure for recording parent-child interactions. *Journal of Consulting and Clinical Psychology*, 1973, *40*, 163-164. Copyright 1973 by the American Psychological Association. Reprinted by permission.

Classroom observation   Children often experience social and psychological problems that manifest themselves in fearful, aggressive, disruptive, noncompliant or off-task behaviors at school. Since the school is one of the prime settings for most children, it is not surprising that many children who are referred to clinical psychologists for assessment and treatment are experiencing difficulties at school. Observational assessment has been employed in classroom settings with students of various ages, in public and private schools, as well as with retarded clients or adult outpatients who are participating in classroom programs at day hospitals.

O'Leary has utilized a classroom observation system that he and his colleagues developed (Kent, Miner, & Ray, 1974). Sample categories are provided in Table 10-5. This coding system is designed for use in classrooms for elementary-age children.

Similar codes have been developed by Patterson, Cobb, and Ray (1973), and Hops and Nicholes (1974). While these codes are useful in research where several experimenters wish to compare their data using a single standard observational measure, researchers and practitioners are sometimes interested in gathering observational data that are designed specifically for their needs. For example, if the clinician is working with a disruptive child, the observations could include "interrupts," "calls out," and "out of seat." In contrast, the clinician whose classroom contains outpatient adults may want to assess very different behaviors, such as "appropriate social interactions," "responds to requests," and "initiates positive socializing." By following the procedures we have discussed for the development of observational measures, each clinician can use naturalistic observation with this flexibility.

Inpatient hospital observation   Observational codes have been developed to assess the behaviors of clients who reside in institutions for the retarded or the psychologically impaired (Agras, 1976; Kazdin & Straw, 1976; Wallace, 1976). As in the observational assessment systems used in the home and in the classroom, the types of functioning that have been assessed in hospitals are quite varied and include self-care skills, work skills, interpersonal skills, delusional or hallucinatory speech, physical and verbal disruption, language skills, and attendance at therapeutic activities.

Paul and his colleagues have developed the Time Sample Behavioral Checklist as a naturalistic observation code for assessing inpatients' behavior in psychiatric hospitals (Mariotto & Paul, 1974). Instead of observing patients for several consecutive minutes, observers make only one two-second observation for each patient—but this is done once in every waking hour so as to produce a behavioral profile for the complete day. In this way, all time points in the day are sampled, as well as a variety of activities and situations.

The Time Sample Behavioral Checklist involves a large number of categories, each of which describes a specific behavior from one of four general areas. "Hostile-Belligerent" behaviors include such actions as cursing, injuring self or others, or destroying property. "Cognitive Distortion" categories include verbalized delusions, incoherent speech, or smiling without a stimulus. The

Table 10-5 Sample Categories from O'Leary's Classroom Observation Code Manual

Category	Definition
Interference	
I. Physical	A. Banging on desk, purposeful banging or dropping of chair, exaggerated foot stomping, noise made by what seems to be an accidental dropping of books, etc., noise made by pushing books off desk.
	B. Tapping on another student or teacher.
	C. Throwing things around room (e.g., paper airplane).
	D. Touching someone else's work while child is present.
	Exclude: Target child touches other child's work while other child is not present.
	E. Leaning or sitting on another child's desk while child is present.
	Exclude: Target child leans or sits on another child's desk while other child is not present.
II. Verbal	A. Talking with another child in a loud, extreme manner.
	B. Target child talks to himself in a loud and extreme manner.
	C. Target child calls out in a loud and extreme manner.
	Exclude: 1. Child talks to himself in a low tone of voice.
	2. Child coughs and sneezes—unless loud and in an exaggerated, purposeful manner.
	3. Target child initiates a conversation—unless in a loud, extreme manner.
	D. If during class discussion, where direct instructions were given for children to raise their hands before talking, and the child calls out without complying.
Initiation	A. Child must initiate conversation or direct comments toward another child.
	Examples: Child initiates a conversation.
	Include: Child verbally interrupts another child.
	Exclude: 1. If target child responds, but did not initiate.
	2. If child makes loud, intense vocalization without direction.
	3. If child initiates conversation with teacher.
Aggression	A. Child makes a forceful movement directed at another person either directly or by utilizing a material object as an extension of the hand.
	1. Blocking other with arms or body; tripping, kicking, pinching, biting, or hitting another person.
	2. Throwing objects at another person.
	B. Child curses at another or speaks in a threatening manner.

Adapted from R. N. Kent, G. Miner, and B. Ray, *Clinic observer manual*. State University of New York, Stony Brook, N. Y. Copyright 1974 by K. D. O'Leary. Reprinted by permission.

"Schizophrenic Disorganization" factor is composed of behaviors such as repetitive and stereotypic movements, shaking, pacing, or blank staring. Finally, "Appropriate Behaviors" include such categories as playing games, talking to others, or reading. Observers record the occurrence of any or all of the categories when they make their two-second observations, thus providing nominal-level information. The frequency with which each category occurs during time periods such as a day, a week, or all periods in which a particular activity takes place, can be calculated to provide an ordinal score for individual categories or for the general areas of behavior.

Observers can be trained to rate the Time Sample Behavioral Checklist with excellent reliability, and its scores have been found to be valid indicators of inpatients' level of sociopsychological functioning (Mariotto & Paul, 1974). The checklist provides a thorough description of both prosocial and problematic behaviors that are relevant for treatment programs in inpatient settings. It has also served as the source of data in studies examining methods of gathering observational data with the least bias (Redfield & Paul, 1976).

Ittelson, Rivlin, and Proshansky (1970) have developed a system for observational assessment that, in addition to gathering data on specific behaviors, illustrates how naturalistic observations can provide an assessment of situations as well as of persons.

> All the data were collected through the use of well-trained observers who spend considerable time on the ward becoming thoroughly familiar with the functioning of the ward and, in turn, becoming well-known to the ward occupants. Their presence was known and accepted by all as students of "ward architecture." They were instructed to be friendly with ward personnel and patients, but to avoid any direct involvement in ward activities. . . . Ward personnel reported no difference between periods during which the observers were present and those during which they were absent.
>
> The location and timing of observations typically involved a complete coverage of all physical spaces of the ward on an instantaneous time-sampling basis. What this meant in practice is that all areas of the ward were observed every fifteen minutes, using enough observers so that the total observation time, while not instantaneous, did not exceed three or four minutes. . . .
>
> Observations were recorded on data sheets designed for quick and easy use by the observers and for direct machine punching. . . . It will be noted that the observer (records), in addition to data such as the location and time of observation, the number of participants engaged in each of the various categories of behavior. . . . (pp. 534–535)

Ittelson et al. (1970) have used their observational data to construct "behavioral maps" of the ward environment. The maps profiled patterns of behavior in different areas of the setting, and suggested that, regardless of the specific individuals who were occupying areas on the ward, each area elicited a relatively consistent pattern of behavior. In general, however, observational assessments in hospitals are most often implemented to evaluate the effectiveness of various ward programs.

Observation of psychotherapy process   Research and theory concerning the process of psychotherapy have importance for clinical researchers and practitioners (Gurman, 1977; Kiesler, 1973; Marsden, 1971; Parloff, Waskow & Wolfe, 1978; Orlinsky & Howard, 1978; Pope, 1977). By "process" we mean the cognitive and emotional responses that represent the therapist's and the client's subjective experiencing of psychotherapy and the behavioral interactions of the client and therapist during the actual course of therapy sessions. Through naturalistic observational assessment we can examine what a therapist is saying and doing at different points in therapy and in response to different client behaviors, thus empirically identifying the patterns of therapist-client interactions that facilitate or impede positive outcomes. These patterns can provide the therapist with suggestions concerning what *specifically* to do and say in therapy.

Investigations of the process of individual psychotherapy have utilized several basic observational categories (Mitchell, Bozarth, & Krauft, 1977; Pope, 1977); that fall into two basic types: (1) ordinal ratings of certain therapist characteristics (e.g., empathy) and (2) nominal ratings of the occurrence of specific in-therapy responses (Table 10-6). Most often, highly trained nonprofessional observers listen to 3-10 minute samples of audiotaped therapy sessions and rate scoring units that may range from ten seconds to the entire session.

For group therapy, Bales (1950) has developed an observational assessment system called Interaction Process Analysis (Table 10-7). Research investigations with this assessment system have identified certain consistent patterns of communication, leadership, and group development in structured and unstructured work, therapy, and educational groups (Shaw, 1971). The system can be used to assess the sequences of interactions over intervals that range from 10 seconds to an hour or more, or to focus on the actions of selected individuals in a group and the reactions of other group members. The categories are designed to be broad enough to capture significant interaction themes, yet defined with sufficient precision to enable trained raters to make reliable observations.

Summary   Naturalistic observation measures have been developed for behavioral assessment in homes, classrooms, inpatient hospitals, and psychotherapy interviews. Although observational measures have been most extensively researched in these settings, the methods of developing naturalistic observation systems can be used for assessments in any setting and for a variety of purposes. When naturalistic observations are planned, several issues must, however, be considered.

Issues in Naturalistic Observation   Even when the observational categories are clearly and specifically defined, and observers are trained to achieve high degrees of accuracy, several problems confront the clinical psychologist who wishes to use naturalistic observation as an assessment strategy. Clinicians who spend most of their time delivering services such as therapy or consultation find that detailed observational codes and procedures such as those just described are much too expensive and time consuming. Although researchers must follow carefully standardized procedures for naturalistic observation in order to produce high quality research data, practicing clinicians can scale down existing observational codes or

Table 10-6   Sample Categories for Behavioral Observations of the Process of
Psychotherapy

Therapist Behavior	Examples
Encourages Client to Continue Speaking	
A brief verbal or nonverbal interjection that signals the client that the therapist is listening with interest, but that does not result in the client stopping his or her talking.	"Right." "Mmhmm." "I see."
Probing with Moderate Directiveness and Specificity	
Open-ended requests for information from client —distinguished from closed-ended requests by not constraining the client except to follow a general direction or topic; *not* in the form of multiple-choice, true-false, or fill-in-the-blank questions. May be a statement that is said with intonation patterns that make it a question.	"How do you feel about that?" "What led you to seek therapy at this time?" "What's been happening?" "You think so?"
Direct Guidance	
Explicit instructions for the client to engage in certain activities outside the therapy context. A statement and not a question.	"I want you to talk this over with your wife." "Be sure to follow your contract this week."
Interpretation	
Statement of an inference, assumption, guess or explanation that the therapist has made concerning the client's actions, thoughts, feelings or interactions. Does not include value judgments ("That's right") or normative statements about "people" in general. Includes rhetorical questions.	"You seem very anxious." "This seems to be a definite pattern in your sexual relationships." "Perhaps you learned this style of coping in your family as you grew up?"
Reassurance	
Explicit statement of sympathy, validation, understanding or optimistic expectations concerning the client and the client's feelings, thoughts, actions, or interactions.	"Don't worry." "I can understand why you are feeling hopeless." "I'm sorry to hear that."

Adapted from J. D. Ford, Therapeutic relationship in behavior therapy. *Journal of Consulting and Clinical Psychology*, 1978, *46*, 1302-1314. Copyright 1978 by the American Psychological Association. Reprinted by permission.

create their own behavioral categories in order to apply the naturalistic observation method in clinical assessment (Highlight 10-2). The practitioner can personally visit the client's home, school, work site, hospital, or other settings, or trained therapeutic aides can serve as observers under the clinician's supervision (Kent & O'Leary, 1977). Persons in the client's natural environment, such as parents or spouses, can also be enlisted and trained as observers (e.g., Hall et al., 1972). Whatever the practical method, several precautions are essential.

Table 10-7 Bales' Interaction Process Analysis

Category	Brief Definition
Shows solidarity	Raises other persons' status, gives help, gives reward or praise to individuals or the group
Shows tension release	Jokes, laughs, shows satisfaction
Agrees	Shows passive acceptance, conveys understanding, concurs, complies
Gives suggestion	Gives a directive that implies autonomy and self-direction by other person(s)
Gives opinion	States a belief, analysis, evaluation, feeling, wish
Gives orientation	States information, repeats, clarifies, confirms
Requests orientation	Asks for information, repetition, clarification, confirmation
Requests opinion	Asks for a belief, analysis, evaluation, feeling, wish
Requests suggestion	Asks for direction or courses of action
Disagrees	Shows passive rejection, formality, withholds help, understanding, concurrence, or compliance
Shows tension	Asks for help, withdraws; states unpleasant feelings
Shows antagonism	Deflates other persons' status, aggressively defends or asserts self, criticizes, blames, challenges

Adapted from R. F. Bales, *Interaction process analysis*. Chicago: University of Chicago Press, 1950. Copyright 1950 by the University of Chicago Press. Reprinted by permission.

Highlight 10-2   Clinical Use of Naturalistic Observation

Although the clinician must be cautious in drawing inferences from brief or one-time observations, observing clients in their natural environments can lead to new hypotheses, to a conclusion supporting an established hypothesis, or the disconfirmation of hypotheses. Consider the following hypothetical example.

Mr. and Mrs. Smith have asked a clinical psychologist, Dr. Schulman, to do therapy with their son, Sam, because, as they describe, "Sam is *uncontrollable* at home, always running around and getting into fights with his brother and sister." The Smiths say that Sam is having troubles at school, because despite being 8 years old, he does not appear to be able to tell time and he refuses to read books at home. Mr. and Mrs. Smith describe their other children, Sally (age 10), and Alan (age 12), as "well-adjusted, no problem at home or at school," and their relationship together as "fine, perfectly happy." In fact, they cannot think of a problem in their family except for Sam. Dr. Schulman had asked the Smiths to bring in their entire family to the first session, but only the parents and Sam came because, the parents say, Sally and Alan had had prior commitments to school activities that they had not known about until today. Dr. Schulman noted that Sam sat very quietly between Mr. and Mrs. Smith and did not talk while his parents were in the room except to give single-word answers to questions ("Yeah"; "Okay") which he spoke while looking apprehensively at his father. When Dr. Schulman spoke with Sam alone, the boy relaxed noticeably but would talk avidly only about his interests and activities, not about his family.

Dr. Schulman arranged to visit the Smiths' home for an hour the next week, picking a time when the entire family would be together. Dr. Schulman decided to keep an eye out for any particularly positive, negative, or repeated interactions but also felt that focusing on a few specific behaviors would provide useful data. After talking informally with each family member for a few minutes, Dr. Schulman sat quietly in an inconspicuous area near the living room, den, and kitchen, where all family members could be seen, and began to count how often several actions and interactions occurred. In a 30-minute period, the results were as follows:

	Parents Not Present	Parents Talk to Sally/Alan	Parents Talk to Sam	Parents Argue Quietly
Sam reads/plays quietly	10/15	1/26	0/4	0/15
Sam fights w/siblings	0/15	12/26	0/4	10/15
Sam interrupts parents	—	8/26	0/4	5/15
Sally reads/plays quietly	3/15	6/26	1/4	9/15
Sally fights w/Sam	8/15	0/26	0/4	1/15
Sally interrupts parents	—	14/26	3/4	0/15
Alan reads/plays quietly	2/15	0/26	0/4	0/15
Alan fights w/Sam	7/15	0/26	0/4	5/15
Alan interrupts parents	—	19/26	3/4	0/15

Dr. Schulman made one observation for each of the three children every 30 seconds and noted which of the four predominant actions of the parents were occurring as well. The numbers represent the number of times each child behavior occurred and (on the right of the "/") the total number of times the parents were seen performing each action. Thus, for example, Sam read or played quietly in 10 of the 15 30-second intervals that his parents were in another room, but did so only once in the 26 intervals when they talked to Sally or Alan.

What hypotheses do these observations offer Dr. Schulman? First, it appears that Sam is not the only child who initiates or reciprocates fighting, because Sally and Alan get into the act several times. However, Sally and Alan begin fights when their parents are either not present or arguing, while Sam does so only when his parents are arguing or focusing on Sally or Alan. Dr. Schulman hypothesized that Sam uses fighting as a means of getting his parents' attention, particularly when the parents are themselves fighting. In contrast, Sally and Alan bug Sam when they are alone and keep a "good image" when their parents are present. Sam appears to be able to control his running around and to read quietly, and he does so despite the annoyance of his brother and sister, but the parents simply do not see this behavior.

Second, Mr. and Mrs. Smith talk relatively rarely to Sam (compared to how often they speak to Sally and Alan) and when they do, either Alan or Sally consistently interrupt. Unwittingly, the parents may be communicating to Sam that he will not get their attention unless he misbehaves. Both Alan and Sally make talking difficult for their parents by interrupting frequently, even when they are the ones being talked to, and they seem to be less socially appropriate and controlled than Sam.

Finally, Dr. Schulman noted that Mr. and Mrs. Smith, despite insisting that they were perfectly happy, spent a significant portion of their time arguing in a very quiet, but harsh, manner, tinged with sarcasm and veiled threats. All of the children altered their behavior when this was occurring: Alan tended to pick fights with Sam or leave the vicinity; Sally usually immersed herself in reading; and Sam either initiated fights or interrupted his parents. Dr. Schulman tentatively hypothesized that Sally and Alan withdraw and avoid their parents' anger, while Sam rushes in to "save" the parents by distracting them.

Thus, Dr. Schulman began to view the case as one of family issues, rather than as an instance of a purely dysfunctional child. To be sure, further observations would be needed to verify this family-system perspective, and Dr. Schulman began that process by observing Sam in his school and talking with his teacher. Both the observations and the teacher's report confirmed that Sam was, in fact, doing better than average academically; and that he related very well with his peers. Sam even volunteered the time, at one point, when the teacher asked him if it was time for recess. Dr. Schulman found that Sam's grades, achievement test scores and past reports by teachers were all consistent with the picture of him as a reasonably well-functioning boy.

Dr. Schulman did not conlude that the parents were "at fault," and did not put them on the "hot seat" by telling them that if they would only stop fighting and face up to their own problems that their children would all be fine. He realized that the parents were probably fearful of confronting their dissatisfactions with each other, and that their children were sensitive to the hidden anger, but unable to directly cope with this stress. Thus, all of the family members were experiencing tension that was painful. Therefore, Dr. Schulman insisted that all of the family members needed to come to the sessions.

This was only the beginning, and further assessments revealed new issues that required additional attention, but the example illustrates that direct observation can be a valuable clinical aid.

Reliability   Observational data must be accurate in order to provide meaningful clinical and research conclusions. A key indicator of accuracy is the extent to which two independent observers agree on their observations of the same situation. If both observers report seeing and hearing the same behaviors, then the clinical psychologist can be relatively confident that both observers are accurate. This check on accuracy is called *interobserver reliability*, and most research investigations report that well-trained observers agree on 80% or more of their ratings even though they must make their observations without any help from each other. Although the 80% accuracy rate is often used, the specific percentage is far less important than providing a clear and well-reasoned demonstration that interobserver agreement is sufficient to suggest that the data are clinically and scientifically robust. There is no single formula for this decision, so the clinical assessor must judge the reliability by examining the likely impact of the agreement rate obtained, for each category, on the inferences that are to be made with the data. For example, if a particularly central category is recorded with a near-chance level of agreement (such as 50 to 60%), an overall level of agreement of 80% will obscure the crucial damage that this inaccuracy can cause. However, there are several reasons why observers may produce unreliable data, sometimes even when they appear to be agreeing with each other.

Reactivity is the phenomenon that occurs when people who are being observed alter their actions from their normal patterns because they are either unnerved by the presence of observers or attempting to project a fake image by acting (Johnson & Bolstad, 1973; Kent & Foster, 1977; Patterson, 1977). Although people often react to being observed, clinical researchers have found that the "demand characteristics" (Rosenthal, 1978) that are introduced by the presence of observers cause only small changes from typical interactions *if* the observers establish rapport with the subjects at the outset and then fade into the woodwork while collecting data, and *if* there are no obvious contingencies to motivate the subjects to fake their actions.

Observer bias occurs when observers know the status of the people whom they are observing (for example, knowing whether the subjects are in the treatment group or the control group in a study of the effects of intervention), or any other information that might lead them to alter their observations because of assumptions about how the people "should" be acting (Johnson & Bolstad, 1973; Kent & Foster, 1977). If the clinician creates behavior categories that are clear and specific, however, research has shown that observers' expectations do not bias their observations *unless* they are given feedback directly encouraging them to alter the observations (O'Leary, Kent, & Kanowitz, 1974). Observers also tend to be more accurate when they know that they are (or could be) checked by another observer at any time (Kent & Foster, 1977).

Observer drift is a subtle distortion of data that can occur when observers work together in fixed groups over a time period. Each group is likely to gradually develop its own idiosyncratic rules for interpreting the observational categories and for making difficult observations, and, thus, to "drift" away from the original category definitions and from the other groups (Johnson & Bolstad, 1973; Kent & Foster, 1977). Observers in a group may show a high rate of agreement with each other, but yet be producing inaccurate data. The best solution for drift is to regularly change the groupings of observers, and to frequently retrain observers and check their accuracy against a preset criterion that has been agreed on by several experienced observers.

Validity   Observational data must be evaluated for validity as well as reliability. It is first important to demonstrate that the behavior categories are truly representative of significant real-life behaviors. This is called *content validity* and can be handled by conducting preliminary observations or surveying people in the natural environment to determine what behaviors occur most frequently or with the greatest impact. In a similar vein, the observational procedure must be shown to have *external validity*. The requirement here is that a complete and representative sample of persons, situations and time periods must be observed. For example, if the clinician desires information about a family's home interactions, it would be important to observe the family at several typical time points during the day when as many people as possible are present (Patterson, 1977).

Concurrent validity and *predictive validity* must be demonstrated for observational instruments just as for other psychological assessment measures. This can be done by comparing the data from naturalistic observation with ratings by the target-person's significant others, scores on psychometric or projective tests, institutional records such as school grades, or any other measure that aims to measure the same phenomenon as the observational code. For example, Mariotto and Paul (1974) compared data from the Time Sample Behavioral Checklist with scores from a structured psychological interview and global ratings by nurses on an inpatient psychiatric ward. Behaviors from the checklist that were designed to measure such dimensions as "schizophrenic disorganization" or "appropriate behavior" were significantly correlated with parallel factors from the interview and nurses' ratings data, thus demonstrating that the behavior observations were producing meaningful information. In addition, Mariotto and Paul showed that the checklist categories were *un*related to other categories that should theoretically be distinct: for example, patients who were observed to behave aggressively should, in theory, be just as likely to show signs of "schizophrenic disorganization" (based on behavior observations, interview data or nurses' ratings) as not, because aggressive behavior and disorganized behavior are two very different types of actions. In fact, Mariotta and Paul found this to be true, thus demonstrating *discriminant validity* for their Time Sample Behavioral Checklist.

Most naturalistic observation codes in wide use by clinical researchers have been at least tentatively shown to possess adequate reliability and concurrent validity (Mariotto & Paul, 1974; Mitchell et al., 1977; Patterson, 1977; Pope, 1977). However, reliability must be rechecked every time that an observational instrument is used anew, because it is not only the code but also the procedures that guide its use that assure its accuracy. Furthermore, systematic demonstrations of content, external, predictive or discriminant validity have been rare. Finally, when an observational code is used to evaluate changes in people over time, for instance, before and after therapy, the observational data must be shown to be sufficiently sensitive to change in people to accurately reflect all true changes.

This is generally found with observational codes because they provide very specific information about behaviors that are likely to change if an intervention has had a real impact (see also Cone & Foster, 1982).

Self-Monitoring

When people serve as the observers of their own actions and interactions, this is called *self-monitoring* (Ciminero, Nelson, & Lipinski, 1977; Thoresen & Mahoney, 1974). Although a person's biases and blind spots may interfere with accurate observation, self-monitoring is more economical than monitoring by an external observer, and more immediate and focused than retrospective self-report. Research comparing self-monitoring with data from unobtrusive observers has shown that self-monitoring is moderately to highly accurate with noninteractional behaviors such as nervous gestures, but that more complex interpersonal interactions such as parenting, teaching, or public speaking are self-monitored with questionable reliability (Lipinski & Nelson, 1974). However, both children and adults can self-monitor many behaviors quite accurately if they are carefully trained, liable to reliability checks at any time, provided with systematic and immediate reminders and feedback, and highly motivated (e.g., Kaufman & O'Leary, 1972; Lipinski, Black, Nelson, & Ciminero, 1975).

Self-monitoring requires that the person *discriminate* whether certain behaviors or thoughts or feelings have occurred, then *record* the data, and finally *display* the data in a form that permits its use in assessment and intervention (Thoresen & Mahoney, 1974). Several devices have been created or adapted to provide readily available, inexpensive, and unobtrusive self-monitoring. For example, wrist counters look much like wristwatches, except that they display numbers in digital form and enable the person to simply press a button each time the target behavior occurs. In a similar fashion, stopwatches or other portable timing devices can be employed, if the goal is to record the time durations of behavioral events. Another device for quick-and-easy frequency counts is a self-monitoring card, which is typically a wallet or pocket-sized piece of thin, but firm, cardboard on which the person can quickly note events by keeping tally with a pen or pencil. Cards can be less accessible and more awkward than wrist counters, but they enable the person to record multiple behaviors. Behavioral diaries are somewhat less efficient but more informative, as illustrated in Table 10-8. Diaries enable the person to record entire events rather than just response frequencies or durations.

Self-monitoring can serve as a clinical or research assessment procedure in a variety of cases. Most often, it is used to evaluate clients' or research subjects' status and improvement on specifically defined responses. Wrist counters or cards are often used in assessment and treatment programs with, for example, smokers, to record the number of cigarettes smoked at different times of the day and the number and intensity of urges to smoke (e.g., Danaher & Lichtenstein, 1977). Similarly, they can be used to monitor exercise, studying, weight change, alcohol consumption, assertive behaviors, tics, self-injurious actions, positive parenting behaviors, and a range of other clinically relevant actions and interactions.

Date	Situation	Self Statements	Behavior	Outcomes
Jan. 2	Getting coffee at the morning break.	I'd sure like a smoke with my coffee, but I want to quit.	Did not have a cigarette.	Left the coffee room early and went back to work.
Jan. 2	Working on an account for Mr. X and I find that he left out some information. I'll have to go back over everything.	What an idiot! He should have given me all the data.	Lit a cigarette.	Put the cigarette out after smoking half of it.

Table 10-8 Sample Behavioral Diary for Recording Smoking Behavior and Its Antecedents and Consequences

Because the act of monitoring one's own actions can lead the person to initiate a change in those actions, self-monitoring can be used as an aid for therapeutic change as well as in assessment (Ciminero et al., 1977). Clinical case studies (see Highlight 10-3) and a few recent controlled research investigations (e.g., Lipinski et al., 1975) indicate that self-monitoring can produce improvements in certain problem behaviors. However, self-monitoring is rarely alone sufficient for clinical improvement and must usually be supplemented with other therapeutic interventions. The person must be highly motivated to change in order for self-moni-

---

Highlight 10-3   Self-monitoring as a Treatment for Depression[1]

The client, L.M., was a 22-year-old housewife who had been married two years to a clerical worker. During that time, she had consulted several therapists "because of feelings of depression, worthlessness, inactivity and frequent negative self-statements." The therapist concluded that "L.M. was extremely harsh with herself to the point of restricting herself from pleasurable experiences. Her activities were carried out in a quasimechanical manner with an apparent unfavorable distortion to feedback in terms of considerable sensitivity only to unacceptable performances." He decided to select a task that L. M. did frequently and considered important, and to have her monitor her performance and give herself positive feedback when she attained goals that she set for herself. L. M. selected housekeeping activities and, with the therapist helping her to establish performance expectancies that were realistic and yet somewhat challenging, she contracted to reinforce herself with a compliment, a cigarette, or a telephone call to an interesting friend when she met the goals.

[1]From Jackson, 1972.

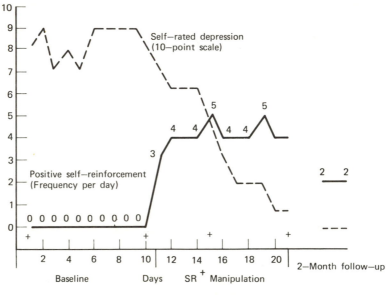

Daily records of depression and frequency of positive self-reinforcement (SR +). (Adapted from B. Jackson, Treatment of depression by self-reinforcement. *Behavior Therapy*, 1972, *3*, 298–307. Copyright 1972 by Academic Press. Reprinted by permission.)

The Figure shows that during the 10-day baseline period in which L. M. only monitored her self-reinforcement frequencies and her feelings of depression, the latter remained at zero and the former stayed very strong. However, when the self-reinforcement motivation program was instituted, her feelings of depression began to subside. In two weeks, she reported that she no longer felt depressed and she terminated therapy. When contacted two months later, L. M. had continued the self-monitoring and self-reinforcement and was still not feeling markedly depressed. Instead, she described herself as not at all depressed.

This case illustrates that a combination of realistic goals, self-monitoring, and self-reinforcement can, indeed, reactivate clients who are experiencing mild to moderate clinical depression. In combination with more intensive treatment methods such as milieu, pharmacological, group or one-to-one therapy, self-monitoring may add to therapeutic efficacy.

toring to effect change, and even then the resultant changes usually vanish shortly after self-monitoring has been discontinued. To attempt to reduce the short-lived quality of the self-monitoring effects, the self-monitoring must be gradually faded out or some other intervention used to maintain the improved behavior.

In sum, self-monitoring offers an economical means of assessing the person's own direct observations of his or her actions and interactions, but it must be arranged so as to be minimally inconvenient and intrusive and to be maximally accurate. Used judiciously, self-monitoring may be a component in clinical intervention, although not a complete therapeutic intervention by itself.

Self-Report in Behavioral Assessment

Self-report assessment differs from self-monitoring, although both rely on the subject as the source of data: self-report is more retrospective and summative, relying on the person's recall of general patterns of behavior, while self-monitoring emphasizes immediate recording of specific responses. Research investigations have demonstrated that the information that people report about themselves can be accurate and valid, and behavioral assessors add that this is particularly true if the questions that are used to elicit self-report data are focused on *specific behaviors that occur in specific settings* (Ajzen & Fishbein, 1977; Mischel, 1968; Morganstern, 1976; Tasto, 1977; Walsh, 1967; Wiggins, 1973). Self-report occurs in behavioral assessment through the use of questions such as, "When giving a speech, do you find yourself growing dizzy and stuttering?" rather than with global questions such as "Do unimportant thoughts run through your mind and bother you?" An array of guides for clinical interviews (e.g., Cautela & Upper, 1976; Holland, 1970; Meyer, 1977; Wahler & Cormier, 1970) and questionnaires (see Table 10-9) have been developed to enable behavioral assessors to probe for specific interactions that may be problematic or facilitative in specific situations.

Self-report measures have been developed to assess aspects of *situations* as well as to assess behavior. For example, Moos and his colleagues (Moos, 1974, 1975, 1976; Moos & Insel, 1974) have developed self-report questionnaires that enable persons in a variety of settings to describe the social climate. These scales include the Family Environment Scale, the Work Environment Scale, the Community Oriented Programs Environment Scale, the Ward Atmosphere Scale, and the Classroom Environment Scale (see Table 10-10 for an example). In each setting, three basic dimensions are assessed: Relationships, Personal Growth, and Systems Maintenance and Change. The relevant subdimensions for Relationships include such environmental characteristics as cohesiveness, supportiveness, expressiveness, and patterns of conflict resolution. Personal Growth subdimensions include such aspects as the setting's tolerance for and encouragement of achievement, autonomy, intellectual interests, religious pursuits, and self-discovery. The Systems Maintenance and Change dimension is manifested in such factors as the patterns of organization, the clarity and comprehensiveness of communication, and the degree of innovation in the setting.

Research examining the psychometric properties of these scales is encouraging. For example, the Family Environment Scale, one of the most often used of these scales, shows high internal consistency and retest reliability, and concurrent and discriminant validity (Bromet & Moos, 1977; Moos, 1974). The Family Environment Scale has also been found to be sensitive to changes in families who have received marital communication training (Ford, Bashford, & DeWitt, 1980) and

Table 10-9 Sample Self-Report Questionnaires for Behavioral Assessment

Target Area	Instrument	Reference
Fears	Fear Survey Schedule	Wolpe and Lang (1964)
		Lang and Lazovik (1963)
		Geer (1965)
Anxiety	Stimulus-Response Inventory of Anxiousness	Endler, Hunt, and Rosenstein (1962)
		Endler and Hunt (1968)
		Endler and Okada (1975)
	Zuckerman Inventory of Personal Reactions	Zuckerman (1978)
Assertiveness	Adult Self-Expression Scale	Gay, Galassi, and Hollandsworth (1975)
	Rathus Assertiveness Schedule	Rathus (1973)
	Conflict Resolution Inventory	McFall and Lillesand (1971)
	Assertion Inventory	Gambrill and Richey (1975)
	Dating and Assertion Questionnaire	Levenson and Gottman (1978)
Depression	Beck Depression Inventory	Beck (1972)
	Zung Self-Rating Depression Scale	Zung (1965)
	Pleasant Events Schedule	MacPhillamy and Lewinsohn (1972)
Sexual arousal and pleasure	Sexual Interaction Inventory	LoPiccolo and Lobitz (1974)
	Sexual Functioning Inventory	Derogatis (1976)
Marital satisfaction and communication	Areas of Change Questionnaire	Weiss, Patterson, and Hops (1973)
	Marital Activities Inventory	Weiss, Patterson, and Hops (1973)
	Pleases and Displeases	Weiss, Patterson, and Hops (1973)
	Marital Adjustment Test (Locke-Wallace)	Locke and Wallace (1958)
	Marital Communication Inventory	Bienvenu (1970)
	Marital Precounseling Inventory	Stuart and Stuart (1972)
Dysfunctions of hospitalized patients	Minimal Social Behavior Scale	Farina, Arenberg, and Guskin (1957)
	Inpatient Multi-Dimensional Psychiatric Scale	Lorr and Klett (1966)

Table 10-10 Moos' (1974) Family Environment scale

Subscale	Definition	Sample Item
Cohesion	The extent to which family members are concerned and committed to the family and helpful and supportive	Family members will help and support one another
Expressiveness	The extent to which family members are allowed and encouraged to act openly and express feelings directly	Family members will often keep their feelings to themselves
Conflict	The extent to which the open expression of anger and aggression and generally conflictual interactions are characteristic	Family members often criticize one another
Independence	The extent to which family members are encouraged to be assertive, self-sufficient, and self-directed	In our family, we are strongly encouraged to be independent
Achievement orientation	The extent to which activities are cast into an achievement context	Getting ahead in life is very important in our family
Intellectual-cultural orientation	The extent to which the family is concerned about political, social, intellectual, and cultural activities	We often talk about political problems
Active-recreational orientation	The extent to which the family participates actively in varied recreational and sporting activities	We often go to movies, sporting events, camping, etc.
Moral-religious orientation	The extent to which the family actively discusses and emphasizes moral and religious issues	Family members attend church, synagogue, Sunday School fairly often

Table 10-10 *Continued*

Subscale	Definition	Sample Item
Organization	The extent to which order and organization are important in structuring family activities, financial planning, and the explicitness and clarity of rules and responsibilities	Activities in our family are pretty carefully planned
Control	The extent to which the family is organized in a hierarchical manner, the rigidity of rules and procedures, and the extent to which family members order each other around	There are very few rules to follow in our family

Adapted from R. Moos, *The Family, Work & Group Environment Scales Manual.* Reproduced by special permission of the publisher, Consulting Psychologists Press, from The Family, Work & Group Environment Scales Manual by Rudolph H. Moos et al. Copyright 1974.

family therapy (Fuhr, Ford, & Moos, 1980). The social climate scales thus represent an advance in the assessment of settings, providing the clinician or researcher with a method for examining the impact of the social environments on their participants.

Analogue Assessment

An "analogue" is a facsimile of reality, a scaled-down version that contains certain basic characteristics of the real thing in a simplified and controlled manner. The game "Monopoly" is an analogue for the world of finance, big business, industry, and real estate. The theater presents us with a multitude of analogues for all kinds of human experiences. In similar fashion, psychologists have created a variety of analogues that serve as substitutes for significant real-life situations in assessment with clients or research participants. When naturalistic observation is too expensive or too time consuming, the clinical psychologist may wish to obtain a direct sample of behavior in response to an analogue situation.

Analogue assessment may be conducted in the following ways: *paper-and-pencil* tests, *audiotape* or *videotape* tests, *enactment* tests, *role play* tests, and *simulations* (Nay, 1977). These methods differ in the means by which the analogue situations are presented to the client or research participant and in the type of response that is requested from the client or research participant. In each case, however, the subject is directly observed in a simulated situation.

Paper-and-pencil tests present the person with a written situation and ask for a written response. In some cases the person may select from several response alternatives in a multiple-choice format, as in this example:

> *Your son has not cleaned up his room for two weeks, although you have repeatedly asked him to do so. What would you do?*

> *1.   Say nothing and clean the room for him.*
> *2.   Scold and spank him and then again insist that he clean the room.*
> *3.   Talk with him to learn why he has not cleaned it thus far.*
> *4.   Tell him that he must clean it today or else lose a privilege.*

Such tests can also be done in a more open-ended fashion, so as to determine the person's unprompted response or to learn about the sequences of actions that the person might take in responding to a complex problem. For instance:

> *Describe exactly what you would do in the following situation: You have asked a woman whom you would like to get to know to go out with you for dinner that night. Unexpectedly, your parents arrive in town from across the country, saying that they can only stay for the evening.*

Audiotape or *videotape* tests present the person with auditory or audiovisual cues to make the situation more lifelike (Fiedler & Beach, 1978). For example, an analogue situation to test for dating skills (e.g., Arkowitz, Lichtenstein, McGovern, & Hines, 1975) might require the person to listen to the following audiotaped instructions and to then respond:

You have been sitting at a party with a man whom you are dating for the first time, when he turns to you and says: "This is really a boring party, isn't it?"

Similarly, the person might be presented with situations that require refusals of invitations to have a drink (for alcoholics), a cigarette (for smokers), or a delicious food (for weight-loss clients). Taped tests present the person with the additional auditory or visual cues that would be missing from written tests, as well as typically requiring a behavioral rather than written response.

Enactment tests bring the person directly in contact with the relevant stimulus object in a controlled laboratory or clinic setting. For example, the Behavioral Avoidance Test (Bernstein & Paul, 1971; Lang & Lazovik, 1963) requires the person to walk toward a feared stimulus such as a snake or a spider and to stop when at the point of fear, or, if possible, to touch and even hold the feared stimulus. The examiner measures the distance between the person and the stimulus and whether the person touches or holds it. Because these tests hinge on the person's willingness to move into proximity with a typically feared object or situation in an obviously safe and controlled setting, the participant may act in a more fearless manner than in less secure situations. Borkovec, Weerts, and Bernstein (1977) describe the problems that these "demand characteristics" of enactment tests can cause and suggests that the likelihood that participants will behave with false confidence can be reduced by (1) identifying behaviors that are not easy to "fake," such as speech disfluencies, and measure these instead of, or in addition to, more alterable actions and (2) assessing subjective discomfort and coping skills as well as approach behavior.

Role play tests present the person with another individual "playing a role" and ask the client or research participant to interact as if it were "for real." For example, Behavioral Assertiveness Tests (McFall & Marston, 1970) present the individual with a "confederate," a trained actor or actress, who enacts certain preprogrammed "lines."

A role play situation to assess assertiveness might run as follows:

You answer the doorbell and suddenly a man walks in and says,

CONFEDERATE: "Excuse me, but I understand that you need encyclopedias."

The participant must then say and do whatever is most representative of his or her real-life handling of such situations. If the participant should ask the confederate to leave, the confederate might then reply:

CONFEDERATE: "I'm afraid I can't. I'm here to show you a very special deal, so I have to go ahead with it."

Once again, the participant must respond. The confederate may have a series of preset statements if the respondent continues to reply assertively, but the situation would end if the participant gives in.

Role play tests have the advantage of creating a more complete and demanding situation than other analogue measures, although the possibility of contamination from demand characteristics remains strong because the participant knows that it's just "acting." At present the scientific validity of role play tests is equivocal (Bellack, Hersen, & Lamparski, 1979), although they are widely used as informed therapy aids by clinical psychologists of many theoretical orientations.

Finally, *simulation* tests require the person to actually interact with significant others such as children, relatives, or friends, but in a context that is somewhat more limited than daily interactions. Sometimes the interactions are themselves gamelike and artificial (e.g., Olson & Strauss, 1972), but more often participants are asked to engage in real, but time-limited, conversations (e.g., Patterson, Weiss, & Hops, 1976; Robin, O'Leary, Kent, Foster, & Prinz, 1977). For example, simulation behavioral assessment might ask a family to decide, as a group, how to spend a $100 gift they just received. Observers could record the family's interactions to produce data that are similar to data collected by naturalistic observation. However, the family is focused on the single task for a brief time period, rather than observed without instructions for a longer period in the natural setting. Simulation tests more closely approximate the demands and stresses of real-life than any other analogue modality, thus having the greatest potential for both valid and useful information.

In summary, analogue observation is a useful method of behavioral assessment for obtaining limited samples of clients' or research participants' knowledge or skills, and may be particularly useful when naturalistic observation or self-monitoring cannot be conducted. Paper-and-pencil, taped and enactment tests may not, however, serve as effective predictors of what people will actually do in real life (Borkovec et al., 1977; Nay, 1977), most likely because there is a significant gap between having the knowledge or even the capability and actually undertaking a difficult or anxiety-evoking action in risky and confusing naturalistic settings. There is tentative evidence that role play and simulation tests can validly predict real-life actions (e.g., McFall & Marston, 1970; Patterson et al., 1976), but, here again, the clinician or researcher is best advised to use analogue observation data as only one of several assessment modalities in order to get a fully complete and accurate assessment.

Behavioral Observations and Behavioral Ratings From Significant Others

Peers, parents, teachers, and psychiatric ward staff are often asked to directly observe or retrospectively rate the behaviors of clients or research participants. These methods represent a worthwhile data source because the way that a person is viewed by significant others strongly influences that person's behaviors and self-perceptions. Data provided by significant others can also tell the clinician a great deal about a client's social environment, as well as suggesting possible problem areas for the client to consider changing. The potential for bias, especially if the significant others are angry with the person or have already labeled the person as "crazy" (e.g., Farina & Ring, 1965), must be taken seriously and the data should be balanced with data from a variety of other sources. Nevertheless, the behavioral observations and ratings of significant others offer an important additional perspective for the assessor.

Peers of all ages have been asked to rate, rank, or nominate other persons as a method of assessment (Kane & Lawler, 1978; Wiggins & Winder, 1961). Peer nominations involve having each member of a group, such as a classroom, designate a certain number of their peers as highest or lowest on a particular characteristic or performance dimension. For example, you might be asked to nominate three persons in your class who are the most friendly and three who are the least, excluding yourself. Peer reports can also be obtained by having peers give numerical ratings or rankings to certain target persons. Peer nominations and rankings have been found to have good test-retest and interrater reliability, while peer ratings are strong on the former but weak on the latter (Kane & Lawler, 1978). The reports of peers do not always agree with those of other sources such as teachers or supervisors, but this is not unexpected, given the differing vantage points of the various groups.

Parents and *teachers* are often asked to provide descriptions of their children. Requests are usually in the form of structured behavioral checklists and ratings (e.g., Achenbach, 1978; Conners, 1969; Gesten, 1976; Miller, 1972; Ross, Lacey, & Parton, 1965; Walker, 1970), although personality inventories have been adapted for this purpose (e.g., Wirt, Lachar, Klinedienst, & Seat, 1977). Checklists provide the parent or teacher with a series of specific behaviors, such as "cries," "fights," or "leaves assignments unfinished," and ask the respondent to indicate whether or not, and to what degree, the child displays each of the behaviors (e.g., on a rating scale from 1 = never to 5 = almost always).

Achenbach's (1978; Achenbach & Edelbrock, 1979) Behavior Problems Checklist exemplifies the behavior checklist approach to obtaining data from parents. It contains 118 specific behaviors that are grouped into nine subscales (e.g., Immature, Hyperactive, Aggressive, Delinquent, Social Withdrawal). Based on administering the checklist to 1800 parents from 25 East Coast (U.S.A.) locations, norms have been established for boys aged 12 to 16, girls aged 12 to 16, boys aged 6 to 11, and girls aged 6 to 11. All subscales were identified through factor analyses, and each subscale was shown to be temporally reliable and to yield high agreement for parents rating the same child (interrater reliability). Evidence for the concurrent validity of all subscales was demonstrated by comparing scores for children who had been referred for psychological treatment versus comparable "nonproblem" peers.

Gesten's (1979) Health Resources Inventory illustrates the use of teacher ratings for the assessment of *competency*, rather than dysfunction. The inventory describes 54 behaviors indicative of effective personal functioning, and is scored with factor-analytically derived subscales for "good student," adaptive assertiveness, peer sociability, rule adherence, and frustration tolerance. While not normed as extensively as Achenbach's checklist, the inventory has been shown to be temporally reliable, to have interrater reliability, and to distinguish children referred for psychological treatment from "normal" peers. Achenbach's checklist also includes three subscales to assess personal competency, reflecting a trend in clinical assessment toward gathering data concerning clients' strengths as well as their dysfunctions.

The *ward staff* in psychiatric hospitals are also frequently asked to provide ratings of their patients' functioning (e.g., Achenbach, 1966; Gruenberg, Brandon, & Kasius, 1966; Honigfeld, Gillis, & Klett, 1966; Lorr, O'Connor, & Stafford,

1960). For example, the Nurse's Observational Scale for Inpatient Evaluation (NOSIE-30) is a 32-item questionnaire that Honigfeld et al. (1966) have developed for ward staff to make ratings on patients' conduct over three-day periods. The NOSIE-30 (Table 10-11) is scored for subscales including Total Assets, Social Competence, Personal Neatness, Irritability, Manifest Psychosis, and Retardation. Although the NOSIE-30, like most other ward staff rating forms, is not as situation-specific as most behavioral assessment methods, these rating scales provide valuable insights concerning the views of the therapeutic staff who have the most direct contact with psychiatric patients. Ward staff may provide additional data by completing rating scales that identify patients' primary behavioral dysfunctions or symptoms.

ADDITIONAL AREAS OF BEHAVIORAL ASSESSMENT

The assessment of specific *physiological* responses and the assessment of specific *cognitive* responses represent two additional areas within behavioral assessment. Although still in the formative stages, both psychophysiological assessment and cognitive-behavioral assessment can be of benefit in a comprehensive assessment.

Psychophysiological Assessment

According to Kallman and Feuerstein (1977), psychophysiological measurement can be defined as "the quantification of biological events as they relate to psycho-

Table 10-11 Sample Items From The NOSIE-30 (Nurse's Observational Scale for Inpatient Evaluation)

Instructions to raters: For each of the following items you are to rate this patient's behavior during the last THREE DAYS ONLY.

Items	Ratings				
	Never	**Sometimes**	**Often**	**Usually**	**Always**
Is impatient	1	2	3	4	5
Shows interest in activities around him	1	2	3	4	5
Hears things that are not there	1	2	3	4	5
Has trouble remembering	1	2	3	4	5
Is slowmoving and sluggish	1	2	3	4	5
Quick to fly off the handle	1	2	3	4	5
Refuses to speak	1	2	3	4	5
Says that he is no good	1	2	3	4	5

Adapted from G. Honigfeld, R. Gillis, and C. Klett, *Nurse's Observational Scale for Inpatient Evaluation.* Copyright 1966 by G. Honigfeld. Reprinted by permission.

logical variables'' (p. 329). Essentially then, the focus of the assessment is on the recording of bodily reactions to certain environmental stimuli. The reactions that are typically a part of such an assessment include muscle tension, heart rate, blood pressure, and skin resistance. Precise measurement instruments are required for psychophysiological assessment because these responses are often subtle and minute (see Table 10-12).

Psychophysiological assessment is classified as behavioral assessment both because of the specificity of the situation or stimuli to which the assessor measures the physiological response, and because the target for the assessment is often the quantification of discrete responses.

The physiograph (Lykken, 1979) is the usual device used for psychophysiological assessment. A physiograph is a physiological recording instrument that has sensing components that pick up certain signals, amplifiers to adjust the potency of the signal, and an output system to convert the electrical signal to an observable printout. For example, a cuff on the person's arm would be the sensing device to measure blood pressure. The readings are amplified and converted to a numerical reading that can be observed by the assessor.

Psychophysiological assessment has been used in both clinical treatment and research (see Katkin & Hastrup, 1982). In treatment, the physiograph can be used to trace changes that occur in certain physiological systems over the course of therapy, to assess whether certain stimuli arouse the client physiologically, or to function itself as an important part of the treatment. Biofeedback would be an example of this latter case. In biofeedback, specific psychophysiological responses are monitored, displayed, and fed back to the subject. For example, a physiograph that is prepared to monitor muscle tension may be attached to a patient with severe muscle tension. Using the feedback from the recorder to provide discriminative cueing and reinforcement to the client, muscle tension can be identified and reduced. Each client develops different internal methods for ac-

Table 10-12 A Sample of the Physiological Responses, the Recording Instrument, and the Physiological Basis of the Response

Electromyogram (EMG)	Electromyograph	Muscle Action Potentials
Electrocardiogram (EKG)	Electrocardiograph	Cardiac muscle action potentials
Blood pressure (BP)	Sphygmomanometer (i.e., pressure cuff)	Systolic: force of blood leaving the heart
		Diastolic: residual pressure in the vascular system
Galvanic Skin response (GSR)	Low-level D.C. amplifier	Sweat gland activity
Sexual responses	Plethysmograph	Engorgement of penis/ vagina with blood

Adapted from W. M. Kallman and M. Feuerstein, Psychophysiological procedures. In A. R. Ciminero, K. S. Calhoun, and H. E. Adams (Eds.), *Handbook of behavioral assessment*. New York: Wiley, 1977. Copyright 1977 by John Wiley & Sons, Inc.; adapted by permission.

complishing this (e.g., thinking, *"relax"*), but the (bio) feedback is the teaching tool to help clients learn what works best for them.

Recently, a variety of portable and relatively inexpensive devices have appeared on the market as alternatives to the physiograph. These devices can measure responses such as heart rate, skin conductance, or muscle tension, although usually each instrument can measure only one or two separate indexes. The portability and the reasonable cost of such equipment can allow individual clients to make use of these instruments as part of their treatment in places other than the professional's office (e.g., at home).

Psychophysiological assessment is more often used as part of a research project. For example, in the study of anxiety, subjects' psychophysiological responses have been used to assist in the development and validation of paper-and-pencil measures of anxiety (e.g., Alexander & Husek, 1962), as dependent measures in their own right (e.g., Hodges & Speilberger, 1966), or in conjunction with other types of measures of anxiety (e.g., Holmes & Houston, 1974). The literature on the use of psychophysiological devices to assess anxiety is, however, not clear-cut. One problem is that each physiological index (heart rate, skin resistance) has an idiosyncratic relationship with anxiety and so their concurrent use can lead to discrepant findings. Another problem is that some individuals' physiological anxiety response appears on only one index (e.g., skin resistance). That is, there are individual differences in the physiological manifestation of anxiety.

Physiological assessments are central to the detection of deception using the so-called "lie detector." While some suggest that these tests are highly beneficial (Podlesny & Raskin, 1977), Lykken (1979) points out that the polygraph (lie detector) has an accuracy of only 64 to 77%—not very impressive in relation to a 50% accuracy based on chance alone. These accuracy rates were gathered when polygraph charts were scored blindly and are thus "clean" of any subjective impressions of the person taking the test. Despite the controversies surrounding the specifics of physiological responding associated with anxiety and deception, it is generally accepted that some form of physiological arousal is associated with the experience of anxiety.

Cognitive-Behavioral Assessment

The targets of cognitive-behavioral assessment are specific responses, but these responses are the cognitive activities of the clients or subjects and are not observable events. In this one sense, cognitive events do not belong within behavioral assessment. However, in several other ways, the assessment of specific cognitive responses within specific situations, either as an aid for treatment or a dependent variable in research, is an important addition to behavioral assessment (see Kendall & Hollon, 1981a; Kendall & Korgeski, 1979).

There are numerous possible methods for assessing cognitive-behavioral responses (see Kendall & Hollon, 1981b; Merluzzi, Glass, & Genest, 1981). Two such methods are *thought sampling* and *self-statement inventories*. Thought sampling is an assessment procedure that requests that the individual, at various times, report on his or her thoughts. This approach has been taken by Klinger

(1978), who makes use of a portable "beeper" that is carried by subjects and which goes off at varied intervals. When it goes off, the person stops and records "current thoughts" on a questionnaire. This procedure provides the clinician with a sample of the thoughts that the individual had during the period when the beeper was carried. Allowing the client or subject to take the beeper into the real world can provide a naturalistic assessment of cognitive events. In addition, having the client or subject specify the situation in which each of the recorded cognitive events took place provides the assessor with situational specificity. It appears then that this approach can be viewed an an important new direction in behavioral assessment.

Self-statement inventories are another way to collect cognitive-behavioral data (see Table 10-13). This type of an inventory includes a series of thoughts or "things that people say to themselves" and requires the individual to indicate how frequently he or she has had the thoughts that are listed. While the structure and length of self-statement inventories vary, the clinician is generally interested in assessing what the client says to him or her. For example, Schwartz and Gottman (1976) studied the specific role of self-statements in the ability of individuals to perform assertive behaviors. These researchers found that while subjects did not differ with respect to knowledge of assertive responses, the low-assertive subjects reported significantly more negative and fewer positive self-statements than

Table 10-13 Sample items from a Self-Statements Inventory Used to Assess Patients' Self-Statements During a Stressful Medical Procedure

Instructions to subjects:

> Listed below are several statements that people make to themselves (their thoughts) during medical procedures. Please read each self-statement and indicate how frequently these self-statements characterized your thoughts during the catheterization procedure. Please read each item carefully and then circle the appropriate number as it relates to your thoughts.

Sample Items	Hardly Ever				Very Often
I was thinking that the procedure could save my life	1	2	3	4	5
I kept thinking how much I dislike the smell of being in a hospital.	1	2	3	4	5
I was thinking about the things I need to do to be a good patient (like staying still and following the doctor's instructions).	1	2	3	4	5
I was worried about the bad things that the doctor said might happen to me.	1	2	3	4	5
I was concerned that the doctor looked too young and inexperienced.	1	2	3	4	5
I was listening and expecting them to say something bad about my health.	1	2	3	4	5
I kept reminding myself about all the times in the past when I had been successful in coping with stress and pain and that this was not any worse than those situations.	1	2	3	4	5

Sample items from self-statement inventory used in P. C. Kendall, L. Williams, T. Pechacek, L. Graham, K. Shisslak, and N. Herzoff. Cognitive-behavioral and patient education interventions in cardiac catheterization: The Palo Alto medical psychology project. *Journal of Consulting and Clinical Psychology*, 1979, *47*, 49–58.

did subjects who were moderately or highly assertive. Use of an inventory to assess self-statements led to the researcher's ability to identify "interfering self-statements" as an important component of nonassertive behavior. Similar self-statement inventories have been developed to assess the "automatic thoughts" associated with depression (Hollon & Kendall, 1980) and anxiety (Glass, Merluzzi, Biever, & Larsen, in press).

Meichenbaum (1976) has proposed a "cognitive functional analysis" to incorporate cognitions as antecedents, behaviors, and consequences in the functional analysis paradigm. A thought may serve as the antecedent or consequence, just as can an event or stimulus in the external environment. For example, the thought "I hate myself" may regularly precede a target behavior such as yelling at one's spouse. In contrast, a thought such as "What a relief" may serve as the reinforcing consequence for a target behavior such as admitting a mistake. Similarly, the target behavior can be cognitive rather than, or in addition to, an external behavior. Clinicians emphasize the importance of careful assessment of "suicidal ideation" (i.e., thoughts about suicide, such as a plan for taking one's life or the idea that life is worthless) because such thoughts can begin a chain of thinking and behavior that may lead to actual suicide attempts. Meichenbaum's conceptualization thus underscores the importance of assessing internal/cognitive stimuli and behaviors along with assessments of external environmental events and actions.

BEHAVIORAL ASSESSMENT: RETROSPECT AND PROSPECT

Although every clinician assesses relationships between clients' actions (behavioral, physiological, and/or cognitive) and their life situations, systematic behavioral assessment is a recent phenomenon. Nevertheless, the range of innovative methods and instruments pioneered or adapted by behaviorally oriented assessors is large. Behavioral assessors have moved from the mechanical measurement of simple responses toward the application of a rigorous and science-based paradigm to the assessment of complex and subtle functional relationships among people, behaviors, and the internal and external environment (see Nelson & Hayes, 1979a; 1979b). The scientific process of behavioral assessment has been gradually merging with the multifaceted clinical constructs that have been assessed via "traditional" approaches, producing a positive integration.

Liberation by M. C. Escher, 1955.

This work by Escher symbolically suggests change (metamorphosis).

IV

CLINICAL PSYCHOLOGICAL
INTERVENTIONS

Illustration by John Tenniel, from *Through the Looking Glass* by Lewis Carroll.

The ideal condition
Would be, I admit, that men should be right by instinct.
But since we are all likely to go astray,
The reasonable thing is to learn from those who can teach.

Sophocles

11

INTERVENTION: PROFESSIONAL AND SCIENTIFIC CONCERNS

Clinical intervention involves applying psychological principles to help people overcome problems and develop more satisfying lives. Clinical psychologists utilize their knowledge of human functioning and social systems in combination with the results of their clinical assessment to formulate ways to help clients change for the better. For example, individual therapy might be conducted to aid a client in overcoming debilitating anxiety, or family therapy might be provided to help family members relate more effectively with one another. Or, a clinician may serve as a consultant assisting a community group in its attempts to improve their community's mental health facilities. Each example illustrates a form of clinical intervention.

In this chapter, we consider the basic reasons for clinical intervention, the goals of clinical interventions, the basic methodology clinicians use to guide their intervention, the types of intervention, the basic phases of clinical intervention, the legal and ethical issues involved in clinical intervention, and the methods used by clinical psychologists to determine when interventions are effective.

REASONS FOR CLINICAL INTERVENTION

Clinical interventions are conducted for three basic reasons: amelioration, prevention, and enhancement. *Amelioration* involves helping people or social systems to overcome problems that already exist. For example, a person may undergo therapy to remove distressing feelings of anxiety and failure. *Prevention* involves attempts to forestall problems before they develop. For instance, a clinician might help a community design recreational programs to prevent teenagers from turning to juvenile delinquency. *Enhancement* involves aiding people in improving their personal skills, relationships, and life environments. The aim of enhancement is to increase life quality, rather than to resolve problems or dysfunctions. For example, marital enrichment groups are conducted in order to help satisfied couples develop even better relationships.

409

Ameliorative, preventive, and enhancement interventions are essential to a comprehensive system of psychological services. Each approach has unique advantages (Harper & Balch, 1975), and all three are complementary and integral components of a fully effective service delivery system. Existing problems must be resolved, potential future dilemmas must be anticipated, and quality of life must be maximized—although in most cases any single clinical psychologist functions in at most one or two of these roles.

A variety of additional practical reasons may lead clinical psychologists to intervene. Therapy and consultation are often conducted on the direct request of the client, the parent or family of a client, a school system or community organization that wishes to receive consultation from the clinical psychologist, or many other kinds of concerned individuals and groups. It is essential that the clinical psychologist always clearly recognize and respond in accord with the stated goals of the requestor of services: although the clinical psychologist's values and goals may differ from the client's, it is presumptuous for any clinician to take the paternal attitude of "I know what's best for the client even if this contradicts the client's wishes" (Bergin, 1980). In reality, therapy or consultation goals reflect a blend of the client's hopes and the clinician's professional assessment, but it is incumbent on the clinician to assure that the client's goals are meaningfully incorporated.

Clinical psychologists are also asked to intervene by a "third party." Teachers, courts of law, physicians in general practice, and other clinical psychologists or mental health professionals all frequently request therapy and/or consultation services from clinical psychologists. Psychological assessment and therapy may be sought on behalf of a child who is failing in school and exhibiting fearful or antisocial behavior, or on behalf of adults who have committed crimes that may stem (at least in part) from psychological dysfunctions, among many examples. Consultation may be requested by a mental health professional who wishes a second opinion about a difficult therapy case, or by a hospital that is having staff morale and service delivery problems, among many examples.

Clinical psychologists intervene to ameliorate, prevent, and/or enhance, and they do so in response to a variety of practical needs. Once a clinician has offered to provide professional help to a client, the goals of the intervention must be established.

GOALS OF INTERVENTION

Clinical psychologists have two basic alternatives when they seek to create goals for a clinical intervention. First, the clinician can choose to *help clients make a better adjustment to their current life situation.* For example, the psychologist could provide a therapeutic intervention to help a client adjust to an antagonistic family, without attempting to bring about any change in the family itself. Second, interventions can be conducted to *help clients alter their life situations.* For instance, the clinician could teach a family new ways to communicate and more effective ways to make decisions so as to change the entire family environment.

Facilitating Adjustment

A clinician may help clients to establish a better "fit" with their social environments. Clients may be aided in adjusting their expectations and evaluations of themselves to be more in line with their real capabilities, interests, and needs. Clients may also be seen individually in therapy in order to improve their self-acceptance, social skills, or problem-solving abilities, among a long list of other possible personal assets for adjusting effectively to the requirements, resources, and limitations of the social environment.

Potential Problems   Although it is important for people to fit in with their current life situations and to accept themselves in a realistic fashion, "adjustment" is a sham if the person must deny critical needs or values in order to make this adaptation. A prerequisite to setting a goal of better adjustment is a thorough and honest exploration of the client's abilities, interests, aspirations, and values. For example, a clinician might help a depressed woman to clarify both the benefits and limitations of her current role as a housewife and to examine any discrepancies between this life situation and her longer-range goals for herself (e.g., re-education), before setting specific goals for therapy.

Another danger in helping clients to adjust themselves to their current social environments is that these life situations may be physically or psychologically harmful or inadequate. Physical threats are somewhat easier to appraise than psychological dangers, but two characteristics of social environments that are widely held to be important for psychological "health" are (1) *openness to diversity* and (2) *encouragement of self-determination* (Krasner, 1976; Rappaport, 1977; Sarason, 1972). Social systems that require all members to fit into a single "correct" mold are likely to develop problems that are detrimental for those involved. Similarly, social systems that seek to dictate all decisions for their members are likely to engender apathetic, excessively dependent, or aggressive responses from their members. Thus, social environments that prohibit or punish diversity and self-determination create restrictive, stagnant, and sometimes even dangerous life situations for their members. In such cases, it may be preferable to either change the social system or remove the client from that setting, rather than aiding the client to adjust to a destructive life situation.

A third problem arises when there is no way to remove the client from the dysfunctional social system nor to effectively improve the system. For example, a client may report that conflict with his family is making life miserable, but the family may be unwilling to be involved in therapy and the client may have no way of leaving the famly at present (e.g., an adolescent who is legally a minor; an adult whose religious beliefs proscribe divorce). In such cases, Freud (1935) alerts the clinician to an important issue:

> . . . those (persons) nearest to the patient frequently show less interest in his recovery than in keeping him as he is. When as so often occurs the neurosis is connected with conflicts between different members of a family, the healthy person does not make much of putting his own interest before the patient's recovery. (p. 400)

When the only alternative is to help the client adjust to a bad situation, the clinician must anticipate the ways in which the client's significant others may "sabotage" any positive changes in the client. For example, the client may learn to take a more relaxed and self-confident approach to dealing with family conflicts, only to have family members accuse him of being "cold and uncaring." If such backlash effects can be predicted in advance, the client can be prepared to handle them with aplomb. In our example, the clinician might help the client to develop assertive replies to such deprecating remarks from family members, for instance, "It's not that I don't care, but rather that I want to deal with our conflicts in a calmer and fairer way."

A final potential problem with the adjustment approach to clinical intervention has been labelled "symptom substitution" by Freud (1920). Clients may be provided with short-term and superficial relief from their pain and behavioral symptoms at the expense of dealing more thoroughly and honestly with deeper personal issues. If basic psychological dysfunctions remain unchanged then the client may simply "substitute" new symptoms when the original ones are removed. For example, if a husband is fighting with his wife about conflicts that he has fought over with his parents and every woman with whom he has ever been seriously involved, then helping the couple to reach specific agreements might not fully aid the husband to overcome the more deep-seated feelings of anger, frustration, and hopelessness. It might be more important to first have the husband examine how and why the same issues arise for him in every intimate relationship and to help him alter his basic fears and prejudices about trusting a loved person.

Not all clinical psychologists agree that symptom substitution occurs when clients are aided in establishing better adjustments to their current life situations. Bandura (1969) presented an alternative view that "symptom substitution" occurs only when the client has not made a truly complete adjustment. Bandura stressed that psychological dysfunctions can be treated if the client achieves a reinforcing adjustment to the current social setting. In our example, Bandura might take the position that by helping the client and his wife to establish a more reinforcing relationship the client will be provided with important real-life learning experiences that will help him to unlearn any irrational past feelings, beliefs, or behaviors.

Both viewpoints have merit. For our purpose, it is important to remember that a "good" adjustment must be based on a thorough understanding of the client and the client's current life situation, so that a good "fit" can be achieved without glossing over important problems in the person or the social environment.

Restructuring Social Systems

Although it often seems difficult to "change the system," clinical psychologists frequently work with clients with the goal of changing the client's social environments. This goal can be achieved by (1) teaching clients new skills with which they can have a positive effect on their life situations, or (2) directly intervening to alter the clients' social systems.

Skills For Self-Management   Clinical psychologists teach their clients a variety of skills that aid the clients in changing social systems. Such skills include *facilita-*

tion, consequation, conceptualization, and *problem solving* (Ford, 1980). Facilitation skills enable clients to set the stage so that desired results are attained. For instance, a client may learn to model the appreciative behaviors that she wants her husband to display, in order to encourage the husband and to remind him of her desire. Consequation skills involve providing feedback to significant others after they have displayed an important behavior to motivate them to respond in a desirable fashion in the future. For example, an employer could be taught to genuinely praise her workers when they are efficient and productive. Conceptualization skills are strategies for cognitively processing information from the environment to make change possible. For example, a parent might be taught to reinterpret his son's behavior as a sign of insecurity rather than hostility, so that the parent can then respond in a caring fashion rather than with anger. Finally, problem-solving skills enable clients to make effective decisions and plan strategies for future action. For example, members of a citizen's group could be taught new ways to analyze their community's mental health services so that they can more effectively plan strategies for lobbying for improvements. Clinicians thus help clients to take a more active and effective role in determining the course of their lives by teaching them skills for influencing their social environment.

Direct Social Change Clinical psychologists can also deal directly with social systems in order to create positive changes. In therapy, clinicians may work with an entire family in order to help the family members communicate more clearly. For example, Heard (1978) reported a family therapy case in which the mother and father were assisted in developing a more complementary and honest relationship with one another, to establish a better home environment for each other and their son. All family members were involved in the effort to create an improved family system.

Similarly, as consultants, clinical psychologists may bring together all members of a school's faculty or all employees and managers in a business, in order to change their patterns of interacting with one another. For example, Lawler (1973) described the process of helping workers and executives collaborate in designing job requirements that promote both productivity and employee satisfaction. The "group-on-group" exercise is one such tactic: several persons representing both management and labor sit in a circle and discuss how to create the best work situation, while an equal number of persons sit outside the inner circle and pair up with a member of the inner circle to provide the inner-circle member with encouragement and feedback. All members of the organization can thus be represented in the attempt to design an improved business organization.

Potential Problems As with adjustment interventions, several potential problems may crop up when a clinician seeks to help clients to change their life situations. First, clients may hope to achieve changes without considering the needs and priorities of other persons in their social environments. For example, a child may want his parents to do away with all rules and requirements, ignoring the fact that parents want to have some say in their children's lives. The optimal goal is an *equitable* social system (Walster, Walster, & Berscheid, 1978). Such systems enable all participants to get a fair share of both the rewards and responsibilities. In our example, an equitable parent-child relationship might be one where the parents provided their child with some meaningful choices, but where they were able to maintain effective policies concerning family issues.

Psychologists have questioned whether we have the right, the expertise, or the technology to attempt to alter social systems (Albee, 1977b; Dunham, 1965; Halleck, 1969). Concerning rights, it has been argued that social systems ought to be left to make their own decisions autonomously, rather than having their choices dictated by an "outsider" such as a clinical psychologist. However, it is noteworthy that even radical activists (e.g., Alinsky, 1971) do *not* view the social change agent as a dictator or final authority. Instead, clinicians function as *advisors* who help clients explore options, *teachers* who aid clients in acquiring the skills to make their own decisions, and *guides* who help clients carry out their own plans.

Concerning expertise, commentators have observed that clinical psychologists are not trained as lawyers, politicians, or businesspersons. Thus, clinicians cannot expect to provide effective therapy or consultation unless they (1) gain a thorough assessment of the social systems that make up their clients' life situations and (2) team up with experts in other fields when special expertise is required. For example, Fairweather, Sanders, Cressler, and Maynard (1969) worked with community officials and businesspersons to identify a small business venture that could be handled by former mental patients and that could successfully make money by meeting a real need in the community. They decided to initiate a janitorial service, rather than a business such as a restaurant or store that would have had to compete with other similar firms that already existed in the community. As a result, the business prospered, and thus provided a means for a group of former psychiatric patients to live autonomously outside the confines of a mental institution.

Critics of both therapy and consultation have cautioned that there is insufficient evidence of the efficacy of social change interventions to permit psychologists to undertake them (e.g., Rappoport & Kren, 1975). A great controversy is raging concerning the ethical, economic, and therapeutic appropriateness of delivering psychological interventions (see, for example, recent issues of *Science* or the American Psychological Association *Monitor*): on the one hand, can clinical psychologists (*and* all other psychotherapists and psychological consultants) offer interventions to consumers fairly when the scientific evidence validating these interventions is not definitive? On the other hand, can we suspend therapeutic and consultative interventions and leave prospective clients adrift? Economic pressures and the pain of psychological dysfunctions are two principal reasons why therapeutic and consultative interventions continue to be requested and provided. These forces will continue to play a powerful role, thus suggesting that the ultimate question is, "How best to offer therapy and/or consultation, for the benefit of the client and society," rather than, "Can we 'allow' psychotherapy and consultation to be delivered?" We explore new roles for clinical psychologists—such as developers of nonprescriptive self-improvement services and community or family enhancement specialists—as well as well as more traditional niches, in the next four chapters. No simple or single answer will suffice, and this question of the viability and ethical justifiability of clinical psychological interventions must be kept in mind at all times.

THE EMPIRICAL-CLINICAL METHODOLOGY

Clinical psychologists gather data from multiple perspectives and then draw on their professional knowledge to formulate, implement, and evaluate intervention programs for each unique client. In these efforts, clinical psychologists are hypothesis testers who utilize *empirical* data from both their assessments and their acquaintance with prior research and theory, and *clinical* data from both their inferences in assessment and their past experiences with clients. They then develop and carry-out *clinical* interventions to aid each client, as well as conducting *empirical* evaluations of the effectiveness of these strategies. Although the specific data sources, inferences, interventions, and evaluations may vary from psychologist to psychologist, all clinical psychologists aspire to reach the ideal that this *empirical-clinical methodology* represents (Goldfried & Davison, 1976; Strupp, 1977).

For example, consider the following hypothetical clinical case. Sam B. is a 9-year old Caucasian boy who has been brought to see a clinical psychologist because his parents feel that "He will not go to school." The clinician talks with Sam to explore his feelings about family, friends, and school, and gives Sam a battery of psychological tests. The parents are interviewed to explore their relationships with one another and all other family members, as well as to get an initial evaluation of their current status as individuals and spouses. Sam's teacher is interviewed concerning Sam's academic performance and social relationships, and the school psychologist is consulted concerning Sam's performance on standard tests of achievement. Finally, the clinician observes Sam and his family and friends in the B.'s home.

With these data, the clinical psychologist is able to evaluate the likely pros and cons of several intervention strategies. Individual therapy might be undertaken to help Sam overcome anxiety or emotional conflicts concerning school, family, or social relationships. Family or marital therapy might be warranted if there is evidence of strife between Mr. and Mrs. B. that could be motivating Sam to avoid school—as often is the case (Oltmanns, Broderick, & O'Leary, 1977). The clinician could also involve Sam in group therapy to help him develop new social skills and relationships. The parents and teacher could be aided in developing a motivational program to encourage Sam to attend school and (if needed) improve his academic performance. The psychologist might also consult with the teacher concerning ways to restructure the classroom setting if it appears to be deficient in providing consistent and interesting learning experiences and emotional support for the students.

The clinical psychologist thus formulates several hypotheses about what intervention strategies might be advisable. These are evaluated in light of the assessment data, and the interventions that best suit the needs of Sam, his family, and the school are selected. This decision is based on the clinician's knowledge of clinical research, as well as on prior experience with similar clients and discussions with colleagues. When the appropriate interventions are chosen, this represents the clinician's best professional judgment, but it is never a "sure bet." Therefore, the clinical psychologist subsequently evaluates the results of the interventions to determine (1) if the outcomes are satisfactory to those involved, and (2) how the interventions can be improved.

The empirical-clinical methodology provides the basic guidelines for the process of clinical intervention that are compatible with differing theoretical orientations. This model enables clinicians to make the best possible use of their knowledge of clinical research, their past experience in conducting clinical interventions, and the data from their clinical assessment (Schover, 1980). It also encourages psychologists to be creative and thorough in designing interventions, as well as consistent and accurate in evaluating them.[1]

TYPES OF CLINICAL INTERVENTION

Therapy and consultation are the two basic types of clinical intervention. Therapy involves aiding individual clients to explore and resolve personal dilemmas such as depression or marital unhappiness. Consultation involves aiding members of social systems such as schools or clinics to evaluate and improve the policies and processes that guide these systems.

Therapy

When clinical psychologists conduct therapy, they apply principles that are derived from psychological theory and research, and from their past training and clinical experience, to aid individual clients in recognizing, defining, and overcoming personal and interpersonal problems. As Strupp (1977) noted:

> In broadest terms, the enterprise called "psychotherapy" encompasses a person who has recognized that he is in need of help, an expert who has agreed to provide that help, and a series of human interactions, frequently of highly intricate, subtle, and prolonged character, designed to bring about beneficial changes in the patient's feelings and behavior that the participants and society at large will view as therapeutic. (p. 3)

Although therapy is a complicated and demanding endeavor, the basic definitions that clinicians of different theoretical orientations have formulated for therapy are often remarkably similar. For example, consider the following description of psychoanalytic therapy and behavior therapy (these two approaches to therapy are often thought to be quite dissimilar).

> . . . psycho-analytic treatment is a kind of re-education. The patient's mental life is permanently changed by overcoming (inner) resistances, is lifted to a higher level of development, and remains proof against fresh possibilities of illness. (Freud, 1935, p. 392)

---

[1]The interested reader is referred to the first seven articles in the April 1981 issue of the *Journal of Consulting and Clinical Psychology* in which the topic of empirical clinical practice is discussed.

Behavior therapy involves primarily the application of principles derived from research in experimental and social psychology for the alleviation of human suffering and the enhancement of human functioning. Behavior therapy emphasizes a systematic evaluation of the effectiveness of these applications. Behavior therapy involves environmental change and social interaction rather than the direct alteration of bodily processes by biological procedures. The aim is primarily educational. The techniques facilitate improved self-control. (Franks & Wilson, 1975, p. 2)

"Therapy" has a common emphasis on helping clients overcome personal problems and attain more mature and satisfying lives through the application of psychological principles. Therapy seeks to aid clients in acquiring autonomous self-determination through an educative process.

Consultation

Consultation involves the application of psychological principles to providing members of social systems with skills and knowledge that will enable them to create positive change in their social systems. Rather than helping clients to explore and resolve personal problems, consultants assist their consultees in more effectively understanding and managing systems such as schools, businesses, community organizations, or entire communities.

Four approaches to consultation have been delineated (Caplan, 1970; Cormick & Love, 1976). Clinicians can work with individuals who seek to resolve problems that prevent them from fulfilling their role responsibilities in their social environments. For example, Dorr (1977) described a behavioral approach to consulting with teachers concerning more effective ways to deal with aggressive or low-achievement students. Clinicians can also teach individuals new skills so that the clients can prevent future problems in their social roles. For example, Drotar (1976) used a weekly problem-solving group format to teach psychological skills to the medical staff in a pediatric hospital.

Alternately, the consultant can focus on helping clients improve their social systems rather than only their own personal capabilities. Lepkin (1975) utilized this approach to ameliorate employee-management conflict in a large industrial firm. Negotiations were conducted to restructure basic personnel policies in order to improve the morale and work environment for workers, supervisors, and management.

Finally, the consultant may serve as an advocate for a particular group or organization, providing guidance and training for the express purpose of enhancing that client's efficacy. For example, Chesler, Bryant, and Crowfoot (1976) described taking an explicit stand to promote the rights and interests of low-income groups. The client groups were organized and trained to lobby more effectively for change in their communities, and the consultant directly negotiated on behalf of these groups with more powerful agents such as school administrators and community government leaders.

Clinical psychologists are less often provided with the full range of skills for consultation than they are with expertise as psychotherapists. Either training in, or collaborative work with, professionals from such disciplines as industrial, school, organizational, consulting, community, and social psychology, business administration, organizational development, and management systems is essential for the clinical psychologist who seeks to serve as an organizational consultant.

BASIC PHASES OF CLINICAL INTERVENTION

In both therapy and consultation, the basic phases of intervention are preentry, rapport establishment and contract negotiation, assessment, goal formulation, the intervention per se, and termination.

Preentry

This phase of the clinical intervention process raises issues concerning appropriateness of the clinician's skills and expertise, and the nature of the client's needs.

Therapy   Before commencing therapy, clinical psychologists carefully consider several questions involving the following theme: "Am I and my (potential) client prepared to work productively together?" Therapy is most likely to succeed if the clinician has determined that therapy is in fact the most appropriate intervention. Clients may come to a therapist with problems that are more in the province of physicians, lawyers, pastoral or vocational counselors, or self-help groups (see Table 11-1). The therapist's first task is to ascertain whether the client could benefit more from these services than from psychological therapy, and whether these alternatives might be required as adjuncts even if psychological therapy seems appropriate.

Therapists must also consider their professional competency. A central principle of professional ethics is that clinicians do not conduct therapy if their training and experience have not fully prepared them to deal competently with a client's particular needs and issues (American Psychological Association, 1977a). For example, if a client presents a sexual problem and the therapist has little or no experience in providing sexual therapy, then referral to an experienced sex-therapist would be called for. Although general experience per se is not always related to therapeutic effectiveness (Auerbach & Johnson, 1977; Parloff, Waskow, & Wolfe, 1978), it is important that the therapist has had supervised experience doing therapy to aid clients with the presenting type of dysfunction.

Personal competency, as exemplified by such qualities as self-confidence, freedom from interfering psychological conflicts, and genuine caring and respect for other people, is equally important in an effective therapist. For example, Fromm-Reichman (1950) states:

> *Where there is a lack of security, there is anxiety; where there is anxiety there is fear of the anxieties in others. The insecure (therapist), therefore, is liable to . . . thwart the patient's tendency to submit (personally significant) experiences to psychotherapeutic investigation by feeling called upon to give premature reassurance to patients because he needs reassurance himself. . . . Moreover . . . the patient may take (the therapist's anxiety) as a confirmation of his own fear of being threatening, that is, "bad." (pp. 24–25)*

Table 11-1   Examples of Alternative Helping Systems

Individual Self-Help

Changes in social relationships, marital status, or life-style

Changes in work, place of residence, or child-care arrangements

Recreational activities

Acquiring additional education

Use of self-help reading materials

Religious activities

Training for Personal Effectiveness

Parent effectiveness training

Marriage encounter

Assertiveness training

Relaxation training (Transcendental Meditation, yoga, biofeedback)

Peer Self-Help Groups

Alcoholics Anonymous

Weight Watchers, Take Off Pounds Sensibly (TOPS), etc.

Widow-to-Widow

Parents Without Partners

Consciousness-raising groups

Reevaluation counseling

Support groups for child abusers

Support groups for persons with specific physical or mental disabilities (e.g., after mastectomy, after mental hospitalization)

Crisis Intervention Systems

Rape crisis centers

Drug addiction centers

Suicide hotlines

Pregnancy and abortion counseling

Shelters for abused wives

Psychological/Psychiatric Helping Systems

Hospitalization, partial hospitalization, day programs

Mood-modifying drugs or other physical interventions

Other systems of therapy or other therapists

Other Institutional Helping Systems

Social welfare agencies

Vocational counseling

Legal assistance

Medical care

Pastoral counseling

From R. T. Hare-Mustin, J. Maracek, A. G. Kaplan, and M. Liss-Levinson, Rights of clients, responsibilities of therapists. *American Psychologist*, 1979, *34*, 3–16. Copyright 1979 by the American Psychological Association. Reprinted by permission.

Thus, both professional and personal competency are crucial in the therapist.

The clinician must also consider whether or not the client seems prepared to work effectively in therapy. Clients who are forced to undertake therapy, for instance as a consequence of committing a crime or due to pressure from family members, may have little motivation to work towards personal change. Even when clients actively seek therapy for themselves, they may still be confused and uncertain about what to expect from therapy. Fortunately such persons can still benefit greatly from therapy when they are given information about what generally happens in therapy, reassurance that therapy is not dangerous, and reason to believe that therapy can have a meaningful personal payoff. For instance, Heitler (1973) describes pretherapy groups that are conducted to provide a supportive orientation to therapy for low-income clients. When such clients are given an explanation of their responsibilities, the therapist's role, and the general process of therapy, they tend to benefit more from individual therapy than similar clients who received no preparation. Similarly, Strupp and Bloxom (1973) report the successful use of a film to prepare lower-class patients for group psychotherapy.

Consultation   As in therapy, there are several issues that should be considered at the preentry phase in consultation (Cherniss, 1976; Glidewell, 1959). Consultants must examine the values of the organization that is seeking service. For example, a clinician might prefer to decline to consult with a firm that uses advertising strategies that are at odds with the clinician's personal values. Consultants also check to assure that they have the resources and skills needed to satisfy the consultee's requests. Such resources include time, money, official approvals, cooperation from all participants, equipment, and technical expertise. Last, but not least, consultants must consider whether consultation is the most appropriate intervention. Therapy, political advocacy, or investigative reporting are three alternatives that merit consideration as alternatives to, or complements for, consultation.

Rapport Establishment And Contract Negotiation

In both therapy and consultation, the second phase of the intervention follows the clinician's decision to accept the case. At this point, the clinician seeks to establish a warm and respectful relationship with the client, and to develop a contract that describes the responsibilities of both the clinician and the client.

Clinicians have found that communicating with clients in a reserved yet friendly, interested, and understanding fashion can reduce clients' anxieties and gain their trust. Rogers (1957) has proposed that clinicians must convey understanding, caring, and honesty to clients in order to provide effective therapy. Several studies (e.g., Ford, 1978; Gurman, 1977) have reported that clients tend to stay in therapy all the way to the end and to benefit maximally when they view their therapists as warm, genuine, and understanding. Consultants also recommend the establishment of good rapport with all clients, particularly when attempting to help serve groups in conflict (Rhodes, 1974).

In order to provide a clear agreement concerning the rights and responsibilities of both clinician and client, many clinicians recommend negotiating a contract at the outset. The clinician cannot promise to alleviate all of the client's problems completely, but a contract can state the clinician's intentions to provide the most effective intervention possible. Similarly, the contract can state the client's needs and intentions. While the format of intervention contracts can be determined by each individual client-clinician-dyad, the topic areas that have been recommended for contracts include: (1) the goals of therapy, (2) the length, frequency, and cost of therapy sessions, (3) the duration of treatment, (4) the general approach to therapy that will be provided, (5) the client's responsibility for participation in sessions, and (6) the provisions for keeping information private and confidential (Goldberg, 1977; Goldfried & Davison, 1976; Weiner, 1975).

Assessment

From the first moment of contact with the client, the clinician is gathering assessment data by observing the behavior patterns that the client displays. The majority of assessment data is gathered according to the assessment strategies and techniques described in Chapters 6 to 10. Typically, a battery of psychological tests, observations, and interviews are employed.

Among the important questions for which psychological assessments are undertaken is "why has this client sought therapy or consultation at *this particular time?*" Although inquiry may reveal that the client has enduring problems and has been seeking a solution for many months or years, it is important to know what current crises, pressures, or incentives have led the client to seek help at this time.

Goal Formulation

Once the clinician and client have developed a clear picture of the central problems and issues, they must work together to formulate the specific goals of the intervention.

Therapy   Goal formulation begins with a comparison of the discrepancies between clients' current beliefs, feelings, or actions and the beliefs, feelings, or actions that they want to be experiencing. From this starting point, goal formulation is a gradual process that has five defining characteristics: (1) progressive clarification and refinement, (2) moving from the general to the specific, (3) establishing both interim and terminal objectives, (4) establishing constructive rather than negative goals, and (5) collaboration between client and therapist.

Progressive clarification and refinement   The goals that the client or clinician might first suggest are not always the goals that are ultimately most important. For example, a client might insist that he has problems dealing with his boss and co-workers, and that all other areas of his life are fine. As a result of the assessment it might become clear that the client's angry behavior at work is largely an offshoot of feelings of frustration experienced in relation to his wife and his parents. These more basic problems may result from deeply ingrained misconceptions about his role as a husband and father and a fear of asserting his needs in his family. It may still be important for this client to learn skills for coping with work, but this now appears to be secondary in importance to the more pervasive issues concerning his family.

From the general to the specific   Few clients are able to state goals that are sufficiently specific to permit effective intervention at the outset. General goals, such as "helping me to feel less depressed," or "helping me to live with my family," are an important aid to help the clinician to learn the depth and extent of the client's needs and troubles. However, the therapist must work with the client to define the goals more exactly. This is facilitated when the goals are stated in observable terms such that there is a basis for judging how to intervene and how to measure progress. Thus, "behavioral objectives" (Mager, 1962), which are statements of specific and observable goals, are valuable aids to the implementation and evaluation of therapy (see Table 11-2 for examples).

Interim and terminal goals   According to Mager (1962), interim goals are the steps that the client must take in order to gradually attain the ultimate or terminal goals. Ideally, each interim goal is a step that is small enough to be within the client's capability to reach, yet sufficiently productive to challenge the client to move forward. If a client fails to succeed on an interim goal, the clinician may need to divide this goal into two or more smaller steps that will be within the client's capability. For example, for a terminal goal of "relaxed interaction with members of the other sex," a few of the interim goals might include: "imagines talking with a person of the other sex without experiencing anxiety," "joins a group of persons of both sexes without talking," and "talks to a person of the other sex about a familiar topic."

Constructive goals   Constructive goals specify the positive changes that can be instituted instead of describing only what should *not* happen. For example, a con-

Table 11-2   Examples of Behavioral Objectives

Vague Goal	Behavioral Objective
Make my child behave	Increase the percentage of parental commands that the child follows within 15 minutes, and decrease the frequency of parental commands
Make my boss listen to me	Increase the frequency with which the boss restates what his or her employees have said to him or her, and the frequency of "I" statements by employees
Give life new meaning	Increase the frequency of interpersonal interactions in which the client receives positive feedback and provides self with positive feedback
Create a smoothly running decision-making system for the mental health clinic	Decisions will be made within one week of their initiation

structive alternative to the goal of "removing anxiety" would be "increasing the frequency of relaxed interaction." If therapy is aimed at doing away with a negative behavior pattern, such as aggressive fighting, it is essential to establish constructive goals that provide the client with positive ways to obtain the same payoffs (such as attention from parents) that the dysfunctional behavior had served to provide in the past.

Collaborative goal setting   Both the therapist and the client contribute to the formulation of goals in most cases, so that the goals reflect the psychologist's therapeutic expertise *and* include the client's unique needs and personal understandings. When the therapist involves clients as coparticipants in formulating goals, this can serve to provide the clients with guided practice in controlling their own lives. Thus, goal formulation is a scaled-down experience in effective problem solving and self-determination that in itself can bolster the client's skills and self-confidence.

Consultation   As in therapy, consultation goals must be developed in a gradual, constructive, collaborative, and specific fashion. If for example, a consultant aims to help a teacher deal more effectively with a "problem" student, both the teacher *and* the student have goals that cannot be overlooked. If only the teacher's goals are considered, the consultation may result in changes that create a "quiet, still, and docile" student, but this may be at the expense of the student's learning and future adjustment (Winett & Winkler, 1972).

In consulting with an organization, it is important to get inputs from all participants. Ford and Hutchison (1974) describe a model for soliciting and processing the disparate goals of all participants in a clinical training program. The basic strategy is to systematically collect the specific priorities of groups such as students, trainers, administrators, and community representatives, and then to create a forum in which the consultant helps these groups negotiate compromise goals that adequately reflect each group's general priorities. Thus, clear and constructive goals are formulated, and all participants have a positive stake in achieving these objectives.

Intervention

Although the detailed descriptions of specific approaches to clinical intervention are reserved for the upcoming chapters, there are several *practical arrangements* that are important aspects of any clinical intervention.

There are no hard and fast rules for when, where, how often, or for how long therapy or consultation should be conducted. The times and places are usually dictated by the clinician's and client's schedules, although therapy is generally conducted in a professional office. However, some therapists might occasionally meet with their clients in the actual situations that are of principal concern in the client's dysfunctions. For example, if a client fears heights, the therapist may accompany the client to a skyscraper.

The frequency of therapy sessions varies from three to five times per week in some treatments to once a week or every two weeks in others. Outpatient therapy, where the clients live at home and visit the therapist's office, is typically conducted on a once-a-week basis. Inpatient therapy, where the clients reside in a hospital or other treatment facility, usually occurs between one and three times a week. Here too, a therapist may choose to see a client for an intensive time period (e.g., three to four hours every day for two weeks) in order to maximize the therapy's effects. Alternately, treatment sessions may be spaced out over several weeks if the aim is to provide continuing contact. Similarly, the frequency of consultations varies according to the desired goals, ranging from intensive all-day sessions for a week to monthly 50-minute sessions.

The duration of therapy or consultation varies from a single session to numerous sessions over several years. Crisis intervention involves helping people who are experiencing severe but temporary stress to get back on their feet, and may be limited to a single phone call or office visit (Butcher & Maudal, 1976). Some therapists purposely limit therapy to a brief duration, for example 5 to 10 sessions total (Pittman, 1967; Watzlawick, Weakland, & Fisch, 1974). Some research evidence indicates that time-limited brief therapy is equally as effective as lengthier open-ended therapy. For example, Shlien (1957, 1964) compared time-limited therapy with time-unlimited therapy of two varieties and with a client group that received only minimum contact (a brief introductory interview and the promise of future therapy). All three therapy groups were found to show significantly more self-acceptance after therapy than did the minimal contact control group. None of the three therapy approaches proved superior to the others, and Shlien concluded that time-limited therapy is just as effective, and more efficient (due to the fewer number of sessions), compared to lengthier time-unlimited therapy. Although similar comparisons between time-limited and open-ended therapies are needed, time-limited therapy seems viable in many cases. Many therapists take a middle-ground approach by establishing a contract to work with their clients for a limited number of sessions, and agreeing to then negotiate whether or not further therapy seems desirable.

Consultation is often conducted for brief and time-limited periods when the goal is to teach the client problem-solving and self-management skills (e.g., Spielberger, 1974). Other consultation interventions may require extensive work over a long time period. For instance, a consultant who agrees to assist a hospital director in developing a new clinic for treating outpatient clients should plan on making regular contact with the director throughout the creation of the clinic, and on into the first months of its operation in order to troubleshoot the difficulties of a new program.

Termination

The questions of how and when to terminate a clinical intervention are complex. Most clinicians agree that the best time is when the client has acquired the capability to handle problems autonomously. Freud (1937) put this issue in perspective:

> Our aim will not be to rub-off every peculiarity of human character for the sake of a schematic "normality," nor yet to demand that the person who has been "thoroughly analysed" shall feel no passions and develop no internal conflicts. The busi-

ness of analysis is to secure the best possible psychological conditions for the function of the ego; with that it has discharged its task. (p.250)

As in all phases of intervention, the ideal process for terminating involves a collaborative decision by both clinician and client. Therapists and consultants usually introduce the idea of termination several weeks in advance, to allow time for a discussion of the client's feelings and for a gradual winding down of the interventions.

Although clients do sometimes terminate before their clinicians feel the intervention should end (Baekeland & Lundwall, 1975), the clinician and client usually reserve at least one session for dealing with three termination issues: relationship concerns, maintenance, and, reentry.

Relationship Issues   Clients often feel great distress at the prospect of separating from such an intimate and supportive confidant as the therapist. Feelings of being abandoned, and a resultant mixture of fear and anger, are not uncommon. Regardless of the type of therapy interventions that have been utilized, it is important to explore these feelings, both to help the client confront the responsibility of controlling life independently, and to reassure clients that the therapist continues to genuinely care about them. Relationship concerns are less salient in consultations, although it remains important to reserve some time for a personal goodbye to the client.

Maintenance Issues   Clinicians attempt to help their clients maintain the gains that have been made in therapy or consultation in several ways. Feedback is given to the client concerning the improvements that can be seen, the barriers that have been overcome, and the specific changes that the client has made to accomplish these positive results. In addition, clients are often asked to evaluate their own progress and plan for the future. The client is asked to anticipate future problems and to plan self-directed approaches to handling such stresses, as a means to preparing for autonomous functioning. Some clinicians actually ask clients to make old problems reemerge for a limited time, so that the clients can see that such dilemmas are solvable setbacks and not catastrophes (Dell, 1981; Fisher, Anderson, & Jones, 1981; Haley, 1976; Marlatt, 1979).

Reentry Issues   Although it is important to encourage clients to handle new problems as self-sufficiently as possible, clinicians reassure their clients that further therapy or consultation can be arranged if necessary. No promises are made, except that the clinician will be available in the event the client wishes to discuss the possibility of recommencing therapy or consultation or to get help in making contact with other therapeutic or educational resources.

ETHICAL AND LEGAL ISSUES IN CLINICAL INTERVENTION

Several ethical issues in clinical intervention have already been discussed, including the importance of establishing a relationship aimed at protecting the client's values and welfare, the value of a contract specifying all participants' responsibilities and rights, and the requirement that clinical psychologists only provide services when they have sufficient skill and experience. In this section, several specific legal and ethical concerns involving clinical work in residential institutions and in outpatient settings will be considered.

Ethical and Legal Issues in Residential Treatment

Clinical psychologists provide consultation and therapy services in residential treatment institutions such as mental hospitals, as well as in residential incarceration settings such as prisons. Several legal and ethical concerns arise in such situations: Who is the client? What legal rights do patients or prisoners have to treatment? What constitutes an informed consent to a treatment?

Who Is The Client?   When clinicians provide interventions in patient institutions they must gain the approval of the institution. Therefore, every clinical intervention in a residential treatment facility is influenced by the goals and values of the sponsoring institution. These priorities are not always shared by those in the institution, such as prisoners, patients, or staff. For example, prison administrators may place a high value on reducing costs, while the guards may value security and order, and the prisoners may prefer meaningful counseling and recreation programs. How then can a clinician conform to the institution's requirements and goals while also meeting the needs of prisoners and staffpersons?

Monahan (1978) and Stolz (1977) believe that psychologists can and must serve both the system and the individuals. While stressing that this is a very difficult challenge, they suggest that clinicians should (1) attempt to develop treatment programs that address all participants' needs, (2) safeguard certain inviolable rights of both the system and the participants in all cases, and (3) notify all clients in advance when they may have to sacrifice these rights due to legal requirements. For instance, the clinician might contract with a prison to establish an assessment and counseling program that would reduce costs by replacing a less efficient existing procedure. The program could be geared to bringing together prisoners and guards in problem-solving sessions that would help both groups share feelings, resolve conflicts, and create practical routines for maximizing both security and humane living. The program could also offer private groups for prisoners for confidential personal counseling and training in useful social skills, thus making use of the assessment information specifically to provide meaningful help for prisoners and not for punishment or perfunctory routine (Monahan, 1978).

Right To Treatment   In 1972, more than 40% of the 250,000 persons in state and county mental hospitals were involuntarily confined (Stone, 1975b). This means that these patients have been required to stay in the institution because they are judged to either (1) require care which they are not capable of receiving outside the hospital, (2) be dangerous to themselves or others, or (3) be an excessive burden on their families (Stone, 1975a). The original request for such involuntary hospitalization often comes from a family member or the police, and most states permit mental hospitals to detain new patients for between 48 and 72 hours without their consent just on this initial complaint. Usually, one or two professionals must then judge whether the patient requires continued hospitalization. If their verdict is ''yes,'' then the patient may be held indefinitely, although periodic reviews (e.g., every three months) are typically required to be sure that the patient is not simply forgotten.

In recent years, both individual patients (e.g., *O'Connor* v. *Donaldson*) and representatives of many patients (e.g., *Wyatt* v. *Stickney*, a class action case) have brought legal suits against mental hospitals with the charge that they have been detained excessively without meaningful treatment (Bernard, 1977; Friedman, 1975). Although the outcomes of these cases are difficult to interpret due to many appeals, the most recent and definitive statement by the U. S. Supreme Court held that (Bernard, 1977, p. 1085):

> *treatment is a* quid pro quo *for confinement. . . . before anyone many be confined against his or her will, be it in a prison or hospital, two criteria of fairness must be met: (a) procedures insuring a fair hearing (notice of the hearing, the right to be present at the hearing and to be represented by counsel, etc.) must be followed, and (b) the law justifying commitment must be fair and just.*

As Bernard (1977) and Stone (1975a) have noted, the courts have not defined what constitutes "adequate treatment." Rather, this has been left to mental hospitals to determine, with the understanding that future court cases may challenge certain forms of treatment as "inadequate."

Informed Consent   Ideally, all persons in residential institutions would have the right to refuse treatment as well as to receive it. However, for several reasons, patients and prisoners may not be in a position to give a truly informed consent (Friedman, 1975; Stone, 1975a). First, informed consent must be made by a *competent* person. It is very difficult to determine when a person is sufficiently rational and intellectually skilled to be considered competent. The decision usually rests with the mental health professionals who are responsible for treating the patient. While cases where the treatment is said to be effective and is needed to prevent dangerous acts by the patient (e.g., suicide) are more straightforward, most judgments of competency are more complex. The pressures on a psychologist to override a patient's preference must be carefully weighed against the possibility that (1) the patient might in fact "know best," and (2) the patient might later bring a law suit against the clinician or the institution for malpractice. When a patient objects to a treatment, it is wise for the psychologist to consult at least one professional colleague and, if possible, to consult impartial laypersons who can take the patient's view (American Psychological Association, 1977a, 1977b).[2]

Second, informed consent must be *free* from pressure and coercion. It has been argued that prisons and mental hospitals are inherently coercive, because their residents often think that they must conform to institutional policies or else be punished or prevented from being released (Friedman, 1975; Stolz, 1977). Patients or prisoners may consent to treatments that they might otherwise decline in the hope of receiving better care or an earlier release. Davison and Stuart (1975) propose that, in such cases, all treatments be approved by an ethics committee that is constituted by impartial professionals and laypersons as well as institution-

---

[2]These standards have recently received reaffirmation in a statement of guidelines specific to clinical psychology (American Psychological Association, 1981b).

al officials and patient representatives. Individual clinicians could then select interventions from those that were previously approved by the ethics committee, while also double checking with their own assessment that the benefits accrued by participants will outweigh any costs of participation.

Finally, informed consent must be made with *knowledge* of both the treatment that is to be provided and alternative treatments. Clinicians can serve a valuable role by developing alternative interventions within and outside residential settings, and by being careful to appraise participants in their programs of the realistic alternatives.

Ethical and Legal Issues in Outpatient Treatment

Similar ethical and legal challenges face clinicians who conduct interventions in outpatient settings such as private practice, community mental health centers, or hospital outpatient clinics (Goldberg, 1977; Van Hoose & Kottler, 1975). Protection of the client's welfare is always the top priority (American Psychological Association, 1977a),[3] but specific dilemmas can make this task a difficult task or even render psychologists incapable of serving prospective clients. The following issues are important: limitations on confidentiality and malpractice.

Limitations on Confidentiality   Clinical psychologists strive to protect their clients' *right of privacy* at all times (American Psychological Association, 1977a). It is considered ethically acceptable to discuss personal information concerning a client only with other professionals who are providing services to the client (e.g., a physician or social worker), unless the client gives written informed consent to release this information elsewhere. Thus, for example, it is not ethically appropriate to discuss a client's personal disclosures with his or her spouse, unless the couple was informed in advance that this will happen. Whenever such privileged information is to be communicated outside the client-clinician relationship, it is important to frankly discuss the pros and cons of such action with the client in advance.

Certain practical pressures limit confidentiality. An extreme instance is where a client threatens to, or reports having already, harmed some person (including self). It is difficult to know when such statements really foreshadow a danger, or when they are simply emotional expressions with no real implication for harmful actions. Consider, for instance, the case of *Tarasoff* v. *Regents of the University of California* (*Pacific Reporter*, 529, P 2d, 553, 1975). A client at a university counseling center told his therapist that he intended to kill an ex-girlfriend when she returned from a summer trip. The therapist informed the campus police, and the client was held briefly but released because the woman was still away. Unfor-

---

[3]A revised version of the *Ethical Principles of Psychologists* was adopted by the American Psychological Association's Council of Representatives effective January 24, 1981 (see *American Psychologist*, 1981a, *36*, 633–636). Changes in both wording and substance are included, warranting the reader's careful attention. For example, in Principle 4 on Public Statements, the psychologist is advised in section "k." that "personal advice" may be given by such means as radio, television, magazine articles or demonstrations if "the highest level of professional judgment" is exercised (p. 635). In the past, such relatively impersonal and imprecise means of counseling were prohibited because of their grave potential for misuse and misunderstanding.

tunately, the parents were not informed, and the client subsequently killed the woman. The parents sued the university, the police, and the therapist, and the California Supreme Court eventually upheld the parents' claim of negligence. The court ruled that the therapist had a legal responsibility to warn appropriate persons sufficiently to avert any danger:

> Public policy favoring protection of the confidential character of patient-psycho-therapist relationship must yield in instances in which disclosure is essential to avert danger to others; the protective privilege ends where the public peril begins.

Clinicians rely on their best judgment to determine when a threat should be reported to the authorities and other persons involved, although it is worse to err by being too lenient. Where this question arises, consulting with professional colleagues is the recommended first step. The clinician must also discuss the implications of threats with their clients, so that the client is warned that confidentiality cannot be maintained in such instances.

When working with families, parents may want to be told what their child has said during therapy sessions. The clinician must establish ground rules from the start to clarify exactly what will and what will not be disclosed. Often, the clinician agrees to provide a general summary that will help parents relate more positively with their child, but without revealing anything specific. Thus, the parents are informed, but the child's right to privacy is still respected.

Finally, clinical psychologists report many illustrative interventions as case studies in professional journals. When this is done, the client(s) must be forewarned and given the opportunity to refuse. Confidentiality is always protected by disguising clients' names and specific identifying information, and it is a good policy to let the client(s) read the final report before the case study is submitted for publication.

Malpractice   If clients feel that they have been mistreated or provided with inadequate services by a clinical psychologist they can file suit for malpractice. Such legal action is civil rather than criminal in nature because (unless the clinician has broken a law) the client is suing for redress of damages rather than attempting to prove that the clinician has committed illegal acts (Knapp, 1980). The basis for a malpractice suit lies in the laws of each state ("statutory laws"). Every state has specific laws to protect clients from malpractice. The statutory law that clients can use to bring suit against a clinician usually states that monetary remuneration (in amounts to be determined by a judge) is due to any client who can prove that he or she received treatment that was either harmful or grossly deficient compared to the normal standards maintained by other clinicians in that state. These "normal standards" are not written into the law, but rather must be determined by calling several experts to testify concerning whether they believe that the treatment in question was adequate.

The professional practices that appear most risky for malpractice are those that in any way endanger, humiliate, or violate the values of the client. Several specific practices are almost certainly unethical: sexual relations with clients; depriving clients of constitutional rights, for instance withholding basic food or shelter, or imprisoning a person with no chance for a fair appeal; pressuring clients to engage in acts that violate their personal values or the law; and physically harming a client. Consistent emphasis on the protection of clients' rights, values, and welfare is the best safeguard against malpractice.

APPROACHES TO CLINICAL EVALUATION

The clinician who engages in the practice of therapy, in addition to the issues discussed earlier in this chapter, must face the issue of *evaluation*. The major scientific concern pertaining to clinical intervention is the evaluation of the effectiveness of the procedures that are employed. The evaluation process is, however, not a simple one.

Highlight 11-1   Sexual Relations Between Client and Clinician

The American Psychological Association's (1977a) Ethical Standards of Psychologists states that "sexual intimacies with clients are unethical" (p. 4). This ethic is endorsed because sexual relations with a client can have several damaging effects on the client (American Psychological Association Task Force on Sex Bias and Sex Roles in Psychotherapeutic Practice, 1975; Taylor & Wagner, 1976): the therapist's ability to be objective is reduced by such a personal relationship; the client is being exploited because the therapist is using expertise and power to influence the client to engage in sex; and the therapy termination is far more likely to be plagued by issues of abandonment, disrespect, and a deflation of the client's self-worth.

A recent survey of clinical psychologists concluded that only 4% viewed erotic sexual contact with an other-sex client as even possibly beneficial, and many of these respondents apparently meant sex with a surrogate partner and not with the therapist (Holroyd & Brodsky, 1977). Sexual surrogates are persons who engage in sexual activities required by some treatments for sexual dysfunctions when the client has no partner to fill this role (Wolfe, 1971). The great majority of sex therapists, however, do *not* endorse the use of sexual surrogates, but rather feel that all sexual activities should take place only between partners in an ongoing intimate relationship.

In Holroyd and Brodsky's survey (1977), sexual contact between client and clinician was soundly rejected. However, male clinicians were slightly more likely to endorse erotic relations with clients than female clinicians (6% versus 1%). When asked whether they actually had engaged in sexual relations with clients, 5% of the men responded that they had had intercourse with clients while fewer than 1% of the women had done so. The 5% figure is comparable to that found in an earlier survey of psychiatrists (Kardener, Fuller, & Mensh, 1973). Thus, both clinical psychologists and their psychiatric colleagues reject sexual relations with clients as unethical and potentially harmful to the client.

Internal Validity and its Threats

It is important that the clinician be able to determine that the treatment was responsible for any observed changes and be able to rule out the effects of variables other than the intervention. These other variables, such as unanticipated changes in clients' lives, or natural maturation, are said to be threats to the internal validity of the analysis (Campbell & Stanley, 1963). An evaluation possesses *internal validity* to the extent that it demonstrates the effects of only the intervention by ruling out the effects of other variables. Several important threats to internal validity are the passage of time, the decay of measuring instruments, statistical regression, and the simultaneous occurrence of outside events.

Passage of time simply refers to the client's growing older, maturing, or any process that changes with time. A clinician may notice a marked increase in a child's school achievement and while this may be attributed to treatment, it may actually be the result of the maturation that leads all children to increase their cognitive capacities.

Measurement instruments may become less accurate due to decay over time. Changes in a client's anxiety level, measured by psychophysiological equipment such as an electromyograph or electrocardiograph, may for example appear to indicate improvement when it is really only the result of the decaying sensitivity of the equipment.

Statistical regression refers to the mathematical concept that extreme scores are more likely to "regress to the mean" than they are to remain the same or become more extreme. That is, people who score extremely high or low on a dependent variable seem to have hit the ceiling or floor, respectively. Having nowhere to go but down or up, they tend to do just that, and score closer to the average if they are measured a second time. For clinical work, this principle could apply when, for example, a given client has hit an extremely low depression score, perhaps even near the bottom of the scale that measures depression. It would then be more likely that the patient will have a less depressed score on retesting regardless of any clinical intervention.

Many life events can have therapeutic effects and thus become sources of internal invalidity. Perhaps a depressed client who begins treatment on Monday receives a long phone call from a former roommate on the same day. The clinician's evaluation of the effects of treatment will be confounded by the patient's changes that result from the uplifting phone conversation.

Clinicians often evaluate the effects of their therapy interventions using either *single-subject* or *group-comparison* designs. Both approaches utilize specific procedures to control sources of internal validity, thus permitting the clinical researcher to clearly determine the impact of clinical interventions.

Single-subject Experimental Designs

The single-subject research methodology (Sidman, 1960; Skinner, 1953) grew largely from behavioral psychology but has had an impact on clinical psychologists with diverse backgrounds. It involves specification of the client's problem behavior(s) to be treated and the monitoring and recording of the naturally occurring frequency of these problem behavior(s). The problems that are monitored need not be observable behaviors: they could be disturbing thoughts, unwanted feelings, or levels of insight. In any case, the assessments continue across time as the clinician intervenes, to see if the intervention affects the naturally occurring rate of the problem. If the data indicate desirable changes only when the treatment is introduced, then the treatment is said to be responsible for the observed changes. Single-subject experimental design strategies (see Hersen & Barlow, 1976; Kazdin, 1982) have been used to provide the clinician with some indication that the observed changes were related to treatment. Within the literature on single-subject designs, A denote's the baseline while B, C, and D, etc. denote each new treatment.

Baselines   The A phase, baseline, consists of an initial period of recording the natural occurring frequency of the problem(s), to provide a standard of comparison with the frequency of the problem under treatment conditions. Without a baseline, the clinician cannot be certain that any changes in the client were a function of the treatment. Moreover, baseline assessment allows for an evaluation of the magnitude of the problem(s) and provides an accurate description of the trend of occurrence over time of the problem before treatment is begun.

Baselines vary with respect to the precise number of times that the problem has to be monitored and the recommended duration. However, it is the accepted rule of thumb that baseline data are collected on numerous occasions and for a period of time that produces a relatively *stable* rate. If a stable rate of the problem is not demonstrated at baseline, the researcher cannot be sure that it was the treatment, or just a random fluctuation, that was causing changes during the treatment.

The A-B-A-B Design   In an A-B-A-B design baseline periods (A) are alternated with intervention phases (B) (see Figure 11-1). After the first intervention period, the clinical researcher can identify changes in client problems, but it is as yet unclear as to whether the treatment was responsible or if one (or more) of the sources of internal invalidity were responsible. Returning to baseline, indicated by the second A phase, requires a temporary termination of treatment. If the rate of the problem behavior returns to its natural frequency then several of the sources of internal invalidity can be dismissed as alternate explanations. Following the second baseline, the second provision of the treatment allows the clinician to further determine that the treatment, and not the sources of internal invalidity, were responsible for the observed changes.

The data in Figure 11-1 indicate desirable changes in the target problem that resulted from the provision of treatment (Phase B). That is, the initially high levels of the problem, also observed during the return to baseline, were reduced by the provision of treatment. All threats to internal validity can be ruled out as a contribution to change because no positive change occurred in the second A phase and positive change clearly occurred in both B phases. For example, if decay in measurement instruments caused the change from A_1 to B_1, it should have also continued that trend from B_1 to A_2. Instead, the change reversed between B_1 and A_2, indicating that decay was not the key factor.

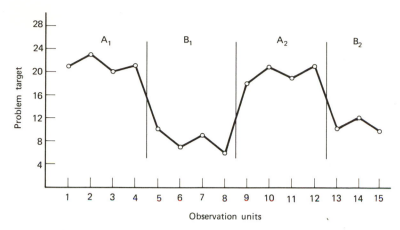

Figure 11-1 Hypothetical data indicating the changes in the target behavior-problem via an A-B-A-B design.

However, the A-B-A-B design is not without some shortcomings. The return to baseline phase is often quite difficult for the clinician to accomplish. First, the absence of a treatment during the initial baseline is not likely to be identical to the absence of a treatment some time after there had been a treatment in effect (A_2, the second baseline). Clients are likely to look upon the second baseline as distinctly different from the first as the result of treatment having been provided in between. Second, when the treatment has had a positive effect, it may be difficult to get both the client and the client's social environment to actually return to the conditions that were present when the problem existed. Ethically, it seems inappropriate to restore a problem that the client wants ended. Finally, when the treatment is withdrawn and the problem returns to its baseline level, a demonstration of treatment control, this also suggests that the treatment effects were not maintained after the therapy was removed. That is, the treatment is producing only temporary results, where clinicians seek to provide interventions that provide lasting benefits. For these reasons clinical researchers often utilize other designs, such as multiple baseline designs, to help evaluate the effects of interventions.

Multiple Baseline Designs In a multiple baseline two or more baselines are simultaneously recorded. When the intervention is begun, it is applied to only one of the baselines but not the others. For example, family therapy might be provided for a boy's disobedience at home with no intervention for school problems. The other remaining baseline(s) serve as a control representing what the treated baseline might have looked like had intervention not taken place. The nontreated baselines control against the potentially confounding effects of the sources of internal invalidity because, if the clinician observes a change in the treated behavior and no specific changes in the other baselines, then this suggests that the treatment was responsible for the change. A reliable treatment effect is one that is demonstrated when each of the baselines changes only when the treatment is applied to it.

Figures 11-2 and 11-3 provide two examples of the use of multiple baseline designs to evaluate interventions. Figure 11-2 depicts a multiple baseline "across-

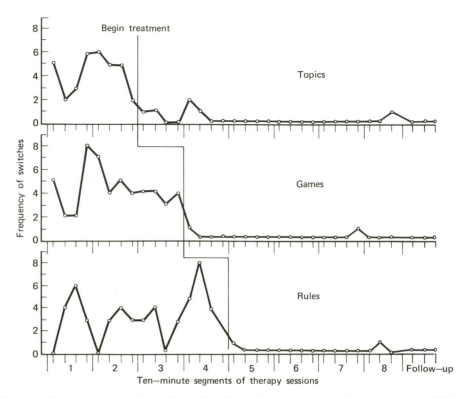

Figure 11-2 An example of a multiple baseline design across three behaviors in one child. This figure represents the actual data from a study that used self-instructional training along with a response-cost contingency to treat the impulsive switching of a 9-year-old boy. Adapted from P. C. Kendall and A. J. Finch, Jr., A cognitive-behavioral treatment for impulse control: A case study. *Journal of Consulting and Clinical Psychology*, 1976, *44*, 852–857. Copyright 1976 by the American Psychological Association. Reprinted by permission.

behaviors" design. In this type of design the treatment of one client is being evaluated by recording the rate of three different problem behaviors—switches in *topics* of conversation, switches in *games* played with, and switches in *rules* of play. Glancing at Figure 11-2 one can readily see that each of the problematic "switching" behaviors, and *only* that behavior, was markedly reduced as the treatment was begun for each separate behavior. Moreover, the strength of the treatment is seen in the immediacy of the reduction of the problem behaviors.

A multiple baseline "across-situations" design is illustrated in Figure 11-3. In this design the same problem behavior is recorded in different settings (classrooms) during baseline and treatment. However, the treatment is introduced in one setting at a time. The untreated settings provide the baselines against which the clinician can compare the effects observed in the setting that receives treatment. The data in Figure 11-3 illustrate positive treatment effects since the amount of verbal aggression is reduced only in the treated setting while it remains

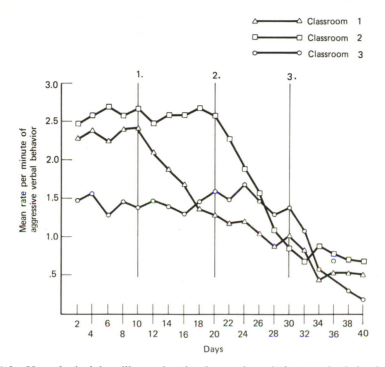

Figure 11-3 Hypothetical data illustrating the changes in verbal aggressive behavior via a multiple baseline across classrooms design. 1. The treatment begins in classroom 1. 2. The treatment begins in classroom 2. 3. The treatment begins in classroom 3. From P. C. Kendall and W. R. Nay, Treatment evaluation strategies. In W. R. Nay, *Multimethod clinical assessment*. New York: Gardner Press, 1979. Copyright 1979 by Gardner Press; reprinted by permission.

relatively unchanged in the untreated setting. After all classroom settings have initiated the treatment (Day 30) all classrooms show a reduction in the amount of verbal aggression.

The multiple baseline designs do not involve ethical and practical problems caused by withdrawing treatment. However, one issue merits consideration. This major problem concerns the relationship between the different problematic behaviors or settings that serve as untreated baselines. If they are related to the treated problem, then it may be expected, and even desirable, that when one change occurs the related baselines will show the effects of a generalized change. This means that one treatment can produce multiple positive changes, which is a very desirable form of treatment outcome. In contrast, when the problems are unrelated or independent of each other the treatment would not be expected to affect all of them at once (Kazdin & Kopel, 1975), and here a multiple baseline design may be entirely appropriate.

The Simultaneous Treatment Design   The fundamental characteristic of the simultaneous treatment design is the simultaneous application of two or more treatments to *one single client*. The effects of the different treatments are monitored separately and, after a period of time, the more effective treatment is continued. The simultaneous treatment design can be depicted as:

$$A - \left[\begin{matrix} B \\ C \\ D \end{matrix} \right. - B \text{ or } C \text{ or } D$$

Again, A represents the baseline period and B, C, and D each represent separate treatments.

McCullough, Cornell, McDaniel, and Mueller (1974) provided an example of the simultaneous treatment design. In this experimental analysis of a single client the authors simultaneously introduced two different treatments following a five-day baseline (Figure 11-4). The two treatments were provided in a counter-balanced order by two different teachers. The first treatment, labeled Condition B, was social reinforcement for cooperative behavior and the ignoring of uncooper-

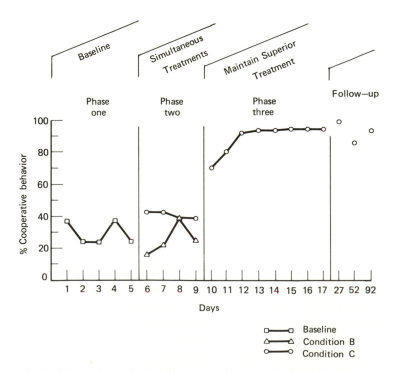

Figure 11-4 An illustration of a simultaneous treatments design. The data presented are the percentages of the observation periods during which the subject emitted cooperative behavior. Adapted from J. P. McCullough, J. E. Cornell, M. H. McDaniel, and R. K. Mueller, Utilization of a simultaneous treatment design to improve student behavior in a first grade classroom. *Journal of Consulting and Clinical Psychology*, 1974, *42*, 288–292. Copyright 1974 by the American Psychological Association. Reprinted by permission.

ative behavior. The second treatment, labeled Condition C, included social reinforcement for cooperative behavior and a two-minute time-out from the classroom for uncooperative behavior.

As reported by McCullough et al., (1974) the simultaneous treatment design compared the treatment effects of two types of treatment (with one client) and allowed the clinician to utilize this data in making a decision as to what treatment should be maintained. As seen in Figure 11-4, Condition C was superior to Condition B in the improvement of cooperative behavior (Phase Two) and was therefore maintained for the remainder of the study. However, it should be pointed out that the simultaneous treatment design does not rule out some of the sources of internal invalidity (e.g., time, regression), and is not suited for all types of intervention.

The importance of the various single-subject research designs is that they can be done by practicing clinical psychologists without the major investments of time, energy, and money that are necessary for larger-scale research projects. They are also useful in providing evidence of the effectiveness of therapy that can be presented to the client, those paying for the service, or future consumers. Single-subject designs are limited, however, in that only one therapist and one client are involved and the results from each case cannot always be directly generalized to other therapists or clients who, by virtue of their unique personal characteristics, learning histories, and social environments, may be differentially affected by the treatment. Thus, the treatment must be reevaluated for each new client.

Therefore, single-subject designs are valuable clinical tools, but they are limited to telling the clinician what outcomes were produced by a single treatment conducted by a single therapist with a single client.

Group Comparison Designs

A second strategy for the evaluation of clinical interventions involves the experimental comparison of two or more groups of clients in which each group receives a different treatment (or control conditions). At its most basic level, the group comparison design (see *factorial designs*, Chapter 3) entails the arrangement of two distinct groups that are subsequently compared on measures of therapeutic gain. Several issues must be considered: What type of clients should constitute the groups? What types of therapy should be studied? What types of therapists? What scores should be obtained? And, how long should the study take? Although it would be easiest if we could simply assign clients to either a control or treatment group and then compare the outcomes, there are several problems with this simplistic view, as described in Kiesler's (1966; 1971) discussion of the "myths of psychotherapy."

Uniformity Myths   The "patient uniformity myth" (Kiesler, 1966) refers to the assumption that, at the start of therapy, clients are more alike than different— they can be lumped together as similar without concern for differences in their personal characteristics. Research that makes this assumption will be markedly hampered by enormous individual differences that will interfere with the evaluation of therapy. To avoid this, group comparison studies should include at least one independent variable that separates clients into meaningful groups based on personal characteristics (manipulation by selection)—thus accounting for some of the differences between clients.

The "therapist uniformity myth" refers to the assumption that all therapists of the same school of therapy provide the same treatment—one therapist would behave in therapy exactly as another. However, therapists who share the same theoretical orientation often differ greatly in their actual therapeutic actions (Sundland, 1977). If psychotherapy is to advance it must first identify and measure therapist variables that are related to outcome. Different therapists may produce different types of change in their clients, so every clinical evaluation should utilize several therapists and examine how each one fares on outcome.

Finally, the "outcome uniformity myth" (Kiesler, 1971) suggests that there is one uniform and homogenous client dimension that can be measured to assess the effects of psychotherapy. Quite the contrary, there are numerous variables that can be measured to evaluate therapy. Multimethod assessment is essential to identify the ways in which different kinds of intervention create different types of change.

Grid Model   These uniformity myths can lead clinicians to ignore the important differences that exist in the types of clients, types of clinicians, and types of psychosocial change that can occur. Only when these variations are taken into account will clinically meaningful and useful findings result. Kiesler (1971) describes a grid model (see Figure 11-5) for the design of group comparison studies of the effects of psychotherapy that incorporate and evaluate differences in patients, therapists, and outcome measures. Kiesler suggested that psychotherapy research designs make consistent use of factorial designs in which patient, therapist, and outcome are independent variables and dependent variables are examined over time (repeated measures). Kiesler's formulation of a grid model has had positive effects on the field of psychotherapy research, providing the researcher with an opportunity to begin to answer the critical question raised by several workers in the field (Kiesler, 1966; Paul, 1969; Strupp & Bergin, 1969): What therapist behaviors are effective with which types of clients in producing which kinds of patient change?

In Figure 11-5 there are several important dimensions. First, all clients are not lumped together. The independent variable A defines a least two different groups of clients (person variables). It is important here that these groups be homogeneous in nature. After all, the purpose for the different patient groups is to reduce the "noise" (unwanted variance) generated by client differences and therefore the groups should be composed of subjects who are very similar to each other. The B variable is similarly important. This grouping of therapists prevents "noise" due to therapist differences. Again, the groupings are successful to the extent that they result in homogeneous clusters of therapists.

The C variable merely indicates that the effects of therapy need to be evaluated over time and that several measurements be taken. This dimension of the grid describes what is often referred to as pretreatment, posttreatment, and follow-up. Finally, the D variable are dependent variables which, in the case of psychotherapy, are the different behaviors, test scores, or ratings that will be examined to assess the effects of psychotherapy.

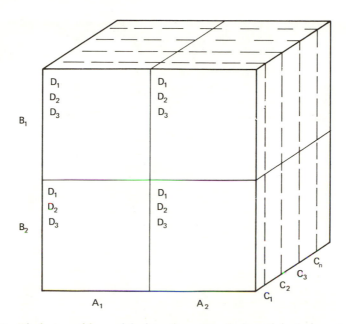

Figure 11-5 Kiesler's grid model for the use of factorial designs to evaluate psychotherapy. A = Different homogeneous groups of subjects (clients). B = Different homogeneous groups of therapists. C = Different times of assessment. D = Different behaviors that are being monitored to assess change. Adapted from D. J. Kiesler, Experimental design in psychotherapy research. In A. E. Bergin and S. L. Garfield (Eds.), *Handbook of psychotherapy and behavior change.* New York: Wiley, 1971. Copyright 1971 by John Wiley and Sons, Inc. Reprinted by permission.

Our knowledge about the outcome of clinical interventions will be advanced as we accumulate information gathered according to the grid model. At times, however, the conduct of just one experimental study of psychotherapy can become an onerous task as the clinician tries to include all the important variables in one study. For this reason, psychotherapy researchers have typically addressed portions of the grid, one at a time, in a series of *programmatic* studies that, taken together, begin to fill in several cells in the grid.

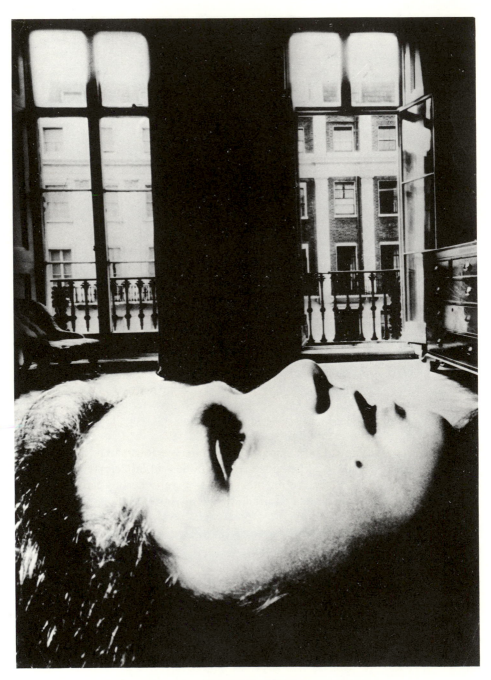

O Captain! my Captain! our fearful trip is done,
The ship has weathered every rack, the prize we sought is won,
The port is near, the bells I hear, the people all exulting.

Walt Whitman

12

INTERVENTIONS WITH INDIVIDUALS: PSYCHOANALYTIC, CLIENT-CENTERED, EXISTENTIAL, GESTALT, AND CRISIS THERAPIES

Assessment is often conducted to provide a basis for defining the problem to be treated and determining the best treatment. Many interventions are currently available, as we describe in this and the following chapters. We focus, in the first two of these chapters, on interventions that deal with clients on an individual basis, that is, where a clinician meets with one client to help that one person. Such interventions are applicable across a variety of types of clients and types of problems, and indeed, persons of all ages, sexes, and socioeconomic classes are involved in individual therapy.

SOURCES OF HYPOTHESES ABOUT INDIVIDUAL INTERVENTIONS

Individual interventions can vary in the degree to which the therapist (1) tries to help the client by acting directively or nondirectively, (2) aims to understand the person by focusing on the past or the present, and (3) evaluates therapy based on insight or behavior change. The sources of these different therapeutic approaches include *experience*, *theory*, and *research*.

Therapy methods are often developed through experience within clinical work. Since the practicing therapist has to decide for each case the appropriate approach to take, a therapist may acquire extensive experience that leads to his or her formulation of a novel method of therapy. Experience outside of the clinical situation can also germinate an approach to therapy. That is, methods of therapy can be developed from intensive reflection on personal experiences with life and/ or life's problems, or from literary/dramatic analogues of life.

Experience as the source of therapy methods can be subject to certain biases. The experience that serves as the foundation is a select sample of life. This limitation affects the applicability of the resulting clinical methods in that the restricted sample reduces one's ability to generalize to other people in other situations.

Theory can also serve as a source of intervention hypotheses. For instance, behavioral theory suggests that behavior is maintained by reinforcement—the clinician would search for the rewards that maintain the problem. Theory itself has a variety of sources (e.g., clinical experience, research), but a well-developed theoretical formulation can, on its own, be a valuable resource for the therapist.

Another source of therapeutic hypotheses is provided by the results of research studies. Data from research fields such as experimental, social, learning, developmental, and cognitive psychology and others, provide evidence that can lead to therapeutic methods. Studies of human cognition that indicate how we forget offer suggestions to help understand how clients "forget" or suppress emotionally laden material.

These different sources of hypotheses about clinical interventions, although not independent, each have something to offer the practicing clinician. However, the key to the usefulness of any hypothesis is the test to see if it works. There are numerous types of therapy that have emerged from the full range of sources: existential therapy arose largely from a philosophical position, behavior therapy largely from the learning and experimental social psychology literatures, and psychoanalysis from extensive clinical experience. In this and the upcoming chapters, each of the different types of therapy will be described and their research evaluations considered.

PSYCHOANALYTIC THERAPY

Psychoanalytic therapy is conceptualized as a process during which unconscious feelings, thoughts, and needs become conscious through the therapist's interpretations of client behavior (Freud, 1920). It is theorized that clients have, since childhood, overutilized defense mechanisms to reduce anxiety. The defense mechanisms are immature attempts at coping with anxiety, because they are thought to lead the person to avoid rather than confront and resolve the conflicts that produce anxiety. These conflicts become banished to the unconscious, never to be fully resolved unless the client is assisted in consciously recognizing and coping with them. Psychoanalytic therapists believe that "insight," the conscious knowledge of one's conflicts, is crucial to effective therapy. Psychoanalysts help their clients gain insight by first aiding them to reveal their unconscious impulses and defenses, and then offering interpretations designed to help the client understand and accept them.

Clients are aided in revealing their unconscious conflicts in several ways. They may be asked to "free associate," that is, to express thoughts and feelings as they come into consciousness without censure. Projective tests may be used. The client may be encouraged to describe dreams and fantasies (Freud, 1939). Or, the therapist may observe the client's reactions and note instances where transference leads the client to express significant feelings concerning parent figures. All of these approaches are thought to get around the client's defenses, thus freeing the client to express him or herself without anxiety.

Interpretations play an important role in psychoanalytically oriented therapies. According to Weiner (1975), "the main tool for communicating understanding in psychotherapy is interpretation'' (p. 115). Weiner goes on to define an interpretation as a statement that refers to something the patient has said or done in such a way as to identify features of his or her behavior that he or she has not been fully aware of. Therefore, interpretations are intended to increase the client's self-understanding (Highlight 12-1). Weiner (1975) contrasts interpretation with other

---

Highlight 12-1   An example of the psychoanalytic approach

PATIENT (PT.): We had a salesman's meeting, and a large group of us were cramped together in a small room and they turned out the lights to show some slides, and I got so jumpy and anxious I couldn't stand it.

THERAPIST (TH.): So what happened? [Question]

PT.: I just couldn't stand it. I was sweating and shaking, so I got up and left, and I know I'll be called on the carpet for walking out.

TH.: You became so anxious and upset that you couldn't stand being in the room even though you knew that walking out would get you into trouble. [Clarification]

PT.: Yeah. . . What could have bothered me so much to make me do a dumb thing like that?

TH.: You know, we've talked about other times in your life when you've become upset in close quarters with other men, once when you were in the army and again in your dormitory at college. [Confrontation]

PT.: That's right, and it was the same kind of thing again.

TH.: And if I'm correct, this has never happened to you in a group of men and women together, no matter how closely you've been cramped together. [Further confrontation]

PT.: Uh. . .Yes, that's right.

TH.: So it appears that something especially about being physically close to other men, and especially in the dark, makes you anxious, as if you're afraid something bad might happen in that kind of situation. [Interpretation]

PT.: (Pause): I think you're right about that . . . and I know I'm not physically afraid of other men. Do you think I might get worried about something homosexual taking place?[1]

This excerpt is from a psychoanalytically oriented therapy. The client is sharing thoughts and feelings, and the therapist interprets this material for the client. The therapist listens to the client, tries to be penetrating, confronts the client with issues, and presents an interpretation. The goal of such procedures is to help clients achieve insight into their problems and thus prepare them to more effectively deal with the anxiety that the problems cause. Some aspects of the treatment, such as clarification, are not uniquely psychoanalytic.

[1]From I. B. Weiner, *Principles of Psychotherapy*. New York: Wiley, 1975. Copyright 1975 by John Wiley & Sons, Inc. Reprinted by permission of John Wiley & Sons, Inc.

therapeutic techniques by noting that interpretations deal with unconscious material rather than actual behavior, seek to explain rather than describe behavior, and consist of inferences and possibilities rather than observations and facts.

Interpretations are offered in tentative terms, stated concisely, and timed carefully. Since interpretations can elevate a client's anxiety and discomfort, they should be kept to a tolerable level, be focused on the behaviors causing the client's problems, and be deferred until a later time if necessary. In addition, initial interpretations should refer to behaviors closest to the client's awareness. Although interpretations are important, they are not used excessively by experienced therapists.

Attempts to overcome the traumatic experiences of early childhood or to facilitate more in-depth self-understanding by bringing certain facts into conscious awareness may run into *resistance*. That is, the client may not be willing to express his or her true feelings, to divulge his or her actual thoughts, or to accept the interpretations of the therapist. Early in therapy, psychoanalysts may make a silent note of such resistance but at a later point they more often interpret hesitations, digressions, or slips of the tongue as indicating underlying conflicts.

One of the sources of resistance in psychoanalytic therapy is the *transference* relationship. In the transference relationship, the client tends to relive the earlier feelings and experiences of the principal figures remembered from childhood. The therapist serves as a substitute figure, and the client reenacts as yet unresolved conflicts. For example, if the client mistrusted his father, he may display a similar mistrust of the therapist. "Working through" the transference requires that the patient recognize these unconscious motives, cast them aside, and come to relate to the therapist in a more positive fashion.

Countertransference refers to the positive and negative feelings that the therapist experiences toward his or her clients. These feelings may interfere with the accuracy of the therapist's interpretation and are essentially undesirable. Therefore, therapists must be prepared for the experience of such feelings and skilled to recognize them when they occur.

Psychoanalytic therapists assume that complete *insight* will dramatically alter the client's psychological experience of self and the world. Insight denotes an emotional understanding (and for some an intellectual understanding as well) of basic intrapsychic conflicts, and thus represents the key to a positive outcome. Change in overt behavior is regarded as secondary in importance, because it is thought that insight will automatically lead the client to make any behavioral changes that are necessary for self-enhancement. This position has been a source of controversy for several decades (Hobbs, 1962).

The psychoanalytic approach to therapy is multifaceted. Freud, the founder and most influential psychoanalyst, has been challenged over the years by others who are in varying degrees discontented with Freud's theories. Jung (1934) disagreed with Freud's premise that psychological energy was primarily sexual and with the view that very early childhood experiences are irrevocable. In contrast, Jung emphasized symbolic analyses of the unconscious that are aimed at identifying the positive as well as negative features in the client's unconscious. Adler (1917) also rejected Freud's emphatic position about the central role of sexuality, but underscored the role of the total individual striving to overcome inferiority and to live a more complete life. Adlerian therapists emphasize helping clients to recognize their inferiority conflicts and to refocus on developing themselves in positive ways. Sullivan (1953) also departed from Freud when he emphasized the role of interpersonal relationships in individual analysis. Sullivan utilized the therapist-client relationship as a sample of the client's interpersonal experience and further used it to examine the client's interpersonal difficulties. Other modifications of Freudian psychoanalysis were proposed by neo-Freudians such as Fromm, Horney, Lewin, and Maslow, among many others. Though these neo-Freudians have helped to expand the psychoanalytic perspective, they have produced a state of affairs where one can no longer justify a single description of "the" psychoanalytic viewpoint. Indeed, Wachtel (1977) has advanced an integration of psychoanalytic and behavioral therapies and Horowitz (1979) has developed short-term analytic treatment. Nevertheless, we have attempted to describe those aspects of psychoanalysis that are relatively acceptable to psychoanalytic therapists of varying persuasions.

Research Evaluation

Freud's position on the merits of the experimental enterprise is evident in Luborsky and Spence's (1971) account of a comment by Freud. When asked to comment on an experimental study of repression, Freud replied,

> "I have examined your experimental studies for the verification of the psychoanalytic assertions with interest. I cannot put much value on these confirmations because the wealth of reliable observations on which these assertions rest make them independent of experimental verification. Still, it can do no harm." (p. 408) (Quoted also in MacKinnon and Dukes, 1962.)

Essentially, Freud was stating that his method of clinical observation produced sufficiently reliable observations such that experimental investigations were not necessary to confirm his theory.

Some of the real obstacles that interfere with the experimental study of psychoanalysis include its lack of quantification and operationalization of key concepts and its emphasis on clinical rather than research functions. Both difficulties seriously detract from controlled scientific efforts. Practical difficulties, such as the separateness of psychoanalytic settings from most academic environments and the length of psychoanalytic treatments (some three to five years) also interfere. Nevertheless, there have been several studies of the characteristics of patients who are most suitable for psychoanalysis. In a large-scale evaluation undertaken at the Menninger Clinic (Kernberg, Burnstein, Coyne, Applebaum, Horowitz, & Voth, 1972), the researchers identified the neurotic individual, who is currently suffering psychologically (high anxiety) but who has a capacity for insight (high ego strength) as likely to benefit more from psychoanalysis than low-anxiety/low-ego-strength clients.

The research literature on the effectiveness of psychoanalytically oriented therapy is limited. The current data on the timeliness of interpretations, the value and meaning of free association and transference, and other variables that are most salient within the therapy process are minimal. There have been some efforts, for example, to capture behavior that could be called "transference," but the absence of quantitative studies remains (Luborsky & Spence, 1978).

The Kernberg et al. report (1972) provides some information about the changes that take place as a result of psychoanalysis. Patients showed resolution of the transference, an increase in ego strength, and global psychological improvement (rated by the therapist). Just what this means in regard to the patient's reduction of problem symptoms and improved personal life is not clear. Furthermore, the changes cannot be definitively attributed to the therapy since no control groups were utilized.

In one of the more carefully controlled studies of psychoanalytically oriented treatment, Sloane, Staples, Cristol, Yorkston, and Whipple (1975) evaluated the effectiveness of short-term psychoanalytic therapy in relation to short-term behavior therapy and a waiting-list control group. The patients (classified as neurotic and personality disorder) were seen for four months by expert therapists. At the end of the treatment, clients in both behavior therapy and psychoanalytic therapy were significantly more improved than the waiting-list group, but neither therapy approach appeared superior to the other. Similarly, following a careful review of all available studies evaluating psychotherapy, Prochaska (1979) concluded that to date, "no study has found either psychoanalysis or psychoanalytically oriented psychotherapy to be significantly more effective than either a placebo treatment or some alternative form of therapy" (p. 61).

Nevertheless, the impacts of the theory of psychoanalysis have been far reaching. Many, if not all of the social sciences have been affected by psychoanalytic writers and scholars and, until not long ago, the vast majority of clients seen for therapy were in some form of psychoanalysis. Psychoanalytic therapists have offered clinicians a wealth of hypotheses concerning psychological dysfunctions and psychotherapy, but these notions must be considered tentative in view of their limited scientific support.

CLIENT-CENTERED THERAPY

Client-centered therapy emphasizes the client's psychological experiencing in the present moment and is based on the "humanistic" belief that all people are motivated to, and capable of, improving themselves. Individuals are seen as solving their problems if the therapist establishes a warm and understanding relationship. The central therapeutic strategy involves encouraging clients to guide their own therapy. To facilitate this independent decision making, the therapist does not actively direct the client but seeks to create a therapeutic atmosphere that is *nondirective* and *facilitative*.

Rogers (1957), the originator of client-centered therapy, contends that if certain definable therapist conditions are present then clients will self-actualize and overcome their problems. Self-actualization, according to Rogers (1959) is "the inherent tendency of the organism to develop all its capacities in ways which serve to maintain or enhance the organism" (p. 196). The specific therapist conditions that are desired are *genuineness or congruence, accurate empathy,* and *unconditional positive regard.*

Therapist genuineness or congruence requires therapists to allow their inner feelings and inner experiences to emerge honestly and openly and become apparent within the therapeutic relationship. Genuineness or congruence is often thought to be the most basic of the three conditions and is the base for the entire therapy process. For genuineness to be experienced, the therapist must be his or her actual self, communicating honestly his or her feelings when appropriate. There is no room for facade.

Accurate empathy is seen as the therapist's active immersion of himself or herself in the client's world by imagining what it would be like to actually be in the client's position. The therapist tries to understand the client's perceptions of the world and works to be sensitive to the client's personal, private situation.

Last, nonpossessive caring and an acceptance of the client's individuality both constitute unconditional positive regard. Nonpossessive caring involves an acceptance of the client without evaluation or judgment and unconditional positive regard requires that the therapist trusts that the client's own actualizing process will lead to positive change.

These three conditions are not thought to be independent but rather are clearly recognized as logically related. The basic hypothesis in the client centered approach to therapy is that if these conditions are present in the therapist, then positive growth will take place in the client.

Unlike the psychoanalytic theory of therapy, the client-centered position is stated in hypotheses that are amenable to scientific verification. Also in contrast to psychoanalytic views, Rogerian therapists accept the client's self-reports as valid, reliable sources of information, no matter how they appear to the therapist. Accordingly, therapists rarely interrupt the client except to perhaps verify or amplify some understanding, and they seek to *never* interpret except to perhaps summarize what the client has said (Highlight 12-2). Rogers rejected interpretations as too directive and pejorative, for they imply that the therapist knows more about the client than the client does. The therapist also attempts not to blame, praise, or advise, nor seek to achieve insight or overcome transference. Rogerians are also noted for rejecting the traditional psychiatric diagnostic classification system on the grounds that it sets up the therapeutic relationship with potential limits that hinder the client's actualization process. They focus on client's strengths rather than their deficits, seeking to promote personal growth and not to "cure" a "mental illness."

Research Evaluation

Interestingly, there is research suggesting that Rogerian therapists, indeed Rogers himself, systematically shape the verbal behavior of their clients through reinforcing certain client statements. For example, Truax (1966) analyzed audiotape transcripts from therapy sessions conducted by Rogers and found evidence that empathic and positive regard statements were consistently made by Rogers immediately after the client made remarks that involved positive expectations, expressed a positive self-image, or agreed with the therapist. It appears then that "nondirective" therapy can be subtly influencing the client in a therapeutically desirable fashion.

A central strength of the client-centered approach is its recognition and use of the methods of science in the study of the process of psychotherapy. Client-cen-

Highlight 12-2   A portion of a client-centered therapy session

The following example of the Rogerian (client-centered) approach to therapy has been called "a silent young man" and has been reproduced on several occasions as an illustrative example. We present selected portions of the interview here.

T: Everything's lousy, huh? You feel lousy?
(Silence of 39 seconds)

T: Want to come in Friday at 12 at the usual time?

C: [Yawns and mutters something untelligible.]
(Silence of 48 seconds)

T: Just kind of feel sunk way down deep in these lousy, lousy feelings, hm? Is that something like it?

C: No.

T: No?
(Silence of 20 seconds)

C: No. I just ain't no good to nobody, never was, and never will be.

T: Feeling that now, hm? That you're just no good to yourself, no good to anybody. Just that you're completely worthless, huh? Those really are lousy feelings. Just feel that you're no good at all, hm?
[. . .and from later in the session]

C: I just want to run away and die.

T: M-hm, m-hm, m-hm. It isn't even that you want to get away from here to something. You just want to leave here and go away and die in a corner, hm?
(Silence of 30 seconds)

T: I guess as I let that soak in I really do sense how, how deep that feeling sounds, that you—I guess the image that comes to my mind is sort of a— wounded animal that wants to crawl away and die. It sounds as though that's kind of the way you feel that you just want to get away from here and, and vanish. Perish. Not exist.
(Silence of 1 minute)

C: [almost inaudibly] All day yesterday and all morning I wished I were dead. I even prayed last night that I could die.

T: I think I caught all of that, that for a couple of days now you've just wished you could be dead and you've even prayed for that, I guess that— One way this strikes me is that to live is such an awful thing to you, you just wish you could die, and not live.
(Silence of 1 minute, 12 seconds)

T: So that you've been just wishing and wishing that you were not living. You wish that life would pass away from you.
(Silence of 30 seconds)

C: I wish it more'n anything else I've ever wished around here.

T: M-hm, m-hm, m-hm. I guess you've wished for lots of things but boy! It seems as though this wish to not live is deeper and stronger than anything you ever wished before.
(Silence of 1 minute, 36 seconds)[2]

Note in this example the absence of analytic interpretations. Rather, the therapist is reflecting the client's feelings back to him in order to facilitate the client's own development.

[2]Reproduced by permission of the publisher, F. E. Peacock Publishers, Inc., Itasca, Ill. From B. D. Meador and C. R. Rogers, Person-centered therapy, in Raymond J. Corsini and Contributors, *Current Psychotherapies*, 2nd ed., 1979, pp. 155–158.

tered therapy is one of the most extensively researched psychotherapies, both in elaborate clinical projects and smaller analogue studies. One monumental effort tested the client centered approach with hospitalized schizophrenic patients (Rogers, Gendlin, Kiesler, & Truax, 1967). The findings from this study indicated that: (1) the patients who received psychotherapy did not differ *as a group* from untreated control patients in average constructive personality change and subsequent hospitalization; (2) however, patients whose therapists exhibited high levels of genuineness, accurate empathy, and unconditional positive regard showed significant positive personality and behavior change; and (3) patients whose therapists offered low levels of these conditions showed deterioration in personality and behavioral functioning. Thus, the three therapist conditions were found to be related to therapy outcome, but since some therapists did not provide the three conditions to some patients, the average treated subject appeared similar to the average control subject (Truax & Mitchell, 1971).

In addition to this large-scale evaluation of the client-centered approach, numerous studies with more specific foci have been conducted. According to Truax and Mitchell (1971), when these studies are taken together they suggest that helping professionals who are accurately empathic, unconditionally positive, and genuine are indeed effective therapists. These findings seem to be consistent across a variety of patient types, a variety of therapist orientations, and a variety of therapeutic settings. Figure 12-1 depicts Truax and Mitchell's summary of an earlier study (Truax, Wargo, Frank, Imber, Battle, Hoehn-Saric, Nash, & Stone, 1966) that had investigated therapist empathy, genuineness, and warmth as related to therapy outcome. The client with the single most improvement was assigned a value of 100% and the change in each other client was described as a percentage of that. The two groups that are compared are those clients that received a high degree of the three therapist conditions (summed together) versus those that received low levels of the therapist conditions. As can be seen in Figure 12-1, the majority of the clients who improved had received high levels of therapist warmth, genuineness, and accurate empathy.

However, a more recent review by Mitchell, Bozarth, and Krauft (1977) reevaluated the research concerning the relationship between empathy, unconditional positive regard, and genuineness and therapeutic outcome, and concluded that *"the relationship between the interpersonal skills and client outcome has not been investigated adequately, and, consequently, nothing definitive can be said about the relative efficacy of high and low levels of empathy, warmth, and genuineness"* (p. 488, authors' italics). Mitchell et al. (1977) support this position by noting that few studies demonstrated that their therapists were truly high or low in these three skills, and that fewer than 25% of all analyses from all studies did in fact support the effectiveness of the therapeutic conditions. It must be noted that empathy, regard, and genuineness were measured by trained observers' ratings in these studies, and studies that use a more theoretically relevant measurement source—the *client's* perception of therapist empathy, warmth, and genuineness—do consistently find these therapeutic conditions to be predictive of positive therapy outcomes in several types of therapy (Gurman, 1977). However, clients who tend to perceive therapists as empathic, warm, and genuine may differ *a priori* from those who do not and hence may do better whether or not they actually re-

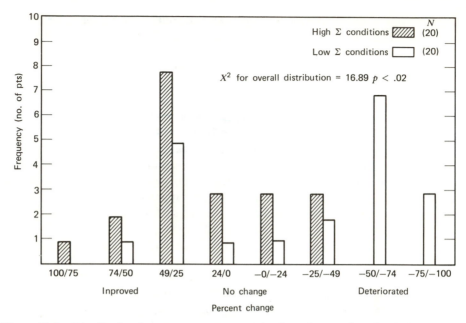

Figure 12-1   Distribution in outcome measures: Number of cases changing in higher versus lower sum of conditions for Johns Hopkins outpatients. From C. B. Truax and K. M. Mitchell, Research on certain therapist interpersonal skills in relation to process and outcome. In A. E. Bergin and S. L. Garfield (Eds.), *Handbook of psychotherapy and behavior change.* New York: Wiley, 1971. Copyright 1971 by John Wiley & Sons, Inc. Reprinted by permission of John Wiley & Sons, Inc.

ceive client-centered therapy. It is also possible that clients who improve may, as a result, feel that their therapists were warm and empathic. Thus, the evidence in support of the Rogerian therapeutic conditions is mixed. When one considers all the data, there is some evidence to suggest that empathy, warmth, and genuineness may be important factors in effective psychotherapy but the evidence is not conclusive.

EXISTENTIAL THERAPY

The existential approach to therapy is philosophically based upon the writing of several "existentialists" such as Kierkegaard (1954), Buber (1948), and Heidegger (1963). Focusing on each individual's psychological experience of his or her own existence, therapists of an existential orientation seek to analyze the patient's "human condition." Therapists are enjoined to avoid theoretical entanglements so as to accept the client's personal experience of the current world and to more fully understand the "being" of the client. The "being" is the inner nature, the uniquenesses, the special values, and human unity. Existential therapy is nonacademic, nonscientific, nontheoretical, and often not concerned with the details of the specific therapy that is utilized. The emphasis is rather on achieving therapeutic understanding of the client's mode of immediate existence. The therapist's role is that of a deeply aware, authentic, and understanding individual who helps clients to lead themselves to initiate their own therapeutic changes in their inner selves.

The therapist helps clients to focus more fully and actively on their feelings, thoughts, behaviors, and environment through what Gendlin (1979) calls *focusing instructions*:

> *Focusing instructions, instead of telling people to do something that only invites their same manner once again, tells them something totally different they can do. They are asked to pay attention and wait . . . (so as to live) in the body's own manner, rather than in the usual ways. . . . One receives and accepts, with some kind of interest, whatever comes up. . . . Psychotherapy is based on the assumption that if one talks about, and becomes aware of, one's unlovely aspects, these will change. . . . if one can remain and respond peaceably, both to one's own reactions, whatever they are, and to the other person's, if one can give the other person room for whatever comes up, however unlovely, then what will eventually come up will be helpful. (pp. 356–357)*

For example, Gendlin (1979) described a brief case example:

> *One client complained of a persistent feeling of tension in his chest. The therapist said, "Let yourself feel everything that goes with that tension, all of its meaning and feeling quality." . . . Several times the client tried but failed to let himself get closer to it. "I hate it," he said, in explanation of why it was difficult for him to feel all that went with the tension. The therapist said, "You have to approach it in a friendly way. Welcome it in so we can ask what all goes with it." This time the method succeeded and the client sat quietly for a moment. When he spoke again, he said, "It's funny, but when I welcome it, I feel it dissolving." (pp. 355–356)*

Thus, clients are helped to overcome problems by accepting their troublesome feelings and living more fully rather than attempting to fight or avoid life.

Frankl (1959) developed a similar existential approach called *logotherapy*. In this approach, therapists focus on helping clients to overcome feelings of meaninglessness ("existential vacuum") by exploring "spiritual" issues such as their values and life goals. Clients are aided in finding meaning and importance in even the smallest or most painful experiences.

Two practical techniques are at the heart of logotherapy: dereflection and paradoxical intention. Dereflection is used when clients are pressuring themselves to perform, for instance in sex, to the point where the natural desire to achieve pleasure for self and partner becomes an anxiety-evoking obsession. Clients are asked to "dereflect" by focusing instead on the pleasurable (or painful) feelings that occur naturally, so that spontaneous positive interactions can occur.

In contrast, paradoxical intention requires clients to focus in an exaggerated fashion on unpleasant feelings or situations in order to reduce the fear that such events will be catastrophic. For example, Frankl (1959) describes telling a client who feared excessive perspiration to try and show people how much he could sweat on purpose. The result was that the client was able to overcome the fear that had bothered him for quite some time.

Unlike traditional psychoanalysts who view human desires and conflicts as neurotic hangups, existentialists accept these at face value and consider them simply a part of life. Also in contrast with traditional psychoanalysts, existential therapists work in the present and downplay the past.

Existential therapists put their faith in human freedom and reject notions of determinism. Accordingly, clients are invited to take responsibility for changing themselves. Existential therapy is a description of a form of interpersonal interaction, a system that does not deliberately try to change the patient but rather seeks to understand the patient and *allow* the patient to change.

Research Evaluation

The approach to therapy taken by the existentialists has not been evaluated through scientific inquiry. Although the dearth of research in this area leaves the question of the efficacy of the treatment unanswered, existential therapists would be neither impressed nor depressed by either positive or negative outcomes because they discount entirely such scientific methods and their results.

GESTALT THERAPY

The theme of gestalt therapy has consistently centered on the promotion of the individual's growth processes and "human potential." Perls (1969), the founder of gestalt therapy, speaks of becoming real, learning to take a stand, and understanding the basis of existence—"you are you and I am I."

The notions of gestalt psychology were very influential to Perls' thinking. As a science of perception, gestalt principles include "closure" (the tendency to perceive figures as complete when they are actually incomplete), and the relationship of figures (salient features) and ground (background). Perls captured the implications of these perceptual phenomenon for psychotherapy. For example, people naturally seek closure: when an experience is incomplete it demands the attention of the person. Clients will return to important themes in their lives because these themes represent unfinished business demanding closure. Figure-ground relationships, where things that are important for the client will stand out while other aspects of the environment will fall into the background, suggest that problems may occur because a person or an issue psychologically in the background for a client needs to be seen more clearly as an important part of the client's life.

Gestalt principles also include the belief in human motivation to be self-actualized. People are seen as seeking to have their bodily, emotional, and thought processes in unison and to be aware of all of these activities. People feel a psychological havoc when they lose awareness of how and why their bodies, feelings, thoughts, or behavior are as they are, when there are unfinished activities that seek closure, or when the self is dichotomized or fragmented and the individual identifies with only a part of him or herself.

A fundamental goal of the gestalt approach is to produce growth through personal *awareness*. Awareness is viewed as a full understanding of all that is being sensed, felt, and thought within the person. Because such awareness can only be achieved in the "here-and-now," it is the therapist's job to assist clients to realize why and how their behavior is as it is right in the therapy session. Awareness in the here-and-now cannot be programmed or forced, so the gestalt therapist tries to reach this goal through facilitating the person's own needs for actualization.

A second goal is to achieve integration. Complete integration includes closure of unfinished business, recognition of all parts of the self, and unity of verbal and nonverbal behaviors.

The gestalt therapist has a series of techniques or exercises that are used to achieve the goals. For one, the therapist has to set an "aware" example for the client. The therapist actively participates and demonstrates awareness of behavior. At times, for the sake of demonstration, the therapist will exaggerate and do to clients what the therapist perceives clients to be doing to themselves. Gestalt therapists also focus attention on the congruence of verbal and nonverbal behavior. For example, imagine a young female client who is slouched back in the chair, one leg is across the arm of the chair, while one hand is stroking her knee. At the same time she is saying that she's not a seductress and that she doesn't try to be sexy. The therapist would highlight the discrepancy between the verbal and the nonverbal behavior: "Look at what you are doing right now, look at the way you are sitting, do you know that you are stroking your leg? What do these positions suggest?"

Clients may also be aided to role play both positions in a dialogue between themselves and their conflicted feelings or significant others. The therapist may have a client sit in one chair to portray themselves, and then change chairs and "become" their spouse, parent, or painful feeling, in each case conversing with the other person or feeling in the "empty chair." Similarly, dreams can be acted out with the client playing two or more roles in the dream (see Highlight 12-3).

Highlight 12-3   An Excerpt from Gestalt Therapy: The Therapist Is Fritz Perls

MARY: Did you want a dream? (laughter)

FRITZ: You see, the first step is—I always listen especially to the first sentence. In the first sentence she put responsibility on to me.

M: All right. I'm in a—there's sort of a war going on, and I'm in Ohio and I'm trying to get home to Michigan, to Grand Rapids. And ah—it's like the second world war—you know, you gotta show the ID and everything—or like movies I saw of the second world war. For some reason I haven't got the ID and I'm with another woman; I don't know who this woman is, I can't remember. But anyway we have an awful time and we're arranging to go across Lake Erie, and we snuck in like we were the French underground or something. And I'm trying to get—I'm trying to get home is the main thing, and I can't seem to get there. That's it.

F: Okeh. Can you play the frustrator here?

M: Frustrator?

F: Yah, You see, there are two kinds of dreams: wish-fulfillment, in the Freudian sense, and there are frustration dreams—nightmares. You can already see how full of frustration this dream is. You try to get home and something always prevents you. But at the same time, it's your dream—you are frustration yourself. So play the frustrator, "Mary, I don't let you get home. I put obstacles in your way.''

M: O.K. I'm not gonna let you get home . . . just keep talking?

F: Yah. It's *your* frustrating part of yourself. Get this out. See how well you can frustrate Mary to prevent her from getting home.

M: Gee, I don't know. Ah—well you gotta take this route or that route or—or some other way, and I'm going to keep you from getting there. I'm not gonna let you remember how to get there, I'm going to get you doing too many other things to get there—too many other activities. I'm not gonna let you cross the lake. . . I'm just gonna keep you all up tight— (puts up right hand as if pushing away).

F: Do this again.

M: I'm gonna keep you from doing it.

F: Do this to Mary.

M: Do it to me?

F: Yah, sure. You're the frustrator.

M: All right, stay back where you are. Don't go ahead.

F: Now change seats and be Mary.

M: But I wanna go ahead.

F: Say this again. . .

M: But I want to get there. . .

F: Change seats.

M: I'm not gonna let you. I'm too angry at you. I am not going to let you get there. . .

F: Go on writing the script. Go on with the dialogue.

M: Back and forth? /F: Yah./ I'm not sure where I'm going at the moment. Ah. . .

F: What's your right hand doing? I've noticed it a few times.

M: What's my what?

F: Right hand doing?

M: It's scratching my head because I—I . . . Well, I think where I wanna get is, I—I want to find, to get to myself. That's the home.[3]

In this sample of Gestalt therapy we find Perls, the therapist, conversing with Mary, the client, about a dream. Perls spends time dealing with the content and meaning of the dream, but more importantly, has the client get into the role of the person in the dream. The client takes two positions, the frustrator and the frustrated, and acts out the interaction. The therapist stays in the ''here and now'' so that the client will gain from the actual in-session experiences that are being generated based on the content of the dream. His goal is to help the client resolve some ''unfinished business'' by acting out her dream.

[3]From F. S. Perls, *Gestalt Therapy Verbatim*. Moab, Utah: Real People Press, 1969, 213–215. Copyright 1969, Real People Press. Reprinted by permission.

Gestalt therapists do not interpret what the client says during the exercises. Instead, gestalt therapists focus on client's nonverbal expressions (e.g., tone of voice, posture) and comment on what they hear and see in order to increase the client's awareness. If the therapist's feedback does not result in increased awareness or change, the therapist may challenge the client to get more involved in the exercises. While gestalt therapists seem to agree with client-centered therapists that accurate empathy is important, gestalt therapists are more actively concerned with increasing the client's awareness, integration, and personal responsibility.

Research Evaluation

There are few scientific inquiries into the nature and effect of gestalt therapy. Most reports deal with growth experiences in persons who are not seeking therapy. Conclusions drawn from the few studies of the gestalt approach are not entirely encouraging, and are mostly based on group therapy (see Chapter 14).

PLAY THERAPY WITH CHILDREN

Play therapy has been practiced in a variety of ways with individual children. As in many of the adult therapies, there are differing theoretical rationales for the use of play therapy. However, most advocates would agree that play, an expressive activity that often captures the child's attention and effort, can be used to tap the emotions that are pent up within the child. Through play, the child may be capable of expressing feelings that may otherwise remain painfully hidden.

Another area of agreement among many play therapists is the use of play sessions to assess the problems of the individual child. Children may be asked to draw pictures, play with dolls or other toys, make up stories, or play and listen to music in order to help them reveal their inner feelings and conflicts, much as adults are given projective tests or asked to free associate.

Play therapists differ in their *directiveness*. Directive play therapists take an active role by selecting toys, stating rules, and making interpretations. Nondirective play therapists refrain from setting constraints and making interpretations, giving the child greater responsibility for action and reaction.

Directive Play Therapy

The directive play therapy technique of Klein (1932) is derived largely from psychoanalytic notions. Klein contends that through the observation of children's play one can derive the origin of the child's sense of guilt. Through play, Klein believes the child symbolically expresses desires, fantasies and true-life experiences, thus releasing inner tension. As the therapy sessions proceed, Klein makes interpretations of the child's behavior and shares these with him or her. For example, she might tell the child who just broke a toy "You did that to get back at your parents." The goal of the interpretative play is to assist the child in achieving an acceptance of self and reality.

The similarity of this psychoanalytic approach to adult psychoanalysis is evident in Klein's (1932) statement:

> . . . the main principles of analysis are the same. Consistent interpretation, steady resolution of the resistances, constant reference back to the transference, whether positive or negative, to earlier situations—these establish and maintain a correct analytic situation with the child no less than with the adult. (pp. 35-36)

Play activity is considered to be the language of the child, and just as the psychoanalytically oriented therapist guides talking therapy with adults, Klein recommends a guiding approach with children.

A second proponent of directive play therapy is Anna Freud (1946b), although she would not totally agree with Klein that child psychotherapy is similar to adult psychotherapy because she does not view the play activity of the child as the same as the adult's verbal free associations. Anna Freud states that the child is too young to accept therapist's interpretations and she relies less on the symbolic meanings of children's play.

Nondirective Play Therapy

In marked contrast to the directive play therapist's concern for the psychoanalytic process, the nondirective play therapist takes a more child-centered approach. Both Axline (1947) and Moustakas (1973) are supporters of the nondirective, child-centered strategies of play therapy.

Axline (1947) maintains that each child has a drive for self-realization, and that this self-realization signifies a strength and maturity that is built on independence. Axline recommends that the play setting be designed so that the children have the opportunity to express themselves freely and without constraint, and that the playroom should be secure for the child and should help build the child's trust in the therapist. Axline prescribes a permissive and accepting therapist, and would not even direct the child to a toy to play with. The therapist's role is to encourage personal growth by helping the child make independent decisions consistently throughout the therapy. Central to Axline's nondirective play therapy are the following basic principles: child-therapist rapport, a permissive and accepting environment, the child leads the session, and the therapist refrains from prompting the child.

The therapeutic play described by Moustakas (1973) is child centered and oriented to developing a positive child-therapist relationship—much like Axline's procedures. Moustakas considers three attributes to be important in the therapy process: faith, acceptance, and respect. Faith is communicated by the therapist allowing the child to take the directing role in the play sessions. Acceptance centers around the therapist's permissiveness and the absence of standards in the playroom. Finally, respect is achieved when the child recognizes that the therapist genuinely cares about his or her welfare.

These approaches to nondirective play therapy are similar to the nondirective therapy espoused by Rogers. Theoretical rationales for nondirective therapy with both children and adults are based upon the notion of self-actualization. However, some clinicians question this viewpoint on the ground that permissiveness may teach the child that it is acceptable to act out without self control or concern for other persons. For example, behavior therapists suggest that the child's environment should be structured and consistent in order for the child to learn what is and what is not acceptable behavior. Since the research literature contains few controlled studies of the efficacy of play therapy, little can be said about the scientific status of these methods. Some evidence does suggest that severely disturbed children are not likely to show as marked improvements as a result of play therapy as they would from a more structured behavioral approach (Ney, Palvesky, & Markely, 1971).

In tracing the recent history of therapeutic approaches with children, Davids (1975) points out that the traditional schedule of two one-hour sessions of play therapy per week is no longer typical. Although play therapy from the psychoanalytic perspective was once believed to be the essential aspect of child treatment (circa 1950s-early 1960s), current treatment approaches are more likely to emphasize the family and the use of more structured behavior therapy principles.

CRISIS INTERVENTION/BRIEF THERAPY

Unlike the interventions with individuals that have been described thus far, crisis interventions are designed to be brief and to be implemented in times of emergency; when the pressure of the stress may be leading to what laypersons call a "breakdown." The therapist is typically concerned first with the alleviation of the current psychological crisis. Such brief therapies have been undertaken from a variety of therapeutic systems (Butcher & Maudel, 1976), but most efforts can be classified as either psychoanalytic, behavioral (see Chapter 13), systems (see Chapter 14), or crisis oriented (Butcher & Koss, 1978).

In the psychoanalytically oriented brief therapy, the therapist continues to use interpretations, but they are more concerned with the present problem than with childhood experiences (Alexander & French, 1948; Horowitz, 1979). Nevertheless, the therapist does try to provide the client with some understanding of why the person is having the problem. For example, Merrill and Cary (1975) discuss the use of interpreting dreams to facilitate adjustment in brief psychotherapy.

Within the crisis-oriented therapies, four levels of intervention are described (Butcher & Koss, 1978; Jacobson, Strickler, & Morley, 1968). At the first level the therapist serves as a referral source, helping clients to find an appropriate psychological or medical treatment service. At the second level the helper provides support by listening to the client, so as to help the client regain a sense of self-worth and support. The third level is characterized by the therapist's seeking to solve the specific crisis—without reference to the client's personality. For example, the therapist might assist a client through an unpleasant and upsetting LSD trip, but without trying to modify the person's drug-dependent personality. The fourth level deals with understanding the person and helping the person to understand why the problem has developed. In this case, for example, the therapist may focus on the problem of an abused child and also on the client's understanding of the reasons for the child abuse.

The level of the intervention in the case of a crisis is sometimes determined by the length of contact that the therapist and client expect to have. Regardless of the level of the intervention, however, crisis intervention is an important component of the clinical psychologist's social function (see Highlight 12-4). By helping clients to overcome temporary problems due to divorce, death, or natural disaster, the public is shown the utility of clinical services.

Highlight 12-4   Crisis Intervention: Two Cases

EXAMPLE 1

Paul, a middle-aged man, was brought to the crisis center from the hospital's emergency room by security guards. Paul had gone to the emergency room after he learned that his wife had been taken there following a suicide attempt. When he arrived at the crisis center he was very angry and unable to say anything other than "Why, why did she do something so stupid?" He was gradually able to calm down and relate his story.

He and his wife, Marie, had an argument earlier in the evening when he wanted to have a drink with friends. Paul left the house and when he returned neither Marie nor his children were there. The police arrived shortly (they were looking for the pills Marie had taken) and took Paul to the hospital. By that time, Marie, who was 8½ months pregnant, had been admitted to the intensive care unit of the hospital. Paul was tremulous, had difficulty organizing his thoughts, and difficulty deciding what to do next. At that point the security guard suggested he get help from the crisis center.

The crisis center psychologist aided Paul in determining what he needed to do: (1) locate his children, (2) get information about his wife's condition, (3) get transportation home. She was also able to get him to talk about his feelings and eventually gain control over them. Whenever Paul would direct the conversation toward solving his longstanding marital problems or the futility of trying to solve his problems, the psychologist would redirect the session to the more pressing, immediate problems (e.g., how his children were, what he was going to do the rest of the evening). Paul went home in his wife's car after about two hours in the crisis center, planning to get some sleep and to pick up his children at his neighbor's house in the morning.

The psychologist followed up with several phone calls over the next week. Marie had her baby and both were in good condition. The psychologist gave Paul several referrals for marital therapy and he agreed to contact them, although he had not done so at the last follow-up call.

EXAMPLE 2

Eva first came to the crisis center at 4 A.M., the morning after she had admitted her husband George to the hospital. George was dying of cancer. Eva was brought to the hospital's Emergency Room for a "nervous heart," a condition she stated was apt to get worse while under stress. The doctors in the emergency room determined no physical basis for her complaint and referred her to the crisis center. Eva was judged to be in situational stress and was given a three-day supply of a sleeping medication by the crisis center's psychiatrist. Eva was told that she could come back to the crisis center if she needed to and several follow-up contacts were planned.

Eva returned later that same afternoon. She had just visited George and became sick when he vomited blood. She was feeling guilty about not being able to stay with him. A psychiatric nurse spent over an hour with her, offering her an opportunity to discuss her feelings. The psychiatrist again evaluated her and gave her a week's supply of a minor tranquilizer (Valium). Close phone contact was maintained over the next few days.

Four days later Eva returned to the crisis center. Her husband George had just died. Eva was unable to locate her daughter who had promised to make all the funeral arrangements. Eva "just didn't know what to do" and was afraid she would have trouble with her heart. Although her son was present, Eva appeared to want to talk with someone other than family.

Eva was then interviewed by a psychologist. She cried several times during the session, but later appeared to be responding fairly well to the stress. She expressed much concern about her heart, and feared that she was "going crazy." The psychologist reassured her that she was not "going crazy," but that she was experiencing normal anxiety and grief similar to what many people felt when they experienced a loss. After consultation with a physician, Eva's dosage of Valium was increased temporarily. She was told the Valium should help her feelings of nervousness and heart palpitations. The psychologist suggested that if she were unable to sleep during the night, that she should not worry about it but get up and talk with the many relatives staying with her.

An attempt was made to keep Eva functioning independently of mental health professionals and to have her rely on her friends and relatives for support during her grief period. The psychologist arranged for Eva's daughter to meet her at the crisis center and later take her home. However, it was emphasized that both Eva and her daughter could return if she felt a need. If she had returned to the crisis center, she would have been referred to a mental health center for more long-term care. A last follow-up phone call was made. Eva reported that she had been able to talk with some of her relatives and was feeling somewhat better.

These examples, from Williams (1978), illustrate the immediacy of the client's psychological problems and the therapist's need to keep a focus on the problem at hand.

Research Evaluation

There has, to date, been little systematic research into the efficacy of crisis intervention efforts (Auerbach & Kilmann, 1977). Moreover, surveys indicate that many crisis centers are lax in gathering the necessary follow-up data for evaluation (Bloomfield, Levy, Kotelchuck, & Handleman, 1971). Nevertheless, there has been some relevant research concerning telephone hotlines for suicide prevention, and the provision of crisis-oriented therapy for emergency psychiatric patients.

Shneidman and Farberow (1968) have described the development of the Los Angeles Suicide Prevention Center and this model program has served as the impetus for many other crisis programs throughout the United States. There are, however, several problems in researching the effectiveness of suicide prevention crisis centers. Should accurate referral be the primary goal of the crisis center (McGee, 1974)? Should clients be considered failures if they do not show up for appointments that they have scheduled? The prime goal of crisis therapy is the patient's self-reported emotional state: that is, does the patient report feeling less in crisis after having received the intervention? One study (Knickerbocker, 1973) examined the phone caller's level of anxiety and depression during the first and last 30 seconds of the call and found that a reduction in the caller's negative emotional states was related to the quality of the relationship established by the crisis worker. Unfortunately, few evaluations of crisis hotlines have employed measures of client change or satisfaction (Auerbach & Kilmann, 1977).

Direct face-to-face crisis service can be provided for clients who seek help at psychiatric hospitals. For example, Gottschalk, Fox, and Bates (1973) assigned clients who came to a crisis intervention clinic to either a crisis oriented treatment or a waiting list control. Both groups showed comparable improvement after six weeks on a rating scale completed by a trained interviewer. However, the use of a waiting list control is not especially appropriate for crisis therapy evaluation since many of the clients may have sought help elsewhere during the waiting period or the crisis could have resolved itself (spontaneous remission) during the six weeks.

In a series of studies, Langsley and colleagues have evaluated the effectiveness of family crisis intervention in comparison to inpatient psychiatric treatment (Langsley, Flomenhaft, & Machotka, 1969; Langsley, Pittman, Machotka, & Flomenhaft, 1968). Clients, all of whom would have potentially been admitted as inpatients, were either given crisis therapy (for an average of 24 days) in which they stayed in their homes, or the inpatient treatment. While the two groups showed comparable degrees of improvement on measures of personal adjustment and social adjustment, crisis clients were reported to have returned to their jobs sooner, to have required fewer days of later hospitalization, and to have been meaningfully less expensive than the subjects who received hospitalization. It should be noted that while this treatment was crisis oriented and dealt with the client for only a few visits (average of 4.2), there were phone calls (5.4), and home visits (1.3), and that the treatment did cover a 24-day span.

Crisis Intervention With Children

A recent example of crisis intervention with children was reported by Dallas (1978) to describe the services that were provided following an incident where a son murdered (stabbed to death) his father in front of some 50 children witnesses.

Within a few hours after the incident had occurred, those organizing the crisis intervention stopped regular classes and had the teachers lead discussion groups. These discussion groups were designed to allow the children to openly express their feelings. In addition, parents were told to consider altering a vast array of events, including the route the child took to school, having fathers come home from out-of town business trips, and canceling summer camp plans to be replaced by family vacations.

Although Dallas should be commended for the efforts that were put forth to help those persons involved, this example of crisis intervention is not without criticism. For instance, was the "total push" approach, which involved all students (not just witnesses), parents, and teachers, necessary or called for? Glenwick, Jason, Copeland, and Stevens (1979) pointed out that perhaps less global, more focused services might have been more effective and economical. Glenwick et al. also questioned the "catharsis" model that was employed. The "catharsis" model suggests that allowing children to ventilate, experience, and express their feeling will provide a needed outlet. The criticism is that having involved all children and having focused so much attention on the event may have further sensitized the children to the murder rather than helping them to cope with this event. Also, the lengthy discussion groups may also have increased the likelihood that the children would nonadaptively dwell on the event.

Glenwick et al. suggested a different approach, emphasizing the identification of children needing assistance (or at risk), providing individualized services for those children, and evaluating the intervention. Such a proposal is more in line with the scientist-professional model because of the focus on proper subject identification, provision of individualized service, and evaluation of the crisis intervention.

FACTORS INFLUENCING THE OUTCOME OF INDIVIDUAL INTERVENTIONS

Several reviews have been written to summarize the existing research (Highlight 12-5) on evaluation of nonbehavioral therapy (e.g., Baekeland & Lundwall, 1975; Bergin & Lambert, 1978; Garfield, 1978; Luborsky, Singer, & Luborsky, 1975; Meltzoff & Kornreich, 1970; Parloff, Waskow, & Wolfe, 1978; Wilkins, 1977). Therapist factors, client factors, and therapy process factors are variables that may interact with treatment method to determine therapy outcome (Kiesler, 1966).

Highlight 12-5   The Effectiveness of Psychotherapy: An Historical Controversy

In a stimulating and controversial article published in 1952, Eysenck reviewed the available literature on the evaluations of therapy and concluded that the data had failed to prove that psychotherapy facilitates the recovery of neurotic patients. Instead, he stated, "two-thirds of a group of neurotic patients will recover or improve to a marked extent within about two years of the onset of their illness, whether they are treated by means of psychotherapy or not" (p. 322). Thus, Eysenck concluded that certain people with neuroses or behavior disorders appear to improve significantly without the benefit of psychotherapy, and he called this "spontaneous remission." The argument being made was that psychotherapy should be considered effective only when therapeutic efforts result in treatment gains that are appreciably greater than the gains that result from spontaneous remission.

While this argument is a sound one, there is some controversy surrounding the evidence that Eysenck presented to support the spontaneous recovery rate.

Two studies were used to establish the "base rate" (i.e., percent of persons who show spontaneous remission; Landis, 1937 and Denker, 1946, 1947). Landis' report considered the discharge rate of hospitalized neurotics and suggested that 72% were discharged as recovered or improved. Although these individuals were hospitalized, the assumption is that they received essentially custodial care and no psychotherapy. Denker's estimate was based on the improvement seen in disability claimants who were suffering from psychoneurosis and who were treated by general practitioners. Although the general practitioners were likely to use sedatives, suggestions, and reassurances to treat their patients, there was no attempt "at anything but the most superficial type of psychotherapy" (Eysenck, 1952). Denker's results included the finding that, in all, 72% of the cases recovered.

These conclusions regarding spontaneous remission have been questioned for a variety of reasons. For example, Subotnik (1972) considered spontaneous remission to be nothing but artifact and that these artifacts result from the use of poor criteria and misleading statistics. Subotnik also suggested that what appears as spontaneous remission may be cyclical variations that are part of the disorders themselves—the "fluctuation hypothesis." The spontaneous remission rate reported in Eysenck's paper has also been criticized for lumping all the neurotic disorders together and for assuming that the changes reported in Landis and Denker were not due to other events, events that might have been similar to psychotherapy (e.g., seeing a clergyman) (Bergin, 1971).

In a recent consideration of the spontaneous remission issue, Bergin and Lambert (1978) reviewed 34 studies and presented their data in two summary tables: one for studies where subjects received minimal treatment and a second for studies where subjects were untreated. The average spontaneous remission rate from the minimal treatment studies was 43% (range from 18 to 67 percent). From the untreated studies, a 50% rate was identified. Bergin and Lambert (1978) proposed that a two-thirds (66%) spontaneous remission estimate is unrepresentative and unrealistic.

Although the Eysenck (1952) article is over 25 years old and has been said to have used a dubious methodology, the question it raised remains important. The issue is not so much whether psychotherapy is effective, but more a question of the efficacy of psychotherapy in comparison to base rates of improvement. Future research must continue to address this issue.

Therapist Factors

Research on therapist factors that are related to therapy outcome has not yet been very productive. Literally dozens of personality variables have been investigated, but no one has yet been able to identify the personality characteristics of "good" or "bad" therapists. This is not surprising in view of the global nature of the personality measures used, and because many promising characteristics (e.g., tolerance of ambiguity; locus of control) have received little attention. Two promising predictors have been identified, although they await cross validation: personal values that favor an egalitarian and optimistic approach toward other persons

(Lerner, 1973) and credibility as seen by the client (Beutler, Johnson, Neville, El-kins, & Jobe, 1975).

In a recent review of the research on therapist variables related to the outcome of psychotherapy, Parloff et al. (1978) concluded that "the therapist variables most frequently selected by the researcher for study are, unfortunately, such simplistic, global concepts as to cause this field to suffer from possible terminal vagueness" (p. 273). Parloff et al. (1978) pointed out that variables such as personality, sex, experience, and race are not likely to be the relevant therapeutic variables that characterize therapists. Instead, factors such as the congruence of client and therapist values, expectations, and cognitive styles, are viewed as offering a more promising research direction (Berzins, 1977; Parloff et al., 1978).

Client Factors

Client factors have been more extensively researched than therapist factors, but with equally unclear results. Again, personality variables are poor or at best inconsistent predictors of outcome, although adequacy of overall personality functioning (Luborsky, Chandler, Auerbach, Cohen, & Bachrach, 1971) and ego strength (Lerner, 1973; Meltzoff & Kornreich, 1970) have shown promise. Socioeconomic status, motivation, and expectancy of gain are factors that have received mixed but generally positive support as predictors of outcome. Mixed and inconclusive data have appeared in evaluations of IQ, age, education, and initial level of psychological disturbance. Sex, marital status, race, and social environment have either not received sufficient research or have been generally shown to be poor predictors of therapy outcome. As a result, the clinician cannot, as yet, turn to any single client variable and make confident predictions about therapy outcome. Research on client-therapist similarity in personality, values, socioeconomic status, and A-B status (Highlight 12-6), while still equivocal, appears to be a fruitful direction (Berzins, 1977; Parloff et al., 1978). Nevertheless, there are certain client characteristics that therapists consider a part of the "ideal client" (Schofield, 1964): young, educated, and married females (see Table 12-1).

Highlight 12-6   A- and B-Type Therapists

In studying the experience of psychotherapy with schizophrenic patients, Whitehorn and Betz (1960; see also Betz, 1962) researched the personality characteristics of therapists who were highly successful versus those therapists whose success rate was very poor. They found that they could differentiate between the two groups based on their responses to the Strong Vocational Interest Blank. A 23-item measure, the A-B scale, was developed from the items on the Strong Vocational Interest Blank. "A" therapists score high on items relating to occupations involving public service, and have been characterized by active participation in therapy and an ability to establish a trusting relationship. "B" therapists, in contrast, score high on items for mechanical aptitude and are sometimes described as tending toward passive permissiveness and the use of interpretations and instructions in therapy. "A" therapists were found to be more successful with schizophrenic clients than "B" therapists.

The A-B distinction was clouded when McNair, Callahan, and Lorr (1962) reported that for a sample of outpatients, "B" therapists produced better outcomes. Although this finding apparently contradicted earlier results of Whitehorn and Betz, the subject populations that were treated in the two studies were different: McNair et al. (1962) were working with predominantly *neurotic* patients. These findings, in combination, led to the *interaction hypothesis*: "A" therapists work best with schizophrenics while "B" therapists work best with neurotics.

Reviews of the research have varied in their degree of enthusiasm for the A-B variable (Carson, 1967; Razin, 1971, 1977), but the more recent evidence does seem to seriously question the validity of the interaction hypothesis. For example, Tuma, May, Yale, and Forsythe (1978) reported that the A-B distinction made no significant contribution to the effective treatment of schizophrenia. Here again, further research is necessary to elucidate and evaluate an interesting, but as yet tentative, hypothesis concerning the optimal combination of therapists and clients.

Therapy Process

A final crucial determinant of therapy outcome is the process of therapy, that is, the specific behavioral interactions between client and therapist and the cognitive interpretations that client and therapist formulate about one another and their interaction. It might seem that different therapy treatments would require completely different therapist-client interactions, and this is to some extent true. However, there is evidence that therapists and clients can interact in very *similar* ways even when undergoing very different therapies. For instance, therapists of three different orientations (i.e., behavioral, analytic, humanistic) have been found to be comparable in their levels of empathy, warmth, and genuineness (e.g., Fischer, Paveza, Kickerts, Hubbard & Grayston, 1975). Furthermore,

Table 12-1 The Ideal Patient for Psychotherapy as Viewed by Three Professions

	Social Worker's Patient	Psychologist's Patient	Psychiatrist's Patient
Sex	Female[a]	Female[a]	Female
Age	20–40	20–40	20–40
Marital status	Married	Married-single[b]	Married
Education	High school plus	Some college or degree	Some college or degree
Occupation	(no clear preference)	Professional-managerial	Professional-managerial

From W. Schofield, *Psychotherapy: The purchase of friendship*. Copyright 1964, p. 131, Table 5. Reprinted by permission of Prentice-Hall, Inc., Englewood Cliffs, N.J.

[a]Slight margin of preference.

[b]Equally occurring preferences.

widely variable therapist-client interactions can occur even when all are involved in the same therapy treatment (e.g., Ford, 1978).

Therefore, the moment-to-moment interactions of client-therapist dyads have been examined as determinants of therapy outcome (Orlinsky & Howard, 1978). Relatively little research has focused on client behavior per se. No client-response mode has been found to be consistently related to positive or negative therapy outcomes, although the intensity and clarity of the client's focusing on personal issues (Gendlin, 1979) has shown some promise as a predictor. Research on therapist behavior is more prevalent (e.g., Ford, 1978; Marsden, 1971), but no conclusive findings have emerged.

Therapy process also includes the client's and therapist's perceptions of one another and the therapeutic relationship. Therapist perceptions have consistently been found to be unrelated to therapy outcome (e.g., Lerner & Fiske, 1973), but the client's perception of the therapeutic relationship has been found to be inversely related to client's dropping out and positively associated with the client's short-term gains, in a variety of therapy types (Gurman, 1977).

Summary

Despite extensive research, it seems that predictors of therapy outcome are difficult to identify (see Highlight 12-7). This may well be due to the fact that different factors will probably be predictive for different therapy types, therapy settings, client populations, and therapist populations. A recent study by Dougherty (1976) suggests that what we need is not a cookbook of universal predictors, but rather a methodology for empirically identifying optimal matchings of therapists, clients, therapy types and settings that can be efficiently utilized independently by the many different service settings to develop predictors that fit their unique groups of clients, therapists and treatment types. Dougherty developed and evaluated a system whereby a clinic's best and worst cases were examined each year to determine the client-therapist matchings that were repeatedly associated with success or failure. These results were then used to create client-therapist matchings during the subsequent year, and once again evaluated. In this way, a scientific-professional methodology can be established to promote effective therapy in any psychological clinic.

Premature Termination

The research on predictor's of one type of outcome—premature termination—is somewhat more encouraging. However, dropping out of therapy cannot automatically be given a negative valence since many clients who discontinue therapy before their therapists feel finished may have benefited greatly. Nevertheless, dropping out is generally seen in a negative light, and a comprehensive review of the empirical data by Baekeland & Lundwall (1975) identified three classes of predictors: socially isolated or unaffiliated clients; therapists who are ethnocentric, reluctant to utilize medications, introverts, and who dislike or are apathetic about the client and behave in a detached or unprofessional manner (e.g., frequently cancel appointments, fail to instruct clients adequately concerning medications);

Highlight 12-7   Fees and Therapy

According to Dightman (1970), a commonly held belief by practicing therapists is that having clients pay for their treatment will positively affect psychotherapy outcome. Different therapeutic rationales handle the issue somewhat differently but the psychoanalytic perspective is an illustrative example. From this vantage point, the client's having to pay for therapy is viewed as a symbolic commitment to therapy. With the current trend toward third-party payments (insurance for psychotherapy) the question of fee assessment becomes of special importance. If someone other than the client pays the fee, will this undermine therapy?

The question of fee assessment and psychotherapy outcome was addressed in a research project by Pope, Geller, and Wilkinson (1975). These researchers gathered data from the records of 434 clients who had received individual outpatient psychotherapy. They then examined whether the clients' fees, diagnoses, or socioeconomic statuses were predictive of three measures of outcome: number of appointments, attendance, and posttherapy adjustment. The fee variable consisted of no fee, welfare, insurance, scaled payment, and full payment. The diagnoses consisted of psychosis, neurosis, personality disorder, transient situational disturbance, and other. There were five levels of socioeconomic status.

Diagnosis was the only variable that was significantly related to therapy outcome, number of appointments, and attendance. Thus, when the effects of socioeconomic status and diagnosis are controlled for, fee, by itself, does not affect psychotherapy outcome.

Balch, Ireland, and Lewis (1977) also addressed the issue of the relationship of source of payment to the process of therapy, in this instance focusing on number of client contacts, length of stay, and type of discharge (i.e., agreed on by client and therapist or not). In their report, the source of payment was related to the clients' number of contacts and length of stay, with the relationship being one of *longer* stay and *increased* contact from those whose payments were made only in part by the client than when the client paid the entire fee!

In general, fee assessment does not appear related to outcome when diagnosis and socioeconomic status are accounted for. Furthermore, when a relationship does appear, it is *not* in the direction of personal payment facilitating therapy. These data have implications for the current increase in third-party payments for psychotherapy: having third-party payments should not have a deleterious effect on psychotherapy outcome. Moreover, DeMuth and Kamis (1980) studied the relationship of payment source to service utilization and found that third-party reimbursements did *not* lead to excessive utilization.

and cases where the therapist and client have discrepant initial expectations. These factors were found to be predictive of dropping out in every research study conducted to evaluate their effects. Several client factors were also effective predictors of dropping out in three-quarters or more of the available studies: drug dependence, passive-aggressive personality, independence, low motivation, a lack of psychological mindedness, sociopathy, and family system pathology. Finally, client age, sex, social stability, and socioeconomic status were predictive in only about 50% of the relevant investigations.

THE UNDESIRABLE EFFECTS OF THERAPY

If we assume that the psychotherapeutic enterprise has the ability to produce meaningful changes in those who participate as clients, then we must recognize that not all of the effects will necessarily be positive. Some outcomes for some clients may, unfortunately, be negative. Examples of possible negative effects are (1) a worsening of the symptoms for which the client sought treatment, (2) the appearance of new problems that were not evident prior to treatment, (3) the client's misuse or abuse of therapy, and (4) the loss of trust in the therapist or therapeutic process (see Hadley & Strupp, 1976). These undesirable effects of therapy have been termed "deterioration effects" (Bergin, 1963; 1971) or "negative effects" (Hadley, & Strupp, 1976) and fall in the general category of *iatrogenic effects* (i.e., problems that are *caused,* not cured, by treatment).

Some of the important evidence for deterioration effects comes from the careful examination of studies of the positive effects of psychotherapy. As Bergin (1966) has illustrated (see Figure 12-2), the average amount of change that occurs in the treatment and the control groups may not differ, but the amount of variability in the reactions of individual subjects may still differ meaningfully. The significant increase in the variability of changes seen in the treatment groups suggests that while some are getting better, others are deteriorating.

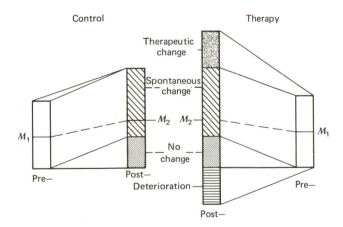

Figure 12-2 The deterioration effect. Schematic representation of pre- and post-test distributions of criterion scores in psychotherapy outcome studies. M = gm From A. E. Bergin, Some implications of psychotherapy research for therapeutic practice. *Journal of Abnormal Psychology*, 1966, *71*, 235–246. Copyright 1966 by the American Psychological Association. Reprinted by permission.

Summarizing a survey of the leading psychotherapists in the United States, Hadley and Strupp (1976) listed a variety of factors that their respondents said were associated with negative effects. This list included an inaccurate or deficient assessment, poor clinical judgment on the part of therapist, pretherapy weaknesses within the patient, misapplication of the therapeutic procedures, and problems within the patient-therapist relationship. Furthermore, more specific aspects of the treatment procedures were identified. These included false assumptions concerning therapy, expecting too much from therapy, overly intense therapy, misuse of interpretations or insights in therapy, and fostering an overdependency on therapy. Each of these concerns can be the source of the negative effects of psychotherapy.

Though the potential sources for iatrogenic effects are diverse, there is nevertheless, one common sentiment among the psychotherapists surveyed by Hadley and Strupp (1976); "Perhaps the most compelling finding of the survey was strong support of the need for systematic research into the problem of negative effects" (p. 1302). Negative effects occur (Bergin & Lambert, 1978), but research is needed to identify exactly when and for whom.

MEASURES OF THERAPEUTIC CHANGE

When a clinical psychologist asks the question, "Did the treatment procedures that I used show beneficial change for my client?" there must be a standard by which outcome can be judged. What are the best measures to use in the evaluation of psychotherapy? Although assessment measures should be sensitive to the specific type of clients and treatments being evaluated, several general recommendations, organized by the type of measure, appear valuable (Waskow & Parloff, 1975).

Personality Tests

In terms of psychological tests that measure relevant characteristics of the patient, Dalstrom (1975) recommends the California Psychological Inventory (CPI; Gough, 1957) and the Minnesota Multiphasic Personality Inventory (MMPI; Hathaway & McKinley, 1942) (see Chapter 8). The CPI is useful in that it contains measures of social reponsibility, effectiveness, sensitivity to others, impulse control, and stability. In addition, the CPI gives scores of social and emotional maturity. These measures, along with the entire list of characteristics measured by the CPI, should make the CPI a valuable tool in psychotherapy research. For purposes of evaluating client changes in the degree to which they were impaired or disturbed, the MMPI may be the instrument of choice.

Patient Self-Report

When the patient is used as the direct self-reporter of the effects of therapy, Imber (1975) and Cartwright (1975) both recommend the Hopkins Symptom Checklist (HSCL). The HSCL consists of 58 items that are characteristic complaints of psychiatric outpatients. On a four-point scale, the patient rates the extent to which each complaint has been bothersome. The checklist takes approximately 15 minutes for the patient to complete all the items and only a matter of a few minutes for the examiner to calculate several scores reflecting the type and intensity of the patient's dysfunctions.

A second patient-report measure is the Profile of Mood States (POMS), a 65-item adjective rating scale that requires the client to rate subjective aspects of affect and mood on a 1 to 5 scale (McNair, Lorr, & Droppleman, 1971). The client is told that the list includes a number of words that people use to describe their feelings, and is then instructed to indicate how he or she has been feeling over the past week including today. The results can be scored for six subscales representing six factors from a factor-analytic study: tension-anxiety, depression-dejection, confusion, anger-hostility, vigor, and fatigue.

Both of the self-report measures (symptom checklists) have some potential shortcomings. The client may present an unusual symptom or specific complaint that is not provided among those on the checklists. This requires that the clinician be alert to inquire if the client has any particularly unique or troublesome concerns or symptoms. These checklists also focus on the symptoms of dysfunction, and, while they may be sensitive to change in terms of the removal of dysfunctions, they are not useful for studies that seek to provide human growth experiences or life-enhancement training. Nevertheless, these checklists are useful instruments since have been shown to be relatively reliable, reasonably valid, and sensitive to the changes that result from several types of psychotherapy.

Projective Tests

Although the use of projective tests has decreased over the years, the Holtzman Inkblot Technique (HIT) and the Thematic Apperception Test (TAT) are considered to be the most useful projective measures for therapy outcome research (Endicott & Endicott, 1975). The HIT is considered more useful than the Rorschach because there are two alternate forms of the test that are matched on the major determinants of people's perceptions and because the test administration is more standardized. Also, only one response per card is required with the HIT. However, a moderately valid measure of ego strength can be obtained from the Rorschach (Lerner, 1973). Both TAT and HIT offer clinicians many intriguing assessment hypotheses, but less in the way of valid conclusions concerning therapy outcome.

Therapist Measures

The assessment of therapy outcome would be incomplete without a consideration of the therapist as a source of data regarding client change (Mintz, 1977). However, the therapist is not an unbiased observer and thus may not give entirely accurate evaluations. Biases notwithstanding, the clinical psychologist who provided the treatment is certainly in a good position to be aware of data from within the actual therapy and, as a trained observer, should be capable of providing accurate ratings.

Strupp and Bloxom (1975) recommend the Health-Sickness Rating Scale (Luborsky, 1962), which was developed by the Adult Psychotherapy Research Committee of the Menninger Clinic in order to provide therapists with a relatively simple instrument to record information about individual clients. The scale was devised to be useful in evaluating the changes observed in a single case over time and in the recording of the client's status when observed by a variety of professionals. There are several subscales to the Health-Sickness Rating Scale: ability to function autonomously, seriousness of symptoms, degree of discomfort, effect on the environment, utilization of abilities, quality of interpersonal relationships, and breadth and depth of interests. However, as Strupp and Bloxom (1975) point out, the subscales reflect the clinician-researcher's own value judgments about the criteria for mental health, and may not be a valid outcome measure for clients of other social and cultural backgrounds.

Strupp and Bloxom (1975) recommend that therapist ratings of the client's specific target complaints be utilized, as is done in Goal Attainment Scaling. Goal Attainment Scaling (Kiresuk & Sherman, 1968; Kiresuk & Lund, 1975) is a methodology for developing personalized and multivariable descriptions that can be used for setting objectives in therapy outcome (see also Mintz & Kiesler, 1982). The basic goal attainment scaling procedures relevant to outcome evaluation include (1) collecting information about the person for whom goals will be scaled, (2) specifying the major areas where change would be feasible and helpful, (3) developing specific predictions for each major area, and (4) scoring the outcomes at the conclusion of therapy. A sample goal attainment scale is provided in Figure 12-3.

In the first column of the goal attainment scale, the various goal attainment levels are described. These levels range from the most *unfavorable* treatment outcome to the most *favorable* treatment outcome. The remaining columns are for the client's different problem areas. After gathering information the client and therapist describe the most favorable and unfavorable outcomes for each problem, and intermediate outcomes as well. The middle of the range of attainment levels is labeled the expected level. This level is usually developed first and it should reflect the *most likely* outcome. Each outcome level is specified by an observable outcome that is hoped for within a specific period of therapy (e.g., six months). Therapy durations can vary and should be designed for the individual needs of the particular client and agency.

The goal-attainment scaling procedure allows the therapist to document the client's problems and predict possible outcomes and, when treatment is completed, to evaluate outcome with precision. The flexibility of the goal-attainment scaling procedure allows for its application to a wide variety of clients and in a diverse number of settings.

Ratings by Significant Others

People who interact with the client in his or her day-to-day environment are sources of valuable information about the effects of therapeutic interventions. As outlined by Fiske (1975), these peer rating assessments can be gathered by having the clinician interview one of the client's significant others, having the significant

Figure 12-3 Goal Attainment Follow-Up Guide

	Scale Headings and Scale Weights				
Scale Attainment Levels	Scale 1: Employment (Interest in work) self-report $(w_1 = 10)$	Scale 2: Self-concept (physical appearance) patient interview $(w_2 = 15)$	Scale 3: Interpersonal Relationships (in training program as judged by receptionist) (do not score if he does not go to training program. $(w_3 = 5)$	Scale 4: Interpersonal relationships (report of client's spouse) $(w_4 = 8)$	Scale 5: $(w_5 = \quad)$
a. Most unfavorable treatment outcome thought likely	Client states he does not want to ever work or train for work	Client (1) has buttons missing from clothes, (2) unshaven (but says he is growing beard), (3) dirty fingernails, (4) shoes unshined (if wearing shoes needing shine), (5) socks don't match	Never spontaneously talks to anyone. May answer if spoken to.	No friends and no close friends (i.e., "close" equals friends with which he can talk about serious, intimate topics and who he feels like his company)	
b. Less than expected success with treatment	Client states that he may want to work "someday" (a year or more later) but not now, and no training	4 of the above 5 conditions	Spontaneously talks to his own therapists or caseworkers, but no other clients	One person who is a friend or acquaintance but not a close friend	

Figure 12-3 *Continued*

Scale Attainment Levels	Scale Headings and Scale Weights				
	Scale 1: Employment (Interest in work) self-report $(w_1 = 10)$	Scale 2: Self-concept (physical appearance) patient interview $(w_2 = 15)$	Scale 3: Interpersonal Relationships (in training program as judged by receptionist) (do not score if he does not go to training program. $(w_3 = 5)$	Scale 4: Interpersonal relationships (report of client's spouse) $(w_4 = 8)$	Scale 5: $(w_5 = \ )$
c. Expected level of treatment success	Client states that he might be interested in working within the next 12 months, but only if no training is required	3 of the above 5 conditions	Spontaneously talks to therapists, caseworkers and one other client	Two or more persons who are friends, but not close friends	
d. More than expected success with treatment	Client states that he might be interested in working within the next 12 months and training for no more than 30 work days	2 of the above 5 conditions	Spontaneously talks to therapists, caseworkers and 2 or 4 other clients	One close friend, but no other friends	
e. Most favorable treatment outcome thought likely	Client states that he might be interested in working within the next 12 months. Will train for as many days as are necessary	One of the above 5 conditions	Spontaneously talks to therapists, caseworkers and 5 or more other clients	One or more close friend, plus one or more other friends or acquaintances	

Reprinted from P.E.P. Report, 1969–1973, Chapter 1, T. J. Kiresuk, Ph.D., by permission of the publisher, Minneapolis Medical Research Foundation.

others complete a questionnaire about the client, or through the acquisition of factual records (e.g., favorable changes in living situations, release from hospitalization, incidences with the courts). Wolf (1978) and Kazdin (1977a) also recommend social validation as a technique to demonstrate the effects of treatment. For instance, a group of laypersons can judge the degree of improvement shown by the client.

Large numbers of others (nonclients) can also assist in therapy evaluation through normative comparisons (Kendall & Norton-Ford, 1982). In normative comparisons, the scores of a representative sample of normal people on the measures used to evaluate treatment are gathered and compared to the scores obtained by the treated subjects. The researcher, with the aid of statistical tests, thus seeks to determine if the treated subjects are nonsignificantly different from the normal group.

Multimethod Assessment

It is apparent at the present juncture that the clinician who is interested in therapy research is not hampered by an absence of available instruments and methods for the assessment of outcome. It is also apparent that there are an abundance of different therapy approaches. If the researcher were to use all of them, any one study would prove to be prohibitive. It is therefore necessary for the individual clinician to review the measurement materials and select those that are appropriate for the study in question. *Multimethod assessment* is usually the best approach, including assessments of client self-report, performance on diagnostic tests or tasks, ratings by therapists and significant others, and some observational data on the frequency of specific symptoms (see Chapter 10). Multimethod assessment affords the clinical researcher a variety of hypotheses to be tested and allows for the analysis of the breadth and specificity of the treatment effects. In each study, the clinician must also be attentive to the type of treatment that is being evaluated in order to be sure to include measures that will be sensitive to potential client change.

Learning without thought is labor lost; thought without learning is perilous.

Confucious

13

INTERVENTIONS WITH INDIVIDUALS: BEHAVIORAL, COGNITIVE, AND COGNITIVE-BEHAVIORAL THERAPIES

BEHAVIOR THERAPY

Behavior therapy is a field that is increasingly difficult to pinpoint in a single definition (Wilson, 1978b). Behavior therapy was originally defined as the application of learning principles to the treatment of maladaptive behavior (cf. Krasner, 1971). Behavior therapy has also been viewed as a variety of specific techniques developed from various paradigms: systematic desensitization from classical conditioning, modeling treatments based on observational learning, and assertion training and biofeedback based on instrumental conditioning.

Characteristic of the behaviorally oriented therapist is an interest in *pinpointing* the client's exact presenting complaint and *teaching* the client new skills for controlling his or her life more effectively. Psychological dysfunctions are thought to result from maladaptive learning experiences in which environmental forces shape and maintain undesirable behaviors. As a result, behavior therapists perform a careful analysis of the variables that are maintaining the client's maladaptive bahavior pattern—a "functional analysis." In a functional analysis the behavior therapist will assess the frequency and/or duration of the client's troublesome behaviors, and then provide new learning experiences for the client in order to examine whether or not these therapeutic interventions cause an improvement in the problematic behaviors. These learning experiences usually involve attempts by the client (while guided by the therapist) to perform new behavior after having been given instructions and demonstrations by the therapist. Thus, the behavior therapist seeks to achieve observable changes in behavior through performance-based treatment. (see Highlight 13-1.)

Recently, behavior therapists have widened their scope to include a larger variety of guiding principles (cf. Bandura, 1969, 1977a; Franks & Wilson, 1977; Goldfried & Davison, 1976; Lazarus, 1976). Research areas such as social psychology, personality psychology, and cognitive psychology, are included as sources of data and hypotheses for a science of behavior change.

It is also not uncommon for behavior therapy to be defined more in terms of its scientific methodology than its specific techniques or procedures or its reliance on principles of learning. In such cases, behavior therapy is defined as an empirical-clinical methodology (Goldfried & Davison, 1976). The fundamental guidelines for the empirical-clinical methodology include (1) an openness to new and diverse

Highlight 13-1   A Behavior Therapy Sampler

Following is an excerpt from a behavior therapy session illustrating the therapist's desire to pinoint the problem and to provide the client with guided learning experiences.

CLIENT: The basic problem is that I have the tendency to let people step all over me. I don't know why, but I just have difficulty in speaking my mind.

THERAPIST: [My immediate tendency here is to reflect and clarify what the client said, adding a behavioral twist. In paraphrasing what she has already said, I can cast it within a behavioral framework by introducing such terms as "situation," "respond," and "learn."] So you find yourself in a number of different situations where you don't respond the way you would really like to. And if I understand correctly, you would like to learn how to behave differently.

C: Yes. But you know, I have tried to handle certain situations differently, but I just don't seem to be able to do so.

T: [Not a complete acceptance of my conceptualization, seemingly because she has tried to behave differently in the past and nothing has happened. What I should do, then, is somehow provide some explanation of why previous attempts may have failed, and use this to draw a contrast with a potentially more effective treatment strategy that we'll be using in our sessions.] It's almost as if there is a big gap between the way you react and the way you would like to react.

C: It seems that way, and I don't know how to overcome it.

T: Well, maybe you've tried to do too much too fast in the past, and consequently weren't very successful. Maybe a good way to look at the situation is to imagine yourself at the bottom of a staircase, wanting to get to the top. It's probably too much to ask to get there in one gigantic leap. Perhaps a better way to go about changing your reaction in these situations is to take it one step at a time.

C: That would seem to make sense, but I'm not sure if I see how that could be done.

T: Well, there are probably certain situations in which it would be less difficult for you to assert yourself such as telling your boss that he forgot to pay you for the past four weeks.

C: (Laughing.) I guess in that situation, I would say something. Although I must admit, I would feel uneasy about it.

T: But not as uneasy as if you went in and asked him for a raise.

C: No. Certainly not.

T: So, the first situation would be low on the staircase, whereas the second would be higher up. If you can learn to handle easier situations, then the more difficult ones would present less of a problem. And the only way you can really learn to change your reactions is through practice.

C: In other words, I really have to go out and actually force myself to speak up more, but taking it a little bit at a time?

T: [This seems like an appropriate time

to introduce the function of behavior rehearsal. I won't say anything about the specific procedure yet, but instead will talk about it in general terms and maybe increase its appeal by explaining that any failures will not really "count." If the client goes along with the general description of the treatment strategy, she should be more likely to accept the details as I spell them out.] Exactly. And as a way of helping you carry it off in the real-life situation, I think it would be helpful if we reviewed some of these situations and your reactions to them beforehand. In a sense, going through a dry run. It's safer to run through some of these situations here, in that it really doesn't "count" if you don't handle them exactly as you would like to. Also, it can provide you an excellent opportunity to practice different ways of reacting to these situations, until you finally hit on one which you think would be best.

C: That seems to make sense.

T: In fact, we could arrange things so that you can actually rehearse exactly what you would say, and how you would say it.

C: That sounds like a good idea.[1]

[1]From Marvin R. Goldfried and Gerald C. Davison, *Clinical Behavior Therapy*. Copyright 1976 by Holt, Rinehart and Winston. Reprinted by permission of Holt, Rinehart and Winston.

methods to promote change, rather than placing confidence in any single tradition, (2) a reliance on the methods of scientific evaluation for the validation of clinical hypotheses, and (3) a commitment to teaching clients the skills that they need in order to control their own lives. Behavior therapists attempt to continuously develop innovative, but empirically validated, methods for helping people to become the masters of their own destinies.

Recognizing the ever-broadening scope of behavior therapy, we now present a sampling of some of the most widely used and researched therapeutic strategies that have been identified as falling within the rubric of behavior therapy. More extensive and detailed coverage of the multifaceted field of behavior therapy is provided by Craighead, Kazdin, & Mahoney (1981), Franks and Wilson (1979), Goldfried and Davison (1976), Leitenberg (1976), O'Leary and Wilson (1975), and Rimm and Masters (1979).

Systematic Desensitization

Systematic desensitization is one of a variety of treatment methods that have been developed to remediate the behavioral and affective distress associated with problems involving persistent anxiety (Wolpe, 1973). The treatment procedure is based largely on the learning principle of counterconditioning. In counterconditioning, a response that is incompatible with an undesirable response is substituted for this undesirable response as a result of repeated training. In desensitization, counterconditioning principles are usually applied by teaching the client to gradually perform a relaxation response as a substitute for the anxiety response elicited by problematic situations such as public speaking or heights.

Within Wolpe's (1958) systematic desensitization, the patient is first taught to relax via Jacobsonian relaxation procedures (see Highlight 13-2). Wolpe (1973) described teaching the client to relax in about six interviews with home practice for two 15-minute periods a day. Once clients have acquired relaxation skills, they are instructed to relax deeply while imagining the anxiety-producing situation(s). In order to guarantee that relaxation will replace the anxiety response, the client imagines the anxiety "scenes" in a predetermined hierarchy.

Highlight 13-2   Progressive Muscle Relaxation

In 1929, Edmond Jacobson published a book entitled *Progressive Relaxation* (2nd ed., 1938). The procedures described by Jacobson have been adopted by many behavior therapists as an adjunct component of systematic desensitization.

Jacobson's (1938) procedures were designed to train the patient to use his own initiative to learn to "localize tensions when they occur during nervous irritability and excitement and to relax them away" (p. 40). Jacobson suggested that while the length of treatment varies greatly, two or three sessions are often sufficient especially if the individual also practices for an hour or two each day. When undergoing progressive relaxation the subject should be lying or sitting in a comfortable position, for instance, in a recliner chair. In Jacobson's time, a canvas couch without sides was recommended. The room should be quiet and dimly lit. The subject should wear comfortable clothes and remove distractions such as glasses or contact lenses.

The procedures of progressive relaxation are designed to teach the subject to recognize the presence of muscular contractions (i.e., tension). After subjects are able to recognize contractions, they are shown how to relax the muscles. The cultivation of the "muscle sense" is a gradual process in which the subject learns to recognize contractions in various parts of the body in a certain order. The large muscle groups are studied first. As the subject learns to recognize contractions and relax these muscles, other parts of the body are included.

Jacobson's progression begins with the muscles in the arm area (forearm, biceps, hand), and then goes to other muscle groups in a sequence something like the following: feet, ankles, legs, thighs, abdominal muscles, respiratory muscles, shoulders, back muscles, neck muscles, facial muscles, and eye muscles. As each muscle group is focused on, the therapist tries to develop the subject's ability to localize tensions for that group of muscles. First the subject is instructed to flex the muscles, for example, in the left arm. The flex is done steadily and the therapist may provide some slight pressure against the arm. The subject is taught to recognize the "tenseness" of the muscles, not whether they are or are not contracting. In the absence of the tenseness the patient is informed that relaxation involves no effort.

Jacobson recognized the therapeutic potential of progressive relaxation and suggested its use in the treatment of a variety of neuroses and physical disorders. Muscular relaxation is also a pleasant and valuable skill for all people in our increasingly stressful world.

"An anxiety hierarchy is a list of stimuli on a theme, ranked according to the amount of anxiety they evoke" (Wolpe, 1973, p. 108). The therapist acquires detailed information about the client's anxiety and its situational determinants from a thorough assessment. When a variety of sources of anxiety have been identified, they are classified into themes and rank ordered according to the degree of anxiety associated with each situation. An example of anxiety hierarchies is presented in Table 13-1.

The least anxiety-provoking item on the hierarchy is presented first to the relaxed client. The anxiety associated with the hierarchy item should be weak enough to be inhibited by the state of relaxation. Gradually, the more and more anxiety-producing stimuli are presented to the client. Caution is observed in moving up the hierarchy in a very gradual fashion.

Thus, a potential dilemma for the therapist is to determine reasonably spaced differences between items on the hierarchy. When the client fails to maintain relaxation (i.e., anxiety has overpowered the relaxation) the therapist should ask the client to repeat earlier items in the hierarchy. The troublesome item may also have to be divided into two or more smaller steps. For example, an item in the hierarchy for a test-anxious client (Table 13-1), "The examination paper lies face down before her," may have to become two items: "The exams are being distributed" and "Your exam booklet is on your desk."

Desensitization need not be presented imaginally. The therapist can use the systematic desensitization procedures in the client's actual environment and in the presence of the feared stimulus (or situation). Contact or *in situ* desensitization is the name for these procedures by which the client engages in graduated exposure in the naturalistic setting. For instance, a person fearful of leaving the safety of home ("agoraphobia") may be accompanied by the therapist on outings of gradually increased duration and distance.

Research Evaluation   The therapeutic effectiveness of systematic desensitization has received a great deal of research attention. Perhaps the most noted demonstration of the effectiveness of systematic desensitization was reported by Paul (1966). Paul's study focused on college students who were identified as being under high distress when speaking in public. Participants were ranked according to the severity of their problem and then assigned to one of four groups: systematic desensitization, insight-oriented psychotherapy, an attention-placebo control group, and a test-retest control group. Subjects in the desensitization condition were taught to relax and were then presented imaginally with a hierarchy of anxiety items that began with reading about a speech and culminated with delivering a speech before a large audience. The insight-oriented therapy used interpretive methods to pursue the reasons for the anxiety and to seek self-understanding on the part of the client. The attention-placebo group received sessions where they performed a task and were administered a drug (placebo). The test-retest subjects constituted a no-treatment control.

The therapists in this study were five clinicians who had extensive experience in the insight-oriented therapy. Therefore, the study was somewhat biased in favor of the insight therapy. The treatment lasted for five sessions distributed over six weeks. The results of this study indicated that, in general, systematic desensitization was superior to the other treatment conditions. Specifically, though all groups improved in comparison to the test-retest controls, the desensitization proved to be the most beneficial. The results for behavior ratings, self-reports,

Table 13-1   Several Sample Desensitization Hierarchies, from Wolpe (1973). Hierarchies in Descending Order of Reaction Intensity

A. Examination Series
   1. On the way to the university on the day of an examination.
   2. In the process of answering an examination paper.
   3. Standing before the unopened doors of the examination room.
   4. Awaiting the distribution of examination papers.
   5. The examination paper lies face down before her.
   6. The night before an examination.
   7. One day before an examination.
   8. Two days before an examination.
   9. Three days before an examination.
   10. Four days before an examination.
   11. Five days before an examination.
   12. A week before an examination.
   13. Two weeks before an examination.
   14. A month before an examination.
B. Scrutiny Series
   1. Being watched working (especially drawing) by 10 people.
   2. Being watched working by 6 people.
   3. Being watched working by 3 people.
   4. Being watched working by one expert in the field. (Anxiety begins when the observer is 10 feet away and increases as he draws closer.)
   5. Being watched working by a nonexpert. (Anxiety begins at a distance of 4 feet.)
C. Devaluation Series
   1. An argument she raises in a discussion is ignored by the group.
   2. She is not recognized by a person she has briefly met three times.
   3. Her mother says she is selfish because she is not helping in the house. (Studying instead.)
   4. She is not recognized by a person she has briefly met twice.
   5. Her mother calls her lazy.
   6. She is not recognized by a person she has briefly met once.
D. Discord Between Other People
   1. Her mother shouts at a servant.
   2. Her young sister whines to her mother.
   3. Her sister engages in a dispute with her father.
   4. Her mother shouts at her sister.
   5. She sees two strangers quarrel.

From J. Wolpe, *The practice of behavior therapy.* (2nd ed.) New York: Pergamon Press, 1973. Reproduced by permission of the publisher. Note that in this case, in the examination series, the hierarchical order of the top 5 items does not correspond with the temporal order.

and physiological measures are presented in Figure 13-1. Further evidence of tne effectiveness of the desensitization procedures was provided by Paul's two-year follow-up (1967a). In this report, desensitization yielded the highest percentage of subjects still evidencing improvements (85% in comparison to 50% and below). Other studies have reported similarly impressive findings in support of the therapeutic effectiveness of systematic desensitization (cf. Kennedy & Kimura, 1974; Lang & Lazovic, 1963; McGlynn, Reynolds, & Linder, 1971). Systematic desensitization appears strongly supported by empirical research. However, while we can be confident that it works with phobias, it is not necessarily effective with other disorders.

Nor are we certain of exactly how disensitization works (Kazdin & Wilcoxon, 1976). Few studies have evaluated the effects of desensitization when the client's expectancy for success has been controlled or when subjects received an alternate treatment that was presented in an equally plausible fashion. We must also recall that the majority of research evaluations of desensitization have been done with research volunteers serving as clients, rather than with persons who are seeking psychotherapy on their own. Although the utility of systematic desensitization as a behavior change procedure has been demonstrated, it remains to be confirmed for severely distressed clients.

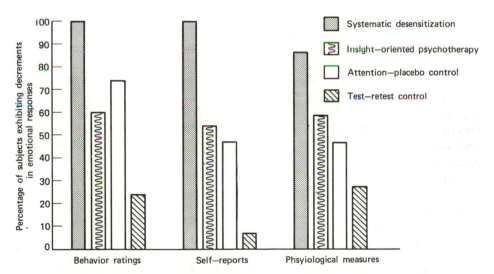

Figure 13-1 Percent of subjects in each of the four conditions who displayed decreases in anxiety as measured by behavior ratings, self-reports of emotional disturbance, and measures of physiological arousal. Adapted from Albert Bandura, *Principles of Behavior Modification. Copyright* © 1969 by Holt, Rinehart and Winston, Inc. Reprinted by permission of Holt, Rinehart and Winston.

Operant Conditioning

The application of the principles of positive and negative reinforcement, response cost, shaping by successive approximations, and discrimination/generalization represent a widely used approach within behavior therapy. Historically, the laboratory studies and educational applications of Watson and Thorndike have been elaborated on in the behavior change technologies for which Skinner is the popular proponent in the 1950 to 1980s decades (Kazdin, 1978a; Krasner, 1971). Operant methods are at the heart of behavioral interventions and have been viewed as equally important for psychodynamic, client centered, and other models of clinical intervention (Bandura, 1969).

Positive reinforcement principles are utilized in behavior therapy for depressive disorders (e.g., Lewinsohn et al., 1974; McLean, 1976). Clients are aided in developing "menus" of "pleasant events" that can serve as reinforcers for engaging in self-enhancing behaviors such as maintaining social relationships, exercising, and working productively. Specific positive reinforcement contingencies are established to increase the frequency of such mood-promoting actions. For instance, a depressed individual might develop a plan to get up and work on a meaningful project each morning, rather than sleeping excessively. The enjoyment of the project serves as a positive reinforcer to sustain the renewing habit of rising each morning.

Positive reinforcement is also an essential element in the therapeutic relationship between client and therapist (Ford, 1978). Genuine expressions of praise and encouragement are important sources of ongoing personal support and, from a behavioral viewpoint, positive reinforcers for optimistic effort and positive self-statements on the client's part. For example, a therapist might reply to this statement—"I'm discouraged but still trying", by saying "It is a difficult road, yet I admire your strength and persistence."

Negative reinforcement, the provision of positive reinforcers contingent on *not* engaging in a negative behavior, is illustrated in one behavioral approach to treating "tics" or stuttering. The technique of negative practice involves a combination of overpractice (engaging in a behavior until beyond the point of satiation) and negative reinforcement. For instance, a client might be instructed to make the undesirable behavior happen excessively (under controlled circumstances), to the point that the relief and relaxation of stopping is a reinforcer. If a positive activity is instigated immediately after the negative practice, this can be an additional positive reinforcer for *not* stuttering. A similar method has been applied, with careful medical supervision, to aid smokers to kick that habit (Leventhal & Cleary, 1980).

Response cost, the repossession of positive reinforcers contingent on a negative behavior, is exemplified in the "treatment contract" often used as an incentive for clients to participate fully in an educational or therapeutic program. For instance, participants in a program to teach parenting skills (e.g., Patterson, 1976) might be asked to submit a deposit equal to their fee (but separate), which would be refunded to them when they complete the entire intervention. If, however, the clients fail to attend sessions, a designated portion of the deposit would be forfeited (typically by donation to a worthy charity) as a "cost." The key issue of adherence to therapeutic programs (cf. Matarazzo, 1980; Stachnik, 1980) can thus be addressed, providing clients with a self-determined incentive to maintain participation.

When a complex skill must be acquired by a client, the shaping by successive approximations methodology is often effective. A clear example comes from behavior modification of psychiatric patients' social skills (Hersen, 1979). Beginning with each patient's initial social capabilities, which are often minimal due to institutionalization, a hierarchical sequence of interim objectives are established, and each of these successive steps is encouraged and positively reinforced. The sequence might include the following steps: (1) establishes eye contact for 5+ seconds, (2) nods to answer Yes or No, (3) says Yes or No audibly in response to questions, (4) restates questions, and (5) initiates Yes-No questions. Gradual learning is promoted through realistic yet challenging stages that bring positive reinforcement on attainment.

Discrimination training and its counterpart, programmed generalization, are exemplified by behavioral approaches to stress management and health education (e.g., Matarazzo, 1980; Meyer, Nash, McAlister, Maccoby, & Farquhar, 1980). Clients are first taught to distinguish between stress/tension and relaxation, in terms of their bodily and cognitive-behavioral reactions. This *discrimination* can be reinforced by role playing stressful versus relaxing situations, by contrasting tension and relaxation in progressive muscular relaxation, or by self-monitoring stress over a week's time. Coping skills can be applied in specific stress situations (e.g., Novaco, 1976, 1977a), but this depends on a *generalization* of the skills and the ability to recognize stressors from the training context to everyday independent living. From the many available approaches to fostering this generalization (cf. Stokes & Baer, 1977), a sampling might include encouraging clients to practice frequently on their own in-between training sessions, aiding clients to set up salient reminders in their natural environments (e.g., posted notes in a central home or work location), and teaching clients to positively reinforce themselves when they identify and/or cope effectively with a stressor.

Research Evaluation   The data from dozens of single-subject and group experimental investigations clearly indicate that operant methods are usually effective in altering specific responses or behavior chains (Hersen, 1979, 1981; Kazdin, 1978b, 1979; Kazdin & Wilson, 1978). However, there are many cases where clients (and/or significant others in their school, home, work, or hospital settings) appear to resist the well-intentioned application of operant techniques (e.g., Hersen, 1979). Still more problematic, however, are the data concerning long-term maintenance of changes produced through operant intervention: psychiatric patients tend to regress, smokers tend to be recidivists (Leventhal & Cleary, 1980), overweight persons tend to regain the lost pounds or kilograms (Dahlkoetter, Callahan, & Linton, 1979), and cardiovascular-risk persons tend to return to their unhealthy habits (Meyer et al., 1980), to mention a few examples. In other words, operant procedures have been demonstrated to have specific and direct impact, but they are not unequivocal cures. Nevertheless, in cases calling for specific alteration of specific responses, in settings permitting control of relevant contingencies (e.g., hospitals), operant techniques are ideal for rapid and direct behavior change.

Modeling

Modeling (observational learning) has been used to produce such diverse therapeutic and educational outcomes as the elimination of behavioral deficits, the reduction of excessive fears and inhibitions, and the facilitation of social behavior (Bandura, 1969; 1971; Rosenthal & Bandura, 1978). The therapeutic use of modeling entails the exposure of a client to an individual (or individuals) who actually demonstrates the behaviors to be learned by the client. The manner in which the modeling is presented can be quite varied. Such methods as graduated, live, symbolic, filmed, and participant modeling describe some of these distinctions. Graduated modeling refers to a step-by-step demonstration of the behavior to be learned. Live modeling, as opposed to symbolic modeling where the demonstration may be filmed, refers to the actual ongoing quality of the demonstrated behavior. Participant modeling involves both modeled demonstration and client participation.

An important differentiation concerns whether the model displayed "coping" or "mastery" behavior. A *mastery* model demonstrates ideal (fearless) behavior; for example, in the case of snake avoidance this would include approaching and touching or holding a snake. In contrast, a *coping* model initially demonstrates apprehension, but subsequently overcomes the fear and performs effectively (fearlessly). In terms of the effectiveness of the model in helping clients reduce avoidance behavior, a *coping* model has been found to be superior to a mastery model (e.g., Kazdin, 1974; Sarason, 1975). Moreover, Meichenbaum (1971) has shown (see Figure 13-2) that a coping model who also models self-verbalizations such as, "I can handle this," provides the most effective modeling strategy by adding these cognitive coping skills.

Other characteristics of the model have been shown to enhance the effects of observational learning. For instance, subjects are more influenced by a model who is positively rewarding, has high status, and is perceived as similar, than they are by nonrewarding, low status, dissimilar models (Bandura, 1969). It has also been shown that multiple models are more effective that single models (Bandura & Menlove, 1968) and that a live model produced more lasting effects than a symbolic (filmed) model, although both live and symbolic models altered the target behavior (Bandura & Mischel, 1965).

Also important in the acquisition of imitative responses are the consequences of behavior that are experienced by the model. When a model is rewarded, this is called vicarious reinforcement if (as usually is the case) this induces the client to imitate the modeled behavior. Vicarious reinforcement has consistently been found to enhance therapeutic modeling.

Research Evaluation   Modeling has been successfully incorporated into therapy programs that treat autistic children (Lovaas, 1966), phobic patients (Bandura & Menlove, 1968), and retardates (Whalen & Henker, 1971), to mention a

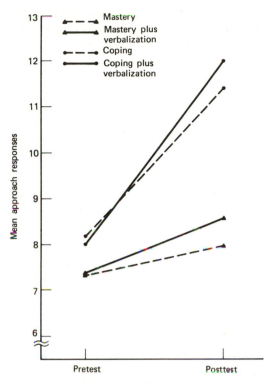

Figure 13-2 Results of Meichenbaum's study comparing mastery and coping models with and without self-verbalization. From D. Meichenbaum, Examination of model characteristics in reducing avoidance behavior. *Journal of Personality and Social Psychology*, 1971, *17*, 298–307. Copyright 1971 by the American Psychological Association. Reprinted by permission.

few. In general, observational learning is not employed as a sole clinical technique but instead as a part of a more comprehensive intervention program. The bulk of the research on modeling has compared different types of models rather than comparing modeling against other types of treatment, so the research validation for modeling techniques is not yet conclusive.

In a study by Blanchard (1970), several components of the participant modeling procedure were compared. The three components that were isolated were (1) nonverbal modeling, (2) verbal information, and (3) direct contact. In an ingenious fashion, Blanchard had four snake-phobic subjects involved in his study at one time. First, the therapist administered a participant modeling procedure to one subject while two other subjects observed from behind a one-way mirror. One of these observers also had earphones and could hear, while the other merely observed. Thus, one subject received modeling plus information plus contact, one received modeling plus information, and one received only the modeling. A fourth subject did not observe the session.

The effectiveness of the different components of the modeling procedure were evaluated by having subjects attempt to approach a live (harmless) snake. The results indicated that the entire participant modeling treatment was the most effective in reducing the subjects fear toward the snake used in treatment. Modeling appears most effective when both verbal and nonverbal modalities, and direct participation, are utilized.

Assertion Training

Many people experience difficulty in taking the initiative with other persons, expressing their opinions and positive and negative feelings, standing up for their reasonable rights, and refusing unreasonable requests. Assertion training encompasses several behavioral methods that have been designed to help clients improve their interpersonal competence without being overly aggressive *or* submissive.

Assertion training (AT) has been used in the treatment of obsessive-compulsive disorders, alcoholism, sexual deviations, dating anxiety, aggressive and explosive behaviors, and a wide range of social skill deficits (Heimberg, Montgomery, Madsen, & Heimberg, 1977; Rich & Schroeder, 1976).It has been used with chronic psychiatric patients as well as with less severely debilitated persons exhibiting "neurotic" dysfunctions or simply desiring a "growth experience." Literally thousands of AT groups for adults and children have been offered by universities, schools, community centers, religious groups, and mental health clinics across the country.

AT typically involves the following behavioral techniques. *Shaping by successive approximations* is perhaps the fundamental method, involving the provision of positive reinforcement to clients as they gradually learn to perform more and more assertive behaviors. Similar to desensitization, a hierarchy of assertion skills is often constructed by the therapist and client, with each successive skill building on all previous ones. The client is rewarded usually by sincere praise from the therapist and by the satisfaction of seeing improvement, for successively mastering each skill. The more specific training techniques include *modeling*, where the client views demonstrations of effective assertion; *behavior rehearsal*, where the client practices the new behaviors in a nonthreatening setting; *coaching*, where the therapist guides the client in rehearsing the behaviors; *feedback*, where the therapist provides reinforcement and suggestions for improvement after the client has engaged in rehearsal; and detailed *instructions* describing how to behave assertively. Clients may also view their practice responses on *videotape*, as an additional source of feedback. Although modeling or behavior rehearsal with coaching and feedback have been found to be moderately effective alone (McFall & Twentyman, 1973), best results are found, in research evaluations, when all these techniques are combined in a complete treatment package.

Research Evaluation   AT has consistently been found to be superior to no-treatment or placebo-control conditions but has been found to be neither consistently superior nor inferior to alternative treatments (Heimberg, et al., 1977). Thus, as with desensitization, much research has shown positive effects due to treatment, but it remains unclear exactly which clients with what problems will benefit most from the possible different approaches to AT. Important future directions for AT research include (Heimberg et al., 1977; Rich & Schroeder, 1976): evaluation of the *long-term* impact of AT, development of guidelines for constructing the best assertion rehearsal scenes for each unique client, evaluation of AT with out-patient psychotherapy clients, and evaluation of the effects of AT on clients' family and friendship relationships (e.g., does becoming more assertive lead to improvement or disruption in such relationships?).

A recent study involving AT illustrates several directions in which research and clinical work in behavior therapy are moving. Linehan, Goldfried, and Goldfried (1979) and Ford (1978) describe an AT program in which clients received one of three types of treatment: interactive, in which therapists focused on providing nondirective support to the client; instigation, in which nondirective support was supplemented by homework assignments to engage in assertive behaviors; and rational restructuring, in which cognitive therapy techniques (Ellis, 1962) were added to the support and homework components. All clients were also taught assertion skills by means of instructions and modeling. The clients, women between the ages of 22 and 60, received eight weekly therapy sessions with one of 13 therapists.

Outcomes were assessed in two ways. First, a comparison of the relative effectiveness of the three treatments (Linehan, Goldfried, & Goldfried, 1979) indicated that rational restructuring was consistently the most effective approach, in terms of helping clients improve their perceptions of their own assertiveness and their actual assertion skills. Instigation was slightly (not statistically significant) less effective, but both instigation and rational restructuring were significantly superior to the interactive approach. Thus, the addition of behavioral and cognitive treatments markedly enhanced AT compared to a more nondirective approach (see also Linehan, 1979).

Second, the importance of the specific actions of the therapist and the client's perception of the therapist's empathy, warmth, and genuineness were evaluated (Ford, 1978). Results indicated that, *regardless* of the treatment type, clients who perceived a *non*supportive therapeutic relationship in the early stages of therapy quickly dropped out of therapy, and those who viewed the therapists as most supportive in middle sessions tended to gain the most from AT. At different points in therapy, different actions by the therapists produced this favorable client reaction: for example, early in therapy, communicating concern and involvement appeared essential, while talking less and encouraging the client to review her successes in being more assertive seemed more important later in AT. However, the client's perception of therapist empathy, warmth, and genuineness had no effect on the long-term gains in assertiveness made by clients.

This study suggests the importance of evaluating both treatment methods *and* the elements in the therapy process that can be found in all treatment programs. A positive therapeutic relationship, as emphasized by "client centered" therapists, appears to be important in AT, but behavioral and cognitive methods also seem necessary in order to provide for lasting gains in assertiveness.

Biofeedback

Following the demonstration that laboratory animals could be instrumentally conditioned to control the functioning of their autonomic nervous system (Miller & DiCara, 1967), investigators have studied the clinical utility of training humans

---

Highlight 13-3   Multimodal Behavior Therapy

Multimodal behavior therapy is the broad spectrum approach to clinical treatment developed by Lazarus (1976). As in all behavior therapy strategies, multimodal behavior therapy is concerned with specifying observable problems and goals, designing individualized treatment techniques, and systematic outcome evaluations. Lazarus developed the multimodal approach around the premise that the more the client learns in therapy the more lasting the change will be after therapy. In Lazarus' own words "durable results are in direct proportion to the number of specific modalities deliberately invoked by any therapeutic system: (1976, p. 13)." In order to maximize what the client can learn, the multimodal approach tries to identify the salient issues in each of seven "modalities." These dimensions include *behavior, affect, sensation, imagery, cognition, interpersonal* relationships and *drugs.*[2] Multimodal behavior therapy, with behavioral principles and a social learning framework, thus seeks to provide clinical treatment by correcting irrational beliefs, deviant behavior, unpleasant feelings, stressful relationships, negative sensations, and possible biochemical imbalances (Lazarus, 1976).

The multimodal approach represents an expansion that currently has great influence with behavior therapists. No longer are behaviors the sole target for therapeutic intervention: according to the multimodal position, there are at least six other modalities that are potential treatment targets. However, although multimodal behavior therapy offers a useful heuristic for clinical intervention, many of the premises of multimodal behavior therapy are in need of systematic evaluation.

[2]As Lazarus pointed out, if you take the first letter of each of the underlined words you have the acronym BASIC ID.

---

to control certain problematic autonomic responses. The instrumental conditioning of human autonomic behavior has come to be known as *biofeedback.*

The general paradigm for biofeedback treatment involves the use of recording instruments that continually monitor the physical responses of the subject and displays these responses back to the subject. For example, a monitor can be attached to record and display the subject's heart rate or muscle tension, and the subject can watch the display and receive feedback. A variety of physical maladies such as tension headaches, migraines, essential hypertension, and seizures have all been treated with biofeedback.

Research Evaluation   Tension headaches are a very common problem related to sustained contraction of the scalp and neck muscles. Biofeedback applications to remedy tension headaches involve electromyogram recordings of muscle tension in the frontalis and occipitalis muscles with subsequent training in relaxation of these muscles. Budzynski, Stoyva, Adler, and Mullaney (1973) compared eight weeks of biofeedback training (two 30-minute sessions a week) with control groups receiving false feedback and no treatment. The results of this study indicated that four of the six subjects treated with biofeedback reported an absence of headaches following treatment while only one of six false feedback subjects and none of the no treatment controls reported a remission of headaches. While these results support the effectiveness of the biofeedback, it should be noted that subjects also received training in home relaxation so the changes may not be entirely due to the biofeedback procedure.

High blood pressure is said to disturb 15 to 30% of the population of the United States and is known to be related to an increased risk of arteriosclerosis, coronary artery disease, and heart attack. Blood pressure is measured using a pressure cuff and the reading can be produced on a screen and "fed back" to the subject who then receives reinforcement for achieving the desired change in blood pressure. An application of biofeedback to hypertensive patients was reported by Benson, Shapiro, Tursky, and Schwartz (1971). These researchers had their patients achieve a relaxed resting blood pressure for five consecutive sessions. Next, biofeedback training to lower their blood pressure was begun and continued until the patient could no longer produce additional decreases. The results indicated that five of the seven subjects showed marked decreases in their blood pressure (systolic). Although these results are impressive, the absence of a control group prevents clear-cut interpretations of the data.

While numerous studies have been conducted to examine the effectiveness of biofeedback procedures (cf. Blanchard & Epstein, 1978), there are many issues in biofeedback that have not been sufficiently examined. Perhaps most compelling is the comment of Blanchard and Young (1973) that biofeedback seems capable of producing statistically significant group differences but *not* of helping most individuals with serious clinical problems. That is, subjects are capable of producing muscle tension or blood pressure changes but these changes may not be of sufficient quantity or duration to be clinically useful. Nevertheless, psychologists and other professionals are enthusiastic about biofeedback because it has in some cases helped clients overcome otherwise insoluble physical and psychological problems.

Aversive Conditioning

Aversive conditioning, also called aversive counterconditioning, involves teaching clients to avoid responses such as smoking or drug misuse through the use of noxious stimulus materials. Aversion therapy is based on the assumption that repeated pairings of the undesirable response with aversive stimuli will diminish the response's reinforcement value and thus induce the person to stop performing it. Aversion therapy has been used to treat such problems as excessive alcohol consumption, smoking, sexual disorders, and self-destructive behavior.

In the area of excessive alcohol consumption, for example, chemicals that induce nausea can be paired with alcoholic beverages. Thus, the alcoholic beverage is the conditioned stimulus, and the nausea-producing agent is the unconditioned stimulus. Through the repeated pairing of alcohol with a nausea-producing agent, it is believed that the alcohol will come to elicit the noxious nausea. As a

Highlight 13-4   Clinical Hypnosis

Hypnosis, unlike most other therapeutic techniques, is not the special province of any particular school of therapy. The processes loosely assembled under the term "hypnosis" have been used by therapists of all persuasions in the attempt to relieve their clients' personal distress. Although there is controversy among psychologists as to the nature of the trance state that is induced, hypnosis is generally agreed to produce a temporary state of highly focused attention and unusual suggestibility.

Modern medical and therapeutic interest in hypnosis can be traced as far back as the 1700s and a European physician by the name of Franz Anton Mesmer. Mesmer's theory of "animal magnetism" posited a sort of magnetic fluid in the bodies of organisms that could be controlled and guided by certain hand gestures of the physician. This gave rise to a frenzied trance state, culminating in a "crisis"—a fit—that sometimes was associated with cures of such problems as bodily pains, numbness, paralysis, and epilectic fits.

Mesmer's theory has gone by the wayside, but the phenomena maintained interest. Braid is often credited (see Sarbin & Andersen, 1967) with developing the famous hypnotic induction technique of ocular fixation on a single object. He is also credited with using the term "neurohypnotism" and later "hypnotism," and with introducing the idea of a trance state instead of animal magnetism. Charcot's positon was different. He thought that the hypnotic state was artificial hysteria, a form of neurological disorder. Although this position did not receive support, Charcot's prominence in medicine at the time helped the theory to endure (Pattie, 1967).

Another person often associated with hypnosis is Freud. Freud actually studied hyposis from Charcot in Paris before attempting its use with his own patients. While able to relieve the symptoms of many patients with direct suggestions, Freud claimed that the effects of the treatment were unstable and tended to dissipate rapidly. Free association and dream interpretation replaced hypnosis in Freud's psychoanalytic practice as the preferred method for tapping the unconscious.

More recently, hypnosis has been increasingly employed by a variety of therapists as an adjunct to other techniques. A blend of hypnotic and behavioral approaches might be, for example, direct suggestions to the client that he or she will no longer desire cigarettes combined with self-monitoring and self-reinforcement for abstinence or the induction of a light trance prior to systematic desensitization rather than muscle relaxation exercises. Self-hypnosis has been suggested as useful along these same lines for such ends as helping clients to learn to deliberately relax in formerly anxiety-provoking situations, for directly suggesting to oneself changes in behaviors or desires, and for developing skills in concentration. The use of self-hypnosis as part of the treatment regimen fits in well with behavior therapists' frequent use of "homework assignments."

Although there are a variety of methods that are used to induce a hypnotic state, and despite arguments that hypnosis does not produce a unique "state," the following illustrates one approach to hypnotic induction. It is called the eye-fixation technique.

Basic to the eye-fixation method is the instruction to the subject to look at a specific object. This object may be a watch, a coin, a spot on the wall, or anything in the room that is not obstructed by other objects. As the eyes tire, the hypnotist initiates an induction monologue that may take many forms, for example: "You look very comfortable. You are getting very relaxed. As you relax even more I'd like you to take a deep breath. Keep staring at the tack on the wall and as your eyes go out of focus continue to relax. Your eyes will blink and you will find your vision blurring. Your eyelids are becoming heavier and heavier. As they become so heavy that you can no longer keep them open, go ahead and close your eyes. As your eyes close you find yourself feeling more and more relaxed. Soon your head will become so heavy that you will no longer be able to support it. You will let it fall forward. Go ahead and relax. You are now in a very relaxed state. If you would like to continue with this relaxed state, nod your head." At this point, a trained hypnotist working with a cooperative subject is likely to have induced a light trance.

Further hypnotic induction procedures can then be used to both deepen the trance and check that the subject has achieved a deeper level. There are many "deepening" techniques but we will discuss only one. Here, the hypnotist instructs the subject to clasp both hands together in a "handshake" of sorts. The subject is then told to try to separate his or her hands. "The harder you try, the harder they will clamp together." If the subject is unable to separate the hands then a deeper level of hypnosis has been achieved. However, if the subject breaks the hand clasp the trance is often broken.

Of particular interest in recent years has been the work of Hilgard and Hilgard (1975) on the use of hypnosis in pain control. These authors have studied the ability of hypnotized subjects to, for instance, maintain their hand and forearm in circulating ice water ("cold-pressor response"). Using the subject's self-reported level of pain as a dependent variable, hypnosis with analgesic suggestions was found to increase subjects' cold-pressor endurance. When pain is caused by ischemia (blood pressure cuff cutting off blood flow to the hand), subjects given analgesic hypnotic suggestions endure the ischemia longer and report less pain.

Therapeutically, hypnosis has been used as an analgesic long before the twentieth century. For example, Esdaile employed hypnosis in India to prevent pain during surgery. More recently, hypnosis has been applied to hypertension (Friedman & Taub, 1977), childbirth (Davenport-Sleek, 1975), and stressful dental and/or medical procedures (e.g., Field, 1974; McAmmond, Davidson, & Kovitz, 1971). Readers interested in personality characteristics associated with hypnotic susceptibility are referred to Tellegen and Atkinson (1974). Readers interested in the relationships between hypnosis and psychopathology are referred to a special issue of the *Journal of Abnormal Psychology* on this topic (1979, *88*, No. 5). There are also several recent studies of posthypnotic amnesia (see for example, Kihlstrom & Evans, 1977).

result, alcohol is no longer associated with pleasure, but rather with very unpleasant experiences.

Research Evaluation   While some reported evidence supports the utility of aversive conditioning for reducing the alcohol consumption of problem drinkers, Rachman and Teasdale (1969) reviewed the pertinent research and concluded that there was no convincing evidence that clinical aversion is an effective treatment for alcoholic patients. In particular, there has been no proof that an aversion learned in therapy will stop clients from drinking in real-life situations.

Similar aversion procedures have been applied with sexual disorders. Marks and Gelder (1967) have described the use of aversive conditioning with clients who were suffering from fetishism and/or transvestism. Their conditioning procedures included the delivery of shock after the patient imagined himself in a sexually provocative but deviant act. Alternately, the noxious stimulus can be an unpleasant mental image. For instance, Callahan and Leitenberg (1973) had clients imagine themselves vomiting while imagining themselves in sexually arousing deviant behaviors. Although recent research (Barlow, 1973; Marks, 1978) suggests that aversion therapy is effective in reducing sexual deviance, several other less aversive procedures have proven equally effective. For example, Barlow and Agras (1973) had male homosexual clients view slides of male and female nudes in a procedure called "fading." Gradually, the male slides were faded out and the female slides faded in, until the clients became aroused by imagining women.

There are also several ethical and professional concerns that have reduced psychologists' interest in aversive conditioning procedures. The extensive physical harm that can result from self-destructive behavior, as well as the intractible quality of these behaviors to other forms of treatment, have led some research clinicians to evaluate aversion procedures for problems such as head banging, flesh tearing, and gouging with objects. Although sometimes found to be effective, many clinicians remain reluctant to use aversion therapy with children because of the fear that such methods are not humane. However, the alternative for these children is often a lifetime of hospitalization in restraints, and this is sometimes seen as more unfortunate and inhumane than a brief period of aversion therapy.

Aversion therapy, although it enjoyed a brief period of research interest, is probably the behavior therapy procedure employed least often. Ethical issues, informed consent, and our culture's changing definition of what is deviant have all contributed to the lessened interest in aversion therapy.

Behavior Therapy With Children

The application of behavior therapy to children has a relatively well-established history. Several procedures have been found effective including, contingent reinforcement, shaping by successive approximations, modeling, and time-out from reinforcement.

The use of contingent reinforcement to increase the social interactions of a withdrawn preschooler was reported by Allen, Hart, Buell, Harris, and Wolf (1964). Initially, the child was found to spend inordinate time seeking adult attention and little time interacting with other children. As part of the treatment, adults paid attention to the child only when she interacted with other children.

Adult attention served as a positive reinforcement for interacting with other children and soon the child was spending approximately two-thirds of the day with other children.

Shaping, by rewarding successive approximations, is also illustrated in the Allen et al. (1964) report. Since there was virtually no peer interaction in the child's typical behavior pattern, the child's behavior had to be shaped toward interaction with other children. That is, the child would first be rewarded for standing near other children, then for talking with them, and finally for continuing to interact.

Modeling has been effective in a variety of interventions with children such as the reduction of fears and the modification of socially withdrawn behavior. Melamed, Weinstein, Hawes, and Katin-Borland (1975) have employed symbolic modeling (a film) with children who show a fear of the dentist. Their modeling film depicted a child successfully going through the dental procedures. The children who were exposed to the film were found to have experienced less trauma during the dental procedures. Bandura, Grusec, and Menlove (1967) employed graduated modeling to treat children who were excessively fearful of dogs. Small groups of children observed a model who, on successive occasions, interacted more closely with the dog. After the completion of eight 10-minute sessions, the modeling procedures were found to have increased the treated children's approach to and interaction with dogs.

Socially withdrawn behavior has also been modified using modeling procedures (O'Connor, 1969). In the O'Connor study, a film of children who progressively engaged in more social interactions was shown to socially withdrawn children. Immediately after the showing of the film, behavioral observations in the classroom indicated that the formerly socially withdrawn children displayed more social behavior than children in the control group and that they were indistinguishable in terms of social behavior from their normal classmates.

Time-out from reinforcement entails the systematic removal of the child from a reinforcing situation when the child engages in inappropriate behavior. When a child is in a playroom with other children and is seen starting a fight, the child can be placed briefly in a quiet and nonrewarding area. This brief "time-out" (often one or two minutes) has been found to reduce such inappropriate behavior as tantrums, and climbing on furniture (Wolf, Risley, & Mees, 1964).

Behavior therapy procedures have also been applied to mentally retarded (Thompson & Grabowski, 1972), hyperactive (Pelham, 1978), and conduct-problem (Kent & O'Leary, 1976) children, as well as a wide variety of other childhood disorders (see also Browning & Stover, 1971; Graziano, 1975; Ross, 1978). Indeed, the use of behavior therapy approaches to child treatment is not restricted to any particular problem or age group but is one of the most often used and most effective strategies for treating children.

COGNITIVE THERAPY

The cognitive therapies are derived from conceptualizations that focus upon the person's cognitions or thoughts as one of the main sources of psychological dysfunctions. Cognitive therapy aims to modify the client's feelings and behaviors by

Highlight 13-5   Behavior Therapy with Autistic Children

Autism remains one of the most serious of the disorders of childhood. Autistic children have been described as (1) incapable of developing a close relationship with others from a very early age, (2) desirous that things in the environment constantly remain the same, (3) lacking in appropriate communication skills, and (4) preoccupied with their own self-stimulating behavior and repetitive play with small objects (Kanner, 1943). Although autism is relatively rare, the prognosis for those children who are considered autistic is not good. Indeed, many approaches to the treatment of childhood autism have been unsuccessful. Behavioral methods have, in contrast, shown moderate success.

The use of behavior therapy procedures with autistic children is based on the early research of Ferster and DeMyer (1962). These researchers developed a structured and controlled environment in which autistic children were able to learn some new behaviors.

Lovaas and his colleagues (Lovaas, Koegel, Simmons, & Long, 1973) have reported on the results of a more extensive behavioral treatment program for autistic children. These researchers utilize a variety of treatment strategies in order to improve the behavior and verbal abilities of their autistic children. For example, the Lovaas treatment includes the use of contingent rewards (i.e., food), contingent aversive events (i.e., slap on the wrist), removal of attention (i.e., turning eyes away from the child), and modeling (e.g., of appropriate language). In order for these procedures to be maximally effective, the therapist sits directly in front of the child and the treatment takes place in an environment that lacks distracting stimuli.

The results of the behavioral treatment for autistic children indicate that the procedures are effective in teaching the children to begin to use language (Lovaas, Beckevich, Perloff, & Schaeffer, 1966) and in eliminating bizarre tantrums and self-destructive behaviors (Lovaas, Freitag, Gold, & Kassorla, 1965). In some studies, the autistic children that received the treatment and were discharged to their parents were found to have maintained their gains and even improved further (Lovaas et al., 1973). Although the treatment appears to have great promise for the otherwise difficult group of children, not all of the treated children show marked improvement and even the successful cases do not return to a normal level of development. Nevertheless, behavior therapy is perhaps the most effective approach with autistic children.

modifying the client's thoughts. Cognitive therapists hypothesize that changes in clients' cognitions will produce positive changes in their problematic behaviors.

Cognitive therapy is different from the more traditional approaches that are also somewhat "cognitive" (e.g., psychoanalysis) because there is more structure, a greater focus on overt symptoms, little attention given to the client's childhood experiences, and less concern with insight into the origins of the problem (Beck, 1970). Although there are an increasing number of clinical psychologists who subscribe to similar theoretical systems, we limit our discussion to three representative cognitive approaches: rational-emotive therapy (Ellis, 1962; Ellis & Harper, 1968), Beck's (1967, 1976) cognitive therapy for depression, and cognitive training with children. As we shall discuss in the next section on cognitive-behavioral therapies, some of the cognitive approaches have recently incorporated several of the intervention strategies of the behavioral therapies.

Rational Emotive Therapy

Rational emotive therapy (RET) is based on helping clients to become aware of self-defeating beliefs (Table 13-2) and to replace these with more self-enhancing self-statements. Ellis hypothesizes that people learn to talk to themselves in order to cope with stress, and these self-statements often cause more problems than they solve if they are "irrational." According to this system, it is the manner in which the person interprets the environment that produces psychological dysfunction or well-being.

The essence of RET can be summarized by a consideration of Ellis' "ABC" model. "A" refers to the *a*ctivating event, the situation that the client is exposed to, whereas "C" stands for the *c*onsequences (both emotional and behavioral) that the client reports resulted from A. The central factor is "B," the *b*eliefs that the client holds regarding the situation in question. It is the existence of and self-reflection on these irrational beliefs, in the form of irrational self-talk, that result

Table 13-2 Ellis's Irrational Ideas

1. The idea that it is a dire necessity for an adult human being to be loved or approved by virtually every significant other person in his community.
2. The idea that one should be thoroughly competent, adequate, and achieving in all possible respects if one is to consider oneself worthwhile.
3. The idea that certain people are bad, wicked, or villainous and that they should be severely blamed and punished for their villainy.
4. The idea that it is awful and catastrophic when things are not the way one would very much like them to be.
5. The idea that unhappiness is externally caused and that people have little or no ability to control their sorrows and disturbances.
6. The idea that if something is or may be dangerous or fearsome one should be terribly concerned about it and should keep dwelling on the possibility of its occurring.
7. The idea that it is easier to avoid than face certain life difficulties and responsibilities.
8. The idea that one should be dependent on others and need someone stronger than oneself on whom to rely.
9. The idea that one's past history is an all-important determiner of one's present behavior and that because something once strongly affected one's life, it should indefinitely have a similar effect.
10. The idea that one should become quite upset over other people's problems and disturbances.
11. The idea that there is invariably a right, precise, and perfect solution to human problems and that it is catastrophic if this perfect solution is not found.

From Dr. Albert Ellis, Ph.D., *Reason and Emotion in Psychotherapy*. Published by arrangement with Lyle Stuart. Copyright 1962 by the Institute for Rational Living, Inc.

in the emotional consequences experienced at point C. A does not cause C, C is the result of the mediating beliefs.

The ABC model can be expanded to include treatment. "D" refers to the process whereby the therapist *d*isputes the client's irrationality. Lastly, "E" stands for the *e*ffects of confronting the client's irrational beliefs. As is evident in Ellis' ABC model, it is not the activating event that makes a client emotionally upset, but rather the client's irrational beliefs, expressed as irrational self-talk, that produces the unwanted emotional consequences.

Consider the following example often used by several cognitive psychotherapists. Suppose you are giving a talk before a reasonably large audience. You are now in front of the group and just a few minutes into your presentation when several members of the audience rise from their seats and leave. Now you can say one of several things to yourself. You could say "My god! I must be doing something wrong, I must be boring! I knew I would do poorly and this proves it." Or, you could think that maybe they are in the wrong room and they simply didn't want to miss another presentation in another room. Now, depending on what has gone through your head, you may become emotionally upset and your presentation may go downhill because of the anxiety that *you* have created. Or you may remain quite calm and give a sterling performance, unaffected by the environmental events.

As a therapy, RET seeks to alter the clients' problematic behavior by actively attacking the person's beliefs that are seen as producing the maladaptive consequences. The therapist challenges the client, requires explanations for all sorts of assumptions, and expresses disbelief and disapproval when the client describes irrational beliefs. However, the attack is directed at the irrational beliefs and *not* at the client personally. In fact, RET prescribes full acceptance and tolerance of the client as an individual. The client's beliefs however, are directly challenged and actively dismantled by the therapist.

Other ancillary procedures within RET are somewhat varied. Although we have classified it as a cognitive therapy, there are several aspects of the approach that appear emotionally evocative, and others that are more behavioral. Some of the emotionally evocative techniques, such as falsification and dramatization, use overemphasis to point out to the client that certain beliefs are entirely unrealistic. The therapist may also try to persuade the client to abandon irrational beliefs or direct the client to straighten up and start thinking more efficiently. (See Highlight 13-6.)

Many behavioral principles are embedded within the RET procedures as well. The therapist may require a client to role play a particular scene, to observe the therapist modeling appropriate behavior, and to complete homework assignments. RET also uses feedback and reinforcement by rewarding the client as changes in the client's irrational beliefs and behavior are observed.

Research Evaluation   An evaluation of treatments for speech anxious subjects was conducted by Meichenbaum, Gilmore, and Fedoravicius (1971). In this study, Meichenbaum et al., compared the effectiveness of an RET-like treatment, desensitization, RET and desensitization, an attention placebo condition, and a

Highlight 13-6 Rational Emotive Therapy: An Illustration[3]

Here, Albert Ellis, the developer of rational emotive therapy, is the therapist.

THERAPIST: What's the main thing that's bothering you?

CLIENT: I have a fear of turning homosexual—a real fear of it!

T: A fear of becoming a homosexual?

C: Yeah.

T: Because "if I became a homosexual," what?

C: I don't know. It really gets me down. It gets me to a point where I'm doubting every day. I do doubt everything, anyway.

T: Yes. But let's get back to—answer the question: "If I were a homosexual, what would that make me?"

C: (Pause) I don't know.

T: Yes, you do! Now, I can give you the answer to the question. But let's see if you can get it.

C: (Pause) Less than a person?

T: Yes. Quite obviously, you're saying: "I'm bad enough. But if I were homosexual, that would make me a total shit!"

C: That's right.

T: Now, why did you just say you don't know?

C: Just taking a guess at it, that's all. It's—it's just that the fear really gets me down! I don't know why.

T: (Laughing) Well, you just gave the reason why! Suppose you were saying the same thing about—we'll just say—stealing. You hadn't stolen anything, but you thought of stealing something. And you said, "If I stole, I would be a thorough shit!" Just suppose that. Then, how much would you then start thinking about stealing?

C: (Silence)

T: If you believed that: "If I stole that, I would be a thorough shit!"—would you think of it often? Occasionally?

C: I'd think of it often.

[And later in the same session. . .]

T: But the reason you're obsessed is the same reason you'd be obsessed with anything. I see people who are obsessed with five thousand different things. But in every single case, just about, I can track it down; and they're saying, "If I were so-and-so—" For example, "if I got up and made a public speech and fell on my face, I'd be a shit!"—"If I went to school and failed, I'd be a shit!"—"If I tried for a better job and failed, I'd be a shit!" Now, you're doing the same thing about homosexuality: "If I ever did fail heterosexually and became a homosexual, I'd be an utter worm!" Now that will obsess you with homosexuality.

C: And that obsession brings me to doubt myself.

T: Well—no. It's part of your general obsession. Your real obsession is: "If (1) I failed at something big, like heterosexuality, and (2) other people didn't like me—they really didn't like me—then I'd be no damned good!" Now, as a subheading under that, you've got the homosexuality. Your general fear is of being worthless—isn't it?

C: Yeah.

T: And you don't only have it in the homosexual area—that's only dramatic and outstanding. What are you working at, at present?

C: I'm a commercial artist.

T: Now, how do you feel about that, when you work at it?

C: Well, I made supervising artist. But I really didn't feel it was good enough. And I just keep going on and on—.

T: Oh. You see: "I made supervising artist, but if I'm not outstanding, I'm a shit!" Is that what you're really saying?

C: (Silence)

T: Think about it, now. Don't agree because I said so. Isn't it something like that?

C: (Pause) I'll go along with it. Because I doubt just everything!

T: Right! But why does anybody doubt everything? Suppose I introduce you to another guy and—I can show you guys who have Ph.D.'s, who have M.D.'s, who are outstanding painters or sculptors, and they feel the same way as you. And some of them have got reputations in their field; they're doing well. They still think they're shits. Now, why do you think they do?

C: (Pause)

T: There's one main reason for shithood. Now what do you think it is?

C: (Pause) Their goals are set too high?

T: Exactly! They're not saying, "I'd like to succeed." They're saying "I've got to! I need an absolute guarantee that I always will succeed. And since there's always a good chance I won't, I'm no damned good!"

C: They're foolish for that.

T: Right. But you're believing that, aren't you?

C: (Pause) Yes, I am.

T: Now the problem is: How are you going to give up that crap?[3]

In rational emotive therapy (RET) the emphasis is on helping the client think more clearly and effectively. In this sample we saw how the therapist asked direct questions and challenged the client's beliefs. The therapist seeks to demonstrate to the client that an irrational belief is directly affecting behavior.

[3]From A. Ellis, *Growth through reason*. Palo Alto: Science & Behavior Books and Hollywood: Wilshire Books, 1971. Copyright by the Institute for Rational Living. Reprinted by permission.

waiting-list control. All treatments were conducted in a group format. On both objective measures and self-report measures, the RET and desensitization subjects evidenced the most improvement. The waiting-list control group showed the least change while the attention control and combined RET/desensitization group showed only moderate changes. The relative ineffectiveness of the combined treatment was attributed to the limited amount of time that could be allowed for each of the treatments (all treated subjects received eight one-hour sessions). Interestingly, Meichenbaum et al., (1971) also measured the speech performance scores of people who were *low* in speech anxiety, and reported that the treated subjects were able to perform as well as these "nonanxious" persons by the end of the study. These findings, along with evidence for the maintenance of the treatment effects at a three-month follow-up period, are evidence for the therapeutic utility of RET (see also Fremouw & Zitter, 1978).

RET was compared to relaxation training and a waiting-list control in the treatment of speech anxious college students (Trexler & Karst, 1972). RET was found to be superior to the waiting-list control and, to a lesser degree, superior to the relaxation training. That is, while several indices supported the superiority of RET over both other conditions, the support provided by the behaviors of the treated subjects observed while giving a speech was not as clear cut.

Another study evaluated the effects of a cognitive therapy for test anxiety. In both of these studies, the cognitive therapy was modeled after RET. Holroyd (1976) conducted an investigation to compare the effectiveness of cognitive therapy, systematic desensitization, combined cognitive therapy and systematic desensitization, "pseudotherapy," and waiting-list control with test-anxious persons. The dependent measures in this study include self-report, an analogue test situation, and grade-point average. Holroyd (1976) found that the cognitive therapy procedure was more effective in reducing anxiety in the testing situation and in improving grade-point average than any of the other procedures. These findings were evident at posttreatment and at a short, one-month follow-up. It is also noteworthy that the systematic desensitization, combined systematic desensitization and cognitive therapy, and control conditions were not significantly different from each other. Only the cognitive therapy produced gains, and these occurred for actual grade-point average, as well as more indirect measures.

A recent study of the effectiveness of RET with a sample of actual clinical cases was reported by Lipsky, Kassinove, and Miller (1980). These authors reported that "on each dependent variable used, RET, either alone or in combination with rational role reversal or rational-emotive imagery (these are two strategies sometimes employed by RET therapists) was superior to both no-contact and a realistic alternative treatment condition" (p. 371, parenthetical comment added). One unfortunate limitation of this study, however, was the sole reliance on client self-reports as the measures of outcome.

In general, the therapeutic benefits of rational emotive procedures have received some empirical support as treatments for varied forms of anxiety. However RET has been evaluated primarily with volunteer subjects and/or with self-report measures, so its utility requires additional study.

Beck's Cognitive Therapy For Depression

Beck hypothesizes that psychological dysfunctions, in this case depression, are the result of the way people have come to think about themselves. That is, it is hypothesized that there are typical self-defeating thoughts or cognitive distortions that characterize the depressed person. While the cognitive approach to depression highlights the role of depressive thoughts, it also recognizes a whole host of additional signs of depression. These depressive indicants include a sad and gloomy mood, some trouble with getting to sleep or staying asleep despite a constant sense of being tired, a loss of appetite, a sense of helplessness, a lack of satisfaction, difficulty making decisions, and a generally negative self-image.

Beck believes that depressed persons feel depressed because they have evaluated themselves as inadequate and they systematically misinterpret events in their lives to confirm this negative self-image. Beck and Greenberg (1974) suggest that the depressed person must recognize the negative thoughts and self-evaluations and correct them by substituting more realistic thoughts.

The first step in cognitive treatment for depression is an accurate assessment of the negative thoughts that are influencing the client. Generally, the typical negative thoughts of depressed clients fit into one of the following three categories described by Beck: negative ideas about the world, negative thoughts about the self, and negative perceptions of the future. These three areas of concern are often referred to as the negative triad. Some of the typical negative thoughts include negative self evaluations brought about by self-comparisons with more successful others, self-criticism and self-blame resulting from an overemphasis on personal shortcomings, inaccurate negative evaluations of even the simplest event, and a sense of being overwhelmed by typical responsibilities to the point of helplessness. The client who reports debilitating depression is likely to be thinking overcritically and in an automatic rather than deliberate fashion, as well as exaggerating the negative, overgeneralizing from nonrepresentative events, and ignoring the positive.

The therapist next guides the client to a more attentive position, reflecting on the thoughts that run through the client's mind while stressful events are happening. As a part of this process, clients are instructed to correct their thoughts by replacing overly negative ones with more accurate and positive ones. A useful procedure for this process is the double-column technique for recording thoughts. In this procedure the client is instructed to write down automatic negative thoughts in one column and to record the corrected (more positive) thoughts in the second column. This procedure provides the therapist with valuable assessment data as well as an indication of the client's progress in therapy.

The general strategy employed by the therapist has been called "collaborative empiricism." This collaboration refers to teaming the client and therapist together in the effort to identify problems and gather data to test the logic and rationality of the client's thinking and beliefs. Self-monitoring is an important skill that is taught to the client—important because it is the client's self-monitored mood, activities, and thoughts that are examined collaboratively by therapist and client.

Each client is asked to monitor his or her experiences carefully so that the therapist can help determine if the client is incapable of feeling pleasure or if the client is being overly critical and harshly discounting pleasurable experiences. Activity scheduling offers a valuable tool. Often, depressed clients have withdrawn from activities and ruminate about this lack of interest. Via activity scheduling, the therapist guides the client in planning and participating in some potentially enjoyable events. Corresponding to the tendency of depressed clients to withdraw from activities, they also fail to engage in or complete routine tasks. Again, the therapist and client work together to set up tasks that are broken down into separate small steps. Progress along these graded task assignments is then required of the client.

Throughout the activity scheduling and graded task assignments the therapist has the client self-monitor his or her thoughts. These thoughts can be recorded on a dysfunctional thoughts record—a record-keeping form provided to the client to keep track of situations, his or her thoughts, and his or her feelings at the time. The full array of the client's self-monitored data is then examined in collaboration with the therapist. Together, they evaluate day-to-day experiences in a more logical and rational fashion than is typically done by the client and in so doing teach the client new cognitive skills for evaluating future situations (see Beck, Rush, Shaw, & Emery, 1979; Hollon & Beck, 1979).

Research Evaluation   Shaw (1977) contrasted Beck's cognitive treatment to the behavioral approach of Lewinsohn (1974). The behavioral program focused on teaching clients to engage in more pleasant events in their daily lives, and to develop better social skills to improve their interpersonal relationships. Subjects were assessed on a variety of measures, including client self-report, objective and subjective clinical ratings, and assigned to one of four groups. In addition to the cognitive therapy and the behavioral therapy groups, Shaw used a nondirective intervention and a waiting-list control. The results of Shaw's study indicated that, immediately and one month after therapy, the cognitive therapy intervention was the most effective in alleviating depression as measured by the client's self-report and the objective rating of depression. Subjects in the behavioral treatment and the nondirective method evidenced greater improvement in their self-report of depression than did the waiting-list control subjects.

Additional experimental investigations have compared cognitive therapy to imipramine, a drug that is often prescribed for depressive symptomotology and often used in the research on pharmacotherapy for depression. A study that made just such a comparison was reported by Rush, Beck, Kovacs, and Hollon (1977). In the Rush et al. study, 41 depressed outpatients were randomly assigned to either a cognitive therapy group or an imipramine (drug) group. Unlike some of the other studies of the cognitive therapy for depression, the patients in this study were seriously depressed. By and large, patients had been intermittently or chronically depressed for over eight years and 75% were suicidal. The cognitive therapy involved a maximum of 20 sessions over a period of 12 weeks while the drug group received up to 250 milligrams a day of imipramine for 12 weeks.

The outcome of the comparisons of cognitive therapy and drug treatment were quite favorable in that both treatment groups showed meaningful reduction in the symptoms of depression. However, the cognitive therapy procedure resulted in significantly greater improvement than did the imipramine treatment on both a self-report measure of depression and two clinical rating scales. Both treatments were found to be successful at a one-year follow-up, with self-rated depression being lower for the cognitive therapy group (Kovacs, Rush, Beck, & Hollon, 1981).

Several other outcome studies have examined the effects of cognitive/cognitive-behavioral treatments for depression and the results are supportive, though not without some restrictions. For instance, Zeiss, Lewinsohn, and Muñoz (1979) compared cognitive therapy, interpersonal skills training, and pleasant events scheduling for the treatment of depression. All treatments were found to have significantly alleviated depression, thus providing support for the cognitive approach but failing to endorse its superiority over the comparison approaches. Note, however, that the Zeiss et al. (1979) "cognitive therapy" was not a direct implementation of the Beck procedures but a combination of related strategies labeled cognitive therapy.

McLean and Hakstian (1979) treated clinically depressed outpatients with either (a) short-term, insight-oriented psychotherapy, (b) relaxation therapy, (c) behavioral therapy, or (d) drug therapy. Since the behavioral therapy incorporated a cognitive rationale and some cognitive methods, this form of treatment might be considered a cognitive-behavioral approach. The results indicated that, on self-report measures, the behavioral therapy was superior to the other forms of intervention. The short-term insight therapy fared the most poorly, and there were no significant differences between relaxation and drug treatment. The successful therapy in this study appears to have relied more on the behavioral strategies that exist in cognitive-behavioral therapy than on the cognitive strategies, and therefore provides supportive evidence for the behavioral strategies employed in the treatment of depression. In general, evidence supports a cognitive-behavioral approach to treating depression (see also Fuchs & Rehm, 1977; Taylor & Marshall, 1977).

Cognitive Training with Children

Recent research interest within the field of child psychotherapy has also centered on cognitive training procedures to remediate the psychological dysfunctions of childhood. One strength of this research is that the cognitive deficits in certain groups of children are first identified and the cognitive training procedures are then designed and implemented to remediate these known deficits. Two examples follow.

Douglas (1975) has conducted research on hyperactive children and has noted that these children's problems, in part, result from two factors: (1) an inability to reflect before acting, and (2) deficient skill in maintaining focused attention on work tasks. With these deficits in mind, Douglas, Parry, Marton, and Garson (1976) designed an intervention that focused on teaching strategies for developing and sustaining attention. The children received 24 one-hour training sessions. In order to help the children learn task strategies by continuing the procedures outside treatment, parents and teachers observed several of the sessions. Following the training, hyperactive children who had received treatment were found to have scored significantly better than hyperactive controls on several psychological measures.

In studying young aggressive boys, Camp (1977) identified one aspect of these children's deficit as a lack of effective use of verbal mediation. That is, despite normal verbal intellectual skills, these children evidenced more immature forms of private speech than nonaggressive boys, and their private speech was less adequate for self-regulation on a variety of tasks. The intervention program, called "Think Aloud," focused on the teaching of verbal mediational abilities (Camp, Blom, Herbert, & VanDoorninck, 1977) and involved the child's being taught to solve problems by answering four questions "What is my problem? What is my plan? Am I using my plan? How did I do?" In order to get the children to engage in the questions and their answers, the therapist would go first and model for the children—a "copycat" strategy. In answering the questions, the children would "think out loud" along with the therapist on a variety of problems. Following six weeks of 30-minute daily sessions, the 12 aggressive second graders who were treated were improved on ratings of aggression, but no more so than the untreated aggressive children. However, the treated children evidenced an improvement in the number of appropriate prosocial behaviors that was not seen in the untreated aggressive controls, and improvement over the controls on certain psychological tests.

Other approaches, although similar in several respects (see Kendall, 1981; Urbain & Kendall, 1980), include training in perspective-taking (role-taking) skills (Chandler, 1973) and interpersonal, cognitive, problem-solving skills (Shure & Spivack, 1978; Spivack & Shure, 1974).

COGNITIVE-BEHAVIORAL INTERVENTIONS

Cognitive therapies and behavioral therapies have recently been integrated in the form of cognitive-behavioral interventions (Kendall & Hollon, 1979; Mahoney, 1974; Meichenbaum, 1977). Intervention procedures that reflect a cognitive-behavioral position are based on the principles that (1) the human organism responds to cognitive representations of the environment, and not the environment per se, (2) these cognitive representations are related to the processes of learning, (3) most human learning is cognitively mediated, and (4) thoughts, feelings, and behaviors are causally interactive (Mahoney, 1977). Integrated cognitive-behavioral interventions have been developed for both adults and children.

Cognitive-Behavioral Interventions with Adults

In practice, cognitive methods such as Beck's cognitive therapy for depression are actually cognitive-behavioral (cf. Hollon & Beck, 1979). Although these procedures place an emphasis on the cognitive processes of the client, therapists use behavioral procedures as part of the treatment as well. Procedures such as homework assignments, rehearsal, self-monitoring, and reinforced practice turn cognitively oriented treatments into cognitive-behavioral ones. In current practice, the treatments described as "cognitive therapy" are actually cognitive-behavioral.

One treatment approach that grew directly from the field of cognitive-behavioral interventions is the stress-inoculation training procedure (Meichenbaum, 1977; Meichenbaum & Cameron, 1973; Meichenbaum & Turk, 1976). Stress-inoculation training, designed for the control of anxiety, stress, and anger, has three phases: the educational phase, the rehearsal phase, the application phase. During the educational phase the therapist provides the subject with a conceptual framework for understanding the nature of stress. Within this framework, behavioral and cognitive coping skills are taught to the subject and they are then practiced during the rehearsal phase. For example, the therapist might induce anxiety in the client and require that the client actually practice the use of the newly acquired coping skills. In the last phase, the therapist encourages the client to apply the cognitive and behavioral coping skills in the stressful conditions.

One important aspect of the rationale underlying the stress inoculation procedures concerns the effort to teach clients that they will not become overwhelmed by stress because they will learn to cope with stress in small doses. Clients are ''inoculated'' against uncontrollable levels of stress by having been helped in coping with milder levels of stress.

Novaco has described how the phases of stress inoculation training can be adapted for the treatment of anger problems (Novaco, 1975, 1976). In Novaco's intervention the client is presented with an explanation of anger in cognitive, emotional, and behavioral terms. Clients are then asked to identify anger-producing situations, keep a diary of anger experiences, and describe the self-statements that mediate the anger. Client and therapist collaborate to set up a hierarchy of anger-inducing situations. Clients are then given opportunities to learn and rehearse coping self-statements and gradually move up the anger hierarchy while remaining relaxed. Not all anger is unwanted, and the Novaco strategy recognizes this fact and treats only debilitating and unwanted anger.

Cognitive restructuring strategies also grew from the increased interest in cognitive-behavioral interventions. Cognitive restructuring has been used by some writers to describe any of a variety of treatments that seek to modify the client's thinking, and in so doing they make the term almost synonymous with cognitive-behavioral therapy. The more specific association pertains to a technique developed by Goldfried, Decenteceo, and Weinberg (1974) called systematic rational restructuring—a more systematic RET-like strategy for treating anxiety disorders.

Systematic rational restructuring has four phases: presentation of the rationale, overview of irrational asumptions, analysis of the client's problems in rational-emotive terms, and teaching the client to modify his or her internal self-statements. During the rationale phase clients are presented with an explanation of how their beliefs, assumptions, and self-talk have an effect on their emotions. It is not that clients deliberately give themselves debilitating demands, but that they have learned to behave in certain ways that reflect their underlying unwanted self-talk. During the overview of irrational assumptions phase the therapist describes, in general rather than in reference to the specific client, the unreasonable and unrealistic nature of certain beliefs. Next, the therapist examines with the client the nature of the client's problems within the framework of the rationale and understandings gained thus far. Last, the client is taught to use the experience of anxiety as a cue for engaging in new and different (less anxiety-producing) self-talk. Clients are provided with guided practice in the form of behavioral role play and imagery. Therapists also serve as cognitive coping models by demonstrating the use of coping self-talk.

Research Evaluation   A cognitive-behavioral intervention modeled after stress inoculation procedures has been applied to the anxiety and stress associated with invasive medical procedures (Kendall, Williams, Pechacek, Graham, Shisslak, & Herzoff (1979). In the Kendall et al. study, adult males who were scheduled to undergo an invasive medical procedure (i.e., cardiac catheterization) were provided with either a cognitive-behavioral treatment, a patient education intervention, an attention/placebo control, or the standard hospital conditions. The cognitive-behavioral treatment focused on labeling the stress, helping the patient to identify stress-related cues, discussing the use of positive self-talk as a cognitive coping strategy, and the modeling and rehearsing of these coping skills. Subjects receiving patient education were taught about the heart, heart disease, and the procedures of the upcoming catheterization. The attention/placebo group discussed their current concerns with the therapist.

Levels of subjective anxiety, as reported by the patients, and ratings of adjustment, provided by the cardiologists and nurses, were used to evaluate the interventions. The results indicated that the cognitive-behavioral intervention was the most effective in terms of both anxiety reduction and adjustment during the catheterization procedure. (For a review of the stress-inoculation outcome literature see Jaremko, 1979.)

Evaluations of the stress inoculation procedures for the treatment of anger and pain have also appeared in the literature. Novaco (1976) reported on an evaluation of the treatment of anger. Thirty-four clients with anger-control problems were treated with cognitive-behavioral strategies and relaxation in a design that allowed for the separate evaluation of each component. A variety of assessments were gathered, including self-report, physiological indicies, and ratings of coping in a planned provocation situation. On several measures, the combined treatment significantly reduced anger and improved anger management. Also, clients receiving the cognitive-behavioral training alone showed improvements greater than clients in the control condition (see also Novaco, 1979). In reference to the control of pain, the application of these procedures and their outcomes are described in Turk and Genest (1979).

Recent research has provided data supporting the utility of cognitive restructuring (or systematic rational restructuring). For instance, Goldfried, Linehan, and Smith (1978) reported that the reevaluation of cognitions was an important component of the treatment of test anxiety. Specifically, clients receiving systematic rational restructuring were found to fare better on self-report measures of test anxiety and anxiety in social situations than both clients receiving prolonged exposure to the anxiety-arousing cues and clients in the control condition. Based on the work of Glogower, Fremouw, and McCroskey (1978), one can maximize the effectiveness of cognitive restructuring interventions by emphasizing coping self-statements and identifying and altering negative self-statements.

Research on the utility of cognitive-behavioral procedures for adults (see also Foreyt & Rathjen, 1978; Kendall & Hollon, 1979; Mahoney & Arnkoff, 1978) has produced some supportive evidence. Given the data and the existence of a general trend toward the integration of varying approaches to treatment (e.g. Goldfried, 1980), additional efforts in the development, evaluation, and application of cognitive-behavioral interventions seems warranted (see Highlight 13-7).

Cognitive-Behavioral Interventions with Children

Perhaps one of the most noteworthy results of the cognitive-behavioral blend is an intervention procedure described as *self-instructional methods* (Meichenbaum, 1975; 1977). Meichenbaum emphasizes that the therapist's ability to change what clients say to themselves is an important component of any interven-

Highlight 13-7   Self-efficacy Theory

Bandura (1977b) has provided a unifying theory of behavioral change labeled self-efficacy theory. The theory comes from the social learning/cognitive-behavioral perspective. In essence, Bandura has described how psychological interventions alter the level, strength, and generality of client self-efficacy and that it is the client's self-efficacy expectations that determine the ultimate success of the treatment.

The degree to which individuals develop the expectancy that they will be able to perform desired behaviors is an important cognitive factor in behavioral change. The expectancy factor has two components: *self-efficacy expectations* and *response outcome expectations*. Self-efficacy expectations have to do with anticipated personal mastery of problem behaviors. In contrast, response outcome expectations pertain to an individual's anticipation that if a behavior is performed (by anyone) it will have the proposed effect. The response outcome expectation has to do with the likelihood of a behavior having an effect, but this is not as important as the self-efficacy expectation—the client's personal expectation that he or she can perform the necessary behaviors. Bandura underscores the importance of behavioral, performance based treatment procedures in producing beneficial change, but identifies changes in self-efficacy expectations as the cognitive process underlying change. Bandura, Adams, and Beyer (1977), for example, reported a strong correspondence between treated subjects' (formerly snake phobics) self-efficacy expectations and the degree to which these persons evidenced fearless performance.

The theory appears to offer a bridge between cognition and behavior. Recently, there have been numerous commentaries on the value of self-efficacy theory and while some take positive positions (e.g., Rosenthal, 1978; Wilson, 1978c), some others are somewhat less favorably inclined (e.g., Borkovec, 1978; Eysenck, 1978). Note, however, that self-efficacy is not purported to be *the* unique source of behavioral change. Bandura has written that his statement that different experiences alter coping ability through the mechanism of self-efficacy is a proposal not an empirical fact, and that while self-efficacy is an influential factor in determining behavior it is not the sole determinant of behavior (Bandura, 1978b). Clearly, Bandura's position is one of reciprocal determinism where multiple interlocking factors combine to cause behavior and behavior change. Self-efficacy expectations are proposed as the cognitive mechanism associated with behavioral change.

tion. As in cognitive therapy, the client's thinking style is the focus of treatment. However, self-instructional methods also utilize the performance-based procedures of behavioral therapy. That is, the client is not simply "talked with" about self-statements; instead, the therapist models appropriate self-statements, has the client role play these statements, and uses reinforcements to strengthen the new self-dialogue.

Self-instructional procedures have been applied to a variety of maladaptive behavior patterns and the results have been generally supportive of treatment effectiveness. Meichenbaum and Goodman (1971) developed a procedure to train children to use self-talk to control their impulsiveness. In this strategy, the therapist models the performance tasks of several while stating several self-instructions out loud for the child. Then the child is asked to self-instruct out loud. Later, the therapist self-instructs in a low voice and asks the child to do likewise. Finally, the therapist performs the task without talking out loud and then requires the child to do similarly (see Table 13-3). The treatment is designed to teach impulsive children to use verbal mediational strategies before responding.

Kendall and Finch (1979) describe the integration of the self-instructional procedures with a behavioral contingency and have conducted a series of evaluations of treatment effectiveness. The behavioral contingency is called response cost; the child is first given some chips or coins and informed that these are his or hers to spend later for a reward but that he or she can lose one for each task error, going too fast, or failing to use the self-instructions. Positive social reinforcements are also used for appropriate behavior. The results from several evaluations indicate that the integration of cognitive and behavioral procedures was effective in reducing impulsive task performance and impulsive classroom behavior.

Table 13-3 Content and sequence of self-instructional procedures with impulsive children.

Type of Self-Statement	Content of Self-Instructions
	Sample Self-Statement
Problem definition	"Let's see, what am I supposed to do?"
Problem approach	"Well, I should look this over and try to figure out how to get to the center of the maze."
Focusing of attention	"I better look ahead so I don't get trapped."
Coping statements	"Oh, that path isn't right. If I go that way I'll get stuck. I'll just go back here and try another way."
Self-reinforcement	"Hey, not bad. I really did a good job!"

Sequence of Self-Instructions

• The therapist models task performance and talks out loud while the child observes.
• The child performs the task, instructing himself or herself out loud.
• The therapist models task performance while whispering the self-instructions.
• The child performs the task, whispering to himself or herself.
• The therapist performs the task using covert self-instructions with pauses and behavioral signs of thinking (e.g., stroking beard or chin, raising eyes briefly).

Adapted from P. C. Kendall and A. J. Finch, Jr., Developing nonimpulsive behavior in children: Cognitive-behavioral strategies for self-control. In P. C. Kendall and S. D. Hollon (Eds.), *Cognitive-behavioral interventions: Theory, research, and procedures*. New York: Academic Press, 1979. Copyright 1979, Academic Press; reprinted by permission. Modeled after Meichenbaum and Goodman (1971).

The examples here pertain to performance on maze tasks during training.

In a study by Kendall and Wilcox (1980), two types of self-instructional strategies were compared: concrete self-instructions, those that are relevant only to the task at hand, and conceptual self-instructions, those that are general and can be applied to any situation. Again, blind teacher ratings of self-control and hyperactivity indicated improvement for the treated children over an attention/placebo control group. Moreover, the results favored the conceptual self-instructional approach. Additional research is required to further our understanding of these procedures but the evidence to date suggests its continued investigation. Indeed, the training of clients to use appropriate self-statements has been described as an important component of several cognitive-behavioral interventions (for children; see also Craighead, Wilcoxon-Craighead, Meyers, 1978; & Kendall, 1981; and for adults (see also Craighead, 1979; Glass, Gottman, & Shmurak, 1976).

NONPRESCRIPTIVE BEHAVIOR THERAPIES

Our last section on strategies for individual intervention deals with what Rosen (1976) has termed the nonprescriptive behavior therapies. These interventions are self-help programs or manuals that can be purchased at the bookstore and self-administered without professional consultation.

All of us are probably familiar with at least one of these do-it-yourself books. Each purports to contain the special information to fulfill your inner-most desire to change, if you only buy and read the book and follow the instructions and advice. Some of the most common nonprescriptive therapies are the assertion books, weight loss manuals, smoking abatement pamphlets, and guides to more sensual sex. Not all of them are to be dismissed as useless. Some self-help manuals are nothing more than faddish manifestos, but others are solid professional advice distilled into popular paperback style.

Although it is *not* necessarily the case that all nonprescriptive therapies are unfounded, the majority lack specific evidence to document their effectiveness when administered through the manuals in which they are marketed. It is important, though as yet infrequently true, that self-administered programs be experimentally demonstrated to be effective when read by consumers without any professional supervision. Even the most effective clinician-administered intervention must still independently be shown to be effective in book form.

The goals of the over-the-counter therapies can range from the mercenary to the missionary. On the energetic marketplace, the motivation is often to sell a product for the highest price that the market will bear. The application of sales pitches to manuals that are designed to assist the troubled individual can be unsettling. However, the missionary service of self-help manuals is basically to provide a service to a greater number of individuals than would be capable of getting the service without a mass-produced manual or guidebook. This is consistent with the goals of clinical psychology as a helping profession, and easily purchasable manuals offer an efficient means to disseminate our knowedge and help many people. This position is not universally accepted. Some practicing clinical psychologists feel that an overabundance of cure-yourself manuals may decrease the public's faith in the efficacy or necessity of actual clinicians—''Why seek professional help when I can buy a manual?'' The public should be warned that the guidance of an expert clinician is essential when complex human problems are being treated, and that harm may come to naive book buyers. There are differences of opinion concerning the value of nonprescriptive therapies, and, due to their relatively recent appearance on the marketplace, many of the concerns are unresolved. Although we make neither a profit nor a prophecy, we will turn our discussion now to some of the current books on psychological self-help.

Overweight individuals can presently select from over 100 books on weight control. Of these, the manual by Stuart and Davis entitled *Slim Chance in a Fat World* (1972) is a good example. This manual provides the reader with a behavioral analysis of how people become overweight, and specific methods for losing weight without losing good health or using drugs. These methods, which are often used by clinical psychologists with overweight clients (Leon, 1975), include interventions such as eating more slowly, putting food out of sight and reach, keeping records of food eaten and calories consumed, developing new ways for coping with stress (e.g., relaxation, self-statements), setting up an exercise program, and reinforcing oneself (but not with food) for making these changes and losing weight. A series of studies have been conducted to evaluate the effectiveness of the Stuart and Davis manual, and, although the findings are positive, the actual number of pounds lost by the subjects (5 to 15 pounds) are often unimpressive in light of the seriousness of their overweight problem (50 to 100 pounds).

Sexual dysfunction is not a new topic for the authors of do-it-yourself manuals but the emergence of the women's rights movement has spurred on these self-help guidebooks. *Becoming Orgasmic: A Sexual Growth Program for Women,* is one such self-help manual (Heiman, LoPiccolo, & LoPiccolo, 1976), in which techniques originally developed by Masters and Johnson (1970) and often prescribed by clinicians for their clients are described.

Many guides to improved assertiveness have been marketed, beginning with Alberti and Emmons' (1974) *Your Perfect Right,* and culminating in more recent volumes such as Bower and Bower's (1976) *Asserting Yourself* and Lange and Jakubowski's (1976), *Responsible Assertive Behavior.* These books present material that reeducates the reader by providing role playing and modeling experiences, assigning homework, and engaging the reader in cognitive restructuring. The desired end product is that the individual will be adquately trained to perform responsible assertive behaviors.

Popular primers on "how-to" raise children are particularly widely available. Also, there are numerous approaches that are espoused by a diverse list of authors (Clarke-Stewart, 1978). Griffore (1979) suggests that the authors be more concerned with telling the parent-readers about the effects of the procedures that they are recommending—both positive and limiting. Along these lines, research is needed to determine what, if any, are the results of (1) parental self-education and (2) the specific approaches that are endorsed by different authors.

The relative effectiveness of these and numerous other nonprescriptive guidebooks has been reviewed by Glasgow and Rosen (1978). Since the overall quantity and quality of the evaluative data on these nonprescriptive packages is slim, flags of caution must be raised. However, studying the methods and procedures that are involved in getting people to maintain participation in self-help programs would appear to be a valuable arena for future research.

EVALUATION OF INDIVIDUAL INTERVENTION PROGRAMS

In addition to the variety of methods that are available for the appraisal of the effects of therapeutic interventions, the research-clinician may wish to assess the effectiveness of the overall clinic, or a particular hospital program. No longer is the interest focused on one client's change, but on the effects of a more general program.

The purpose of program evaluation is to measure the effects of a program, for instance, a clinic that provides individual therapies to outpatient clients, against the goals that it set out to accomplish as means of contributing to subsequent decision making about the program (Weiss, 1972). In the attempt to be maximally effective, the program evaluator should seek to clarify the program goals, develop multiple measures that will be used to evaluate the extent to which the goals have been achieved, analyze and report the results of the evaluation, and adjust the program according to the findings.

First, we need to be aware of the clinic goals. For example, we are dealing with a mental health center that was opened in a rural area in order to serve the economically struggling inhabitants of the area. Knowing this one goal produces a meaningful evaluation question—were the economically struggling members of the rural community served by the clinic? In this instance, the evaluator would want to accumulate demographic data from the files of the clients who were seen in the clinic over a specified period of time. If clients are categorized according to income and residence, the program evaluation could determine whether economically disadvantaged clients were seen more, less, or equally often, compared to community members of other social classes.

Although the first question appears answered, a critic may say "So, the clients you served were poor and rural. You only reached 10% of the problem cases that exist in the community!" Here, another question is being asked. What percentage of these persons needing psychological help were able to receive treatment as a function of the clinic? To answer this question, the evaluator must gather data on the incidence of psychological disturbance in the geographic region of interest and then determine what percentage of those were able to receive treatment at the facility.

Other program evaluation questions of relevance for a clinic include the following. How swiftly were clients treated and discharged? How long do clients have to wait before being treated? Are certain types of clients forced to wait longer or discharged more quickly? To what extent do the various professionals who may work together to help a client (e.g., psychologist, psychiatrist, social worker, vocational counselor) in fact work in harmony? How efficiently are services being provided, and where can costs be lowered without detracting from service? As you can see from this brief sampling, many important issues must be answered in program evaluation.

CUMULATIVE ANALYSES OF STUDIES
OF INTERVENTION WITH INDIVIDUALS

Research on therapy has utilized many evaluation methods and, for the most part, has produced evidence that therapy helps many clients improve their lives. However, most of the studies of therapy are, like the majority of scientific investigations, published as individual reports amongst numerous other reports in professional journals. When students and scholars are interested in reviewing the literature on the effects of therapy they must search through a variety of journals, obtain copies of the relevant articles, read them, and try to make sense of a diversity of studies. This review procedure is quite productive in that it is likely to be educational for the reviewer and informative for the future reader. Nevertheless, different reviewers can reach different conclusions, and there are several methods that can be utilized in conducting such a cumulative analysis (or "meta" analysis).

The clearest dichotomy in the methods for meta analyses pits subjective "voting" versus statistical "operations." One cumulative review of the voting variety was reported by Luborsky, Singer, and Luborsky (1975). In this review, the authors report on approximately 40 studies that compared different psychotherapies. Since not all therapy outcome studies are of equal scientific merit, the authors devised a list of 12 criteria with which they evaluated the various reports. Interventions were then categorized as significantly "better," "tied," or "worse" than comparison treatment procedures in each study. These studies were summarized under various headings: group versus individual therapy, time limited versus time unlimited therapy, client-centered therapy versus other traditional therapies, and behavior therapy versus psychotherapy. In comparing group and individual therapy, time limited and time unlimited treatment, and client-centered and psychotherapy, most studies showed that the approaches were tied. A similar finding occurred when behavior therapy was compared with psychotherapy (13 of 19 studies were ties) but the remaining 6 indicated that behavior therapy was superior. Luborsky also calculated "box scores" for the results of studies comparing pharmacotherapy plus psychotherapy with pharmacotherapy alone. The results indicated that the combined treatment was superior in the majority of studies, some were ties, but there were no cases where the single therapy was superior to the combined therapies. When clients in psychotherapy were compared to the subjects in the control groups, 20 of the 33 reported studies indicated that psychotherapy "won," 13 were classified as "ties," and there were no cases where the controls were superior. Although Luborsky et al.'s (1975) cumulative analysis provides some reasonably sound evidence that therapy is effective but no one approach is superior, the validity of the box-score system used is highly questionable because counting numbers of "winning" studies does not necessarily demonstrate the goodness of a therapy method.

Smith and Glass (1977) conducted another cumulative analysis of the effects of therapy. These authors employed statistical operations to evaluate nearly 400 studies. The reasons that there are more studies in this comprehensive analysis than in the paper by Luborsky et al., (1975) is that the present authors used a wider variety of therapy studies. Luborsky et al. had, for example, selected only those outcome studies that used actual patients, thus, eliminating analogue therapy studies. Smith and Glass, on the other hand, included therapy analogues as well as studies of actual psychotherapy and counseling.

Smith and Glass conducted their analysis by calculating an "effect size" score for each of the dependent variables reported in the outcome studies. This score indicates the degree to which the treated group improved with respect to the control group. Since several dependent variables are often reported in each therapy study, Smith and Glass's procedures resulted in 875 effect-size scores. Using these scores, it was possible to analyze how much change occurs in different dependent variables in all therapies. For instance, the effect size was found to be quite large for outcome measures that assessed fear or anxiety reduction and for outcome measures of self-esteem. Measures of adjustment produced a moderate effect size, whereas school or work achievement as an outcome measure had a rather low effect size. Overall, it appears that either clients tend to change more in some areas than others in *all* therapy approaches, or that some measures (e.g., of anxiety) are more sensitive to change than others (e.g., school achievement).

An examination of the different types of therapy and their effect sizes resulted in some interesting findings. These scores are presented in Table 13-4. An inspection of the findings shows that systematic desensitization, rational emotive therapy, and behavior modification produced the largest effect sizes. From the number of effect sizes that were calculated, the reader can see that there are numerous studies done on systematic desensitization and relatively few done on gestalt therapy. Also, the reader can refer to the last column in Table 13-4 and discover that, for rational emotive therapy, the average (median) treated subject is at the 78th percentile in the respective control group. This means that the average treated subject was functioning better than 78% of all untreated subjects.

Smith and Glass' report (1977) also includes an analysis of the effect sizes for the different therapies when they are classified as behavioral versus nonbehavioral. Here, the behavioral treatments produced an effect size of .80 while the nonbehavioral interventions produced a .60 effect size. This comparison is tinged with some artifacts that, when removed, reduce the difference between these two classes of therapy; particularly the fact that behavioral studies used the change measures that consistently showed the most change in all therapies, while studies of other approaches used measures that uniformly reflected less change. The authors' conclusion therefore was that the behavioral and nonbehavioral therapies produce positive effects but that they are not meaningfully different from each other.

The actual meta analysis of the effects of therapy was a combining of all the data from all the experiments on therapy outcome. The average effect size for this data was .68. This information led Smith and Glass to conclude that "the average client receiving therapy was better off than 75% of the untreated controls" (p.754). The statistical integration of the data from numerous studies led Smith and Glass to state that "the findings provide convincing evidence of the efficacy of psychotherapy" (p. 752). Thus, despite their different methodologies, the Luborsky et al. (1975) and Smith and Glass (1977) reviews are in substantial agreement: therapy helps many of the people much of the time. Note, however, that the methodological and substantive value of both approaches to meta-analysis has been questioned by several commentators. For example, Rachon & Wilson (1980) stated that "the claim is often made that poor data is better than no data at all." However, poor data from faulty studies can mislead and confuse (page 256). The criticisms of the meta-analysis approach includes: (A) the analysis is overgeneral, crossing over significant difference between therapy and (B) recommendation concerning the type of therapy best for different individuals are needed but lacking.

Table 13-4   Effects of Ten Types of Therapy on Any Outcome Measure

Type of Therapy	Average Effect Size	No. of Effect Sizes	Standard Error of Mean Effect Size	Median Treated Person's Percentile Status in Control Group
Psychodynamic	.59	96	.05	72
Adlerian	.71	16	.19	76
Eclectic	.48	70	.07	68
Transactional analysis	.58	25	.19	72
Rational emotive	.77	35	.13	78
Gestalt	.26	8	.09	60
Client centered	.63	94	.08	74
Systematic desensitization	.91	223	.05	82
Implosion	.64	45	.09	74
Behavior modification	.76	132	.06	78

From M. L. Smith and G. V. Glass, Meta-analysis of psychotherapy outcome studies, *American Psychologist*, 1977, *32*, 752-760. Copyright 1977 by the American Psychological Association. Reprinted by permission.

One of the surest evidences of friendship that one can display to another, is telling him gently of a fault. —If any other can excel it, it is listening to such a disclosure with gratitude, and amending the error.

Bulwer

14

GROUP INTERVENTIONS

Clinical psychologists conduct interventions with groups as well as with individuals. The group may be composed of people who already are involved with one another, such as a family, or people who do not know one another in advance but who are all seeking therapy. Additionally, clinicians provide educational and growth experiences for groups of people who are reasonably well functioning. For instance, "encounter" or "T-groups" can be used to help people explore new feelings and ways of interacting with others. In all of these cases, the clinical psychologist is acting as a direct facilitator of change by helping to create an interpersonal system (the group) that aids each individual participant to resolve problems, acquire skills, and learn new ways of relating.

In this chapter, we consider the rationales for group intervention, and the different major approaches to group intervention. Group intervention strategies are discussed for (1) intervening with couples and families and (2) conducting growth or therapy groups.

RATIONALE FOR GROUP INTERVENTION

Clinical psychologists use two basic approaches to group intervention. In some instances, the clinician may determine that an individual client will be best able to change if that person's partner or complete family become involved in therapy. Here, the group is a natural one that provides the context for the client's life, and the psychologist seeks to restructure the group system for the betterment of both the client and the other group members. Family therapy, couples therapy, sexual therapy, and marital enrichment programs are prime examples of intervention with natural groups.

Alternately, the clinical psychologist may create a group by bringing together previously unacquainted individuals in order to aid them to resolve personal issues. The special therapeutic forces that are uniquely available in a group context

515

are utilized to help each member learn new skills, gain new confidence, and develop more satisfying and effective interpersonal relationships.

Several common rationales underlie both of these approaches to group intervention. When people gather together in a group, they create an interpersonal system. Every group provides rules for conduct, roles for the performance of social tasks, new interactions and relationships to be experienced, and an often powerful emotional atmosphere. As such, groups offer a potentially valuable vessel for change and medium for growth.

Even if the group is a family that has been the same for many years, meeting with a clinical psychologist automatically changes the system (Haley, 1976; Minuchin, 1974). With both natural and newly formed groups, the clinician attempts to establish new norms that facilitate honest and caring communication. For example, a policy such as "Everyone must talk only for themselves, and not to express the thoughts or feelings of another person," may help clients to accept the responsibility for asserting their own needs without leaning on other people for help. This can relieve their family members of this burden, while simultaneously teaching the clients new ways to function more autonomously.

Clinical psychologists also utilize the events and processes that emerge naturally in groups. By observing how each individual interacts with other group members, a great deal of useful assessment data can be obtained. Even when a group involves people who have no prior shared relationships, members often display patterns of interpersonal interactions in the group that closely parallel their relationships outside the group. For example, a member who has difficulty in being assertive with persons of the other sex outside the group is likely to behave in a similar nonassertive fashion in the group. As group members develop patterns of interacting with one another, the clinician finds these interactions to be valuable indicators of their typical interpersonal strengths, weaknesses, and problems.

Group members can learn a great deal about themselves by watching and listening to one another. Every individual contributes a unique set of abilities, personal difficulties, and viewpoints. The clinical psychologist will often encourage group members to use each other as both positive and negative models. For example, the clinician might say, "Hey, Bill, did you just see how Sally asked the group to help her? She was pretty indirect at first, and the group gave her a hard time (negative model). But then she asked clearly and directly, and she got what she was after (positive model.)" The clinician may also provide direct feedback to a group member about that person's behavior, as well as encouraging group members to exchange constructive feedback with one another. For instance: "You have been silent all session Al, even though you left some important loose ends dangling at the end of last session. I'm feeling uncomfortable about that, and I wonder if other group members are reacting too?" This amplification of the positive modeling and feedback processes in the group serves as a further means to providing learning experiences for members.

A group can serve as a special place where members feel sufficiently safe and secure to take risks and try out new ways of feeling, thinking, and interacting.

Groups often develop an atmosphere of caring and mutual respect as their members come to know and value one another. Even with a family or couple where the members initially dislike and distrust each other, the clinical psychologist can help them to be genuinely supportive and appreciative. Once some group cohesiveness has developed, the group members can provide encouragement that may help one another to confront painful personal issues and take the risk of giving up old habits in favor of difficult but beneficial new changes. By mobilizing group support, the clinician can use the group to move a "stuck" client toward therapeutic change. If it were only the clinician who was challenging the client to change, there might not be sufficient support and incentive to induce the client to take the risk.

In sum, a group situation provides several unique resources that can facilitate therapeutic change and growth. Clinicians can utilize the natural processes of modeling, communication, and support as sources of assessment and intervention, as well as restructuring the group system to further generate improvements in the individual members. Although the ultimate goal is to help each individual participant, the clinical psychologist seeks to achieve this objective by using the group as the direct agent of change.

INTERVENTIONS WITH COUPLES AND FAMILIES

Importance of the Family in Therapy

The central interpersonal system in almost every person's life is the family. Several decades ago Ackerman (1937) described the importance of the family:

> None of us live our lives utterly alone. Those who try are doomed to a miserable existence. It can fairly be said that some aspects of life experience are more individual than social, and others more social than individual. Nevertheless, principally we live with others, and in early years almost exclusively with members of our own family. (p. 1)

Infants learn how to live and what to expect of life almost exclusively through interactions with their families. The intense emotional bonds and the fundamental beliefs about self and the world that result from early family interactions are carried by every person into future relationships (Framo, 1976). As children grow and mature, they change in many ways and their families change as well, but the family's impact remains significant. When children make the transition to adolescence and adulthood, and form their own families, they continue to be influenced by their family of origin; added in, however, is the impact of the new family system that they are creating. Thus, families play a central role in every individual's functioning throughout the life span.

When children (e.g., Oltmanns, Broderick, & O'Leary, 1977), adolescents (e.g., Alexander & Parsons, 1973), or adults (e.g., Turkewitz & O'Leary, 1976) experience psychological dysfunctions, these problems may derive from unresolved conflicts in their current or past families (see also Jackson, 1965). For example, a married couple may bring their young child in for therapy, only to reveal that their problems with the child are secondary to marital conflicts. It may be the case that the child is "caught in the middle" between two warring parents, thus developing symptoms such as anxiety, disobedience, or school failures due to the stresses in the family situation. Similarly, an adult client may seek to overcome feelings of depression by acquiring greater self-esteem, and it may emerge that marital conflicts are the principal area in which his self-confidence is undermined.

Even when an individual client is dealing with issues that do not appear to be caused by family dysfunctions, the family can be an important resource to aid the therapeutic process. Thus, a clinician might seek to enlist the support and encouragement of family members when an individual client is attempting to try out new ways of thinking or acting as a result of therapeutic exploration. Direct intervention with an entire family can serve, therefore, as either the primary means for aiding clients to overcome problems or achieve new growth, or as a valuable adjunct to individual therapy.

When clinical psychologists intervene with families or couples, the entire family is often seen together. This is referred to as *conjoint* therapy, because all relevant persons are seen as a single group. When family problems are discussed by only one family member with a therapist, this would be *individual* therapy if only one family member is involved, and *concurrent* therapy if two or more family members are each seen separately by a therapist. Conjoint family interventions have the advantage of bringing all family members directly into the therapy process. This establishes a commitment to work together for change, as well as minimizing the chance that each family member will be given different guidance (as could happen if each member sees a separate therapist). It also enables the clinician to witness the family "in action" right in the therapy session, rather than having to rely on family members' retrospective report of how the family functions.

Three general approaches have been developed for intervening with couples and families (Beels & Farber, 1969; Ritterman, 1977): systems/communication, psychodynamic, and behavioral therapies. We first discuss representative interventions from each perspective, highlighting their similarities and differences, and then consider the sexual therapy procedures that may be necessary in therapy with couples.

Systems/Communication Approaches

Views on Adjustment and Maladjustment   The system/communication orientation to family and couples therapy is based on the view that family members' well-being hinges on the nature and quality of subtle patterns of interaction that define each family member as a person and the family as a system (Haley, 1976; Jackson, 1965; Minuchin, 1974; Satir, 1964). It is hypothesized that dysfunctional families are unable to create an intimate pattern of interactions that enhances all members' self-awareness, self-esteem and feeling of belongingness. Effective family functioning is seen as depending on (1) effective self-regulation systems, (2) an adaptive family structure, and (3) facilitative communication.

Self-regulation systems   Systems/communication therapists emphasize *family rules* (Jackson, 1965) when conceptualizing and intervening to change family systems. Families are seen as preventing change by creating repeated patterns of interaction. Although family members might not be consciously creating these patterns, they behave as if following a rule that dictates the particular interaction patterns. For example, if a family's interactions repeatedly involve one person expressing a need and others replying with criticism or indifference, we might infer that the unspoken rule is: "Family members are not allowed to openly express their feelings or requests." When family rules are rigid, secretive, or enforced by blaming one member as a "scapegoat" (Zuk, 1967), family dysfunction is thought to be imminent.

Structure   Family structure is defined by both the natural boundaries that separate different generations (e.g., parents versus children) and the informal boundaries that are created when family members join one another in *coalitions* (Minuchin, 1974). When two family members from different generations form a coalition this creates rigid boundaries that prevent them from establishing positive relationships with one another or other family members. Similarly, when boundaries are ambiguous, family members may be caught in the bind of trying to act, think, and feel "just alike." Members' right to privacy and individuality may be obscured, to the detriment of the entire family.

Bowen (1978) and Fogarty (1978) postulate a similar structural formation—the triangle. When a dyad finds conflict intense or intimacy painful, it is hypothesized that a third person (or object or event) is drawn into the system to artificially stabilize the twosome at a safe emotional distance. The problem is that this static triangle formation greatly limits the freedom and flexibility of movement of all persons involved, often leading to feelings of isolation, anger, and helplessness.

Communication   Systems/communication therapists focus on several specific dimensions of family communication (Doane, 1978). Families are believed to be dysfunctional when their communication patterns involve (1) blaming and criticizing rather than genuine acceptance of responsibility for making the family a better system, (2) mindreading in which members act as though they know what other members are thinking or feeling without having to ask, (3) making incomplete statements, such as saying "I'm angry" without saying at whom or about what, (4) making statements that describe alterable events as fixed and permanent, such as when a parent says "I cannot get respect from my children," and (5) overgeneralizing such as "I *never* get *any*thing that's important to me" (Bandler, Grinder, & Satir, 1977).

Therapeutic Strategies   Several systems/communications strategies have been developed for dealing with problems in families. These strategies include validation, reframing, structural change, detriangulation, symptom prescription, and communication training.

Validation   Validation by the therapist involves expression of understanding and acceptance of each family member's feelings, beliefs, and aspirations (Satir, 1964). Validation can be done by finding something important that each family member has said and agreeing with it, or in more subtle ways, that include making sure to speak directly and respectfully to each member, disclosing similar feelings or ideas, or reassuring a member that, although their actions or feelings are unpleasant, they are understandable given the person's current situation. For example, a therapist might respond to a client's anguished appeal for security by saying: "I know that you want to be the master of your own destiny in the long run, but I see that you are in so much pain right now that you couldn't help but feel despondent and insecure." This conveys the idea that it is not any other person's responsibility to make this person feel better, but yet provides the kind of genuine support that may in fact be the greatest comfort to that person. Fulweiler goes one step further and makes sure the family understands that therapy is a "no man's land" (Haley & Hoffman, 1967, p. 72) by insisting that each family member agree to *not* punish any other member in any way for anything that is said or done in family sessions. This can be very important when family members are likely to feel angry but not express this hostility until the family has left the therapist to go home, as well as to facilitate open and direct communication while the family is with the therapist.

Reframing   Systems/communication therapists teach families new ways to conceptualize by reframing problems as a family responsibility, rather than as any one person's fault, and as the result of good intentions and caring feelings that have been distorted by a stressful social environment. The therapist *reframes* psychological dysfunctions in a way that helps family members feel better about one another and themselves (Jackson, 1965). Reframing may be done by simply requiring all family members to attend therapy sessions and participate actively in all homework assignments (Haley, 1976), or by reinterpreting apparently "angry" or "deficient" or "crazy" actions as reflecting more genuinely positive feelings or attributes. For instance, a mother's refusal to participate in house cleaning may be reframed as communicating self-enhancing assertiveness rather than a lack of caring or responsibility. Similarly, the act of criticizing can be reframed as an indirect expression of insecurity and neediness on the part of the critic. Reframing is never used as an excuse for family members to shirk responsibility for relating together in a caring and accepting manner. Instead, it is used as a cognitive restructuring technique (a new and different way to think of things): if family members can begin to label each other in more positive ways, they may have less incentive to fight and greater reason and willingness to work together for positive change.

Structural change   Structural change involves restructuring coalitions. The therapist at first attempts to join forces with all family members so as to gain their trust and confidence. For example, Bell (1976) describes agreeing with both parents and children that *family* problems exist, and suggesting that the parents ought to have more authority but that children also ought to get their way more often. In this manner, the conflicting persons are indirectly shown that they are fighting for a common goal—a better family—and that cooperative action offers a greater promise for all family members to achieve their goals. Then the therapist seeks to realign family members in more positive relationships with one another. Top priority is given to disentangling persons who are overinvolved with one another in intergenerational coalitions, but all family members are aided in developing more self-enhancing positions in the family. For example, with a mother-son coalition, Minuchin (1974) would suggest that the father take over the disciplinarian role so as to take the burden off his wife and to become more actively involved in the family. At the same time, he would help the father and son plan some positive activities together. To avoid leaving the mother without sources of involvement, Minuchin might propose that she pursue personal interests outside the family, such as career interests, hobbies, or friends. She might also be advised to develop new ways to share positive experiences with her daughters.

The essential final component in such a restructuring intervention would be a gradual encouragement of the parents to begin exploring simple and satisfying ways to enjoy being together, for instance a quiet dinner date without their children. Such a specific and direct prescription is used to induce family members to adopt more positive relationships with one another. Family members are not confronted or asked to do anything that is inconsistent with their basic shared goal of creating a better family, so resistance is minimized and the clients' motivation to change is maximized (Highlight 14-1).

Detriangulation   Systems/communication therapists use a detriangulation strategy when one family member is caught as the scapegoat between two other members who are fighting but pretending to not be in conflict (Bowen, 1978; Zuk, 1967). For example, if two parents insist that their marriage is happy but still find themselves engaged in quiet conflict over how to discipline a "problem" child, the therapist may attempt to have the parents shift their attention away from the child and on to their own disagreements as a couple. In so doing, the therapist is replacing the child as the "go-between" (Zuk, 1967) so that the parents will stop blaming and pressuring their child and work toward a more honest marital relationship. The parents are not accused of such misdeeds, but rather encouraged to take a "vacation" from worrying about their child in order to enjoy one another more fully. Only after they have begun to communicate directly to each other, rather than in a triangle fashion with their child as the go-between, will the therapist suggest that the triangle pattern is problematic—and by then the parents can directly observe the benefits of a detriangulated relationship, as well as giving themselves credit for changing.

Symptom prescription   Systems/communication therapists utilize a special form of therapeutic instructions that are called *symptom prescriptions* or *paradoxical directives* (Dell, 1981; Haley, 1971, 1976). Such instructions are paradox-

Highlight 14-1   A Case Example of Systems/Communication Family Therapy

Minuchin's therapy session with the family of an anorectic 14-year-old named Laura exemplifies the systems/communication approach to restructuring troubled families (Aponte & Hoffman, 1973). Anorexia nervosa, a dysfunction that is manifested by a discontinuation of food intake (and often resulting in life-threatening weight loss), traditionally has been very difficult to remediate with psychotherapy. Minuchin's (1974) structural approach has proven far more successful (Gurman & Kniskern, 1978). The goal as stated by the authors of this case study (Aponte & Hoffman, 1973), is to:

> . . . *assist the family to reorganize itself so that its dysfunctional structure will not support the symptom of the child. Throughout the interview they (the therapists) probe the characteristic interaction patterns of the family and engage with the family subsystems, making changes in the husband-wife relationship, the parent-child relationships, and the sibling relationships. The connection between the anorectic symptom and the structural organization of the family becomes clearer as the interview unfolds,* with the result that the child's eating at the end seems incidental compared to the many changes in family relationships. (p. 1)

Minuchin's initial interview with the family, with a cotherapist, is presented verbatim with commentary by Aponte and Hoffman (1973). The family includes parents (Mr. and Mrs. R.); Laura; Jill, age 12; and Steven, age 10. Minuchin's preplanned strategy was to eat lunch with the family during the session, so that the family's handling of the identified problem (Laura's eating) could be directly observed and explored in the context of all relationships among family members.

Before lunch was served, the history of the family and of the problem was explored by asking family members to discuss these topics among themselves. It was learned that Laura had been taken to a psychologist eight years before due to school problems, and that the therapist had told them that Laura was fine but that she was caught in the middle of parental disagreements. In order to "defuse" this blaming, Minuchin took no stand on the subject, but asked the family to reenact how they handle Laura's refusal to eat (p. 4):

DR. M.: (to Laura) When you get annoyed, how do you express your annoyance? What do you say to Dad? Say it now, the way you said it then.

LAURA: (to father) No I don't want any food. (Pause)

DR. M.: What do you do then? (pause)

Dad, what do you do then, when she says that? . . . O.K. Make believe it's happening.

— — —

DR. M.: (to Laura) Do the same thing with Mom. How does it go? (to Mrs. R) It goes also with you similar?

Shortly thereafter, the group orders lunch. Minuchin orders a sandwich that is the same as the mother's, and a drink that is the same as the kids'. Aponte interprets this as an attempt to selectively and symbolically "take sides," first with the mother because she is less aggressive than Mr. R. (so an alignment by the therapist strengthens her position in the family), and then with the children to indicate that they are separate from the parents: "He is splitting the family into camps and setting the stage for disagreement" (Aponte & Hoffman, 1973, p. 7).

Minuchin next shifts the focus to the other daughter, Jill, by asking her what happens when she disagrees with her parents:

What Minuchin is doing is to accept that framework of agreement that the family offers . . . He's aligning himself with the children, separating them from the parents. . . . And he's doing another thing. By going to the other daughter, he's lining up an ally for the identified patient. Laura can't openly differ with her father, but Jill can. (p. 8)

In the ensuing discussion, Mr. R. denies that anyone in the family ever really disagrees with anyone else, and describes them as all "cuddling" and sharing much closeness. In fact, it appears that he and the children "cuddle" while Mrs. R. is relatively uninvolved. Aponte states:

There is no boundary between this father and his kids. Family therapists who think along structural lines see a "healthy" family as one where there are clear demarcations between the generations. . . . In an . . . "enmeshed" family, there is a blurring of generation lines . . . what you often find in these enmeshed families is that there is a hiatus between mother and father but it isn't openly expressed. Mother depends on the kids to console Dad for the fact that she isn't very interested in him. (pp. 11–12)

With this formulation in mind, Minuchin shifts again to discuss privacy in the family. Privacy appears to be taboo, in an unspoken fashion.

DR. M.: Laura do you close the door of your bedroom?

LAURA: No.

DR. M.: Don't you want . . . some privacy sometimes?

LAURA: No—yeah, I do, but I get enough leaving the door open.

— — —

DR. M.: When Daddy enters without knocking, do you tell him that you would like him to knock?

LAURA: No.

— — —

DR. M.: Would it bother Dad to tell him that you want the door closed, and you want him to knock at the door? . . . I have a feeling that it would bother Dad because he is a very loving kind of Dad that likes always to have people respond to him and he responds to people—to the children certainly. That's my hunch—ask him. Ask Dad . . .

LAURA: (to Mr. R.) Would it bother you if I asked you to knock at my door?

Mr. R.: Probably so (Laura laughs), because I like to have all the doors open (Jill and Mrs. R. laugh and exchange looks).

— — —

DR. M.: (to Jill) And do you want sometimes for your door to be closed?

JILL: Yes.

— — —

DR. M.: (to Steve) And you?

STEVE: Yes.

Minuchin uses the specific issue of open versus closed doors to metaphorically discuss the father's reluctance to let his children have privacy. By asking each child, and drawing them all together in support of their right of privacy, Minuchin has also solidified the alliance of the children—and removed the burden of blame from Laura's shoulders. However, Minuchin also takes care to "reframe" the father's desire for open doors as an outgrowth of Mr. R.'s "loving" nature—thus avoiding direct criticism.

Next, Minuchin turns to a cautious exploration of the husband-wife relationship, using the "cuddling" and the open doors as the ostensible issues:

DR. M.: Mom doesn't like her back to be rubbed. What's your thinking (Mrs. R.) about this question of the closed doors? For your grown up—growing up—daughters?

MRS. R.: I don't mind if their doors are closed. I don't like them to lock them, but I don't mind if their doors are closed.

— — —

MRS. R.: The only thing that bothers me is the phone calls, like at dinner time. Dave gets a lot of phone calls at dinner time . . . and I find it disturbing. . .

DR. M.: But why—why doesn't that change? You don't like it.

MRS. R.: I don't know, I guess you get —just get into a pattern and— just don't do anything about it.

DR. M.: Yes, but what? Could you talk to Dave about it? . . . Talk with him now. . . . If it is important, you will need to tell Dave in ways that he will think it is important.

— — —

At this point, Minuchin has initiated a direct dialogue between the parents by having them talk to each other (not to him or the kids) about their relationship (rather than about Laura or Jill or Steve). This results in the "discovery" that (p. 26):

DR. M.: . . . you (Mrs. R) are saying that you and Dave are so busy that there is very little time that you have together without the children. Is that so?

MRD. R.: Yes, I would say so.

DR. M.: (touching Mr. R on the knee) Come back, Dave, now—I want you to come with your wife, you belong here. (Gets up and exchanges chairs with Mr. R.) The kids are going to grow up and some day go away and then you will be all alone with your wife and not know what to do with her. Now what kind of things have you lately done together without the children?

Minuchin emphasizes the importance of the parents learning to develop their relationship independently of the children, changing the seating arrangement to bring Mr. and Mrs. R. together (and sitting between them and their children, to highlight the importance of some separation between the parental and children's generations). However, Minuchin shifts focus again before the parents feel excessively "on the spot," noting that Laura's parents seem to treat her "just the same" as her brother and sister even though she is older than them. He challenges her by suggesting that she is behaving like a 12-year-old (Jill's age), even though she wants to be treated like a 14-year-old. But

Minuchin does not blame her, noting that it appears that her father does not want her to grow up—because then she might "be interested in rubbing the back of someone else" (p. 34) and Mr. R. would have to rely on his wife for "cuddling."

During this conversation, lunch is served, and Minuchin makes sure that the conversation never turns to Laura's eating until he can say (pp. 35–36):

DR. M.: I don't think we have any problems with Laura's eating— she will eat. (Laura, watching him, takes a bite.) ". . . At the point at which you are 14, Laura, you will eat without any problems. . . . But I think that it is good that you are not eating now, because I think that what's happening is that this is the only area in your family, Laura, in which you have a say-so. And at 14 you'll need to have a say-so in another way. . . . What about— there are some, some other things, Laura—some other areas about which you have a say-so? . . . Around food, at least, you can fight. You can say, "That's my body, and that's what I want to eat." Isn't that what you are saying?

LAURA: Um hmm. (continues to eat)[1]

Minuchin has succeeded in reframing the problem: what was seen as "Laura (for some crazy reason) won't eat" now can be viewed as a series of *family issues*, including Laura's legitimate need for self-assertion and the parents' need to rediscover their relationship. Although Laura began eating with no difficulty, the therapy was by no means ended. Instead, the family was helped in subsequent sessions to explore the patterns of interacting with one another and the feelings that were previously hidden by their controversy over Laura's eating. Minuchin thus began to help the family open new doors, while showing them that each family member has the right to keep some doors closed in order to have autonomy.

[1]From H. Aponte and L. Hoffman, The open door: A structural approach to a family with an anorectic child. *Family Process*, 1973, *12*, 1-44. Copyright 1973 by *Family Process*. Reprinted by permission. All names have been changed by Aponte and Hoffman to insure confidentiality.

ical because, on the surface, they seem to be a prescription for the clients to do more, not less, of the problematic behaviors that led the clients to seek therapy. For example, a paradoxical directive for an entire family of four clients might go as follows:

I want Mom and Dad to continue ignoring each other, just as you both have been doing recently. I know that you both want to enjoy being together, but I think it's too soon for that to happen yet. You both need time to get a better feeling for how that will be different, and so do your kids. Now, Tom and Mary (children), I want you to keep fighting together, so that Mom and Dad will be too busy to be tempted to be together. I know that you two are really tired of all the fighting, but it's important for you to keep doing it this week.

The therapist has conveyed empathy for all family members' feelings of discontent, but also highlighted how all of them really want things to be better. Rather than adding to the pressure that family members are already placing on themselves and each other to "shape up," the therapist gives them all permission to continue their misbehavior until they feel ready to make their own decision to change for the better. As a result, family members are relieved of any guilt that they may feel for not being ready to take the risks involved in a change, and they can no longer blame anyone but the therapist, because he or she is now responsible for instructing them to misbehave.

Paradoxical directives are not a blank check for interminable family conflict, but rather a brief respite from guilt, anger, and despair, in which the family members finally are given a chance to take their lives into their own hands rather than staying in a vicious cycle of blame and hostility. If, however, the clients feel unwilling to take any advice from their therapist—as will happen when clients are resistant—then they may actually rebel by doing the best thing possible: the family may change for the better, just to show the therapist "who's boss." In any event, paradoxical directives give the clients permission to make an independent decision about when and how to change by freeing them from the painful conflicts that have become associated with the psychological dysfunctions they are experiencing.

Communication training   In order to improve the clarity, genuineness, and supportiveness of the manner in which family members interact with one another, systems/communication therapists use several *communication training strategies*. These strategies include asking family members to speak only for themselves as individuals (rather than speaking for other members), and/or to talk directly to one another rather than to the therapist. Additional strategies may involve asking clients to use structured communication patterns such as "I" statements or "Fair Fight" exercises (Bach & Bernhard, 1971; Bach & Wyden, 1970). "I" statements require that the speaker take the responsibility for what is said and not blame someone else (see Table 14-1). "Fair Fight" exercises allow family members to release inner feelings and tensions during brief time periods. For example, the Fair Fight exercise called "Vesuvius" enables family members or couples to express pent-up anger by taking turns as a quiet "listener" and a "yeller" for brief time periods (e.g., one minute). Fair Fight exercises are designed to change threatening and personally attacking communications into a mutually acceptable process for dealing with difficult feelings.

The therapist may also ask the family members a series of questions that are designed to point out unobtrusively the basic beliefs and assumptions in their style of communication (Bandler, Grinder, & Satir, 1977; Sorrells & Ford, 1969): (1) "What are you seeing and hearing that is important to you?" (2) "What do you say to yourself to make sense of what you are seeing and hearing?" (3) "When you make that interpretation of what you are seeing and hearing, how do you feel?" (4) "Have you checked out the truth of that interpretation by trying a new way of looking at this situation or behaving in it?" Using this communication strategy, clients are encouraged to distinguish between what they see and hear and how they cognitively construe these perceptions. They are also taught to recog-

Table 14-1   "I" Statements Versus "You" Statements

"I" Statement: Constructive	"You" Statement: Blaming
I disagree with what you said.	You are a fool.
I prefer that you not make jokes.	You should never say that.
I disagree with what you did.	You are absolutely wrong.
I would like to go now.	You had better take me home now.
I would be happiest if you would come with me.	You had better come with me or else.
I like time by myself.	Leave me alone; you get on my nerves.
I feel hurt and sad.	You make me feel hurt and sad.
I would like to know how you feel.	You ought to confide in me more.
I am going to the show.	You better leave me alone.

nize that even seemingly hopeless situations can be changed if they are willing to try changing their interpretations or to communicate directly with one another rather than making untested assumptions.

Research Evaluation   Recent research reviews suggest that systems/communication interventions with families or couples can produce positive gains and that the improvements are seen in approximately 65 to 70% of all clients (Gurman & Kniskern, 1978a, 1978b; Strelnick, 1977; Wells & Dezen, 1978). Controlled experimental evaluations with comparable attention-placebo or wait-list control groups are relatively rare, but the existing studies support the efficacy of systems/communication therapies with couples or families whose members have psychosomatic problems. In one of the few controlled experimental evaluations, Stanton and Todd (cited in Wells & Dezen, 1978) used Minuchin's (1974) structural therapy with "hard-core" drug addicts at a Veterans Administration outpatient center. Clients and their families received standard drug counseling treatment, including group therapy, detoxification and methadone maintenance, and occupational therapy. They were also assigned to one of four groups: structural family therapy with payment (to the clients) for participation and staying drug free, structural family therapy with no payment, attention-placebo groups that involved viewing anthropological movies about families in other cultures, or no additional treatment. Results at a six-month posttreatment follow-up showed that both family therapy treatments were more effective than the control conditions on measures including employment and absence of drug use. The family therapy-plus-payment group gained the most, suggesting the importance of reinforcement for improvement. Further research is needed to more clearly document the efficacy of systems communication therapies.

Psychodynamic Approaches

Views on Adjustment and Maladjustment   Several psychoanalytically trained clinicians have shifted their focus from individual psychotherapy to family and couples interventions (Ackerman, 1958; 1966; Bowen, 1976b; 1978; Framo,

1976). Their psychodynamic approach involves a focus on the intrapsychic conflicts that people are believed to have learned in their early family experiences, with the central hypothesis that these unresolved issues are at the root of people's current problems. Families and couples are seen conjointly in therapy because it is believed that the current family social environment both helps to maintain and exemplifies these psychological dysfunctions.

Psychodynamic family therapists hypothesize that troubled families share a common but lethal flaw: none of the members has developed the personal resources and skills that are necessary to function as an autonomous adult. Such families are "undifferentiated ego masses" (Bowen, 1978), that is, collages of people who are painfully stuck together without the ability to grow as separate individuals. As a result, family members are seen as never having developed sufficient trust in themselves to create their own independent life-styles, relying instead on their families' traditional rules, norms, and values. Communication is usually muddled within the family, because everyone assumes that either all family members think and feel just alike, or, that no one but yourself cares about your needs and feelings. If these people marry and start their own families, it is hypothesized that they will unconsciously recreate a highly similar and dysfunctional family system (Framo, 1976).

Therapeutic Strategies   Two primary strategies are used to discover and alter the psychological distortions that are believed to underlie unresolved personal and interpersonal conflicts: family-of-origin exploration, and confrontation.

Family-of-origin exploration   In order to encourage adult family members to free themselves from the bondage of their past family conflicts, Bowen (1978) and Framo (1976) aid them in exploring their feelings and recollections about the interactions in the families in which they grew up. Such exploration may be done in regular therapy sessions, or by actually meeting with one's family of origin with the therapist as a mediator. The adult family members are first encouraged to identify parallels between problems in their current and original families, and to delineate the feelings and interactions that are painful carryovers. They are then asked to raise both distressing and joyful issues and past experiences with their families of origin, in order to assert their rights to their own individual beliefs and feelings and to establish more genuine and open communication in their original families. The aim is to have clients enlist the aid of their families as places where caring and support are possible. This realistic and optimistic perspective is thought to pave the way for constructive change by the clients in their current families.

Confrontation   The second general psychodynamic strategy is one of confrontation within the current family. The primary agenda is to uncover family "secrets" and "pathogenic defenses" (Ackerman, 1966; Highlight 14-2). Such "secrets" are really unspoken fears, feelings, and foibles—the family skeletons that are conspicuously hidden to everyone's dismay right in the front-hall closet. No one will admit it, but everyone knows about these "secrets." Pathogenic defenses are self-defeating tactics for coping with stress that a family evolves when it is unable

Highlight 14-2   Ackerman's Psychodynamic Family Therapy

Nathan Ackerman (1966) describes a troubled family in therapy as a result of the parents' concern about their youngest son's delinquent behavior. Henry, aged 14, has confessed to having planned to rob a store with his two older brothers (away at college) and his younger sister (aged 12), Henry is also doing poorly in school and has been reported as a discipline problem by his teachers. The parents are extremely hard working and responsible:

> Mr. N. has channeled his emotional needs largely toward the children and has chosen for himself the role of solicitous, martyred parent, partly to live down his guilt-ridden memory of his own irresponsible gambler father. He is an angry servant to his children, since he never can obtain from them sufficient satisfaction of his own strong cravings for a generous parent, and he experiences their growing away from him as a threat. Mrs. N. has been assigned the role of "commander" in this family and has been given authority to wield, but she has on a deep level experienced her husband as shutting her out from any real emotional closeness with him or with the children; she feels thwarted in her own longing for emotional warmth and support from her environment. Both parents are thus repeating in their marriage aspects of their early family experiences, in which there was extreme deprivation, a need to suppress resentment in order to preserve security, and a precocious assumption of adult responsibility at a young age. (p. 213)

Ackerman's goal is thus to help the parents realize that Henry's misbehavior is an indirect expression of their own longings to be nurtured and their own anger at their parents for having deprived them of emotional support.

Transcript of Therapy Session

FATHER: All parents want to make their children happy. (Cliche)

HENRY: I want to make him happy too.

DR. A.: But you haven't made your parents happy, Henry. You've made them unhappy and worried them very much. Yet you say you want to make your father happy.

HENRY: That was past, and this is the present

DR. A.: you're not going to worry him any more?

HENRY: No.

(*Father begins to weep uncontrollably.*)

DR. A.: Now, Papa, you are worrying Henry.

Ackerman's Comments

Father and son each claim desire to please the other.

Therapist challenges them.

Son claims a change of heart. He is going to be a good boy now. No more stealing.

This opens the floodgates.

Therapist turns the tables on father. He points out instantly that father's sobbing now worries son.

FATHER: Excuse me. (*Sits down.*)

DR. A.: You feel you should apologize for crying?

FATHER: Yes, it's just an emotion. (*He breaks down again.*)

Father makes defensive gesture of suppressing emotion.

MOTHER: My husband always takes it more emotionally than I. I agree with Henry, it's in the past. What troubles me now is his reason for doing this. . . . We're not rich, but if Henry came to us we'd always try to give him anything. His father especially would do everything . . .

Mother compensates with intellectual formulation of problem.

DR. A.: I want to go back to what just happened. When Pop cried, Henry looked at him and there was the first feeling I've seen on his face.

Therapist counters father's exhibitionism, calling attention to the son's show of feeling.

— — —

DR. A.: (After pause.) You know, Henry, I don't think your parents understand you even now. You're a big mystery. . .

At this point, therapist shifts gears from presenting symptom to barrier between Henry and his parents.

MOTHER: I do understand him. Well to a certain extent he is a mystery. He's entirely different from the other children. We'd like to help him.

At first, mother denies barrier, then admits that somehow Henry is different and she does not understand him.

DR. A.: Is it true, Henry, are you different?

HENRY: Yes. I like hunting and fishing. Father doesn't like it, can't go with me.

Henry is now more open. He responds to the therapist's support by expressing his difference from his father. Through this difference, his urge to fish, hunt, and shoot, he loses his father. He leaves the living space of the family to find a father substitute.[2]

Ackerman continues to explore Henry's "uniqueness," uncovering what he believes to be significant sexual symbolism in the father's reluctance to hunt or fish: he sees the father as symbolically castrated by the domineering wife and, more importantly, by his fear of and anger toward his own father. By retracing the parents' problems with their families of origin, Ackerman helps them to see that Henry is expressing feelings that they have shut off in themselves, particularly the needs for nurturance and for autonomy. Over the next 18 months the family continued in therapy, enabling the parents to develop a more meaningful marital relationship, which in turn helped them to be more accepting and caring toward Henry. Henry had no further troubles with thefts, and began to do excellent work in school. Both he and his younger sister requested individual therapy as well, to help them resolve their emotional conflicts that had built up over the years from family tension.

²From N. Ackerman, *Treating the troubled family*. New York: Basic Books, 1966. Copyright 1966 by Basic Books. Reprinted by permission.

to use open communication and effective problem solving. For example, one member may be "scapegoated" and punished for misdeeds that are actually equally or more the responsibility of other members.

Ackerman (1966) colorfully labeled his confrontive method "tickling the defenses," and described it as follows:

> This is a tactic of catching the family members by surprise, by exposing dramatic discrepancies between their self-justifying rationalizations and their subverbal attitudes. (The therapist) challenges empty cliches and static or pat formulae for meeting the problems of family living. He halts fruitless bickering over routine, external, or unimportant matters. Watchful for each cue, he reaches out for more honesty and meaningful kinds of communication. (p. 97)

Family members are challenged to disclose true feelings and needs that they communicate only indirectly through innuendo and metaphorical hints at present. They are encouraged to experience the relief that comes from revealing "secrets" and abandoning pathogenic defenses, and to then begin to work together to create a satisfying and growth-enhancing family environment. To facilitate the latter goal and to provide a safe atmosphere for the family throughout therapy, Ackerman also sought to act as a role model exemplifying effective parenting. He described the therapist as "fulfill(ing) in part the role of a true parent figure—a controller of danger and a source of emotional support and satisfaction-supplying elements that the family needs but lacks" (1966, p. 101).

Whitaker (1976) advocates a confrontive approach in which humor and aggression are emphasized. He sees therapy as a process in which the therapist helps family members to shift from self-defeating to self-enhancing perspectives by startling them—much as a sudden noise can jar a person out of a daydream, or as an eyeblink can change one's perception of a surrealistic painting. Surprise is introduced by responding to humorous, aggressive, or symbolic client statements in ways that reveal the client's deeper feelings, rather than in the shallow fashion dictated by social etiquette. For example, Whitaker (in Haley & Hoffman, 1967) recounts replying to a statement by the daughter in a client family that her mother needed to take some "Contac" (a decongestant) by asking, "How long has your mother been *cold* toward your father?" Whether right or wrong, such probing questions are likely to activate the family and perhaps move them to change. Such evocative and confrontive approaches must be used with caution.

Research Evaluation   Although it has been stated that approximately two in every three clients derive some benefit from psychodynamic couples or family therapy, very few experimental studies exist in which a specifically defined psychodynamic therapy was contrasted with appropriate control conditions (Gurman & Kniskern, 1978a, 1978b; Wells & Dezen, 1978). Even when such investigations have been reported, the psychodynamic family therapy is typically found to be no better (or even worse) than control groups (e.g., Alexander & Parsons, 1973). The evidence supporting this approach is insufficient at present.

Behavioral Approaches

Views on Adjustment and Maladjustment   Behavioral clinicians conceptualize both functional and dysfunctional families as social environments that provide key learning experiences for their members. Families that are satisfying and growth enhancing are seen as creating reinforcement contingencies that promote positive interactions, while dysfunctional families are believed to be suffering because positive interactions are punished, penalized or extinguished and problematic behaviors are reinforced. Therefore, behavioral clinicians assert that family dysfunctions can best be remedied by increasing family members' rates of reciprocal positive reinforcement and by clarifying their communication messages (Jacobson & Martin, 1976, Patterson, 1976; Patterson, Weiss, & Hops, 1976).

Therapeutic Strategies   Two distinct behavioral approaches to family interventions have evolved: behavioral marital therapy (Goldiamond, 1965; Stuart, 1969) and behavioral family therapy (Hawkins, Peterson, Schweid, & Bijou, 1966; Patterson, 1966).

Behavioral marital therapy   Working directly with the couple, behavioral marital therapists teach clients new ways to utilize explicit communication and positive reinforcement to reduce their frequency of unclear, nonreinforcing, nonassertive, and aversive interactions. Several techniques are utilized: pinpointing, communication training, problem-solving training, contingency contracting, and homework assignments.

   Pinpointing (also called discrimination training) involves training couples to define their complaints and desires in specific and constructive terms, rather than as vague statements of anger or blame. This requires that each client clarify exactly what it is that is sought from the other partner in positive terms. For example, a wife might be asked to translate "He never acts like he loves me," into a constructive goal such as, "I want him to embrace me warmly at least once each day."

   Behavioral communication training involves providing clients with instructions and demonstrations concerning ways to communicate in a more assertive and mutually reinforcing manner. Behavior therapists have taken communication exercises from the systems/communication approaches and refined the training methods in several ways. The couple is also asked to rehearse these skills by talking directly with each other, and the therapist provides feedback to help them improve after every practice talk. The feedback often takes the form of specific verbal comments, such as "John, you made two positive comments in response to Cindy, but you missed four opportunities and made critical replies in two other cases." Additionally, the couple may be videotaped while they converse, and the tape can be replayed to provide further feedback.

Negotiation and problem-solving training involves teaching couples to develop consensually acceptable plans for achieving their joint and separate goals. Building on their pinpointing and communication skills, the partners are shown straightforward methods for brainstorming and bargaining. The aim is to produce solutions that are equally satisfactory to each partner.

Contingency contracting follows directly from the couple's problem solving, and involves the establishment of an explicit contract, which states what each partner will do for the other, and what positive consequences will follow if the contract is upheld. Penalities for failure to comply are also specified. The simplest form of contract would be, "Husband agrees to do X and wife agrees to do Y," where X refers to the wife's request and Y to the husband's. Weiss, Birchler, and Vincent (1974) recommend the "Good Faith Contract" as an alternative approach. This contract involves separating the husband's and wife's requests, so that they will not be caught in the bind of "I won't do it until *you* do it." A good faith contract takes the following form: "Husband agrees to do X and he will receive a reward if he complies, while wife agrees to do Y and she will receive a reward if she complies." Contracts can be used to induce the couple to engage in positive activities that will replace their negative encounters. For example, if the spouses argue incessantly, the contract might focus on getting them to increase the frequency of sharing recreational activities or quiet conversation, both of which are incompatible with hostile arguing.

Homework assignments are used to help couples to transfer their new skills from the therapy session to their daily lives. Couples may be given the assignment to engage in time-limited communication sessions at home to practice their pinpointing, communication, and negotiation skills. They may also be asked to monitor their own, or their partner's, positive and negative behaviors throughout the week. The couple may also be assigned the task of creating a contract for an issue that has not yet been negotiated.

Behavioral family therapy   Although behavior therapists have trained entire families to use communication, problem solving, and contracting skills (e.g., Alexander, Barton, Schiavo, & Parsons, 1976; Alexander & Parsons, 1973; Kifer, Lewis, Green, & Phillips, 1974; Robin, Kent, O'Leary, Foster, & Prinz, 1977), behavioral family therapy often involves training only the parents (Berkowitz & Graziano, 1972; O'Dell, 1974; Patterson, 1976). Behavioral parent training involves teaching clients skills for managing their children's behavior more effectively through the application of positive and negative reinforcement, extinction, punishment, or response cost.

Positive reinforcement techniques that are taught to parents include the systematic use of attention, privileges, and material items such as candy or toys. Parents are shown how to define behaviors that they view as positive, such as compliance with requests, studying for school, or quiet conversation. They are then trained to utilize a variety of reinforcers so as to increase the frequency of positive behaviors. For example, if parents wish to have their daughter study at least one hour every evening, they might be aided in establishing a system whereby they seek out the child at least once while she is studying to praise her. The principle of secondary reinforcement can also be applied, for example, by having the parents reward their daughter with 10 points for every hour of study, and making these "points" redeemable for more tangible reinforcers such as an extended bedtime or a special treat.

Although *negative reinforcement* is less frequently used in behavioral parent training, parents may be instructed to cease reminding their children about their responsibilities when the children show evidence of fulfilling such tasks on their own. Since parental reminders are often aversive (e.g., "nagging"), this constitutes a negative reinforcement paradigm: as long as the child meets parental expectations, the unpleasant reminders are discontinued.

Extinction is applied in two ways. Most simply, parents are often trained to ignore their children when they are misbehaving, in hopes that the children will grow tired of such actions if the actions fail to irk their parents. However, when children behave in extremely aggressive ways, the *time-out* technique is taught to parents. Time-out constitutes a specified time period (e.g., two minutes) during which the child receives no reinforcers—a "time-out" from reinforcement as it were. The child must also calm down, thus enabling the entire family to have a "breather" and a chance to start afresh.

Punishment is taught as a technique to be used in rare instances. Many parents attempt to utilize punishment excessively, often by making threats that they have no intention of carrying out. Behavioral training emphasizes the cautious application of punishment, so that all warnings are enforced and negative consequences are used only as a last resort. For example, Risley (1968) demonstrated a judicious use of punishment to a mother whose daughter behaved with uncontrolled aggressiveness at times. Although no prior methods had ever effectively restrained the child, a brief electric shock delivered to the girl's arm immediately after she had exploded in a tantrum produced a dramatic positive result. The child recoiled with surprise, but calmed down. The procedure had to be repeated a few times, but within one treatment session the use of a simple "No!" command sufficed to halt the destructive behavior. This improvement permitted Risley to quickly begin to work with the mother on more positive goals for the child through the application of positive reinforcement techniques.

Response cost is also taught as a means of reducing undesirable child behaviors. Here again, parents are trained to use this procedure in moderation and only when more positive interventions are not sufficient. The parents must clearly specify to their children exactly what penalties will apply to what specific misbehaviors, as well as consistently enforcing this policy. For example, a child might be fined 10¢ from his 50¢ allowance every time that he engages in a physical fight with a playmate.

Parents are also taught to employ behavioral principles to teach their children academic skills. Ryback and Staats (1970), for instance, trained parents to tutor their dyslexic children in basic reading skills. The parents where shown how to shape behaviors such as appropriate attending to a book, recognition of words and sounds, and clear pronunciation through the gradual application of positive reinforcement. In this way, the parents were able to help their children increase these crucial skills without placing a heavy burden on teachers or the school system.

Parents have recently been taught to utilize self-control skills with which *they* can better cope with the stresses of parenting (Brown, Gamboa, Birkimer, &

Brown, 1976). In one case, parents were trained to reinforce themselves for dealing effectively with their children, as well as to use cognitive self-statements in order to reduce anxiety or anger. Thus, parents can be aided to better control their own behavior as well as their children's.

Research Evaluation   Several controlled experimental evaluations support the efficacy of behavioral marital therapy (Gurman & Kniskern, 1978b; Jacobson & Weiss, 1978) and parent training (O'Dell, 1974; Patterson, 1976). However, these investigations were almost always conducted with research volunteers rather than actual clients. Three exceptional studies that dealt with seriously dysfunctional families illustrate the importance of working with "real" clients.

Patterson (1974) offered training in child management skills to the parents and/or teachers of 27 boys who had been referred by the juvenile court, schools, or community mental health agencies due to serious emotional and behavioral problems. Families were referred by community agencies such as juvenile court or mental health clinics because at least one boy in the family was identified as having a history of aggressive and disobedient behavior. Each family's parents received at least one month of training from 1 of 11 trainers. Parents were provided with a programmed text on behavioral principles of parenting, individualized training in defining and monitoring problematic child behaviors, contingency contracting, and tutoring their child, and group training in behavioral child management procedures. Teachers were aided in establishing a reinforcement program to induce the target child to study quietly.

Naturalistic observation data in the home and school settings showed that deviant behavior such as fighting or disobedience declined significantly, and appropriate behavior such as quiet studying increased significantly at follow-up intervals as long as 12 months. Ratings by parents and teachers corroborated these positive changes. However, methodological problems may have led to more promising conclusions than are warranted: in particular, the most disturbed boys were not included in the follow-up data (Kent, 1976). Reid & Patterson (1976) also noted that the fairest overall conclusion is that parent training alone is *not* sufficient with very distressed families. He recommends involving the entire family in behavior therapy rather than only the parents.

Alexander and Parsons (1973) evaluated a behavioral problem-solving method for family therapy with clients who had been referred from juvenile court. Reasoning that children exert an important influence on their parents, and that children may participate more fully and effectively in family changes if they are directly involved in planning and implementing these alterations, the entire family was taught communication, negotiation, and contracting skills. At an 18-month followup, only 26% of the clients in the behavioral treatment had been rearrested, compared to 47% for a client-centered group, 50% for a wait-list group, and 73% for a psychodynamic condition. Although the treatment method actually represented a blend of behavioral *and* systems/communication strategies, the results suggest that the treatment was quite effective with seriously distressed families if all family members are directly involved.

Turkewitz and O'Leary (1976) recruited couples who were interested in marital counseling, and provided each couple with training in either contingency contracting or communication skills. Although the clients were recruited, rather than people who sought therapy on their own, their initial scores on questionnaire measures of marital satisfaction and anologue observational measures of communication behavior showed that they were generally very distressed. Each couple met with one of four therapists in eight weekly sessions. Posttest scores on the assessment measures revealed that younger (mean age = 29) clients benefited more from therapy focusing on contingency contracting, while older (mean age = 42) couples gained more when the focus was on improving communication skills. Thus, behavioral treatments are likely to be maximally effective if each therapy strategy is matched with the kind of clients who can benefit most from it.

Sexual Therapy

Many family and couples therapy cases involve sexual dysfunctions, and clinical psychologists have developed a variety of methods for sexual therapy (LoPiccolo, 1978; Masters & Johnson, 1970). Sexual problems are often presented by clients as the "fault" or "burden" of only one partner, as for example when a woman cannot achieve orgasm (i.e., orgasmic dysfunction) or when a man cannot maintain an erect penis (i.e., erectile dysfunction). However, treatment focuses on helping both partners change their attitudes and actions regarding sexuality.

Therapeutic Strategies   Three basic strategies are utilized in sexual therapy: information, skill training, and anxiety reduction.

Sexual information is often very helpful in reorienting couples toward a more satisfying sexual relationship. Many couples suffer from a lack of knowledge about issues such as the location and function of sexual organs or the normal phases of sexual arousal (Masters & Johnson, 1966). Even more debilitating are the many "myths" or misconceptions about sexuality (Table 14-2). Books, movies, and frank conversation can help to dispel such misinformation.

Although sexual interactions are ideally spontaneous and playful, a host of *skills* are necessary to achieve this goal. Through vicarious aides such as films or guidebooks (Annon & Robinson, 1978; Nemetz, Craig, & Reith, 1978) and homework exercises developed by the therapist, each partner is encouraged to teach his or her mate new ways to touch for sensual or erotic pleasure, to communicate requests, feedback, and appreciation, and to help promote a relaxed atmosphere. For example, the *sensate focus* exercise involves having each partner take turns in either gently caressing the other person or being the recipient of this sensual touching (Masters & Johnson, 1970). The *squeeze* exercise is a treatment for men who feel unable to delay ejaculation as long as they and their partners desire ("premature ejaculation"), requiring the couple to simply cease all direct stimulation of the man's penis when he senses that ejaculation is imminent (Seemans, 1956). The man or his partner then squeeze his penis firmly so as to reduce his sexual arousal without causing pain. Through these and similar exercises, the couple is aided in developing new skills that lead to a greater enjoyment of sex.

Anxiety, worry, and feelings of being under pressure to "perform" often hamper people's sexual functioning. The most frequently utilized intervention in sexual therapy is a simple prescription that helps clients take a more relaxed ap-

Table 14-2 Myths Concerning Sexual Functioning

The Myth	Clinical and Research Findings
There is one and only one "right way" to please a partner sexually.	Every person enjoys different kinds of sexual pleasuring; part of the fun of sex is discovering new ways for yourself and your partner.
A person should know what his or her partner wants without asking.	Asking your partner for suggestions and feedback is an essential part of a quality sexual relationship.
Masturbation is unhealthy; married couples who do it must have marital problems.	Most people, married and unmarried, can enjoy masturbation; it signals a problem only if it is an exclusive substitute for other sex activities.
Homosexuality is caused by, or is a sure sign of, psychological dysfunction.	Homosexuality is an atypical sexual preference that is linked with psychological problems in some but not all homosexuals. Many people report some attraction to people of their sex, although few are homosexual.
The size of man's penis is an indication of his manliness or sexual prowess.	Penile size is unrelated to a man's or woman's sexual pleasure in most cases.
A "vaginal" orgasm, that is one which occurs with no direct stimulation of the clitoris, is most "mature."	While women may experience orgasms due to the man's thrusting or due to direct clitoral stimulation, neither type is in any way "better."

Source: Masters and Johnson, 1970; Kinsey, Pomeroy, and Martin, 1948; Kinsey, Pomeroy, Martin, and Gebhard, 1953; Singer and Singer, 1972.

proach to sexual interaction: the client couple is *prohibited* from trying to achieve any goal, especially that of producing an orgasm or an erect penis, during their private sexual encounters. Instead, they are instructed to give and receive caresses of all kinds purely for the pleasurable relaxation that such sensual activity can provide. They may be asked to engage in a "teasing" technique (Masters & Johnson, 1970) by ceasing any stimulating activity if it produces erotic arousal. The purpose of these prescriptions is to reduce anxiety by having the clients focus on pleasure rather than on what they "should" be doing or feeling. Sexual arousal occurs naturally unless it is inhibited by anxiety, so the anxiety reduction instructions are an attempt to substitute a natural focus on pleasure for the artificial and self-defeating fear of performance failure. Structured techniques such as systematic desensitization or gradual shaping or erotic activities are also often used to reduce anxiety and increase sexual enjoyment.

Research Evaluation   Although sex therapy is done only in the context of individual or couples therapy in most real clinical cases, evaluations of sex therapy alone have been reported (Hogan, 1978; Marks, 1978). Masters and Johnson

(1970) conducted the first and most extensive clinical evaluation of sexual therapy, reporting improvement rates ranging from 60% for erectile dysfunction cases and 75% for certain orgasmic dysfunction cases, to 95% for clients who were treated for premature ejaculation and problems of pain during intercourse. Masters and Johnson describe the treatment of 510 couples who were referred by physicians or mental health professionals. Each couple received daily therapy sessions over a two-week period at the Saint Louis Reproductive Biology Research Foundation. One of several male-female cotherapy teams treated each couple, to assure that both partners have a same-sex translator/advocate. Therapy begins with an extensive social and sexual history assessment and proceeds gradually through informational sessions, sensate focus and sexual retraining homework exercises, and specialized interventions tailored to each couple's needs and problems. In addition, 54 men and 3 women were treated without any permanent partner through the use of surrogate partners.

Based on interviews at the end of therapy, 81% of Masters and Johnson's (1970) clients reported alleviation of their sexual dysfunctions. Intensive interviews were conducted at a five-year follow-up with the first 313 couples treated, revealing a 95% long-term success rate. The reliability and validity of these interview self-report data are questionable, and no control group was monitored, so these results must be considered tentative although impressive.

Two experiments have contrasted sexual therapy with alternative interventions. Crowe (cited in Marks, 1978) contrasted sex therapy with "interpretive" therapy for couples experiencing a variety of marital and sexual problems. Sex therapy clients improved significantly more than interpretive therapy clients on measures of sexual satisfaction and performance, but both groups improved equivalently on measures of marital satisfaction and communication. Although neither intervention was sufficiently clearly described to permit replication, the study suggests that specific sexual retraining may be necessary in addition to supportive or interpretive therapy to remedy specific sexual dysfunctions.

Everaerd (cited in Marks, 1978) compared the guided practice approach to sexual therapy with a treatment that emphasized teaching couples general communication skills. The presenting problem for all clients was the female partner's orgasmic dysfunction. Although sexual therapy was generally superior to communication training on self-report measures of sexual functioning, only those couples who initially reported satisfaction with their marriages improved in sexual therapy. Thus, therapy that addresses the broader relationship issues may be important as a prerequisite, or concurrent treatment, for sexual therapy (Kilmann, 1978). This is consistent with the typical clinical practice of conducting sexual therapy in the framework of individual or marital therapy, rather than as an isolated intervention.

Ethical Concerns   Although all group and individual interventions raise ethical issues, including the importance of guarding against casualties and of ensuring that each client receives effective individualized treatment, both professionals and laypersons have expressed particular concern about sexual therapy. For instance, Bailey (1978, p. 1502) has expressed the position that sexual therapy may be no more than "massage parlor technology." Szasz (1980) offers an even more sweeping criticism portraying sexual therapy as a moralistic tool of social control that robs individuals of their right to privacy and freedom to be different.

Clinicians who are experienced in conducting sexual therapy have responded by noting that "all therapies involve value judgments" (Wagner, 1978, p. 1507) that require that the clinician carefully involve the client in all treatment decisions. Wilson (1978a) notes that no adverse effects have been documented with sex therapy, and that no alternative treatment approach has yet demonstrated anywhere near the positive value that research evaluations show with direct sexual therapy. This controversy reminds us that *all* clinical interventions must be conducted with great care to protect the client's rights. Bailey's (1978) closing comments seem reasonable: interventions are "appropriate and desirable when performed by a *psychotherapist* who combines sensitivity to philosophical, moral, and theological issues with his or her armamentarium of technological skills" (p. 1507, italics in original).

GROUP THERAPY AND ENCOUNTER GROUP INTERVENTIONS

When several clients are joined together for group therapy, an interpersonal setting is created that offers several potential therapeutic forces not available in individual therapy. As early as 1905, a physician named Joseph Pratt was conducting group sessions with tuberculosis patients to teach personal and vocational skills in an atmosphere of interpersonal caring. By the 1920s psychoanalysts were translating their methodology to group work (Burrows, 1927; Schilder, 1939), and a minority of analysts have continued the psychoanalytic approach to group therapy (Slavson, 1964). However, group interventions first flourished when Lewin, an eminent social psychologist, collaborated with Bradford, Benne, and Lippit to develop training groups as a means of preparing community leaders to deal more effectively with interracial tensions (Bradford, 1967; Marrow, 1967). These training groups, or "T-groups" as they have become known, emphasized engaging all members in open and honest dialogues among themselves to promote learning of new modes of action and problem solving and to "unfreeze" or disconfirm rigid beliefs. The results were described anecdotally as impressive, from the perspective of both the trainees and trainers, and the T-group model has been disseminated to provide growth experiences for educators, business leaders, politicians, clinicians, and laypersons through an organization called the National Training Labs (Campbell & Dunnette, 1968; Phares & Campbell, 1971). From these diverse origins, several approaches to group intervention have evolved. Following an overview description of the special "curative factors" provided by group interventions (Yalom, 1975), eight distinct approaches to group intervention are described.

Curative Factors in Group Therapy

Group interventions can take any of three basic orientations (Parloff, 1968): *client-therapist* interactions may be the focus, with the goal of exploring each client's individual psychosocial needs and dysfunctions; *client-client* interactions may be emphasized through the discussion of members' current feelings and reactions to each other; or *group* interactions may be the central topic, with an emphasis on discussing the central issues or themes in the group's development. Each approach provides several special therapeutic experiences that cannot be found in individual therapy. Yalom (1975) labels these experiences the "curative factors" (Table 14-3), and describes their nature and effects as follows.

The encouragement and support that group members frequently offer one another can *instill hope* that otherwise might be seen as only "part of the job" when provided by a therapist. Learning that other group members also experience painful and puzzling personal problems gives each client a sense of *universality,* a feeling of "welcome to the human race, you are not a freak." These two factors make the group a secure and energizing milieu.

The group can also *impart information* to each member when participants share their experiences and expertise. The advice and instructions that are often exchanged by group members enables them to gain both by serving as teachers and learners. Similarly, when group members interact with one another, this provides three further sources of gain: *imitative behavior* is facilitated when members model different actions and ways of thinking and feeling, *development of social skills* is also enhanced because members have many opportunities to practice new ways of relating and to then receive extensive feedback from both peers and therapist, and *interpersonal learning* takes place as members test out their self-defeating beliefs and gain a less distorted view of themselves and their social relationships. Yalom (1975) calls the group a "social microcosm" that is, a miniature version of each member's interpersonal milieus. It can thus be a safer place in

Table 14-3   Curative Factors in Group Interventions

Factor	Representative Response
Instillation of hope	"I can really change!"
Universality	"I am not alone."
Imparting information	"I can learn from others' advice."
Altruism	"I can really be important to someone else!"
Corrective recapitulation of the primary family group	"I can relearn new ways to handle old issues."
Development of social skills	"I can learn to get along with others."
Imitative behavior	"I can learn from watching others."
Interpersonal learning	"I can overcome self-defeating misconceptions."
Cohesiveness	"The group is important to me."
Catharsis	"I can ventilate my feelings."
Existential factors	"I must live my own life."

Adapted from I. Yalom, *The theory and practice of group psychotherapy.* (2nd Ed.) New York: Basic Books, 1975. Copyright 1975 by Basic Books. Reprinted by permission.

which to take risks and test new behaviors, as well as a setting where feelings are valued and problems are considered solvable.

Although group members may be marginal, or even outcasts, in their day-to-day social environments, every member is important in the group. The therapist underscores this validation by including all group members in the interaction, as well as by commenting on the roles that each member plays (see Highlight 14-3). Perhaps even more importantly, the group provides a setting where members can experience the benefits of *altruism*: "patients receive from giving . . . (It is) a refreshing, self-esteem boosting experience to find that they can be of importance to others" (Yalom, 1975, p. 13). Helping other members can thus enable a participant to overcome feelings of worthlessness in a unique experiential fashion.

Highlight 14-3   Roles in Group Interventions

When clinicians bring together several persons who have had no prior relationships with one another, the resultant group system parallels natural groups (such as families, friendship circles, and classes) in many ways. In particular, certain roles seem to appear, regardless of the specific persons who enter the group. These roles can cause problems for the group leader when they center on issues of conflict or resistance, but they can also provide useful self-knowledge and even a chance to learn new skills for the group members. Here then is a sampling of some of the recurrent group roles (Bach, 1954; Rosenthal, Frank, & Nash, 1954; Yalom, 1975).

GUARDIAN OF DEMOCRACY

This person makes certain that all group interactions and decisions are fair to one and all. Underneath the apparent egalitarianism and selflessness often is found a resentment of authority and difficulties with personal assertiveness.

STAR

This member grabs the spotlight frequently, seeking to gain acclaim for openness, difficult problems, impressive therapeutic gains, or talent. The star often has difficulties in relating empathically or genuinely with others.

SELF-RIGHTEOUS MORALIST

This person is often pompous and condescending, criticizing other members for their weaknesses of character and lack of scruples. The rigid and irritating insistance on dictating moral standards for all group members often hides painful self-doubt and even self-hate.

SILENT

The member who withdraws from group interactions in a cloak of silence can, paradoxically, be a very powerful figure in the group. Other members may direct a great deal of attention to sympathizing with, attacking, or seducing this member, as well as guessing frantically why "she or he won't talk!" Many motives may underlie a stance of silence, including anxiety, depression, low self-confidence, or manipulativeness.

PROVOCATEUR

This person incites the group through spicy and even aggressive statements, accusations, and insinuations. The provacative stance can provide a shield behind which a person who fears rejection can hide.

SCAPEGOAT

Just as in families, one person often emerges in a group on whom all anger, fear, and blame is focused. The scapegoat may oblige by misbehaving, thus helping the group members to project their negative feelings on to this external target. This person may feign innocence but, even when he or she truly does not understand why he or she is being attacked, the scapegoat has often learned that the only way to get attention from others is through martyrdom. It is important to both help the scapegoat learn new ways of getting social validation and aid members to take more honest responsibility for their feelings.

JESTER

This person is witty and urbane, yet cynical and cryptic. The jester expresses metacommunications about the group process and group members in veiled jokes and antics. Despite serving a valuable tension reduction and process observer role, the jester often fears facing personal issues and conflicts directly and honestly.

HELP-REJECTING COMPLAINER

This person is full of complaints, but dismisses every attempt by others to help as inadequate, misdirected, or foolish. The prototypical statement by this person is, "yes, but:" for instance, "Yes I do feel sad, but what you suggest won't help." Such a person is caught in a vicious double bind of desperately seeking to change but believing firmly that nothing can really help.

These are some of the roles that evolve in groups. Other roles might include "the group stud," "the social secretary," "the romantic," "the time keeper," and "the doctor's helper." As group members take on the various roles, they can learn a great deal about themselves and the ways that they do or do not handle their interpersonal relationships.

Group *cohesiveness* is also important. Cohesiveness refers to "the attractiveness of the group for its members" (Yalom, 1975, p. 46). It is thus the counterpart in groups for the therapeutic relationship in individual interventions. The sense of belongingness and warmth that characterize cohesiveness can be very important in keeping members coming back despite the emotional and challenging nature of many groups.

The highly emotional atmosphere that often develops in groups can lead to two further curative factors. First, members have an unusual opportunity to openly ventilate their feelings, both positive and negative. Such *catharsis* is not always thought to be sufficient for therapeutic change (e.g., Hobbs, 1962), but it can relieve and energize the members. Second, the group can recreate many experiences that closely parallel ones from members' original families. Thus, just as in family therapy (cf. Framo, 1976), members may have the opportunity for a *"corrective recapitulation of the primary family group"* (Yalom, 1975). That is, new feelings, beliefs, and behaviors can be learned in areas that have been problems for the members since they were children or adolescents. This may include the opportunity to resolve issues such as dependency, rebellious defiance of authority figures, sibling rivalries, or reification of parent figures.

Finally, Yalom (1975) asserts that group members often learn several important new general rules for living. He calls these the *existential factors*. For instance, group members may learn that life is sometimes fair and sometimes unjust, even though we wish it were not. Or, they may finally gain the conviction that every person must face life alone in the end, and that there is no escape from either life's pain or death. In this way, group members can change their basic approach to life toward greater personal responsibility for their own lives.

Each approach to group interventions emphasizes some curative factors and downplays other ones. However, all 11 factors can contribute significantly to therapeutic change in group members. Eight orientations to group intervention are described, including psychoanalytic, behavioral, Synanon, gestalt, transactional analysis, psychodrama, encounter, and marathon. Although every approach shares common elements with several others, each distinct orientation reflects a unique blend of the curative factors.

Psychoanalytic Group Therapy

Psychoanalysts at Britain's Tavistock Clinic have been, in the past 35 years, some of the major proponents of psychoanalytic group therapy (e.g., Ezriel, 1973; Malan, Balfour, Hood, & Shooter, 1976). Much as in the case of individual psychoanalysis, the aim is to help each member to recognize, confront, and accept unconscious impulses that are thought to have originated due to inadequate psychosexual development. However, the group as a whole is treated as the client in the following fashion:

> . . . *the therapist avoids getting drawn into the discussion, answering questions, or giving direct support or advice, and he tries to confine his interventions to interpretations of a psychoanalytic nature. In each session, he seeks to wait until a group theme develops; he then makes the working assumption that this expresses an unconscious feeling, often anxiety, that the group members have in common . . . and he seeks to make use of interpretations to bring this unconscious feeling into the open . . . the group is usually put before the individual . . . since only if a common*

theme is found can the individual members speak in a receptive and supportive at-
mosphere, otherwise there is the danger of the situation degenerating into a series of
separate sessions, with the other members listening in politely concealed boredom,
waiting for their turn to speak. (Malan et al., 1976, p. 1304, emphasis in original)

Thus, the Tavistock approach represents a systematic attempt to go beyond the format of one-to-one therapy in a group setting. The special therapeutic forces in a group are thought to come from members sharing common unconscious problems that can be explored in a less threatening way by talking about the group instead of any individual client. As in one-to-one psychotherapy, however, the transference relationship between the group and their therapist is the focus, rather than the relationships between group members.

Behavior Therapy Groups

A variety of therapeutic interventions have been translated from one-to-one behavior therapy to a group format (Hastorf, 1965; Lawrence & Walter, 1978; Lazarus, 1968; Liberman, 1970). Systematic desensitization (Lazarus, 1961) and assertion training (Wolpe & Lazarus, 1966), have been conducted in groups with adult clients. Behavioral programs have been established for parent training (Rose, 1974), marital enrichment or therapy (Weiss & Margolin, 1977), weight problems (Stunkard, 1972), and smoking cessation (Schmahl, Lichtenstein, & Harris, 1972) as well.

Although behavioral groups vary in their specific formats, several common elements can be elucidated. The therapist provides didactic instruction in techniques of behavior change, usually accompanied by demonstrations and opportunities for group members to rehearse the new skills. For example, the leader might describe the "broken record" (Lange & Jakubowski, 1976) method of assertion, which involves persistent repetition of a request or statement until it is acknowledged. The therapist could then employ *modeling* and *role playing* with group members, as for example:

CLINICIAN: "Let's see how the broken record approach works. Joe, would you play the role of a person who is cutting in front of me in line?"

JOE: (Gets up, walks over in front of the clinician as if cutting-in in a cash register line) "Excuse me, but I'm in a rush."

C: "Please go to the end of the line."

J: (Pointedly ignores the assertion)

C: "Please go to the end of the line."

J: "I'm in a hurry."

C: "I said, please go to the end of the line!"

J: "Oh come off it."

C: "Please go back to the end of the line!"

J: "Well, all right."

C: (Turning to the group) "So, what comments do you have about this?

Following this demonstration and discussion, group members would be encouraged to practice the technique by role playing with one another. The clinician is then likely to lead a discussion of the pros and cons on this skill when applied to a variety of real-life situations. Finally, group members would probably be assigned a homework exercise in which they would try out the technique during the week and record their results for discussion in the next session. In this way, behavioral groups integrate systematic training methods and facilitative group interaction, with a focus on producing specific behavior changes in members.

Synanon Groups

Synanon is a self-help organization for drug abusers (Enright, 1971). Although the total program includes a highly structured and supportive therapeutic milieu in a residential treatment facility, confrontive group experiences play an important role in Synanon. In Synanon groups, "the game" is "put on" each participant: every member is singled out, one at a time to be confronted by the entire group. The target person is aggressively challenged to face up to weaknesses and problems without "copping out" and hiding behind a self-serving social facade. Group members may sarcastically denounce and attack the target person as a fraud, attempting to break through psychological defenses so that the target person will honestly admit personal inadequacies.

The Synanon approach is designed to provide a form of intense group confrontation—forcing each member to recognize and accept their flaws without shame or denial. It is hoped that such a bedrock personal confrontation will bolster the members' strength in their weakest areas, thus helping them to cope better with all stresses. Synanon groups are called "games" because every effort is made to keep a clear distinction between the time-limited attacks in the group and the warm and supportive atmosphere that is the norm throughout the rest of the day. There are, however, serious concerns about the excessive confrontation and aggression that can potentially harm participants. The Synanon approach has not been widely used by clinical psychologists.

Gestalt Group Therapy

Gestalt groups focus on the here and now with an emphasis on helping each member to integrate their feelings with their more intellectual beliefs and cognitive controls (Perls, Hefferline, & Goodman, 1951). In a fashion somewhat like the Synanon games (but *less* confrontive), each member is placed on "the hot seat" and confronted by the leader and members. The target person is encouraged to identify current sensations and emotions, particularly ones that are painful or incongruent. The clinician often comments on nonverbal cues that are thought to reveal special conflict areas in the target person. For example, after Vivian has been asked to occupy the hot seat, a Gestalt group interaction might proceed as follows:

CLINICIAN: "I notice that your hands are clenched, Vivian. What are your hands saying to you about your feelings right now?"

VIVIAN: (Looks startled, quickly relaxes hands, slumps forward slightly) "I don't know. Maybe I'm tense about what my mother has been doing to me."

C: "Hold on, let's focus on what's happening *now*. You're slumped over; is your body expressing a feeling that you need to be aware of?"

V: (Starts to cry softly) "I can't seem to feel anything, not really. It's like I'm all stopped up inside. It hurts."

C: (Gently puts a hand on Vivian's arm.) "Now you've hit something. It's like you've swallowed some feelings that have got you all plugged up, as if your mother had forced you to eat when you just couldn't swallow another bite. In a moment I'll want you to fantasize yourself with your mother. But right now, let's stay with feeling the pain."

Many emotion-charged experiential exercises are used in Gestalt groups, to vividly confront members with their unconscious feelings and needs, and to help them to accept and assert those repressed "pieces" of themselves. In our example, the clinician alluded to the "empty chair" technique, which involves having the member confront some important person by talking as if that person were sitting in an empty chair right in the room. Although members who are not currently on the hot seat usually observe quietly, the intensity generated through these exercises is thought to provide for important vicarious learning.

Transactional Analysis Groups

Transactional analysis (Berne, 1970; 1972) involves an intensive examination of the "transactions" that people enact within themselves and with other persons. Each person is seen as having three separate mental agencies that must be kept in balance: a "parent" (paralleling the superego), an "adult" (similar to the psychoanalytic concept of ego), and a "child" (similar to the id, but with more attention paid to the positive playfulness of children). When any one of these internal forces takes excessive control, psychological dysfunction is thought to occur. For example, a person who is experiencing extreme guilt might be said to have too much "parent" control, at the expense of the reality-oriented "adult" and the pleasure-oriented "child."

Transactional analysis also deals with interpersonal transactions, focusing on "the games people play" (Berne, 1970) and the "scripts" that people use in their attempts to cope with life (Berne, 1972). According to Berne, a "game is a repeated and often destructive interaction between two or more people." For example, the "alcoholic" game involves five roles: the "alcoholic" who drinks to escape tension and involvement, the "persecutor" who blames and attacks the alcoholic, the "rescuer" who tries to save the alcoholic from disaster, the "patsy'' who is taken advantage of by the alcoholic, and the ''connection'' who supplies the alcoholic with both liquor and encouragement to continue drinking. While not all five roles are involved in every instance of alcoholism, these roles can be used to clarify the often confusing situation that can cause or maintain this self-destructive condition.

A ''script'' is a narrow and self-defeating strategy for coping with life. Rather than utilizing a flexible and effective approach to handling life's challenges, a person who is relying on a single script has taken a single life plan as the method for dealing with relationships. For example, the ''Sisyphus'' script is based on the Greek myth of a man who was doomed to an eternity of frustration in which he had to push a boulder up a steep mountain only to have it roll back over him to the bottom each time that he approached the peak. This script might be said to occur when a person consistently strives to be successful, but always seems to fail just at the brink of success.

Transactional analysis is readily adapted to group intervention. Group members are encouraged to develop honest relationships with one another, and then helped to identify the scripts and games that lead to conflict. The clinician may also comment on instances when a member's mental agencies seem to be out of balance, or where one member is talking through one mental agency and yet addressing another member at a different level. For example, a member may criticize another participant for being irresponsible, much as a parent might unfairly blame a child. The therapist would encourage both members to interact at the same level: as ''parent'' to ''parent,'' ''adult'' to ''adult,'' or even ''child'' to ''child.'' For example, a group interaction might go as follows:

JACK: ''I think you're an idiot to ignore me, Bob.'' (Critical Parent)
BOB: ''I don't care what you say, you SOB. Bug off!'' (Agressive Child)
CLINICIAN: ''I wonder if you could talk more to Bob's parent, Jack?''
J: ''Well, look Bob, we both want to benefit from being in this group. I'm not comfortable with the way that we give each other feedback.'' (Nonblaming Parent)
B: ''All right, let's work out a plan so that we can be honest without intimidating each other. (Nurturant Parent) Let's relax and try to enjoy the group.'' (Child)
J: ''Say, I can get behind that idea. I'd like to relax too.'' (Child)
C: ''I'm impressed by how you two were able to get your ''parents'' and your ''childs'' in sync. The last time we reached this point, it looked to me like you got sidetracked in a ''Now see what you've done'' game. Maybe the group can point out what happened to make this transaction work today?''

Transactional analysis groups thus focus on the here-and-now interactions between group members. The therapist may relate the group interaction patterns to issues that members face in their daily lives, but the emphasis is on recognizing and changing the games and scripts that occur right within the group.

Psychodrama Groups

Moreno (1946) originated the psychodrama approach to group intervention. In psychodrama, one group member takes the role of the "protagonist," and the clinician serves as a "director." With the aid of other group members as supporting actors and actresses, vignettes from the protagonist's life or dreams are enacted. The intent is not to recreate the precise events, but rather to use theatre as a medium through which the protagonist can act out needs and feelings that might otherwise be unconscious. When such unrecognized insights are literally brought to life in the psychodrama the impact can be much greater than in therapy that relies strictly on talking.

Although the focus is on the protagonist, members who serve as contributors are encouraged to relate their feelings and reactions. This provides an approximation to direct feedback from significant others in the protagonist's life, adding a new dimension to the enactment. The protagonist may also be asked to experiment with a role reversal, that is, to take the role of one of the other persons in the vignette in order to experience different perspectives.

Encounter Groups

While the prior group interventions are utilized both as ameliorative interventions with therapy clients and as enhancement experiences for well-functioning individuals, encounter groups have been developed explicitly to provide persons who are *not* seeking remedial therapy a group setting for self-exploration. In practice, the distinction between group therapy and encounter groups is not clear. Both experiences offer opportunities for both personal growth and the resolution of psychological problems. However, the contract between members and leader is different in the two approaches, because group therapy is definitely intended to help in the alleviation of dysfunctions, while encounter groups promise to offer a safe and honest setting for growth.

Rogers (1968; 1970) has been a major proponent of encounter groups. Rogers' client-centered approach to counseling and therapy can be used to create a stimulating and supportive group milieu. The clinician serves as a facilitator of interaction, encouraging members to focus on empathic, positive, and genuine interactions with one another. As in transactional analysis and gestalt groups, the emphasis is on here-and-now relationships between group members. While it is expected that most members will not continue these relationships outside the group, the hope is to aid each member in exploring new feelings and new ways of interacting with other people. Honest self-disclosure of emotions, conflicts, and personal goals is encouraged. For many, this group experience may be a refreshing or even stunning change from the superficiality and anonymity of their daily interpersonal existence. Encounter groups seek to increase members' sense of personal security and worth, as well as their willingness to reach out and develop meaningful relationships.

Some encounter groups utilize sensory awareness exercises in the model developed at the Esalen Institute in California (Schutz, 1967). These experiences offered a structured way for deepening and extending the person's self-awareness and relationships. For example, one sensory awareness exercise involves having a group member stand in the middle of a circle formed by the other members. The central person closes his or her eyes and falls backward while retaining a straight posture. The encircling members then pass this person around the circle, keeping his or her feet centered. This exercise calls for a relinquishment of personal control and can help the person experience a renewed sense of confidence and trust.

Encounter groups are often reported to be powerful experiences by their participants. Although there are dangers of potential harm (Hartley, Roback, & Abramowitz, 1976), the powerful experience can work toward positive personal growth. A group member's appraisal offers an illustration of the best features of encounter groups:

> For the first time in my life, I felt really safe and protected. I've always hidden the "real me" behind a facade of being strong and totally self-assured, but doubts gnawed away inside me. In this group, I was terrified of being seen for the coward that I feel I really am. After many moments of uncertainty, I found that the openness and honesty of other members brought forth some courage that I didn't realize I had. I crawled out of my shell, and shared my feelings of pain and fear with the group. The reaction stunned me: they weren't angry or disgusted, but they seemed to really care about me. I can't say for sure, but I think that was the beginning of a new self-confidence for me.

Safety and honesty are the key in encounter groups. When the facilitator establishes a pattern of group interactions that enables group members to "encounter" both themselves and each other in this manner, the experience can be both exciting and enhancing. Given the documented potential for harm, however, encounter groups warrant special care and caution.

Marathon Groups

When encounter groups are conducted in a single continuous session, running for as long as 16 to 48 hours consecutively, they have been called marathon groups (Bach, 1966). "Marathon" is used to describe the intensive and prolonged nature of the one-session experience. Rare marathon groups are conducted in the nude to further potentiate the impact (Bindrim, 1968), but most are simply modifications of the encounter approach to a single lengthy meeting (Rogers, 1970). The goal in marathon groups is to use the combination of time limits (only one session) and exhausting time length to promote the expression of intense emotions. Social niceties are abandoned in an attempt to generate spontaneity and honest self-disclosure. Members are often not allowed to withdraw from group participation throughout the marathon, thus creating a stressful social environment that encourages a loosening of one's defenses and a reliance on other members for support. Marathon groups offer a "massed practice" approach to learning, seeking to amplify the effects of encounter groups that meet at spaced intervals. Marathon groups are not routine and caution must be exercised.

Research Evaluation

Group interventions offer a variety of experiences aimed at helping clients achieve such diverse goals as intrapsychic exploration and insight, behavioral skills, increased self-awareness and receptivity to intimate relationships, and enhanced coping skills in previously deficient personality areas. Encounter groups, both when conducted in a marathon format (Kilmann & Sotile, 1976), in weekly sessions (Bednar & Kaul, 1978), and in behavioral groups (Marks, 1978; Rich & Schroeder, 1976) have been found to be more effective than no treatment or attention-placebo control conditions. However, experimental evaluations of the other approaches are rare, and the limited evidence suggests that these group therapies with adults (Bednar & Kaul, 1978) or children (Abramowitz, 1976) are *not* reliably effective. Further research is needed to more fully evaluate all group therapy approaches, and studies that investigate the parameters of group intervention offer a particularly promising direction. Relevant parameters include leadership style, time format, group structure, cohesiveness, self-disclosure, type of feedback, pregroup preparation, cotherapy, and group composition.

Leadership Style   Lieberman, Yalom, and Miles (1973) provided 10 different group interventions for 200 undergraduate volunteers, with each subject randomly assigned to one group: T-group, Rogerian encounter group, sensory awareness encounter group, gestalt, transactional analysis, psychodrama, Synanon, psychoanalytic, marathon encounter, and videotapes that presented a Rogerian encounter group for subjects to view. Subjects were assessed on a variety of personality questionnaires and ratings by group leaders and participants and close acquaintances of the subjects, before, immediately after, and six months after participating. Differences were not consistently found in the gains made by participants in different groups, but analyses of observational data concerning the group leaders' actual in-session behavioral styles yielded significant findings. Although the leaders were all experienced in doing group work in the group orientation that their group was supposed to provide, their actual behavior was generally not different from one another except in four respects: leaders varied in the extent to which they focused on communicating (1) *caring*, that is, emotional support and protection, affection, and genuine and empathic understanding; (2) *meaning attributions*, that is, explaining, clarifying, interpreting, and providing cognitive labels to help members intellectually understand their experiences; (3) *emotional stimulation,* that is, confrontive challenges to group members to take risks that were balanced by self-disclosures by the leader about his or her own feelings, conflicts, and needs; and (4) an *executive function*, that is, setting limits, rules, and goals to make sure that the group was efficient and productive.

Lieberman et al. (1973) found that the leaders' supposed orientations did *not* correlate with their actual leadership behaviors. Thus a "gestalt" leader might use the caring style as much as an emotional stimulation approach, or a "transactional analysis" leader was as likely to take an executive function style as a meaning attribution approach. What the leaders *said* they do with groups was not equivalent with what they actually *did* do.

However, the observed leadership styles did play an important role in producing positive or negative outcomes. Leaders who actually focused only on emotional stimulation, meaning attribution, or the executive function were least likely to promote positive changes in group members and most likely to have group members who deteriorated. Fully 8% of all members scored worse on the assessment measures at the six-month follow-up than they had before participating, and most of these casualties came from groups where the leader took a narrow confrontive, interpretive, or businesslike style. In contrast, members whose leaders focused on communicating caring, especially when added to an equal emphasis on meaning attribution, were uniformly and highly successful. Thus, regardless of the clinician's stated orientation, effective group leadership appears to require the creation of a group milieu where emotional confrontation is balanced by genuine caring and the teaching of new cognitive or behavioral skills for social problem solving. Further research with "real" therapy clients, rather than volunteers, is needed before this conclusion can be applied to group therapy as well as to encounter groups.

Time Format When marathon groups are contrasted with comparable interventions conducted on a spaced-session basis (e.g., one three-hour session per week), the results appear equivalent (Kilmann & Sotile, 1976). For example, Shapiro (1971) assigned participants who were matched on age, sex, previous group experience, and level of self-disclosure to either a twice-weekly group or an 18-hour marathon group. After participating, the two groups did not differ in their scores on personality questionnaires, although marathon participants reported more negative feelings as a result of the experience. Thus, while marathon formats may arouse more intense negative emotions, there is no evidence that they have more or less positive effects on participants' longterm psychological functioning than spaced-session groups.

Structure Group leaders can introduce structure by actively regulating the group interaction, for example by using structured gestalt or behavioral exercises or by intervening frequently when members are talking. Two studies, one employing a marathon format (Kilmann, Albert, & Sotile, 1975), and the other using a series of shorter sessions (Abramowitz, Abramowitz, Roback, & Jackson, 1974), both indicate that participants who believe they control their own lives (internal locus of control) respond better to a group with less structure, while members who believe that external forces dominate their lives (external locus of control) gain more from groups where the leader provides a great deal of structure. Group structure can be beneficial, but the degree of structure should be tailored to fit the locus of control (and perhaps also other aspects of the interpersonal and cognitive styles) of group members.

Cohesiveness Cohesiveness refers to the extent to which members identify with and emotionally support each other. Jeske (1973) observed counseling groups at a university clinic and found that the frequency with which members identified with each other was strongly correlated with their gains from therapy. Identification was measured by asking participants to rate their degree of empathy for other group members, while outcome was assessed via MMPI scores. Further research is needed with clients other than students, with varied types of group interventions, and with experimental manipulations of group cohesiveness to confirm this initial finding.

Self-Disclosure   When leaders talk about their own feelings and experiences, this self-disclosure inclines group members to view them as helpful and friendly, but the impact that this has on group effectiveness remains uninvestigated (Bednar & Kaul, 1978). One study has examined the relationship between self-disclosure by group members and their gains or deterioration. Stassberg, Roback, Anchor, and Abramowitz (1975) rated the level of self-disclosure of psychiatric patients in group therapy, based on audiotapes of the group sessions, and measured patients' prepost changes on the MMPI and clinicians' ratings of symptoms and adjustment. Results indicated that patients who disclosed *less* tended to gain more, while high self-disclosure was correlated with no change or even deterioration. The correlational research design prevents us from knowing whether the self-disclosure, or some other factor correlated with self-disclosure, produced the unfavorable outcomes. However, the study converges with Lieberman et al. (1973) to recommend caution by group leaders in eliciting emotional self-disclosure from clients.

Feedback   Feedback from the leader or group members can potentially help participants to learn new strategies for feeling, thinking, and behaving, as well as possibly increasing their trust in other persons. Experimental studies have demonstrated that positive feedback is more believable and persuasive than negative feedback (Jacobs, Jacobs, Cavior, & Burke, 1974), while feedback about behavior is perceived by group members to be more effective than emotional feedback (Jacobs, Jacobs, Feldman, & Cavior, 1973). Perhaps most importantly, when undergraduates in encounter groups were provided with both positive and negative feedback—as occurs in most real groups—the order in which the two types of feedback was presented was significant (Jacobs, Jacobs, Gatz, & Schaible, 1973). When negative feedback preceded positive feedback, the participants were more willing to accept the feedback and change their attitudes than when positive feedback was delivered first. Thus, starting out with the "bad news" and following with the "good news" appears most effective. However, further research is needed to verify these findings with "real" clients in group therapies.

Preparation   Many group members enter therapy with great uncertainty and trepidation, particularly if they have had no prior exposure to the concepts and methods of group intervention. For this reason, Hoehn-Saric, Frank, Imber, Nash, Stone, and Battle (1964) developed a "Role Induction Interview" to teach prospective clients how therapy can help them, what they can expect to have happen in therapy, and how they will be expected to contribute in group sessions. Strupp and Bloxom (1973) provided 40 low-socioeconomic-status clients with such a supportive and informative interview, and had 40 other similar clients view a videotape of the same type of preparation interview. Compared to 40 other clients who received no preparation, the prepared clients were better informed and more motivated at the beginning of therapy, and they perceived themselves as having gained more at the end of the group therapy. Interestingly, the interview seemed best for conveying factual information, while the film had the strongest positive effect on client motivation. These findings converge with the results of similar investigations (e.g., Yalom, Monte, Newell, & Rand, 1967) to show that preparation can enhance group interventions.

Cotherapy   When two (or more) therapists are working as a team this is called cotherapy. Although greater professional manpower is used by cotherapy than with only one therapist, cotherapy offers several potential advantages: two therapists have greater leverage and better coverage than one; each therapist can more flexibly take on different roles in therapy, such as observing while the cotherapist takes charge; cotherapists can also model effective communication and negotiation by talking openly with one another during group sessions; in emotionally charged interventions such as sex therapy, a male-female cotherapist team can provide clients of both genders with a same-sex advocate. Despite the clinical importance of determining when cotherapy's extra costs are warranted by its potential advantages, only one study has been reported which compares single therapist versus cotherapist interventions. Bancroft (cited in Marks, 1978) found cotherapy slightly (but nonsignificantly) more effective in sexual therapy. Comparable research is needed with other forms of group intervention.

Group Composition   The concern here is with the question of what types of persons can join together to form the best milieu for group intervention. In couples therapy, the superiority of conjoint over individual approaches indicates that both partners should be fully involved in treatment sessions. In family therapy, studies indicate that clients are more likely to continue in treatment (Shapiro & Suchman, 1973) and to show improvement (Love, Kaswan, & Bugental, 1972; Martin, 1977) if the father is directly present in therapy sessions. The importance of including children and other family members such as grandparents has not been empirically established (Gurman & Kniskern, 1978), but the evidence does indicate that full involvement by both parents is very important.

In group therapy and encounter groups, Yalom (1975) hypothesized that an optimal composition would include members who share sufficient commonalities to enable them to trust and identify with one another but who also bring differences in viewpoints, backgrounds, and problems to add spice and newness to the group. Homogeneous groups can become stagnant and superficial because members share so much empathy and mutual support that they never challenge one another to take risks and try new ways of feeling, thinking, and behaving. Hetereogeneous groups offer members a variety of new models and perspectives, but they can become so embroiled in conflict that emotional support and caring may be lacking. Research is needed to evaluate this hypothesis.

So many worlds, so much to do,
So little done, such things to be.
Ring out the want, the care, the sin
The faithless coldness of the times.
Ring out the thousand wars of old,
Ring in the thousand years of peace.

Alfred, Lord Tennyson

15

MILIEU AND COMMUNITY INTERVENTIONS

Clinical psychologists' interventions sometimes involve the design and implementation of two types of alterations in their clients' sociophysical environments. *Milieu interventions* are systematic changes in existing social institutions, such as a new therapeutic program that improves the social environment of a mental hospital ward or training teachers to incorporate preventive psychological concepts in their curricula. *Community interventions* involve the development of new educational and therapeutic service and support networks as alternatives to the existing ones, such as the creation of a treatment center for drug addiction that provides community-based services or the development of self-help groups for troubled parents. In each case, changes in both the social and physical aspects of clients' environments are being undertaken in order to make peoples' life settings more educational and therapeutic.

Milieu and community interventions can be designed to ameliorate or prevent psychological dysfunctions, or to enhance interpersonal relationships, just as was true for individual and group interventions. However, milieu and community interventions are unique in that they aim to directly restructure the sociophysical environment for groups of people who live in the same community or institution. The primary goal in individual and group interventions is to help each individual *client*, but the focus in milieu and community interventions is on changing clients' *environments* for the betterment of many people rather than for only one client or a small group. The ultimate goal is to help people live fuller lives, but the strategy of milieu and community interventions is to work with large groups who share the same life setting to make that setting a better place to live.

The situations that we encounter in our daily lives can have detrimental effects on our psychological well-being. For example, a physical environment that is excessively crowded, polluted, and noisy places its residents under constant stress (Cohen, 1980). Or a social environment where people are rewarded for passively following orders and keeping quiet may be teaching its residents a way of life that is helpless, lonely and stagnant (Schmidt & Keating, 1979).

Alternately, our life settings can help us to overcome or prevent problems and even to expand our interests and competencies. For example, a physical environment that is not crowded, yet filled with resources such as tools, books, and convenient meeting places, is likely to stimulate its residents to become involved with one another and to undertake meaningful social and occupational roles. Or, a social environment that is governed by rules that have been formulated and agreed on by all residents is helping its residents to learn and use leadership and problem solving skills in a self-determined fashion. Milieu and community interventions are designed to change problematic environments in the positive directions that the latter two examples suggest.

STRATEGIES OF MILIEU AND COMMUNITY INTERVENTIONS

There are several strategies that are often employed when a clinical psychologist provides interventions for milieus and communities. Although these strategies are typically employed together within a comprehensive program, each is examined separately.

Increasing the Quality of Environments

When people live in environments that are unpredictable, unrewarding (or even punishing), and detrimental in what they teach residents to do and think, psychological dysfunctions are likely to result. For example, Lewinsohn and Libet (1972) and Lewinsohn and Graf (1973) found a correlation between participation in events that were rated by subjects as "pleasant" and self-rated depression. Subjects included depressed, nondepressed but psychologically impaired, and "normal" (not receiving therapy) adults, who completed a checklist of pleasant events (see Table 15-1) and the Depression Adjective Checklist daily. For all groups, it was shown that failing to create a pleasant social environment by engaging in attractive events was clearly related to feelings of depression. While experimental tests of this finding are needed (Blaney, 1977), the study demonstrates that psychologically distressed persons perceive their environment as bleak and themselves as negative contributors to this situation.

Clinical interventions can have an important positive impact if they help to make detrimental environments more predictable, rewarding, and educational. Thus, several milieu interventions have been designed to improve mental hospital wards by (1) creating clear and systematic rules for both patients and staff (i.e., increasing predictability), (2) training ward staff to spend more time talking and listening to patients in a mutually rewarding fashion, and also encouraging patients to do the same with one another (i.e., increasing rewardingness), and (3) training both staff and patients to serve as teachers for the patients and to foster the learning of personal, social, and vocational skills.

Special Services for High-Risk Persons

Research has been underway for several years in an effort to identify those persons who are likely to develop certain psychosocial problems, such as those asso-

Table 15-1   Samples of the Activities Found to Correlate Inversely with Depressive Mood[a]

1. Laughing (IA)
2. Being relaxed (IA)
3. Being with happy people (S)
4. Having people show interest in what you have said (S)
5. Doing a project in my own way (E)
6. Planning or organizing something (E)

From P. M. Lewinsohn, A. Biglow, and A. M. Zeiss, Behavioral treatment of depression. In P. O. Davidson (Ed.), *The behavioral management of anxiety, depression, and pain.* New York: Brunner/Mazel, 1976. See original source for a complete list.

[a] S = Social; IA = Internal Affect; E = Effectiveness oriented.

ciated with the diagnosis of schizophrenia (e.g., Mednick & Schulsinger, 1968). Persons whose parent(s) has been diagnosed as schizophrenic are designated as "high risk," because such people have been found to be more likely to incur schizophrenia than any other persons. Measurements of psychological, social, academic and physiological functioning are then obtained from these individuals at regular intervals (e.g., every year) beginning as early in life as possible. The ultimate goal is to identify the genetic and environmental factors that produce the schizophrenic syndrome, so that prospective parents who have risky genetic makeups can be forewarned. High-risk identification also facilitates the development of improved life settings for children who are "at risk," such as home and school programs that teach skills for coping with stress. Similar programs have been developed to identify and aid children who are at risk for other problems such as school maladjustment.

Creating New Settings

The design and creation of a new setting for the benefit of residents in a community is a complicated and problematic endeavor, but one which clinical psychologists have found themselves called on to undertake when existing mental health, community service, and educational institutions do not appear to be amenable to positive change.

Sarason (1972) states that the creator of a new setting must recognize several basic issues:

> . . . that a new setting has a prehistory, local and national; that locally many different individuals and groups have a role in its birth; that much of its past is in the living present and must be dealt with; that resources are always limited and usually over-estimated because of a sense of mission and boundless enthusiasm; that conflict within the setting (and between settings) is a fact of social life exacerbated by conflicts between ideas; that verbal agreement about values is no substitute for foregoing a constitution that anticipates and helps deal with differences in values, ideas and change; that the leader is inevitably a model for the thinking and action of others and that in the usual unthinking course of things the leader visits on others his

increasing sense of privacy, fear of openness, dependence on extrinsic factors as cri-
teria of worth, and boredom; that the usual structure of settings as well as the defi-
nition of and credentials for work tend rather quickly to extinguish curiosity and the
sense of challenge. (p. 277)

With these issues in mind, clinicians have attempted to create new settings that
are innovative alternatives to existing institutions, such as community mental
health centers or self-help programs that enable laypersons to join together to
solve psychosocial problems.

Development of Community Resources

Resources in the community are utilized and improved by clinical psychologists
when developing milieu and community interventions (Highlight 15-1). For example, in the past two decades, clinical psychologists have increasingly enlisted
the aid of laypersons to serve as paraprofessional mental health agents (Anthony
& Carkhuff, 1977). A paraprofessional is a person who has not received a formal
degree such as a Ph.D., M.A., Psy.D., M.S.W., R.N., etc., but who has been
carefully trained by professionals such as clinical psychologists to conduct counseling, tutoring, or some other community service.

Reiff and Reissman (1960) made an important differentiation between
paraprofessionals who are not from the community that is being helped—for example, middle-class housewives or college students—and ones who are "indigenous," that is, members of the target community. The first group, called "ubiq-
uitous" paraprofessionals, share the middle-class values and language of the
professionals, thus permitting a good working relationship. However, indigenous
paraprofessionals have closer ties with the community residents who are being
served and can thus provide liaisons between professionals and the community.
When indigenous persons are trained as mental health or community service
agents, this also strengthens the community by providing new jobs and developing the skills and knowledge of both the paraprofessionals and the other residents.

Highlight 15-1   Environmental Conservation

The growing concern about deficiencies in our expected standards for environmental quality and our energy sources' capabilities has led to several
developments in psychological research on environmental conservation.
Everett, Hayward, and Meyers (1974) provided an early example on their experimental modification of bus ridership. A token economy procedure was instituted on a college-town bus such that riders earned tokens (tickets) worth
between 5¢ and 10¢ (and stamped with a thanks for "being ecological") on
each bus trip. Compared to baseline periods and to a comparable "control"
bus, the token intervention raised ridership 150%. The cost for a week was less
than $150, with an increase of nearly 150 riders per day. The method was
strongly endorsed by local merchants who redeemed the tokens for goods such
as record albums, movies, and food treats, because this encouraged shopping
and served as an inexpensive advertisement source.

Chapman and Risley (1974) evaluated two approaches to promoting litter cleanup in an urban area. Noting the health and aesthetic damage caused by city littering, the authors first simply requested, and subsequently offered monetary reinforcement for help from low-income neighborhood children in collecting litter in their 390-family apartment complex. For a cost of approximately $50 per week, notable reduction in litter (producing a litter level almost comparable to that of a middle-income neighborhood) was achieved. Verbal exhortations had little effect, but small rewards were sufficient to promote community involvement by the children and improved environmental quality.

Another issue of environmental concern is the use of electrical energy. Hayes and Cone (1977) reported that monetary payments, energy information, and daily feedback on consumption were employed to reduce the use of electricity in four units of a university housing complex. Initially, the baseline level of electrical consumption was objectively recorded, followed by the participants in the study recording their own baseline usage. A comparison of these baseline records indicated that, in this instance, there were no appreciable differences due to the reactivity of data recording. Payments to the participants depended on the weekly current reduction from the original baseline. For example, participants could earn from $3.00 for a 10 to 19% reduction to $15 for a 50% or greater reduction. This daily feedback consisted of the distribution of a flier that described (1) the amount of electricity consumed the previous day, (2) the amount conserved so far that week, (3) the amount that would be conserved for the week if the current rate were maintained, and (4) the percent above or below the baseline. The provision of energy information consisted of a poster that described ways to reduce consumption of electricity and gave the amounts of electricity used by various household devices. Comparisons of the different facets of the intervention indicated that the monetary payments were successful in producing immediate and substantial reductions in the consumption of electricity. This positive finding was also evident even after the payments were reduced considerably. The feedback about daily consumption was helpful in reducing consumption, while the information about the method of conservation did not produce any meaningful differences in the use of electricity.

Although environmental conservation is only one area for community intervention, it is an important concern for all of us who share the limited sources of energy that are available. Clinical psychologists are among those in the current effort to apply behavioral science methods to this significant goal (Nietzel, Winett, MacDonald, & Davidson, 1976).

For example, Weinman, Sanders, Kleiner, and Wilson (1970) recruited retired people to serve as volunteer "enablers" for chronic mental patients who had been released from a hospital to the community. The enablers were extensively trained and supervised over the course of a year, and during this time they either took a patient into their homes or visited a patient who was living in his or her own apartment (10 hours per week). Compared to hospitalized patients, the patients who lived in the community with the help of enablers were found to be more likely to successfully live in their community without returning to the hospital over the year following the program.

Enhancement of Community Self-Determination

Clinical psychologists also create programs that directly increase residents' control over the decision-making mechanisms that shape the entire community. This strategy has been undertaken in two ways. First, community persons have been taught new skills that enable them to more effectively participate in the community's existing political and educational institutions. For instance, Briscoe, Hoffman, and Bailey (1975) trained nine low-income and educationally disadvantaged persons to utilize systematic problem-solving skills in fulfilling their mandate as elected members of the community planning board. The board members were responsible for "identifying and solving community problems, such as arranging to have repairs made to the community center, organizing social and educational events, discovering and distributing social welfare resources to the community, finding and providing medical care . . ." (p. 158). Individualized training for each member resulted in dramatic increases in the board's ability to identify, evaluate, and solve community issues (Figure 15-1).

A second strategy for increasing community self-determination has been called social activism. Here the members of a community are aided in organizing themselves as an effective lobbying group. For example, Alinsky (1971) described working with the leaders of the black community in a major city to influence a large department store to hire black employees. Extensive training and planning was required to unite these traditionally powerless persons, and the climax came when the group exerted pressure on the store by buying and then immediately returning large amounts of merchandise. Shortly after this chaotic scene, the store finally rescinded its prejudicial hiring policies. Although psychologists have only infrequently used the social activist approach, the clinician's skills in communication, decision making, and interpersonal influence could be a valuable asset for community organizers who hope to improve the system for the benefit of the less powerful residents in the community. However, social/political activism requires experience and training often not provided in clinical psychology: forays into this arena require caution, ethics, and preparation (cf. Dunnette, 1976).

ROLE OF THE CLINICAL PSYCHOLOGIST IN MILIEU AND COMMUNITY INTERVENTIONS

Clinical psychologists can participate in the design and development of sociophysical environments by employing any or all of the strategies just described. Their goal in conducting milieu and community interventions is to develop life settings that offer opportunities for growth, personal satisfaction, and achievement, and meaningful interpersonal relationships for the many different kinds of people who reside in the institution or community. In so doing, clinical psychologists can offer several unique contributions based on their scientific and professional expertise (see Table 15-2). Again, it is important to note that special skills are essential to the role of social change agent: organizational development, systems management, program consultation, program evaluation, and advocacy are

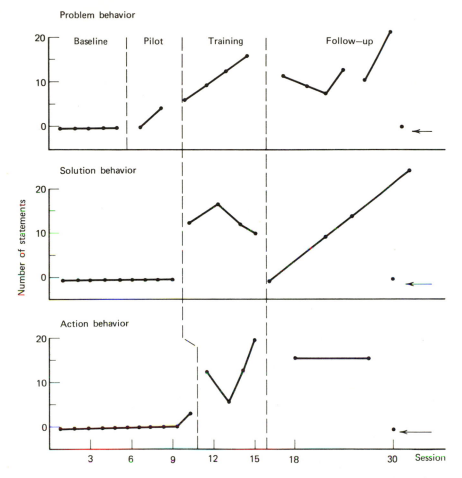

Figure 15-1 Number of problem solving statements made during the board meetings by all nine subjects. In the pilot condition, the training program utilized a lecture and discussion approach. This approach was attempted during one training session with all subjects and the next session with only the chairperson. In the training condition, the programmed instructional model was utilized as the training procedure with the chairperson and individual subjects. In the followup condition, the subjects no longer received training but were observed during the meetings. The arrow at meeting 30 indicates that during this meeting several outsiders and the first two authors attended the meeting and participated extensively. The participation of the subjects appeared to decrease greatly as a result. Adapted from R. B. Briscoe, J. B. Hoffman, and J. S. Bailey, Behavioral community psychology: Training a community board to problem solve. *Journal of Applied Behavior Analysis*, 1975, *8*, 157–168. Copyright 1975 by the Society for Experimental Analysis of Behavior. Reprinted by permission.

examples of areas of expertise that can be acquired through specialized training in fields such as community psychology, law, business administration, or public health. With such preparation, some clinical psychologists can and do move beyond one-to-one and group therapy and into the realm of social change.

Table 15-2 Sample Roles for Clinical Psychologists in Milieu and Community Interventions

Role	Description	Reference
Human development liaison	A go-between who brings together the many and varied groups and organizations in a community in order to help them to coordinate their services	Dokecki (1978)
Facilitator of innovation	A guide who establishes a supportive and challenging social environment for group or organizational planners and leaders can explore new goals and methods	Perlman and Gurin (1971)
Catalyst	An activator who sparks members of communities or groups to take action by helping them mobilize their resources and showing them clear needs for change	Perlman and Gurin (1971)
Educator	A teacher who listens to members of communities or groups and provides learning experiences to help them develop new skills and knowledge to better control their own lives and environments	Guerney, Stollak, and Guerney (1971)
Social policy evaluator	A research and evaluation specialist who aids community groups and organizations to scientifically and ecologically monitor the effects and effectiveness of their services	Goodwin (1971)
Advocate	A spokesperson who uses power and persuasion to influence established social institutions to improve their policies and actions toward community people and organizations	Perlman and Gurin (1971)
Tactician	A planner of strategy and tactics to help communities and groups increase their resources and scope of influence	Perlman and Gurin (1971)
Systems analyst	A conceptualizer who develops practical understandings of community and organizational networks in order to enhance community and organizational environments	Sarason (1976)

The clinician can teach skills, facilitate communication and organization within the community, evaluate current and prospective programs, or even directly represent the community in bargaining with politicians, businesspersons, or administrators. Representing a community may be the chosen tack because psychologists believe that positive change in a total milieu or community requires complementary changes on the part of all persons and organizations involved. A noteworthy "failure" experience exemplifies this view. Klaus and Gray (1968) developed a program to prepare low-income black preschoolers for elementary school. They found that two or three years of systematic teaching for both the children and their mothers were able to produce higher IQ scores than those attained by two untreated control groups when the children entered the first grade (Gray & Klaus, 1970). However, these gains had all but disappeared by the fourth grade, and reviewers have suggested that a lasting positive impact could only have been produced by intervening to improve the *schools* that the children entered (in addition to the programs for the children and mothers) (Baratz & Baratz, 1970). While this position remains controversial, our example does suggest the importance of altering all relevant environmental systems when comprehensive milieu and community interventions are being undertaken.

INTERVENTIONS IN EXISTING INSTITUTIONS

Three important institutions that deal with people are mental hospitals, schools, and correctional institutions. Clinical psychologists have developed milieu interventions in each of these settings.

Milieu Interventions in Mental Hospitals

The treatment regimen provided within a mental hospital varies, but often consists primarily of medication and individual or group therapy. Anthony, Buell, Sharratt, and Althoff (1972) have reviewed several studies that indicate that inpatient facilities with this approach were effective in helping only about 50% of the patients to return to their communities without requiring further hospitalization. Fewer than 30% of the patients were reported to have secured full-time employment at a one-year followup. Although recidivism and employment are not always the best measures of the effects of hospital treatment, the report of Anthony et al. (1972) does suggest that mental hospitals may be in need of additional programs to assist the patient in returning and adjusting to the environment.

Clinical psychologists have developed three particular types of milieu interventions in an effort to make hospital treatment more effective: the therapeutic community, the token economy, and the day hospital.

The Therapeutic Community A century ago, a "moral" treatment approach was developed to replace prisons and madhouses for the insane (Grobb, 1973). Gradually, however, new economic and political pressures led to the evolution of massive mental institutions in which patients were once again relegated to passive and dependent roles. Jones (1953; 1968), a psychiatrist, is often credited with having pioneered the milieu intervention that has come to be called the "therapeutic community.'' The basic idea was to change mental hospital wards into cohesive communities in which each patient is a valued contributor and a recipient of social support. The therapeutic community utilizes principles from clinical, social, and environmental psychology. Staff and patients are treated as valued individuals who contribute to a microcosm community. Natural incentives, such as the pleasure of conversation or the satisfaction of having a positive impact on a troubled person, are made available to all participants who join in the counseling, ward government, and recreation activities.

Establishing a therapeutic community requires staff training, changing the roles of the staff and the patients, changing the ward rules, and, when possible, altering the physical environment of the ward. Since the therapeutic community utilizes nurses and attendants as paraprofessional counselors and activity organizers for the patients, staff training focuses on personnel skills for developing rapport with, and facilitating communication between, patients. Training focuses on increasing the ward staff's sensitivity to the needs, problems, and capabilities of their patients and fostering a more humanitarian and respectful attitude toward the patients. In this way, ward staff are trained to be valuable therapeutic aides who help to plan and implement more effective therapy programs for patients.

Self-determination is restored within the therapeutic community by encouraging patients to participate meaningfully in ward decision making. This is accomplished through community meetings for recreation, crafts, and self-government. For example, ward policies can be based on recommendations from the patient government, and staff persons can serve as advisors and facilitators of communication and problem solving. Patients are thus given responsibility for running their own lives.

The physical environment can be changed to foster interaction and physical activity. Comfortable furniture can be arranged in small circles to facilitate conversation. Staff can encourage patients to make decorations for the ward and wards can be unlocked to stimulate outdoors activity and to remove the stigma of imprisonment. Wards can also be made coed to permit normal social contact between men and women. Suitable lighting, a range of appealing colors, and good ventilation are also essential.

Research evaluation   Research on the effectiveness of the therapeutic community is sparse (Manning, 1976). However, the few studies that exist show it to be more effective than hospital programs that rely primarily on drug therapy and sporadic individual or group counseling. For example, Fairweather, Simon, Gebhard, Weingarten, Holland, Sanders, Stone, and Reahl (1960) contrasted a therapeutic community with inpatient treatments of three types: (1) group therapy and an individual work assignment, (2) individual therapy and an individual work assignment, and (3) individual work assignment with no therapy. Program effectiveness was assessed through administering several personality assessment instruments such as the MMPI and TAT before and after treatment, and by means of a follow-up questionnaire that the patients completed to describe their living and work situations six months later. Overall, the four treatments did not produce significantly different results. Interestingly, patients who received individual or group therapy, or participated in the therapeutic community tended to improve most, if they were not diagnosed as severely and chronically psychotic, while chronic patients were the ones who gained the most from the program of only work assignments. The differential outcome for chronic psychotics versus other patients suggests that more limited and practically oriented treatments may be best initially for severely disabled persons, and then more sophisticated milieu therapies may be most appropriate once patients have regained basic self-care skills.

More recently, Bromet, Moos, Bliss, and Wirthman (1977) reported that five separate therapeutic community programs for alcoholics were all able to produce decreases in drinking and increases in overall psychosocial functioning and employment success that were maintained as long as eight months after clients graduated from treatment. Clients who participated most actively in treatment were those who gained the most, as is predicted from the principles that guide therapeutic communities. While it appears that therapeutic communities can be effective, additional empirical evaluations are still much needed.

Token Economy   When systematic reinforcement contingencies are established through the use of a simulated economic system, this is called a token economy (Atthowe & Krasner, 1968; Ayllon & Azrin, 1968). On a mental hospital ward, this usually takes the form of (1) an explicit statement of the behaviors that can earn reinforcers and (2) a simulated monetary currency that is used as the mechanism for actually distributing reinforcers. The desired behaviors typically include actions relevant to personal hygiene (e.g., bathing, clean clothes), ward maintenance (e.g., chores such as washing floors), social interaction (e.g., conversation with another patient), self-improvement (e.g., participation in educational or therapy groups), and vocational skills (e.g., holding a job outside the ward in the hospital cafeteria). When the desired behavior is satisfactorily completed, the patient is credited with a fixed number of reinforcement points through the use of "tokens" (e.g., poker chips, point cards, scrip money). These tokens can later be exchanged for reinforcers like snacks, day or weekend passes out of the hospital, special time for meetings with the ward psychologist, or advancement to a higher status level in the ward program. The latter reinforcer refers to the fact that many token economies use "level systems": patients are placed in one of several hierarchical levels depending on their earnings and performance in the token economy, with each level affording greater freedom and access to luxuries.

Token economy programs are designed to teach patients that responsible and autonomous action has a positive payoff. With patients who often manifest a great deal of disorientation and personal distress, the initial behaviors must be extremely specific and limited. For example, the beginning of a token economy program may simply require that the patient "make eye contact with an adult." However, the ultimate goal is to help the client to autonomous living in the community and the designers of token economies advocate that the behaviors be consistently geared toward preparing the patient to leave the hospital. Patients are, therefore, able to earn token reinforcers for behaviors such as maintaining a ward

job, participating in a ward government, evaluating one another's work performance, and formulating specific plans for a residence and employment outside the
hospital. At each higher level in the system, patients learn to depend less and less
on token reinforcers and more on the natural social reinforcers inherent in a self-
determined life-style. For instance, patients at a high level within the token economy might be paid on a weekly basis and only for vocational behaviors to simu-
late jobs in the real world.

Several guidelines have been formulated for use of a token economy. As was
the case for a therapeutic community, staff training is required to maintain a consistent reinforcement program. Often, negative attitudes toward patients or fears
that the token economy will increase the work load must be overcome (Gardner,
1972; Paul & McInnis, 1974). It is also important for tokens to be delivered concurrently with social rewards such as praise or encouragement, so that social interaction will gradually be a sufficient reinforcer for patients (Atthowe & Krasner, 1968; Theobold & Paul, 1976).

Problems with the token economy may also crop up. The informal peer group
of patients sometimes reinforces the very behaviors that the token economy is designed to replace (e.g., bizarre or rebellious actions) and such competition must
be minimized. Patients may also save up large quantities of tokens and then return to a sedentary life-style. This may be prevented, for example, by requiring at
least a minimum performance level before patients can spend their token savings
(Stahl & Leitenberg, 1976). A range of legal complications may arise as well, including potential violations of minimum wage legislation and the constitutional
right to refuse treatment (Schwitzgebel & Schwitzgebel, 1980).

Research evaluation   Rather extensive positive evidence has been reported concerning the superiority of token economy programs over traditional hospital
treatment (Kazdin, 1977b). When the outcome measures focus on in-hospital behaviors such as self-care, participation in activities, or social interaction, token
economy programs are uniformly more effective than comparable wards with no
formal milieu program (Gershone, Errickson, Mitchell, & Paulson, 1977; Gripp
& Magaro, 1971; Maley, Feldman, & Ruskin, 1973; Schaefer & Martin, 1968;
Schwartz & Bellack, 1975; Shean & Zeidberg, 1971). Studies that have used recid-
ivisim, employment, or freedom from medication as criteria of successful functioning outside the hospital similarly find token economy patients to fare better
than no program (Birky, Chambliss, & Wadsen, 1971; Heap, Boblitt, Moore, &
Hord, 1970; Schaefer & Martin, 1968; Shean & Zeidberg, 1971), although there is
still the concern that the behaviors that are developed within the token economy
are specific to the setting and personnel of the ward program (Kazdin, 1975).

Nevertheless, the data do indicate that token economies can produce desirable
behaviors. When patients who were rated as most dysfunctional were placed in a
token economy program, the token economy resulted in significantly lower recidivism rates at a six-month follow-up after patients were discharged. In 35 months
of operation, the token economy treated 478 patients and discharged 68% of
them with only 14% returning to the hospital; in contrast, other wards in that
hospital treated and released fewer patients and had a much higher recidivism
rate (50%) in the patients who were discharged. Thus, token economy programs

appear to have promise as methods of rehabilitating even severely and chronically distressed patients—and it is worth noting that a token economy program for an entire hospital ward may cost as little as only $425 more than traditional hospital programs over an entire year (Stahl & Leitenberg, 1976).

Comparisons of token economy and the therapeutic community   Two recent studies have contrasted these two types of milieu interventions. Milby, Pendergrass, and Clarke (1975) asked both staff and patients on two comparable wards to rate their wards' social climates. Both staff members and patients on the token economy ward gave higher ratings for interpersonal involvement and spontaneity than did their counterparts on the therapeutic community ward. Staff persons also rated the token economy as better in its practical orientation than the therapeutic community. However, very few subjects were involved in this study (i.e., fewer than 20 patients in total), and many of the above differences were not statistically significant. Furthermore, token economy participants rated their ward as higher in anger, aggression, and personal problems than did the therapeutic community subjects. Thus, the study suggests that token economy programs may facilitate involvement and spontaneity, but therapeutic community programs may be more effective in reducing individual patients' distresses.

Mishara (1978) described a more extensive and methodologically sophisticated investigation. Eighty inpatients who were elderly (average age = 69) and chronic "failures" (average length of hospitalization = 21.4 years) and of whom only 38% were communicating verbally, were randomly assigned to either a token economy or a therapeutic community. Based on reliable behavior observations by staff members, approximately 40% of the patients on each ward improved and 40% became worse in their social and psychological functioning. The token economy seemed to work best for patients who were more actively rebellious (as opposed to apathetic "institutionalized" persons), while the therapeutic community was optimal for patients who were most amenable to social interaction from the start. The therapeutic community was also more successful than the token economy in reducing patients' incontinence. Given the extreme problems presented by these patients, the finding of improvement in the in-hospital functioning of a large majority of patients by both programs is impressive. Future directions for more individually tailored programs are also suggested by the findings.

Highlight 15-2   Psychosocial Treatment of Chronic Mental Patients

One of the most impressive evaluations of psychological treatments for the chronic mental patient was reported by Paul and Lentz (1977). In their comprehensive report, Paul and Lentz describe their background and procedures and present the result and discussion of a comparison of two psychosocial treatments, milieu treatment and social learning treatment, versus standard hospital procedures. The overall goal was to examine treatment effectiveness in terms of reduction of the number of individuals remaining chronic mental patients.

According to the authors, the milieu approach focused on increased social interactions, planned group activities, group pressure toward normal functioning, freedom of movement, goal-directed communication, and treating the patient as a responsible individual rather than a custodial case. The social learning treatment utilized a token economy program to promote learning. The social learning therapy employed response-contingent consequences (e.g., rewards for appropriate behaviors and no rewards for inappropriate behaviors) and a systematic control of the patients' physical and social environment. The patients who were initially assigned to these treatments and the standard hospital procedures condition were matched for age, sex, socioeconomic status, symptoms, and duration of hospitalization. (As new patients were integrated into the project they were assigned to keep groups comparable.)

The Paul and Lentz report includes analyses of numerous sets of data—time-sampled patient behaviors, patient use of available resources, staff attitudes, staff behaviors, program costs. Although all of the detailed outcomes deserve examination, it is fair to summarize and conclude, as the authors have, that the social learning therapy proved to be the most effective treatment. Indeed, an examination of the changes in overall functioning for subjects in the three conditions across a four and 1/2 year period indicated that the social learning program had the superior effects. In terms of hospital release, the social learning treatment was significantly better than the milieu treatment and standard hospital treatment, and the milieu treatment was better than the standard hospital treatment. That is, both psychosocial treatments resulted in a significant increase in the number of releases from the hospital over the standard hospital treatment procedures: 96% of the patients were released from the social learning program, 68% from the milieu program, and 46% from the standard hospital program. This pattern of outcome data remained at follow-up.

These results are most impressive, not only because the chronic mental patient received meaningful interventions, but also because the report identifies one form of intervention—the social learning approach—as the most efficacious. However, do not assume that all facilities for chronic patients will immediately adopt the successful approach: a great many factors dictate against program initiation (e.g., lack of awareness of such research results, concern about costliness of changing hospital care). In his commentary on the future of research in clinical psychology, Garmezy (1982) refers to Paul and Lentz's work as an "extraordinary program of research that . . . has brought forth from psychiatry the most nonbenign neglect it has been my displeasure to witness over the past 30 years." Garmezy's concerns are shared by many mental health professionals who also wish to see research results translated into effective treatment.

The Day Hospital   In an effort to develop a middle ground between complete inpatient hospitalization and outpatient treatment, mental health professionals have developed the day hospital (Meltzoff & Blumenthal, 1966). Patients spend

INTERVENTIONS IN EXISTING INSTITUTIONS 569

part or all of each day in the hospital but continue to return to their homes in the evening. This schedule permits patients to benefit from a variety of treatment programs while still retaining their status as participating adults in their communities and families. Where outpatient therapy is usually restricted to no more than a few hours per week, the day hospital provides up to a full week of varied activities for each patient.

The specific treatment programs within day hospitals varies from setting to setting. However, group and individual therapy, vocational training and counseling, training in skills such as assertiveness or self-relaxation, and informal recreational programs are usually provided. Therapeutic community and token economy programs are frequently used to integrate these treatments.

Research evaluation Day hospital programs have been shown to be more effective than custodial inpatient treatments. Washburn, Vannicelli, Longabaugh, and Scheff (1976) randomly assigned 30 patients to an inpatient ward and 29 to a day treatment center, and assessed patients' mental status, personality functioning and family and community adjustment before and 6 and 12 months following treatment. Day hospital patients improved at least equally, and sometimes significantly more, when compared to the inpatient group on all measures. In addition, day hospital treatment cost significantly less for the patient and required significantly shorter amounts of time than inpatient hospitalization. Washburn et al. concluded that day hospital programs are superior because they enable patients to maintain their connection with family and community support systems, as well as due to their lesser financial drain on patients and their families. Working with a less well-educated patient group, Penk, Charles, and VanHoose (1978) found that a seven-week day hospital program resulted in significantly better ratings by significant others in the community (e.g., friends) of patients' social activity, employment and anxiety than did a comparable inpatient treatment. The evidence thus favors day hospital treatment over standard inpatient treatment for most patients.

Combining Milieu Interventions Therapeutic community, token economy, and day hospital programs need not be conducted separately. In fact, a combination offers many advantages: token economy guidelines offer a means to creating a consistent, challenging, and rewarding milieu, while the therapeutic community provides a method for facilitating social interaction and autonomous decision making by patients. Two studies by Greenberg and his colleagues (Greenberg, Scott, Pisa, & Friesen, 1975; Olson & Greenberg, 1972) suggest that a combination is preferable to either program singly. The therapeutic community ward involved a patient government, daily work assignments, and individual, group, and occupational therapies. Patients were also placed in five- to seven-person groups in which they met twice weekly to develop individualized treatment programs for one another; these recommended programs were ratified in weekly community meetings of all patients and staff, but staff members participated in the small groups only when specially requested. On the token economy ward, staff members formulated individualized reinforcement programs for each patient, and also dispensed tokens for four standard behaviors: grooming, social interaction, ward work, off-ward jobs. Thus, the token economy was controlled by staff members, while the therapeutic community encouraged independent problem solving and decision making by patients. Systematic reinforcement contingencies were established in the token economy to promote behavior change by patients, while no formal contingencies were utilized in the therapeutic community.

In the combined program, patients not only took on decision-making responsibility in small groups and received reinforcement contingent on performing the desired behaviors, but they also received tokens based on the quality of their treatment proposals. Patients were thereby reinforced for working together effectively as a group, as well as for their individual behaviors. In both studies, a combined program was most effective in discharging patients without recidivism. For example, Greenberg et al. (1975) found that patients from the combined program spent an average of 219 days out of the hospital during a year's time, while patients from a token economy program were out of the hospital for only 130 days on average.

Further evidence for the compatibility of the three milieu interventions comes from programs where a token economy or a therapeutic community was used in a day hospital setting. For example, Liberman, King, and De Risi (1976) described a day treatment center token economy that enabled patients to earn token reinforcers for target behaviors such as participation in occupational therapy, joining in group activities, setting and meeting individual goals for self-improvement, and helping to run the token economy. Educational workshops teaching skills for personal effectiveness, including assertion, coping with anxiety and depression, and consumer awareness were also made available. Compared to a "traditional" day treatment ward, the token economy produced significantly more social interaction. A judicious integration of the best features of all three types of milieu interventions has great promise.

Milieu Interventions in Schools

Perhaps one of the most common ameliorative milieu interventions in the school system is the token economy. However, preventive programs have also been developed for the schools.

Token Economy in School Classrooms   Token economy programs in the school use the same basic principles as those we described as important in mental hospitals, including the definition of specific desirable behaviors and the provision of token reinforcers contingent on performance of or improvements in the target behaviors.

O'Leary and Becker (1967) are said to have pioneered the token economy program as a milieu intervention for schools. Working with the teacher of 17 9-year-old students who had been assigned to a special "adjustment" class because of disruptive and aggressive conduct, they established six target behaviors: "In Seat, Face Front, Raise Hand, Working, Pay Attention, and Desk Clear." After placing observers in the classroom for three weeks to allow the children and teacher to get used to them, baseline data were gathered on the children's behavior for four weeks while the teacher was asked to teach as she normally did. Then the token program was instituted, and for a week the psychologist announced each day that the students could earn points for the six behaviors. He then observed them while the teacher taught, and gave each child from 1 to 10 points based on their overall behavior. The teacher actually dispensed the tokens to the children (by writing the number of points in a special booklet that each child kept as a record), and provided "prizes" such as comics or kites that the children could purchase with their points. The teacher was asked to praise each child for specific improvements as she distributed token points. Finally, the children also received points as a group, based on their overall performance.

In order to help the children behave appropriately after the token program was discontinued, the announcements and the token points were gradually given less frequently. First, the number of ratings made each day was decreased from five to three, and the number of points required to purchase prizes was increased. Second, points were gradually required to be kept for a day, then two days, and finally for four days before they could be exchanged for prizes. These are two methods of "fading" out the token program so that gradually the children are responding more to natural cues in the classroom than to the tokens. After a week, the teacher also took complete control of the program.

Behavior observation data on the eight most disruptive children's "deviant" behavior (e.g., name calling, fighting, talking out of turn) showed a dramatic change from the baseline period to when the token system was instituted (Figure 15-2). Deviant behavior occurred in an average of 76% of the observation periods during baseline, but in only 10% once the token program was in effect. Over the 10 weeks of the token economy, all eight children consistently reduced their deviant behavior, and reports from teachers in other classrooms and school settings indicated that the children developed more effective and pleasant interpersonal styles even when not in the token class. O'Leary, Becker, Evans, and Saudargas (1969) subsequently replicated these positive findings with other children.

Several special features have been found to be important in school token economy programs. Clearly stated goals, rules, and reinforcement contingencies are essential. Praise for positive behaviors and either ignoring or firmly penalizing disruptive behavior are two additional components. When negative behavior cannot be ignored, soft reprimands (and not loud criticisms or threats) or time out from reinforcement have been found to be necessary (O'Leary & O'Leary, 1976). Careful training of the teacher is essential both to teach methods of warm and consistent reinforcement and to instill a positive attitude toward the program. For example, when Kuypers, Becker, and O'Leary (1968) asked a teacher to run a token economy with only brief practical instructions, the program failed and the teacher subsequently refused to undergo further training. It is also important to short circuit any competing reinforcement contingencies, such as peer praise for disruptive behavior.

The reinforcement contingencies can also be designed so that each student is rewarded only for his or her own behavior, or such that the class earns tokens as a group. Along these lines, Rosenbaum, O'Leary, and Jacob (1975) found that a group contingency was somewhat more effective than an individual contingency in reducing disruptive behavior in hyperactive children—perhaps because the group contingency utilizes peer pressure as an incentive in addition to tokens.

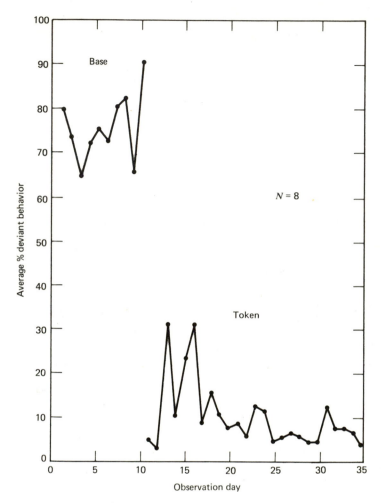

Figure 15-2 Average percentages of deviant behavior during the base and token periods. Adapted from K. D. O'Leary and W. C. Becker, Behavior modification of an adjustment class: A token reinforcement program. *Exceptional Children*, 1967, *33* 637–642. Copyright 1967 by the Council for Exceptional Children. Reprinted by permission.

Students can also be taught to run their own token economy, as for example, where Drabman (1973) showed that a token economy managed by students was more effective in producing lasting behavior change than one run by the teacher.

There are several other ways that a token economy can be modified to increase the likelihood that the resultant improvement in students' behavior will be maintained even after the token program is discontinued. One, parents can be involved by sending home daily reports from the teacher which the parents use to reward their children with token points (Bailey, Wolf, & Phillips, 1970). Two, parents and teachers can be trained to establish parallel token programs at home and at school (Kent & O'Leary, 1976). Three, children can be trained and reinforced for accurately evaluating and rewarding themselves (Johnson & Bolstad, 1973). Most ambitiously of all, token programs can be set up in every classroom in an entire school to create a consistent environment (Boegli & Wasik, 1978).

Research evaluation of classroom token economies   Token economy programs have consistently been found to reduce disruptive behavior and increase quiet studying behavior in classes for children with special problems (e.g., hyperactivity, retardation) as well as in regular school settings (O'Leary & O'Leary, 1976). Token systems that combine several incentives and contingencies are usually most effective. For example, Walker, Hops, and Fiegenbaum (1976) demonstrated in two experiments with underachieving elementary school students that a combination of contingent social reinforcement (i.e., praise by the teacher), token economy, and response cost (i.e., students lose tokens for disruptive behavior) was more effective than praise alone or praise plus the token economy.

A major problem with token economy interventions in the schools, however, has been the difficulty in producing improved student behavior that is maintained after the token system is discontinued. Durable changes are important for at least two reasons: when students go to another classroom every day, we would hope that they would generalize their new positive behaviors to these nontoken economy settings; and, when students move on to new classes and new teachers each year, we would hope that the positive changes would persist. Several methods for "programming generalization and maintenance" have been found to be somewhat successful (Bolstad & Johnson, 1972; Walker & Buckley, 1972), for instance, training students to serve as self-evaluators and self-reinforcers and, group contingencies in the token economy that encourage the peer group to reward positive behavior. Additional research is required to determine how these procedures can produce more durable and persistent behavior change.

School-Based Prevention Programs   Programs have been developed for both *primary* and *secondary* prevention in the schools. Children who are at risk for school and interpersonal problems are identified and given special help in secondary prevention programs, whereas primary prevention interventions are designed to aid all children develop new skills without singling out a special "problem" group (Zax & Specter, 1974).

Secondary prevention   Cowen's Primary Mental Health Project (Cowen, Trost, Lorion, Dorr, Izzo, & Issacson, 1975) is an example of secondary prevention. Cowen et al. (1975) created a two-step intervention for identifying and aiding "high-risk" kindergarten and first-grade students. The first phase in the PMHP is accomplished through an assessment that centers on teacher ratings of all students on an 11-item screening checklist that produces reliable scores for *ag*gressive behavior, *m*ood dysfunction, and *l*earning disability (AML). Approximately 1 child in 10 is found to show signs of serious maladjustment, and these children are guided into the project's second phase. Housewife volunteers who have been trained as tutors and nondirective counselors then meet with the children on a one-to-one basis from one to several times per week, under the supervision of a school psychologist. The children thus receive individualized attention and training where before they might just have been anonymous "faces in the crowd" or labeled "problem children."

Research evaluation   Cowen et al. (1975) reported that children who were identified as "at risk" but not aided by mental health volunteers showed serious academic deficits in the third and seventh grades and often required special psychotherapy services. In contrast, treated children were functioning significantly better on measures including teacher ratings, achievement tests, self-reported anxiety, and the number of referrals to school nurses. Housewives were found to be more effective than college students in producing positive results, although both types of prevention agents were able to help the children achieve rather long-lasting freedom from academic and interpersonal problems. The children who made the most gains as a result of the program were those who were initially shy and anxious, young, and high in family social status. Overall, Cowen et al. concluded that the project requires a 40% increase in school costs, but it provides as much as 1000% improved services.

More recently, Cowen, Gesten, and Wilson (1979) reported an evaluation of the PMHP's revised procedures (Cowen, Lorion, & Dorr, 1974) from the 1975–1976 year. Children were seen for an average of 28 45-minute sessions over the school year, with greater attention paid to dealing with acting-out problems. Two hundred and fifteen participants (150 boys, 65 girls) were assessed before and after the year on four measures: (1) teacher ratings of problem behaviors, (2) teacher ratings of social competence, (3) counselors' ratings of problem behaviors, and (4) school psychologists' ratings of psychological adjustment. On all measures, the participants showed significant improvements. Compared to a matched group of children who did not receive intervention, participants improved significantly more on 5 of the 11 outcome scores obtained from the four measures (and improved more, but not quite statistically significantly, on all other scores). Although the control group was assessed in the previous year for practical reasons, and thus is not exactly comparable to the participant group, the evidence is consistent and favorable (see also Weissberg, Gesten, Rapkin, Cowen, Davidson, de Apodaca, & McKim, 1981).

At present, the Cowen model is being utilized by at least 20 school systems across the United States. For example, Durlak (1977) describes a program where 31 boys and 35 girls in the second grade were identified as at risk using the AML. These children met in five- to seven-person groups for eight one-hour weekly sessions in which a counselor or college or high school volunteer led them in recreational, arts and crafts, or storytelling activities. In the meetings, individualized behavior-change goals were established for each child, and a token system was used to reward increasingly prosocial behavior. When these students were compared with a matched high-risk group on the AML, teacher ratings, and ratings by their group leaders, the treated children showed significantly more improvement than the untreated control group. This positive finding was maintained at a seven-month follow-up, suggesting very durable changes. The evidence for this secondary prevention model appears quite favorable.

Primary prevention   A primary prevention program with some promise is the problem-solving curriculum of Spivack and Shure (1974). Students are taught skills for interpersonal problem solving by means of stories and role-play games that can be used in 30-minute sessions by teachers: (1) how to delay impulsive responding, (2) how to define problems in specific terms, (3) how to brainstorm to create alternative solutions, (4) how to anticipate the positive and negative consequences of each solution, (5) how to break a selected solution into "doable" action steps, and (6) how to combine all these skills in real-life situations. For example, students might listen to a story about a child who must choose between the conflicting requests of two friends. After discussing the steps that the child had to go through in making a decision, they might role play making a different choice to explore the consequences of different solutions. The training method and materials are readily adaptable for integration into teachers' regular academic curriculum at a relatively small cost in time and effort. The Spivack and Shure program focuses on training interpersonal cognitive problem-solving (ICPS) skills and represents an intervention that can enable teachers to prepare their students for interpersonal functioning.

Research evaluation   Concerning the problem-solving approach to primary prevention, Spivack and Shure (1974) reported several studies showing significant increases in preschoolers' abilities.

> First, it *enhances alternative, consequential, and cause-and-effect thinking*. Second, it *decreases superfluous and irrelevant thinking*. Third, it *enhances problem-solving* ability among those who need it most (those who are behaviorally abberant). Fourth, it *shifts the priority away from aggressive solutions and trains children to see nonforceful as well as forceful possibilities*. (p. 98)

For example, in a study of 20 preschool classes from nine inner-city Philadelphia schools, 113 children from 10 classes received 12 weeks of training by teachers who were simultaneously receiving three hours of weekly supervision. Independent of their initial IQs, trained children showed significantly greater increases on such tests of interpersonal problem solving as stories that require the child to create an appropriate middle when given the beginning and end (the Means-Ends Test). Trained children generated more and better solutions, including less coercive or aggressive ones, and also were better able to anticipate the consequences of their proposed solutions. In addition, children who were initially rated as impulsive or inhibited by their teachers were significantly more often rated as adjusted at the end of the study if they had received the training compared to if they had not. Perhaps most important, the children were subsequently rated by their kindergarten teachers nine months later. Eighty-three percent of the trained children who had changed from maladjusted to adjusted as a result of the program were also rated as adjusted by these new teachers.[1] Furthermore, regardless of their initial status 86% of the trained children who had been rated as adjusted after training were still seen as adjusted by the kindergarten teachers, but only 66% of the control children who had been rated as adjusted at the end of the study were similarly viewed as adjusted by their kindergarten teachers.

---

[1]Although the teachers in the first portion of the evaluation were not ignorant of the children's status in the study, these later teachers did not know (i.e., were blind raters) whether or not the child had participated.

Milieu Interventions in Correctional Settings

Ameliorative milieu interventions within correctional settings have focused on token economies and therapeutic communities. Also, preventive milieu interventions have developed such as diversion programs and special police training.

Token Economy and Therapeutic Community Programs

Interventions based on token economy or therapeutic community principles have been attempted in both prison and reform school settings. For example, McCorkle, Elias, and Bixby (1958) describe a therapeutic community program conducted at the Highfields juvenile detention center. The inmates were organized into small groups for counseling and problem-solving training, and an inmate government was established to promote autonomous self-evaluation and increased social effectiveness. Kennedy (1976) described a token economy program run by John McKee and colleagues at an adult prison in Alabama, which is notable in its emphasis on reinforcing independent self-management and assertive problem solving rather than docility and orderliness. Meaningful reinforcers were offered: for example, visits to a women's prison, interviews with parole board members, or fishing trips could be earned through participation in educational, personal development, and housekeeping activities (Highlight 15-3).

Research evaluation Experimental investigations typically do not support the efficacy of either token economy or therapeutic community programs in adult prisons (Kennedy, 1976; Martinson, 1974). For example, the exemplary token system developed by McKee (cited in Kennedy, 1976) was unable to produce lower recidivism rates than a no-treatment control condition when prisoners' records were examined 18 months after the token economy. Similarly, Kasenbaum, Ward, and Wilner (1971) found that inmates who had participated in mandatory large-group or small-group counseling, or in voluntary small-group counseling, were no more likely than comparable control subjects to be successfully paroled 36 months after their release. Thus, while such programs may help make prisons more humane, they do not promote rehabilitation (Martinson, 1974).

In contrast, there is some evidence that both therapeutic community and token economy programs can facilitate rehabilitation in juvenile correctional institutions. Although early evaluation (e.g., McCorkle et al., 1958) used research designs that can be considered flawed and therefore prevent us from accepting their positive findings, a recent study by Jessness (1975) yields promising results with good methodological precautions. Nine hundred and eighty-three 15- to 17-year-old male juvenile offenders were randomly assigned to one of two 400-person residential schools. One school was run using transactional analysis guidelines, thus creating a therapeutic community in which the students met twice weekly in small groups to evaluate and encourage one another. These students also developed individualized "life scripts" and contracts for changes in conference with staff counselors to help them understand and resolve the personal

---

Highlight 15-3   Innovative Uses of Token Economy Programs

Token economy systems can be applied to create more consistent, educational, and rewarding milieus in many social settings (Kazdin, 1977b). Three recent extensions of token economy principles exemplify this idea.

Wang (1976) describes an integrated token economy and therapeutic community program in community aftercare facilities for chronic mental patients. Patients were released from the hospital to homes in which small groups of ex-patients lived under the supervision of trained paraprofessionals. In these aftercare residences, group meetings were regularly held to foster social relationships and independent decision making, and a simulated monetary system was used to teach money-management skills and other personal development target behaviors. Compared to aftercare homes with no such program, the treated subjects gained significantly in self-reported and staff-rated self-concepts and social adjustment.

In a medical setting, Magrab and Papadopoulou (1977) established token economy systems to encourage four hemodialysis patients to stop gaining weight by exercising and eating more appropriately. The hemodialysis team administered the token economy with their child patients, and found that both weight gains and fluctuations were reduced. The childrens' body levels of important chemicals associated with kidney functioning also returned to normal levels.

Further afield, Bookwalter (1978) describes a token system implemented in a moving and storage company. Moving van drivers were rewarded with points for prompt service, appropriate call-ins to dispatchers, van maintenance, and overall company productivity. Although no control group was employed, results showed dramatic increases to all-time highs in productivity and worker satisfaction.

Our examples illustrate how creativity and careful attention to the needs and preferences of special situations can result in innovative and effective token economy programs in diverse settings.

---

and interpersonal dilemmas that had gotten them in trouble. The second school utilized token economy systems to provide contingent reinforcement for students as they achieved individualized and standard desired behaviors that were designed to contribute to improved academic performance and social relationships.

Both before participating and at a 7- to 25-month follow-up students were assessed on standardized achievement tests, an objective personality questionnaire (the Jessness Inventory), staff ratings (the Jessness Behavior Checklist), a projective test of ego strength (Sentence Completion), and records of parole violations. Significant improvements were demonstrated on all measures for students in both programs, although the specific programs each worked best with specific subgroups of students. Transactional analysis was most successful with students who were initially moderately well adjusted according to the Jessness Inventory and the Sentence Completion test, while the token economy was more effective with either very poorly or very well-adjusted students. Transactional analysis was generally viewed as producing a more therapeutic and personalized social climate, although low-adjustment students showed an opposite view by favoring the token economy. In sum, the Jessness (1975) study suggests that both milieu programs can create an environment conducive to educational and social rehabilitation within juvenile correctional institutions.

Diversion Programs   The courts and prisons are overburdened to the point where people are often detained for days or weeks without a trial and then given only brief hearings (Mullen, 1974). It has been proposed that preventive interventions, such as diverson programs, be established so that certain persons could be identified as "low risks," and then released on their own recognizance while awaiting trial (without having to pay the often costly bail) and possibly even given suspended sentences (i.e., not required to serve a prison term). Potential low-risk persons could be identified by brief interviews with paraprofessional volunteers who would use basic information such as past record, type of offense, local friends or family, employment, and length of residence in the current community to predict the potential benefits of employing the diversion program.

Seidman, Rappaport, and Davidson (1976) describe a comprehensive program for juvenile offenders that attempted to develop viable methods for police officers to use in deciding when a reprimand would suffice and when referral to juvenile court seemed necessary to prevent further illegal acts. College undergraduates were trained to serve as advocates for adolescents who would otherwise have been sent to juvenile court. In this role, the advocates helped their clients, on a one-to-one basis, to develop behavioral contracts with their families and schools such that more consistent expectations and means of obtaining reinforcers were established. Advocates also negotiated directly with community resources such as local schools, social service agencies, and employers to help their clients make better use of their social settings. Eight to 10 hours per week were spent in these informal guidance sessions, in an attempt to reorient the clients toward more effective independent decision making and better social, familial, and work interactions.

Research evaluation   Controlled experimental evaluations of diversion programs are rare, but results from the few careful investigations are promising. Mullen (1974) reviews four studies that compared pretrial diversion to normal bail procedures concluding that persons who are released on their own recognizance are no more likely to commit another crime than are bailed persons. She notes that only one program designed to divert adults by giving them suspended sentences has been evaluated. In this case, only 6% of the diverted persons were rearrested, but a control group was not used so firm conclusions cannot be drawn.

Two diversion projects for juvenile offenders have been carefully researched. The first used what Rappaport (1977) calls "intensive probation," that is, a procedure where adolescents who are having school or family problems are provided with crisis-oriented family counseling rather than the typical procedure of a trial and brief monthly one-to-one meetings with a probation officer. At a seven-month follow-up, the diverted adolescents were 25 to 30% less likely to have been rearrested. However, this positive finding held true primarily for females, most of whom came from lower-middle-class white families. Furthermore, the probation office was overburdened by the extra work required by thorough family crisis counseling, and the adolescents were still enmeshed in the criminal justice system rather than truly being diverted.

The Seidman et al. (1976) project represents the only experimentally evaluated program that aims to prevent trials and imprisonment by meeting the individual needs of juvenile offenders. With two separate sets of police-referred adolescents, the advocacy program resulted in a significant reduction in number of police contacts, seriousness of the police contacts, and number of court hearings. The gains seen in the diverted group were not made by the control group, and they were maintained as long as two years after the program. The advocacy group became more involved in positive ways with their families and schools, suggesting that improvement is facilitated by getting the adolescents away from the correctional system and back into more effective relationships (Davidson, 1975).

Training Police as Crisis Counselors   Conflicts between family members or friends are often first dealt with by police officers, and the possibility of harm to the persons and the officer is significant when a crisis has precipitated violence or harsh verbal exchanges. It is estimated that 80 to 90% of police officers' work involves mediating such disputes (Wilson, 1969), and that 22% of police deaths and 40% of police injuries sustained while on duty result during intervention in family conflicts (Bard, 1970). Therefore, it has been proposed that programs designed to teach crisis intervention skills to police officers could provide a valuable service: broad-scale training could lead to more frequent satisfactory resolution of these frequent social disputes without harm to either citizens or police officers.

Bard (1970) has developed a systematic program for training police officers as crisis counselors. Nine black and nine white New York City police officers participated in lectures, discussion groups, and role-play exercises that taught communication, negotiation, and crisis defusing techniques. Thereafter, these officers were specially called in when family crises were reported in their precinct. They received weekly supervision from advanced clinical psychology graduate students, and met in small groups to share and evaluate their successes and difficulties in crisis incidents. Bard's program attempted to utilize and develop the special skills of an existing community service group—the police—to resolve frequently occurring family crises without harm or imprisonment.

INTERVENTIONS IN ALTERNATIVE SETTINGS

Although several programs within existing mental health, educational, and correctional institutions show promise as means to ameliorate or prevent psychosocial dysfunctions, other clinical interventions, in alternative settings, have been developed. These alternatives aim to more directly help people right in their own communities in order to reduce the stigma of mental health treatment and to achieve greater effectiveness (Rappaport, 1977). Such "community psychology" programs are based in communities rather than in special institutions, and they emphasize building stronger and more supportive community systems for the benefit of all residents.

There are a variety of community psychology interventions: community mental health centers, residential treatment settings, preschool prevention programs, paraprofessional and self-help programs, and resource development projects. Each intervention represents an attempt to create an alternative setting that fosters personal effectiveness in individual clients and social resources in their community.

Community Mental Health Centers (CMHCs)

Initiated by an act of Congress in 1963, CMHCs are designed so that "*all* mental health services would be available to *all* people" (Korchin, 1976, p. 488). More than 500 CMHCs are currently in operation, each serving a "catchment area" (i.e., a community area designated as the CMHC's responsibility) of between 75,000 and 200,000 persons. Each CMHC must provide a diversity of basic services in order to receive federal funding (described in Chapter 1).

CMHCs have typically been established in conjunction with existing mental health institutions or through an integration of several existing social and clinical service agencies in a community. Despite admirable "outreach" efforts (e.g., storefronts and rural clinics), CMHCs have been severely criticized as merely superficially altering the location of clinical services rather than helping to establish more effective community support systems (Nassi, 1978). For example, an early position paper issued by the American Psychological Association (Smith & Hobbs, 1966) recommended several improvements in CMHCs: (1) a greater emphasis on providing interventions that change social systems, such as consultation to community citizens' organizations, (2) greater control by the community of the types and delivery of mental health services, (3) a greater emphasis on developing interventions and not buildings, (4) greater flexibility in tailoring services to each community's needs, (5) a greater emphasis on services for disadvantaged groups, (6) a greater emphasis on training, research, and evaluation, (7) increased utilization of paraprofessionals, and (8) increased emphasis on competency rather than professional credentials in assigning responsibilities to staff members. Nevertheless, CMHCs represent an important attempt to provide a broader range of clinical services to more people at a lower cost.

Research Evaluation   Community mental health centers have been soundly criticized by consumer activists (Chu & Trotter, 1974) and clinical psychologists (Sarason, 1972) alike. Data from evaluation studies indicate that CMHCs have made positive strides by redirecting clients from inpatient hospitals to outpatient and day treatment facilities (Windle, Bass, & Taube, 1974). However, any change in the numbers of mental hospital residents is more likely due to political pressure to "deinstitutionalize" (Slotnick & Jaeger, 1978; Stone, 1975a)—that is, to cut hospital costs by returning patients to the community with or without good aftercare (Bloom, 1973). Furthermore, at most 50% of the people in the communities that have CMHCs are able to identify the center, its location, or its services (Windle et al., 1974). And only 3% chose the CMHC as their preferred place for mental health services—describing problems such as long waiting lists, fees, and concern about being labeled as "crazy" as their reasons (Windle et al., 1974). It also appears that most CMHCs do not actively encourage participation from community residents in their planning and evaluation, and that few provisions have been made for assuring that clients receive all necessary services in a prompt and continuous fashion (Windle et al., 1974). There are almost no data concerning the effectiveness of CMHC services in preventing or ameliorating the community problems that they are designed to deal with. In sum, CMHCs offer a potential for better services that remains unrealized.

Residential Treatment Centers

Many clinical psychologists are concerned that clients who are placed in inpatient hospital treatment programs will lose the skills, the motivation, and the social support systems that help them to function effectively in their natural communities (Rappaport, 1977). For this reason, clinicians have developed residential treatment centers that are situated in a homelike setting right in the community. These centers are often called *halfway houses* (Raush & Raush, 1968) because they are designed to serve as a halfway point between hospitalization or incarceration and a completely independent life in the community. Three influential models for residential treatment have evolved: Synanon, Achievement Place, and the Community Lodge.

Synanon   Therapeutic community principles have been used to guide many residential centers for drug addicts (Glaser, 1974). Perhaps the most widely publicized program of this type is Synanon (Enright, 1971). While some addiction treatment centers permit or even encourage clients to continue to use substitute drugs such as methadone or minor tranquilizers, Synanon requires all participants to remain drug free. The centers are run on a day-to-day basis by ex-addicts who are successful graduates of the program, and they help the participants to provide support for one another. A wide variety of educational, vocational development, recreational, and house-maintenance activities are required of all participants. The central treatment method is carried out in small groups that meet daily to confront each participant with his or her personal responsibilities and the ways these are being shirked or mishandled (see "Synanon Games" in Chapter 14).

Achievement Place   Token economy principles have been used to develop the Achievement Place model for community-based residential treatment of adolescents who have been sent to juvenile court for offenses such as truancy, vandalism, or theft (Phillips, Phillips, Fixsen, & Wolf, 1971). An adult couple, called the "teaching parents," coordinates all activities for six to eight youths living in a house in the community. The goals and procedures are as follows:

> . . . *(teaching parents) educate their youths in a variety of social, academic, prevocational and self-help skills. Their goal is to equip each youth with an alternative, more adaptive skill repertoire and to thereby increase his chances of survival and*

success in his community. The family-style setting allows the teaching parents to tailor their teaching to the individual needs of each youth.

Teaching parents utilize a flexible motivation system to enhance their effectiveness as teachers. In that motivation system a youth earns points for learning and engaging in appropriate, adaptive behavior and loses points for inappropriate, maladapative behaviors. These points are exchanged by the youth at first on a daily, and later on a weekly basis for privileges such as watching television, an allowance, and returning to his natural home on the weekend. Success in the motivation system advances a youth to the merit system in which points are no longer required for privileges. If the youth maintains his appropriate behavior while on the merit system, he begins to spend more and more time with his natural or foster family before being released from the program. (Braukmann, Fixsen, Kirgin, Phillips, Phillips, & Wolf, 1975)

In addition to the token economy system, teaching parents have experimentally demonstrated that innovations such as a self-government program and policies encouraging the youths to take over complete management of the token economy result in increased participation and fewer problems in the system (Fixsen, Phillips, & Wolf, 1973; Phillips, Wolf, & Fixsen, 1973).

Community Lodge   The Community Lodge program utilizes principles from therapeutic communities, behavior modification, and practical economics to provide a halfway-house setting for former chronic mental patients (Fairweather, Sanders, Maynard, & Cressler, 1969; Fairweather, Sanders, & Tornatzky, 1974). Patients who had participated in a problem-solving-oriented therapeutic community in a mental hospital were placed, as a group, in a large house in the community (the lodge). They received extensive training and supervision in handling the basic responsibilities of autonomous living: shopping, cooking, cleaning, group decision making, bookkeeping, follow through with prescribed medications, recreational activities, and even managing a self-supporting business. Extensive preparations were made to assure that the community residents would accept such a lodge in their community, and to guarantee the economic feasability of the lodge business (a janitorial service). Over a two-year period, all professional supervisors were phased out (with the exception of biweekly visits from a public health nurse), and the lodge residents assumed full responsibility for themselves, their lodge, and their business. Considering that these were chronic mental patients with no families to go to in the community, and little hope of successful reintegration into their communities with even the best in-hospital preparation (Fairweather et al., 1969), the lodge system provided a unique opportunity for sheltered community living.

Research Evaluation   Evaluation results are encouraging for the residential treatment programs that we have described. Although centers for drug addiction treatment have not been shown to be effective—often because their clients leave shortly after entering the program (Glaser, 1974)—the Achievement Place and Community Lodge models have emphasized quality-control evaluation to demonstrate their efficacy. The Achievement Place self-government (Fixsen et al., 1973) and resident-managed token economy (Phillips et al., 1973) systems have been experimentally shown to improve the residents' social participation and individualized behaviors. Furthermore, Achievement Place youths fared significantly better after treatment on measures such as recidivism, school attendance and grades, and police contact, compared to similar youths who had been placed on probation or in an industrial school. While the latter finding must be viewed as only tentative because the boys were not randomly assigned to treatments (Phillips et al., 1973), it does appear that Achievement Place has the potential for long-term positive effects.

Fairweather et al., (1969) present substantial data supporting the Community Lodge program. Compared to randomly assigned control patients, the lodge residents were 4 times as likely to be living in the community 40 months after discharge from the hospital (80% versus 20%), and 40 times more likely to be employed full time (40% versus 1%). This was accomplished at a daily cost of between $5 and $10 per resident, compared to a cost of between $15 and $55 for inpatient hospital treatment (Figure 15-3). There appears to be strong evidence that programs designed to facilitate ex-patients' adjustment to community life when the patients return to the community are effective, as long as the assistance is consistent and continuous.

Preschool Prevention Programs

Much like the milieu interventions in school systems, preschool prevention programs are designed to help children develop skills and confidence they might otherwise have missed out on. Unlike the programs that are provided in the existing school institutions, these programs take place in alternative settings.

Based on the finding that poor and minority group children often fare poorly in the traditional public school system, and on the belief that children's early life experiences play a major role in causing this problem (Hunt, 1960), several preschool interventions were developed. The most widely publicized preschool program is the Head Start project, which created federally funded learning centers across the United States (Westinghouse Learning Corporation/Ohio University, 1969). Several specific educational models were utilized by different centers, and three factors distinguish the diverse models from one another: (1) the opportunity for children to initiate their own learning experiences, (2) the focus on academic versus emotional and interpersonal skills, and (3) the involvement of parents.

Some preschool programs provided the children with carefully preprogrammed learning activities, such as specific primers that are to be read in a set order (e.g., Bereiter & Engelmann, 1966; Bushell, 1971). In contrast, other projects encouraged children to choose from a variety of traditional and innovative learning experiences ranging from books to science projects to educational games (e.g., Weikart, 1972). In both types, teachers played an active role in providing basic learning resources and a supportive social climate, although children have more responsibility for self-direction in the latter programs.

Preschool programs also fall on a second spectrum that ranges from total emphasis on formal school skills such as reading, spelling, and arithmetic (e.g., Bereiter & Engelmann, 1966) to an exclusive focus on free-play and social-

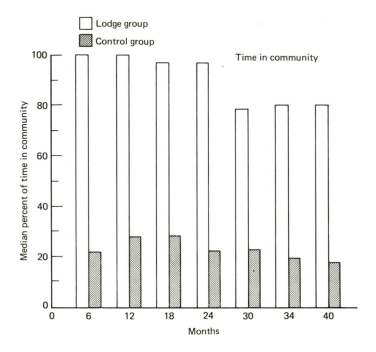

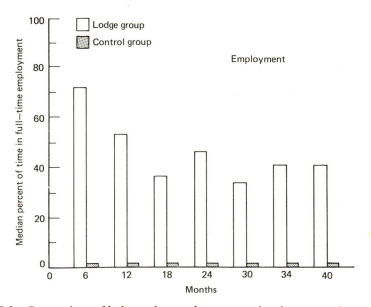

Figure 15-3   Comparison of lodge and control groups on time in community and employment for 40 months of follow-up. Adapted from G. W. Fairweather and L. G. Tornatzky, *Experimental methods for social policy research*. New York: Pergamon Press, 1977. Copyright 1977 by Pergamon Press. Reprinted by permission.

emotional growth (e.g., Shapiro & Biber, 1972). Most projects provide learning experiences of both types (e.g., Gray & Klaus, 1970).

Finally, several preschool programs have sent workers into the children's homes to provide the parents with encouragement, brief counseling, and training in tutoring skills (e.g., Gray & Klaus, 1970; Karnes, Teska, Hodgins, & Badger, 1970; Weikert, 1972). The aim is to establish consistent and educational environments in both the home and the preschool. Most often, mothers are the focus, but involvement of the father is also important (Gurman & Kniskern, 1978b). Mothers are taught skills ranging from informal ways to initiate verbal interactions with their children to techniques of contingency management and academic tutoring.

Preschool programs are designed to help children who are at risk for academic and personal difficulties to master the skills that will enable them to successfully enter and advance through public schools. Similar preschool centers have been created in many areas for children whose parent(s) require daily child care, thus permitting wives who would otherwise stay at home to take on new careers, as well as extending this special preparation to children from all backgrounds.

Research Evaluation   A study of 104 randomly selected Head Start programs, comparing treated children versus matched children who neither volunteered for nor participated in Head Start, concluded that the preschool intervention made no difference in children's success in the first, second, or third grades (Westinghouse Learning Corporation/Ohio University, 1969). However, Smith and Bissell (1970) found that Head Start children from urban black neighborhoods were significantly more likely to score well on reading readiness tests at the beginning of the first grade than were untreated controls. These positive gains had disappeared by the second and third grades, suggesting that preschool preparation may not be effective in the long run.

Evaluations of more specifically defined preschool interventions generate the same conclusions regardless of whether the programs emphasize child-initiated activities or preprogrammed curricula, academic or emotional development, and parents or only the preschool. By the end of the programs, children have made significant gains in IQ and achievement test scores, but these gains dissipate as they move on to regular public schools (Engelmann, 1970; Gray & Klaus, 1970; Karnes et al., 1970; Weikart, 1972).

It is clear that preschool programs make a difference, but innovations in regular schools seem needed to maintain these improvements. To the extent that schools teach skills that are meaningful for their students in a fashion that is tailored to the style of learning and behaving which best fits these children, *all* students could benefit from such innovations.

Paraprofessional and Self-Help Programs

Virtually all innovative interventions in alternative settings are directly amenable to implementation by carefully trained paraprofessionals, and most in fact depend on such mental health agents to provide effective services more economically than would be possible with professional clinicians. A parallel development has been that of the self-help groups, in which laypersons band together to support and educate one another. In both cases, clinical psychologists can provide a valuable contribution by helping organize, train and supervise, and evaluate the laypersons who actually administer the programs.

Paraprofessionals have been trained to serve as counselors or behavior therapists in settings such as outpatient clinics or crisis intervention telephone hotlines, as well as to provide companionship and tutoring for children. For example, Rioch, Elkes, Flint, Usdansky, Newman, and Silber (1963) trained housewives to utilize nondirective and supportive therapy with outpatient clients similar to themselves. Tharp and Wetzel (1969) taught nurses, social workers, teachers, community volunteers, and college students behavioral assessment, modeling and shaping techniques so that they could serve as consultants to parents and teachers who were experiencing conduct and emotional problems with their children. Goodman (1972) trained college students to serve as "big brothers" and "big sisters" to children from poor families who were running into trouble at school and/or home. Thus, paraprofessionals can play an important part in ameliorating or preventing psychosocial problems by offering friendship, emotional support, and tutoring in academic or parenting skills to persons who are in, or on the verge of, distress.

Self-help groups have evolved on a large scale since the 1930s, to the point where Tracy and Gussow (1973) estimate that more than 20,000 such organizations exist in communities across the world. The largest self-help group is Alcoholics Anonymous, numbering more than 18,000 separate chapters. Similar groups have developed for relatives of alcoholics (Alanon), persons seeking to lose weight (Weight Watchers), parents who fear they are abusing their children (Parents Anonymous), ostomy patients (United Ostomy Clubs), former mental patients (Recovery, Inc.), open heart surgery patients (Mended Hearts), mastectomy patients (Reach to Recovery), and compulsive gamblers (Gamanon), among others (Tracy & Gussow, 1973). Self-help groups serve several functions, including reducing feelings of loneliness and isolation, motivating members to overcome problems and achieve personal growth, facilitating friendships, increasing members' feelings of competence and self-worth, helping members to deal more effectively with professionals such as physicians and teachers, providing members with opportunities to learn through helping other persons, and educating professionals concerning the special needs of the groups' members. Self-help group members rightfully consider themselves the experts on their own needs and problems, but consultation from clinicians concerning strategies for peer counseling, and group communication and decision making, is often warmly received by these groups (see Highlight 15-4).

Research Evaluation   Paraprofessionals have been shown to be effective in providing behavioral or supportive counseling and companionship to children and adolescents, although their efficacy with inpatient and outpatient adults is equivocal (Anthony & Carkhuff, 1977; Balch & Solomon, 1976; Ford, 1980; Karlsruher, 1974; Seigel, 1973). For example, Fo and O'Donnell (1974) trained community volunteers to utilize three techniques in serving as "buddies" for children with school and home problems. Using truancy as the dependent

Highlight 15-4 Mental Health Professionals' Views of Self-Help Groups

If clinical psychologists are to effectively integrate their services with the resources provided by self-help groups, both a clear understanding of the appropriate applications and basic limitations of self-help programs and positive expectations concerning the effectiveness of such programs will be necessary. A national survey of mental health professionals working in outpatient psychological facilities was conducted by Levy (1978) to explore the views that psychologists, social workers, psychiatrists, and psychiatric nurses have about self-help groups.

Levy defined self-help groups using five criteria:

1. *Purpose.* Its express, primary purpose is to provide help and support for its members in dealing with their problems and in improving their psychological functioning and effectiveness.
2. *Origin and sanction.* Its origin and sanction for existence rest with the members of the group themselves, rather than with some external agency or authority. (This would not exclude, however, groups which were initiated by professionals—such as some chapters of Make Today Count— but which are then taken over by group members as the group becomes functional.)
3. *Source of help.* It relies upon its own members' efforts, skills, knowledge, and concern as its primary source of help, with the structure of the relationship between its members being one of peers, so far as help giving and support are concerned. Where professionals do participate in the group's meetings, as, for example, in the case of Parents Anonymous, they do so at the pleasure of the group and are cast in an ancillary role vis-à-vis group members.
4. *Composition.* It is generally composed of members who share a common core of life experience and problems.
5. *Control.* Its structure and mode of operation are under the control of members although they may, in turn, draw upon professional guidance and various theoretical and philosophical frameworks. (Levy, 1978, p. 306)

Twenty self-help groups dealing with psychosocial issues such as Alcoholics Anonymous, Schizophrenics Anonymous, and Solo Parents were identified on a questionnaire that asked respondents to answer five questions about each self-help group. (1) Utilization—How often does the respondent's clinic or agency refer clients to the group? (2) Source of referrals—How often does the respondent's clinic or agency receive referrals from the group? (3) Evaluation of effectiveness—How effective is the group in helping its members resolve their problems and achieve increased personal competence? (4) Potential role—How important is the group as a part of the total mental heath service system? (5) Probability of integration—How likely is it that the respondent's clinic or agency would wish to, and be able to, work closely with the self-help group in providing mental health services? The questionnaire was mailed to approximately 1800 outpatient psychological facilities across the United States, and replies were received from nearly 750 professional representatives of those clinics and agencies.

Levy chose not to report results for any single self-help group, but rather summarized the data to examine mental health professionals' general views about all self-help groups. Although more than half of the respondents had *never* referred a client to a self-help group (52%) or received a referral from a self-help group (70%), more than 40% of the respondents evaluated self-help groups as "very high" or "high" in effectiveness and only 16% saw self-help groups as "very low" or "low" in effectiveness. This finding indicates that clinical professionals have positive expectations concerning self-help groups' ability to provide support and basic mental health education but that consistent lines of communication do not yet exist between professionals and self-help programs in a majority of communities. The difficulty of developing a close working relationship between professional and self-help programs is reflected in the finding that more than 30% of the professionals felt that the probability of integration with self-help groups was "very low" or "low." Yet, another 31% of the professionals were "very high" or "high" in optimism concerning such an integration of professional and self-help services, so this goal appears to be a distinct, although challenging, possibility.

In all, Levy's survey demonstrates that most mental health professionals in outpatient psychological facilities have a positive interest in the potential of self-help groups, but that much work is needed to define the roles of, and processes of coordination linking, professional clinicians and self-help services. In particular, Levy notes that research is needed to examine (1) the actual effectiveness of self-help groups for people from different backgrounds who have varied psychosocial dysfunctions or needs and (2) the expectations that self-help groups have about when and how linkages could be established with mental health professionals and psychological clinics and agencies. The self-help group phenomenon is growing rapidly in the United States, and clinical psychologists will be in the best position to offer comprehensive and effective services to clients and communities if they make a concerted effort to develop appropriate interfaces with the self-help movement.

measure, they found that buddies were significantly more effective when they contingently reinforced their child for target behaviors such as studying or appropriate socializing than when they assumed a nondirective counseling approach, and the former technique was more effective than a no-treatment control. Use of monetary reinforcers (i.e., $10 per month) further enhanced buddies' efficacy. These results, when combined with Goodman's (1972) and Dicken, Bryson, and Kass's (1977) findings that nondirective "companionship therapy" was only moderately effective in improving teacher- and parent-rated problem behaviors, suggest that paraprofessionals are most effective with children when they have skill in behavior modification. The establishment of a warm personal relationship with the child also appears to be important in most cases (Dicken et al., 1977; Karlsruher, 1976), but this must be done in different ways with different kinds of children. For instance, aggressive children may benefit from an informal consultant who quietly helps them to achieve greater self-control and self-confidence, while withdrawn children may profit from a more actively supportive companion.

Studies have found paraprofessionals to be effective as nondirective counselors (e.g., Carkhuff & Truax, 1965) and contingency managers (e.g., Paul & McInnis, 1974) with inpatients and outpatients, but appropriate control groups were rarely utilized and the outcome measures were often based on the paraprofessional's behavior rather than improvement in their clients. Other investigations find paraprofessionals to be only mildly effective (e.g., Peterson, 1972; Poetter, Alvarez, Abell, & Krop, 1974). Systematic experiential training (as opposed to brief or lecture-oriented preparation), continued supervision (Quiltch, 1975), and careful selection of applicants (Paul & McInnis, 1974) appear to be the crucial ingredients that can lead to effective paraprofessional programs with adult clients. In some cases, paraprofessionals may be equally as effective as professional clinicians (e.g., Carkhuff & Truax, 1965; Karlsruher, 1976; Poser, 1966), although the studies that suggest this have involved two major limitations: (1) experimental controls such as random assignment of subjects and equivalent treatment types and durations were often lacking and (2) the paraprofessionals utilized only a few basic techniques rather than providing extensive psychotherapy. Thus, paraprofessionals may be the optimal treatment agent for some clients and some problems, but further research is needed to specify when a more highly trained clinician is needed.

Self-help groups have achieved great popularity, but experimental evaluations of their efficacy are rare. However, Barrett's (1978) controlled evaluation of three types of groups for widows illustrates the value of careful program evaluation. A self-help group based on Silverman's (1972) Widow-to-Widow project was contrasted with groups that were oriented to helping members develop a close confidant or to raising their consciousness concerning women's issues pertinent to widowhood. Compared to a waiting-list control group, all three treatments led to significant positive changes in self-reported index of optimistic expectations and actual life changes. All three approaches appear to offer valuable help to women who are making the stressful transition of widowhood, and a combination might be optimal. Similar investigations of the effectiveness of different self-help treatments are clearly needed.

Resource Development

When psychologists serve as program consultants to organizations such as community mental health centers or self-help groups, they are helping to develop community resources. Other avenues also exist for clinical interventions that focus on resource development: *community development* and *dissemination projects*.

Most communities could benefit from extending, expanding, or strengthening resources such as recreational or educational facilities and activities. Knapp and McClure (1978) describe the *community development* approach:

> . . . *by providing the community with various recreational, vocational, counseling,*
> *or other activities, participants will develop important skills and positive self-*
> *concepts, which will permit them to acquire satisfaction from their environment in*
> *more socially acceptable ways. (p. 280)*

Knapp and McClure helped the residents in a southern city's public housing projects to develop resources such as a youth club, Cub Scout and Girl Scout clubs,
athletic teams, academic tutoring, and Saturday night dances for children and
adolescents. Monthly drug awareness community meetings were held, and counseling and referral services were offered for adults. Thus, the community environment was altered to provide more positive opportunities and reinforcers for residents who might otherwise turn to drugs and crime, or incur psychological or
physical dysfunctions.

   A second way that clinicians can help to build better communities is through
the *dissemination of interventions* that have previously been shown to be effective. For example, Fairweather, Sanders, and Tornazky (1974) sought to persuade federal and state mental hospitals to adopt the Community Lodge program. They contrasted three different persuasion approaches: (1) descriptive
brochures, (2) workshops, and (3) demonstration projects in which a consultant
aided the hospital in actually creating a sample lodge for its patients. The first
method requires the least work, but brochures are also easily ignored by hospital
officials. Demonstration projects provide living evidence of the program, but
they are expensive for both the consultant and the hospital. Workshops represent
a middle-ground tactic, establishing a stronger commitment from the hospital
than the brochures but not requiring the total investment of a full demonstration.
Additional methods for dissemination also exist, including training sessions for
staff members from several hospitals in a central location and enlisting a citizen's
group or political organization as lobbyists for the program. The important idea
is that psychologists can provide an important public service by using their skills
to induce communities to utilize interventions that have been experimentally
tested and found effective.

Research Evaluation   Resource development projects are underresearched.
Although social activists continue to develop exciting methods for organizing
community groups and improving resources in community environments (e.g.,
O.M. Collective, 1971), few experimental evaluations have been conducted.
Knapp and McClure (1978) provide one of the few studies in this area. These researchers offer an illustrative study in which they assessed community members'
locus of control, awareness of community resources, and vandalism and police
arrest rates before and after initiating several new community groups and
facilities. Compared to persons from a similar public housing project, youths in
the experimental project significantly increased their belief in personal power and
their awareness of resources, and the arrest rate for the experimental group
declined sharply. Adults in the experimental condition did not gain in locus of
control, but they did stay the same while the control group showed a significant
decline in perceived personal power. Thus, we have initial evidence that community development may be a viable intervention.

Finally, *dissemination projects* are a recent phenomenon, because mental health and educational professionals have been content to simply report their findings in books and journals without actively attempting to persuade other institutions and communities to make use of their innovations. However, Fairweather and Tornatzky (1977) have developed a systematic experimental strategy for disseminating innovative and empirically tested programs, as illustrated by their efforts to get the Community Lodge project accepted in 255 mental hospitals across the United States. The Fairweather et al. (1974) study showed that the brochure and the workshop tactics were more likely to help them get a "foot-in-the-door" (i.e., successful entry in 65% and 68% of attempts) than the demonstration project method (i.e., 14%) but that the workshop and demonstration project tactics were more effective in eventually getting the lodge program adopted (i.e., in 12% and 11% of attempts) than the brochures (i.e., 5%). Thus, face-to-face contact with hospital personnel appears important in gaining acceptance. Further analyses showed that such contacts were equally effective regardless of whether the contact person was an administrator, psychiatrist, psychologist, social worker, or nurse, but that greatest efficacy was achieved when the dissemination consultant spent a substantial proportion of the contact time discussing their working relationship. This is consistent with results from 35 studies reviewed by Mannino and Shore (1975) in which a collaborative consultant-consultee team appears to be a crucial ingredient in effective consultation.

ISSUES IN MILIEU AND COMMUNITY INTERVENTIONS

Clinical psychologists have been involved in the development of a wide range of interventions both within and outside the existing mental health, educational, and correctional settings. What are the specific clinical skills that are required for an effective intervention at this level? Many clinical skills that are integral in interventions with individuals and groups appear important in the design and coordination of milieu interventions. For example, competencies in interpersonal communication and problem solving are vital. Additionally, special competency in dealing with social systems is required. Not all clinicians are qualified to conduct milieu interventions, but those with the background skills and interest often find them a rewarding professional task.

Several issues should be considered by the clinical psychologist prior to providing milieu and community interventions. To what extent, and in what ways, should community laypersons participate in the planning, implementation, and evaluation of interventions? CMHCs are required by law to solicit and utilize feedback from their community constituencies. However, unless community members have direct veto power over the decisions of administrators and CMHC professional staff persons, their role may be limited to that of an advisory board that may be largely ignored. Such illusory "community control" may have several negative effects, including leading community people to fight among themselves while administrators and professionals quietly continue to run the mental health program without regard to the needs and priorities of the community (Nassi, 1978; Reissman & Gartner, 1970). Even clinicians with the best training and intentions can find themselves involved in interventions that meet only the goals of the middle-class, Caucasian, and male-dominated "establishment," because these are the people who usually control funding, hiring, and political votes. They are also people who are from the same background as most professionals, and thus their values and priorities are the easiest for most clinicians to identify with (Klein, 1978). Nevertheless, community members from all social strata and cultural backgrounds are equally deserving of excellent clinical services, and they are likely to gain the most if they develop new skills and resources by directly participating in the development of their community's clinical interventions (Reissman & Gartner, 1970; Sarason, 1974; Zacker & Bard, 1973). Therefore, it is essential that clinical psychologists consider the issues of control and utilize their skill in establishing collaborative consultation teams to develop milieu interventions in which community persons have a meaningful input.

Clinicians must also attempt to anticipate the longterm generalized impacts that milieu and community interventions may have (Trickett, Kelly, & Todd, 1972; Willems, 1975). For example, Wolfred and Davidson (1977) report on the effects of an individualized residential treatment center program for children who refuse to stay in school or in their homes. Although this intervention was successful in reducing specific behavior problems that had caused the children to be in conflict with teachers and parents, it *increased* the likelihood that the children would eventually be placed in juvenile institutions rather than in foster homes. Thus, the short-term goal was accomplished, but a longer range outcome was decidedly negative. Criticisms of milieu interventions in schools (Winett & Winkler, 1972) and mental hospitals (Krasner, 1976) have focused on the fact that some of these programs teach their clients how to be compliant and orderly rather than how to create a successful autonomous life for themselves. It appears that clinicians must be careful not to lose sight of the basic goal for milieu interventions: to help people and their communities develop life-styles and environments that maximize long-term personal growth and positive relationships.

Although no program can forsee all possible future impacts, milieu interventions can be designed to gather feedback during their operation that will permit the coordinators to modify the intervention as unexpected outcomes become apparent. Consistent program evaluation is thus essential in these interventions. However, clinicians have been warned that even the most scientifically rigorous evaluation findings may be used to simply perpetuate bad programs rather than to stimulate positive changes (Feldman & Wodarski, 1974; Silverman, Beech, & Reister, 1976). Weiss (1972) states the dilemma:

> Some evaluators have found only after their study was done that they had unwittingly played a role in a larger political game. They found that nobody was particularly interested in applying their results to the decisions at hand, but only using them (or any quotable piece of them) as ammunition to destroy or justify. (p. 13)

Program evaluation can be an invaluable tool for creating effective milieu interventions, but only to the extent that it is used without prejudice to generate better services for all clients rather than to merely justify the denouncement of certain persons (e.g., clients who need special programs or clinicians who attempt to speak for such persons) or the perpetuation of the *status quo*.

Clinical psychologists have the opportunity to help a broad range of people through the development of milieu and community interventions. A risk also exists: these interventions impact on many people, so any harmful effects that result may be widespread. For example, the failure of Head Start programs to produce long-term benefits for disadvantaged children has led critics to argue that money should not be allocated for *any* programs for minority persons because these people are "incapable" of ever being more than "second-class" citizens. Such victim blaming (Ryan, 1971) is harmful and unwarranted, because the Head Start experiment points as much to the failure of our traditional school systems as it does to any deficiency in preventive programs or their clients. Yet, the danger for such political misuses of milieu and community interventions exists and must be recognized. We hope that clinical psychologists will nevertheless continue to develop increasingly effective milieu and community interventions for the benefit of their clients, society, and the communities in which we all live.

REFERENCES

Abraham, K. (1911) Notes on the psychoanalytical investigation and treatment of manic-depressive insanity and allied conditions. In *Selected papers of Karl Abraham*. London: Hogarth Press, 1949.

Abramowitz, C. V. The effectiveness of group psychotherapy with children. *Archives of General Psychiatry,* 1976, *33,* 320–326.

Abramowitz, C. V., Abramowitz, S. I., Roback, H. B., & Jackson, C. Differential effectiveness of directive and nondirective therapies as a function of client internal-external control. *Journal of Consulting and Clinical Psychology,* 1974, *42,* 849–853.

Abramowitz, S. I. Internal-external control and social-political activism: A test of the dimensionality of Rotter's internal-external scale. *Journal of Consulting and Clinical Psychology,* 1973, *40,* 196–201.

Abramson, L. Y., Seligman, M. E. P., & Teasdale, J. D. Learned helplessness in humans: Critique and reformulation. *Journal of Abnormal Psychology,* 1978, *87,* 49–74.

Achenbach, T. M. The classification of children's psychiatric symptoms: A factor analytic study. *Psychological Monographs,* 1966, *80,* Whole No. 615.

Achenbach, T. M. The child behavior profile: I. Boys aged 6–11. *Journal of Consulting and Clinical Psychology,* 1978, *46,* 478–488.

Achenbach, T. M., & Edelbrock, C. S. The child behavior profile: II. Boys aged 12–16 and girls aged 6–11 and 12–16. *Journal of Consulting and Clinical Psychology,* 1979, *47,* 223–233.

Ackerman, N. The family as a social and emotional unit. *Bulletin of the Kansas Mental Hygiene Society,* 1937, *29,* 1–7.

Ackerman, N. *The psychodynamics of family life.* New York: Basic Books, 1958.

Ackerman, N. *Treating the troubled family.* New York: Basic Books, 1966.

Adams, K. M. In search of Luria's battery: A false start. *Journal of Consulting and Clinical Psychology,* 1980, *48,* 511–516.

Adler, A. *Study of organ inferiority and its physical compensation.* New York: Nervous and Mental Diseases Publishing Co., 1917.

Adler, A. *Practice and theory of individual psychology.* New York: Harcourt, Brace and World, 1927.

Adler, P. T. Evaluation of the figure drawing technique: Reliability, factorial structure, and diagnostic usefulness. *Journal of Consulting and Clinical Psychology,* 1970, *35,* 52–57.

Adler, P. T. Ethnic and socioeconomic status differences in human figure drawings. *Journal of Consulting and Clinical Psychology*, 1971, *36*, 344-354.

Adler, P. T. Will the Ph.D. be the death of professional psychology? *Professional Psychology*, 1972, *3*, 69-72.

Agras, W. S. Behavior modification in the general hospital unit. In H. Leitenberg (Ed.), *Handbook of behavior modification and behavior therapy*, New York: Appleton-Century-Crofts, 1976.

Agras, W. S., & Berkowitz, R. Clinical research in behavior therapy: Halfway there? *Behavior Therapy*, 1980, *11*, 472-487.

Aiken, M. Community power and community mobilization. *Annals of the American Academy of Political and Social Science*, 1969, *385*, 76-88.

Ajzen, I., & Fishbein, M. Attitude-behavior relations: A theoretical analysis and review of empirical research. *Psychological Bulletin*, 1977, *84*, 888-918.

Akiskal, H. S., & McKinney, W. T. Depressive disorders: Toward a unified hypothesis. *Science*, 1973, *182*, 20-29.

Akiskal, H. S., & McKinney, W. T. Overview of recent research in depression: Integration of ten conceptual models into a comprehensive clinical frame. *Archives of General Psychiatry*, 1975, *32*, 285-305.

Albee, G. W. The uncertain future of clinical psychology. *American Psychologist*, 1970, *25*, 1071-1080.

Albee, G. W. Emerging conceptions of mental illness and models of treatment. *Professional Psychology*, 1971, *2*, 129-144.

Albee, G. W. Does including psychotherapy in health insurance represent a subsidy to the rich from the poor? *American Psychologist*, 1977, *32*, 719-721. (a)

Albee, G. W. The protestant ethic, sex and psychotherapy. *American Psychologist*, 1977, *32*, 150-161. (b)

Albee, G. W. The uncertain future of the MA clinical psychologist. *Professional Psychology*, 1977, *8*, 120-122. (c)

Alberti, R. E., & Emmons, M. *Your perfect right.* (2nd ed.) San Luis Obispo, Ca.: Impact, 1974.

Alderidge, P. Hospitals, madhouses and asylums: Cycles in the care of the insane. *British Journal of Psychiatry*, 1979, *134*, 321-334.

Alexander, F., & French, T. M. *Psychoanalytic therapy.* New York: Ronald, 1946.

Alexander, J. F., Barton, C., Schiavo, R. S., & Parsons, B. V. Systems-behavioral intervention with families of delinquents: Therapist characteristics, family behavior, and outcome. *Journal of Consulting and Clinical Psychology*, 1976, *44*, 656-664.

Alexander, J. F., & Parsons, B. V. Short-term behavioral intervention with delinquents: Impact on family process and recidivism. *Journal of Abnormal Psychology*, 1973, *81*, 219-225.

Alexander, S., & Husek, T. R. The anxiety differential: Initial steps in the development of a measure of situational anxiety. *Educational and Psychological Measurement*, 1962, *22*, 325-348.

Alinsky, S. *Rules for radicals.* New York: Random House, 1971.

Allen, F. H. Therapeutic work with children. *American Journal of Orthopsychiatry*, 1934, *4*, 193-202.

Allen, K. E., Hart, B., Buell, J. S., Harris, F. G., & Wolf, M. M. Effects of social reinforcement on isolate behavior of a nursery school child. *Child Development*, 1964, *35*, 511–518.

Allport, G. W. *Patterns and growth in personality*. New York: Holt, Rinehart and Winston, 1961.

Allport, G. W., & Odbert, H. S. Trait names: A psychological study. *Psychological Monographs*, 1936, *47*, (1, Whole No. 211).

Amante, D., Van Houten, V. W., Grieve, J. G., Bader, C. A., & Margules, P. H. Neuropsychological defects, ethnicity, and social economic status. *Journal of Consulting and Clinical Psychology*, 1977, *45*, 524–535.

American Psychiatric Association. *Diagnostic and statistical manual of mental disorders (2nd ed.): DSM II*. Washington, D. C.: American Psychiatric Association, 1968.

American Psychiatric Association. *Diagnostic and statistical manual of mental disorders (3rd ed.): DSM III*. Washington, D. C.: American Psychiatric Association, 1980.

American Psychological Association. Clinical Section. The definition of clinical psychology and standards of training for clinical psychologists. *Psychological Clinics*, 1935, *23*, 2–8.

American Psychological Association. *Technical recommendations for psychological tests and diagnostic techniques*. Washington, D. C.: American Psychological Association, 1954.

American Psychological Association. *Casebook on ethical standards of psychologists*. Washington, D. C.: American Psychological Association, 1967.

American Psychological Association. *Ethical principles in the conduct of research with human participants*. Washington, D. C.: American Psychological Association, 1973.

American Psychological Association. *Publication manual of the American Psychological Association*. Washington, D. C.: American Psychological Association, 1974. (a)

American Psychological Association. *Standards for educational and psychological tests*. Washington, D. C.: American Psychological Association, 1974. (b)

American Psychological Association. *Casebook on ethical standards of psychologists*. Washington, D. C.: American Psychological Association, 1974. (c)

American Psychological Association. Report of the task force on sex bias and sex role stereotypes in psychotherapeutic practice. *American Psychologist*. 1975, *30*, 1169–1175.

American Psychological Association. Task force on health research. Contributions of psychology to health research: Patterns, problems, and potentials. *American Psychologist*, 1976, *31*, 263–274.

American Psychological Association. *Ethical standards of psychologists*. Washington, D. C.: American Psychological Association, 1977. (a)

American Psychological Association. *Standards for providers of psychological services*. Washington, D. C.: American Psychological Association, 1977. (b)

American Psychological Association. Task force on the role of psychology in the criminal justice system. Report of the task force. *American Psychologist*, 1978, *33*, 1099–1113.

American Psychological Association. Task force on continuing evaluation in national health insurance. Continuing evaluation and accountability controls for a national health insurance program. *American Psychologist*, 1978, *33*, 305–313.

American Psychological Association. *Criteria for accreditation of doctoral training programs and internships in professional psychology.* Washington, D. C.: American Psychological Association, 1979.

American Psychological Association. APA-approved doctoral programs in clinical, counseling, and school psychology: 1980. *American Psychologist*, 1980, *35*, 1116–1118.

American Psychological Association. Ethical principles of psychologists. *American Psychologist*, 1981, *36*, 633–638. (a)

American Psychological Association. Specialty guidelines for the delivery of services by clinical psychologists. *American Psychologist*, 1981, *36*, 640–651. (b)

Anastasi, A. *Psychological testing.* (3rd ed.) New York: Macmillan, 1968.

Annon, J. S., & Robinson, C. H. The use of vicarious learning in the treatment of sexual concerns. In J. LoPiccolo & L. LoPiccolo (Eds.), *Handbook of sex therapy.* New York: Plenum, 1978.

Anthony, W. A. Psychological rehabilitation: A concept in need of a method. *American Psychologist*, 1977, *32*, 658–662.

Anthony, W. A., Buell, G., Sharrott, S., & Althoff, M. G. Efficacy of psychiatric rehabilitation. *Psychological Bulletin,* 1972, *78*, 447–456.

Anthony, W. A., & Carkhuff, R. R. The functional professional therapeutic agent. In A. S. Gurman & A. M. Razin (Eds.), *Effective psychotherapy: A handbook of research.* New York: Pergamon, 1977.

Aponte, H., & Hoffman, L. The open door: A structural approach to a family with an anorectic child. *Family Process*, 1973, *12*, 1–44.

Argyris, C. Some unintended consequences of rigorous research. *Psychological Bulletin*, 1968, *70*, 185–197.

Argyris, C. Dangers in applying results from experimental social psychology. *American Psychologist*, 1975, *30*, 469–485.

Aries, P. *Centuries of childhood.* (Translated by R. Baldids.) New York: A. A. Knopf, 1962.

Arkowitz, H., Lichtenstein, E., McGovern, K., & Hines, P. The behavioral assessment of social competence in males. *Behavior Therapy,* 1975, *6*, 3–13.

Asch, S. Forming impressions of personality. *Journal of Abnormal and Social Psychology*, 1946, *41*, 258–290.

Asch, S. Studies of independence and conformity. A minority of one against a unanimous majority. *Psychological Monographs*, 1956, *70* (9, Whole No. 416).

Astrachan, B. M., Levinson, D. J., & Adler, D. A. The impact of national health insurance on the tasks and practice of psychiatry. *Archives of General Psychiatry*, 1976, *33*, 785–794.

Atkinson, J. W., & McClelland, D. C. The projective expression of needs. II. The effect of the different intensities of the hunger drive on thematic apperception. *Journal of Experimental Psychology*, 1948, *38*, 643–658.

Atkinson, R. C., & Shiffrin, R. M. The control of short-term memory. *Scientific American,* 1968, *225*, 89–90.

Atthowe, J. M., & Krasner, L. Preliminary report on the application of contingent reinforcement procedures (token economy) on a "chronic" psychiatric ward. *Journal of Abnormal Psychology*, 1968, *73*, 37–43.

Auerbach, A. H., & Johnson, M. Research on the therapist's level of experience. In A. S.

Gurman & A. M. Razin (Eds.), *Effective psychotherapy: A handbook of research*. New York: Pergamon, 1977.

Auerbach, S. M., & Kilmann, P. R. Crisis intervention: A review of outcome research. *Psychological Bulletin*, 1977, *84*, 1189–1217.

Averill, J. R. Autonomic response patterns during sadness and mirth. *Psychophysiology*, 1969, *5*, 399–414.

Averill, J. R. A semantic atlas of emotional concepts. *JSAS Catalog of Selected Documents in Psychology*, 1975, *5*, 330 (Ms. 421).

Ax, A. F. The physiological differentiation between fear and anger in humans. *Psychosomatic Medicine,* 1953, *15*, 433–442.

Axline, V. M. *Play therapy*. New York: Ballantine Books, 1947.

Ayllon, T. & Azrin, N. *The token economy*. New York: Appleton-Century-Crofts, 1968.

Azrin, N., Sneed, T. J., & Foxx, R. M. Dry-bed training: Rapid elimination of childhood enuresis. *Behaviour Research and Therapy*, 1974, *12*, 147–156.

Bach, G. R. Intensive group psychotherapy. New York: Ronald Press, 1954.

Bach, G. R. The marathon group: Intensive practice of intimate interactions. *Psychological Reports*, 1966, *18*, 995–1002.

Bach, G. R., & Bernhard, Y. M. *Aggression lab*. Dubuque, Iowa: Kendall/Hunt, 1971.

Bach, G. R., & Wyden, P. *The intimate enemy*. New York: Avon Books, 1970.

Backman, C. W., Secord, P. F., & Pierce, J. R. Resistance to change in the self-concept as a function of consensus among significant others. *Sociometry*, 1963, *26*, 102–111.

Baekeland, F., & Lundwall, L. Dropping out of treatment: A critical review. *Psychological Bulletin,* 1975, *82*, 738–783.

Baer, D. M., Wolf, M. M., & Risley, T. R. Some current dimensions of applied behavior analysis. *Journal of Applied Behavior Analysis*, 1968, *1*, 91–97.

Bailey, J. S., Wolf, M. M., & Phillips, E. L. Home based reinforcement and modification of predelinquents' classroom behavior. *Journal of Applied Behavior Analysis,* 1970, *3*, 223–233.

Bailey, K. G. Psychotherapy or massage parlor technology?: Comments on Zeiss, Rosen and Zeiss' treatment procedure. *Journal of Consulting and Clinical Psychology*, 1978, *46*, 1502–1506.

Balch, P., Ireland, J. F., & Lewis, S. B. Fees and therapy: Relation of source of payment to course of therapy at a community mental health center. *Journal of Consulting and Clinical Psychology*, 1977, *45*, 504.

Balch, P., & Solomon, R. The training of paraprofessionals as behavior modifiers: A review. *American Journal of Community Psychology*, 1976, *4*, 167–180.

Bales, R. F. *Interaction process analysis*. Reading, Mass.: Addison-Wesley, 1950.

Baltes, P. B., Reese, H. W., & Lipsett, L. P. Life span developmental psychology. *Annual Review of Psychology*, 1980, *31*, 65–110.

Baltes, P. B., & Schaie, K. W. On the plasticity of intelligence in adulthood and old age: Where Horn and Donaldson fail. *American Psychologist,* 1976, *31*, 720–725.

Bandler, R., Grinder, J., & Satir, V. *Changing with families*. Palo Alto: Science and Behavior Press, 1977.

Bandura, A. *Principles of behavior modification*. New York: Holt, Rinehart and Winston, 1969.

Bandura, A. Psychotherapy based upon modeling principles. In A. E. Bergin & S. L. Garfield (Eds.), *Handbook of psychotherapy and behavior change.* New York: Wiley, 1971.

Bandura, A. Self-efficacy: Toward a unifying theory of behavior change. *Psychological Review*, 1977, *84*, 191–215. (a)

Bandura, A. *Social learning theory.* Englewood Cliffs, N. J.: Prentice-Hall, 1977. (b)

Bandura, A. The self system in reciprocal determinism. *American Psychologist*, 1978, *33*, 344–358. (a)

Bandura, A. Reflections on self-efficacy. *Advances in Behavioural Research and Therapy*, 1978, *1*, 237–269. (b)

Bandura, A., Adams, N. E., & Beyer, J. Cognitive processes mediating behavioral change. *Journal of Personality and Social Psychology*, 1977, *35*, 125–139.

Bandura, A., & Mischel, W. Modification of self-imposed delay of reward through exposure to live and symbolic models. *Journal of Personality and Social Psychology*, 1965, *2*, 698–705.

Bandura, A., Grusec, J. E., & Menlove, F. L. Vicarious extinction of avoidance behavior. *Journal of Personality and Social Psychology*, 1967, *5*, 16–23.

Bandura, A., & Menlove, F. L. Factors determining vicarious extinction of avoidance behavior through symbolic modeling. *Journal of Personality and Social Psychology*, 1968, *8*, 99–108.

Banner, H. *Group dynamics: Principles and applications.* New York: Ronald Press, 1959.

Baratz, S., & Baratz, J. Early childhood intervention: The social science base of institutional racism. *Harvard Educational Review*, 1970, *40*, 29–50.

Barbarick, P. Fixed-force intervention strategies: Changing the educational status quo in a community. *American Journal of Community Psychology*, 1975, *3*, 47–58.

Bard, M. *Training police as specialists in crisis intervention.* Washington, D. C.: U.S. Government Printing Office, 1970.

Bard, M., & Berkowitz, B. Training police as specialists in family crisis intervention: A community psychology action program. *Community Mental Health Journal*, 1967, *3*, 315–317.

Barker, R. G., & Gump, P. V. *Big school, small school.* Stanford, Cal.: Stanford University Press, 1964.

Barker, R. G. *Ecological psychology.* Stanford, Cal.: Stanford University Press, 1968.

Barker, R. G., Gump, P. V. *Big school, small school.* Stanford, Cal.: Stanford University Press, 1964.

Barker, R. G. & Schoggen, P. *Qualities of community life.* San Francisco: Jossey-Bass, 1973.

Barlow, D. H. Increasing heterosocial responsiveness in the treatment of sexual deviation: A review of the clinical and experimental evidence. *Behavior Therapy*, 1973, *4*, 655–671.

Barlow, D. H., & Agras, W. S. Fading to increase heterosexual responsiveness in homosexuals. *Journal of Applied Behavior Analysis*, 1973, *6*, 355–366.

Baron, R. A., & Bell, P. A. Aggression and heat: The influence of ambient temperature, negative affect, and a cooling drink on physical aggression. *Journal of Personality and Social Psychology*, 1976, *33*, 245–255.

Baron, R. A., & Lawton, S. F. Environmental influences on aggression. The facilitation of modeling effects by high ambient temperature. *Psychonomic Science*, 1972, *26*, 80–82.

Baron, R. A., & Ronsberger, V. M. Ambient temperature and the occurrence of collective violence: The "long, hot summer" revisited. *Journal of Personality and Social Psychology*, 1978, *36*, 351–360.

Barrett, C. J. Effectiveness of widows' groups in facilitating change. *Journal of Consulting and Clinical Psychology*, 1978, *46*, 20–31.

Barron, F. An ego-strength scale which predicts response to psychotherapy. *Journal of Consulting Psychology*, 1953, *17*, 327–333.

Barron, F., & Leary, T. F. Changes in psychoneurotic patients with and without psychotherapy. *Journal of Consulting Psychology*, 1955, *19*, 239–245.

Barthell, C. N., & Holmes, D. S. High school yearbooks: A nonreactive measure of social isolation in graduates who later became schizophrenic. *Journal of Abnormal Psychology*, 1968, *73*, 313–316.

Bates, F. L., & Harvey, C. C. *The structure of social systems.* New York: Gardner Press, 1975.

Bateson, G. *Steps to an ecology of mind.* New York: Ballantine, 1972.

Bateson, G., Jackson, P. D., Haley, J., & Weakland, J. Toward a theory of schizophrenia. *Behavioral Science*, 1956, *1*, 251–264.

Battersby, W. S., Bender, M. R., Pollack, M., & Kahn, R. L. Unilateral "spatial agnosia" ("inattention") in patients with cortical lesions. *Brain*, 1956, *79*, 68–93.

Baum, A., Aiello, J. R., & Calesnick, L. E. Crowding and personal control: Social density and the development of learned helplessness. *Journal of Personality and Social Psychology*, 1978, *36*, 1000–1011.

Bauman, G., & Roman, M. Interaction product analysis in group and family diagnosis. *Journal of Projective Techniques and Personality Assessment*, 1964, *32*, 331–337.

Baumeister, A. A. Use of the WISC with mental retardates: A review. *American Journal of Mental Deficiency*, 1964, *69*, 183–194.

Baxter, B. (Ed.) American Psychological Association, Task Force on Employment Testing of Minority Groups. Job testing and the disadvantaged. *American Psychologist*, 1969, *24*, 637–650.

Bayley, N. Comparisons of mental and motor test scores for ages 1–15 months by sex, birth order, race, geographical location, and education of parents. *Child Development*, 1965, *36*, 379–411.

Beck, A. T. Thinking and depression: II. Theory and therapy. *Archives of General Psychiatry*, 1964, *10*, 561–571.

Beck, A. T. *Depression: Clinical, experimental and theoretical aspects.* New York: Harper & Row, 1967.

Beck, A. T. Cognitive therapy: Nature and relation to behavior therapy. *Behavior Therapy*, 1970, *1*, 184–200.

Beck, A. T. *Depression: Causes and treatment.* Philadelphia: University of Pennsylvania Press, 1972.

Beck, A. T. The development of depression: A cognitive model. In R. J. Friedman & M. M. Katz (Eds.), *The psychology of depression: Contemporary theory and research.* Washington, D, C.: V. H. Winston, 1974.

Beck, A. T. *Cognitive theory and the emotional disorders.* New York: International Universities Press, 1976.

Beck, A. T., & Greenberg, R. L. *Coping with depression.* New York: Institute for Rational Living, Inc., 1974.

Beck, A. T., Rush, A. J., Shaw, B. F., & Emery, G. *Cognitive therapy of depression.* New York: Guilford, 1979.

Beck, A. T., Ward, C. H., Mendelson, M., Mock, J. E., & Erbaugh, J. K. Reliability of psychiatric diagnosis: II. A study of consistency of clinical judgements and ratings. *American Journal of Psychiatry*, 1962, *119*, 351–357.

Beck, S. J. *Rorschach's test.* (Vol. 1) *Basic processes.* New York: Grune and Stratton, 1944.

Beck, S. J. *Rorschach's test. II: A variety of personality pictures.* New York: Grune and Stratton, 1945.

Beck, S. J. *Rorschach's test. III: Advances in interpretation.* New York: Grune and Stratton, 1952.

Becker, J. *Depression: Research and theory.* New York: Halsted, 1974.

Bednar, R. L., & Kaul, T. J. Experimental group research: Current perspectives. In S. L. Garfield & A. E. Bergin (Eds.) *Handbook of psychotherapy and behavior change.* (2nd ed.) New York: Wiley, 1978.

Bednar, R. L., Melnick, J., & Kaul, T. Risk, responsibility and structure. A conceptual framework for initiating group counseling and psychotherapy. *Journal of Counseling Psychology*, 1974, *21*, 31–37.

Beels, C., & Farber, A. Family therapy: A view. *Family Process*, 1969, *8*, 280–332.

Bell, J. E. A theoretical framework for family group therapy. In P. J. Guerin (Ed.), *Family therapy.* New York: Gardner Press, 1976.

Bellack, A. S., Hersen, M., & Lamparski, D. Role-play tests for assessing social skills: Are they valid: Are they useful? *Journal of Consulting and Clinical Psychology*, 1979, *47*, 335–342.

Bellak, L. *A guide to the interpretation of the Thematic Apperception Test.* New York: Psychological Corporation, 1947.

Bem, D. J. Constructing cross-situational consistencies in behavior. Some thoughts on Alker's critique of Mischel. *Journal of Personality*, 1972, *40*, 17–26.

Bem, D. J., & Allen, A. On predicting some of the people some of the time: The search for cross-situational consistencies in behavior. *Psychological Review*, 1974, *81*, 506–520.

Bem, S. L. The measurement of psychological androgyny. *Journal of Consulting and Clinical Psychology*, 1974, *42*, 155–162.

Bender, L. *A visual-motor Gestalt test and its clinical use.* New York: American Orthopsychiatric Association, 1938.

Benedict, R. Continuity and discontinuity in cultural conditioning. *Psychiatry,* 1938, *1*, 161–167.

Bendix, R., & Lipset, S. M. *Class, status and power.* New York: Macmillan, 1953.

Bennett, C. C., Anderson, L. S., Cooper, S., Hassol, L., Klein, D. L., & Rosenblum, G. (Eds.), *Community psychology.* Boston: Boston University Press, 1967.

Bennis, W. G., & Shepard, H. A. A theory of group development. *Human Relations*, 1956, *9*, 415–437.

Bensman, J., & Rosenberg, B. Socialization: Fitting man to his society. In P. I. Rose (Ed.), *The study of society.* New York: Random House, 1967.

Benson, H., Shapiro, D., Tursky, B., & Schwartz, G. E. Decreased systolic blood pressure through operant conditioning techniques in patients with essential hypertension. *Science*, 1971, *173*, 740–742.

Benton, A. L. *Test of three-dimensional construction praxis manual.* Neurosensory Center Publication No. 286, University of Iowa, 1973.

Benton, A. L. *The Revised Visual Retention Test* (4th ed.). New York: Psychological Corporation, 1974.

Benton, A. L., & Van Allen, M. W. *Test of facial recognition manual.* Neurosensory Center Publication No. 287. University of Iowa, 1973.

Bereiter, C., & Englemann, S. *Teaching disadvantaged children in the preschool.* Englewood Cliffs, N. J.: Prentice Hall, 1966.

Berger, L., Bernstein, A., Klein, E., Cohen, J., & Lucas, G. Effects of aging and pathology on the factorial structure of intelligence. *Journal of Consulting Psychology,* 1964, *28,* 199–207.

Bergin, A. E. Psychotherapy and religious values. *Journal of Consulting and Clinical Psychology,* 1980, *48,* 95–105.

Bergin, A. E. The effects of psychotherapy: Negative effects. *Journal of Counseling Psychology,* 1963, *10,* 244–250.

Bergin, A. E. Some implications of psychotherapy research for therapeutic practice. *Journal of Abnormal Psychology,* 1966, *71,* 235–246.

Bergin, A. E. The evaluation of therapeutic outcomes. In A. E. Bergin & S. L. Garfield (Eds.), *Handbook of psychotherapy and behavior change.* New York: Wiley, 1971.

Bergin, A. E., & Lambert, M. J. The evaluation of therapeutic outcomes. In S. L. Garfield & A. E. Bergin (Eds.), *Handbook of psychotherapy and behavior change.* (2nd ed.) New York: Wiley, 1978.

Berkowitz, B. P., & Graziano, A. M. Training parents as behavior therapists: A review. *Behaviour Research and Therapy,* 1972, *10,* 297–317.

Bernal, E. M., Jr. A response to "Educational uses of tests with disadvantaged students." *American Psychologist,* 1975, *30,* 93–95.

Bernard, J. L. The significance for psychology of O'Connor vs. Donaldson. *American Psychologist,* 1977, *32,* 1085–1088.

Berne, E. *Games people play.* (2nd ed.) New York: Grove Press, 1970.

Berne, E. *What do you say after you say hello?* New York: Grove Press, 1972.

Bernstein, D. A., & Paul, G. L. Some comments on therapy analogue research with small animal "phobias." *Journal of Behavior Therapy and Experimental Psychiatry,* 1971, *2,* 225–237.

Bersoff, D. In house counsel seeks true "friend" of the court role for APA. *American Psychological Association Monitor,* 1980, *11*(4), 13.

Berzins, J. I. Therapist-patient matching. In A. S. Gurman & A. M. Razin (Eds.), *Effective psychotherapy: A handbook of research.* New York: Pergamon Press, 1977.

Bettleheim, B., & Sylvester, E. A therapeutic milieu. *American Journal of Orthopsychiatry,* 1948, *18,* 191–206.

Betz, B. J. Experiences in research in psychotherapy with schizophrenic patients. In H. H. Strupp & L. Luborsky (Eds.), *Research in psychotherapy.* Vol. 2. Washington, D. C.: American Psychological Association, 1962.

Beutler, L. E. Toward specific psychological therapies for specific conditions. *Journal of Consulting and Clinical Psychology,* 1979, *47,* 882–897.

Beutler, L. E., Johnson, D. T., Neville, C. W., Jr., Elkins, D., & Jobe, A. M. Attitude similarity and therapist credibility as predictors of attitude change and improvement in psychotherapy. *Journal of Consulting and Clinical Psychology*, 1975, *43*, 90–91.

Bevan, W. The sound of the wind that's blowing. *American Psychologist*, 1976, *31*, 481–491.

Bevan, W. On getting in bed with a lion. *American Psychologist*, 1980, *35*, 779–789.

Bieber, I. A discussion of "Homosexuality: The ethical challenge." *Journal of Consulting and Clinical Psychology*, 1976, *44*, 163–166.

Biederman, L., & Cerbus, G. Changes in Rorschach testing. *Journal of Personality Assessment*, 1971, *35*, 524–526.

Bievenu, M. J. Measurement of marital communication. *Family Coordinator*, 1970, *19*, 26–31.

Bijou, S. W. Development in the preschool years: A functional analysis. *American Psychologist*, 1975, *30*, 829–837.

Bindrim, P. A report on a nude marathon. *Psychotherapy: Theory, Research and Practice*, 1968, *5*, 180–188.

Binet, A., & Simon, T. Methodes nouvelles pour le diagnostic du niveau intellectial des anormaux. *L'Anneé Psychologigue*, 1905, *11*, 191–244. (a)

Binet, A., & Simon, T. Application des méthodes nouvelles are diagnostic du niveau intellectual chez des infants normaux et anormaux d'hospice et d'ecole primaire. *L'Anneé Psychologigue*, 1905, *11*, 245–336. (b)

Binet, A., & Simon, T. Sur la necessite d'etablir un diagnostic scientifique des etats inferieurs de l'intelligence. *L'Anneé Psychologigue*, 1905, *11*, 162–190. (c)

Birky, M. J., Chambliss, J. E., & Wadsen, R. A comparison of residents discharged from a token economy and traditional psychiatric programs. *Behavior Therapy*, 1971, *2*, 46–51.

Birnbauer, J. S. Mental retardation. In H. Leitenberg (Ed.), *Handbook of behavior modification and behavior therapy*. New York: Appleton-Century Crofts, 1976.

Bishop, D. V. M. The P scale and psychosis. *Journal of Abnormal Psychology*, 1977, *86*, 127–134.

Blanchard, E. B. The relative contributions of modeling, information influences, and physical contact in the extinction of phobic behavior. *Journal of Abnormal Psychology*, 1970, *76*, 55–61.

Blanchard, E. B., & Epstein, L. H. *A biofeedback primer*. Reading, Mass.: Addison-Wesley, 1978.

Blanchard, E. B., & Young, L. D. Self-control of cardiac functioning: A promise as yet unfulfilled. *Psychological Bulletin*, 1973, *79*, 145–163.

Blaney, P. H. Contemporary theories of depression: Critique and comparison. *Journal of Abnormal Psychology*, 1977, *86*, 203–223.

Blashfield, R. K., & Draguns, J. G. Evaluative criteria for psychiatric classification. *Journal of Abnormal Psychology*, 1976, *85*, 140–150.

Bleuler, E. The physiogenic and psychogenic in schizophrenia. *American Journal of Psychiatry*, 1930, *10*, 203–211.

Block, J. *Challenge of response sets*. Appleton-Century Crofts, 1965.

Block, J. The Eysencks and psychoticism. *Journal of Abnormal Psychology*, 1977, *86*, 653–654. (a)

Block, J. P scale and psychosis: Continued concerns. *Journal of Abnormal Psychology*, 1977, *86*, 431–434. (b)

Bloom, B. Letter to the editor. *Harvard Educational Review*, 1969, *39*, 419–421.

Bloom, B. L. The domain of community psychology. *American Journal of Community Psychology*, 1973, *1*, 8–11.

Bloom, B. L., & Parad, H. J. The psychologist in the community mental health center. An analysis of activities and training needs. *American Journal of Community Psychology*, 1978, *6*, 371–379.

Bloom, L. J., Weigel, R. G., & Trautt, G. M. "Therapeugenic" factors in psychotherapy: Effects of office decor and subject-therapist sex pairing on the perception of credibility. *Journal of Consulting and Clinical Psychology*, 1977, *45*, 867–873.

Bloomfield, C., Levy, H., Kotelchuck, R., & Handelman, M. Free clinics. *Health PAC Bulletin*, 1971, No. 34, 1–16.

Boegli, R. G., & Wasik, B. H. Use of a token economy system to intervene at a school wide level. *Psychology in the Schools*, 1978, *15*, 72–78.

Boll, T. J. Behavioral correlates of cerebral damage in children aged 9–14. In R. M. Reitan & L. A. Davison (Eds.), *Clinical neuropsychology: Current status and applications*. Washington, D. C.: Winston, 1974.

Boll, T. J. Prognosing brain impairment. In B. Wolman (Ed.), *Clinical diagnosis of mental disorders*. New York: Plenum, 1978.

Boller, F., & Vignolo, L. A. Latent sensory aphasia in hemisphere-damaged patients: An experimental study with the token test. *Brain*, 1966, *89*, 815–831.

Bolstad, O. D., & Johnson, S. M. Self regulation in the modification of disruptive classroom behavior. *Journal of Applied Behavior Analysis,* 1972, *5*, 443–454.

Boneau, C. A., & Cuca, J. H. An overview of psychology's manpower: Characteristics and salaries from the 1972 APA survey. *American Psychologist*, 1974, *29*, 821–840.

Bookwalter, S. T. The application of behavioral psychology in an industrial environment. *Dissertation Abstracts International*, 1978, *38*(B), 4440.

Boring, E. G. *A history of experimental psychology*. New York: Appleton-Century-Crofts, 1950.

Borkovec, T. D. Self-efficacy: Cause or reflection of behavior change? *Advances in Behaviour Research and Therapy*, 1978, *1*, 163–170.

Borkovec, T. D., Weerts, T., & Bernstein, D. Assessment of anxiety. In A. Ciminero, K. Calhoun, & H. Adams (Eds.), *Handbook of behavioral assessment*. New York: Wiley, 1977.

Boshes, B., & Myklebust, H. R. A neurological and behavioral study of children with learning disorders. *Neurology*, 1964, *14*, 7–12.

Bouchard, T. J. *Differential psychology*. New York: Wiley, in preparation.

Bouchard, T. J., & McGue, M. Familial studies of intelligence: A review. *Science*, 1981, *212*, 1055–1059.

Bowen, M. Principles of multiple family therapy. In P. J. Guerin (Ed.), *Family therapy*. New York: Wiley, 1976. (a)

Bowen, M. Theory in the practice of psychotherapy. In P. J. Guerin (Ed.), *Family therapy*. New York: Gardner Press, 1976. (b)

Bowen, M. *Family therapy in clinical practice*. New York: Jason Aronson, 1978.

Bower, S., & Bower, G. *Asserting yourself*. Menlo Park, Cal.: Addison-Wesley, 1976.

Bowers, K. S. Situationism in psychology: An analysis and a critique. *Psychological Review*, 1973, *80*, 307–336.

Bowlby, J. *Attachment and loss*. Vol. 1. New York: Basic Books, 1969.

Bowlby, J. The making and breaking of affectional bonds—1. Aetiology and psychopathology in the light of attachment theory. *British Journal of Psychiatry*, 1977, *130*, 201–210.

Boyd, R. D. *The Boyd Developmental Progress Scale*. San Bernadino, Cal.: Inland Counties Regional Center, 1974.

Brackbill, G. Studies of brain dysfunction in schizophrenia. *Psychological Bulletin,* 1956, *53*, 210–226.

Bradford, L. P. Biography of an institution. *Journal of Applied Behavioral Science*, 1967, *3*, 127–144.

Bradford, L. P., Stock, P., & Horowitz, M. How to diagnose group problems. In National Training Labs, *Selected Reading Scenes: Vol. 1, Group Development*. Washington, D. C.: NTL, 1961.

Bramel, D. A. A dissonance theory approach to defensive projection. *Journal of Abnormal and Social Psychology*, 1962, *64*, 121–129.

Braukman, C. J., Fixsen, D. L., Kirgin, K. A., Phillips, E. A., Phillips, E. L., & Wolf, M. M. Achievement Place: The training and certification of teaching parents. In W. S. Wood (Ed.), *Issues in evaluating behavior modification*. Champaign, Ill.: Research Press, 1975.

Bredemeier, H. C., & Stephenson, R. M. *The analysis of social systems*. New York: Holt, Rinehart and Winston, 1962.

Brim, O. G., Jr., & Kagan, J. (Eds.). *Constancy and change in human development*. Cambridge, Mass.: Harvard University Press, 1980.

Briscoe, R. B., Hoffman, J. B., & Bailey, J. S. Behavioral community psychology: Training a community board to problem solve. *Journal of Applied Behavior Analysis*, 1975, *8*, 157–168.

Britt, S. H., & Morgan, J. P. Military psychologists in World War II. *American Psychologist*, 1946, *1*, 423–427.

Broadbent, D. E. The current state of noise research: Reply to Poulton. *Psychological Bulletin,* 1978, *85*, 1052–1067.

Broadhurst, A. Clinical psychology in the community: Initial services in Britain. *Professional Psychology*, 1980, *11*, 733–740.

Bromet, B., & Moos, R. H. Environmental resources and the posttreatment functioning of alcoholic patients. *Journal of Health and Social Behavior*, 1977, *18*, 326–338.

Bromet, B., Moos, R. H., Bliss, F., & Withman, C. Posttreatment functioning of alcoholic patients. Its relation to program participation. *Journal of Consulting and Clinical Psychology*, 1977, *45*, 829–842.

Brown, J. H., Gamboa, A. M., Jr., Birkimer, J., & Brown, R. Some possible effects of parent self-control training of parent-child interactions. In E. J. Mash, L. C. Handy, & L. A. Hamerlynck (Eds.), *Behavior modification approaches to parenting*. New York: Brunner/Mazel, 1976.

Browning, R. M., & Stover, D. O. *Behavior modification in child treatment*. Chicago: Aldine Atherton, 1971.

Brunswick, E. *Systematic and representative design of psychological experiments*. Berkeley: University of California Press, 1947.

Buber, M. *Between man and man*. New York: Macmillan, 1948.

Buck, J. N. The H-T-P Technique: A qualitative and quantitative scoring manual. *Journal of Clinical Psychology*, 1948, *4*, 319–396.

Budzynski, T. H., Stoyva, J. M., Adler, C. S., & Mullaney, T. EMG biofeedback and tension headaches. *Seminars in Psychiatry*, 1973, *5*, 397–410.

Burchard, J. D., & Lang, P. T. Behavior modification and juvenile delinquency. In H. Leitenberg (Ed.), *Handbook of behavior modification and behavior therapy*. New York: Appleton-Century-Crofts, 1976.

Burns, T., & Stalker, G. M. *The management of innovation*. London, England: Tavistock Publications, 1961.

Burrows, T. The group method of analysis. *Psychoanalytic Review*, 1927, *19*, 268–280.

Bush, L. E. Individual differences in multidimensional scaling of adjectives denoting feelings. *Journal of Personality and Social Psychology*, 1973, *25*, 50–57.

Bushell, D. J. *Reinforcement principles in education: Large-scale application in project follow through.* Paper presented in the University of Oregon Symposium on the uses of reinforcement principles in education. Washington, D. C.: 1971.

Buss, A. H. *Psychopathology*. New York: Wiley, 1966.

Buss, A. H., & Gerjuoy, H. The scaling of adjectives descriptive of personality. *Journal of Consulting Psychology*, 1957, *21*, 366–371.

Butcher, J. N. *Objective personality assessment*. New York: General Learning Press, 1971.

Butcher, J. N. Present status of computerized MMPI reporting devices. In O. Buros (Ed.), *Eighth mental measurements yearbook*. Highland Park, New Jersey: Gryphon Press, 1978.

Butcher, J. N., & Koss, M. P. Research on brief and crisis-oriented therapies. In S. L. Garfield & A. E. Bergin (Eds.), *Handbook of psychotherapy and behavior change*. (2nd ed.) New York: Wiley, 1978.

Butcher, J. N., & Maudal, G. R. Crisis intervention. In I. B. Weiner (Ed.), *Clinical methods in psychology*. New York: Wiley, 1976.

Butcher, J. N., & Owen, P. L. Objective personality inventories: Recent research and some contemporary issues. In B. B. Wolman (Ed.), *Clinical diagnosis of mental disorders: A handbook*. New York: Plenum Press, 1978.

Butler, O. T., Coursey, R. D., & Gatz, M. Comparison of the Bender Gestalt test for both black and white brain-damaged patients using two recovering systems. *Journal of Consulting and Clinical Psychology*, 1974, *44*, 280–285.

Calhoun, K., Adams, H., & Mitchell, K. (Eds.), *Innovative treatment methods in psychopathology*. New York: Wiley, 1974.

Callahan, E. F., & Leitenberg, H. Aversion therapy for sexual deviation: Contingent shock and covert sensitization. *Journal of Abnormal Psychology*, 1973, *81*, 60–73.

Cameron, N. *Personality development and psychopathology: A dynamic approach*. Boston: Houghton Mifflin, 1963.

Camp, B. W. Verbal mediation in young aggressive boys. *Journal of Abnormal Psychology*, 1977, *86*, 145–153.

Camp, B. W., Blom, G. E., Herbert, F., & Van Doorninck, W. J. "Think Aloud": A program for developing self-control in young aggressive boys. *Journal of Abnormal Child Psychology*, 1977, *5*, 157–169.

Campbell, D. T., & Fiske, D. W. Convergent and discriminant validation by the multitrait-multimethod matrix. *Psychological Bulletin,* 1959, *56,* 81–105.

Campbell, D. T., & Stanley, J. C. *Experimental and quasiexperimental designs for research.* Chicago: Rand McNally, 1963.

Campbell, J. P., & Dunnette, M. D. Effectiveness of T-group experiences in managerial training and development. *Psychological Bulletin,* 1968, *70,* 73–104.

Cancro, R. (Ed.). *Intelligence: Genetic and environmental influences.* New York: Grune and Stratton, 1971.

Cannon, W. B. The James-Lange theory of emotions: A critical examination and an alternative theory. *American Journal of Psychology,* 1927, *39,* 106–124.

Caplan, G. *The theory and practice of mental health consultation.* New York: Basic Books, 1970.

Carkhuff, R. R., & Traux, C. B. Training in counseling and psychotherapy: An evaluation of an integrated didactic and experiential approach. *Journal of Consulting Psychology,* 1965, *29,* 333–336.

Carson, R. C. A and B therapist "types." A possible critical variable in psychotherapy. *Journal of Nervous and Mental Disease,* 1967, *144,* 47–54.

Cartwright, D. S. Patient self-report measures. In I. E. Waskow & M. B. Parloff (Eds.), *Psychotherapy change measures.* Washington, D. C.: U. S. Government Printing Office, 1975.

Cartwright, R. D. Effects of psychotherapy on self-consistency. *Journal of Counseling Psychology,* 1957, *4,* 15–22.

Cartwright, R. D., & Zander, H. (Eds.) *Group dynamics: Research and Theory.* (3rd ed.) New York: Harper & Row, 1968.

Cattell, J. M. Retrospect: Psychology as a profession. *Journal of Consulting Psychology,* 1937, *1,* 1–13.

Cattell, P. *The measurement of intelligence of infants and young children.* New York: Psychological Corporation, 1947.

Cattell, R. B. *Culture Fair Intelligence Test.* Institute for Personality and Ability Testing, Inc., 1949.

Cattell, R. B. *Personality and motivation, structure and measurement.* New York: World Book, Yonkers-on-Hudson, 1957.

Cattell, R. B. Theory of fluid and crystal intelligence: A critical experiment. *Journal of Educational Psychology,* 1963, *54,* 1–22.

Cattell, R. B., Eber, H. W., & Tatsuoka, M. M. *Handbook for the Sixteen Personality Factor Questionnaire* (16PF). Champaign, Ill.: Institute for Personality and Ability Testing, 1970.

Cattell, R. B., & Scheier, I. H. The nature of anxiety: A review of 13 multivariate analyses comparing 814 variables. *Psychological Reports,* Monograph Supplement, 1958, *5,* 351–388.

Caudra, C. A. A scale for control in psychological adjustment (Cn). In G. W. Welsh and W. G. Dahlstrom (Eds.), *Basic readings on the MMPI in psychology and medicine.* Minneapolis: University of Minnesota Press, 1953.

Cautela, J., & Upper, D. The Behavioral Inventory Battery: The use of self-report measures in behavior analysis and therapy. In M. Hersen & A. Bellack (Eds.), *Behavioral assessment: A practical handbook.* New York: Pergamon, 1976.

Chandler, M. J. Egocentrism and antisocial behavior: The assessment and training of social perspective-taking skills. *Developmental Psychology*, 1973, *9*, 326–332.

Chapman, C., & Risley, T. R. Anti-litter procedures in an urban high-density area. *Journal of Applied Behavior Analysis,* 1974, *7*, 377–383.

Chapman, L. Illusory correlation in observational report. *Journal of Verbal Learning and Verbal Behavior*, 1967, *6*, 151–155.

Chapman, L., & Chapman, J. Genesis of popular but erroneous psychodiagnostic observations. *Journal of Abnormal Psychology*, 1967, *72*, 193–204.

Chapman, L., & Chapman, J. Illusory correlation as an obstacle to the use of valid psychodiagnostic signs. *Journal of Abnormal Psychology*, 1969, *74*, 271–280.

Chelune, G. J., Heaton, R. K., Lehman R. A. W., & Robinson, A. Level versus pattern of neuro-psychological performance among schizophrenic and diffusely brain damaged patients. *Journal of Consulting and Clinical Psychology*, 1979, *47*, 155–163.

Cherniss, C. Pre-entry issues in consultation. *American Journal of Community Psychology*, 1976, *4*, 13–24.

Chesler, M. A., Bryant, B. I., Jr., & Crowfoot, J. E. Consultation in the schools: Inevitable conflict, partisanship, and advocacy. *Professional Psychology*, 1976, *8*, 637–645.

Chinoy, E. *Automobile workers and the American dream*. New York: Random House, 1955.

Chu, F. O., & Trotter, S. *The madness establishment: Ralph Nader's study group on the National Institute of Mental Health*. New York: Grossman, 1974.

Churchill, W. D., & Smith, S. E. Relationship between the 1960 Stanford-Binet Scale and group measures of intelligence and achievement. *Measurement and Evaluation in Guidance*, 1974, *7*, 40–45.

Cicchetti, D. V., & Ryan, E. R. A reply to Beutler at al.'s study. Some sources of variance in accurate empathy ratings. *Journal of Consulting and Clinical Psychology*, 1976, *44*, 858–859.

Ciminero, A. R., Calhoun, K. S., & Adams, H. E. (Eds.) *Handbook of behavioral assessment*. New York: Wiley, 1977.

Ciminero, A. R., Nelson, R. O., & Lipinski, D. Self-monitoring procedures. In A. R. Ciminero, K. S. Calhoun, & H. E. Adams (Eds.), *Handbook of behavioral assessment*. New York: Wiley, 1977.

Clark, R. A. The projective measurement of experimentally induced levels of sexual motivation. *Journal of Experimental Psychology*, 1952, *44*, 391–399.

Clarke-Stewart, K. A. Popular primers for parents. *American Psychologist*, 1978, *33*, 359–369.

Cleary, T. A., Humphreys, L. G., Kendrick, S. A., & Wesman, A. Educational uses of tests with disadvantaged students. *American Psychologist*, 1975, *30*, 15–41.

Clemons, R. Proposed legal regulation of applied behavior analysis in prisons. Consumer issues and concerns. *Arizona Law Review*, 1975, *17*, 127–131.

Cohen, J. Factors underlying Wechsler-Bellevue performance of three neuropsychiatric groups. *Journal of Abnormal and Social Psychology*, 1952, *47*, 359–365. (a)

Cohen, J. A factor-analytically based rationale for the Wechsler-Bellevue. *Journal of Consulting Psychology*, 1952, *16*, 272–277. (b)

Cohen, J. A factor-analytically based rationale for the Wechsler Adult Intelligence Scale. *Journal of Consulting Psychology*, 1957, *21*, 452–457. (a)

Cohen, J. The factorial structure of the WAIS between early adulthood and old age. *Journal of Consulting Psychology*, 1957, *21*, 283–290. (b)

Cohen, S. Aftereffects of stress in human performance and social behavior: A review of research and theory. *Psychological Bulletin*, 1980, *88*, 82–103.

Cole, J., & Magnussen, M. Where the action is. *Journal of Consulting Psychology*, 1966, *30*, 539–543.

Collins, B. E., & Ashmore, R. D. *Social psychology*. Reading, Mass.: Addison Wesley, 1970.

Comrey, A. L. *A first course in factor analysis*. New York: Academic Press, 1973.

Cone, J., & Foster, S. Direct observation in clinical psychology. In P. C. Kendall & J. N. Butcher (Eds.) *Handbook of research methods in clinical psychology*. New York: Wiley, 1982.

Conners, C. K. A teacher rating scale for use in drug studies with children. *American Journal of Psychiatry*, 1969, *126*, 152–154.

Conry, R., & Plant, W. T. WAIS and group predictions of an academic success criterion: High school and college. *Educational and Psychological Measurement*, 1965, *25*, 493–500.

Copeland, B. A. Hospital privileges and staff membership for psychologists. *Professional Psychology*, 1980, *11*, 676–683.

Coriat, I. H. The experimental synthesis of the dissecrated memories in alcoholic amnesia. *Journal of Abnormal Psychology*, 1906, *1*, 109–122.

Cornell, E. L. The psychologist in the school system. *Journal of Consulting Psychology*, 1942, *6*, 185–195.

Corsini, R. Functions of the prison psychologist. *Journal of Consulting Psychology*, 1945, *9*, 101–104.

Corsini, R. J. (Ed.) *Current psychotherapies*. (2nd ed.) Itasca, Ill.: Peacock, 1979.

Corwin, R. G. Patterns of organizational conflict. *Administrative Science Quarterly*, 1969, *14*, 507–520.

Coser, L. A. Social conflict and the theory of social change. *British Journal of Sociology*, 1957, *8*, 197–207.

Costello, C. G. A critical review of Seligman's laboratory experiments on learned helplessness and depression in humans. *Journal of Abnormal Psychology*, 1978, *87*, 21–31.

Cowen, E. L., Gesten, E. L., & Wilson, A. B. The Primary Mental Health Project (PMHP): Evaluation of current program effectiveness. *American Journal of Community Psychology*, 1979, *7*, 293–303.

Cowen, E. L., Lorion, R., & Dorr, D. Research in the community cauldron: A case report. *Canadian Psychologist*, 1974, *15*, 313–325.

Cowen, E. L., Trost, M. A., Lorion, R., Dorr, D., Izzo, L., & Issacson, R. V. *New ways in school mental health*. New York: Human Sciences Press, 1975.

Coyne, J. C. Depression and the response of others. *Journal of Abnormal Psychology*, 1976, *85*, 186–193.

Craighead, L. W. Self-instructional training for assertion-refusal behavior. *Behavior Therapy*, 1979, *10*, 529–542.

Craighead, W. E , Kazdin, A. E., & Mahoney, M. J. *Behavior modification: Principles, issues, and applications*. (2nd ed.) Boston: Houghtin Mifflin, 1981.

Craighead, W. E., Wilcoxon-Craighead, L., & Meyers, A. W. New directions in behavior modification with children. In M. Hersen, R. Eisler, & P. Miller (Eds.), *Progress in behavior modification.* Vol. 6. New York: Academic Press, 1978.

Crissey, M. S. Mental retardation: Past, present, and future. *American Psychologist,* 1975, *29,* 800–808.

Cronbach, L. J. Response sets and test validity. *Educational and Psychological Measurement,* 1946, *6,* 475–494.

Cronbach, L. J. Coefficient alpha and the internal structure of tests. *Psychometrika,* 1951, *16,* 297–334.

Cronbach, L. J. Assessment of individual differences. In P. R. Farnsworth (Ed.), *Annual review of psychology.* Vol. 7. Stanford, Cal.: Annual Reviews, Inc., 1956.

Cronbach, L. J. The two disciplines of scientific psychology. *American Psychologist,* 1957, *12,* 671–684.

Cronbach, L. J. Beyond the two disciplines of scientific psychology. *American Psychologist,* 1975, *30,* 116–127.

Cronbach, L. J. & Meehl, P. E. Construct validity in psychological tests. *Psychological Bulletin,* 1955, *52,* 281–302.

Cummings, N. A. The anatomy of psychotherapy under national health insurance. *American Psychologist,* 1977, *32,* 711–718.

Cummings, N. A. Editorial. *American Psychological Association Monitor,* 1979, *10*(12), 3.

Cummings, N. A., & Follette, W. T. Brief psychotherapy and medical utilization: An eight year follow-up. In H. Dorken & Associates (Eds.), *The professional psychologist today. New developments in law, health insurance, and health practice.* San Francisco: Jossey-Bass, 1976.

D'Amato, M. R. *Experimental psychology: Methodology, psychophysics, and learning.* New York: McGraw-Hill, 1970.

Dahlkoetter, J., Callahan, E. J., & Linton, J. Obesity and the unbalanced energy equation. *Journal of Consulting and Clinical Psychology,* 1979, *47,* 898–905.

Dahlstrom, W. G. Recommendations for patient measures in evaluating psychotherapy: Test batteries and inventories. In I. E. Waskow & M. B. Parloff (Eds.), *Psychotherapy change measures.* Washington, D. C.: U. S. Government Printing Office, 1975.

Dahlstrom, W. G., Welsh, G. S., & Dahlstrom, L. E. *An MMPI Handbook.* Vol. 1 *Clinical Interpretation.* Minneapolis: University of Minnesota Press, 1972.

Dallas, D. Savagery, show and tell. *American Psychologist,* 1978, *33,* 388–390.

Dana, R. H. The perceptual organization TAT score, number, order, and frequency. *Journal of Projective Techniques,* 1959, *23,* 307–310.

Danaher, B., & Lichtenstein, E. *Become an ex-smoker.* Englewood Cliffs, N.J.: Prentice-Hall, 1977.

Darley, J. G., & Wolfe, D. Can we meet the formidable demand for psychological services? *American Psychologist,* 1946, *1,* 179–180.

Darwin, C. R. *The expression of emotions in men and animals.* London: John Murray, 1872.

Davenport-Sleek, B. A comparative evaluation of obstetrical hypnosis and antenatal childbirth training. *International Journal of Clinical and Experimental Hypnosis,* 1975, *23,* 266–281.

Davids, A. Therapeutic approaches to children in residential treatment: Changes from the mid-1950's to the mid-1970's. *American Psychologist*, 1975, *30*, 809–814.

Davidson, W. S. *The diversion of delinquents*. Unpublished doctoral dissertation, University of Illinois at Champaign-Urbana, 1975.

Davis, H. R., & Salasin, S. E. The utilization of evaluation. In E. L. Stivening & M. Guttentag (Eds.), *Handbook of evaluation research*. Beverly Hills, Cal.: Sage, 1975.

Davis, K. *Human society*. New York: Macmillan, 1949.

Davis, K., & Moore, W. E. Some principles of stratification. *American Sociological Review*, 1945, *10*, 242–249.

Davison, G. C. Homosexuality: The ethical challenge. *Journal of Consulting and Clinical Psychology*, 1976, *44*, 157–162.

Davison, G. C. Not can but ought: The treatment of homosexuality. *Journal of Consulting and Clinical Psychology*, 1978, *46*, 170–172.

Davison, G. C., & Stuart, R. G. Behavior therapy and civil liberties. *American Psychologist*, 1975, *30*, 755–763.

Dean, C. W., & Reppucci, N. D. Juvenile correctional institutions. In D. Glaser (Ed.), *Handbook of criminology*. New York: Rand McNally, 1974.

DeCaprio, N. S. *Personality theories: Guides to living*. Philadelphia: W. B. Saunders, 1974.

Deleon, P. H. Implications of national health policies for professional psychology. *Professional Psychology*, 1977, *8*, 263–268.

Dell, P. F. Some irreverent thoughts on paradox. *Family Process*, 1981, *20*, 37–41.

De Muth, N. M., & Kamis, E. Fees and therapy: Clarification of the relationship of payment source to service utilization. *Journal of Consulting and Clinical Psychology*, 1980, *48*, 793–795.

Denker, P. G. Results of treatment of psychoneuroses by the general practitioner. *New York State Journal of Medicine*, 1946, *46*, 2164–2166.

Denker, P. G. Results of treatment of psychoneuroses by the general practitioner: A follow-up study of 500 cases. *Archives of Neurology and Psychiatry*, 1947, *57*, 504–505.

Depue, R. A., & Monroe, S. M. Learned helplessness in the perspective of the depressive disorders: Conceptual and definitional issues. *Journal of Abnormal Psychology*, 1978, *87*, 3–20. (a)

Depue, R. A., & Monroe, S. M. The unipolar-bipolar distinction in the depressive disorders. *Psychological Bulletin*, 1978, *85*, 1001–1029. (b)

Derogatis, L. R. *The Derogatis Sexual Functionary Inventory*. Baltimore: Johns Hopkins University Press, 1975.

Derr, C. B. Conflict resolution in organizations: Views from the field of educational administration. *Public Administrative Review*, 1972, *22*, 495–502.

Detre, T. P., & Kupfer, D. J. Psychiatric history and mental status examination. In A. M. Freedman, H. I. Kaplan, & B. J. Sadock (Eds.), *Comprehensive textbook of psychiatry*. (2nd ed.) Baltimore: Williams and Wilkins, 1975.

Dicken, C., Bryson, R., & Kass, W. Companionship therapy: A replication in experimental community psychology. *Journal of Consulting and Clinical Psychology*, 1977, *45*, 637-646.

Dightman, C. R. Fees and mental health services: Attitudes of the professional. *Mental Hygiene*, 1970, *54*, 401-406.

Dimond, R. E., Havens, R. A., Rathnow, S. J., & Colliver, J. A. Employment patterns of subdoctoral clinical psychologists. *Professional Psychology*, 1977, *8*, 114-119.

Doane, J. A. Family interaction and communication deviance in disturbed and normal families: A review of the literature. *Family Process*, 1978, *17*, 357-376.

Doehring, D. G., & Reitan R. M. MMPI performance of aphasic and non-aphasic brain-damaged patients. *Journal of Clinical Psychology*, 1960, *16*, 307-309.

Dokecki, P. R. A transactional perspective on the interrelationship of the society power structure, the mental health establishment, the individual and the community: A commentary on Nassi. *Journal of Community Psychology*, 1978, *6*, 19-21.

Doll, E. A. A genetic scale of social maturity. *American Journal of Orthopsychiatry*, 1935, *5*, 180-190.

Doll, E. A. The social basis of mental diagnosis. *Journal of Applied Psychology*, 1940, *24*, 160-169.

Doll, E. A. *Vineland Social Maturity Scale: Manual of direction.* (Rev. ed.) Minneapolis: American Guidance Service, 1965.

Dollard, J., & Auld, F., Jr. *Scoring human motives: A manual.* New Haven, Conn.: Yale University Press, 1959.

Dollard, J., Doob, L. W., Miller, N. E., Mowrer, O. H., & Sears, R. R. *Frustration and aggression.* New Haven, Conn.: Yale University Press, 1939.

Dollard, J., & Miller, N. E. *Personality and psychotherapy.* New York: McGraw Hill, 1950.

Doppelt, J. Estimating the full scale score on the Wechsler Adult Intelligence Scale from scores on 4 subtests. *Journal of Consulting Psychology*, 1956, *20*, 63-66.

Dörken, H. Avenues to legislative success. *American Psychologist*, 1977, *32*, 738-745.

Dörken, H. National Health Insurance: Implications for mental health practitioners. *Professional Psychology*, 1980, *11*, 664-671.

Dörken, H. Coming of age legislatively: In 21 steps. *American Psychologist*, 1981, *36*, 165-173.

Dörken, H., & Cummings, N. A. A school of psychology as innovation in professional education: The California School of Professional Psychology. *Professional Psychology*, 1977, *8*, 129-149.

Dorr, D. Some practical suggestions on behavioral consulting with teachers. *Professional Psychology*, 1977, *9*, 130-137.

Dougherty, F. E. Patient-therapist matching for prediction of optimal and minimal therapeutic outcome. *Journal of Consulting and Clinical Psychology*, 1976, *44*, 889-897.

Douglas, V. I. Are drugs enough? To train or to treat the hyperactive child. *International Journal of Mental Health*, 1975, *5*, 199-212.

Douglas, V. I., Parry, P., Marton, P., & Garson, C. Assessment of a cognitive training program for hyperactive children. *Journal of Abnormal Child Psychology*, 1976, *4*, 389-410.

Drabman, R. S. Child versus teacher-administered token programs in a psychiatric hospital school. *Journal of Abnormal Child Psychology*, 1973, *1*, 68-87.

Drotar, D. Psychological consultation in a pediatric hospital. *Professional Psychology*, 1976, *8*, 77-83.

Dubois, P. *The psychic treatment of mental disorders.* New York: Funk & Wagnalls, 1908.

Dudek, S. Z., Lester, E. P., Goldberg, J. S., & Dyer, G. B. Relationship of Piaget measures to standard intelligence and motor scales. *Perceptual and Motor Skills*, 1969, *28*, 351-362.

Duncan, R. B. Characteristics of organizational environments and perceived environmental uncertainty. *Administrative Science Quarterly*, 1972, *17*, 313-327.

Dunham, H. W. Community psychiatry: The newest therapeutic bandwagon. *Archives of General Psychiatry*, 1965, *12*, 303-313.

Dunn, L. M. *Peabody Picture Vocabulary Test Manual.* Minneapolis: American Guidance Service, 1959.

Dunn, L. M. *Expanded manual for the Peabody Picture Vocabulary Test.* Minneapolis: American Guidance Service, 1965.

Dunnette, M. (Ed.) *Handbook of industrial and organizational psychology.* Chicago: Rand McNally, 1976.

Durlak, J. Description and evaluation of a behaviorally oriented school-based preventive mental health program. *Journal of Consulting and Clinical Psychology*, 1977, *45*, 27-33.

D'Zurilla, T. J., & Goldfried, M. R. Problem solving and behavior modification. *Journal of Abnormal Psychology*, 1971, *78*, 107-126.

D'Zurilla, T., & Nezu, A. Social problem solving in adults. In P. C. Kendall (Ed.) *Advances in cognitive-behavioral research and therapy.* Vol. 1. New York: Academic Press, 1982.

Edinger, J. D., Kendall, P. C., Hooke, J. F., & Bogan, J. B. The predictive efficacy of three MMPI short forms. *Journal of Personality Assessment*, 1976, *40*, 259-265.

Edinger, J. D., & Norwood, P. E. Relative efficacy of Wechsler Adult Intelligence Scale short forms with outpatients. *Journal of Consulting and Clinical Psychology*, 1975, *43*, 591.

Edlund, C. V. The effect on the behavior of children, as reflected in the IQ scores, when reinforced after each correct response. *Journal of Applied Analysis*, 1972, *5*, 317-319.

Edney, J. J. Human territoriality. *Psychological Bulletin*, 1974, *81*, 959-975.

Edwards, A. L. *Manual for Edwards Personal Preference Schedule.* New York: Psychological Corporation, 1953.

Edwards, A. L. *The social desirability variable in personality assessment and research.* New York: Dryden, 1957.

Edwards, D. W., Greene, L. R., Abramowitz, S. I., & Davidson, C. V. National health insurance, psychotherapy, and the poor. *American Psychologist*, 1979, *34*, 411-419.

Eisler, R. M., Miller, P. M., Hersen, M., & Blanchard, E. B. Situational determinants of assertive behaviors. *Journal of Consulting and Clinical Psychology*, 1975, *43*, 330-341

Ellis, A. *Reason and emotion in psychotherapy.* New York: Lyle Stuart, 1962.

Ellis, A. *Growth through reason.* Hollywood, Cal.: Wilshire Book Co., 1971.

Ellis, A., & Harper, R. A. *A guide to rational living.* New York: Lyle Stuart, 1968.

Endicott, N. A., & Endicott, J. Assessment of outcome by projective tests. In I. E. Waskow and M. B. Parloff (Eds.), *Psychotherapy change measures.* Washington, D. C.: U. S. Government Printing Office, 1975.

Endler, N. S. A person-situation interaction model for anxiety. In C. D. Spielberger and I. G. Sarason (Eds.), *Stress and anxiety.* Vol. 1. Washington, D. C.: Hemisphere Publications, 1975.

Endler, N. S., & Hunt, J. McV. S-R inventories of hostility and comparisons of the propositions of variance from persons, responses, and situations for hostility and anxiousness. *Journal of Personality and Social Psychology*, 1968, *9*, 309-315.

Endler, N. S., Hunt, J. McV., & Rosenstein, A. J. An S-R inventory of anxiousness. *Psychological Monographs*, 1962, *76* (Whole No. 536).

Endler, N. S., & Magnusson, D. (Eds.) *Interactionism in psychology*. New York: Wiley, 1976.

Endler, N. S., & Okada, M. A multidimensional measure of trait anxiety: The S-R Inventory of General Trait Anxiousness. *Journal of Consulting and Clinical Psychology*, 1975, *43*, 319-329.

Englemann, S. The effectiveness of direct instruction on IQ performance and achievement in reading and arithmetic. In J. Hellmuth (Ed.), *Compensatory education: A national debate*. Vol. III. *The disadvantaged child*. New York: Brunner/Mazel, 1970.

Enright, J. B. On the playing fields of Synanon. In L. Blank, G. B. Gottseger, & M. G. Gottseger (Eds.), *Confrontation*. New York: Macmillan, 1971.

Epstein, N., & Jackson, E. An outcome study of short-term communication training with married couples. *Journal of Consulting and Clinical Psychology*, 1978, *46*, 207-212.

Erdelyi, M. H. A new look at the new look: Perceptual defense and vigilance. *Psychological Review*, 1974, *81*, 1-25.

Ericksen, S. C. Responsibilities of psychological science to professional psychology. *American Psychologist*, 1966, *21*, 950-953.

Erickson, K. T. Notes on the sociology of deviance. *Social Problems*, 1962, *9*, 307-314.

Erikson, E. *Childhood and society*. New York: Norton, 1950.

Erlenmeyer-Kimling, L., & Jarvik, L. P. Genetics and intelligence: A review. *Science*, 1963, *142*, 1477-1479.

Eron, L. D. A normative study of the Thematic Apperception Test. *Psychological Monograph*, 1950, *64* (Whole No. 9).

Esser, A. Environment and mental health. *Science, Medicine and Man*, 1974, *1*, 181-193.

Everett, P. B., Hayward, S. C., & Meyers, A. W. The effects of a token reinforcement procedure on bus ridership. *Journal of Applied Behavior Analysis*, 1974, 7, 1-9.

Exner, J. E. *The Rorschach: A comprehensive system*. New York: Wiley, 1974.

Exner, J. E. Projective techniques. In I. B. Weiner (Ed.), *Clinical methods in psychology*. New York: Wiley, 1976.

Exner, J. E., & Clark, B. The Rorschach. In B. B. Wolman (Ed.), *Clinical diagnosis of mental disorders: A handbook*. New York: Plenum Press, 1978.

Exner, J. E., Weiner, I. B., & Schuyler, W. *A Rorschach workbook for the comprehensive system*. Bayville, New York: Rorschach Workshops, 1976.

Eysenck, H. J. The effects of psychotherapy: An evaluation. *Journal of Consulting Psychology*, 1952, *16*, 319-324.

Eysenck, H. J. Psychiatric diagnosis as a psychological and statistical problem. *Psychological Reports*, 1955, *1*, 3-17.

Eysenck, H. J. *The biological basis of personality*. Springfield, Ill.: Charles C Thomas, 1967.

Eysenck, H. J. Expectations as causal elements in behavioural change. *Advances in Behaviour Research and Therapy*, 1978, *1*, 171-175.

Eysenck, H. J., & Eysenck, S. B. G. *Psychoticism as a dimension of personality*. London: Hodder & Stoughton, 1976.

Eysenck, H. J., & Eysenck, S. B. G. *Eysenck personality inventory.* San Diego: Educational and Industrial Testing Service, 1968.

Eysenck, H. J., & Eysenck, S. B. G. Block and psychoticism. *Journal of Abnormal Psychology*, 1977, *86*, 651-652.

Ezriel, H. Psychoanalytic group therapy. In L. R. Wolberg & E. K. Schwartz (Eds.), *Group therapy 1973.* New York: Intercontinental Medical Book Corp., 1973.

Fairweather, G. W., Sanders, D. H., Cressler, D. L., & Maynard, M. *Community life for the mentally ill.* Chicago: Aldine, 1969.

Fairweather, G. W., Sanders, D. H. & Tornatzky, L., *Creating change in mental health organizations.* New York: Pergamon, 1974.

Fairweather, G. W., Simon, R., Gebhard, M. E., Weingarten, E., Holland, J. L., Sanders, R., Stone, G. B., & Reahl, J. E. Relative effectiveness of psychotherapeutic programs: A multicriteria comparison of four programs for three different patient groups. *Psychological Monographs*, 1960 (Whole No. 492).

Fairweather, G. W., & Tornatzky, L. G. *Experimental methods for social policy research.* New York: Pergamon, 1977.

Farina, A., Arenberg, D., & Guskin, S. A scale for measuring minimal social behavior. *Journal of Consulting Psychology*, 1957, *21*, 265-268.

Farina, A., & Ring, K. The influence of perceived mental illness on interpersonal relations. *Journal of Abnormal and Social Psychology*, 1965, *70*, 47-51.

Farina, A., Thaw, J., Lovern, J., & Mangone, D. People's reactions to a former patient moving into their neighborhood. *Journal of Community Psychology*, 1974, *2*, 108-112.

Faschingbauer, T. R. A 166-item written short form of the group MMPI: The FAM. *Journal of Consulting and Clinical Psychology*, 1974, 42, 654-655.

Feinberg, M. R. The powers and pitfalls of the clinical and industrial psychologist as administrator. In L. E. Abt & B. F. Reiss (Eds.), *Clinical psychology in industrial organizations.* New York: Grune and Stratton, 1971.

Feldman, R. A., & Wodarski, J. S. Bureacratic constraints and methodological adaptations in community based research. *American Journal of Community Psychology*, 1974, *2*, 211-224.

Fenichel, O. *The psychoanalytic theory of neurosis.* New York: Norton, 1945.

Ferenzi, S. *Thalasia: A theory of genitality.* New York: Psychoanalytic Quarterly, 1938.

Ferster, C. B. A functional analysis of depression. *American Psychologist*, 1973, *28*, 857-870.

Ferster, C. B., & DeMyer, M. K. A method for the experimental analysis of behavior of autistic children. *American Journal of Orthopsychiatry*, 1962, *32*, 89-98.

Ferster, C. B., & Skinner, B. F. *Schedules of reinforcement.* New York: Appleton-Century-Crofts, 1957.

Fichter, M. M., & Wittchen, H. U. Clinical psychology and psychotherapy: A survey of the present state of professionalization in 23 countries. *American Psychologist*, 1980, *35*, 16-25.

Fichter, M. M., Wittchen, H. U., & Dvorak, A. Psychologen im Beruf: Ergebnisse einer empirischen Untersuchung. In V. Birtsch & D. Tscheulin (Eds.), *Universitaesausbildung in Klinischer Psychologie: Ziele-Methoden-Evaluation.* Weinheim, West Germany: Beltz, in press.

Fiedler, D., & Beach, L. R. On the decision to be assertive. *Journal of Consulting and Clinical Psychology*, 1978, *46*, 537-546.

Fiedler, F. E. *A theory of leadership effectiveness.* New York: McGraw-Hill, 1967.

Field, P. B. Effects of tape-recorded hypnotic preparation for surgery. *International Journal of Clinical and Experimental Hypnosis*, 1974, *22*, 54-61.

Fields, F. R. J., & Whitmyre, J. W. Verbal and performance relationships with respect to laterality of cerebral involvement. *Diseases of the Nervous System*, 1969, *30*, 177-179.

Filskov, S., & Goldstein, S. G. Diagnostic validity of the Halstead-Reitan Neuro-psychological Battery. *Journal of Consulting and Clinical Psychology*, 1974, *42*, 382-388.

Filskov, S., & Locklear, E. A multidimensional perspective on clinical neuropsychology research. In P. C. Kendall & J. N. Butcher (Eds.) *Handbook of research methods in clinical psychology.* New York: Wiley, 1982.

Finch, A. J., Jr., Childress, W. B., Wilkins, K. A., & Kendall, P. C. WISC short forms with emotionally disturbed children. *Journal of Abnormal Child Psychology*, 1974, *2*, 337-341.

Finch, A. J., Jr., Kendall, P. C., Spirito, A., Entin, A., Montgomery, L. E., & Schwartz, D. J. Short form and factor-analytic studies of the WISC-R with behavior problem children. *Journal of Abnormal Child Psychology*, 1979, *7*, 337-344.

Finch, A. J., Jr., Ollendick, T. H., & Ginn, F. W. WISC short forms with mentally retarded children. *American Journal of Mental Deficiency*, 1973, *78*, 144-149.

Finch, A. J., Jr., Thornton, L. S., & Montgomery, L. E. WAIS short forms with hospitalized psychiatric patients. *Journal of Consulting and Clinical Psychology*, 1974, *42*, 469.

Fine, R. Interpretation: The patient's response. In E. F. Hammer (Ed.), *Use of interpretation in treatment.* New York: Grune and Stratton, 1968.

Finlayson, M. A. J., Johnson, K. A., & Reitan, R. M. Relationship of level of education to neuropsychological measures in brain-damaged and non-brain-damaged adults. *Journal of Consulting and Clinical Psychology*, 1977, *45*, 536–542.

Fischer, J., Paveza, G. J., Kickertz, N. S., Hubbard, L. J., & Grayston, S. B. The relationship between theoretical orientation and therapists' empathy, warmth and genuineness. *Journal of Counseling Psychology*, 1975, *22*, 399-403.

Fisher, L. On the classification of families. *Archives of General Psychiatry*, 1977, *34*, 424-433.

Fisher, L., Anderson, A., & Jones, J. E. Types of paradoxical interventions and indications/contraindications for clinical practice. *Family Process*, 1971, *20*, 25-36.

Fisher, R. J. Third party consultation: A skill for professional psychologists in community practice. *Professional Psychology*, 1976, *8*, 344-351.

Fiske, D. W. The use of significant others in assessing the outcome of psychotherapy. In I. E. Waskow & M. B. Parloff (Eds.), *Psychotherapy change measures.* Washington, D. C.: U. S. Government Printing Office, 1975.

Fitts, W. *Manual: Tennessee self-concept scale.* Nashville, Tenn.: Counselor Recordings and Tests, 1964.

Fixsen, D. L., Phillips, E. L., & Wolf, M. M. Achievement place: Experiments in self-government with predelinquents. *Journal of Applied Behavior Analysis,* 1973, *6*, 31-49.

Fleming, P., & Ricks., D. F. Emotions of children before schizophrenia and before character disorder. In M. Roff & D. F. Ricks (Eds.), *Life history research in psychopathology*. Vol. 1. Minneapolis: University of Minnesota Press, 1970.

Flippo. J. R., & Lewinsohn, P. M. Effects of failure on the self-esteem of depressed and nondepressed subjects. *Journal of Consulting and Clinical Psychology*, 1971, *36,* 151.

Fo, W. S., & O'Donnell, C. R. The buddy system: Relationship and contingency conditions in a community intervention program for youths with nonprofessionals as behavior change agents. *Journal of Consulting and Clinical Psychology*, 1974, *42*, 163-169.

Fogarty, T. F. On emptiness and closeness. In P. J. Guerin (Ed.), *The best of the family 1973-1978*. New Rochelle, N.Y.: Center for Family Learning, 1978.

Follette, W. T., & Cummings, N. A. Psychiatric services and medical utilization in a prepaid health plan setting. *Medical Care*, 1967, *5*, 25-35.

Ford, J. D. Training in clinical psychology. Reappraisal based on recent empirical evidence. *The Clinical Psychologist,* 1977, *30*, 14-16.

Ford, J. D. Therapeutic relationship in behavior therapy: An empirical analysis. *Journal of Consulting and Clinical Psychology*, 1978, *46*, 1302-1314.

Ford, J. D. Research on training counselors and clinicians. *Review of Educational Research*, 1979, *49*, 87-130.

Ford, J. D. Training in environmental design. In L. Krasner (Ed.), *Environmental design and human behavior*. New York: Pergamon, 1980.

Ford, J. D., Bashford, M. B., & DeWitt, K. Prediction of outcome in marital enrichment communication training. In R. Moos (Ed.), *Social climate scales bibliography*. Palo Alto, Cal.: Stanford University, 1979.

Ford, J. D., & Hutchinson, W. R. *Elements of an effective and responsive training program for community-based psychologists*. Paper presented at the CUNY Psychology in Action Conference, New York, 1974.

Ford, J. D., & Migles, M. The role of the school psychologist: Teacher's preferences as a function of personal and professional characteristics. *Journal of School Psychology*, 1980, *17*, 372-378.

Forehand, R., & Atkeson, B. M. Generality of treatment effects with parents as therapists: A review of assessment and implementation procedures. *Behavior Therapy*, 1977, *8*, 575-593.

Foreyt, J. P., & Rathjen, D. P. (Eds.) *Cognitive behavior therapy: Research and application*. New York: Plenum, 1978.

Foucalt, M. *Madness and civilization*, New York: Random House, 1965.

Fowler, R. D., Jr. Automated interpretation of personality test data. In J. N. Butcher (Ed.), *MMPI: Research developments and clinical applications*. New York: McGraw-Hill, 1969.

Foxx, R. M., & Hake, D. F. Gasoline conservation: A procedure for measuring and reducing the driving of college students. *Journal of Applied Behavior Analysis*, 1977, *10*, 61-74.

Fozard, J. L., & Popkin, S. J. Optimizing adult development: Ends and means of an applied psychology of aging. *American Psychologist*, 1978, *33*, 975-989.

Framo, J. L. Marriage therapy in a couples' group. In P. A. Block (Ed.), *Techniques of family psychotherapy: A primer*. New York: Grune and Stratton, 1973.

Framo, J. L. Family of origin as a therapeutic resource for adults in marital and family therapy: You can and should go home again. *Family Process*, 1976, *15*, 193-210.

Frankl, V. Logos and existence in psychotherapy. *American Journal of Psychotherapy*, 1953, *7*, 8-15.

Frankl, V. *Man's search for meaning.* Boston: Beacon Press, 1959.

Franks, C. M., & Wilson, G. T. (Eds.) *Annual review of behavior therapy: Theory and practice.* Vol. 3. New York: Brunner/Mazel, 1975.

Franks, C. M., & Wilson, G. T. (Eds.) *Annual review of behavior therapy: Theory and practice.* Vol. 5. New York: Brunner/Mazel, 1977.

Franks, C. M., & Wilson, G. T. *Annual review of behavior therapy: Theory and practice.* Vol. 7. New York: Brunner/Mazel, 1979.

Franz, S. I. Observations on the functions of the association areas (cerebrum) in monkeys. *Journal of the American Medical Association*, 1906 (November 3).

Freeman, M. Of cults and communication. A conversation with Margaret Singer. *APA Monitor*, 1979 (July-August), 6-7.

Fremouw, W. J., & Zitter, R. E. A comparison of skills training and cognitive restructuring-relaxation for the treatment of speech anxiety. *Behavior Therapy*, 1978, *9*, 248-259.

French, J. R. P., Jr., & Raven, B. The bases of social power. In N. Cartwright (Ed.), *Studies in social power.* Ann Arbor, Mich.: Institute for Social Research, 1959.

Freud, A. *Technique of child analysis.* New York: Nervous and Mental Disease Publishing Company, 1928.

Freud, A. *The ego and the mechanisms of defense.* New York: International Universities Press, 1946. (a)

Freud, A. *The psychoanalytic treatment of children.* New York: International Universities Press, 1946. (b)

Freud, S. *A general introduction to psychoanalysis.* New York: Liveright, 1920.

Freud, S. *The psychopathology of everyday life.* New York: New American Library, 1904.

Freud, S. *Essays on the theory of sexuality.* New York: Basic Books, 1905/1959.

Freud, S. The origin and development of psychoanalysis. *American Journal of Psychology*, 1910, *21*, 181–218.

Freud, S. *The ego and the id.* London: Hogarth Press, 1923.

Freud, S. *The problem of lay analysis.* New York: Brentano's, 1927.

Freud, S. *A general introduction to psychoanalysis.* New York: Liveright, 1935.

Freud, S. Analysis terminable and interminable. *Standard Edition*, Vol. XXIII. London: Hogarth, 1937.

Freud, S. *The basic writings of Sigmund Freud.* New York: Modern Library, 1938.

Freud, S. *The interpretation of dreams.* New York: Macmillan, 1939.

Freud, S. (1917) Mourning and melancholia. *Standard edition.* Vol. XIV. London: Hogarth Press, 1957.

Frick, T., & Semmel, M. I. Observer agreement and reliabilities of classroom observational measures. *Review of Educational Research*, 1978, *48*, 157–184.

Friedman, H., & Taub, H. A. The use of hypnosis and biofeedback procedures for essential hypertension. *International Journal of Clinical and Experimental Hypnosis*, 1977, *25*, 335-347.

Friedman, P. R. Legal regulation of applied behavior analysis in mental institutions and prisons. *Arizona Law Review*, 1975, *17*, 39–104.

Fromm-Reichman, F. *Principles of intensive psychotherapy.* Chicago: University of Chicago Press, 1950.

Fuchs, C. Z., & Rehm, L. P. A self-control therapy program for depression. *Journal of Consulting and Clinical Psychology*, 1977, 45, 206-215.

Fuhr, R., Ford, J. D., & Moos, R. H. Family social climate and family therapy. In R. Moos (Ed.), *Social climate scales bibliography.* Palo Alto, Cal.: Stanford University, 1980.

Gadlin, M., & Ingle, G. Through the one-way mirror. The limits of experimental self-reflection. *American Psychologist*, 1975, *30*, 1003-1010.

Gagnon, J., & Davison, G. C. Asylums, the token economy, and the metrics of mental life. *Behavior Therapy*, 1976, 7, 528-534.

Galton, F. *Hereditary genius: An inquiry into its laws and consequences.* London: Macmillan, 1869.

Gamble, K. R. The Holtzman inkblot technique: A review. *Psychological Bulletin*, 1972, 77, 172-194.

Gambrill, E. D., & Richey, C. A. An assertion inventory for use in assessment and research. *Behavior Therapy*, 1975, *6*, 550-561.

Gans, H. J. Urbanism and suburbanism as ways of life: A re-evaluation of definitions. In A. Rose (Ed.), *Human behavior and social processes.* Boston: Houghton Mifflin, 1962.

Gantt, W. H. *Experimental basis for neurotic behavior.* New York: Harper, 1944.

Gantt, W. H. Experimental basis for neurotic behavior. In H. D. Kimmel (Ed.), *Experimental psychopathology: Recent research and theory.* New York: Academic Press, 1971.

Garber, J., & Seligman, M. E. P. (Eds.) *Human Helplessness: Theory and applications.* New York: Academic Press, 1980.

Gardner, J. M. Selection of nonprofessionals for behavior modification programs. *American Journal of Mental Deficiency*, 1972, 76, 680-685.

Garfield, S. L. *Psychotherapy: An eclectic approach.* New York: Wiley, 1980.

Garfield, S. L. Research on client variables in psychotherapy. In S. L. Garfield & A. E. Bergin (Eds.), *Handbook of psychotherapy and behavior change.* (2nd ed.) New York: Wiley, 1978.

Garfield, S. L., & Bergin, A. E. (Eds.) *Handbook of psychotherapy and behavior change.* (2nd ed.) New York: Wiley, 1978.

Garfield, S. L., & Kurtz, R. Clinical psychologists in the 1970's. *American Psychologist*, 1976, *31*, 1-9. (a)

Garfield, S. L., & Kurtz, R. Personal therapy for the psychotherapist: Some findings and issues. *Psychotherapy: Therapy, Research and Practice*, 1976, *13*, 121-127. (b)

Garmezy, N. Process and reactive schizophrenia: Some conceptions and issues. *Schizophrenia Bulletin*, 1970, *2*, 30-67.

Garmezy, N. Emerging conceptions of mental illness and models of treatment. *Professional Psychology*, 1971, *2*, 129-144.

Garmezy, N. Children at risk: The search for the antecedents of schizophrenia. Part I: Conceptual models and research methods. *Schizophrenia Bulletin*, 1974, *8*, 14-92.

Garmezy, N. DSM III: Never mind the psychologists: Is it good for the children? *The Clinical Psychologist*, 1978, *31*, 1-6.

Garmezy, N. Research in clinical psychology: Serving the future hour. In P. C. Kendall & J. N. Butcher (Eds.) *Handbook of research methods in clinical psychology*. New York: Wiley, 1982.

Gaskill, H. The closing phase of the psychoanalytic treatment of adults and the goals of psychoanalysis: The myth of perfectability. *International Journal of Psycho-Analysis*, 1980, *61*, 11-23.

Gatchel, R. J., Paulus, P. B., & Maples, C. W. Learned helplessness and self-reported affect. *Journal of Abnormal Psychology*, 1975, *84*, 732-734.

Gay, M., Hollandsworth, J. G., & Galassi, J. P. An assertiveness inventory for adults. *Journal of Counseling Psychology*, 1975, *22*, 340-344.

Gazzaniga, M. S. Brain mechanisms and behavior. In M. S. Gazzaniga & C. Blakemore (Eds.), *Handbook of psychobiology*. New York: Academic Press, 1975.

Geer, J. H. The development of a scale to measure fear. *Behaviour Research and Therapy*, 1965, *3*, 45-53.

Gendlin, E. T. Experiential psychotherapy. In R. J. Corsini (Ed.), *Current psychotherapies* (2nd ed.), Itasca, Ill.: Peacock, 1979.

Gerbasi, K. C., Zuckerman, M., & Reis, H. T. Justice needs a new blindfold: A review of mock jury research. *Psychological Bulletin*, 1977, *84*, 686-713.

Gershone, T. R., Erickson, E. A., Mitchell, J. E., & Paulson, G. A. Behavioral comparison of a token economy and a standard psychiatric treatment ward. *Journal of Behavior Therapy and Experimental Psychiatry*, 1977, *8*, 381-385.

Gesell, A. *The mental growth of the preschool child*. New York: Macmillan, 1925.

Gesell, A., & Associates. *Gesell developmental schedules*. New York: Psychological Corporation, 1949.

Gesten, E. A health resources inventory: The development of a measure of the personal and social competence of primary grade children. *Journal of Consulting and Clinical Psychology*, 1976, *44*, 775-786.

Ghiselli, E. E. The validity of aptitude tests in personnel selection. *Personnel Psychology*, 1973, *26*, 461-477.

Gilberstadt, H., & Duker, J. *A handbook for clinical and actuarial MMPI interpretation*. Philadelphia: Saunders, 1965.

Glaser, F. B. Some historical aspects of the drug-free therapeutic community. *American Journal of Drug and Alcohol Abuse*, 1974, *1*, 37-52.

Glasgow, R. E., & Rosen, G. M. Behavioral bibliotherapy: A review of self-help behavior therapy manuals. *Psychological Bulletin*, 1978, *85*, 1-23.

Glass, C. R., Gottman, J., & Shmurak, S. Response acquisition and cognitive self-statements modification approaches to dating skills training. *Journal of Counseling Psychology*, 1976, *23*, 520-526.

Glass, C. R., Merluzzi, T. V., Biever, J. L., & Larsen, K. L. Cognitive assessment of social anxiety: Development and validation of a self-statement questionnaire. *Cognitive Therapy and Research*, in press.

Glass, D. C., & Singer, J. E. *Urban stress*. New York: Academic Press, 1972.

Glenwick, D. S., Jason, L. A., Copeland, A. P., & Stevens, E. Crisis intervention with children. *American Psychologist*, 1979, *34*, 183-185.

Glidewell, J. The entry problem in consultation. *Journal of Social Issues*, 1959, *15*, 51–59.

Glogower, F. D., Fremouw, W. J., & McCrosky, J. C. A components analysis of cognitive restructuring. *Cognitive Therapy and Research*, 1978, *2*, 209-223.

Goebel, R. A. & Satz, P. Profile analysis and the abbreviated Wechsler Adult Intelligence Scale: A multivariate approach. *Journal of Consulting and Clinical Psychology*, 1975, *43*, 780-785.

Goffman, I. *Asylums*. Garden City, N.Y.: Doubleday, 1961.

Goldberg, I. D., Krantz, G., & Locke, B. Z. Effect of a short-term outpatient psychiatric therapy benefit on the utilization of medical services in a prepaid group practice program. *Medical Care*, 1970, *8*, 419-428.

Goldberg, L. R. Diagnosticians versus diagnostic signs: The diagnosis of psychosis versus neurosis from the MMPI. *Psychological Monographs*, 1965, *79*(Whole No. 602).

Goldberg, L. R. *Therapeutic partnership*. New York: Springer, 1977.

Golden, C. J. Validity of the Halstead-Reitan neuropsychological battery in a mixed psychiatric and brain impaired population. *Journal of Consulting and Clinical Psychology*, 1977, *45*, 1043-1051.

Golden, C. J. *Diagnosis and rehabilitation in clinical neuropsychology*. Springfield, Ill.: Charles C Thomas, 1978.

Golden, C. J., Hammeke, T. A., & Purisch, A. D. Diagnostic validity of a standardized neuropsychological battery derived from Luria's neuropsychological tests. *Journal of Consulting and Clinical Psychology*, 1978, *46*, 1258-1265.

Goldfried, M. R. toward the delineation of therapeutic change principles. *American Psychologist*, 1980, *35*, 991-999.

Goldfried, M. R., & Davison, G. C. *Clinical behavior therapy*. New York: Holt, Rinehart and Winston, 1976.

Goldfried, M. R., Decenteceo, E. T., & Weinberg, L. Systematic rational restructuring as a self-control technique. *Behavior Therapy*, 1974, *5*, 247-254.

Goldfried, M. R., & Kent, R. N. Traditional versus behavioral personality assessment: A comparison of methodological and theoretical assumptions. *Psychological Bulletin*, 1972, *77*, 409-420.

Goldfried, M. R., Linehan, M. M., & Smith, J. L. reduction of test anxiety through cognitive restructuring. *Journal of Consulting and Clinical Psychology*, 1978, *46*, 32-39.

Goldfried, M. R., & Pomeranz, D. Role of assessment in behavior modification. *Psychological Reports*, 1968, *23*, 75-87.

Goldfried, M. R., Stricker, G., & Weiner, I. B. *Rorschach handbook of clinical and research applications*. Englewood Cliffs, N.J.: Prentice-Hall, 1972.

Goldiamond, I. Self-control procedures in personal behavior problems. *Psychological Reports*, 1965, *17*, 851–868.

Goldstein, A. P. *Therapist-patient expectancies in psychotherapy*. New York: Pergamon, 1962.

Goldstein, A. P. *Structured learning therapy*. New York: Pergamon, 1973.

Goldstein, G., & Neuringer, C. Schizophrenic and organic signs on the trail-making test. *Perceptual and Motor Skills*, 1966, *22*, 347-350.

Goodenough, F. *The measurement of intelligence by drawings.* Yonkers-on-Hudson, N.Y.: World Books, 1926.

Goodman, G. *Companionship therapy: Studies in structured intimacy.* San Francisco: Jossey-Bass, 1972.

Goods, W. J. Community within a community: The professions. *American Sociological Review,* 1957, *22,* 194-200.

Goodwin, L. On making social research relevant to public policy and national problem solving. *American Psychologist.* 1971, *26,* 431-442.

Gorsuch, R. L. *Factor analysis.* Philadelphia: W. B. Saunders, 1974.

Gotkin, J. New words for an old power trip: A critique of behavioral modification in institutional settings. *Arizona Law Review,* 1975, *17,* 29-32.

Gotlib, I. H., & Asarnow, R. F. Independence of interpersonal and impersonal problem solving skills: Reply to Rohsenow. *Journal of Consulting and Clinical Psychology,* 1980, *48,* 286-288.

Gotlib, I. H., & Asarnow, R. F. Interpersonal and impersonal problem-solving skills in mildly and clinically depressed university students. *Journal of Consulting and Clinical Psychology,* 1979, *47,* 86-95.

Gottesman, I. I. Genetic aspects of intelligent behavior. In N. Ellis (Ed.), *The handbook of mental deficiency: Psychological theory and research.* New York: McGraw-Hill, 1963.

Gottesman, I. I. Heredity and intelligence. In W. W. Hartup (Ed.), *The young child.* Vol. 2. Washington, D. C.: National Association for Education of Young Children, 1972.

Gottesman, I. I. Developmental genetics and ontogenetic psychology: Overdue detente and propositions from a matchmaker. In A. D. Pick (Ed.), *Minnesota symposia on child psychology.* Minneapolis: University of Minnesota Press, 1974.

Gottesman, I. I., & Shields, J. *Schizophrenia and genetics: A twin study vantage point.* New York: Academic Press, 1972.

Gottschalk, L. A., Fox, R. A., & Bates, D. E. A study of medication and outcome in a mental health crisis clinic. *American Journal of Psychiatry,* 1973, *130,* 1107-1111.

Gough, H. G. *Manual for the California Psychological Inventory.* Palo Alto, Cal: Consulting Psychologists Press, 1957.

Gough, H. G. Clinical versus statistical prediction in psychology. In L. Postman (Ed.), *Psychology in the making.* New York: Knopf, 1962.

Gough, H. G. Conceptual analysis of psychological test scores and other diagnostic variables. *Journal of Abnormal Psychology,* 1965, *70,* 294-302.

Graham, F. K., & Kendall, B. S. Memory for designs test: Revised general manual. *Perceptual and Motor Skills, Monograph Supplement,* 1960, *11* (No. 2-VII), 147-188.

Graham, J. R. *The MMPI: A practical guide.* New York: Oxford, 1977.

Gray, S. W., & Klaus, R. A. The early training project: A seventh year report. *Child Development,* 1979, *41,* 909-924.

Graziano, A. M. Clinical innovation and the mental health power structure: A social case history. *American Psychologist,* 1969, *24,* 10-18.

Graziano, A. M. (Ed.) *Behavior therapy with children.* Vol. 2. Chicago: Aldine, 1975.

Greenberg, D. J., Scott, S. B., Pisa, A., & Friesen, D. D. Beyond the token economy: A comparison of two contingency programs. *Journal of Consulting and Clinical Psychology.* 1975, *43,* 498-505.

Greist, J. H., Klein, M. H., & Van Cura, L. J. A computer interview for psychiatric patient target symptoms. *Archives of General Psychiatry*, 1973, *29*, 247-253.

Griesinger, W. *The pathology and therapy of psychic disorders*. 1845.

Griffin, W. V., Mauritzen, J. H., & Kasmar, J. V. The psychological aspects of the architectural environment: A review. *American Journal of Psychiatry*, 1969, *125*, 1057–1062.

Griffore, R. J. The validity of popular primers for parents. *American Psychologist*, 1979, *34*, 182-183.

Grinker, R. R. Emerging concepts of mental illness and models of treatment: The medical point of view. *American Journal of Psychiatry*, 1969, *125*, 37-41.

Gripp, R. F., & Magaro, R. F. A token economy program evaluation with untreated control group comparison. *Behaviour Research and Therapy*. 1971, *9*, 137-149.

Griswold, P. M. A family practice model for clinical psychology. *Professional Psychology*, 1980, *11*, 628–636

Grobb, G. N. *Mental institutions in America: Social policy to 1875*. New York: Free Press, 1973.

Gross, S. J. The myth of professional licensing. *American Psychologist*, 1978, *33*, 1009-1016.

Gruenberg, E. M., Brandon, S., & Kasius, R. D. Identifying cases of the social breakdown syndrome. In E. M. Gruenberg (Ed.), *Evaluating the effectiveness of community mental health services*. New York: Milbank, 1966.

Guerney, B., Jr., Stollak, G., & Guerney, L. The practicing psychologist as educator: An alternative to the medical practitioner model. *Professional Psychology*, 1971, *2*, 276-282.

Guertin, W. H., Ladd, C. E., Frank, G. H., Rabin, A. I., & Hiester, D. S. Research with the Wechsler Intelligence Scales for Adults: 1960-1965. *Psychological Bulletin*, 1966, *66*, 385-409.

Guertin, W. H., Rabin, A. I., Frank, G. H., & Ladd, C. E. Research with the Wechsler Intelligence Scales for Adults: 1955-1960. *Psychological Bulletin*, 1962, *59*, 1-26.

Guilford, J. P. The structure of the intellect. *Psychological Bulletin*, 1956, *53*, 267-293.

Gurin, G., Veroff, J., & Feld, S. *Americans view their mental health*. New York: Basic Books, 1960.

Gurman, A. S. The patient's perception of the therapeutic relationship. In A. S. Gurman & A. M. Razin (Eds.), *Effective psychotherapy: A handbook of research*. New York: Pergamon, 1977.

Gurman, A. S., Kniskern, D. P. Enriching research on marital enrichment programs. *Journal of Marriage and Family Counseling*, 1977, *3*, 3-11.

Gurman, A. S., & Kniskern, D. P. Deterioration in marital and family therapy: Empirical, clinical, and conceptual issues. *Family Process*, 1978, *17*, 3–20. (a)

Gurman, A. S., & Kniskern, D.P. Research on marital and family therapy: Progress, perspective, and prospect. In S. L. Garfield & A. E. Bergin (Eds.), *Handbook of psychotherapy and behavior change*. (2nd ed.) New York: Wiley, 1978. (b)

Gurman, A. S., & Knudsen, A. M. Behavioral marriage therapy: I. A psychodynamic-systems analysis and critique. *Family Process*, 1978, *17*, 124-138.

Gurman, A. S., & Razin, A. M. (Eds.) *Effective psychotherapy: A handbook of research*. New York: Pergamon, 1977.

Guthrie, E. G. *The psychology of learning*. New York: Harper, 1935.

Hadley, S. W., & Strupp, H. H. Contemporary views of negative effects in psychotherapy: An integrated account. *Archives of General Psychiatry*, 1976, *33*, 1291-1301.

Hagen, J. V., & Kaufman, A. S. Factor analysis of the WISC-R for a group of mentally retarded children and adolescents. *Journal of Consulting and Clinical Psychology*, 1975, *43*, 661-667.

Hain, J. D. The Bender-Gestalt Test: A scoring method for identifying brain damage. *Journal of Consulting Psychology*, 1964, *28*, 34-40.

Haith, M. M. The response of the human newborn to visual movement. *Journal of Experimental Child Psychology*, 1966, *3*, 235-243.

Haley, J. (Ed.) *Changing families*. New York: Grune & Stratton, 1971.

Haley, J. *Strategies of psychotherapy*. New York: Grune and Stratton, 1963.

Haley, J. *Problem solving therapy*. San Francisco: Jossey-Bass, 1976.

Haley, J., & Hoffman, L. (Eds.) *Techniques of family therapy*. New York: Basic Books, 1967.

Hall, C. S., & Lindzey, G. *Theories of personality*. (3rd ed.) New York: Wiley, 1978.

Hall, E. T. *The hidden dimension*. New York: Doubleday, 1966.

Hall, G. S. Editorial note. *American Journal of Psychology*, 1887, *1*, 1-2.

Hall, R. H. The concept of bureaucracy: An empirical assessment. *American Journal of Sociology*, 1962, *69*, 32-40.

Hall, R. V., Axelrod, S., Tyler, L., Grief, E., Jones, F., & Robertson, R. Modification of behavior problems at home with parent as observer. *Journal of Applied Behavior Analysis*, 1972, *5*, 53-64.

Hallahan, D. P., & Cruickshank, W. M. *Psychoeducational foundations of learning disability*. Englewood Cliffs, N.J.: Prentice-Hall, 1973.

Halleck, S. L. Community psychiatry: Some troubling questions. In L. M. Roberts, S. L. Halleck, & M. B. Loeb (Eds.), *Community psychiatry*. New York: Doubleday, Anchor Books, 1969.

Halleck, S. L. Another response to "Homosexuality: The ethical challenge." *Journal of Consulting and Clinical Psychology*, 1976, *44*, 167–170.

Halperin, K., Neuringer, C., Davis, P. S., & Goldstein, G. Validation of the schizophrenia organicity scale with brain-damaged and non-brain-damaged schizophrenics. *Journal of Consulting and Clinical Psychology*, 1977, *45*, 949-950.

Halstead, W. C. *Brain and intelligence*. Chicago: University of Chicago Press, 1947.

Halstead, W. C., & Wepman, J. M. The Halstead-Wepman aphasia screening test. *Journal of Speech and Hearing Disorders*. 1959, *14*, 9–15.

Hamlin, R. M., & Albee, G. W. Muench's tests before and after nondirective therapy: A control group for his subjects. *Journal of Consulting Psychology*, 1948, *12*, 412–416.

Hammeke, T. A., Golden, C. J., & Purisch, A. D. A standardized, short, and comprehensive neuropsychological test battery based on the Luria neuropsychological evaluation. *International Journal of Neuroscience*, 1978, *8*, 135–141.

Hammen, C. L., & Glass, D. R., Jr., Depression, activity, and evaluation of reinforcement. *Journal of Abnormal Psychology*, 1975, *84*, 718-721.

Hammer, E. F. (Ed.). *The clinical application of projective drawings*. Springfield, Il.: Charles C Thomas, 1958.

Hammer, E. F. The use of imagery in interpretive communication. In E. F. Hammer

(Ed.), *Use of interpretation in treatment*. New York: Grune and Stratton, 1968.

Handlon, J. H. & Parloff, M. B. Treatment of patient and family as a group: Is it group therapy? *International Journal of Group Psychotherapy*, 1962, *12*, 132–141.

Harris, J. G. An abbreviated form of the Phillips rating scale of premorbid adjustment in schizophrenia. *Journal of Abnormal Psychology*, 1975, *84*, 129–137.

Hare-Mustin, R. T., Maracek, J., Kaplan, A. G., & Liss-Levinson, M. Rights of clients, responsibilities of therapists. *American Psychologist*, 1979, *34*, 3–16.

Harper, R. G., & Balch, P. Some economic arguments in favor of primary prevention. *Professional Psychology*, 1975, *7*, 17–25.

Harper, R. G., Weins, A. N., & Matarazzo, J. D. *Nonverbal communication: The state of the art*. New York: Wiley, 1978.

Harris, S. L., & Ersner-Meshfield, R. Behavioral suppression of seriously disruptive behavior in psychotic and retarded patients: A review of punishment and its alternatives. *Psychological Bulletin*, 1979, *85*, 1532–1375.

Harshbarger, D., & Maley, R. F. (Eds.). *Behavior analysis and systems analysis*. Kalamazoo, Mich.: Behaviordelia, 1974.

Hartley, D., Roback, H. R., & Abramowitz, S. F. Deterioration effects in encounter groups. *American Psychologist*, 1976, *31*, 247–255.

Hastorf, A. The reinforcement of individual actions in a group setting. In L. Krasner & L. P. Ullmann (Eds.), *Research in behavior modification*. New York: Holt, Rinehart and Winston, 1965.

Hathaway, S. R., & McKinley, J. C. A multiphasic personality schedule (Minnesota): I. Construction of the schedule. *Journal of Psychology*, 1940, *10*, 249–254.

Hathaway, S. R., & McKinley, J. C. *Minnesota multiphasic personality inventory*. Minneapolis: University of Minnesota Press, 1942.

Hathaway, S. R., & McKinley, J. C. *Manual for the Minnesota Multiphasic Personality Inventory*. New York: Psychological Corporation, 1943.

Hawkins, R., Peterson, R., Schweid, B., & Bijou, S. Behavior therapy in the home: Amelioration of problem-child relations with the parent in a therapeutic role. *Journal of Experimental Child Psychology*, 1966, *4*, 99–107.

Hayduk, L. A. Personal space: An evaluative and orienting overview. *Psychological Bulletin*, 1978, *85*, 117–134.

Hayes, S. C., & Cone, J. D. Reducing residential energy use: Payments, information, and feedback. *Journal of Applied Behavior Analysis*, 1977, *10*, 425–435.

Haynes, S. *Principles of behavioral assessment*. New York: Gardner Press, 1978.

Heap, R. F., Boblitt, W. E., Moore, C. H. & Hord, J. E. Behavior-milieu therapy with chronic neuropsychiatric patients. *Journal of Abnormal Psychology*, 1970, *76*, 349–354.

Heard, D. B. Keith: A case study of structural family therapy. *Family Process*, 1978, *17*, 338–352.

Hearnshaw, L. S. *Cyril Burt: Psychologist*. New York: Cornell University Press, 1979.

Heaton, R. K., Baade, L. E., & Johnson, K. L. Neuropsychological test results associated with psychiatric disorders in adults. *Psychological Bulletin*, 1978, *85*, 141–162.

Heaton, R. K., Smith, H. M., Jr., Lehman, R. A., & Vogt, A. T. Prospects for faking behavioral defects in neuropsychological testing. *Journal of Consulting and Clinical Psychology*, 1978, *46*, 892–900.

Heber, R. F. A manual on terminology and classification in mental retardation. *American Journal of Mental Deficiency*, 1961, *64*, Monograph Supplement.

Heidegger, M. *Being and time* (trans. from Sein and Zeit, Erste Halfte, Jahrbuch fur Philosophic and Phenomenologische Forschung, vol. viii (1927), pp. 1-438 by John Macquarrie & Edward Robinson). New York: Harper & Row, 1963.

Heiman, J., LoPiccolo, L., & LoPiccolo, J. *Becoming orgasmic: A sexual growth program for women*. Englewood Cliffs, N. J.: Prentice-Hall, 1976.

Heimberg, R. G., Montgomery, D., Madsen, C. H., Jr., & Heimberg, J. S. Assertion training: A review of the literature, *Behavior Therapy*, 1977, *8*, 953-971.

Heitler, J. Preparation of lower-class patients for expressive group psychotherapy. *Journal of Consulting and Clinical Psychology*, 1973, *41*, 251-260.

Henry, E., & Rotter, J. B. Situational influences on Rorschach responses. *Journal of Consulting Psychology*, 1956, *20*, 457-462.

Henry, W. E. The Thematic Apperception Technique in the study of culture-personality relations. *Genetic Psychology Monographs*, 1947, *35*, 3-135.

Henry, W. E., Sims, J. H., & Spray, S. L. *The fifth profession*. San Francisco: Jossey-Bass, 1970.

Herman, J. L. The therapeutic act. In E. F. Hammer (Ed.), *Use of interpretation in treatment*. New York: Grune and Stratton, 1968.

Heron, M. J. A note on the concept endogenous-exogenous. *British Journal of Medical Psychology*, 1965, *38*, 241.

Hersen, M. Limitations and problems in the clinical application of behavioral techniques in psychiatric settings. *Behavior Therapy*, 1979, *10*, 65-80.

Hersen, M. Complex problems require complex solutions. *Behavior Therapy*, 1981, *12*, 15-29.

Hersen, M., & Barlow, D. H. *Single-subject experimental designs*. New York: Pergamon, 1976.

Hersen, M., & Bellack, A. S. (Eds.) *Behavioral assessment: A practical handbook*. New York: Pergamon, 1976.

Hess, E. H., & Polt, J. M. Pupil size as related to interest value of visual stimuli. *Science*, 1960, *132*, 349-350.

Hess, H. F. Entry requirements for professional practice of psychology. *American Psychologist*, 1977, *32*, 365-368.

Higgins, J. Process-reactive schizophrenia: Recent developments. *The Journal of Nervous and Mental Disease*, 1969, *149*, 450-472.

Hildreth, G. Psychology as a career. *Journal of Consulting Psychology*, 1937, *1*, 25-28.

Hilgard, E., & Hilgard, J. *Hypnosis in the relief of pain*. Los Altos, Cal.: Kaufman, 1975.

Hobbs, N. Sources of gain in psychotherapy. *American Psychologist*, 1962, *17*, 741-747.

Hoch, E., Ross, A. O., & Winder, C. L. (Eds.) *Professional preparation of clinical psychologists*. Washington, D. C.: American Psychological Association, 1966.

Hodges, W. F., & Spielberger, C. D. The effects of threat of shock on heart rate for subjects who differ in manifest anxiety and fear of shock. *Psychophysiology*, 1966, *2*, 287-294.

Hoehn-Saric, R., Frank, J. D., Imber, S. D., Nash, E. Jr., Stone, A. R., & Battle, C. C. Systematic preparation of patients for psychotherapy: I. Effects on therapy behavior and outcome. *Journal of Psychiatric Research*, 1964, *2*, 267-281.

Hoffman, H., Loper, R. G., & Kammeier, M. L. Identifying future alcoholics with MMPI alcoholism scales. *Quarterly Journal of Studies on Alcohol*, 1974, *35*, 490–498.

Hoffman, N. G., & Butcher, J. N. Clinical limitations of three Minnesota Multiphasic Personality Inventory short forms. *Journal of Consulting and Clinical Psychology*, 1975, *43*, 32–39.

Hogan, D. R. The effectiveness of sex therapy: A review of the literature. In J. LoPiccolo and L. LoPiccolo (Eds.), *Handbook of sex therapy*. New York: Plenum, 1978.

Hogan, R. Development of an empathy scale. *Journal of Consulting and Clinical Psychology*, 1969, *33*, 307–316.

Hogan, R., DeSoto, C. B., & Solano, C. Traits, tests, and personality research. *American Psychologist*, 1977, *32*, 255–264.

Holland, C. An interview guide for behavioral counseling with parents. *Behavior Therapy*, 1970, *1*, 70–79.

Hollandsworth, J. G., Jr. Differentiating assertion and aggression. Some behavioral guidelines. *Behavior Therapy*, 1977, *8*, 347–352.

Hollingshead, A. P., & Redlich, F. C. *Social class and mental illness*. New York: Wiley, 1958.

Hollingsworth, R., & Hendrix, E. M. Community mental health in unreal settings. *Professional Psychology*, 1977, *8*, 232–238.

Hollon, S. D., & Beck, A. T. Cognitive theory of depression. In P. C. Kendall & S. D. Hollon (Eds.), *Cognitive-behavioral interventions: Theory, research, and procedures*. New York: Academic Press, 1979.

Hollon, S. D., & Kendall, P. C. Cognitive self-statements in depression: Development of an Automatic Thoughts Questionnaire. *Cognitive Therapy and Research*, 1980, *4*, 383–395.

Holmes, D., & Houston, K. Effectiveness of situation redefinition and affective isolation in coping with stress. *Journal of Personality and Social Psychology*, 1974, *29*, 212–218.

Holroyd, J. C., & Brodsky, A. M. Psychologists' attitudes and practices regarding erotic and nonerotic physical contact with patients. *American Psychologist*, 1977, *32*, 843–849.

Holroyd, K. A. Cognition and desensitization in the group treatment of test anxiety. *Journal of Consulting and Clinical Psychology*, 1976, *44*, 991–1001.

Holt, R. R. Yet another look at clinical and statistical prediction: Or, is clinical psychology worthwhile? *American Psychologist*, 1970, *25*, 337–349.

Holt, R. R. *Assessing personality*. New York: Harcourt, Brace, & Jovanovich, 1971.

Holt, R. R. *Methods in clinical psychology: Prediction and research*. Vol. 2. New York: Plenum, 1978.

Holzman, P. S. *Psychoanalysis and psychopathology*. New York: McGraw-Hill, 1970.

Holtzman, W. H., Thorpe, J. S., Swartz, J. D., & Herron, E. W. *Inkblot perception and personality*. Austin, Texas: University of Texas Press, 1961.

Honigfeld, G., Gillis, R. O., & Klett, C. J. NOSIE-30: A treatment-sensitive ward behavior scale. *Psychological Reports*, 1966, *19*, 180–182.

Hops, H., & Nicholes, J. S. *Observer training manual*. Eugene, Oregon: Center for Research in the Behavioral Education of the Handicapped, 1974.

Horn, J. L., & Donaldson, G. On the myth of intellectual decline in adulthood. *American Psychologist*, 1976, *31*, 701–709.

Horney, K. *Neurosis and human growth*. New York: Norton, 1950.

Horowitz, M. J. *States of mind: Analysis of change processes in psychotherapy*. New York: Plenum, 1979.

Hugo, J. A. *Abbreviation of the Minnesota Multiphasic Personality Inventory through multiple regression*. Unpublished doctoral dissertation, University of Alabama, 1971.

Hulicka, I. M. Age differences in Wechsler Memory Scale scores. *Journal of Genetic Psychology*, 1966, *109*, 135–145.

Hunt, J. McV. *The challenge of incompetence and poverty*. Urbana, IL: University of Illinois Press, 1969.

Hutt, M. *The Hutt adaptation of the Bender-Gestalt Test*. (2nd ed.) New York: Grune and Stratton, 1969.

Hyman, H. H. The value systems of different classes. In R. Bendix & S. M. Lipset (Eds.), *Class, status and power*. New York: Macmillan, 1953.

Illich, I. *Medical nemesis*. New York: Random House, 1976.

Imber, S. D. Patient direct self-report techniques. In I. E. Waskow & M. B. Parloff (Eds.), *Psychotherapy change measures*. Washington, D. C.: U. S. Government Printing Office, 1975.

Iscoe, I. Community psychology and the competent community. *American Psychologist*, 1974, *29*, 607–613.

Iscoe, I., Bloom, B., & Spielberger, C. (Eds.) *Community psychology in transition*. New York: Hemisphere, 1977.

Isihara, J. *Tests for color-blindness*. (11th ed.) Tokyo: Kanehara, Shuppan, 1964.

Ittelson, W. H., Rivlin, L., & Proshansky, H. M. The use of behavioral maps in environmental psychology. In H. Proshansky, W. Ittelson, & L. Rivlin (Eds.), *Environmental Psychology*. New York: Holt, Rinehart and Winston, 1970.

Ivey, A. *Microcounseling*. Springfield, Ill.: Charles C Thomas, 1971.

Izard, C. *Human emotions*. New York: Plenum, 1977.

Jackson, C. W., Jr., & Wohl, J. A survey of Rorschach teaching in the university. *Journal of Projective Techniques and Personality Assessment*, 1966, *30*, 115–134.

Jackson, D. D. The study of the family. *Family Process*, 1965, *4*, 1–20.

Jackson, D. N., & Messick, S. J. Content and style in personality assessment. *Psychological Bulletin*, 1958, *55*, 243–252.

Jackson, G. D. On the report of the ad hoc committee on educational uses of tests with disadvantaged students: Another psychological view from the Association of Black Psychologists. *American Psychologist*, 1975, *30*, 88–93.

Jackson, R. Treatment of depression by self-reinforcement. *Behavior Therapy*, 1972, *3*, 298–307.

Jacob, T. Family interaction in disturbed and normal families. A methodological and substantive review. *Psychological Bulletin*, 1975, *82*, 33–65.

Jacobs, A., Jacobs, M., Cavior, N., & Burke, J. Anonymous feedback: Credibility and desirability of structured emotional and behavioral feedback delivered in groups. *Journal of Counseling Psychology*, 1974, *21*, 106–111.

Jacobs, M., Jacobs, A., Feldman, G., & Cavior, N. Feedback II—The credibility gap: Delivery of positive and negative emotional and behavioral feedback in groups. *Journal of Consulting and Clinical Psychology*, 1973, *41*, 215–223.

Jacobs, M., Jacobs, A., Gatz, M., & Schaible, T. Credibility and desirability of positive and negative structured feedback in groups. *Journal of Consulting and Clinical Psychology*, 1973, *40*, 244–252.

Jacobson, E. *Progressive relaxation*. Chicago: University of Chicago Press, 1929.

Jacobson, E. *Progressive relaxation*. (2nd ed.) Chicago: University of Chicago Press, 1938.

Jacobson, E. *Depression: Comparative studies of normal, neurotic, and psychotic conditions*. New York: International Universities Press, 1971.

Jacobson, G. F., Stickler, M., & Morley, W. E. Generic and individual approaches to crisis intervention. *American Journal of Public Health*, 1968, *58*, 339–343.

Jacobson, N. S. Problem solving and contingency contracting in the treatment of marital discord. *Journal of Consulting and Clinical Psychology*, 1977, *45*, 92–100. (a)

Jacobson, N. S. Specific and nonspecific factors in the effectiveness of a behavioral approach to the treatment of marital discord. *Journal of Consulting and Clinical Psychology*, 1977, *46*, 442–454. (b)

Jacobson, N. S., & Martin, B. Behavioral marriage therapy: Current status. *Psychological Bulletin*, 1976, *83*, 540–566.

Jacobson, N. S., & Weiss, R. L. Behavioral marriage therapy. III. The contents of Gurman et al. may be hazardous to our health. *Family Process*, 1978, *17*, 149–163.

Jaeger, G., & Selznick, P. A normative theory of culture. *American Sociological Review*, 1964, *29*, 653–669.

Jahoda, M. *Current concepts of positive mental health*. New York: Basic Books, 1958.

James, W. *The principles of psychology*. New York: Holt, 1890.

Janet, P. On the pathogenesis of some impulsions. *Journal of Abnormal Psychology*, 1906, *1*, 1–17.

Jaremko, M. E. A component analysis of stress inoculation: Review and prospective. *Cognitive Therapy and Research*, 1979, *3*, 35–48.

Jastak, J. F., & Jastak, S. R. *The Wide-Range Achievement Test manual*. Wilmington, Del.: Guidance Associates, 1965.

Jenkin, N., Spivack, G., Levine, M., & Savage, W. Wechsler profiles and academic achievement in emotionally disturbed boys. *Journal of Consulting Psychology*, 1964, *28*, 290.

Jelliffe, S. E. Some notes on "transference." *Journal of Abnormal Psychology*, 1913–1914, *8*, 302–309.

Jensen, A. R. How much can we boost IQ and scholastic achievement? *Harvard Educational Review*, 1969, *39*, 1–123.

Jensen, A. R. *Bias in mental testing*. New York: Free Press, 1980.

Jeske, J. O. Identification of therapeutic effectiveness in group therapy. *Journal of Counseling Psychology*, 1973, *20*, 528–530.

Jessness, C. F. Comparative effectiveness of behavior modification and transactional analysis programs for delinquents. *Journal of Consulting and Clinical Psychology*, 1975, *43*, 758–779.

Johnson, D., & Matross, R. Interpersonal influence in psychotherapy. In A. S. Gurman & A. M. Razin (Eds.), *Effective psychotherapy: A handbook of research*. New York: Pergamon, 1977.

Johnson, S. M., & Bolstad, O. D. Methodological issues in naturalistic observation: Some problems and solutions for field research. In L. A. Hamerlynck, L. C. Handy, & E. J. Mash (Eds.), *Behavior change: Methodology, concepts, and practice*. Champaign, Ill.: Research Press, 1973.

Johnson, S. M., & White, G. Self-observation as an agent of behavioral change. *Behavior Therapy*, 1971, *2*, 488–497.

Johnston, J. M. Punishment of human behavior. *American Psychologist*, 1972, *27*, 1033–1054.

Joint Commission on Mental Illness and Health. *Action for mental health*. New York: Basic Books, 1961.

Jones, E. E., & Nisbett, R. E. *The actor and the observer: Divergent perceptions of the causes of behavior*. New York: General Learning Press, 1971.

Jones, M. C. The elimination of children's fears. *Journal of Experimental Psychology*, 1924, *7*, 383–390.

Jones, M. *The therapeutic community*. New York: Basic Books, 1953.

Jones, M. *Social psychiatry in practice: The idea of the therapeutic community*. Middlesex, England: Penguin, 1968.

Jones, M. M. Conversion reaction: Anachronism or evolutionary form? A review of the neurologic, behavioral, and psychoanalytic literature. *Psychological Bulletin*, 1980, *87*, 427–441.

Jung, C. G. On psychophysical relations of the associative experiment. *Journal of Abnormal Psychology*, 1907, *2*, 247–255.

Jung, C. G. *Collected papers on analytical psychology*. New York: Moffatt, Lard, 1917.

Jung, C. G. *Psychological types*. New York: Harcourt, Brace & World, 1933.

Jung, C. G. *The archetypes and the collective unconscious*. Collected works. Vol. 9, Part I. Bollingen Series XX. Princeton, N. J.: Princeton University Press, 1968 (1934).

Kagan, J. *Change and continuity in infancy*. New York: Wiley, 1971.

Kagan, N. Can technology help us toward reliability in influencing human interaction? *Educational Technology*, 1973, *13*, 44–51.

Kagan, N., Krathwohl, D., Goldberg, A., Campbell, R. J., Schankle, P. G., Greenberg, B. S., Danish, S. J., Resnickoff, A., Bowes, J., & Bandy, S. B. *Studies in human interaction: Interpersonal process recall simulated by videotape*. East Lansing: Michigan State University Educational Publication Services, College of Education, 1967.

Kahn, R. L., Goldfarb, A. I., Pollack, M., & Peck, A. Brief objective measures for the determination of mental status in the aged. *American Journal of Psychiatry*, 1960, *117*, 326–328.

Kahneman, D., & Tversky, A. On the psychology of prediction. *Psychological Review*, 1973, *80*, 237–251.

Kallman, F. J. *Heredity in mental health and disorder*. New York: Norton, 1953.

Kallman, W. M., & Feuerstein, M. Psychophysiological procedures. In A. R. Ciminero, K. S. Calhoun, and H. E. Adams (Eds.), *Handbook of behavioral assessment*. New York: Wiley, 1977.

Kane, J. S., & Lawler, E. E., III. Methods of peer assessment. *Psychological Bulletin*, 1978, *85*, 555–586.

Kanfer, F. H., & Phillips, J. S. *Learning foundations of behavior therapy*. New York: Wiley, 1970.

Kanfer, F. H., Phillips, J. S., Matarazzo, J. D., & Saslow, G. Experimental modification of interviewer content in standardized interviews. *Journal of Consulting Psychology*, 1960, *24*, 528-536.

Kanfer, F. H., & Saslow, G. Behavioral analysis: An alternative to diagnostic classification. *Archives of General Psychiatry*, 1965, *12*, 529-538.

Kanfer, F. H., & Saslow, G. Behavioral diagnosis. In C. M. Franks (Ed.), *Behavior therapy: Appraisal and status*. New York: McGraw-Hill, 1969.

Kanner, L. Autistic disturbances of affective contact. *Nervous Child*, 1943, *2*, 217-250.

Kantor, R. E., Wallner, J. M., & Winder, C. L. Process and reactive schizophrenia. *Journal of Consulting Psychology*, 1953, *17*, 157-162.

Kaplan, H. S. *The new sex therapy*. New York: Brunner/Mazel, 1974.

Kardener, S., Fuller, M., & Mensh, I. A survey of physicians' attitudes and practices regarding erotic and nonerotic contact with patients. *American Journal of Psychiatry*, 1973, *130*, 1077-1081.

Karlsruher, A. E. The nonprofessional as a psychotherapeutic agent. *American Journal of Community Psychology*, 1974, *2*, 61-78.

Karlsruher, A. E. The influence of supervision and facilitative conditions on the psychotherapeutic effectiveness of nonprofessional and professional therapists. *American Journal of Community Psychology*, 1976, *4*, 145-154.

Karnes, M. B., Teska, J. A., Hodgins, A. S., & Badger, I. D. Educational intervention at home by mothers of disadvantaged children. *Child Development*, 1970, *41*, 925-935.

Kaswan, J. Manifest and latent functions of psychological services. *American Psychologist*, 1981, *36*, 290-299.

Katkin, E. S., & Hastrup, J. Psychophysiological methods in clinical research. In P. C. Kendall and J. N. Butcher (Eds.) *Handbook of research methods in clinical psychology*. New York: Wiley, 1982.

Katz, M. M., Cole, J. O., & Barton, W. E. (Eds.) *The role and methodology of classification in psychiatry and psychopathology*. Chevy Chase, Md.: National Institute of Mental Health, 1968.

Kaufman, A. S. A short form of the Wechsler Preschool and Primary Scale of Intelligence. *Journal of Consulting and Clinical Psychology*, 1972, *39*, 361-369.

Kaufman, A. S. Comparison of the performance of matched groups of black children and white children on the Wechsler Preschool and Primary Scale of Intelligence. *Journal of Consulting and Clinical Psychology*, 1973, *41*, 186-191.

Kaufman, A. S. Factor analysis of the WISC-R at 11 age levels between 6½ and 16½ years. *Journal of Consulting and Clinical Psychology*, 1975, *43*, 135-147.

Kaufman, K. F., & O'Leary, K. D. Reward, response-cost and self-evaluation procedures for disruptive adolescents in a psychiatric hospital school. *Journal of Applied Behavior Analysis*, 1972, *5*, 293-309.

Kazdin, A. E. Response cost: The removal of conditioned reinforcers for therapeutic change. *Behavior Therapy*, 1972, *4*, 533-546.

Kazdin, A. E. Covert modeling, model similarity, and reduction of avoidance behavior. *Behavior Therapy*, 1974, *5*, 325-340.

Kazdin, A. E. *Behavior modification in applied settings*. Homewood, Il.: Dorsey Press, 1975.

Kazdin, A. E. Assessing the clinical or applied significance of behavior change through social validation. *Behavior Modification*, 1977, *1*, 427–452.(a)

Kazdin, A. E. *The token economy: A review and evaluation*. New York: Plenum, 1977. (b)

Kazdin, A. E. *History of behavior modification*. Baltimore: University Park Press, 1978. (a)

Kazdin, A. E. The application of operant techniques in treatment, rehabilitation, and education. In S. L. Garfield and A. E. Bergin (Eds.), *Handbook of psychotherapy and behavior change* (2nd ed.). New York: Wiley, 1978. (b)

Kazdin, A. E. Fictions, factions, and functions of behavior therapy. *Behavior Therapy*, 1979, *10*, 629–654.

Kazdin, A. E. Single-case experimental designs. In P. C. Kendall & J. N. Butcher (Eds.), *Handbook of research methods in clinical psychology*. New York: Wiley, 1982.

Kazdin, A. E., & Kopel, S. A. On resolving ambiguities of the multiple-baseline design: Problems and recommendations. *Behavior Therapy*, 1975. *6*, 601–608.

Kazdin, A. E., & Straw, M. K. Assessment of behavior of the mentally retarded. In M. Hersen & A. Bellack (Eds.), *Behavioral assessment: A practical handbook*. New York: Pergamon, 1976.

Kazdin, A. E., & Wilcoxon, L. A. Systematic desensitization and nonspecific treatment effects: A methodological evaluation. *Psychological Bulletin*, 1976, *83*, 729–758.

Kazdin, A. E. & Wilson, G. T. *Evaluation of behavior therapy*. Cambridge, Mass.: Ballinger, 1978.

Keeney, B. P. Ecosystemic epistemology: An alternative paradigm for diagnosis. *Family Process*, 1979, *18*, 117–129.

Kelly, E. L. Clinical psychology-1960. *Newsletter: Division of Clinical Psychology of the American Psychological Association*, 1961, *14*, 1–11.

Kelly, G. A. *The psychology of personal constructs*. New York: Norton, 1955.

Kelly, J. G. Naturalistic observations in contrasting social environments. In E. P. Williams & H. L. Raush (Eds.), *Naturalistic viewpoints in psychological research*. New York: Holt, Rinehart and Winston, 1969.

Kelly, J. G. Qualities for the community psychologist. *American Psychologist*, 1971, *26*, 897–903.

Kelly, J. G. Towards an ecological conception of preventive interventions. In J. W. Carter (Ed.), *Research contributions from psychology to community mental health*. New York: Behavioral Publications, 1968

Kendall, P. C. On the efficacious use of verbal self-instructional procedures with children. *Cognitive Therapy and Research*, 1977, 1, 331–341.

Kendall, P. C. Anxiety: States, traits,—situations? *Journal of Consulting and Clinical Psychology*, 1978, *46*, 280–287.

Kendall, P. C. Cognitive-behavioral interventions with children. In B. B. Lahey and A. E. Kazdin (Eds.), *Advances in clinical child psychology*. Vol. 4. New York: Plenum, 1981.

Kendall, P. C., & Finch, A. J., Jr. A cognitive-behavioral treatment for impulsivity: A case study. *Journal of Consulting and Clinical Psychology*, 1976, *44*, 852–857.

Kendall, P. C., & Finch, A. J., Jr. Developing nonimpulsive behavior in children: Cognitive-behavioral strategies for self-control. In P. C. Kendall & S. D. Hollon (Eds.),

Cognitive-behavioral interventions: Theory, research, and procedures. New York: Academic Press, 1979.

Kendall, P. C., Finch, A. J., Jr., Auerbach, S. M., Hooke, J. F., & Mikulka, P. J. The State-Trait Anxiety Inventory: A systematic evaluation. *Journal of Consulting and Clinical Psychology*, 1976, *44*, 406–412.

Kendall, P. C., Finch, A. J., Jr., & Montgomery, L. E. Vicarious anxiety: A systematic evaluation of a vicarious threat to self-esteem. *Journal of Consulting and Clinical Psychology*, 1978, *46*, 997–1008.

Kendall, P. C., & Norton-Ford, J. D. Reasons for clinical research: Characteristics of contributors and their contributions to the *Journal of Consulting and Clinical Psychology. Journal of Consulting and Clinical Psychology,* 1979, *47*, 99–105.

Kendall, P. C., & Hollon, S. D. (Eds.) *Cognitive-behavioral interventions: Theory, research, and procedures.* New York: Academic Press, 1979.

Kendall, P. C., & Hollon, S. D. (Eds.) *Assessment strategies for cognitive-behavioral interventions.* New York: Academic Press, 1981. (a)

Kendall, P. C. & Hollon, S. D. Assessing self-referent speech: Methods in the measurement of self-statements. In P. C. Kendall & S. D. Hollon (Eds.) *Assessment strategies for cognitive-behavioral interventions.* New York: Academic Press, 1981. (b)

Kendall, P. C., & Korgeski, G. P. Assessment and cognitive-behavioral interventions. *Cognitive Therapy and Research*, 1979, *3*, 1–21.

Kendall, P. C., & Little V. L. Correspondence of brief intelligence measures to the Wechsler scales with delinquents. *Journal of Consulting and Clinical Psychology.* 1977, *45*, 660–666.

Kendall, P. C., & Nay, W. R. Treatment evaluation strategies. In W. R. Nay, *Multimethod clinical assessment.* New York: Gardner Press, 1979.

Kendall, P. C., & Norton-Ford, J. Therapy outcome research methods. In P. C. Kendall & J. N. Butcher (Eds.) *Handbook of research methods in clinical psychology.* New York: Wiley, 1982.

Kendall, P. C., & Wilcox, L. E. Cognitive-behavioral treatment for impulsivity: Concrete versus conceptual training with non-self-controlled problem children. *Journal of Consulting and Clinical Psychology*, 1980, *48*, 80–91.

Kendall, P. C., Williams, L., Pechacek, T., Graham, L., Shisslak, C., & Herzoff, N. Cognitive-behavioral and patient education interventions in cardiac catheterization: The Palo Alto medical psychology project. *Journal of Consulting and Clinical Psychology*, 1979, *47*, 49–58.

Kennedy, R. E. Behavior modification in prisons. In W. E. Craighead, A. E. Kazdin & M. J. Mahoney (Eds.), *Behavior modification: Principles, issues and applications.* Boston: Houghton Mifflin, 1976.

Kennedy, T. D., & Kimura, H. K. Transfer, behavioral improvement and anxiety reduction in systematic desensitization. *Journal of Consulting and Clinical Psychology*, 1974, *42*, 720–728.

Kennedy, W. A., Van De Reit, V., & White, J. C. A normative sample of intelligence and achievement of Negro elementary school children in the southeastern United States. *Monographs of the Society for Research in Child Development*, 1963, *28*(Whole No. 6).

Kent, R. N. A methodological critique of "Interventions for boys with conduct problems." *Journal of Consulting and Clinical Psychology*, 1976, *44*, 297–301.

Kent, R. N., & Foster, S. L. Direct observational procedures: Methodological issues in naturalistic settings. In A. Ciminero, K. Calhoun, & H. Adams (Eds.), *Handbook for behavioral assessment*. New York: Wiley, 1977.

Kent, R. N., Miner, G., & Ray, B. *Clinic observer manual*, Stony Brook, N. Y.: State University of New York, 1974.

Kent, R. N., & O'Leary, K. D. A controlled evaluation of behavior modification with conduct problem children. *Journal of Consulting and Clinical Psychology*, 1976, *44*, 586-596.

Kent, R. N., & O'Leary, K. D. Treatment of conduct problem children: BA and/or Ph.D. therapists. *Behavior Therapy*, 1977, *8*, 653-658.

Kernberg, O., Burstein, E., Coyne, L., Appelbaum, A., Horwitz, L., & Voth, H. Psychotherapy and psychoanalysis: Final report of the Menninger Foundation's Psychotherapy Research Project. *Bulletin of the Menninger Clinic*, 1972, *36*, 1-275.

Kety, S. Biochemical theories of schizophrenia. *Science*, 1959, *129*, 1590-1596.

Kierkegaard, S. *Fear and trembling*. New York: Doubleday, 1954.

Kiernan, R. J., & Matthews, C. G. Impairment index versus I-score averaging in neuro-psychological assessment. *Journal of Consulting and Clinical Psychology*, 1976, *44*, 951-957.

Kiesler, C. A. The training of psychiatrists and psychologists. *American Psychologist*, 1977, *32*, 107-108

Kiesler, C. A. Mental health policy as a field of inquiry for psychology. *American Psychologist*, 1980, *35*, 1066-1080.

Kiesler, D. J. Experimental designs in psychotherapy research. In A. E. Bergin and S. L. Garfield (Eds.), *Handbook of psychotherapy and behavior change*. New York: Wiley, 1971.

Kiesler, D. J. Some myths of psychotherapy research and the search for a paradigm. *Psychological Bulletin*, 1966, *65*, 110-136.

Kiesler, D. J. *The process of psychotherapy*. Chicago: Aldine, 1973.

Kiesler, D. J., Mathieu, P. L., & Klein, M. H. Sampling from the recorded therapy interview: A comparative study of different segment lengths. *Journal of Consulting Psychology*, 1964, *28*, 349-357.

Kifer, R. E., Lewis, M. A., Green, D. R., Phillips, E. L. Training predelinquent youths and their parents to negotiate conflict solutions. *Journal of Applied Behavior Analysis*, 1974, *7*, 357-364.

Kihlstrom, J. F., & Evans, F. J. Residual effect of suggestions for posthypnotic amnesia: A reexamination. *Journal of Abnormal Psychology*, 1977, *86*, 327-333.

Kilmann, P. R. The treatment of primary and secondary orgasmic dysfunction: A methodological review of the literature since 1970. *Journal of Sex and Marital Therapy*, 1978, *4*, 155-176.

Kilmann, P. R., Albert, B. M., & Sotile, W. M. The relationship between locus of control, structure of therapy, and outcome. *Journal of Consulting and Clinical Psychology*, 1975, *43*, 588.

Kilmann, P. R., Julian, A., & Moreault, D. The impact of a marital enrichment program on relationship factors. *Journal of Sex and Marital Therapy*, 1978, *4*, 85-91.

Kilmann, P. R., Moreault, D., & Robinson, E. A. The effects of a marital enrichment program in an outcome study. *Journal of Sex and Marital Therapy*, 1978, *4*, 51-57.

Kilmann, P. R., & Sotile, W. M. The marathon encounter group: A review of the outcome literature. *Psychological Bulletin*, 1976, *83*, 827–850.

Kincannon, J. C. Prediction of the standard MMPI scale scores from 71 items: The Mini-Mult. *Journal of Consulting and Clinical Psychology*, 1968, *32*, 319–325.

King, G. D., Hannay, H. J., Masek, B. S., & Burns, J. W. Effects of anxiety and sex on neuropsychological tests. *Journal of Consulting and Clinical Psychology*, 1978, *46*, 375–376.

Kinney, J. M., Madson, B., Fleming, T., & Haapala, D. A. Homebuilders: Keeping families together. *Journal of Consulting and Clinical Psychology*, 1977, *45*, 667–673.

Kinsey, A. C., Pomeroy, W. P., & Martin, C. E. *Sexual behavior in the human male*. Philadelphia: W. B. Saunders, 1948.

Kinsey, A. C., Pomeroy, W. P., Martin, C. E., & Gebhard, P. *Sexual behavior in the human female*. Philadelphia: W. B. Saunders, 1953.

Kiresuk, T. J., & Lund, S. Process and outcome measurement using goal attainment scaling. In J. Zusman & C. W. Wurster (Eds.), *Program Evaluation: Alcohol, drug abuse, and mental health services*. Lexington, Mass.: Lexington Books, 1975.

Kiresuk, T. J., & Sherman, R. E. Goal attainment scaling: A general method for evaluating comprehensive community mental health center programs. *Community Mental Health Journal*, 1968, *4*, 443–453.

Kirkner, F., Wisham, W., & Giedt, F. A report of the validity of the Rorschach Prognostic Rating Scale. *Journal of Projective Techniques*, 1953, *17*, 465–470.

Kittrie, N. *The right to be different*. Baltimore: The Johns Hopkins Press, 1971.

Klaus, R. A., & Gray, S. W. The early training project for disadvantaged children: A report after five years. *Monograph of the Society for Research in Child Development*, 1968, *33*, (4, Serial No. 120).

Klein, D. C. Some reflections on community control: A commentary on Nassi. *Journal of Community Psychology*, 1978, *6*, 16–18.

Klein, D. C., & Seligman, M. E. P. Reversal of performance deficits in learned helplessness and depression. *Journal of Abnormal Psychology*, 1976, *85*, 11–26.

Klein, D. F., & Klein, R. G. Problems in the diagnoses of minimal brain dysfunction and the hyperkinetic syndrome. *International Journal of Mental Health*, 1975, *14*, 45–60.

Klein, M. *The psychoanalysis of children*. London: The Hogarth Press, 1932.

Klinger, E. Consequences of commitment to and disengagement from incentives. *Psychological Review*, 1975, *82*, 1–25.

Klinger, E. Dimensions of thought and imagery in normal waking states. *Journal of Altered States of Consciousness*, 1978, *4*, 97–113.

Klopfer, B., Ainsworth, M. D., Klopfer, W. G., & Holt, R. R. *Developments in the Rorschach technique, Vol. I: Technique and theory*. Yonkers: World Book Company, 1954.

Klopfer, B., & Davidson, H. H. *The Rorschach technique: An introductory manual*. New York: Harcourt, Brace, & World, 1962.

Klopfer, W. G. *The psychological report: Use and communication of psychological findings*. New York: Grune and Stratton, 1960.

Kløve, H. Relationships of differential electroencepholographic patterns to disturbances of Weschler-Bellvue scores. *Neurology*, 1959, *9*, 871–876.

Kløve, H. Validation studies in adult neuropsychology. In R. M. Reitan & L. A. Davison (Eds.), *Clinical Neuropsychology. Current Status and Applications.* Washington, D. C.: Winston, 1974.

Kluckholn, C. The study of culture. In P. I. Rose (Ed.), *The study of society.* New York: Random House, 1967.

Knapp, F., Jr., & McClure, L. F. Quasi-experimental evaluation of a quality of life intervention. *Journal of Community Psychology*, 1978, *6*, 280–290.

Knapp, S. A primer on malpractice for psychologists. *Professional Psychology*, 1980, *11*, 605–612.

Knickerbocker, D. A. Lay volunteer and professional trainee therapeutic functioning and outcomes in a suicide intervention service. (Doctoral dissertation, University of Florida, 1972.) *Dissertation Abstracts International*, 1973, *34*, 416B. (University Microfilms No. 73-15, 510)

Knox, V. J., & Shum, K. Reduction of cold-pressor pain with acupuncture analgesia in high- and low-hypnotic subjects. *Journal of Abnormal Psychology*, 1977, *86*, 639–643.

Koch, S. The nature and limits of psychological knowledge. *American Psychologist*, 1981, *36*, 257–269.

Kohlberg, L. Moral stages and moralization. In T. Lickona (Ed.), *Moral development and behavior: Theory, research and social issues.* New York: Holt, Rinehart and Winston, 1976.

Koocher, G. P. *Children's rights and the mental-health professions.* New York: Wiley, 1976.

Korchin, S. J. *Modern clinical psychology: Principles of intervention in the clinic and community.* New York: Basic Books, 1976.

Korchin, S. J., & Cowan, P. Ethical perspectives in clinical research. In P. C. Kendall and J. N. Butcher (Eds.), *Handbook of research methods in clinical psychology.* New York: Wiley, 1982.

Korman, M. (Ed.) *Levels and patterns of professional training in psychology.* Washington, D. C.: American Psychological Association, 1976.

Kornhauser, W. "Power elite" or "veto group"? In S. G. McNall (Ed.), *The sociological perspective.* Boston: Little, Brown, 1968.

Korzbyski, A. H. *Science and sanity.* Lancaster, Pa.: Science Press, 1941.

Kovacs, M., Rush, A. J., Beck, A. T., & Hollon, S. D. Depressed outpatients treated with cognitive therapy or pharmacotherapy: A one-year follow-up. *Archives of General Psychiatry*, 1981, *38*, 33–39.

Kraepelin, E. *Psychiatrie; ein Lehrbuch fur Studierende und Artzte.* (3rd ed.) Leipzig: Barth, 1887.

Krasner, L. Behavior therapy. *Annual review of psychology*, 1971, *22*, 483–532.

Krasner, L. The ethical and value context of behavior modification. In H. Leitenberg (Ed.), *Handbook of behavior modification and behavior therapy.* New York: Appleton-Century-Crofts, 1976.

Kruglanski, A. W. On the paradigmatic objections to experimental psychology: A reply to Gadlin and Ingle. *American Psychologist*, 1976, *31*, 655–663.

Kubler-Ross, E. *On death and dying.* New York: Macmillan, 1969.

Kuder, G. F., & Richardson, M. W. The theory of estimation of test reliability.

Psychometrika, 1937, *2*, 151–160.

Kurtz, R. M., & Garfield, S. L. Illusory correlation: A further exploration of Chapman's paradigm. *Journal of Consulting and Clinical Psychology,* 1978, *46*, 1009–1015.

Kuypers, D. S., Becker, W. C., & O'Leary, K. D. How to make a token system fail. *Exceptional children,* 1968, *34*, 101–109.

Lachenmeyer, J. R. Mental health consultation and programmatic change. In M. Gibbs, J. Lachenmeyer, & J. Segal (Eds.), *Community psychology.* New York: Gardner Press, 1980.

Lamiell, J. T. Toward an idiothetic psychology of personality. *American Psychologist,* 1981, *36*, 276–289.

Landis, C. Statistical evaluation of psychotherapeutic methods. In S. E. Hinsie (Ed.), *Concepts and problems of psychotherapy.* New York: Columbia University Press, 1937.

Lang, P. J., & Lazovik, A. D. Experimental desensitization of a phobia. *Journal of Abnormal and Social Psychology,* 1963, *66*, 519–525.

Lange, A. J., & Jakubowski, P. *Responsible assertive behavior: Cognitive/behavior procedures for trainers.* Champaign, Ill.: Research Press, 1976.

Langfeldt, G. *The prognosis in schizophrenia and the factors influencing the course of the disease.* London: Milford, 1937.

Langsley, D. G., Flomenhaft, K., & Machotka, P. Follow-up evaluation of family crisis therapy. *American Journal of Orthopsychiatry,* 1969, *39*, 753–759.

Langsley, D. G., Pittman, F. S., Mashotka, P., & Flomenhaft, K. Family crisis therapy: Results and implications. *Family Process,* 1968, *7*, 145–158.

Lanyon, R. I. Development and validation of a psychological screening inventory. *Journal of Consulting and Clinical Psychology,* 1970, *35*, No. 1, Part 2.

Laqueur, H. P. Multiple family therapy. In P. J. Guerin, Jr. (Ed.), *Family therapy.* New York: Gardner Press, 1976.

Lawler, E. J. An experimental study of factors affecting the mobilization of revolutionary coalitions. *Dissertation Abstracts International,* 1973, *33*(A), 7019–7020.

Lawrence, H., & Walter, C. L. Testing a behavioral approach with groups. *Social Work,* 1978, *23*, 127–133.

Lazarus, A. A. Group therapy of phobic disorders by systematic desensitization. *Journal of Abnormal and Social Psychology,* 1961, *63*, 504–510.

Lazarus, A. A. Behavior therapy in groups. In G. M. Gazda (Ed.), *Basic approaches to group psychotherapy and group counseling.* Springfield, Ill.: Charles C Thomas, 1968.

Lazarus, A. A. *Multimodal behavior therapy.* New York: Springer, 1976.

Leitenberg, H. (Ed.) *Handbook of behavior modification and behavior therapy.* New York: Appleton-Century-Crofts, 1976.

Leiter, R. G. Leiter International Performance Scale: Evidence of the reliability and validity of the Leiter tests. *Psychological Service Center Journal,* 1959, *11*, 1–72.

Leon, G. Current directions in the treatment of obesity. *Psychological Bulletin,* 1975, *82*, 557–577.

Lepkin, M. A program of industrial consultation by a community mental health center. *Community Mental Health Journal,* 1975, *11*, 203–210.

Lerner, B. Democratic values and therapeutic efficacy: A construct validity study. *Jour-*

nal of Abnormal Psychology, 1973, *82*, 491–498.

Lerner, B., & Fiske, D. W. Client attributes and the eye of the beholder. *Journal of Consulting and Clinical Psychology*, 1973, *40*, 272–277.

Lerner, R. M., & Ryff, C. Implementation of the life-span view of human development: The sample case of attachment. In P. B. Baltes (Ed.), *Life-span development and behavior*. Vol. 1. New York: Academic Press, 1978.

Leukel, F. *Introduction to physiological psychology*. (3rd ed.) St. Louis: C. V. Mosby, 1976.

Levenson, R. M., & Gottman, J. M. Toward the assessment of social competence. *Journal of Consulting and Clinical Psychology*, 1978, *46*, 453–461.

Leventhal, H., & Cleary, P. The smoking problem. *Psychological Bulletin*, 1980, *88*, 370–405.

Levine, M. Scientific method and the adversary model: Some preliminary thoughts. *American Psychologist*, 1974, *29*, 661–667.

Levinson, D. J. The mid-life transition: A period of psychosocial development. *Psychiatry*, 1977, *40*, 99–112.

Levy, J. Relationship therapy. *American Journal of Orthopsychiatry*, 1938, *8*, 64–69.

Levy, J., & Epstein, N. B. An application of the Rorschach Test in family investigation. *Family Process*, 1964, *3*, 344–376.

Levy, L. H. Self help groups: Types and processes. *Journal of Applied Behavioral Science*, 1976, *12*, 310–322.

Levy, L. H. Self-help groups viewed by mental health professionals: A survey and comments. *American Journal of Community Psychology*, 1978, *6*, 305–313.

Lewin, K. *Field theory in social science*. New York: Harper, 1951.

Lewin, K., Lippitt, R., & White, R. K. Patterns of aggressive behavior in experimentally created social climates. *Journal of Social Psychology*, 1939, *10*, 271–299.

Lewinsohn, P. M. A behavioral approach to depression. In R. J. Friedman & M. M. Katz (Eds.), *The psychology of depression: Contemporary theory and research*. Washington, D. C.: V. H. Winston, 1974. (a)

Lewinsohn, P. M. The behavioral study and treatment of depression. In M. Hersen, R. M. Eisler, & P. M. Miller (Eds.), *Progress in behavior modification*. Vol. 1. New York: Academic Press, 1974. (b)

Lewinsohn, P. M. Clinical and theoretical aspects of depression. In K. S. Calhoun, H. E. Adams, & K. M. Mitchell (Eds.), *Innovative treatment methods in psychopathology*. New York: Wiley, 1974. (c)

Lewinsohn, P. M., Biglan, A., & Zeiss, A. M. Behavioral treatment of depression. In P. O. Davidson (Ed.), *The behavioral management of anxiety, depression, and pain*. New York: Brunner/Mazel, 1976.

Lewinsohn, P. M., Danaher, B. G., & Kikel, S. Visual imagery as a mnemonic device for brain-injured persons. *Journal of Consulting and Clinical Psychology*, 1977, *45*, 717–723.

Lewinsohn, P. M., & Graf, M. Pleasant activities and depression. *Journal of Consulting and Clinical Psychology*, 1973, *41*, 261–268.

Lewinsohn, P. M., & Libet, J. Pleasant events, activity schedules, and depression. *Journal of Abnormal Psychology*, 1972, *79*, 291–295.

Lewinsohn, P. M., & Shaffer, M. Use of home observations as an integral part of the treatment of depression: Preliminary report and case studies. *Journal of Consulting and Clinical Psychology*, 1971, *35*, 87–94.

Lewis, G. P., Golden, L. J., Moses, J. A., Jr., Osmon, D. C., Purisch, A. D., & Hammeke, T. A. Localization of cerebral dysfunctions with a standardized version of Luria's neuropsychological battery. *Journal of Consulting and Clinical Psychology*, 1979, *47*, 1003–1019.

Lezak, M. D. *Neuropsychological assessment*. New York: Oxford University Press, 1976.

Liberman, R. P. A behavioral approach to group dynamics: 1. Reinforcement and prompting of cohesiveness in group therapy. *Behavior Therapy*, 1970, *1*, 141–175.

Liberman, R. P., King, L. W., & De Risi, W. J. Behavioral analyses and therapy in community mental health. In H. Leitenberg (Ed.), *Handbook of behavior modification and behavior therapy*. New York: Appleton-Century-Crofts, 1976.

Lichtenstein, E., & Danaher, B. G. Modification of smoking behavior: A critical analysis of theory, research, and practice. In M. Hersen, R. M. Eisler, & P. M. Miller (Eds.), *Progress in behavior modification*. Vol. 3. New York: Academic Press, 1976.

Liddell, H. S. Conditioned reflex method and experimental neurosis. In J. McV. Hunt (Ed.), *Personality and the behavior disorders*. Vol. 1. New York: Ronald Press, 1944.

Lieberman, M. A., Yalom, I. D., & Miles, S. M. B. *Encounter groups: First facts*. New York: Basic Books, 1973.

Lieberson, S. Residential segregation and ethnic assimilation. *Social Forces*, 1961, *40*, 52–57.

Lieberson, S., & Silverman, A. R. The precipitants and underlying conditions of race riots. *American Sociological Review*, 1965, *30*, 887–898.

Lindzey, G. *Projective techniques and cross-cultural research*. New York: Appleton-Century-Crofts, 1961.

Lindzey, G., & Heinemann, S. H. TAT: Individual and group administration. *Journal of Personality*, 1955, *24*, 34–55.

Linehan, M. Structured cognitive-behavioral treatment of assertion problems. In. P. C. Kendall & S. D. Hollon (Eds.), *Cognitive-behavioral interventions: Theory, research, and procedures*. New York: Academic Press, 1979.

Linehan, M., Goldfried, M. R., & Goldfried, A. P. Assertion therapy: Skill training or cognitive restructuring. *Behavior Therapy*, 1979, *10*, 372–388.

Lipinski, D. P., Black, J. L., Nelson, R. O., & Ciminero, A. R. The influence of motivational variables on the reactivity and reliability of self-recording. *Journal of Consulting and Clinical Psychology*, 1975, *43*, 637–646.

Lipinski, D. P., & Nelson, R. O. The reactivity and unreliability of self-recording. *Journal of Consulting and Clinical Psychology*, 1974, *42*, 118–123.

Lipsey, N. W. Research and relevance. A survey of graduate students and faculty. *American Psychologist*, 1974, *29*, 541–553.

Lipsky, M. J., Kassinove, H., & Miller, N. J. Effects of rational-emotive therapy, rational role reversal, and rational-emotive imagery on the emotional adjustment of community mental health center patients. *Journal of Consulting and Clinical Psychology*, 1980, *48*, 366–374.

Littell, W. M. The Wechsler Intelligence Scale for Children: Review of a decade of research. *Psychological Bulletin*, 1960, *57*, 132–156.

Little, M. Countertransference and the patient's response to it. *International Journal of Psychoanalysis*, 1951, *32*, 32–40.

Lo Piccolo, J. Direct treatment of sexual dysfunction. In J. Lo Piccolo & L. Lo Piccolo (Eds.), *Handbook of sex therapy*. New York: Plenum, 1978.

Lo Piccolo, J., & Steger, J. C. The sexual interaction inventory: A new instrument for assessment of sexual dysfunction. *Archives of Sexual Behavior*, 1974, *3*, 585–595.

Locke, H. M., & Wallace, K. M. Short marital adjustment and prediction tests: Their reliability, and validity. *Marriage and Family Living*, 1959, *21*, 251–255.

Loehlin, J. C., & Nichols, R. C. *Heredity, environment, and personality*. Austin, Texas: University of Texas Press, 1976.

Loevinger, J. Objective tests as instruments of psychological theory. *Psychological Reports*, 1957, *3*(Monograph Supplement 9).

Lorion, R. P. Research on psychotherapy and behavior change with the disadvantaged. In S. L. Garfield & A. E. Bergin (Eds.), *Handbook of psychotherapy and behavior change*. (2nd ed.) New York: Wiley, 1978.

Lorr, M., & Klett, C. J. *Inpatient multidimensional psychiatric scale*. Palo Alto, Cal.: Consulting Psychologists Press, 1966.

Lorr, M., Klett, C. J., McNair, D. M., & Lasky, J. J. *Inpatient Multidimensional Psychiatric Scale manual*. Palo Alto, Cal.: Consulting Psychologists Press, 1962.

Lorr, M., O'Connor, J. P., & Stafford, J. W. The psychotic reaction profile. *Journal of Clinical Psychology*, 1960, *16*, 241–245.

Louttit, C. M. *Clinical psychology*. New York: Harper, 1936.

Louttit, C. M. The nature of clinical psychology. *Psychological Bulletin*, 1939, *36*, 361–389.

Lovaas, O. I. A program for the establishment of speech in psychotic children. In. J. K. Wing (Ed.), *Early childhood autism*. Oxford: Pergamon, 1966.

Lovaas, O. I., Berberich, J. P., Perloff, B. F., & Schaeffer, B. Acquisition of imitative speech by autistic children. *Science*, 1966, *151*, 705–707.

Lovaas, O. I., Freitag, G., Gold, V. J., & Kassorla, I. C. Experimental studies in childhood schizophrenia: Analysis of self-destructive behavior. *Journal of Experimental Child Psychology*, 1965, *2*, 67–84.

Lovaas, O. I., Koegel, R., Simmons, J. Q., & Long, J. S. Some generalization and follow-up measures on autistic children in behavior therapy. *Journal of Applied Behavior Analysis*, 1973, *6*, 131–166.

Love, L. R., Kaswan, J., & Bugental, D. E. Differential effectiveness of three interventions for different socioeconomic groups. *Journal of Consulting and Clinical Psychology*, 1972, *39*, 347–360.

Loveland, N., Singer, M. T., & Wynne, L. C. The family Rorschach: A new method for studying family interactions. *Family Process*, 1963, *2*, 187–215.

Lowenthal, M. F., Thurner, M., & Chiriboga, D. *Four stages of life: A psychological study of men and women facing transitions*. San Francisco: Jossey-Bass, 1975.

Lubin, B., Wallis, R. R., & Paine, C. Patterns of psychological test usage in the United States: 1955–1969. *Professional Psychology*, 1971, *2*, 70–74.

Luborsky, L. Clinicians' judgements of mental health. *Archives of General Psychiatry*, 1962, *7*, 407–417.

Luborsky, L., Chandler, M., Auerbach, A. H., Cohen, J., & Bachrach, H. M. Factors influencing the outcome of psychotherapy: A review of quantitative research. *Psychological Bulletin*, 1971, *75*, 145–185.

Luborsky, L., Singer, B., & Luborsky, L. Comparative studies of psychotherapies: Is it true that "Everyone has won and all must have prizes"? *Archives of General Psychiatry*, 1975, *32*, 995–1008.

Luborsky, L., & Spence, D. P. Quantitive research on psychoanalytic therapy. In A. E. Bergin & S. L. Garfield (Eds.), *Handbook of psychotherapy and behavior change*. New York: Wiley, 1971.

Luborsky, L., & Spence, D. P. Quantitative research on psychoanalytic therapy. In S. L. Garfield & A. E. Bergin (Eds.), *Handbook of psychotherapy and behavior change*. (2nd ed.) New York: Wiley, 1978.

Luria, A. R. *Higher cortical functions in man*. New York: Basic Books, 1966.

Luria A. R. *The working brain: Introduction to neuropsychology*. New York: Basic Books, 1973.

Luria, A. R., & Majovski, L. V. Basic approaches used in American and Soviet clinical neuropsychology. *American Psychologist*, 1977, *32*, 959–968.

Lykken, D. T. The detection of deception. *Psychological Bulletin*, 1979, *86*, 47-53.

Lyle, O., & Quast, W. The Bender-Gestalt: Use of clinical judgement versus recall scores in prediction of Huntington's disease. *Journal of Consulting and Clinical Psychology*, 1976, *44*, 229-232.

MacAndrew, C. The differentiation of male alcoholic out-patients from nonalcoholic psychiatric patients by means of the MMPI. *Quarterly Journal of Studies on Alcohol*, 1965, *26*, 238-246.

Maccoby, E. E., & Maccoby, N. The interview: A tool of social science. In G. Lindzey (Ed.), *Handbook of social psychology*. Reading, Mass.: Addison-Wesley, 1954.

MacCorquodale, K., & Meehl, P. E. On the distinction between hypothetical constructs and intervening variables. *Psychological Review*, 1948, *85*, 99-107.

MacDonald, M. L. The forgotten Americans: A sociopsychological analysis of aging and nursing homes. *American Journal of Community Psychology*, 1973, *1*, 272-294.

MacFarlane, J. W., Allen, L., & Honzik, M. P. *A developmental study of the behavior problems of normal children between 21 months and 14 years*. Berkeley: University of California Press, 1954.

Machover, K. *Personality projection in the drawing of the human figure*. Springfield, Ill.: Charles C Thomas, 1949.

MacKinnon, D., & Dukes, W. F. Repression. In L. Postman (Ed.), *Psychology in the making*. New York: Knopf, 1962.

MacPhillamy, D. J., & Lewinsohn, P. M. Depression as a function of levels of desired and obtained pleasure. *Journal of Abnormal Psychology*, 1974, *83*, 651-657.

Mager, R. F. *Preparing instructional objectives*. Belmont, Cal.: Fearon, 1962.

Magrab, P. R., & Papadopoulou, J. L. The effect of a token economy on dietary compliance for children on hemodialysis. *Journal of Applied Behavior Analysis*, 1977, *10*, 573-578.

Maher, B. A. *Principles of psychopathology: An experimental approach*. New York: McGraw-Hill, 1966.

Maher, B. A. *Introduction to research in psychopathology*. New York: McGraw-Hill, 1970.

Maher, B. A. Stimulus sampling in clinical research: Representative design reviewed. *Journal of Consulting and Clinical Psychology*, 1978, *46*, 643-647.

Mahl, G. F. Gestures and body movements in interviews. In J. M. Shlien (Ed.), *Research in psychotherapy*. Vol. 3. Washington, D.C.: American Psychological Association, 1968.

Mahoney, M. J. *Cognition and behavior modification*. Cambridge, Mass.: Ballinger, 1974.

Mahoney, M. J. *Scientist as subject: The psychological imperative*. Cambridge, Mass.: Ballinger, 1976.

Mahoney, M. J. Reflections on the cognitive-learning trend in psychotherapy. *American Psychologist*, 1977, *32*, 5-13.

Mahoney, M. J., & Arnkoff, D. B. Cognitive and self-control therapies. In S. L. Garfield & A. E. Bergin (Eds.), *Handbook of psychotherapy and behavior change*. (2nd ed.) New York: Wiley, 1978.

Malan, D. H., Balfour, F. G. H., Hood, V. G., & Shooter, A. M. N. Group psychotherapy: A longterm follow-up study. *Archives of General Psychiatry*, 1976, *33*, 1303–1315.

Maley, R. F., Feldman, G. L., & Ruskin, R. S. Evaluation of patient improvement in a token economy treatment program. *Journal of Abnormal Psychology*, 1973, *82*, 141-144.

Mandler, G. *Mind and emotions*. New York: Wiley, 1975.

Mann, P. A. *Community psychology*. New York: The Free Press, 1978.

Manning, N. P. Innovation in social policy: The case of the therapeutic community. *Journal of Social Policy*, 1976, *5*, 265-279.

Mannino, F. V. Task accomplishment and consultation outcome. *Community Mental Health Journal*, 1972, *8*, 102-108.

Mannino, F. V., & Shore, M. F. The effects of consultation: A review of empirical research. *American Journal of Community Psychology*, 1975, *3*, 1-21.

Marañón, G. Contribution a l'etude de l'action 'emotive de l'adrenaline. *Revue Francaise d'Endocrinologie*, 1924, *2*, 301-325.

Margolin, G., & Weiss, R. L. Communication training and assessment. A case of behavioral marital enrichment. *Behavior Therapy*, 1978, *9*, 508-520.

Mariotto, M. J., & Paul, G. L. A multimethod validation of the inpatient multidimensional psychiatric scale with chronically institutionalized patients. *Journal of Consulting and Clinical Psychology*, 1974, *42*, 497-508.

Marks, I. Management of sexual disorders. In H. Leitenberg (Ed.), *Handbook of behavior modification and behavior therapy*. New York: Appleton-Century-Crofts, 1976.

Marks, I. Behavioral psychotherapy of adult neurosis. In S. L. Garfield & A. E. Bergin (Eds.), *Handbook of psychotherapy and behavior change*. (2nd ed.) New York: Wiley, 1978.

Marks, I., & Gelder, M. Transvestism and fetishism: Clinical, and psychological changes during faradic aversion. *British Journal of Psychiatry*, 1967, *119*, 711-730.

Marks, P. A., & Seeman, W. *The actuarial description of abnormal personality: An atlas for use with the MMPI*. Baltimore: Williams & Williams, 1963.

Marlatt, G. A. Alcohol use and problem drinking: A cognitive-behavioral analysis. In

P. C. Kendall & S. D. Hollon (Eds.) *Cognitive-behavioral interventions: Theory, research, and procedures.* New York: Academic Press, 1979.

Marrow, A. Events leading to the establishment of the National Training Laboratories. *Journal of Applied Behavioral Science*, 1967, *3*, 144-150.

Marsden, G. Content analysis studies of psychotherapy. In A. E. Bergin & S. L. Garfield (Eds.), *Handbook of psychotherapy and behavior change.* New York: Wiley, 1971.

Martin, B. Brief family intervention: Effectiveness and the importance of including the father. *Journal of Consulting and Clinical Psychology*, 1977, *45*, 1002-1010.

Martinson, R. What works? Questions and answers about prison reform. *The Public Interest*, 1974, *38*, 22-54.

Maser, J. D., & Seligman, M. E. P. *Psychopathology: Experimental models.* San Francisco: W. H. Freeman, 1977.

Mash, E. J., & Terdal, L. (Eds.) *Behavior therapy assessment.* New York: Springer, 1976.

Mash, E. J., Terdal, L., & Anderson, K. The response-class matrix: A procedure for recording parent-child interactions. *Journal of Consulting and Clinical Psychology*, 1973, *40*, 163-164.

Maslow, A. *Toward a psychology of being.* (2nd ed.) Princeton: Van Nostrand, 1968.

Masserman, J. H. *Behavior and neurosis: A experimental psychoanalytic approach to psychobiologic principles.* Chicago: University of Chicago Press, 1943.

Masters, W. H., & Johnson, V. E. *Human sexual response.* Boston: Little, Brown, 1966.

Masters, W. H., & Johnson, V. E. *Human sexual inadequacy.* Boston: Little, Brown, 1970.

Matarazzo, J. D. *Wechsler's measurement and appraisal of adult intelligence.* (5th and enlarged edition) Baltimore: Williams & Williams, 1972.

Matarazzo, J. D. Higher education, professional accreditation, and licensure. *American Psychologist*, 1977, *32*, 856–859.

Matarazzo, J. D. Behavioral health and behavioral medicine. *American Psychologist*, 1980, *35*, 807-817.

Matarazzo, J. D., Matarazzo, R. G., Wiens, A., & Gallo, A. E., Jr. Retest reliability of the Halstead Impairment Index in a normal, a schizophrenic, and two samples of organic patients. *Journal of Clinical Psychology*, 1976, *32*, 338-349.

Matarazzo, J. D., & Wiens, A. N. *The interview: Research on its anatomy and structure.* Chicago: Aldine-Atheston, 1972.

Matarazzo, J. D., & Wiens, A. N. Black Intelligence Test of Cultural Homogeneity and Wechsler Adult Intelligence Scale scores of black and white police applicants. *Journal of Applied Psychology*, 1977, *62*, 57-63.

Matarazzo, R. G. Research on the training and learning of psychotherapeutic skills. In A. E. Bergin & S. L. Garfield, (Eds.), *Handbook of psychotherapy and behavior change.* New York: Wiley, 1971.

Matarazzo, R. G. Research on the teaching and learning of psychotherapeutic skills. In S. L. Garfield & A. E. Bergin (Eds.), *Handbook of psychotherapy and behavior change* (2nd ed.) New York: Wiley, 1978.

Mathews, C. O. Factors which contribute to undesirable overt behavior. *Journal of Consulting Psychology*, 1937, *1*, 41-48.

Mathews, W. M. Scope of clinical psychology in child guidance. *American Journal of Orthopsychiatry*, 1942, *12*, 388-392.

May, A. R. *Mental health services in Europe: A review of data collected in response to a WHO questionnaire* (Offset publication No. 23). Geneva World Health Organization, 1976.

McAmmond, D. M., Davidson, P. O., & Kovitz, D. M. A comparison of the effects of hypnosis and relaxation training on stress reactions in a dental situation. *American Journal of Clinical Hypnosis*, 1971, *13*, 233-242.

McClelland, D. C., & Apicella, F. S. A functional classification of verbal reactions to experimentally induced failure. *Journal of Abnormal and Social Psychology*, 1945, *40*, 376-390.

McClelland, D. C., Atkinson, J. W., Clark, R. A., & Lowell, E. L. *The achievement motive.* New York: Appleton-Century-Crofts, 1953.

McCord, J. A thirty-year follow-up of treatment effects. *American Psychologist*, 1978, *33*, 284–289.

McCorkle, L. W., Elias, E., & Bixby, F. L. *The Highfields story: An experimental treatment project for youthful offenders.* New York: Holt, Rinehart and Winston, 1958.

McCullough, J. P., Cornell, J. E., McDaniel, M. H., & Mueller, R. K. Utilization of a simultaneous treatment design to improve student behavior in a first-grade classroom. *Journal of Consulting and Clinical Psychology*, 1974, *42*, 288-292.

McDavid, J. W., & Harari, H. *Social psychology: Individuals, groups, societies.* New York: Harper & Row, 1968.

McFall, R. M., & Lillesand, D. V. Behavior rehearsal with modeling and coaching in assertive training. *Journal of Abnormal Psychology*, 1971, *77*, 313-323.

McFall, R. M., & Marston, A. An experimental investigation of behavioral rehearsal in assertive training. *Journal of Abnormal Psychology*, 1970, *76*, 295-202.

McFall, R. M., & Twentyman, C. Four experiments on the relative contributions of rehearsal, modeling, and coaching to assertion training. *Journal of Abnormal Psychology*, 1973, *81*, 198-218.

McGee, R. K. *Crisis intervention in the community.* Baltimore: University Park Press, 1974.

McGlynn, F. D., Reynolds, E. J., & Linder, L. H. Experimental desensitization following therapeutically oriented and physiologically oriented instructions. *Journal of Behavior Therapy and Experimental Psychiatry*, 1971, *2*, 13-18.

McGregor, D. M. *The human side of enterprise.* New York: McGraw-Hill, 1960.

McLean, P. D. Therapeutic decision-making in the behavioral treatment of depression. In P. O. Davidson (Ed.), *The behavioral management of anxiety, depression and pain.* New York: Brunner/Mazel, 1976.

McLean, P. D., & Hakstian, A. R. Clinical depression: Comparative efficacy of outpatient treatments. *Journal of Consulting and Clinical Psychology*, 1979, *47*, 818–836.

McLeod, J. M., & Chaffee, S. R. The construction of social reality. In J. T. Tedeschi (Ed.), *The social influence processes.* Chicago: Aldine, 1972.

McNair, D. M., Callahan, D. M., & Lorr, M. Therapist "type" and patient response to psychotherapy. *Journal of Consulting Psychology*, 1962, *26*, 425–429.

McNair, D. M., Lorr, M., & Droppleman, L. F. *Profile of mood states (POMS).* San Diego, Cal.: Educational and Industrial Testing Service, 1971.

McNamara, J. R., & Woods, K. M. Ethical considerations in psychological research: A comparative review. *Behavior Therapy*, 1977, *8*, 703-708.

McNemar, Q. *The revision of the Stanford-Binet Scale: An analysis of the standardiza-tion data.* Boston: Houghton Mifflin, 1942.

McSweeney, A. J. Including psychotherapy in national health insurance: Insurance guidelines and other proposed solutions. *American Psychologist,* 1977, *32,* 722-730.

Mead, G. H. The genesis of the self and social-control. In A. E. Murphy (Ed.), *The philosophy of the present.* Chicago: Open Court, 1932.

Meador, B. D., & Rogers, C. R. Client-centered therapy. In R. Corsini (Ed.), *Current psychotherapies.* Itasca, Ill.: Peacock, 1973.

Mednick, B. R. Breakdown in high-risk subjects: Family and early environmental factors. *Journal of Abnormal Psychology,* 1973, *82,* 469-475.

Mednick, S. A., & Schulsinger, F. Some premorbid characters related to breakdown in children with schizophrenic mothers. In D. Rosenthal & S. S. Kety (Eds.), *The transmission of schizophrenia.* Elmsford, N. Y.: Pergamon, 1968.

Meehl, P. E. *Clinical versus statistical prediction: A theoretical analysis and a review of the evidence.* Minneapolis: University of Minnesota Press, 1954.

Meehl, P. E. Wanted—A good cookbook. *American Psychologist,* 1956, 11, 263-272.

Meehl, P. E. When shall we use our heads instead of the formula. *Journal of Counseling Psychology,* 1957, *4,* 268-273.

Meehl, P. E. Some ruminations on the validation of clinical procedures. *Canadian Jour-nal of Psychology,* 1959, *13,* 103–128.

Meehl, P. E. The cognitive activity of the clinician. *American Psychologist,* 1960, *15,* 19-27.

Meehl, P. E. Schizotaxia, schizotypy, schizophrenia. *American Psychologist,* 1962, *17,* 827-838.

Meehl, P. E. Seer over sign: The first good example. *Journal of Experimental Research in Personality,* 1965, *1,* 27-32.

Meehl, P. E. Why I don't go to case conferences. In P. E. Meehl *Psychodiagnosis: Selected papers.* Minneapolis: University of Minnesota Press, 1973.

Meehl, P. E., & Rosen, A. Antecedent probability and the efficiency of psychometric signs, patterns, or cutting scores. *Psychological Bulletin,* 1955, *52,* 191-216.

Megargee, E. I. *The California Psychological Inventory handbook.* San Francisco: Jossey-Bass, Inc., 1972.

Mehrabian, A. *Silent messages.* Belmont, Cal.: Wadsworth, 1971.

Meichenbaum, D. Examination of model characteristics in reducing avoidance behavior. *Journal of Personality and Social Psychology,* 1971, *17,* 298-307.

Meichenbaum, D. Self-instructional methods. In F. Kanfer & A. Goldstein (Eds.), *Help-ing people change.* New York: Pergamon, 1975.

Meichenbaum, D. A cognitive-behavior modification approach to assessment. In M. Hersen and A. S. Bellack (Eds.), *Behavioral assessment: A practical handbook.* New York: Pergamon, 1976.

Meichenbaum, D. *Cognitive-behavior modification: An integrative approach.* New York: Plenum, 1977.

Meichenbaum, D., & Cameron, R. *Stress inoculation: A skills training approach to anxie-ty management.* Unpublished manuscript, University of Waterloo, 1973.

Meichenbaum, D., Gilmore, J. B., & Fedoravicious, A. Group insight versus group desensitization in treating speech anxiety. *Journal of Consulting and Clinical Psychology,* 1971, *36,* 410-421.

Meichenbaum, D., & Goodman, J. Training impulsive children to talk to themselves: A means of developing self-control. *Journal of Abnormal Psychology*, 1971, *77*, 115–126.

Meichenbaum, D., & Turk, D. C. The cognitive-behavioral management of anxiety, anger, and pain. In P. O. Davidson (Ed.), *The behavioral management of anxiety, depression, and pain.* New York: Brunner/Mazel, 1976.

Meier, M. J. Some challenges for clinical neuropsychology. In R. M. Reitan & L. A. Davison (Eds.), *Clinical neuropsychology: Current status and applications.* Washington, D. C.: Winston, 1974.

Melamed, B. G., Weinstein, D., Hawes, R., & Katin-Borland, M. Reduction of fear-related dental management problems with use of filmed modeling. *Journal of the American Dental Association*, 1975, *90*, 822-826.

Mellstrom, M., Jr., Zuckerman, M., & Cicala, G. A. General versus specific traits in the assessment of anxiety. *Journal of Consulting and Clinical Psychology*, 1978, *46*, 423.

Meltzer, H., & Stagner, R. (Eds.) Special issue: Industrial/organizational psychology. *Professional Psychology*, 1980, *11*, 347-546.

Meltzoff, J., & Blumenthal, R. L. *The day treatment center: Principles, application, and evaluation.* Springfield, Ill.: Charles C Thomas, 1966.

Meltzoff, J., & Kornreich, M. *Research in psychotherapy.* New York: Atherton Press, 1970.

Mendels, J. *Concepts of depression.* New York: Wiley, 1970.

Mendels, J., & Cochrane, C. The nosology of depression: The endogenous reactive concept. *American Journal of Psychiatry*, 1968, *124*, 1-11.

Mendelson, M. *Psychoanalytic concepts of depression.* (2nd ed.) New York: Spectrum Publications, 1974.

Merluzzi, T. V., Glass, C. R., & Genest, M. (Eds.) *Cognitive assessment.* New York: Guilford, 1981.

Merrill, S., & Carey, G. L. Dream analysis in brief psychotherapy. *American Journal of Psychotherapy*, 1975, *29*, 185-193.

Merton, R. K. *Social theory and social structure.* New York: The Free Press, 1949.

Meyer, A. The interview in behavioral assessment. In A. Ciminero, K. Calhoun, & H. Adams (Eds.), *Handbook for behavioral assessment.* New York: Wiley, 1977.

Meyer, A., Jelliffe, S. E., & Hoch, A. *Dementia praecox: A monograph.* Boston: Gorham Press, 1911.

Meyer, A. J., Nash, J. D., McAlister, A. L., Maccoby, N., & Farquhar, J. W. Skill training in a cardiovascular health education program. *Journal of Consulting and Clinical Psychology*, 1980, *48*, 129-142.

Michener, H. A., & Suchner, R. W. The tactical use of social power. In J. T. Tedeschi (Ed.), *The social influence process.* Chicago: Aldine, 1972.

Milby, J. B., Pendergrass, P. E., & Clarke, J. The token economy vs. control ward: A comparison of staff and patient attitudes toward ward environment. *Behavior Therapy*, 1975, *6*, 22–29.

Milgram, S. The experience of living in cities. *Science*, 1970, *167*, 1461-1468.

Miller, G. A. Psychology as a means of promoting human welfare. *American Psychologist*, 1969, *24*, 1063-1075.

Miller, J. G. *Living systems.* New York: McGraw-Hill, 1979.

Miller, L. C. School behavior check list: An inventory of deviant behavior for elementary school children. *Journal of Consulting and Clinical Psychology*, 1972, *38*, 134-144.

Miller, N. E., & DiCara, L. Instrumental learning of heart-rate changes in curarized rats: Shaping and specificity to discriminative stimulus. *Journal of Comparative and Physiological Psychology*, 1967, *63*, !2-19.

Miller, W. R., & Seligman, M. E. P. Depression and learned helplessness in man. *Journal of Abnormal Psychology*, 1975, *84*, 228-238.

Millon, T. *Theories of psychopathology and personality*. Philadelphia: W. B. Saunders, 1973.

Millon, T. Reflections on Rosenhan's "On being sane in insane places." *Journal of Abnormal Psychology*, 1975, *84*, 456-461.

Mills, C. W. *The power elite*. New York: Oxford University Press, 1956.

Mindess, H. Predicting patients' responses to psychotherapy: A preliminary study designed to investigate the validity of the Rorschach Prognostic Rating Scale. *Journal of Projective Techniques*, 1953, *17*, 327-334.

Mink, O. G. A comparison of effectiveness of nondirective therapy and clinical counseling in the junior high school. *School Counselor*, 1959, *6*, 12-14.

Mintz, J. Survey of patients' and therapists' attitudes toward psychodiagnostic reports. *Journal of Consulting and Clinical Psychology*, 1968, *32*, 500.

Mintz, J. The role of the therapist in assessing psychotherapy outcome. In A. S. Gurman & A. M. Razin (Eds.), *Effective psychotherapy: A handbook of research*. New York: Pergamon, 1977.

Mintz, J., & Kiesler, D. J. Individualized measures of psychotherapy outcome. In P. C. Kendall & J. N. Butcher (Eds.), *Handbook of research methods in clinical psychology*. New York: Wiley, 1982.

Mintz, J., & Luborsky, L. Segments vs. whole sessions: Which is the better unit for psychotherapy process research? *Journal of Abnormal Psychology*, 1971, *78*, 180-191.

Minuchin, S. *Families and family therapy*. Cambridge, Mass.: Harvard University Press, 1974.

Mirels, H. L. Dimensions of internal versus external control. *Journal of Consulting and Clinical Psychology*, 1970, *34*, 226-228.

Mischel, W. *Personality and assessment*. New York: Wiley, 1968.

Mischel, W. On the empirical dilemmas of psychodynamic approaches: Issues and alternatives. *Journal of Abnormal Psychology*, 1973, *82*, 335-344. (a)

Mischel, W. Toward a cognitive social learning reconceptualization of personality. *Psychological Review*, 1973, *80*, 252-283. (b)

Mischel, W. The interaction of person and situation. In D. Magnusson & N. S. Endler (Eds.), *Personality at the crossroads: Current issues in interactional psychology*. Hillsdale, N. J.: Erlbaum, 1977. (a)

Mischel, W. On the future of personality measurement. *American Psychologist*, 1977, *32*, 246-254. (b)

Mischel, W. On the interface of cognition and personality: Beyond the person-situation debate. *American Psychologist*, 1979, *34*, 740-754.

Mischel, W., Ebbesen, E., & Zeiss, A. R. Selective attention to the self: Situational and dispositional determinants. *Journal of Personality and Social Psychology,* 1973, *27*, 129-142.

Mishara, B. L. Geriatric patients who improve in token economy and general milieu treatment programs: A. multivariate analysis. *Journal of Consulting and Clinical Psychology*, 1978, *46*, 1340-1348.

Mitchell, K. M., Bozarth, J. D., & Krauft, C. C. A reappraisal of the therapeutic effectiveness of accurate empathy, nonpossesive warmth, and genuineness. In A. S. Gurman & A. M. Razin (Eds.), *Effective psychotherapy: A handbook of research*. New York: Pergamon, 1977.

Monahan, J. The prediction of violence. In J. Monahan (Ed.), *Community mental health and the criminal justice system*. New York: Pergamon, 1976.

Monahan, J. The prediction of violent ciminal behavior: A methodological critique and prospectus. In P. Blumstein, J. Cohen, & D. Nagin (Eds.), *Deterrence and incapacitation*. Washington, D.C.: National Academy of Science, 1978.

Monahan, J. (Ed.) *Who is the client? The ethics of psychological intervention in the criminal justice system*. Washington, D.C.: American Psychological Association, 1980.

Monson, T. C., & Snyder, M. Actors, observers and the attribution process: Toward a reconceptualization. *Journal of Experimental Social Psychology*, 1977, *13*, 89-111.

Moore, T. G. The purpose of licensing. *Journal of Law and Economics*, 1961, *4*, 93-117.

Moos, R. H. *The social climate scales: An overview*. Palo Alto, Cal.: Consulting Psychologists Press, 1974. (a)

Moos, R. H. *Evaluating treatment environments: A social ecological approach*. New York: Wiley, 1974. (b)

Moos, R.H. *Evaluating correctional and community settings*. New York: Wiley, 1975.

Moos, R. H. *The human context: Environmental determinants of behavior*. New York: Wiley, 1976.

Moos, R. H., & Insel, P. M. (Eds.) *Issues in social ecology*. New York: National Press Books, 1974.

Moos, R. H., & Moos, B. A typology of family social environments. *Family Process*, 1976, *15*, 357–372.

Moreno, J. L. *Application of the group method to classification*. New York: National Committee on Prisons and Prison Labor, 1932.

Moreno, J. L. *Psychodrama*. Beacon, N. Y.: Beacon House, 1946.

Morgan, C., & Murray, H. A. A method for investigating phantasies: The thematic apperception test. *Archives of Neurology and Psychiatry*, 1935, *34*, 289-306.

Morganstern, K. P. Behavioral interviewing. In M. Hersen & A. S. Bellack (Eds.), *Behavioral assessment: A practical handbook*. New York: Pergamon Press, 1976.

Morris, D. P., Soroker, E., & Burruss, G. Follow-up studies of shy, withdrawn children: Evaluation of later adjustment. *American Journal of Orthopsychiatry*, 1954, *24*, 743-755.

Moustakas, C. *Children in play therapy*. New York: Jason Aronson, 1973.

Mullen, J. *Pre-trial services: An evaluation of policy-related research*. Cambridge, MA: ABT Associates, Inc., 1974.

Murnighan, J. K. Models of collition behavior: Game theoretic, social psychological, and political perspectives. *Psychological Bulletin*, 1978, *85*, 1130-1153.

Murray, H. A. *Thematic Apperception Test: Pictures and manual*. Cambridge, Mass.: Harvard University Press, 1943.

Murstein, B. I. *Theory and research in projective techniques (emphasizing the TAT)*. New York: Wiley, 1963.

Mykleburst, M. R. Identification and diagnoses of children with learning disabilities: An interdisciplinary study of criteria. In S. Walzer & P. H. Wolff (Eds.), *Minimal cerebral dysfunctions in children*. New York: Grune and Stratton, 1973.

Nagel, S., & Weitzman, L. Sex and the unbiased jury. *Judicature*, 1972, *56*, 108-116.

Nassi, A. J. Community control or control by the community? The case of the community mental health center. *Journal of Community Psychology*, 1978, *6*, 3-15.

National Institute of Mental Health. *Staffing of mental health facilities, United States, 1976.* Washington, D. C.: U. S. Government Printing Office, 1978. (DHEW No. 78-522.)

Nay, W. R. Analogue assessment methods. In A. R. Ciminero, K. S. Calhoun, & H. E. Adams (Eds.), *Handbook of behavioral assessment:* New York: Wiley, 1977.

Nay, W. R. Comprehensive behavioral treatment in a training school for delinquents. In K. S. Calhoun, H. E. Adams, & K. M. Mitchell (Eds.), *Innovative treatment methods in psychopathology.* New York: Wiley, 1974.

Nebes, R. D. Hemispheric specialization in commissurotomized man. *Psychological Bulletin*, 1974, *81*, 1-14.

Neitzel, M., Winett, R., MacDonald, M., & Davidson, W. S. *Behavioral community psychology.* New York: Pergamon Press, 1977.

Nelson, C. W. *The leadership inventory analyzer.* Chicago: Industrial Relations Center, University of Chicago, 1965.

Nelson, R. O., & Hayes, S. C. The nature of behavioral assessment: A commentary. *Journal of Applied Behavior Analysis*, 1979, *12*, 491-500. (a)

Nelson, R. O., & Hayes, S. C. Some current dimensions of behavioral assessment. *Behavioral Assessment*, 1979, *1*, 1-16. (b)

Nemetz, G. H., Craig, K. D., & Reith, G. Treatment of female sexual dysfunction through symbolic modeling. *Journal of Consulting and Clinical Psychology*, 1978, *46*, 62-68.

Newcombe, F. *Missile wounds of the brain.* London: Oxford University Press, 1969.

Newman, D. E., & Luft, L. L. The peer review process: Education versus control. *American Journal of Psychiatry*, 1974, *131*, 1363-1366.

Newman, W. H. *Administrative action.* Englewood Cliffs, N. J.: Prentice Hall, 1950.

Newmark, C. S., Newmark, L. G., & Cook, L. The MMPI-168 with psychiatric patients. *Journal of Clinical Psychology*, 1975, *31*, 61-64.

Ney, P., Palvesky, A., & Markely, J. Relative effectiveness of operant conditioning and play therapy in childhood schizophrenia. *Journal of Autism and Childhood Schizophrenia*, 1971, *1*, 337-349.

Nisbett, R. E., Caputo, C., Lezant, P., & Marecek, J. Behavior as seen by the actor and by the observer. *Journal of Personality and Social Psychology*, 1973, *27*, 154-165.

Novaco, R. W. *Anger control: The development and evaluation of an experimental treatment.* Lexington, Mass.: Heath, 1975.

Novaco, R. W. Treatment of chronic anger through cognitive and relaxation controls. *Journal of Consulting and Clinical Psychology*, 1976, *44*, 681.

Novaco, R. W. A stress inoculation approach to anger management in the training of law enforcement officers. *American Journal of Community Psychology*, 1977, *5*, 327–346. (a)

Novaco, R. W. Stress inoculation: A cognitive therapy for anger and its application to a case of depression. *Journal of Consulting and Clinical Psychology*, 1977, *45*, 600-608 (b)

Novaco, R. W. The cognitive regulation of anger and stress. In P. C. Kendall & S. D.

Hollon (Eds.), *Cognitive-behavioral interventions: Theory, research, and procedures.* New York: Academic Press, 1979.

Nowicki, S., & Strickland, B. A locus of control scale for children. *Journal of Consulting and Clinical Psychology*, 1973, *40*, 148-154.

O'Connor, R. D. Modification of social withdrawal through symbolic modeling. *Journal of Applied Behavior Analysis*, 1969, *2*, 15-22.

O'Dell, S. Training parents in behavior modification: A review. *Psychological Bulletin*, 1974, *81*, 418-433.

Ogdon, D. P. *Psychodiagnostics and personality assessment: A handbook.* Los Angeles: Western Psychological Services, 1967.

Ogdon, D. P. Extrapolated WISC-R IQ's for gifted and mentally retarded children. *Journal of Consulting and Clinical Psychology*, 1975, *43*, 216.

Olbrisch, M. E. Psychotherapeutic interventions in physical health: Effectiveness and economic efficiency. *American Psychologist*, 1977, *32*, 761-777.

O'Leary, K. D., & Becker, W. C. Behavior modification of a adjustment class: A token reinforcement program. *Exceptional Children*, 1967, *33*, 637-642.

O'Leary, K. D., Becker, W. C., Evans, M. B., & Saudargas, R. A. A token reinforcement program in a public school: Replication and systematic analysis. *Journal of Applied Behavior Analysis*, 1969, *2*, 3-13.

O'Leary, K. D., & Borkovec, T. D. Conceptual, methodological, and ethical problems of placebo groups in psychotherapy research. *American Psychologist*, 1978, *33*, 821-830.

O'Leary, K. D., Kent, R. N., & Kanowitz, J. Shaping data collection congruent with experimental hypotheses. *Journal of Applied Behavior Analysis*, 1974, *7*, 481–490.

O'Leary, K. D., & Turkewitz, H. Methodological errors in marital and child treatment research. *Journal of Consulting and Clinical Psychology*, 1978, *46*, 747-756.

O'Leary, K. D., & Wilson, G. T. *Behavior therapy: Application and outcome.* Englewood Cliffs, N. J.: Prentice-Hall, 1975.

O'Leary, S. G., & O'Leary, K. D. Behavior modification in the school. In H. Leitenberg (Ed.), *Handbook of behavior modification and behavior therapy.* New York: Wiley, 1976.

Olson, D. H., Spenkle, D. H., & Russell, C. Circimplex model of marital and family systems: I. Cohesion and adaptability dimensions, family types, and clinical applications. *Family Process*, 1979, *18*, 3-28.

Olson, D. H., & Strauss, M. A. A diagnostic tool for marital and family therapy: The SIMFAM technique. *The Family Coordinator*, 1972, *21*, 251-258.

Olson, R. P., & Greenberg, D. J. Effects of contingency contracting and decision-making groups with chronic mental patients. *Journal of Consulting and Clinical Psychology*, 1972, *38*, 376-383.

Oltmanns, T., Broderick, J., & O'Leary, K. D. Marital adjustment and the efficacy of behavior therapy for children. *Journal of Consulting and Clinical Psychology*, 1977, *45*, 724-731.

O. M. Collective. *The organizer's manual.* New York: Bantam, 1971.

Opton, E. M., Jr. Institutional behavioral modification as a fraud and sham. *Arizona Law Review*, 1975, *17*, 20-28.

Orlinsky, D. E., & Howard, K. I. The relation of process to outcome in psychotherapy. In S. L. Garfield & A. E. Bergin (Eds.), *Handbook of psychotherapy and behavior change.* (2nd ed.) New York: Wiley, 1978.

Orne, M. T. On the social psychology of the psychological experiment: With particular reference to demand characteristics and their implications. *American Psychologist*, 1962, *17*, 776–786.

Overall, J. E., & Gomez-Mont, F. The MMPI-168 for psychiatric screening. *Educational and Psychological Measurement*, 1974, *34*, 315-319.

Overmier, J. B., & Seligman, M. E. P. Effects of inescapable shock upon subsequent escape and avoidance learning. *Journal of Comparative and Physiological Psychology*, 1967, *63*, 23-33.

Padfield, M. The comparative effects of two counseling approaches on the the intensity of depression among rural women of low socioeconomic status. *Journal of Counseling Psychology*, 1976, *23*, 209-214.

Pallone, N. J., Hennessy, J. J., & Larosa, D. S. Professional psychology in state correctional institutions: Present status and future alternatives. *Professional Psychology*, 1980, *11*, 755-763.

Palmer, J. O. *The psychological assessment of children.* New York: Wiley, 1970.

Papez, J. W. A proposed mechanism of emotion. *Archives of Neurological Psychiatry*, 1937, *38*, 725-743.

Parloff, M. B. Analytic group psychotherapy. In J. Marmor (Ed.), *Modern psychoanalysis.* New York: Basic Books, 1968.

Parloff, M. B., Waskow, I. E., & Wolfe, B. E. Research on therapist variables in relation to process and outcome. In S. L. Garfield & A. E. Bergin (Eds.), *Handbook of psychotherapy and behavior change.* (2nd ed.) New York: Wiley, 1978.

Parsons, O. A., & Klein, M. P. Concept identification and practice in brain-damaged and schizophrenic groups. *Journal of Consulting and Clinical Psychology*, 1970, *35*, 317-323.

Parsons, O. A., & Prigatano, G. P. Methodological considerations in clinical neuropsychological research. *Journal of Consulting and Clinical Psychology*, 1978, *46*, 608-619.

Parsons, T. On the concept of influence. *Public Opinion Quarterly*, 1963, *27*, 37-62.

Parsons, T., & Shils, E. (Eds.) *Toward a general theory of action.* Cambridge, Mass.: Harvard University Press, 1952.

Pascal, G. R., & Suttell, B. J. *The Bender-Gestalt Test: Quantification and validity for adults.* New York: Grune and Stratton, 1951.

Passini, F. T., & Norman, W. T. A universal conception of personality structure? *Journal of Personality and Social Psychology*, 1966, *4*, 44–49.

Patterson, G. R. A learning theory approach to the treatment of the school phobic child. In L. P. Ullmann & L. Krasner (Eds.), *Case studies in behavior modification.* New York: Holt, Rinehart and Winston, 1966.

Patterson, G. R. Interventions for boys with conduct problems: Multiple settings, treatments, and criteria. *Journal of Consulting and Clinical Psychology*, 1974, *42*, 471-480.

Patterson, G. R. The aggressive child: Victim and architect of a coercive system. In E. J. Mash, L. A. Hamerlynck, & L. C. Handy (Eds.), *Behavior modification and families.* New York: Brunner/Mazel, 1976.

Patterson, G. R. Naturalistic observation in clinical assessment. *Journal of Abnormal Child Psychology*, 1977, *5*, 307-322.

Patterson, G. R., Cobb, J. A., & Ray, R. S. A social engineering technology for retraining the families of aggressive boys. In H. Adams & I. P. Unikel (Eds.), *Issues and trends in behavior therapy*. Springfield, Ill.: Charles C Thomas, 1973.

Patterson, G. R., Weiss, R., & Hops, H. Training of marital skills. In H. Leitenberg (Ed.), *Handbook of behavior modification and behavior therapy*. New York: Appleton-Century-Crofts, 1976.

Pattie, F. A. A brief history of hypnotism. In J. E. Gordon (Ed.), *Handbook of clinical and experimental hypnosis*. New York: Macmillan, 1967.

Pauker, J. D. A split-half abbreviation of the WAIS. *Journal of Clinical Psychology*, 1963, *19*, 98-100.

Paul, G. L. *Insight vs. desensitization in psychotherapy: An experiment in anxiety reduction*. Stanford, Cal.: Stanford University Press, 1966.

Paul, G. L. Insight vs. desensitization in psychotherapy two years after termination. *Journal of Consulting Psychology*, 1967, *31*, 333-348. (a)

Paul, G. L., Strategy of outcome research in psychotherapy. *Journal of Consulting Psychology*, 1967, *31*, 109-118. (b)

Paul, G. L. Behavior modification research: Design and tactics. In C. M. Franks (Ed.), *Behavior therapy: Appraisal and status*. New York: McGraw-Hill, 1969.

Paul, G. L, & Lentz, R. J. *Psychosocial treatment of chronic mental patients: Milieu versus social-learning programs*. Cambridge, Mass.: Harvard University Press, 1977.

Paul, G. L., & McInnis, T. L. Additional changes associated with two approaches to training mental health techniques in milieu and social learning programs. *Journal of Consulting and Clinical Psychology*, 1974, *42*, 21-33.

Paul, N. Cross confrontation. In P. J. Guerin (Ed.), *Family therapy*. New York: Gardner Press, 1976.

Pavlov, I. P. *Conditioned reflexes*. (Translated by G. V. Aurep.) London: Oxford, 1927.

Pelham, W. E. Hyperactive children. In R. P. Liberman (Ed.), Symposium on behavior therapy in psychiatry. *Psychiatric Clinics of North America*, 1978, *1*, 227-246.

Peres, H. An investigation of nondirective group therapy. *Journal of Consulting Psychology*, 1947, *11*, 159-172.

Penk, W. E., Charles, H. L., & Van Hoose, T. A. Comparative effectiveness of day hospital and inpatient psychiatric treatment. *Journal of Consulting and Clinical Psychology*, 1978, *46*, 94-101.

Perkins, M. J., Kiesler, D. J., Anchin, J. C., Chirico, B. M., Kyle, E. M., & Federman, E. J. The Impact Message Inventory: A new measure of relationship in counseling/psychotherapy and other dyads. *Journal of Counseling Psychology*, 1979, *26*, 363-367.

Perlman, B. The hunt. Job hunting for the new Ph.D. psychologist. *American Psychologist*, 1976, *31*, 298–302.

Perlman, R., & Gurin, A. *Community organization and social planning*. New York: Wiley, 1971.

Perloff, R., Perloff, E., & Sussna, E. Program evaluation. *Annual Review of Psychology*, 1976, *27*.

Perls, F. S. *Gestalt therapy verbatim*. Moab, Utah: Real People Press, 1969.

Perls, F. S., Hefferline, R. F., & Goodman, P. *Gestalt therapy*. New York: Julian Press, 1951.

Perry, N. W. Why clinical psychology does not need alternative training models. *American Psychologist*, 1979, *34*, 603-611.

Peterson, C. M. An experimental study of the effects of training on the ability of non-professionals to modify the behavior of psychiatric patients. *Dissertation Abstracts International*, 1972, *32*(11-B), 6658-6659.

Peterson, D. R. *The clinical study of social behavior.* New York: Appleton-Century-Crofts, 1968.

Phares, E. J. *Locus of control and personality.* Morristown, N. J.: General Learning Press, 1976.

Phares, E. J., & Campbell, J. P. Sensitivity training in industry: Issues and research. In L. E. Alit & R. F. Reiss (Eds.), *Progress in clinical psychology.* Vol 9. New York: Grune and Stratton, 1971.

Phares, E. J., Ritchie, E. D., & Davis, W. L. Internal-external control and reaction to threat. *Journal of Personality and Social Psychology*, 1968, *10*, 402-405.

Pheysey, D. C., Payne, R. L., & Pugh, D. S. Influence of structure at organizational and group levels. *Administrative Science Quarterly*, 1971, *16*, 61-73.

Phillips, E. L., Phillips, E. A., Fixsen, D. L., & Wolf, M. M. Achievement place: Modification of the behavior of pre-delinquent boys within a token economy. *Journal of Applied Behavior Analysis*, 1971, *4*, 45–60.

Phillips, E. L., Wolf, M. M., & Fixsen, D. L. Achievement place: Development of an elected manager system. *Journal of Applied Behavior Analysis*, 1973, *6*, 541-563.

Phillips, L. Case history data and prognosis in schizophrenia. *The Journal of Nervous and Mental Diseases*, 1953, *117*, 515-525.

Piaget, J. *The construction of reality in the child.* (Translated by M. Cook.) New York: Basic Books, 1954.

Pilisuk, M. Power: The appropriate target for community research. *Community Mental Health Journal*, 1975, *11*, 257-266.

Piotrowski, Z. A new evaluation of the Thematic Apperception Test. *Psychoanalytic Review*, 1950, *37*, 101-127.

Pittman, F., III. Cleaning house. In J. Haley and L. Hoffman (Eds.), *Techniques of family therapy.* New York: Basic Books, 1967.

Podlesny, J. A., & Raskin, D. C. Physiological measures and the detection of deception. *Psychological Bulletin*, 1977, *84*, 782-799.

Poetter, R. A., Alvares, C., Abell, T. V., & Krop, H. Using college students as paraprofessionals. *Hospital and Community Psychiatry*, 1974, *25*, 305-307.

Pope, B. Research on therapeutic style. In A. S. Gurman & A. M. Razin (Eds.), *Effective psychotherapy: A handbook of research.* New York: Pergamon, 1977.

Pope, K. S., Geller, J. D., Wilkinson, L. Fee assessment and outpatient psychotherapy. *Journal of Consulting and Clinical Psychology*, 1975, *43*, 835-841.

Porter, L., & Lawler, E. Properties of organizational structure in relation to job attitudes and job behavior. *Psychological Bulletin*, 1965, *64*, 21-51.

Poser, E. G. The effects of therapists' training on group therapeutic outcome. *Journal of Consulting Psychology*, 1966, *30*, 283-289.

Poulton, E. C. A new look at the effects of noise: A rejoinder. *Psychological Bulletin*, 1978, *85*, 1068-1079.

Powers, E., & Witmer, H. *An experiment in the prevention of delinquency.* New York: Columbia University Press, 1951.

Pressman, R. M. *Private practice. A handbook for the independent mental health practitioner.* New York: Gardner Press, 1979.

Price, R. H., & Bashfield, R. K. Explorations in the taxonomy of behavior setting: Analysis of dimensions and classification of settings. *American Journal of Community Psychology*, 1975, *3*, 335-352.

Prince, M., & Coriat, I. Cases illustrating the educational treatment of the psychoneurosis. *Journal of Abnormal Psychology*, 1907, *2*, 166-177.

Prochaska, J. O. *Systems of psychotherapy: A transtheoretical analysis.* Homewood, Ill.: Dorsey Press, 1979.

Purdue Research Foundation. *Examiner's manual for the Purdue Pegboard.* Chicago: Science Research Associates, 1948.

Purisch, A. D., Golden, C. S., & Hammeke, S. A. Discrimination of schizophrenic and brain-injured patients by a standardized version of Luria's neuropsychological tests. *Journal of Consulting and Clinical Psychology*, 1978, *48*, 1266-1273.

Putnam, J. J. Recent experiences in the study and treatment of hysteria at the Massachusetts General Hospital; with remarks on Freud's method of treatment by "psycho-analysis." *Journal of Abnormal Psychology*, 1906, *1*, 26-41.

Pyle, R. R. Mental health consultation: Helping teachers help themselves. *Professional Psychology*, 1977, *8*, 192-198.

Quattlebaum, L. F. A brief note on the relationship between two psychomotor tests. *Journal of Clinical Psychology*, 1968, *24*, 198-199.

Quay, L. C., & Peterson, D. R. *Manual for the problem behavior checklist.* Champaign, Ill.: University of Illinois Children's Research Center, 1967.

Quiltch, H. R. A comparison of three staff management procedures. *Journal of Applied Behavior Analysis*, 1975, *8*, 159-166.

Rachman, S., & Teasdale J. *Aversion therapy and behavior disorders: An analysis.* Coral Gables, Florida: University of Miami Press, 1969.

Rado, S. The problem of melancholia. *International Journal of Psychoanalysis*, 1928, *9*, 420-438.

Raimy, V. C. (Ed.) *Training in clinical psychology.* Englewood Cliffs, N. J.: Prentice-Hall, 1950.

Rapaport, D., Gill, M., & Schafer, R. *Diagnostic psychological testing. Vol. 1.* Chicago: Yearbook Publishers, 1945.

Rapaport, D., Gill, M., & Schafer, R. *Diagnostic psychological testing.* (Rev. ed., edited by R. R. Holt) New York: International Universities Press, 1968.

Rappaport, J. *Community psychology: Values, research and action.* New York: Holt, Rinehart and Winston, 1977.

Rappaport, J., & Chinsky, J. M. Accurate empathy: Confusion of a construct. *Psychological Bulletin*, 1972, *77*, 400-404.

Rappoport, L., & Kren, G. What is a social issue? *American Psychologist*, 1975, *30*, 838-841.

Rathus, S. A. A 30-item schedule for assessing assertive behavior. *Behavior Therapy*, 1973, *4*, 398-406.

Raush, H. L. Research, practice, and account; bility. *American Psychologist*, 1974, *29*, 678-681.

Raush, H. L., & Raush, C. L. *The halfway house movement.* New York: Appleton-Century-Crofts, 1968.

Raven, J. C. *Progressive matrices: A perceptual test of intelligence, 1938, Individual form.* London: H. K. Lewis, 1938.

Razin, A. M. A-B variable on psychotherapy. A critical review. *Psychological Bulletin*, 1971 *75*, 1–21.

Razin, A. M. The A-B variable: Still promising after twenty years? In A. S. Gurman & A. M. Razin (Eds.), *Effective psychotherapy: A handbook of research.* New York: Pergamon, 1977.

Redfield, J., & Paul, G. L. Bias in behavioral observation as a function of observer familiarity with subjects and typicality of behavior. *Journal of Consulting and Clinical Psychology*, 1976, *44*, 156.

Redfield, R. The folk society. *American Journal of Sociology*, 1947, *52*, 293-308.

Reed, H. B. C., Reitan, R. M., & Kløve, H. Influence of cerebral lesions on psychological test performances of older children. *Journal of Consulting Psychology*, 1965, *29*, 247-251.

Reich, A. On countertransference. *International Journal of Psychoanalysis.* 1951, *32*, 25-31.

Reid, J. B., & Patterson, G. R. Followup analyses of a behavioral treatment program for boys with conduct problems. *Journal of Consulting and Clinical Psychology*, 1976, *44*, 299-302.

Reiff, R., & Reissman, F. The indigenous nonprofessional. A strategy of change in community action and community mental health programs. *Community Mental Health Journal*, 1960, Monograph No. 1, 3-32.

Reik, T. *Listening with the third ear.* New York: Grove Press, 1948.

Reisman, J. M. *The development of clinical psychology.* New York: Appleton-Century-Crofts, 1966.

Reissman, F., & Gartner, A. Community control and radical social change. *Social Policy*, 1970, *1*, 52-55.

Reitan, R. M. Investigation of the validity of Halstead's measures of biological intelligence. *A. M. A. Archives of Neurology*, 1955a, *73*, 28-35.

Reitan, R. M. *The effects of brain lesions on adaptive abilities in human beings.* Unpublished mimeographs, Indiana Neuropsychological Laboratory, 1959.

Reitan, R. M. Certain differential effects of left and right cerebral lesions in human adults. *Journal of Comparative and Physiological Psychology*, 1955b, *48*, 474-477.

Reitan, R. M. Psychological testing of neurological patients. In J. R. Toumans (Ed.), *Neurosurgery: A Comprehensive guide to the diagnosis and management of neurosurgical problems.* Philadelphia: W. B. Saunders Co., 1970.

Reitan, R. M. Methodological problems in clinical neuropsychology. In R. M. Reitan & L. A. Davison (Eds.), *Clinical neuropsychology: Current status and applications.* Washington, D. C.: Winston, 1974. (a)

Reitan, R. M. Psychological effects of cerebral lesions in children of early school age. In R. M. Reitan & L. A. Davison (Eds.), *Clinical neuropsychology: Current status and applications.* Washington, D. C.: Winston, 1974. (b)

Reitan, R. M. Neurological and physiological bases of psychopathology. *Annual Review of Psychology*, 1976, *27*, 189–216.

Reitan, R. M. and Davison, L. A. (Eds.) *Clinical neuropsychology: Current status and applications.* Washington, D. C.: Winston, 1974.

Resnick, R. D., & Entin, A. D. Is an abbreviated form of the WISC valid for Afro-American children? *Journal of Consulting and Clinical Psychology*, 1971, *36*, 97-99.

Reynolds, B. S. Psychological treatment models and outcome results for erectile dysfunction: A critical review. *Psychological Bulletin*, 1977, *84*, 1218-1238.

Rhodes, W. C. Principles and practices of consultation. *Professional Psychology*, 1974, *6*, 287-292.

Rich, A., & Schroeder, M. Research issues in assertiveness training. *Psychological Bulletin*, 1976, *83*, 1081-1096.

Ricksler, C., & Jung, C. J. Further investigations on the galvanic phenomenon and respiration in normal and insane individuals. *Journal of Abnormal Psychology*, 1907-1908, *22*, 189-217.

Riesman, D. *The lonely crowd.* New York: Doubleday Anchor, 1953.

Rimm, D. C., & Masters, J. D. *Behavior therapy: Techniques and empirical findings.* (2nd ed.) New York: Academic Press, 1979.

Rioch, M. T., Elkes, C., Flint, A. A., Usdansky, B. S., Newman, R. G., & Silber, E. National Institute of Mental Health Pilot Study in training mental health counselors. *American Journal of Orthopsychiatry*, 1963, *33*, 678–689.

Risley, T. R. The effects and side effects of punishing the deviant behaviors of an autistic child. *Journal of Applied Behavior Analysis*, 1968, *1*, 21-34.

Ritterman, M. K. Paradigmatic classification of family therapy theories. *Family Process*, 1977, *16*, 29-48.

Roback, H. B. Human figures drawings: Their utility in the clinical psychologist's armamentarium for personality assessment. *Psychological Bulletin*, 1968, *70*, 1-19.

Roberts, R. R. & Renzaglia, G. A. The influence of tape recording on counseling. *Journal of Counseling Psychology*, 1965, 12, 10-16.

Robin, A. L., O'Leary, K. D., Kent, R. N., Foster, S. L., & Prinz, R. An approach to teaching parents and adolescents problem-solving communication skills: A preliminary report. *Behavior Therapy*, 1977, *8*, 639-643.

Robins, E., & Guze, S. B. Classification of affective disorders: The primary-secondary, the endogenous-reactive, and the neurotic-psychotic concepts. In T. A. Williams, M. M. Katy, & J. A. Shields (Eds.) *Recent advances in the psychobiology of the depressive illnesses.* Washington, D. C.: U. S. Government Printing Office, 1972.

Robins, L. N. *Deviant children grown up.* Baltimore, Md.: Williams & Wilkins, 1966.

Roe, A., Gustad, J. W., Moore, B. V., Ross, S., & Skodak, M. (Eds.) *Graduate education in psychology.* Washington, D. C.: American Psychological Association, 1959.

Rogers, C. R. *Counseling and psychotherapy.* Boston, Houghton Mifflin, 1942.

Rogers, C. R. *Client-centered therapy: Its current practice, implications, and theory.* Boston: Houghton Mifflin, 1951.

Rogers, C. R. The necessary and sufficient conditions of therapeutic personality change. *Journal of Consulting Psychology*, 1957, *21*, 95-103.

Rogers, C.R. A theory of therapy, personality and interpersonal relationships, as developed in the client-centered framework. In S. Koch (Ed.), *Psychology: A study of a science*. Vol. III. *Formulations of the person and the social context*. New York: McGraw-Hill, 1959.

Rogers, C. R. *On becoming a person*. Boston: Houghton Mifflin, 1961.

Rogers, C. R. Interpersonal relationships: Year 2000. *Journal of Applied Behavioral Science*, 1968, *4*, 265-280.

Rogers, C. R. *Carl Rogers on encounter groups*. New York: Harper & Row, 1970.

Rogers, C. R., & Dymond, R. *Psycotherapy and personality change*. Chicago: University of Chicago Press, 1954.

Rogers, C. R., Gendlin, E. T., Kiesler, D. J., & Truax, C. B. *The therapeutic relationship and its impact: A study of psychotherapy with schizophrenics*. Madison, Wisc.: University of Wisconsin Press, 1967.

Rohsenow, D. J. Comment on Gotlib and Asarnow's learned helplessness study. *Journal of Consulting and Clinical Psychology*, 1980, *48*, 284-285.

Rorer, L. G. Sixteen personality factor questionnaire. In O. K. Buros (Ed.), *Seventh mental measurements yearbook*. Vol. 1. Highland Park, N. J.: Gryphon Press, 1972.

Rorschach, H. *Psychodiagnostik*. Bern and Leipzig: Ernst Bircher Verlag, 1921.

Rose, S. D. Group training of parents as behavior modifiers. *Social Work*, 1974, *19*, 156-162.

Rosen, G. M. The development and use of nonprescription behavior therapies. *American Psychologist*, 1976, *31*, 139–141.

Rosen, J. C., & Wiens, A. N. Changes in medical problems and use of medical services following psychological intervention. *American Psychologist*, 1979, *34*, 115-121.

Rosen, M. Alice in Rorschachland. *Journal of Personality Assessment*, 1973, *37*, 115-121.

Rosenbaum, A., O'Leary, K. D., & Jacob, R. G. Behavioral interventions with hyperactive children. Group consequences as a supplement to individual contingencies. *Behavior Therapy*, 1975, *6*, 315-323.

Rosenhan, D. L. On being sane in insane places. *Science*, 1973, *179*, 250-258.

Rosenthal, D. *Genetic theory and abnormal behavior*. New York: McGraw-Hill, 1970.

Rosenthal, R. *Experimenter bias in behavioral research*. New York: Appleton-Century-Crofts, 1966.

Rosenthal, R. How often are our numbers wrong? *American Psychologist*, 1978, *33*, 1005-1008.

Rosenthal, R., Frank, J. D., & Nash, E. The self-righteous moralist in early meetings of therapeutic groups. *Psychiatry*, 1954, *17*, 215-223.

Rosenthal, T. L. Bandura's self-efficacy theory: Thought *is* father to the deed. *Advances in Behaviour Research and Therapy*, 1978, *1*, 203-210.

Rosenthal, T. L. & Bandura, A. Psychological modeling: Theory and practice. In S. L. Garfield & A. E. Bergin (Eds.), *Handbook of psychotherapy and behavior change*. (2nd ed.) New York: Wiley, 1978.

Ross, A. O. Behavior therapy with children. In S. L. Garfield & A. E. Bergin (Eds.), *Handbook of psychotherapy and behavior change*. (2nd ed.) New York: Wiley, 1978.

Ross, A. O., Lacey, H. M., & Parton, D. A. The development of a behavior checklist for boys. *Child Development*, 1965, *36*, 1013-1027.

Rotter, J. B. *Social learning theory and clinical psychology*. Englewood Cliffs, N. J.: Prentice-Hall, 1954.

Rotter, J. B. Generalized expectancies for internal versus external control of reinforcement. *Psychological Monographs*, 1966, *80*,(Whole No. 609), 1-28.

Rotter, J. B., Chance, J., & Phares, E. J. (Eds.) *Applications of a social learning theory of personality*. New York: Holt, Rinehart and Winston, 1972.

Rotter, J. B. & Rafferty, J. E. *Manual for the Rotter Incomplete Sentence Blank, College Form*. New York: Psychological Corp., 1950.

Rourke, B. P. Brain-behavior relationships in children with learning disabilities. *American Psychologist*, 1975, *30*, 911–920.

Rush, A. J., Beck, A. T., Kovacs, M., & Hollon, S. D. Comparative efficacy of cognitive therapy and pharmacotherapy in the treatment of depressed outpatients. *Cognitive Therapy and Research*, 1977, *1*, 17-37.

Russell, E. W., Neuringer, C., & Goldstein, G. *Assessment of brain function: A neuropsychological key approach*. New York: Wiley, 1970.

Russell, J. A. Evidence of convergent validity on the dimensions of affect. *Journal of Personality and Social Psychology*, 1978, *36*, 1152-1168.

Ryan, W. *Blaming the victim*. New York: Random House, 1971.

Ryback, D., & Staats, A. W. Parents as behavior therapy technicians in treating reading deficits. *Journal of Behavior Therapy and Experimental Psychiatry*, 1970, *1*, 109-119.

Sahakian, W. S. *Psychopathology today: Experimentation, theory, and research*. Itasca, Ill.: F. E. Peacock Publishers, 1970.

Salter, A. *Conditioned reflex therapy*. New York: Farrar, Straus, 1949.

Sarason, I. G. Test anxiety and the self-disclosing model. *Journal of Consulting and Clinical Psychology*, 1975, *43*, 148-153.

Sarason, S. B. *The creation of settings*. San Francisco. Jossey-Bass, 1972.

Sarason, S. B. *The psychological sense of community: Prospects for a community psychology*. San Francisco: Jossey-Bass, 1974.

Sarason, S. B. Community psychology, networks and Mr. Everyman. *American Psychologist*, 1976, 31, 317-328.

Sarbin, T. R. A contribution to the study of actuarial and individual methods of prediction. *American Journal of Sociology*, 1943, *48*, 593-602.

Sarbin, T. R. The scientific status of the mental illness metaphor. In S. C. Plog & R. B. Edgerton (Eds.), *Changing perspectives in mental illness*. New York: Holt, Rinehart and Winston, 1969.

Sarbin, T. R., & Andersen, M. L. Role-theoretical analysis of hypnotic behavior. In J. E. Gordon (Ed.), *Handbook of clinical and experimental hypnosis*. New York: Macmillan, 1967.

Sargent, H. D. Psychological test reporting: An experiment in communication. *Bulletin of the Menninger Clinic*, 1951, *15*, 175–186.

Satir, V. *Conjoint family therapy*. Palo Alto, Cal.: Science and Behavior Books, 1964

Satterfield, J. H. EEG issues in children with minimal brain dysfunction. In S. Walzee & P. H. Wolff (Eds.), *Minimal cerebral dysfunction in children*. New York: Grune and Stratton, 1973.

Sattler, J. M. *Assessment of children's intelligence*. Philadelphia: W. B. Saunders, 1974.

Sattler, J. M. Scoring difficulty of the WPPSI geometric design subtest. *Journal of School Psychology*, 1976, *14*, 230-234.

Sattler, J. M. & Theye, F. Procedural, situational, and interpersonal variables in individual intelligence testing. *Psychological Bulletin*, 1967, *68*, 347-360.

Satz, P., Fennell, E., & Reilly, C. Predictive validity of six neurodiagnostic tests. *Journal of Consulting and Clinical Psychology*, 1970, *34*, 375-381.

Satz, P., & Mogel, S. An abbreviation of the WAIS for clinical use. *Journal of Clinical Psychology*, 1962, *18*, 77-79.

Sawyer, J. Measurement and prediction, clinical and statistical. *Psychological Bulletin*, 1966, *66*, 178-200.

Schacht, T., & Nathan, P. E. But is it good for the psychologists? Appraisal and status of DSM III. *American Psychologist*, 1977, 32, 1017-1025.

Schachter, S. *Emotion, obesity and crime.* New York: Academic Press, 1971.

Schaefer, M. M., & Martin, P. L. Behavioral therapy for apathy of hospitalized schizophrenics. *Psychological Reports*, 1968, *19*, 1147-1158.

Schaie, K. W., & Strother, C. R. A cross-sequential study of age changes in cognitive behavior. *Psychological Bulletin*, 1968, 70, 671–680.

Schaie, K. W., & Schaie, J. P. Clinical assessment and aging. In J. E. Birren & K. W. Schaie (Eds.), *Handbook of the psychology of aging.* New York: Van Nostrand Rheinhold, 1977.

Schaps, E. Cost, dependency and helping. *Journal of Personality and Social Psychology*, 1972, *21*, 74-78.

Schein, E. *Organizational psychology.* (2nd ed.) Englewood Cliffs, N. J.: Prentice-Hall, 1970.

Schilder, P. Results and problems of group psychotherapy in severe neurosis. *Mental Hygiene*, 1939, *23*, 87-98.

Schildkraut, J. J. The catecholamine hypothesis of affective disorders: A review of supporting evidence. *American Journal of Psychiatry*, 1965, *122*, 509-522.

Schildkraut, J. J., & Kety, S. S. Biogenic amines and emotion: Pharmacological studies suggest a relationship between brain biogenic amines and affective state. *Science*, 1967, *156*, 21-29.

Schless, A. P., Mendels, J., Kipperman, A., & Cochrane, C. Depression and hostility. *Journal of Nervous and Mental Disorders*, 1974, *159*, 91-100.

Schlosberg, M. S. Three dimensions of emotion. *Psychological Review*, 1954, *61*, 81-88.

Schmahl, D. P., Lichtenstein, E., & Harris, D. E. Successful treatment of habitual smokers with warm, smoky air and rapid smoking. *Journal of Consulting and Clinical Psychology*, 1972, *38*, 105-111.

Schmidt, D. E., & Keating, J. P. Human crowding and personal control: An integration of the research. *Psychological Bulletin*, 1979, *86*, 680-700.

Schmidt, F. L., & Hunter, J. E. Racial and ethnic bias in psychological tests: Divergent implications of two definitions of test bias. *American Psychologist*, 1974, *29*, 1-8.

Schneider, W., & Shiffrin, R. M. Controlled and automatic human information processing: I. Detection, search, and attention. *Psychological Review*, 1977, *84*, 1–66.

Schofield, W. *Psychotherapy: The purchase of friendship.* Englewood Cliffs, N. J.: Prentice-Hall, 1964.

Schover, L. R. Clinical practice and scientific psychology. Can this marriage be saved? *Professional Psychology*, 1980, *11*, 268-275.

Schutz, W. *Joy.* New York. Esalen, Cal.: Esalen Center 1967.

Schwartz, J. & Bellack, A. S. A comparison of token economy with standard in-patient treatment. *Journal of Consulting and Clinical Psychology,* 1975, *43*, 107-108.

Schwartz, R. M., & Gottman, J. M. Toward a task analysis of assertive behavior. *Journal of Consulting and Clinical Psychology*, 1976, 44, 910-920.

Scott, W. A. Research definitions of mental health and mental illness. *Psychological Bulletin*, 1958, *55*, 29-45.

Seashore, C. E., Lewis, D., & Soetvert, D. L. *Seashore measures of musical talents.* (Rev. ed.) New York: Psychological Corporation, 1960.

Seeman, J. Deception in psychological research. *American Psychologist*, 1969, *24*, 1025-1029.

Seeman, J. H. Premature ejaculation: A new approach. *Southern Medical Journal*, 1956, *49*, 353-357.

Seidman, E., Rappaport, J., & Davidson, W. S. *Adolescents in legal jeopardy: Initial success and replication of an alternative to the criminal justice system.* Invited address at the American Psychological Association Annual Convention, Washington, D.C., 1976.

Seigel, J. M. Mental health volunteers as change agents. *American Journal of Community Psychology*, 1973, *1*, 138–158.

Seligman, M. E. P. Phobias and preparedness. *Behavior Therapy*, 1971, *2*, 307-320.

Seligman, M. E. P. Depression and learned helplessness. In R. J. Friedman & M. M. Katz (Eds.), *The psychology of depression: Contemporary theory and research.* Washington, D. C.: V. H. Winston, 1974.

Seligman, M. E. P. *Helplessness: On depression, development, and death.* San Francisco: W. H. Freeman, 1975.

Sells, S. Dimensions of stimulus situations which account for behavior variance. In S. Sells (Ed.), *Stimulus determinants of behavior.* New York: Ronald Press, 1963.

Selye, H. *The stress of life.* New York: McGraw-Hill, 1956.

Selz, M., & Reitan, R. M. Rules for neuropsychological diagnosis: Classifications of brain dysfunction in older children. *Journal of Consulting and Clinical Psychology*, 1979, *47*, 258-264.

Selznick, P. Foundations of the theory of organization. *American Sociological Review*, 1948, 13, 25-35.

Shaffer, L. F. Clinical psychology and psychiatry. *Journal of Consulting Psychology*, 1947, *11*, 5-11.

Shah, S. A. The criminal justice system. In S. E. Golann & C. Eisdorfer (Eds.), *Handbook of Community Mental Health.* New York: Appleton-Century-Crofts, 1972.

Shakow, D. An internship year for psychologists: With special reference to psychiatric hospitals. *Journal of Consulting Psychology*, 1938, *2*, 73-76.

Shakow, D. Training in clinical psychology. A note on trends. *Journal of Consulting Psychology*, 1945, 9, 240-242.

Shakow, D. The role of classification in the development of the science of psychopathology with particular reference to research. In M. M. Katy, J. O. Cole, & W. E. Barton (Eds.), *The role and methodology of classification in psychiatry and psychopathology.* Chevy Chase, Md.: National Institute of Mental Health, 1968.

Shakow, D. What is clinical psychology? *American Psychologist*, 1976, *31*, 553-560.

Shakow, D., Brotemarkle, R. A., Doll, E. A., Kinder, E. F., Moore, B. V., & Smith, S.

Graduate internship training in psychology. *Journal of Consulting* Psychology, 1938, 243-266.

Shantz, C. A developmental study of Piaget's theory of logical multiplication. *Merrill-Palmer Quarterly*, 1967, *13*, 121-137.

Shapiro, E., & Biber, B. The education of young children: A developmental-interaction approach. *Teachers College Record*, 1972, *74*, 55-79.

Shapiro, R. J. A comparative investigation of emotionality and multiple outcome criteria in marathon and traditional growth groups. *Dissertation Abstracts International*, 1971, *32*(B), 3652-3653.

Shapiro, R., & Suchman, S. Reflection, termination, and continuation of family and individual therapy. *Family Process*, 1973, *12*, 55-67.

Sharfstein, S. S., Taube, C. A., & Goldberg, I. D. Problems in analyzing the comparative costs of private versus public psychiatric care. *American Journal of Psychiatry*, 1977, *134*, 29-32.

Shaw, B. F. Comparison of cognitive therapy and behavior therapy in the treatment of depression. *Journal of Consulting and Clinical Psychology*, 1977, *45*, 543-551.

Shaw, M. E. *Group dynamics*. New York: McGraw-Hill, 1971.

Shea, M. J. *A follow-up study into adulthood of adolescent psychiatric patients in relation to internalizing and externalizing symptoms.* Unpublished doctoral dissertation, University of Minnesota, 1972.

Shean, G. D., & Zeidberg, Z. Token reinforcement therapy: A comparison of matched groups. *Journal of Behavior Therapy and Experimental Psychiatry,* 1971, *2*, 95-105.

Sheehy, G. *Passages*. New York: Sutton Press, 1976.

Shepherd, M., Oppenheim, B. & Mitchell, S. *Childhood behavior and mental health*. New York: Grune and Stratton, 1971.

Sherif, M., & Sherif, C. W. *An outline of social psychology*. New York: Harper & Row, 1956.

Shields, J. MZA twins: Their use and abuse. In W. E. Nance (Ed.), *Twin studies: Psychology and methodology*. New York: A. R. Liss, Inc., in press.

Shils, E. A. Primordial, personal, racial, and civil ties. *British Journal of Sociology*, 1957, *8*, 130-145.

Shlien, J. M. Time-limited psychotherapy: An experimental investigation of practical values and theoretical implications. *Journal of Counseling Psychology*, 1957, 4, 318–323.

Shlien, J. M. Cross-theoretical criteria in time-limited therapy. *6th International Congress of Psychotherapy*, 1964, 118-126.

Shneidman, E. S., & Farberow, N. I. The suicide prevention center of Los Angeles. In H. L. Resnick (Ed.), *Suicidal behaviors: Diagnosis and management*. Boston: Little, Brown, 1968.

Shuey, A. M. *The testing of Negro intelligence*. (2nd ed.) New York: Social Science Press, 1966.

Shure, M. B. & Spivack, G. *Problem-solving techniques in childrearing*. San Francisco: Jossey-Bass, 1978.

Sidman, M. *Tactics of scientific research*. New York: Basic Books, 1960.

Silberman, C. (Ed.) *The open education reader*. New York: Vintage, 1975.

Silverman, P. R. The widow as a caregiver in a program of preventive intervention with other widows. *Mental Hygiene*, 1970, 54, 540-547.

Silverman, P. R. Widowhood and preventive intervention. *The Family Coordinator*, 1972, *21*, 95-102.

Silverman, W. H. Fundamental role characteristics of the community psychologist. *Journal of Community Psychology*, 1978, *6*, 207-215.

Silverman, W. H., Beech, R. P., & Keister, A. R. Community psychologist as researcher: Hidden and unhidden agenda. *Professional Psychology*, 1976, *8*, 141-146.

Simmel, G. *Conflict.* (Translated by K. M. Wolff) Glencoe, Ill.: The Free Press, 1955.

Simons, R. B., & Wachowiak, D. Psychologists in college counseling centers: A survey of directors. *Professional Psychology*, 1980, *11*, 643-647.

Singer, I. & Singer, J. Types of female orgasm. *Journal of Sex Research*, 1972, *8*, 255-267.

Singer, M. T. The borderline personality. *Archives of General Psychiatry*, 1976, *33*, 1024-1032.

Singer, M. T. Impact vs. diagnosis: A new approach to projective techniques in family research and therapy. In D. Block & C. Sluzki (Eds.), *Family therapy: The widening edge.* New York: Hemisphere, 1977.

Skinner, B. F. *The behavior of organisms.* New York: Appleton-Century-Crofts, 1938.

Skinner, B. F. *Science and human behavior.* New York: Macmillan, 1953.

Skinner, B. F. *Cumulative record: A selection of papers.* New York: Appleton-Century-Crofts, 1972.

Slavson, S. Group therapy. *Mental Hygiene*, 1940, 24, 36–49.

Slavson, S. R. *A textbook in analytic group psychotherapy.* New York: International Universities Press, 1964.

Sloan, W., & Birch, J. W. A rationale for degrees of retardation. *American Journal of Mental Deficiency*, 1955, *60*, 258-264.

Sloane, R. B., Staples, F. R., Cristol, A. H., Yorkston, N. J., & Whipple, K. *Psychotherapy versus behavior therapy.* Cambridge, Mass.: Harvard University Press, 1975.

Sloane, R. B., Staples, F. R., Cristol, A. H., Yorkston, N. J., & Whipple, K. Patient characteristics and outcome in psychotherapy and behavior therapy. *Journal of Consulting and Clinical Psychology*, 1976, *44*, 330-339.

Slotnick, R., & Jaeger, A. *Barriers to deinstitutionalization: An environmental design analysis.* Paper presented at the American Psychological Association Convention, Toronto, 1978.

Smith, M. B. "Mental health" reconsidered: A special case of the problem of values in psychology. *American Psychologist*, 1961, *16*, 299-306.

Smith, M. B., & Hobbs, N. The community and the community mental health center. *American Psychologist*, 1966, *21*, 499-509.

Smith, M. L., & Glass, G. V. Meta-analysis of psychotherapy outcome studies. *American Psychologist*, 1977, *32*, 752-760.

Smith, M. S., & Bissell, J. S. Report analysis: The impact of head start. *Harvard Educational Review*, 1970, *40*, 51-104.

Smith, N. C., Jr. *Factors underlying WISC performance in juvenile public offenders.*

(Doctoral dissertation, Ohio State University) Ann Arbor, Mich.: University Microfilms, 1969, No. 69-15966.

Snow, D. L., & Newton, P. M. Task, social structure, and social process in the community mental health center movement. *American Psychologist*, 1976, *31*, 582–594.

Snyder, W. U. A comparison of one unsuccessful with four successful nondirectively counseled cases. *Journal of Consulting Psychology*, 1949, *11*, 38-42.

Sommer, R. *Personal space*. Englewood Cliffs, N. J.: Prentice-Hall, 1969.

Sorrells, J., & Ford, F. Toward an integrated theory of families and family therapy. *Psychotherapy: Theory, Research and Practice*, 1969, *6*, 150-160.

Soskin, W. F. Influence of four types of data on diagnostic conceptualization in psychological destiny. *Journal of Abnormal and Social Psychology*, 1959, *58*, 69-78.

Spearman, C. "General intelligence," objectively determined and measured. *American Journal of Psychology*, 1904, *15*, 201-293.

Speck, R. V., & Attheave, C. L. Social network intervention. In J. Haley (Ed.), *Changing families*. New York: Grune and Stratton, 1971.

Speer, D. Family systems. *Family Process*, 1970, *9*, 259-278.

Spielberger, C. D. Anxiety as an emotional state. In C. D. Spielberger (Ed.), *Anxiety: Current trends in theory and research*. Vol. 1. New York: Academic Press, 1972.

Spielberger, C. D. Case seminar of group mental health consultation. *Professional psychology*, 1974, *6*, 302-307.

Spielberger, C. D., Auerbach, S. M., Wadsworth, A. P., Dunn, T. M., & Taulbee, E. S. Emotional reactions to surgery. *Journal of Consulting and Clinical Psychology*, 1973, *40*, 33-38.

Spielberger, C. D., Gorsuch, R. C., & Lushene, R. E. *Manual for the State-Trait Anxiety Inventory*. Palo Alto, Cal.: Consulting Psychologists Press, 1970.

Spiro, M. E. Is the family universal?—The Israeli case. *American Anthropologist*, 1954, *56*, 839-846.

Spitz, R. A. Anaclitic depression—inquiry into the genesis of psychiatric conditions in early childhood. *Psychoanalytic Study of the Child*, 1949, *2*, 313-342.

Spitzer, R. L. On pseudoscience in science, logic in remission, and psychiatric diagnosis: A critique of Rosenhan's "On being sane in insane places." *Journal of Abnormal Psychology*, 1975, *84*, 442-452.

Spitzer, R. L. & Endicott, J. The schedule for affective disorders and schizophrenia—Life-time version (SADS-L). (3rd ed.) New York: New York State Psychiatric Institute, Biometrics Research, 1979.

Spitzer, R. L., Fleiss, J. L. Endicott, J., & Cohen, J. Mental status schedule: Properties of factor-analytically derived scales. *Archives of General Psychiatry*, 1967, *16*, 479-493.

Spitzer, R. L. Fleiss, J. L. Burdock, E. I., & Hardesty, A. S. The mental status schedule: Rationale, reliability and validity. *Comprehensive Psychiatry*, 1964, *5*, 384-395.

Spitzer, R. L., Forman, J. B. W., & Nee, J. DSM III field trials: I. Initial interrater diagnostic reliability. *American Journal of Psychiatry*, 1979, *136*, 815-817.

Spitzer, R. L., Sheehy, M., & Endicott, J. DSM-III: Guiding Principles. In V. M. Rakoff, H. C. Stancer, & H. B. Kedword (Eds.), *Psychiatric Diagnosis*. New York: Brunner/Mazel, 1977.

Spreen, O., & Benton, A. L. *Neurosensory center comprehensive examination for aphasia*. Victoria, B. C.: Neuropsychology Laboratory, Department of Psychology, University of Victoria, 1969.

Spivack, G., & Shure, M. B. *Social adjustment of young children. A cognitive approach to solving real-life problems*. San Francisco: Jossey-Bass, 1974.

Spivack, M. Sensory distortions in tunnels and corridors. *Hospital and Community Psychiatry*, 1967, *18*, 12-18.

Sprague, R. L., & Quay, H. C. A factor analytic study of the responses of mental retardates on the WAIS. *American Journal of Mental Deficiency*, 1966, *70*, 595-600.

Stachnik, T. J. Priorities for psychology in medical education and health care delivery. *American Psychologist*, 1980, *35*, 8-15.

Stack, J. T., & Phillips, A. R. Performance of medical, brain-damaged and schizophrenic patients on the Halstead-Reitan Neuropsychological Battery. *Newsletter for Research in Psychology*, 1970, *12*(4), 16-18.

Stahl, J. R., & Leitenberg, H. Behavioral treatment of the chronic mental patient. In H. Leitenberg (Ed.), *Handbook of behavior modification and behavior therapy*. New York: Appleton-Century-Crofts, 1976.

Staples, F. R., Sloane, R. B., Whipple, K., Cristol, A. H., & Yorkston, N. Process and outcome in psychotherapy and behavior therapy. *Journal of Consulting and Clinical Psychology*, 1976, *44*, 340–350.

Stern, M. S. Social class and psychiatric treatment of adults in the mental health center. *Journal of Health and Social Behavior*, 1977, *18*, 317-325.

Stern, W. L. Uber die psychologischen methoden der intelligenyprufung. *Ber. V. Kongress Exp. Psychol.*, 1912, *16*, 1-160. American translation by G. M. Whipple. The psychological methods of testing intelligence. *Educational Psychology Monographs*, No. 13, Baltimore: Warwick & York, 1914.

Stokes, T., & Baer, D. An implicit technology of generalization. *Journal of Applied Behavior Analysis*, 1977, *10*, 71-84.

Stokols, D. On the distinction between density and crowding: Some implications for future research. *Psychological Review*, 1972, *79*, 275-277.

Stolz, S. B. Ethics of social and educational interventions: Historical context and behavioral analysis. In T. A. Brigham & A. C. Catania (Eds.), *Analyses of behavior: Social and education processes*. New York: Wiley, 1977.

Stolz, S. B. *Ethical issues in behavior modification*. San Francisco: Jossey-Bass, 1978.

Stone, A. A. Overview: The right to treatment—Comments on the law and its impact. *American Journal of Psychiatry*, 1975, *132*, 1125-1134. (a)

Stone, A. A. *Mental health and law*. Washington, D. C.: National Institute of Mental Health, 1975. (b)

Storrow, H. A. *Introduction to scientific psychiatry*. New York: Meredith, 1967.

Strassberg, D. S., Roback, H. B., Anchor, K. N., & Abramowitz, S. I. Self disclosure in group therapy with schizophrenics. *Archives of General Psychiatry*, 1975, *32*, 1259-1261.

Streitfeld, M. S. The Aureon encounter: An organic process. In L. Blank, G. B. Gottsegen & M. G. Gottsegen (Eds.), *Confrontation*. New York: Macmillan, 1971.

Strelnick, A. H. Multiple family group therapy. A review of the literature. *Family Process*, 1977, *16*, 307–325.

Stricker, G. On professional schools and professional degrees. *American Psychologist*, 1975, *30*, 1062-1066.

Stricker, G. The doctoral dissertation in clinical psychology. *Professional Psychology*, 1973, *4*, 72-78.

Strickland, A. J. New therapies for the eating disorders: Behavior modifications of obesity and anorexia nervosa. *Archives of General Psychiatry*, 1972, *26*, 391-398.

Strickland, B. R., Hale, W. D., & Anderson, L. K. Effect of induced mood states on activity and self-reported affect. *Journal of Consulting and Clinical Psychology*, 1975, *43*, 587.

Strupp, H. H. Clinical pychology, irrationalism, and the erosion of excellence. *American Psychologist*, 1976, *31*, 561-570.

Strupp, H. H. A reformulation of the dynamics of the therapist's contribution. In A. Gurman & A. Razin (Eds.), *Effective psychotherapy: A handbook of research*. New York: Pergamon, 1977.

Strupp, H. H. & Bergin, A. E. Some empirical and conceptual bases for coordinated research in psychotherapy. *International Journal of Psychiatry*, 1969, *7*, 1-93.

Strupp, H. H., & Bloxom, A. Preparing lower-class patients for group psychotherapy: Development and evaluation of a role induction film. *Journal of Consulting and Clinical Psychology*, 1973, *41*, 373-384.

Strupp, H. H. & Bloxom, A. L. Therapists' assessments of outcome. In I. E. Waskow & M. B. Parloff (Eds.), *Psychotherapy change measures*. Washington, D. C.: U. S. Government Printing Office, 1975.

Stuart, R. B. Operant-interpersonal treatment for marital discord. *Journal of Consulting and Clinical Psychology*, 1969, 33, 675–682.

Stuart, R. B., & Davis, B. *Slim chance in a fat world: Behavioral control of obesity.* Champaign, Ill.: Research Press, Inc., 1972.

Stuart, R. B., & Stuart, F. *Mental pre-counseling inventory*. Champaign, Ill.: Research Press, 1972.

Stufflebeum, D. The use and abuse of evaluation in Title III. *Theory into Practice*, 1967, *6*, 126-133.

Stunkard, A. J. New therapies for the eating disorders. *Archives of General Psychiatry*, 1972, *26*, 391-398.

Sturgis, E. T., & Adams, H. E. The right to treatment: Issues in the treatment of homosexuality. *Journal of Consulting and Clinical Psychology*, 1978, *46*, 165-169.

Subotnik, L. Spontaneous remission: Fact or artifact? *Psychological Bulletin*, 1972, *77*, 32-48.

Sullivan, H. S. *The interpersonal theory of psychiatry*. New York: Norton, 1953.

Sullivan, H. S. *The psychiatric interview*. New York: Norton, 1954.

Sundberg, N. D., Tyler, L. E., & Taplin, J. R. *Clinical psychology: Expanding horizons.* Englewood Cliffs, N. J.: Prentice-Hall, 1973.

Suomi, S. J., Harlow, H. F., & Domek, C. J. Effect of repetitive infant-infant separation of young monkeys. *Journal of Abnormal Psychology*, 1970, *76*, 162-172.

Swensen, C. H. Empirical evaluations of human figure drawings. *Psychological Bulletin*, 1957, *54*, 431-466.

Swensen, C. H. Empirical ,evaluations of human figure drawings: 1957-1966. *Psychological Bulletin*, 1968, *70*, 20-44.

Swiercinsky, D. P., & Warnock, K. Comparison of the neuropsychological key and discriminant analysis approaches in predicting cerebral damage and locating action. *Journal of Consulting and Clinical Psychology*, 1977, *45*, 807-814.

Sykes, R. E. Techniques of data collection and reduction in systematic field observation. *Behavior Research Methods and Instrumentation*, 1977, *9*, 407–417.

Szasz, T. S. *The myth of mental illness*. New York: Harper & Row, 1961.

Szasz, T. S. *The myth of sex therapy*. New York: Doubleday, 1980.

Szasz, T. S. *The manufacture of madness*. New York: Harper & Row, 1970.

Szasz, T. S. Schizophrenia: The sacred symbol of psychiatry. *British Journal of Psychiatry*, 1976, *129*, 308-316.

Talland, G. A. *Deranged memory*. New York: Academic Press, 1965.

Tallent, N. On individualizing the psychologist's clinical evaluation. *Journal of Clinical Psychology*, 1958, *14*, 243-245.

Tallent, N. *Psychological report writing*. Englewood Cliffs, N. J.: Prentice-Hall, 1976.

Tanke, E. D., & Tanke, T. Getting off a slippery slope: Social science in the judicial process. *American Psychologist*, 1979, *34*, 1130-1138.

Tasto, D. Self report schedules and inventories. In A. Ciminero, K. Calhoun, & H. Adams (Eds.), *Handbook of behavioral assessment*. New York: Wiley, 1977.

Taylor, B. J., & Wagner, N. N. Sex between therapists and clients: A review and analysis. *Professional Psychology*, 1976, *7*, 593-601.

Taylor, F. G., & Marshall, W. L. Experimental analysis of a cognitive-behavioral therapy for depression. *Cognitive Therapy and Research*, 1977, *1*, 59-72.

Taylor, J. A. A personality scale of manifest anxiety. *Journal of Abnormal and Social Psychology*, 1953, 48, 285-290.

Tedeschi, J. T., & Bonoma, T. V. Power and influence: An introduction. In J. T. Tedeschi (Ed.), *The social influence process*. Chicago: Aldine, 1972.

Tellegen, A., & Atkinson, G. Openness to absorbing and self-altering experiences ("Absorption"), a trait related to hypnotic susceptibility. *Journal of Abnormal Psychology*, 1974, *83*, 268-277.

Tellegen, A., & Briggs, P. F. Old wine in new skins: Grouping Wechsler subtests into new scales. *Journal of Consulting Psychology*, 1967, *31*, 499-506.

Terman, L. M. *The measurement of intelligence*. Boston: Houghton Mifflin, 1960.

Terman, L. M., & Merrill, M. A. *Stanford-Binet Intelligence Scale: Manual for the third revision, Form L-M*. Boston: Houghton Mifflin, 1960.

Tharp, R. G., & Wetzel, R. T. *Behavior modification in the natural environment*. New York: Academic Press, 1969.

Theobold, D. E., & Paul, G. L. Reinforcing value praise for chronic mental patients as a function of historical pairing with tangible reinforcers. *Behavior Therapy*, 1976, 7, 192–197.

Thomas, E., & DeWald, L. Experimental neurosis: Neuropsychological analysis. In J. D. Maser & M. E. P. Seligman (Eds.), *Psychopathology: Experimental models*. San Francisco: W. H. Freeman, 1977.

Thompson, T., & Grabowski, J. (Eds.) *Behavior modification of the mentally retarded*. New York: Oxford University Press, 1972.

Thompson, V. A. *Bureaucracy and innovation*. University, Ala.: University of Alabama Press, 1969.

Thoresen, C. E., & Mahoney, M. J. *Behavioral self-control.* New York: Holt, Rinehart and Winston, 1974.

Thorndike, E. L. *The fundamentals of learning.* New York: Teacher's College, 1932.

Thorndike, E. L., Lay, W., & Dean, P. R. The relation of accuracy in sensory discrimination to general intelligence. *American Journal of Psychology,* 1909, *20,* 364-369.

Thorndike, R. L. Concepts of culture fairness. *Journal of Educational Measurement,* 1971, *8,* 63-70.

Thorne, F. D. The clinical method in science. *American Psychologist,* 1947, *2,* 159-166.

Tolman, E. Cognitive maps in rats and men. *Psychological Review,* 1948, *55,* 240-252.

Tomkins, S. S. *The Tomkins-Horn Picture Arrangement Test.* New York: Springer, 1957.

Touwen, B. C. L., & Kalverboer, A. F. Neurological and behavioral assessment of children with minimal brain dysfunction. In S. Walzer & P. H. Wolff (Eds.), *Minimal Cerebral dysfunction in children.* New York: Grune and Stratton, 1973.

Tracy, G. S., & Gussow, Z. Self-help groups: A grass-roots response to a need for services. *Journal of Applied Behavioral Science,* 1973, *12,* 381-396.

Trexler, L. D., & Karst, T. O. Rational-emotive therapy, placebo, and no-treatment effects on public-speaking anxiety. *Journal of Abnormal Psychology,* 1972, *79,* 60-67.

Trickett, E. T., Kelly, J. G., & Todd, D. M. The social environment of high school: Guidelines for individual change and organizational redevelopment. In S. E. Golann & C. Eisdorfer (Eds.), *Handbook of community mental health.* New York: Appleton-Century-Crofts 1972.

Truax, C. B. Reinforcement and nonreinforcement in Rogerian psychotherapy. *Journal of Abnormal Psychology,* 1966, *71,* 1-9.

Truax, C. B. The meaning and reliability of accurate empathy ratings. *Psychological Bulletin,* 1972, *77,* 397–399.

Truax, C. B., & Carkhuff, R. R. *Toward effective counseling and psychotherapy: Training and practice.* Chicago: Aldine, 1967.

Truax, C. B., & Mitchell, K. M. Research on certain therapist interpersonal skills in relation to process and outcome. In A. E. Bergin & S. L. Garfield (Eds.), *Handbook of psychotherapy and behavior change.* New York: Wiley, 1971.

Truax, C. B., Wargo, D. G., Frank, I. D., Imber, S. D., Battle, C. C., Hoehn-Saric, R., Nash, E. H., & Stone, A. R. Therapist empathy, genuineness, and warmth and patient therapeutic outcome. *Journal of Consulting Psychology,* 1966, *30,* 395-401.

Tsushima, W. T., & Towne, W. S. Neuropsychological abilities of young children with questionable brain disorders. *Journal of Consulting and Clinical Psychology,* 1977, *45,* 757-762.

Tulchin, S. H. The psychologist. *American Journal of Orthopsychiatry,* 1930, *1,* 39-47.

Tuma, A. H., May, P. R. A., Yale, C., & Forsythe, A. B. Therapist characteristics and the outcome of treatment in schizophrenics. *Archives of General Psychiatry,* 1978, *35,* 81-85.

Tumin, M. Some principles of stratification: A critical analysis. *American Sociological Review,* 1953, *18,* 387-394.

Tupes, E. C., & Christal, R. E. *Recurrent personality factors based on trait ratings.* USAF AFD Technical Report, No. 61-97, 1961.

Turk, D. C., & Genest, M. Regulation of pain: The application of cognitive and behavioral techniques for prevention and remediation. In P. C. Kendall & S. D. Hollon (Eds.), *Cognitive-behavioral interventions: Theory, research, and procedures.* New York: Academic Press, 1979.

Turkewitz, H., & O'Leary, K. D. *Communication and behavioral marital therapy: An outcome study.* Paper presented at the Annual Convention of the Association for Advancement of Behavior Therapy, New York, 1976.

Tylor, E. B. *Primitive culture.* Vol. 1. New York: Appleton-Century-Crofts, 1871.

Ullmann, L. P., & Giovannoni, J. M. The development of a self-report measure of the process-reactive continuum. *Journal of Nervous and Mental Disease*, 1964, *138*, 38-42.

Ullmann, L. P., & Krasner, L. *A psychological approach to abnormal behavior.* (2nd ed.) Englewood Cliffs, N. J.: Prentice-Hall, 1975.

Uzgiris, I. C., & Hunt, J. M. V. *Assessment in infancy: Ordinal scales of psychological development.* Urbana, Ill.: University of Illinois Press, 1975.

Urbain, E. S., & Kendall, P. C. Review of social-cognitive problem-solving interventions with children. *Psychological Bulletin*, 1980, *88*, 109-143.

Urban, R., & Ford, D. Some historical and conceptual perspectives on psychotherapy and behavior change. In A. E. Bergin & S. L. Garfield (Eds.), *Handbook of psychotherapy and behavior change.* New York: Wiley, 1971.

Vale, J. R., & Vale, C. A. Individual differences and general laws in psychology: A reconciliation. *American Psychologist*, 1969, *24*, 1093-1108.

Valfer, E. Double dilemma. *APA Monitor*, February, 1979, p. 17.

Vandenberg, S. G., & Wilson, K. Failure of the twin situation to influence twin differences in cognition. *Behavior Genetics*, 1979, *9*, 55-60.

Van Hoose, W. H., & Kottler, J. A. *Ethical and legal issues in counseling and psychotherapy.* San Francisco: Jossey-Bass, 1975.

Velten, E. A laboratory task for induction of mood states. *Behaviour Research and Therapy*, 1968, *6*, 473-482.

Veroff, J. Development and validation of a projective measure of power motivation. *Journal of Abnormal and Social Psychology*, 1957, *54*, 1-8.

Vidich, A. J., & Bensman, J. *Small town in mass society.* Princeton, N. J.: Princeton University Press, 1958.

von Bertalanffy, L. *General systems theory: Foundation, development, applications.* New York: Braziller, 1968.

Wachtel, P. L. *Psychoanalysis and behavior therapy.* New York: Basic Books, 1977.

Wachtel, P. L. Psychodynamics, behavior therapy, and the implacable experimenter: An inquiry into the consistency of personality. *Journal of Abnormal Psychology*, 1973, *82*, 324-334.

Wade, T. C., & Baker, T. B. Opinions and use of psychological tests: A survey of clinical psychologists. *American Psychologist*, 1977, *33*, 874-882.

Wagner, N. N. Is masturbation still wrong? Comments on Bailey's comments. *Journal of Consulting and Psychology*, 1978, *46*, 1507-1509.

Wahler, R. G., & Cormier, W. H. The ecological interview: A first step in outpatient child behavior therapy. *Journal of Behavior Therapy and Experimental Psychiatry*, 1970, *1*, 279-289.

Wainer, H., Hurt, S., & Aiken, L. Rorschach revisited: A new look at an old test. *Journal of Consulting and Clinical Psychology*, 1976, *44*, 390-399.

Walker, H. M. *Walker Problem Behavior Identification Checklist.* Los Angeles: Western Psychological Services, 1970.

Walker, H. M., & Buckley, N. K. Programming generalization and maintenance of treatment effects across time and setting. *Journal of Applied Behavior Analysis*, 1972, *5*, 209-224.

Walker, H. M., Hops, H., & Fiegenbaum, E. Deviant classroom behavior as a function of combinations of social and token reinforcement and cost contingency. *Behavior Therapy*, 1976, *7*, 76-88.

Wallace, A. F. C. *Culture and personality.* (2nd ed.) New York: Random House, 1970.

Wallace, C. Observational assessment for inpatient token economy programs. In M. Hersen & A. Bellack (Eds.), *Behavioral assessment: A practical handbook.* New York: Pergamon, 1976.

Wallach, M. A., Kogan, N., & Bem, D. J. Group influence on individual risk-taking. *Journal of Abnormal and Social Psychology*, 1962, 65, 75-86.

Wallbrown, F. H., Blaha, J., & Wherry, R. J. The hierarchical factor structure of the Wechsler Preschool and Primary Scale of Intelligence. *Journal of Consulting and Clinical Psychology*, 1973, *41*, 356-362.

Walsh, W. B. Validity of self-report. *Journal of Counseling Psychology*, 1967, *14*, 18-23.

Walster, E., Walster, G. W., & Berscheid, E. *Equity: Theory and research.* Boston: Allyn and Bacon, 1978.

Wang, M. G. Effect of a therapeutic community/token economy program on chronic schizophrenic aftercare patients. *Dissertation Abstracts International*, 1976, *317*(B), 1422.

Ward, C. H., Beck, A. T., Mendelson, M., Mork, J. E., & Erbaugh, J. K. The psychiatric nomenclature: Reasons for diagnostic disagreement. *Archives of General Psychiatry*, 1962, *7*, 198-205.

Waring, M., & Ricks, D. F. Family patterns of children who become adult schizophrenics. *Journal of Nervous and Mental Disease*, 1965, *140*, 351-364.

Warne, M. M., Canter, A. H., & Wincze, B. Analyses and followup of patients with psychiatric disorders. *American Journal of Psychotherapy*, 1953, *7*, 278-288.

Washburn, S., Vannicelli, M., Longabaugh, R., & Scheff, B. J. A controlled comparison of psychiatric day treatment and inpatient hospitalization. *Journal of Consulting and Clinical Psychology*, 1976, *44*, 665-675.

Waskow, I. E., & Parloff, M. B. (Eds.) *Psychotherapy change measures.* Washington, D. C.: U. S. Government Printing Office, 1975.

Watson, C. An MMPI scale to separate brain damaged from schizophrenic men. *Journal of Consulting and Clinical Psychology*, 1971, *36*, 121–125.

Watson, D., & Friend, R. Measurement of social-evaluative anxiety. *Journal of Consulting and Clinical Psychology*, 1969, *33*, 448-457.

Watson, J. B. *Behaviorism.* New York: Norton, 1925.

Watson, J. B., & Rayner, R. Conditioned emotional reactions. *Journal of Experimental Psychology*, 1920, *3*, 1-14.

Watson, R. I. The professional status of the clinical psychologist. In R. I. Watson (Ed.), *Readings in the clinical method in psychology.* New York: Harper, 1949.

Watzlawick, P. *The language of change.* New York: Norton, 1978.

Watzlawick, P., Weakland, J., & Fisch, R. *Change*. New York: Norton, 1974.

Webb, E. J., Campbell, D. T., Schwartz, R. D., & Sechrest, L. *Unobtrusive measures: Nonreactive research in the social sciences*. Chicago: Rand McNally, 1966.

Webb, J. T. Similarities of patients treated by private practice psychologists and psychiatrists. *Professional Psychology*, 1980, *11*, 684-687.

Weber, M. *The theory of social and economic organization*. (Translated by A. M. Hendersen & T. Parsons). Cambridge, Mass.: Harvard University Press, 1947.

Wechsler, D. *The measurement of adult intelligence*. Baltimore: Williams & Wilkins, 1939.

Wechsler, D. The psychologist in the psychiatric hospital. *Journal of Consulting Psychology*, 1944, *8*, 281-285.

Wechsler, D. A standardized memory scale for clinical use. *Journal of Psychology*, 1945, *19*, 87-95.

Wechsler, D. *Wechsler Adult Intelligence Scale Manual*. New York: Psychological Corporation, 1955.

Wechsler, D. *The measurement and appraisal of adult intelligence*. Baltimore: Williams & Wilkins, 1958.

Wechsler, D. *Manual for the Wechsler Preschool and Primary Scale of Intelligence*. New York: Psychological Corporation, 1967.

Wechsler, D. *Wechsler Intelligence Scale for Children—Revised Manual*. New York: Psychological Corporation, 1974.

Wechsler, D. *Personal communication*. American Psychological Association Convention, Montreal, 1980.

Weikart, D. P. Relationship of curriculum, teaching, and learning in preschool education. In J. C. Stanley (Ed.), *Preschool for the disadvantaged*. Baltimore: The Johns Hopkins University, 1972.

Weiner, I. B. Individual psychotherapy. In I. B. Weiner (Ed.), *Clinical methods in psychology*. New York: Wiley, 1976.

Weiner, I. B. *Principles of psychotherapy*. New York: Wiley, 1975.

Weinman, B., Sanders, R., Kleiner, R., & Wilson, S. Community based treatment of chronic psychotics. *Community Mental Health Journal*, 1970, *6*, 13-21.

Weiss, C. H. *Evaluation research: Methods of assessing program effectiveness*. Englewood Cliffs, N. J.: Prentice-Hall, 1972.

Weiss, R. L., Birchler, C. R., & Vincent, J. P. Contractual models for negotiation training in marital dyads. *Journal of Marriage and the Family*, 1974, *36*, 321-330.

Weiss, R. L., Hops, H., & Patterson, G. R. A framework for conceptualizing marital conflict, a technology for altering it, and some data for evaluating it. In F. W. Clark & L. H. Hamerlynck (Eds.), *Behavior modification: Critical issues in research and practice*. Champaign, Ill.: Research Press, 1973.

Weiss, R., & Margolin, G. Marital conflict and accord. In A. Ciminero, K. Calhoun & H. Adams (Eds.), *Handbook of behavioral assessment*. New York: Wiley, 1977.

Weissberg, R. P., Gesten, E. L., Rapkin, B. D., Cowen, E. L., Davidson, E., de Apodaca, R. F., & McKim, B. J. The evaluation of a social problem-solving training program for suburban and inner-city third grade children. *Journal of Consulting and Clinical Psychology*, 1981, *49*, 251-261.

Wells, R. A., & Dezen, A. G. The results of family therapy revisited: The non-behavioral methods. *Family Process*, 1978, *17*, 251-274.

Welsh, G. S. Factor dimensions A and R. In G. S. Welsh & W. G. Dahlstrom (Eds.), *Basic readings on the MMPI in psychology and medicine*. Minneapolis: University of Minnesota Press, 1956.

Wener, A. E., & Rehm, L. P. Depressive affect: A test of behavioral hypotheses. *Journal of Abnormal Psychology*, 1975, *84*, 221–227.

Werner, E. E. Review of the Arthur adaptation of the Leiter International Performance Scale. In O. K. Buros (Ed.) *The sixth mental measurements year-book*. Highland Park, N. J.: Gryphon Press, 1965.

Weschler, M. The self-help organization in the mental health field: Recovery, Inc.—A case study. *Journal of Nervous and Mental Disease*, 1960, *130*, 297–314.

Westinghouse Corporation/Ohio University. *The impact of head start*. Vols. I & II. Springfield, VA: U.S. Department of Commerce, 1969.

Whalen, C. K., & Henker, B. A. Pyramid therapy in a hospital for the retarded: Methods, program evaluation, and long-term effects. *American Journal of Mental Deficiency*, 1971, *75*, 414-434.

Wheeler, L., Burke, C. H., & Reitan, R. M. An application of discriminant functions to the problem of predicting brain damage using behavorial variables. *Perceptual and Motor Skills*, 1963, *16*, 417-440.

Wheeler, L., & Reitan, R. M. Discriminant functions applied to the problem of predicting cerebral damage from behavior testing: A cross-validation study. *Perceptual and Motor Skills*, 1963, *16*, 681-701.

Whitaker, C. A. Psychotherapy of the absurd. With special emphasis on the psychotherapy of aggression. *Family Process*, 1976, *14*, 1-16.

Whitehorn, J. C., & Betz, B. J. Further studies of the doctor as a crucial variable in the outcome of treatment with schizophrenic patients. *American Journal of Psychiatry*, 1960, *117*, 215-223.

Whorf, B. L. *Language, thought, and reality*. New York: Wiley, 1956.

Whyte, W. F. *Street corner society*. Chicago: University of Chicago Press, 1943.

Wicker, A. W., & Kirmeyer, S. From church to laboratory to National Park. In S. Wapner, S. B. Cohen, & B. Kaplan (Eds.), *Experiencing the environment*. New York: Plenum, 1976.

Wiens, A. N. The assessment interview. In I. B. Weiner (Ed.), *Clinical methods in psychology*. New York: Wiley, 1976.

Wiens, A. N., Matarazzo, J. D., & Gaver, K. D. Performance and verbal IQ in a group of sociopaths. *Journal of Clinical Psychology*, 1959, *15*, 191-193.

Wiggins, J. S. *Personality and prediction: Principles of personality assessment*. Reading, Mass.: Addison-Wesley, 1973.

Wiggins, J. S., & Winder, C. L. The peer nomination inventory: An empirically derived sociometric measure of adjustment in preadolescent boys. *Psychological Reports*, 1961, *9*, 643-677.

Wilkins, W. Expectancies in applied settings. In A. Gurman & A. Razin (Eds.), *Effective psychotherapy: A handbook of research*. New York: Pergamon, 1977.

Willens, J. G. Colorado medicare study: A history. *American Psychologist*, 1977, *32*, 746-749.

Williams, C. L. *Crisis cases*. Personal communication, August 1978.

Williams, R. L. *Black intelligence test of cultural homogeneity.* Unpublished manuscript, St. Louis, Missouri, 1972.

Williamson, E. G. Coordination of student personnel services. *Journal of Consulting Psychology*, 1940, *4*, 229-233.

Willis, M. H., & Blaney, P. H. Three tests of the learned helplessness model of depression. *Journal of Abnormal Psychology*, 1978, *87*, 131-136.

Wilson, D. W., & Donnerstein, E. Legal and ethical aspects of nonreactive social psychological research: An excursion into the public mind. *American Psychologist*, 1976, *31*, 765-773.

Wilson, G. T. Ethical and professional issues in sex therapy. Comments on Bailey's— "Psychotherapy or massage parlor technology?" *Journal of Consulting and Clinical Psychology*, 1978, *46*, 1510-1514. (a)

Wilson, G. T. On the much discussed nature of the term "behavior therapy." *Behavior Therapy*, 1978, *9*, 89-98. (b)

Wilson, G. T. The importance of being theoretical: A commentary on Bandura's "Self-efficacy: Towards a unifying theory of behavioral change." *Advances in Behaviour Research and Therapy*, 1978, *1*, 217-230. (c)

Wilson, J. Q. What makes a better policeman? *Atlantic Monthly*, 1969, March, 129-135.

Windle, C., Bass, R. D., & Taube, C. A. PR aside: Initial results from NIMH's service program evaluation studies. *American Journal of Community Psychology*, 1974, *2*, 311-327.

Winett, R. A., & Winkler, R. C. Current behavior modification in the classroom: Be still, be quiet, be docile. *Journal of Applied Behavior Analysis*, 1972, *5*, 499-504.

Winnicott, D. W. *Maturational processes and the facilitating environment.* London: Hogarth Press, 1972.

Winokur, G., Clayton, P. J., & Reich, T. *Manic-depressive illness.* St. Louis: Mosby, 1969.

Winokur, G. Family history studies VIII: Secondary depression is alive and well, and . . . *Diseases of the Nervous System*, 1972, *33*, 94-99.

Winokur, G. The types of affective disorder. *Journal of Nervous and Mental Disorders*, 1973, *156*, 82-96.

Wirt, R. D., Lachar, D., Klinedienst, & Seat, P. D. *Multidimensional description of child personality: A manual for the Personality Inventory for Children.* Los Angeles: Western Psychological Services, 1977.

Wirth, L. Urbanism as a way of life. *American Journal of Sociology*, 1938, *44*, 1-24.

Witmer, L. Clinical psychology. *Psychological Clinics*, 1912, *1*, 1-9.

Wolf, M. M. Social validity: The case of subjective measurement or how applied behavior analysis is finding its heart. *Journal of Applied Behavior Analysis*, 1978, *11*, 203-214.

Wolf, M. M., Risley, T., & Mees, H. L. Application of operant conditioning procedures to the behavior problems of an autistic child. *Behaviour Research and Therapy*, 1964, *1*, 305-312.

Wolfe, D. The reorganized American Psychological Association. *American Psychologist*, 1946, *1*, 3-6.

Wolfe, L. The question of surrogates in sex therapy. *New York Magazine*, 12/3/71, 120-122, 217-218.

Wolfred, T. R., & Davidson, W. S. Evaluation of community based program for the prevention of delinquency: The failure of success. *Community Mental Health Journal*, 1977, *13*, 97-105.

Wolpe, J. *Psychotherapy by reciprocal inhibition.* Stanford, Cal.: Stanford University Press, 1958.

Wolpe, J. *The practice of behavior therapy.* Elmsford, N. Y.: Pergamon, 1969.

Wolpe, J. *The practice of behavior therapy.* (2nd ed.) New York: Pergamon, 1973.

Wolpe, J., & Lang, P. J. A fear survey schedule for use in behavior therapy. *Behaviour Research and Therapy*, 1964, *2*, 27-34.

Wolpe, J., & Lazarus, A. A. *Behavior therapy techniques.* New York: Pergamon, 1966.

Woods, P. *Career opportunities for psychologists.* Washington, D. C.: American Psychological Association, 1976.

Woodworth, R. S. The future of clinical psychology. *Journal of Consulting Psychology*, 1937, *1*, 4-5.

Woo-Sam, J., & Zimmerman, I. L. Note on applicability of the Kaufman formula for abbreviating the WPPSI. *Perceptual and Motor Skills*, 1973, *36*, 1121-1122.

Worchel, S. & Teddlie, C. The experience of crowding: A two-factor theory, *Journal of Personality and Social Psychology*, 1976, *34*, 34–40.

Worell, J. Sex roles and psychological well-being: Perspectives on methodology. *Journal of Consulting and Clinical Psychology*, 1978, *46*, 777-791.

World Health Organization. *International Classification of Diseases (9th Rev.): ICD-9.* Geneva: World Health Organization, 1978.

Wortman, C. B., & Brehm, J. W. Responses to uncontrollable outcomes: An integration of reactance theory and the learned helplessness model. In L. Berkowitz (Ed.), *Advances in experimental social psychology.* Vol 8. New York: Academic Press, 1975.

Wortman, C. B., & Dintzer, L. Is an attributional analysis of the learned helplessness phenomenon viable?—A critique of the Abramson-Seligman-Teasdale reformulation. *Journal of Abnormal Psychology*, 1978, *87*, 75-90.

Wright, C. R., & Hyman, H. H. Voluntary association memberships of American adults. *American Sociological Review.* 1958, *23*, 284-294.

Wyatt, D. F., & Campbell, D. T. On the liability of stereotype or hypothesis. *Journal of Abnormal and Social Psychology*, 1951, *46*, 495-500.

Wyatt, F. What is clinical psychology? In A. Z. Guiora & M. A. Brandwin (Eds.), *Perspectives in clinical psychology.* Princeton, N. J.: Van Nostrand, 1968.

Wynne, L. C. Some guidelines for exploratory conjoint family therapy. In J. Haley (Ed.), *Changing families.* New York: Grune and Stratton, 1971.

Yalom, I. D. *The theory and practice of group psychotherapy.* (2nd ed.) New York: Basic Books, 1975.

Yalom, I. D., Bond, G., Bloch, S., Zimmerman, E., & Freedman, L. The impact of a weekend group experience on individual therapy. *Archives of General Psychiatry*, 1977, *34*, 399-415.

Yalom, I., Monte, P., Newell, G., & Rand, K. Preparation of patients for group therapy: A controlled study. *Archives of General Psychiatry*, 1967, *17*, 416-427.

Yinger, J. M. Contraculture and subculture. *American Sociological Review*, 1960, *25*, 625-635.

Zacker, J. & Bard, M. Adaptive resistance to change in a community. *American Journal of Community Psychology*, 1973, *1*, 44-49.

Zander, A. *Groups at work*. San Francisco: Jossey-Bass, 1977.

Zaltman, G., Duncan, R., & Holbek, J. *Innovations and organizations*. New York: Wiley, 1973.

Zax, M., & Specter, G. A. *An introduction to community psychology*. New York: Wiley, 1974.

Zborowski, M. Cultural components in response to pain. *Journal of Social Issues*, 1953, *8*, 16-31.

Zeiss, A. M., Rosen, G. M., & Zeiss, R. A. Orgasm during intercourse. A treatment strategy for women. *Journal of Consulting and Clinical Psychology*, 1977, *45*, 891-895.

Zeiss, A. M., Lewinsohn, P. M., & Munõz, R. F. Nonspecific improvement effects in depression using interpersonal skills training, pleasant activity scheduling, and cognitive therapy. *Journal of Consulting and Clinical Psychology*, 1979, *47*, 427-439.

Zigler, E., & Phillips, L. Social effectiveness and symptomatic behaviors. *Journal of Abnormal and Social Psychology*, 1960, *61*, 231-238.

Zigler, E., & Phillips, L. Psychiatric diagnosis and symptomatology. *Journal of Abnormal and Social Psychology*, 1961, *63*, 69-75.

Zigler, E., & Phillips, L. Social competence and the process-reactive distinction in psychopathology. *Journal of Abnormal and Social Psychology*, 1962, *65*, 215-222.

Zimmerman, S. F., Whitmyre, J. W., & Fields, F. R. J. Factor analytic structure of the Wechsler Adult Intelligence Scale in patients with diffuse and lateralized cerebral dysfunction. *Journal of Clinical Psychology*, 1970, *26*, 462-465.

Zimbardo, P. The human choice: Individuation, reason and order versus deindividuation, impulse, and chaos. In W. J. Arnold & D. Levine (Eds.), *Nebraska symposium on motivation*. Vol 17. Lincoln: University of Nebraska Press, 1969.

Zubin, J. Discussion of symposium on newer approaches to personality assessment. *Journal of Personality Assessment*, 1972, *36*, 427-434. (a)

Zubin, J. Scientific models for psychopathology in the 1970's. *Seminars in Psychiatry*, 1972, *4*, 283-296. (b)

Zubin, J., Eron, L. D., & Schumer, F. *An experimental approach to projective techniques*. New York: Wiley, 1965.

Zuckerman, M. Development of a situation-specific trait-state test for the prediction and measurement of affective responses. *Journal of Consulting and Clinical Psychology*, 1977, *45*, 513-523.

Zuk, G. The victim and his silencers. In G. Zuk & I. Boszormenyi-Nagy (Eds.), *Family therapy and disturbed families*. Palo Alto, Cal: Science and Behavior Books, 1967.

Zuk, G. Family therapy. In J. Haley (Ed.), *Changing families*. New York, Grune and Stratton, 1971.

Zung, W.K. A self-rating depression scale. *Archives of General Psychiatry*, 1965, *12*, 63-70.

INDEX